Higher Education in American Life, 1636–1986

Recent Titles in
Bibliographies and Indexes in Education

Integrating Women's Studies into the Curriculum: An Annotated Bibliography
Susan Douglas Franzosa and Karen A. Mazza, compilers

Teacher Evaluation and Merit Pay: An Annotated Bibliography
Elizabeth Lueder Karnes and Donald D. Black, compilers

The Education of Poor and Minority Children: A World Bibliography, Supplement, 1979–1985
Meyer Weinberg, compiler

Comparative Reading: An International Bibliography
John Hladczuk and William Eller, compilers

Higher Education in American Life, 1636–1986

A Bibliography of Dissertations and Theses

Compiled by
Arthur P. Young

Bibliographies and Indexes in Education, Number 5

Greenwood Press
New York
Westport, Connecticut
London

Library of Congress Cataloging-in-Publication Data

Young, Arthur P.
　　Higher education in American life, 1636–1986 : a bibliography of
dissertations and theses / compiled by Arthur P. Young.
　　　　p.　cm. — (Bibliographies and indexes in education, ISSN
0742–6917 ; no. 5)
　　Includes index.
　　ISBN 0–313–25352–8 (lib. bdg. : alk. paper)
　　1. Education, Higher—United States—History—Bibliography.
　　2. Universities and colleges—United States—History—Bibliography.
　　3. Dissertations, Academic—United States—Bibliography.　I. Title.
　　II. Series.
　　Z5814.U7Y69 1988
　　[LA226]
　　016.37873—dc19　　　　88–10996

British Library Cataloguing in Publication Data is available.

Library of Congress Catalog Card Number: 88–10996
ISBN: 0–313–25352–8
ISSN: 0742–6917

First published in 1988

Greenwood Press, Inc.
88 Post Road West, Westport, Connecticut 06881

Printed in the United States of America

The paper used in this book complies with the
Permanent Paper Standard issued by the National
Information Standards Organization (Z39.48–1984).

10 9 8 7 6 5 4 3 2 1

To

Daniel Coit Gilman
Librarian and University Builder

Jo Ann Fley
Teacher

Laurence R. Veysey
Scholar

CONTENTS

PREFACE   ix

PART ONE

STATES AND TERRITORIES

Alabama	3	Montana	130
Alaska	8	Nebraska	131
Arizona	9	Nevada	134
Arkansas	11	New Hampshire	135
California	14	New Jersey	136
Colorado	29	New Mexico	141
Connecticut	32	New York	143
Delaware	37	North Carolina	164
District of Columbia	38	North Dakota	171
Florida	42	Ohio	172
Georgia	46	Oklahoma	185
Hawaii	52	Oregon	189
Idaho	53	Pennsylvania	192
Illinois	54	Puerto Rico	205
Indiana	68	Rhode Island	206
Iowa	74	South Carolina	208
Kansas	79	South Dakota	212
Kentucky	83	Tennessee	214
Louisiana	88	Texas	221
Maine	92	Utah	239
Maryland	93	Vermont	243
Massachusetts	98	Virginia	244
Michigan	108	Washington	252
Minnesota	117	West Virginia	256
Mississippi	120	Wisconsin	258
Missouri	124	Wyoming	262

PART TWO

TOPICAL STUDIES

Academic Freedom	263	Humanities	312
Accreditation	264	Intercultural Education	316
Administration	265	Jewish Higher Education	317
Admissions	267	Land-Grant Institutions	317
Adult Education	267	Legislation	318
Agricultural Education	268	Liberal Arts	318
Alumni	268	Libraries and Librarians	319
Architecture	269	Medical Education	322
Associations and Societies	269	Military Education	323
Athletics	270	National University	324
Black Higher Education	274	Native Americans	324
Broadcasting	280	Philosophy of Education	325
Business and Education	280	Politics and Social Policy	326
Business Education	280	Presidents	327
Catholic Higher Education	281	Professions	328
Church and State	283	Protestant Higher Education	330
Colonial Higher Education	284	Public Relations	333
Community Colleges	285	Religion	333
Courts	288	Religious Colleges	334
Curriculum	288	Research	335
Deans	292	Sciences	335
European Influence	292	Social Sciences	340
Examinations	293	State Aid and Coordination	347
Faculty	293	State University	347
Federal Aid	295	Student Activism	347
Fiction, Higher Education in	296	Student Life	349
Finances	299	Student Personnel Services	351
Foreign Higher Education	299	Teacher Education	352
Forensics	300	Teaching, General	356
Foundations	301	Theological Education	356
Fraternities	302	Unions	357
General Education	302	Urban University	357
Graduate Education	303	War and Higher Education	358
Health Sciences	304	Women	358
Higher Education, General	308		

AUTHOR INDEX 363

SUBJECT INDEX 403

ABOUT THE COMPILER 433

PREFACE

The richness, diversity, and cultural significance of higher education in American life is reflected in the literature relating to its history. That literature is vast, scattered and not always recorded in the bibliographic sources. One genre of scholarship, research conducted at the graduate level in the form of doctoral dissertations and master's theses, is sometimes neglected by historians and by those in other specialties. Modest citation activity involving dissertations and theses may be attributable to the complexity of searching the dissertation data base, the inconvenience of physical access, and the elusive nature of the master's thesis. Enhanced bibliographic access to the considerable body of scholarship produced by hundreds of institutions and written about nearly 1,000 colleges and universities is the primary goal of this compilation. Divided into two main sections, citations in Part One are arranged alphabetically by state and then subdivided by institution. Topical studies are arrayed under 69 headings in Part Two. The 4,570 citations were derived from sources published through 1986.

Higher Education in American Life was selected as a rather expansive title to underscore the breadth and variety of influences which characterize the history of academic institutions, curricula, athletics, disciplines, and personalities. Although studies of individual institutions, biographies, and topical works comprise the majority of items, titles pertaining to the emergence and contribution of the various associations and professions and to the history of nonacademic, research-level organizations are also included. To be eligible for selection, titles must have an historical orientation and not just recapitulate a contemporary event or summarize data. For this reason, the hundreds of follow-up studies of graduates from scores of colleges and universities are omitted. *Dissertation Abstracts International* should be consulted for such studies and for other titles which describe a particular institution. Additional biographical information is furnished for 400 citation entries, and thematically related studies are extensively collated in the subject index. Order numbers (UMI#) are provided for all doctoral dissertations which are available from University Microfilms, Inc.

Items listed in this volume were identified from several hundred sources. Anyone undertaking a bibliography of dissertations and theses is indebted to Michael M. Reynolds' *Guide to Theses and Dissertations: An International*

Bibliography of Bibliographies (Oryx Press, 1985) and to Dorothy M. Black's *Guide to Lists of Master's Theses* (American Library Association, 1965). In addition to the use of the indexes and online searching in *Dissertation Abstracts International*, more than 250,000 social science and humanities abstracts were examined to augment entries in the subject index. Every issue of *Master's Theses in Education* and *Master's Theses in the Arts and Social Sciences* was reviewed. Dozens of specialized bibliographies yielded many titles. The extraordinary collection of college and university catalogs held by the University of Illinois Library was indispensable. Personal visits to individual libraries invariably produced results. Despite these efforts to provide comprehensive coverage, experience suggests that some titles may have eluded the compiler's net. Readers are encouraged to forward information about newly discovered items.

Since this bibliography was prepared from computerized records, the bibliometric contours of the literature may be explored in more depth. Of the 4,570 entries, 3,290 are doctoral degrees and 1,280 represent master's theses. Seventy-three percent of the authors are male and 27 percent are female. The top degree-granting institutions are Columbia University (254); New York University (146); University of Michigan (135); Ohio State University (124); University of Chicago (100); George Peabody College for Teachers of Vanderbilt University (92); University of Southern California (86); University of Wisconsin (84); University of Pittsburgh (83); and University of North Carolina–Chapel Hill (78).

Five institutions from that enumeration reappear in the list of universities which are most often the subject of graduate research: Columbia University (70); Harvard University (59); University of Michigan (42); University of Chicago (41); University of Iowa (38); Ohio State University (35); University of Wisconsin (32); Yale University (31); University of North Carolina–Chapel Hill (30); and University of Illinois (29). There is relatively little difference in the proportion of studies emanating from public (2,652) and private (1,918) institutions. Biographies, about 11 percent of the total, are overwhelmingly about male subjects (93%). The modal study was written in 1974 by a Columbia University student about that institution and contained 323 pages.

This compilation has been in preparation for 14 intermittent years, all of them pleasurable and rewarding. Professor Jo Ann Fley, University of Illinios, fired my interest in the history of American educational institutions. The writings of Hugh Hawkins, Frederick Rudolph, Laurence Veysey, and many other scholars invigorated the quest. The interlibrary loan staff at the University of Rhode Island is without peer: Vicki Burnett, Roberta Doran, Marie Rudd.

David Carlson patiently introduced me to the microcomputer. Ronald Desjarlais input the data and indexed much of it with consummate skill. Expert secretarial service was rendered by Barbara George, Sheila Felice, and Virginia Sue Cary. Drawing upon the typographical art and the wizardry of the computer, Robert M. Gutchen has crafted a handsome and readable volume.

Arthur P. Young
Kingston, Rhode Island

Higher Education in American Life, 1636–1986

PART ONE

STATES AND TERRITORIES

ALABAMA

GENERAL STUDIES

1   Day, Robert W. Legal and Historical Development of Public Education in Alabama, 1901-1942. Ph.D., University of North Carolina, 1951. 134p.

2   Dickinson, Augustus C. A Study of the Emergence and Development of Community Service Programs in the Seventeen State Junior Colleges of Alabama. Ph.D., Michigan State University, 1972. 213p. UMI# 73-05360.

3   Dotson, James R. The Historical Development of the State Normal School for White Teachers in Alabama. Ed.D., University of Alabama, 1961. 423p. UMI# 61-04236.

4   Draper, Owen H. Contributions of Governor Braxton Bragg Comer to Public Education in Alabama, 1907-1911. Ed.D., University of Alabama, 1970. 257p. UMI# 71-9080.

5   Freeman, David D., Jr. A Study of the Current Status and History of Title III Programs in Alabama's 2-Year Publicly Funded Junior and Community Colleges. Ph.D., University of Alabama, 1980. 220p. UMI# 81-04068.

6   Granade, Samuel R. Higher Education in Ante-Bellum Alabama. Ph.D., Florida State University, 1972. 262p. UMI# 72-21,313.

7   Harper, James C. A Study of Alabama Baptist Higher Education and Fundamentalism, 1890-1930. Ph.D., University of Alabama, 1977. 148p. UMI# 78-19177.

8   Levy, Roland G. Certain Aspects of the Library Movement in the Southern Association of Colleges and Secondary Schools from 1929 to 1941. Master's thesis, University of Alabama, 1941.

9   Lightfoot, Frank K. The History of the Alabama Collegiate Conference, 1959-1972. Ed.D., University of Alabama, 1978. 131p. UMI# 79-05418.

10   Merritt, Judy M. Junior-Senior Colleges Articulation: A Study of Admission Policies and Practices in Four-Year Colleges and Universities in Alabama, 1963-1973. Ph.D., University of Alabama, 1974. 105p. UMI# 75-09924.

11   Norris, Timmerman H. Public Higher Education and the Alabama Legislature, 1901-1960. Ed.D., University of Alabama, 1973. 141p. UMI# 74-9377.

12   Pannell, William P. A Study of the Variables Influencing the Growth of Alabama Public Junior Colleges. Ed.D., Auburn University, 1973. 269p. UMI# 74-00124.

13   Rowland, David A. A Study of the Decline in the Number of Private Junior Colleges in the State of Alabama (1960-1980) with Contributing Factors Leading to the Decline. Ph.D., University of Alabama, 1983. 276p. UMI# 8327138.

14   Salls, Donald J. Historical Study of the Physical Education Programs in the State Teachers Colleges of Alabama in the Twentieth Century. Ed.D., New York University, 1955. 513p. UMI# 00-12233.

15   Sherer, Robert G., Jr. Let Us Make Man: Negro Education in Nineteenth Century Alabama. Ph.D., University of North Carolina, 1970. 543p. UMI# 70-21229.

16   Van Horn, James E. A History of the Alabama Public Junior Colleges (1958-1970). Ed.D., University of Alabama, 1971. 206p. UMI# 72-08475.

AIR UNIVERSITY

17   Tolson, Billy J. A History of Air University (Alabama). Ph.D., University of Oklahoma, 1983. 317p. UMI# 8404553.

ALABAMA STATE UNIVERSITY

18   Caver, Joseph D. From Marion to Montgomery: A History of Alabama State University. Master's thesis, Alabama State University, 1982.

ALABAMA, UNIVERSITY OF

19   Bradley, Adelbert E. An Historical Analysis of the Speech Activities of the Literary Societies at the University of Alabama from 1831 to 1912. Master's thesis, University of Alabama, 1951.

20   Bradley, Bertha J. A Brief History of Teacher Training at the University of Alabama, 1831-1910. Master's thesis, University of Alabama, 1939. 62p.

21   Hoole, Martha D. William Stanley Hoole, Student-Teacher-Librarian-Author. Master's thesis, Florida State University, 1958. 78p. [director of the University of Alabama Library, 1944-1971].

22   Lorance, Robert T. A History of Speech Activities at the University of Alabama, 1831-1865. Master's thesis, University of Alabama, 1951.

23   McCollom, Marvin G. Robert Earl Tidwell and Public Education in Alabama. Ed.D., University of Alabama, 1962. 244p. UMI# 63-3653. [dean of extension and professor of education, University of Alabama, 1930-1954].

24   Pate, James A. Basil Manly and His Administration at the University of Alabama, 1837-1855. Master's thesis, University of Alabama, 1955.

25   Pollingue, Alice B. The History and Evaluation of the Special Education Doctoral Program at the University of Alabama. Ed.D., University of Alabama, 1985. 204p. UMI# 85-19412.

26   Willmon, Jesse C. A Brief Developmental History and Faculty Evaluation of International Programs of the University of Alabama College of Education. Ph.D., University of Alabama, 1975. 229p. UMI# 76-13949.

ALEXANDER CITY STATE JUNIOR COLLEGE

27   Hall, Reginald W. The History of Alexander City State Junior College: Its Beginning, Foundation, and Progress, 1963-80. Ed.D., Auburn University, 1980. 175p. UMI# 81-07118.

AUBURN UNIVERSITY

28   Kerr, Norwood A. The Alabama Agricultural Experiment Station 1871-1982. Ph.D., Auburn University, 1982. 212p. UMI# 8212663.

29   Morrow, Anne H. A History of Drama at Auburn University from 1915 to 1965. Master's thesis, Auburn University, 1966.

30   Ottinger, Richard E. An Evaluation of the Auburn University Program of Professional Preparation in Physical Education, 1955-1961. Ed.D., Auburn University, 1963. 156p. UMI# 64-04173.

31   Rosene, James. A History of Radio Broadcasting at Auburn University, 1912-1961. Master's thesis, Auburn University, 1968.

32   Smith, Earle R. History of the East Alabama Male College Located at Auburn, Alabama. Master's thesis, Alabama Polytechnic Institute, 1932.

33   Sparks, Robbie S. A Survey of the Development of Auburn College, 1870-1935. Master's thesis, Alabama Polytechnic Institute, 1935.

34   Underwood, Harold L. An Evaluation of Certain Aspects of the Auburn University 1970-71 Junior College Leadership Program. Ed.D., Auburn University, 1971. 106p. UMI# 72-02223.

BLOUNT COLLEGE

35   Murphee, Herbert C. A Brief History of Blount College, Blountsville, Alabama. Master's thesis, University of Alabama, 1941.

COMMUNITY COLLEGE OF THE AIR FORCE

36   O'Connor, Thomas J. The Community College of the Air Force: A History and a Comparative Organizational Analysis. Ph.D., University of Denver, 1974. 284p. UMI# 75-1329.

HUNTINGDON COLLEGE

37   Brasfield, Elizabeth B. History of Alabama Central Female College. Master's thesis, University of Alabama, 1944.

JACKSONVILLE STATE UNIVERSITY

38   Wilson, Jettie L. History of the Jacksonville State Teachers' College. Master's thesis, Alabama Polytechnic Institute, 1937.

JUDSON COLLEGE

39   Epting, James B. A Chronological Review of the Development of Judson College, Marion, Alabama, 1838-1978. Ed.D., University of Alabama, 1978. 159p. UMI# 79-05404.

LIVINGSTON UNIVERSITY

40   Miller, George M. Livingston College: Its Educational Challenge During the Post-Reconstruction Era. Master's thesis, Columbia University, 1967. 42p.

SAMFORD UNIVERSITY

41   Fuller, Katherine B. A History of the Cumberland University School of Law from its Beginning in 1847 to Its Acquisition by Howard College in 1961. Master's thesis, Birmingham-Southern College, 1962.

42   Lancaster, James D. Howard College During the Civil War and Reconstruction, 1860-1873. Master's thesis, Samford University, 1974.

43   Pate, James A. The Development of the Instructional Program at Howard College, 1842-1957. Ed.D., University of Alabama, 1959. 608p. UMI# 60-00282.

44   Willoughby, Avalee. History and Philosophical Foundations of Health, Physical Education, Recreation and Athletics at Samford University, 1900-1970. Ed.D., University of Alabama, 1972. 906p. UMI# 73-08018.

SNEAD JUNIOR COLLEGE

45   Millican, Alta. A History of Snead Junior College Prior to 1940. Master's thesis, University of Alabama, 1948.

STILLMAN COLLEGE

46   Sikes, William M. The Historical Development of Stillman Institute. Master's thesis, University of Alabama, 1936.

TROY STATE UNIVERSITY

47   Bannon, Michael F. A History of State Teachers College, Troy, Alabama. Ph.D., George Peabody College for Teachers, 1955. 105p.

TUSKEGEE INSTITUTE

48   Alverson, Roy T. A History of Tuskegee. Master's thesis, Alabama Polytechnic Institute, 1929.

49   Bennett, Henry W. Tuskegee Institute and Its Influence Upon Negro Education. Master's thesis, University of Iowa, 1936.

50   Blackwell, Velma L. A Black Institution Pioneering Adult Education: Tuskegee Institute Past and Present (1881-1973). Ph.D., Florida State University, 1973. 235p. UMI# 74-18,027.

51   Brazil, Doris J. Curriculum Development in Home Economics at Tuskegee Institute Since 1899. Master's thesis, Tuskegee Institute, 1949.

52   Brooks, Thomas E. The Inception and Development of Student Personnel Services at Tuskegee Institute. Ed.D., Indiana University, 1955. 220p. UMI# 00-13213.

53   Citro, Joseph F. Booker T. Washington's Tuskegee Institute: Black School-Community, 1900-1915. Ed.D., University of Rochester, 1973. 573p. UMI# 73-14844.

54   Clem, Lawrence V. The History of Tuskegee Institute. Master's thesis, Kansas State College, 1938.

55   De Loney, Willie L. A History of Tuskegee Institute. Master's thesis, University of Michigan, 1937.

56   Jackson, McArthur. A Historical Study of the Founding and Development of Tuskegee Institute. Ed.D., University of North Carolina at Greensboro, 1983. 117p. UMI# 8315643.

57   Lassiter, Wright L., Jr. A Historical Review and First Year Application of the Nacubo College Planning Cycle by Tuskegee Institute. Ed.D., Auburn University, 1975. 213p. UMI# 76-2602.

58   Malone, Mark H. William Levi Dawson: American Educator. Ph.D., Florida State University, 1981. 182p. UMI# 8209928. [professor of music education, Tuskegee Institute, 1931-1955].

59   Moniba, Harry F. Booker T. Washington, Tuskegee Institute, and Liberia: Institutional and Moral Assistance, 1908-1969. Ph.D., Michigan State University, 1975. 78p. UMI# 76-5607. [president, 1881-1915].

60   Patience, Alice. Booker T. Washington and Higher Education for Negroes. Master's thesis, University of Scranton, 1954. [president, Tuskegee Institute, 1881-1915].

ALASKA

GENERAL STUDIES

61   Jacquot, Louis F. Alaska Natives and Alaska Higher Education, 1960-1972: A Descriptive Study. Ph.D., University of Oregon, 1973. 264p. UMI# 74-06838.

62   Poole, Charles P. Two Centuries of Education in Alaska. Ph.D., Washington University, 1949.

ALASKA METHODIST UNIVERSITY

63   Goldberg, Barbara L.S. University in Crisis: A Case History of Alaska Methodist University. Ed.D., Harvard University, 1978.

SHELDON JACKSON JUNIOR COLLEGE

64   Armstrong, Neal A. Sheldon Jackson Scenes; A Documentary History of Sheldon Jackson Junior College, Sitka, Alaska, 1878-1967. Educational Specialist, George Peabody College for Teachers, 1967.

ARIZONA

GENERAL STUDIES

65   Gladen, Frank H., Jr. An Historical Survey of Public Land and Public Education in the State of Arizona from 1863 to 1960. Ed.D., University of Arizona, 1962. 472p. UMI# 62-04116.

66   Gustafson, Alburn M. A History of Teachers Certification in Arizona. Ph.D., University of Arizona, 1955. 557p. UMI# 00-12361.

67   Hinsdale, Rosejean C. Maricopa (Arizona) Community College District: First Decade of Growth of a Multicollege District, 1962-1972. Ph.D., Arizona State University, 1973. 184p. UMI# 74-1096.

68   Hondrum, Jon O. The Historical Development of Teacher Education in Arizona. Ph.D., Yale University, 1953. 323p.

69   Konopnicki, William S. The Functions of the State Board of Directors for Community Colleges in Arizona from 1960 through 1973. Ed.D., University of Arizona, 1974. 141p. UMI# 74-21,130.

70   Prince, John F. A Biography of E.W. Montgomery During His Superintendency of the Phoenix Union High School and Phoenix College District, 1925-1953. Ph.D., University of Arizona, 1960. 221p. UMI# 60-02383. [president, Phoenix Junior College].

71   Willson, Michael W.The History of the Arizona Music Educators Association and Its Component Organizations.Ed.D., Arizona State University, 1985. 335p. UMI# 8602830.

ARIZONA STATE UNIVERSITY

72   Barry, John H., Jr. The History of the Arizona State Teachers College at Tempe, 1885-1935. Master's thesis, Stanford University, 1943.

73   Frazier, Robert C. The Origin and Development of an Interdisciplinary Humanities Program at Arizona State University. Ph.D., Arizona State University, 1973. 231p. UMI# 73-20444.

74   Hronek, Pamela C. Women and Normal Schools: Tempe Normal, a Case Study, 1885-1925. Ph.D., Arizona State University, 1985. 209p. UMI# 8526939.

ARIZONA, UNIVERSITY OF

75   Riffe, Terri D. A History of Women's Sports at the University of Arizona. Ph.D., University of Arizona, 1986. 253p. UMI# 8613832.

76   Svob, Roberts S. History of Intercollegiate Athletics at the University of Arizona (1897-1948). Master's thesis, University of Arizona, 1951. 211p.

GRAND CANYON COLLEGE

77   Jenke, James M. The Growth and Development of Grand Canyon College. Ph.D., Arizona
State University, 1983. 451p. UMI# 84-10860.

NAVAJO COMMUNITY COLLEGE

78   House, Lloyd L. The Historical Development of Navajo Community College. Ph.D.,
Arizona State University, 1974. 169p. UMI# 74-21532.

NORTHERN ARIZONA UNIVERSITY

79   Hutchinson, Melvin T. History of Arizona State College at Flagstaff from Its Origin through
a Quarter of a Century. Master's thesis, Arizona State University, 1953.

80   O'Leary, Dennis J. A History of Business Education at Northern Arizona University, 1921-
1971. Master's thesis, Northern Arizona University, 1973.

PHOENIX COLLEGE

81   Bulpitt, Mildred B. The Growth and Development of an Evening Division Program at a
Public Junior College: A Case Study. Ed.D., Arizona State University, 1970. 410p. UMI#
70-20666.

82   Heisser, Wilma A. A Historical Survey of the Phoenix College Library; Phoenix, Arizona,
1925-1957. Master's thesis, Arizona State College, 1958. 80p.

ARKANSAS

GENERAL STUDIES

83   Alderson, Willis B. A History of Methodist Higher Education in Arkansas, 1836-1933. Ed.D., University of Arkansas, 1971. 439p. UMI# 71-19528.

84   Bell, James R. A Descriptive Study of the Impact of Title-VI of the Higher Education Act of 1965 on the Growth and Development of Instructional Media Programs in State Supported Colleges and Universities of Arkansas. Ph.D., Southern Illinois University at Carbondale, 1972. 149p. UMI# 73-06185.

85   Cole, Tommie J. The Historical Development of Junior Colleges in Arkansas. Ed.D., University of Arkansas, 1955. 207p. UMI# 00-12406.

86   Dial, Henry C. Historical Development of School Finance in Arkansas, 1819-1970. Ed.D., University of Arkansas, 1971. 555p. UMI# 71-27651.

87   Gilleland, Diane S. Coordination of Arkansas Public Higher Education, 1961-1978. Ph.D., Southern Illinois University at Carbondale, 1982. 311p. UMI# 8229267.

88   Green, Marvin. The Development and Present Status of the Junior College in Arkansas, 1936. Master's thesis, Texas Christian University, 1936. 61p.

89   Hansbrough, Vivian M. A History of Higher Education in Arkansas. Master's thesis, University of Chicago, 1933.

90   Lee, Lurline M. The Origin, Development, and Present Status of Arkansas' Program of Higher Education for Negroes. Ed.D., Michigan State University, 1955. 295p.

ARKANSAS COLLEGE

91   Homesley, John F. History of Speech Education at Arkansas College, 1872-1962. Master's thesis, Louisiana State University, 1965.

ARKANSAS STATE UNIVERSITY

92   Keller, Jim L. History of Athletics at Arkansas State College. Master's thesis, Arkansas State College, 1965. 124p.

93   Smallwood, Frances. The History of Physical Education at Arkansas State College. Master's thesis, Arkansas State College, 1965.

ARKANSAS, UNIVERSITY OF

94   May, John B. The Life of John Lee Buchanan. Ph.D., University of Virginia, 1937. [president, University of Arkansas, 1894-1902; professor of ancient languages, Emory and Henry College, 1856-1878].

95   Steelman, Bobby J. Teacher Education at the University of Arkansas, 1871-1961. Ed.D., University of Arkansas, 1962. 204p. UMI# 62-2283.

ARKANSAS, UNIVERSITY OF (PINE BLUFF)

96   Chambers, Frederick. Historical Study of Arkansas Agricultural, Mechanical and Normal College, 1873-1943. Ed.D., Ball State University, 1970. 442p. UMI# 71-09046.

97   Dalton, Ulysses G., III. The Music Department of the University of Arkansas at Pine Bluff: Its Development and Role in Music Education in the State of Arkansas, 1873-1973. Ph.D., University of Michigan, 1981. 179p. UMI# 8204634.

98   Johnson, Ted D. History of Art Education at the University of Arkansas at Pine Bluff, 1873-1973. Ed.D., University of Oklahoma, 1985. 156p. UMI# 8601145.

COLLEGE OF THE OZARKS

99   Basham, Robert H. A History of Cane Hill College in Arkansas. Ed.D., University of Arkansas, 1969. 408p. UMI# 70-00373.

COMMONWEALTH COLLEGE

100   Waldrip, William L. History and Policies of Commonwealth College. Master's thesis, George Peabody College for Teachers, 1938. 86p.

HARDING UNIVERSITY

101   Mattox, Fount W. A History of the Development of Harding College, 1905-1939. Master's thesis, University of Oklahoma, 1940.

HENDERSON STATE UNIVERSITY

102   Bledsoe, Bennie G. The Origin and Development of Henderson State College. Ph.D., North Texas State University, 1973. 468p. UMI# 74-14807.

103   Hall, John G. Henderson State College: The Methodist Years, 1890-1929. Ph.D., University of Mississippi, 1972. 364p. UMI# 73-01268.

JOHN BROWN UNIVERSITY

104   Williams, Earl R. John Brown University; Its Founder and Its Founding, 1919-1957. Ed.D., University of Arkansas, 1971. 284p. UMI# 71-27670.

PHILANDER SMITH COLLEGE

105   Gibson, De Lois. A Historical Study of Philander Smith College, 1877 to 1969. Ed.D., University of Arkansas, 1972. 200p. UMI# 72-29699.

QUACHITA BAPTIST COLLEGE

106   Arrington, Michael E. A History of Quachita Baptist College: 1886-1933 (Arkansas). Ph.D., University of Arkansas, 1982. 253p. UMI# 83-05141.

SOUTHERN ARKANSAS UNIVERSITY

107   Skelton, Phillip D. A History of Southern Arkansas University from 1909 to 1976. Ed.D., University of Mississippi, 1979. 230p. UMI# 79-21523.

CALIFORNIA

GENERAL STUDIES

108   Armentrout, William W. The Master's Degree in California. Ed.D., Stanford University, 1953. 288p.

109   Beck, Julian. The History of Legal Education in Los Angeles County. Master's thesis, University of Southern California, 1935.

110   Brenner, Johanna. Public Higher Education in 'Post-Industrial Society': The Case of California. Ph.D., University of California-Los Angeles, 1979. 323p. UMI# 7921373.

111   Brown, Sherman L. The History of the Training and Certification of Secondary School Teachers in California. Ph.D., University of California-Berkeley, 1934.

112   Brundin, Robert E. Changing Patterns of Library Service in Five California Junior Colleges, 1907-1967. Ph.D., Stanford University, 1970. 303p. UMI# 71-12866.

113   Budge, Orla C. A Historical Study of the Development of Student Personnel Services in California Church-Related Liberal Arts Colleges. Ph.D., University of Wyoming, 1963.

114   Chu, Buoy-mun. State Policies and Programs in the Certification of Teachers in California from 1890 to 1940. Ph.D., Stanford University, 1945.

115   Clancy, Lynn R., Jr. The History of the American Federation of Teachers in Los Angeles, 1919-1969. Ph.D., University of California-Los Angeles, 1971. 250p. UMI# 71-19449.

116   Comm, Walter. A Historical Analysis of Vocational Education: Land Grant Colleges to California Junior Colleges, 1862-1940. Doctoral dissertation, University of Southern California, 1967. 190p. UMI# 68-01185.

117   Diederich, Alphonsus F. A History of Accreditation, Certification and Teacher Training in Catholic Institutions of Higher Learning in California. Ph.D., University of California-Los Angeles, 1957.

118   Fox, Frederick G. A History of the Extended Day Programs of the Los Angeles Junior Colleges. Ph.D., University of California-Los Angeles, 1960.

119   Froehlich, Edna P. Historical Antecedents to Contemporary Issues in Cooperative Education in the Community Colleges of California. Ed.D., University of California-Berkeley, 1975. 240p. UMI# 76-15071.

120   Gault, Lon A. California College Professors and the State Loyalty Oath, 1950-1968. Ed.D., Stanford University, 1970. 280p. UMI# 70-22220.

121   Gerth, Donald R. The Government of Public Higher Education in California. Ph.D., University of Chicago, 1963.

122   Harney, Paul J. A History of Jesuit Education in American California. Ph.D., University of California-Berkeley, 1944. 184p.

123   Hedges, Jack R. History of the California State Curriculum Commission. Ph.D., University of California-Los Angeles, 1957.

124   Hurley, Rev. Mark J. Church State Relationships in Education in California. Ph.D., Catholic University of America, 1950.

125   Isaac, Amos. The Development and Status of Black and Brown Studies at the Claremont Colleges, the University of California at Riverside, California State College at San Bernardino, San Bernardino Valley Community College, and University College/Johnston College in Redlands, 1967-1972: A Cross Comparison. Ph.D., Claremont Graduate School, 1972. 384p. UMI# 73-07232.

126   Jackson, George F. The History of Seventh-Day Adventist Education in California. Ph.D., University of California-Los Angeles, 1959.

127   Kenneally, Finbar. The Catholic Seminaries of California as Educational Institutions, 1840-1950. Ph.D., University of Toronto, 1956.

128   Kiefer, Elva. The First Thirty Years of Secondary and Higher Education in Los Angeles County, 1865-1895. Master's thesis, University of Southern California, 1930.

129   Long, Emmett T., Jr. The Background and Effects of Major Studies of Public Higher Education in California, 1947-62. Ed.D., University of Southern California, 1965. 220p. UMI# 65- 9981.

130   Maitland, Christine C. The Campaign to Win Bargaining Rights for the California State University Faculty. Ph.D., Claremont Graduate School, 1985. 300p. UMI# 8523004.

131   Mansfield, Henry. Articulation in California: An Historical Study of the Engineering Liaison Committee of the California Articulation Conference, 1947-1972. Ed.D., University of California-Los Angeles, 1974. 177p. UMI# 74-24,597.

132   McDermott, Genevieve A. The California Association of Student Councils: An Historical Study of Student Participation. Ph.D., University of California-Los Angeles, 1971. 296p. UMI# 72-16348.

133   Merlino, Maxine O. A History of the California State Normal Schools: Their Origin, Growth, and Transformation into Teachers Colleges. Ed.D., University of Southern California, 1962. 378p. UMI# 62-03740.

134   Montgomery, Douglas B. Development of Educational Television in the California State Colleges. Master's thesis, San Diego State College, 1966.

135   Nelson, Fred A. California and Nonpublic Higher Education, the Historical and Current Relationships Between the State of California and Independent Colleges and Universities. Ph.D., Stanford University, 1971. 409p. UMI# 71-19734.

136   Paltridge, James G. California's Coordinating Council for Higher Education: A Study of Organizational Growth and Change. Ph.D., University of California-Berkeley, 1966. 281p. UMI# 67-08621.

137   Park, Hun. Study of Public Junior Colleges in California. Master's thesis, Pepperdine College, 1968.

138   Pruitt, Nero. An Historical Analysis of Vocational Education in the California Public Community Colleges, 1940-1970. Ed.D., University of Southern California, 1976.

139   Ranker, Irene K. Major Studies of Higher Education in California, 1962-1974. Ed.D., University of Southern California, 1976.

140   Reichert, Stephen B., Jr. The Four-Year Junior College Movement in California. Ph.D., University of California-Los Angeles, 1957.

141   Reid, Alban E. A History of the California Public Junior College Movement. Ed.D., University of Southern California, 1966. 746p. UMI# 66-07081.

142   Ryan, James E. The History of Manual Training Teacher Education in the California State Normal Schools. Ed.D., University of California-Los Angeles, 1964. 507p. UMI# 64-09636.

143   Seidel, Robert W. Physics Research in California: The Rise of a Leading Sector in American Physics. Ph.D., University of California-Berkeley, 1978. 603p. UMI# 7904599.

144   Shipp, Frederic T. The Junior College in Its Relationship to the State College in California. Ph.D., Stanford University, 1949.

145   Stanton, Charles M. Student Activism on Three California Campuses During the Years 1930-1940 and 1955-1965. Ph.D., Stanford University, 1967. 344p. UMI# 67-17,510.

146   Thames, Anna-Marie. Women's Studies in Three Institutions of Higher Education in California. Ph.D., University of California- Los Angeles, 1975. 219p. UMI# 75-27,009.

147   Toto, Charles. A History of Education in California 1800-1850. Ph.D., University of California-Berkeley, 1967. 157p. UMI# 67-11670.

148   Vokes, Lee S. A Historical Study of the California Junior College State Athletic Committee: Years 1946-1972. Ph.D., United States International University, 1973. 345p. UMI# 73-22695.

149   Warner, Gordon. A History of the Continuation Education Program in California. Ph.D., University of California-Berkeley, 1954.

150   Welch, Frank G. Freedom of Teaching in California, 1920-1930. Ed.D., University of California-Los Angeles, 1965. 394p. UMI# 65-04707.

151   Zusman, Ami. The Legislature and the University: Conflict in California Higher Education. Ph.D., University of California-Berkeley, 1983. 362p. UMI# 8329110.

AZUSA PACIFIC COLLEGE

152   Brackett, Charles H. The History of Azusa College and the Friends, 1900-1965. Master's thesis, University of Southern California, 1967. 152p.

BAKERSFIELD COLLEGE

153   Harkins, Richard H. The Opportunity Program at Bakersfield College, 1956-1968: A Study Concerning Its Values and Shortcomings as Viewed by the Involved Students and Staff. Ed.D., University of California-Los Angeles, 1970. 264p. UMI# 71-13999.

BERKELEY, UNIVERSITY OF CALIFORNIA

154   Armistead, Timothy W. The Criminalization of Political Protest in Berkeley, 1960-1970. Doctor of Criminology, University of California-Berkeley, 1977. 796p. UMI# 7731242.

155   Austin, Florence O. The History of the Curriculum of the University of California Medical School. Master's thesis, University of California-Berkeley, 1929.

156   Conmy, Peter T. History of the Entrance Requirements of the Liberal Arts Colleges of the University of California, 1860-1927. Master's thesis, University of California-Berkeley, 1928.

157   Elsea, Janet G. The Rhetoric of an Academic President: Clark Kerr, 1958-1964. Ph.D., University of Iowa, 1972. 185p. UMI# 72-17,552. [president, University of California, 1958-1967].

158   Epstein, Sandra P. Law at Berkeley: The History of Boalt Hall. Ph.D., University of California-Berkeley, 1979. 526p. UMI# 80-00334.

159   Fiske, Emmett P. The College and Its Constituency: Rural and Community Development at the University of California, 1875-1978. Ph.D., University of California-Davis, 1979. 490p. UMI# 8016755.

160   Foley, Patrick J. The Antecedents and Early Development of the University of California, 1849-1875. Ph.D., University of California-Berkeley, 1970. 224p. UMI# 71-00772.

161   Gardner, David P. The University of California Loyalty Oath Controversy, 1949-1952. Ph.D., University of California-Berkeley, 1966. 420p. UMI# 68-191.

162   Heirich, Max A. Demonstration at Berkeley: Collective Behavior During the Free Speech Movement of 1964-1965. Ph.D., University of California-Berkeley, 1967. 744p. UMI# 68-00078.

163   Johnson, Loaz W. Evolution of the 'Examination in Subject A' at the University of California. Ph.D., University of California-Berkeley, 1938.

164   King, Kermit C. The Historical Development of University Extension at the University of California, with Particular Reference to Its Organization in the Southern Area. Ph.D., University of California-Los Angeles, 1947. 271p.

165   Murdoch, M.C. Historical Survey of Some Phases of Agricultural Research in the University of California. Master's thesis, University of California-Berkeley, 1944.

166   Muto, Albert H. The University of California Press, 1893-1933. Ph.D., University of California-Berkeley, 1976. 180p. UMI# 77-04550.

167   Oullette, Vernon A. Daniel Coit Gilman's Administration of the University of California. Ph.D., Stanford University, 1952. [president, 1872-1875].

168   Paul, Roschelle Z. Song Tradition of the University of California at Berkeley. Master's thesis, University of California-Berkeley, 1945.

169   Peterson, Kenneth G. The History of the University of California Library at Berkeley, 1900-1945. Ph.D., University of California-Berkeley, 1968. 398p. UMI# 69-03673.

170   Rose, Doreen D. A Study of the Leadership of Clark Kerr and Samuel Hayakawa in the Resolution of Campus Conflict. Ed.D., University of Southern California, 1977.

171   Rowland, James. Un-American Activities at the University of California: The Burns Committee and Clark Kerr, 1952-1967. Master's thesis, San Francisco State University, 1979. [president, 1958-1967].

172   Smith, Dora. History of the University of California Library to 1900. Master's thesis, University of California-Berkeley, 1930.

173   Spindt, Herman A. A History of the Relations of the University of California, 1872-1945. Ph.D., University of California-Berkeley, 1946. 430p.

174   Stuart, Mary C. Clark Kerr: Biography of an Action Intellectual. Ph.D., University of Michigan, 1980. 388p. UMI# 8017376. [president, University of California, 1958-1967].

175   Van Houten, Peter S. The Development of the Constitutional Provisions Pertaining to the University of California in the California Constitutional Convention of 1878-79. Ph.D., University of California-Berkeley, 1973.

176   Walsh, James P. Regent Peter C. Yorke and the University of California, 1900-1912. Ph.D., University of California-Berkeley, 1970. 303p. UMI# 71-00862. [regent, 1903-1913].

177   Wardrip, Mark A. A Western Portal of Culture: The Hearst Greek Theatre of the University of California, 1903. Ph.D., University of California-Berkeley, 1984. 409p. UMI# 85-13034.

178   Watson, James E. A History of Political Science at the University of California, 1875-1960. Ph.D., University of California-Berkeley, 1961.

179   Wedertz, Gilbert C. History of the Origin and Administration of Public Endowments of the University of California. Master's thesis, University of California-Berkeley, 1928. 149p.

CALIFORNIA INSTITUTE OF TECHNOLOGY

180   Gates, Charlynne M.L. The History and Development of the California Institute of Technology. Master's thesis, University of Southern California, 1935.

CALIFORNIA MARITIME ACADEMY

181   McDermott, Louis M. The History of the Deck Curriculum, California Maritime Academy, 1929-1983. Ed.D., University of San Francisco, 1984. 237p. UMI# 8509202.

CALIFORNIA POLYTECHNIC STATE UNIVERSITY

182   Riddell, Steven G. A History of California Polytechnic State University: 1952-1979. Ed.D., Brigham Young University, 1985. 171p. UMI# 8510708.

183   Smith, Morris E. A History of California State Polytechnic College: The First Fifty Years, 1901-1951. Ed.D., University of Oregon, 1958. 299p. UMI# 58-03949.

CALIFORNIA STATE COLLEGE, SAN BERNARDINO

184   Urata, James H. The Development of the California State College at San Bernardino. Master's thesis, San Diego State College, 1967.

CALIFORNIA STATE UNIVERSITY, CHICO

185   Best, Betty J. A History of the Department of Physical Education for Women at Chico State College. Master's thesis, Chico State College, 1968.

186   Calkins, Keith D. The History of Varsity Track at Chico State College. Master's thesis, Chico State College, 1962.

187   Heikkinen, Karena D. A History of the Laboratory School at Chico State College, 1890-1964. Master's thesis, Chico State College, 1965.

188   Moore, Gail E. History of Chico State College. Master's thesis, Oregon State College, 1940.

189   Morris, William M. A History of Baseball at Chico State College, 1896-1963. Master's thesis, Chico State College, 1964.

190   Pihl, Cedric H. A Dramatized History of Chico State College. Master's thesis, Chico State College, 1953.

191   Small, Herbert G. History of Industrial Arts at Chico State College. Master's thesis, Chico State College, 1965.

192   Swartz, Jack H. The First Fifty Years of Varsity Basketball at Chico State College. Master's thesis, Chico State College, 1964.

CALIFORNIA STATE UNIVERSITY, FRESNO

193   Hogan, Fred P. The History of Fresno State Teachers College. Master's thesis, Stanford University, 1930.

194   Keller, Jean. History of Women's Physical Education at Fresno State College, 1911-1970. Master's thesis, California State University at Fresno, 1973.

195   Rowland, Eugenia. Origin and Development of Fresno State College. Ph.D., University of California-Berkeley, 1949. 229p.

CALIFORNIA STATE UNIVERSITY, HAYWARD

196   Williams, John A. A History of the Early Development of California State University,

Hayward, with Emphasis on the Selection of the Site. Master's thesis, California State University at Hayward, 1973.

CALIFORNIA STATE UNIVERSITY, NORTHRIDGE

197   Schneider, Lydia E. The Growth and Development of a California State College. Master's thesis, California State University at Northridge, 1976.

CALIFORNIA STATE UNIVERSITY, SAN DIEGO

198   Boothe, Bradlee J. A History of Baseball at San Diego State College from 1924 to 1971. Master's thesis, San Diego State University, 1971.

199   Cates, David A. A History of Golf at California State University, San Diego, from 1936-1972. Master's thesis, San Diego State University, 1973.

200   Gilliland, John H. The Department of Music of San Diego State College from 1898 to 1972. Master's thesis, San Diego State College, 1972. 101p.

201   Golden, Donna L. History of Theater at San Diego State College from 1926 to 1970. Master's thesis, San Diego State University, 1971.

202   Johnson, Lee A. A History of San Diego State College Track and Field from 1922 to 1966. Master's thesis, San Diego State University, 1968.

203   Nelson, Darryl P. A History of San Diego State College Football from 1921-1968. Master's thesis, San Diego State College, 1970.

204   Scott, Frank L. A Study of the Origin of Recreation Activities of Male Students at San Diego State College. Ph.D., University of Michigan, 1957. 284p. UMI# 58-02012.

205   Skirvin, Emmett E., Jr. A History of the Development of Industrial Arts at San Diego State College from 1902 to 1953. Master's thesis, San Diego State College, 1953.

206   Verner, William S. A History of Tennis at San Diego State University from 1921 to 1973. Master's thesis, San Diego State University, 1973.

CALIFORNIA STATE UNIVERSITY, SAN FRANCISCO

207   Danielson, Melvin D. Origin and Development of Teacher Training in San Francisco State College. Ph.D., University of California-Berkeley, 1960.

208   Hekymara, Kuregiy. The Third World Movement and Its History in the San Francisco State College Strike of 1968-1969. Ph.D., University of California-Berkeley, 1972.

209   Perea, Jacob E. Ethnic Studies in Transition: A Case Study. Ed.D., University of California-Berkeley, 1985. 180p. UMI# 8524858.

210   Persico, Connell F. The Student Movement and Institutional Disruption: An Historical Case Study of San Francisco State College. Ph.D., Stanford University, 1974. 179p. UMI# 74-20223.

211   Roper, Dwight D. Founders and Renovators: Presidents During the Beginning and

Change of a California State College. Ph.D., Stanford University, 1976. 212p. UMI# 76-26067.

CHAPMAN COLLEGE

212   Clover, Haworth A. An Historical Study of Hesperian College, Woodland, California from 1861 to 1896. Master's thesis, College of the Pacific, 1960. 246p.

213   Morris, Marilyn L. A History of the Chapman College Residence Education Center System, 1958-1982. Ph.D., University of Akron, 1984. 304p. UMI# 84-04650.

CHRIST COLLEGE, IRVINE

214   Halm, Dennis R. A History of Christ College Irvine—The First Thirty Years. Ed.D., Pepperdine University, 1986. 289p. UMI# 8616068.

CLAREMONT UNIVERSITY CENTER AND GRADUATE SCHOOL

215   Laudine, Sister Mary. The Honnold Library of Claremont College: Its History and Services 1952-1961. Master's thesis, Immaculate Heart College, 1961. 66p.

COLLEGE OF SAN MATEO

216   Isaacs, Michael. A History of Broadcasting at the College of San Mateo, 1971-1979. Master's thesis, San Francisco State University, 1980.

COLLEGE OF THE DESERT

217   Cheeves, Lyndell D. The Founding of College of the Desert, 1958-1963. Ed.D., University of California-Los Angeles, 1971. 228p. UMI# 72-13592.

EL CAMINO COLLEGE

218   Muck, Steven J. The History of El Camino College, 1946-1966. Ed.D., University of California-Los Angeles, 1971. 358p. UMI# 72-02871.

HUMBOLDT STATE UNIVERSITY

219   Davies, Sarah M. A History of Humboldt State College. Master's thesis, Stanford University, 1947.

220   Ferguson, Janet S. The Development of the Women's Athletic Program at Humboldt State University, 1925-1975. Master's thesis, California State University at Arcata, 1977.

LOMA LINDA UNIVERSITY

221   Otto, Leroy W. An Historical Analysis of the Origin and Development of the College of Medical Evangelists. Ed.D., University of Southern California, 1962. 400p. UMI# 62-06077.

LOMA LINDA UNIVERSITY, LASIERRA

222   Bohl, Jacqueline. The History of Physical Education at Loma Linda University: Lasierra Campus from 1927 to 1981. Master's thesis, Loma Linda University, 1983.

223   Bower, Donald G. Fifty Years of Student Employment at Loma Linda University, Lasierra Campus. Ed.D., University of California-Los Angeles, 1974. 308 p. UMI# 75-14051.

LOS ANGELES CITY COLLEGE

224   Cox, James N. The Urban Community College: A Case Study of Los Angeles City College from 1929 to 1970. Ed.D., University of California-Los Angeles, 1971. 584p. UMI# 72-02794.

LOS ANGELES JUNIOR COLLEGE

225   McAlmon, Victoria M. The Development of Occupational Courses in the Los Angeles Junior College. Master's thesis, University of Southern California, 1931. 88p.

LOS ANGELES PIERCE COLLEGE

226   McHargue, Robert M. The Early History of Los Angeles Pierce College: Its Genesis, Foundation and Transition, 1943-1956. Ed.D., University of California-Los Angeles, 1965. 320p. UMI# 65-04704.

LOS ANGELES SOUTHWEST COLLEGE

227   Wainwright, Frank N. A History of the Early Development of an Urban Community College: The Story of Los Angeles Southwest College: 1967-74. Ed.D., University of Southern California, 1978.

LOS ANGELES TRADE TECHNICAL COLLEGE

228   Lawson, Allen L. Los Angeles Trade-Technical College: 1925-1950. Ed.D., University of California-Los Angeles, 1976. 311p. UMI# 76-28573.

LOS ANGELES, UNIVERSITY OF CALIFORNIA

229   Epler, Stephen M. A History of the University of California Los Angeles (UCLA) Junior College Leadership Program, 1960-1971. Ed.D., University of California-Los Angeles, 1971. 631p. UMI# 72-11883.

230   Florell, David M. Origin and History of the School of Education, University of California, Los Angeles. Ph.D., University of California-Los Angeles, 1946. 430p.

231   Huntley, Richard T. Events and Issues of the Angela Davis Dismissal. Ed.D., University of Southern California, 1976. [professor of philosophy, University of California, Los Angeles].

232   Johnson, John L. Henry Russell Sanders: Coach and Teacher. Ed.D., University of California-Los Angeles, 1965. 311p. UMI# 66-337. [football coach, University of California, Los Angeles, 1949-1958; Vanderbilt University, 1940-1948].

233   Kruszynski, Eugene S. Ernest Carroll Moore, Educational Historian. Ed.D., University of

California-Los Angeles, 1963. 267p. UMI# 64-03057. [University of California at Los Angeles, 1917-1941].

234   La Bougty, High O. Edwin Augustus Lee: Portrait of an Educator. Ph.D., University of California-Los Angeles, 1961. [professor of education and dean, University of California, Los Angeles, 1940-1957].

235   Malnekoff, Jon L. The First Fifty Years: A History of the Department of Physical Education of the University of California, Los Angeles, 1915-1965. Master's thesis, University of California-Los Angeles, 1970. 144p.

236   Nystrom, Richard K. UCLA: An Interpretation Considering Architecture and Site. Ph.D., University of California-Los Angeles, 1968. 309p. UMI# 69-03931.

237   Parker, Craig B. John Vincent (1902-1977): An Alabama Composer's Odyssey. Ph.D., University of California-Los Angeles, 1981. 510p. UMI# 8121029. [professor of music, University of California, Los Angeles, 1946-1969].

238   Phelan, Arthur E. The Administration of the University Elementary School of the University of California at Los Angeles, 1882-1957. Ph.D., University of California-Los Angeles, 1961.

239   Treacy, Robert E. Progressivism and Corinne Seeds: UCLA and the University Elementary School. Ph.D., University of Wisconsin, 1972. 460p. UMI# 72-23340. [principal, 1925-1957].

MIRACOSTA COLLEGE

240   Jorgensen, Sharalee C. Miracosta College: The First Fifty Years. Ed.D., University of San Diego, 1985. 373p. UMI# 85-051527.

MODESTO JUNIOR COLLEGE

241   Luebke, William R., Jr. The Cultural Impact of a Public Community College on Its Community: Modesto Junior College. Ed.D., University of California-Berkeley, 1985. 180p. UMI# 8524857.

242   McClarty, Edward L. Development of Radio Station KRJC at Modesto Junior College. Master's thesis, College of the Pacific, 1952.

PACIFIC, UNIVERSITY OF THE

243   Burns, Robert E. The First Half-Century of the College of the Pacific. Master's thesis, College of the Pacific, 1946.

244   Cooper, Winnie M. A History of the College of the Pacific Speech and Hearing Clinic. Master's thesis, College of the Pacific, 1953.

245   Hogin, James E. Volume I: The Life and Educational Contributions of James William Harris. Volume II: Appendices. Ed.D., University of the Pacific, 1961. 421p. UMI# 62-2427. [dean of education, University of the Pacific, 1924-1944].

PACIFIC UNION COLLEGE

246   Hoffman, Philip G. History of Pacific Union College. Master's thesis, University of Southern California, 1942.

PALOMAR COLLEGE

247   Stevens, Eugene H., Jr. A History of the Administrative Problems of Palomar College. Master's thesis, San Diego State College, 1953.

PASADENA JUNIOR COLLEGE

248   Pfeiffer, Clyde E. A History of Pasadena Junior College. Master's thesis, Occidental College, 1941. 218p.

POINT LOMA NAZARENE COLLEGE

249   Brickley, Donald P. The Life and Work of Phineas F. Bresee. Ph.D., University of Pittsburgh, 1957. 224p. UMI# 00-24734. [founder and president, Point Loma Nazarene College, 1902-1911].

POMONA COLLEGE

250   Sage, George H. A History of Physical Education at Pomona College (1880-1960). Ed.D., University of California-Los Angeles, 1963. 328p. UMI# 63-03875.

251   Ward, Natalie J.S. James Arnold Blaisdell: A Study of His Professional Career. Ph.D., University of California-Los Angeles, 1961. [president, Pomona College, 1910-1926; president, Claremont University Center and Claremont Graduate School, 1926-1936].

REDLANDS, UNIVERSITY OF

252   Sillars, Malcolm S. A History of Intercollegiate Debate at the University of Redlands. Master's thesis, University of Redlands, 1949.

RIO HONDO COLLEGE

253   Huffman, Harold T., Jr. The Early History of Rio Hondo College. Ed.D., Pepperdine University, 1981. 203p. UMI# 8207688.

SACRAMENTO JUNIOR COLLEGE

254   Evans, James M. The Organization and Promotion of Sacramento Junior College, 1916-1940. Ph.D., University of Southern California, 1974. 432p. UMI# 74-23582.

SACRAMENTO STATE COLLEGE

255   Conway, Jerry D. A Brief History of Intercollegiate Football at Sacramento State College from the Period 1954-1963. Master's thesis, Sacramento State College, 1965. 108p.

SAN DIEGO, UNIVERSITY OF

256   Briscoe, Georgia K. Visions and Decisions: History of the University of San Diego School of Law. Master's thesis, University of California-San Diego, 1985.

257   Flaherty, Mary B. A Study of the Merger of Two Academic Institutions. Master's thesis, San Diego State University, 1974.

SAN LUIS OBISPO JUNIOR COLLEGE

258   Jones, Ivan L., Jr. San Luis Obispo Junior College: Demise and Rebirth. Ed.D., University of California-Los Angeles, 1967. 194p. UMI# 67-17372.

SANTA BARBARA, UNIVERSITY OF CALIFORNIA

259   Ellenwood, Theodore S. A Study of the Anna S.C. Blake Manual Training School. Ph.D., University of California-Los Angeles, 1960.

260   Friedman, Henry A. An Analytical History of the Intercollegiate Athletic Administration at the University of California, Santa Barbara. Master's thesis, University of California-Santa Barbara, 1966.

261   McIlwain, James L. A History of Intercollegiate Track and Field Athletics at Santa Barbara State College. Master's thesis, University of California-Santa Barbara, 1965. 202p.

262   O'Reilly, Edmund P. A History of Santa Barbara State Teachers' College. Master's thesis, Stanford University, 1928.

SANTA CLARA, UNIVERSITY OF

263   McKevitt, Gerald. The History of Santa Clara College, a Study of Jesuit Education in California, 1851-1912. Ph.D., University of California-Los Angeles, 1972. 372p. UMI# 72-25811.

SEVEN SEAS, UNIVERSITY OF THE

264   Youngberg, Elizabeth M.The University of the Seven Seas: A Study of the Development of the University of the Seven Seas. Master's thesis, Fresno State College, 1967.

SOUTHERN CALIFORNIA, UNIVERSITY OF

265   Cather, George D. The Trend of Research Studies in Music Education at the University of Southern California, 1924-1949. Master's thesis, University of Southern California, 1950.

266   Gates, Samuel E. A History of the University of Southern California, 1900-1928. Master's thesis, University of Southern California, 1929. 303p.

267   Gay, Leslie F., Jr. History of the University of Southern California. Master's thesis, University of Southern California, 1910. 301p.

268   Hashem, Erfan A. Development of the University Neighborhood: The University of Southern California. Master's thesis, University of Southern California, 1954. 177p.

269   Hungerford, Curtiss R. A Study in University Administrative Leadership: Rufus B. Kleins-mid and the University of Southern California, 1921 to 1935. Ph.D., University of Southern California, 1967. 314p. UMI# 67-17678. [president, 1921-1947].

270   Levitt, Leon. A History to 1953 of the School of Education of the University of Southern California. Ed.D., University of Southern California, 1970. 523p. UMI# 70-23168.

271   Lindgren, Frank E. A Content Analysis of Research Studies in Vocal Music Education at the University of Southern California from 1930-1955, with a View of Establishing Areas of Needful Research. Master's thesis, University of Southern California, 1956.

272   Paxman, Marlys E. The Development of Medical Education at the University of Southern California. Master's thesis, University of Southern California, 1966.

273   Robinson, Giles. An Historical Study of Dramatic Activities at the University of Southern California (1880-1957). Master's thesis, University of Southern California, 1957. 135p.

274   Smart, Ronald E. Ralph E. Rush: A Biography. Doctor of Music Arts, University of South-ern California, 1974. 317p. UMI# 74-14,475. [professor of music and education, University of Southern California, 1957-1965].

275   Turner, Eula D. Eleanor Metheny: Teacher-Scholar. Ph.D., University of Southern Califor-nia, 1974. 166p. UMI# 74-11,715. [professor of physical education, University of Southern California].

STANFORD UNIVERSITY

276   Bienvenu, Harold J. The Educational Career of Grayson Neikirk Kefauver. Ed.D., Stanford University, 1956. 299p. UMI# 00-16003. [dean of education, Stanford University, 1933-1943].

277   Brazee, Annie L. A History of the Theatre at Stanford University (1891-1906). Master's thesis, Stanford University, 1952.

278   Buck, Janet C. David Starr Jordan: His Contribution to American Education. Master's thesis, Smith College, 1935. [president, Stanford University, 1891-1913].

279   Cashel, Patricia M. History and Functions of the Women's Athletic Association at Stan-ford. Master's thesis, Stanford University, 1946.

280   Henderson, Adin D. The Life of Ellwood Paterson Cubberley. Ph.D., Stanford University, 1953. 323p. [professor of education, Stanford University, 1906-1933; dean, 1917-1933].

281   Houghton, Laura L. David Starr Jordan as an Educator. Master's thesis, Stanford Univer-sity, 1936. [president, Stanford University, 1891-1913].

282   Jones, Albert H. The Relation of Historical Thought to Educational Thought as Illustrated by the Works of Ellwood P. Cubberley. Ph.D., Ohio State University, 1966. 351p. UMI# 67-06329. [dean of education, Stanford University, 1917-1933].

283   Kerr, James W. A History of the Stanford University Curriculum. Master's thesis, Stanford University, 1927.

284   Korff, J. Michael. Student Control and University Government at Stanford: The Evolving Student University Relationship. Ph.D., Stanford University, 1975. 255p. UMI# 75-25-558.

285   Leland, Richard W. Stanford University School of Education Under Dean Grayson Neikirk Kefauver. Master's thesis, Stanford University, 1952. [dean, 1933-1943].

286   Medeiros, Frank A. The Sterling Years at Stanford: A Study in the Dynamics of Institutional Change. Ph.D., Stanford University, 1979. 287p. UMI# 7917259. [instructor in history, 1935-1937].

287   Paul, Gary N. The Development of the Hoover Institution on War, Revolution and Peace Library, 1919-1944. Doctor of Library Service, University of California-Berkeley, 1974. 274p. UMI# 74-19,597.

288   Schaap, Eleanor H. The Educational Significance of the Life and Works of David Starr Jordan. Master's thesis, University of Southern California, 1934. [president, Stanford University, 1891-1913].

289   Schmidt, Inge. Stanford's Developing Theatre, 1906-1920. Master's thesis, Stanford University, 1955.

290   Smith, William S. A Rhetorical Criticism of David Starr Jordan's Addresses on Education. Ph.D., Stanford University, 1953. 289p. UMI# 4687. [president, Stanford University, 1891-1913].

291   Stavely, Martha R. A History of Stanford's Program in Education for Women During the Last Fifty Years. Ph.D., Stanford University, 1945. 429p.

292   Trindale, Armando D. Roman Catholic Worship at Stanford University, 1891-1971. Ph.D., Stanford University, 1971. 387p. UMI# 72-06012.

293   Xenakis, William A. The Bruce Franklin Issue: The Dismissal of a Tenured Professor from a Private University and Its Implications Upon Academic Freedom. Ed.D., University of Southern California, 1982.

294   Yarcho, Yvonne V. The Stanford University Theatre: From the Dramatic Council to the Division of Speech and Drama, 1934-1940. Master's thesis, Stanford University, 1959.

295   Young, Alfred C. A History of the Administration of Stanford University. Master's thesis, Stanford University, 1929.

VENTURA COLLEGE

296   Howe, Catherine P. A History of Ventura College, 1925-1958. Master's thesis, University of Southern California, 1958.

WEST COAST CHRISTIAN COLLEGE

297   Smith, Henry J. A History of West Coast Bible College. Master's thesis, Fresno State College, 1971.

WEST LOS ANGELES COLLEGE

298   Horn, Larry. History of West Los Angeles College. Ph.D., University of Southern California, 1971. 722p. UMI# 71-16415.

WESTMONT COLLEGE

299   Hillegas, Lyle C. A History of Westmont College. Ph.D., Dallas Theological Seminary, 1964.

WHITTIER COLLEGE

300   Feeler, William. History of Whittier College. Master's thesis, University of Southern California, 1919. 78p.

COLORADO

GENERAL STUDIES

301   Anderson, William H. A History of the Organization and Operation of Public Junior Colleges in Colorado, with an Analysis of the Laws Governing Them. Master's thesis, University of Denver, 1938. 91p.

302   Gerber, Daniel R. The Public Junior College Movement in Colorado: A History, 1920-1967. Ph.D., University of Denver, 1969. 226p. UMI# 70-14802.

303   Kain, Margaret N. An Evolutionary History of the Colorado Commission for Higher Education with Emphasis on the Conflict in Coordination Between the Commission and Selected Public Four-Year Institutions and State Agencies. Ph.D., University of Maryland, 1980. 332p. UMI# 81-16490.

304   Nelson, David P. A Study of the Inter-Institutional Coordination of Public Higher Education in Colorado, 1937-1965. Ph.D., University of Denver, 1969. 332p. UMI# 70-11928.

ADAMS STATE COLLEGE

305   Williams, Robert L. Development of Intercollegiate Athletics at Adams State College. Master's thesis, Adams State College, 1957.

COLORADO COLLEGE

306   Buckley, Grace L. The History of Colorado College, 1874-1904. Master's thesis, Colorado College, 1935.

307   Westbay, William W. The Historical Development of Forestry Education at Colorado College. Master's thesis, Colorado College, 1925.

COLORADO, UNIVERSITY OF

308   Brier, David H. Bands at the University of Colorado: An Historical Review, 1908-1978. Ph.D., University of Colorado at Boulder, 1983. 243p. UMI# 8317641.

309   Davis, William E. A History of the University of Colorado, 1861-1963. Ed.D., University of Colorado, 1963. 1,889p. UMI# 64-04352.

310   Klausman, Grant J. A History of the University of Colorado College of Music, 1877-1951. Ph.D., University of Colorado, 1967. 270p. UMI# 68-02659.

311   Low, Mortimer E. A History of the Bureau of Audio-Visual Instruction at the University of Colorado, 1923 to 1973. Ph.D., University of Colorado, 1973. 349p. UMI# 73-32568.

312   Riddles, Willard P. The Doctoral Program in Education at the University of Colorado, 1941-1956. Ed.D., University of Colorado, 1959. 270p. UMI# 60-01074.

313   Smith, Glenn R. The Black Studies Program at the University of Colorado (Boulder and Denver Campuses) 1968-1973: Development, Change and Assessment. Ph.D., University of Colorado, 1974. 133p. UMI# 75-13467.

314   Steckman, Mildred C. Harl Roy Douglass: A Biography. Ed.D., University of Colorado, 1970. 353p. UMI# 71-05934. [director of the college of education, University of Colorado, 1940-1958].

COLORADO WOMEN'S COLLEGE

315   Dodge, Norman B. Democracy and the Education of Women: The Colorado Woman's College Story. Ph.D., Columbia University, 1960.

DENVER, UNIVERSITY OF

316   Angel, Donald E. A History of the University of Denver, 1880-1900. Master's thesis, University of Denver, 1961. 187p.

317   Beasley, Joan H. The University of Denver Defines Its Purpose: A History of the Junior College and the Community College, 1940 to 1961. Ph.D., University of Denver, 1985. 262p. UMI# 8606001.

318   Connor, Donald B. The University of Denver: The Buchtel Chancellorship, 1900-1920. Master's thesis, University of Denver, 1961. 115p.

319   Dunleavy, Jeannette J. Early History of Colorado Seminary and the University of Denver. Master's thesis, University of Denver, 1935. 345p.

320   Holland, Ralph T. A Study of Objectives, the Faculty, and the Curriculum of the College of Arts and Science at the University of Denver, as Relating to a Liberal Education, from the Founding of the College until 1965. Ph.D., Denver University of, 1970. 289p. UMI# 70-26395.

321   Kelsey, Harry E., Jr. John Evans. Ph.D., University of Denver, 1965. 474p. UMI# 65-09760. [helped found the University of Denver].

322   Mayer, Gerard E. A History of the University of Denver: 1920-1940. Master's thesis, University of Denver, 1963. 134p.

NORTHERN COLORADO, UNIVERSITY OF

323   Fillinger, Louis C. A History of Educational Field Experiences at the University of Northern Colorado. Ed.D., University of Northern Colorado, 1972. 157p. UMI# 72-23801.

324   Hartman, William F. The History of Colorado State College of Education: The Normal School Period, 1890-1911. Ed.D., Colorado State University, 1951. 213p. UMI# 00-03182.

325   Johnson, Francis M. A History of the Industrial Arts of Colorado State College of Education, 1891-1942. Master's thesis, Colorado State College of Education, 1942.

326   Ogle, Merle F. A History of the Athletic Department of Colorado State College of Education. Master's thesis, Colorado State College of Education, 1936.

327   Pope, Linda T. An Historical Study of the Center for Special and Advanced Programs at the University of Northern Colorado. Ed.D., University of Northern Colorado, 1984. 83p. UMI# 8408153.

328   Travers, Harold E. A History of the Colorado State College of Education, 1890-1935. Master's thesis, Stanford University, 1936.

TRINIDAD STATE JUNIOR COLLEGE

329   Denbo, Philip G. The History of Trinidad State Junior College, 1925-1948. Master's thesis, Western State College of Colorado, 1948.

330   Ross, William R. The History of the Trinidad State Junior College from 1869 to 1939. Ph.D., University of Northern Colorado, 1940. 243p. UMI# 00-00294.

UNITED STATES AIR FORCE ACADEMY

331   Atkins, Jerome A. The United States Air Force Academic Preparatory School: A Historical Perspective and an Analysis of the Performance of Its Graduates. Ed.D., Auburn University, 1979. 159p. UMI# 79-13696.

332   Miller, Edward A., Jr. The Founding of the Air Force Academy: An Administrative and Legislative History. Ph.D., University of Denver, 1969. 482p. UMI# 70-16837.

333   Sands, Gene C. An Administrative History of the U.S. Air Force Academy, 1954-1979. Ed.D., Catholic University of America, 1982. 137p. UMI# 82-21489.

334   Shelburne, James C. Factors Leading to the Establishment of the Air University. Ph.D., University of Chicago, 1954.

335   Spiro, Bernard. Origin and Development of the United States Air Force Academy Curriculum. Master's thesis, University of Maryland, 1960.

336   Wallisch, William J., Jr. The Admission and Integration of Women into the United States Air Force Academy. Ed.D., University of Southern California, 1977.

337   Woodyard, William T. A Historical Study of the Development of the Academic Curriculum of the United States Air Force Academy. Ph.D., University of Denver, 1965. 335p. UMI# 65-09763.

CONNECTICUT

GENERAL STUDIES

338   Averill, Donald C. The Responsibility of the Connecticut State Board of Education for the Education of Teachers in the State from 1865 to 1965. Ph.D., University of Connecticut, 1966. 224p. UMI# 67-4520.

339   Barclay, Kenneth B. The Origins of the Community College Movement in Connecticut, 1946-1961. Ph.D., Kent State University, 1975. 209p. UMI# 76-04910.

340   Bomhoff, Carl B. The Development of State Support of Teacher Education in Connecticut's School-Reform Movement, 1825-1850. (Volumes I-III). Ph.D., New York University, 1952. 476p. UMI# 73-08440.

341   Colucci, Nicholas D., Jr. Connecticut Academies for Females, 1800-1865. Ph.D., University of Connecticut, 1969. 416p. UMI# 70-1248.

342   Lewis, Lenore L. The History and Use of the Book Plate in College Libraries in Connecticut. Master's thesis, Southern Connecticut State College, 1972.

343   Lord, Jerome E. Yale or Storrs? The Land Grant College Controversy in Connecticut, 1885-1986. Ph.D., Columbia University, 1969. 260p. UMI# 73-16224.

344   McKay, Robert B. The History of Citizen Committees in the Development of Connecticut Community Colleges, 1960-1970. Ph.D., University of Connecticut, 1972. 180p. UMI# 72-32235.

345   Pernal, Michael E. A Study of State Legislation in the Development of Public Higher Education in Connecticut from 1849 to 1970. Ph.D., University of Connecticut, 1975. 397p. UMI# 75-18338.

346   Pilver, Erika E. The Politics and Administration of Higher Education in Connecticut (1965-1977). Ph.D., University of Connecticut, 1977. 269p. UMI# 7731213.

347   Pratte, Richard N. A History of Teacher Education in Connecticut from 1639 to 1939. Ph.D., University of Connecticut, 1967. 443p. UMI# 68-01396.

348   Stewart, Gloria P. The Development of Social Sciences Courses for General Studies Students in the Community Colleges of Connecticut, 1965-1972. Ed.D., New York University, 1974. 397p. UMI# 75-08580.

ALBERTUS MAGNUS COLLEGE

349   Kelly, Sister Thomas A. The History, Growth and Development of the Albertus Magnus College Library, New Haven, Connecticut, 1925-1970. Master's thesis, Southern Connecticut State College, 1972. 195p.

ANNHURST COLLEGE

350   Kennett, Sister Marguerite E. Annhurst College Library, South Woodstock, Connecticut 1941-1967. Master's thesis, Southern Connecticut State College, 1968. 145p.

CONNECTICUT COLLEGE

351   Sullivan, Patricia A. Rosemary Park: A Study of Educational Leadership During the Revolutionary Decades. Ph.D., Boston College, 1982. 230p. [professor, dean, and president, Connecticut College, 1935-1962; president, Barnard College, and dean, Columbia University, 1962-1967; vice chancellor and professor of education, University of California, Los Angeles].

CONNECTICUT, UNIVERSITY OF

352   Bosworth, Ruth. The Changing Functions of the University of Connecticut. Ph.D., New York University, 1956. 323p. UMI# 16,583.

353   Lahey, Judith. The University of Connecticut Law School Library: History, Organization and Development 1921-1972. Master's thesis, Southern Connecticut State College, 1972. 72p.

354   Loughlin, William A., Jr. An Historical Study of the Media Program and Services at the University of Connecticut: 1941-1972. Ph.D., University of Connecticut, 1980. 130p. UMI# 81-06717.

355   Shuchman, Hedvah L. Professionalism and Political Influence: A Political History of the University of Connecticut Health Center. Ph.D., George Washington University, 1978. 281p. UMI# 78-10158.

356   Smith, Allan B. The Prediction of Scholastic Success for Freshman Entrants to the University of Connecticut 1933-1951. Ph.D., University of Connecticut, 1953. 241p. UMI# 00-06340.

357   Wyllie, Robert H. Historical Development of Branches of the University of Connecticut. Ph.D., University of Connecticut, 1963. 126p. UMI# 64-03574.

CONNECTICUT, UNIVERSITY OF (TORRINGTON)

358   Sullivan, R. Mark. Examining the Process of Closing Public Colleges: The Case of the Torrington Campus of the University of Connecticut. Ed.D., Harvard University, 1985. 250p. UMI# 8601992.

EASTERN CONNECTICUT STATE COLLEGE

359   Forst, Arthur C., Jr. From Normal School to State College: The Growth and Devlopment of Eastern Connecticut State College from 1889 to 1959. Ph.D., University of Connecticut, 1980. 258p. UMI# 81-03167.

FAIRFIELD UNIVERSITY

360   Preville, Joseph R. Fairfield University: The Emergence of a Modern Catholic Institution. Ph.D., Boston College, 1985. 272p. UMI# 8522288.

ST. JOSEPH COLLEGE

361   Colla, Sister Maria B. A History of the Pope Pius XII Library, St. Joseph College, West Hartford, Connecticut, 1932-1962. Master's thesis, Catholic University of America, 1964. 108p.

UNITED STATES COAST GUARD ACADEMY

362   Perry, Raymond J. A Study of the Problem of Attrition of Cadets at the United States Coast Guard Academy. Ph.D., Harvard University, 1961.

WESLEYAN UNIVERSITY

363   Johnson, Alvin D. A Study of the Place of Religion in Wesleyan University, 1831-1948. Master's thesis, Yale Divinity School, 1949.

364   Markle, David H. Wilbur Fisk, Pioneer Methodist Educator. Ph.D., Yale University, 1935. [president, Wesleyan University, 1831-1839].

YALE UNIVERSITY

365   Blankfort, Joelle R. Madeline Earle Stanton and the Historical Library of the Yale Medical Library. Master's thesis, Southern Connecticut State College, 1976. 102p. [secretary and librarian, 1941-1968].

366   Brooks, Robert E. The Yale University Law Library: Its History, Organization and Development, 1824 to 1962. Master's thesis, Southern Connecticut State College, 1963. 115p.

367   Catlin, Daniel, Jr. Liberal Education at Yale: The Yale College Course of Study 1945-1978. Ph.D., Columbia University, 1981. 309p. UMI# 83-27191.

368   Curtis, Marcia. Autonomy: An Institutional Study: Yale University School of Nursing, 1923-1934. Ed.D., Boston University, 1969. 210p. UMI# 70-12162.

369   Daggy, Robert E. Measures for Yalensia: Naphtali Daggett and Yale College, 1766-1778. Ph.D., University of Wisconsin, 1971. 379p. UMI# 71-25185. [president, 1766-1777].

370   Goode, Elizabeth A. David Stanley Smith and His Music. Ph.D., University of Cincinnati, 1978. 335p. UMI# 7904729. [professor and dean of music, Yale University, 1903-1940].

371   Hall, Julia A.O. C. Vann Woodward: American Educator. Ph.D., University of Mississippi, 1977. 159p. UMI# 78-07982. [professor of history, Johns Hopkins University, 1946-1961; Yale University, 1961-1977].

372   Havner, Carter S. The Reaction of Yale to the Great Awakening, 1740-1766. Ph.D., University of Texas, 1978. UMI# 7807314.

373   Holden, Reuben A., IV. An Educational Experiment in China: The Story of the Development of Yale-in-China. Ph.D., Yale University, 1951.

374   Hovee, Gene H. The Concept of Effective Delivery in the Yale Lectures on Preaching. Ph.D., University of Illinois, 1966. 171p. UMI# 67-6634.

375   James, W.T. The Philosophy of Noah Porter (1811-1892). Ph.D., Columbia University, 1951. 195p. UMI# 00-02823. [president, Yale University, 1871-1886; professor of philosophy, 1846-1892].

376   Johnson, James G. The Yale Divinity School, 1899-1928. Ph.D., Yale University, 1936.

377   Joyce, Walter E. Noah Porter as President of Yale, 1871-1886: A Conservative Response in a Time of Transition. Ph.D., New York University, 1972. 272p. UMI# 73-08173.

378   Kennedy, Peter E. The Life and Professional Contributions of Robert John Herman Kiphuth to Yale and Competitive Swimming. Ph.D., Ohio State University, 1973. 380p. UMI# 74-03219. [swim coach, 1918-1959].

379   Knoff, Gerald E. The Yale Divinity School, 1858-1899. Ph.D., Yale University, 1936.

380   Michelson, Donald D. The Contributions of William Franklin Phelps to Public Education. Ph.D., George Peabody College for Teachers, 1941. 185p. [professor of English, Yale University, 1892-1933].

381   Myres, William V. The Public and Private Political Thought of Ezra Stiles, 1760-1765. Ph.D., University of Dallas, 1973. 381p. UMI# 74-18,753. [president, Yale University, 1778-1795].

382   Nolan, John P. Genteel Attitudes in the Formation of the American Scientific Community: The Career of Benjamin Silliman of Yale. Ph.D., Columbia University, 1978. 235p. UMI# 79-08623. [professor of chemistry and natural history, 1802-1853].

383   Notestein, Robert B. William G. Sumner. Ph.D., University of Wisconsin, 1954. 182p. [professor of political and social science, Yale University, 1872-1908].

384   O'Connor, Thomas F. The Yale University Library, 1865-1931. Doctor of Library Service, Columbia University, 1984. 612p. UMI# 8427442.

385   Prendergast, Michael L. James Dwight Dana: The Life and Thought of an American Scientist. Ph.D., University of California-Los Angeles, 1978. 640p. UMI# 79-01390. [professor of geology, Yale University, 1849-1893].

386   Ray, Harold L. The Life and Professional Contributions of William Gilbert Anderson, M.D. Ph.D., Ohio State University, 1959. 214p. UMI# 60-01208. [director of physical education, Yale University, 1894-1930].

387   Riccomini, Donald R. Literary Indeterminacy and Revolution in the Yale Criticism. Ph.D., University of Wisconsin, 1979. 249p. UMI# 80-08837.

388   Rodes, Harold P. Educational Factors Affecting the Entrance Requirements of Yale College. Ph.D., Yale University, 1948.

389   Stevenson, Louise L. Scholarly Means to Evangelical Ends: The New Haven Scholars, 1840-1890. Ph.D., Boston University, 1981. 275p. UMI# 8126812.

390   Totaro, Joseph V. Curricular Changes in Higher Education: A Case Study of Modern Language Teaching at Nineteenth Century Yale. Ph.D., Syracuse University, 1957. 366p. UMI# 00-24137.

391   Tucker, Louis L. Thomas Clap, First President of Yale College: A Biography. Ph.D., University of Washington, 1957. 464p. UMI# 58-11098. [rector and president, 1740-1766].

392   Tucker, Louis L. Thomas Clap, President of Yale College, 1740-1766: A Study of Early American Conservatism. Master's thesis, University of Washington, 1955. 185p.

393   Vanderhoof, Wesley E. New Doctrine and Old Discipline: New Haven Theology and the Yale Report. Ph.D., State University of New York at Buffalo, 1985. 162p. UMI# 8518781.

394   Warch, Richard. Yale College, 1701-1740. Ph.D., Yale University, 1968. 414p. UMI# 69-13515.

395   Wayland, John T. The Theological Department in Yale College, 1822-1858. Ph.D., Yale University, 1933. 511p. UMI# 64-11903.

396   Wenzke, Annabelle S. Timothy Dwight: The Enlightened Puritan. Ph.D., Pennsylvania State University, 1983. 301p. UMI# 8327571. [president, Yale University, 1795-1817].

DELAWARE

GENERAL STUDIES

397   Schwaneger, Henry. History of Higher Education in Delaware. Ed.D., University of Pennsylvania, 1969. 648p. UMI# 69-21635.

398   Weaver, R.G. The History of Teacher Education in Delaware, 1829-1915. Master's thesis, University of Delaware, 1952.

DELAWARE STATE COLLEGE

399   Satneck, Walter J. The History of the Origins and Development of the Delaware State College and Its Role in Higher Education for Negroes in Delaware. Ed.D., New York University, 1962. 290p. UMI# 63-05380.

DELAWARE, UNIVERSITY OF

400   Bauersfield, Stephanie H. The Growth and Development of the University of Delaware Library, Newark, Delaware, 1833-1965. Master's thesis, Catholic University of America, 1967. 141p.

401   Leeds, Sylvia K. The History of Theatre at the University of Delaware, 1953-1967. Master's thesis, University of Delaware, 1968.

402   Sills, James H., Jr. The Public Service Function at the University of Delaware: A Case Study. Ph.D., Bryn Mawr College, 1981. UMI# 82-15219.

WESLEYAN FEMALE COLLEGE

403   Porter, Louise M. The Wesleyan Female College, Wilmington, Delaware. Master's thesis, University of Delaware, 1958.

DISTRICT OF COLUMBIA

GENERAL STUDIES

404   Dabney, Lillian G. The History of Schools for Negroes in the District of Columbia, 1807-1947. Ph.D., Catholic University of America, 1949. 229p.

405   Hinsley, Curtis M. The Development of a Profession: Anthropology in Washington, D.C., 1846-1903. Ph.D., University of Wisconsin-Madison, 1976. 544p. UMI# 76-18882.

406   Moldow, Gloria M. The Gilded Age, Promise and Disillusionment: Women Doctors and the Emergence of the Professional Middle Class, Washington, D.C., 1870-1900. Ph.D., University of Maryland, 1980. 361p. UMI# 8027122.

CARNEGIE INSTITUTION OF WASHINGTON

407   Cornell, Thomas D. Merle A. Tuve and His Program of Nuclear Studies at the Department of Terrestrial Magnetism: The Early Career of a Modern American Physicist. Ph.D., Johns Hopkins University, 1986. 552p. UMI# 8609316.

CATHOLIC UNIVERSITY OF AMERICA

408   Ahern, Patrick H. The Life of Archbishop John J. Keane, 1839-1918. Ph.D., Catholic University of America, 1954. [rector, Catholic University of America, 1889-1896].

409   Campbell, Kenneth. A Descriptive History of the Origins, Development, and Theoretical Basis of Theatrical Production at the Speech and Drama Department of the Catholic University of America, 1937-1957. Ph.D., University of Denver, 1965. 403p. UMI# 66-11769.

410   Dixon, Blaise P. The Catholic University of America, 1909-1928, the Rectorship of Thomas Joseph Shahan. Ph.D., Catholic University of America, 1972. 403p. UMI# 72-21,566.

411   Fogarty, Gerald P. Dennis J. O'Connell: Americanist Agent to the Vatican, 1885-1903. Ph.D., Yale University, 1969. UMI# 70-2731. [rector, American College in Rome, 1885-1895; Catholic University of America, 1903-1909].

412   Glynn, John J.A. The Educational Theory of Right Reverend John L. Spalding, D.D. Master's thesis, Catholic University of America, 1929. [founder, Catholic University of America].

413   Rodgers, Rosemary T. The Changing Concept of College Theology: A Case Study. Ph.D., Catholic University of America, 1973. 339p. UMI# 74-3506.

414   Weitekamp, Raymond. Maurice Francis Egan: Writer, Teacher, and Diplomat, 1852-1924. Ph.D., Catholic University of America, 1962. 370p. UMI# 63-01937. [professor of English language and literature, Catholic University of America, 1895-1907].

415   Willis, H. Warren. The Reorganization of the Catholic University of America During the

Rectorship of James H. Ryan (1928-1935). Ph.D., Catholic University of America, 1971. 359p. UMI# 72-15962.

CORCORAN SCHOOL OF ART

416   Marsh, Allan T. Washington's First Art Academy, the Corcoran School of Art, 1875-1925. (Volumes I and II). Ph.D., University of Maryland, 1983. 345p. UMI# 8405683.

DISTRICT OF COLUMBIA, UNIVERSITY OF THE

417   Miller, Stephen S. The Emergence of Comprehensive Public Higher Education in the District of Columbia: The Establishment of Federal City College. Ph.D., Catholic University of America, 1970. 137p. UMI# 70-22706.

GALLAUDET COLLEGE

418   Baughman, Robert T. A History of Gallaudet College and Its Service to the Deaf. Master's thesis, Gallaudet College, 1934.

419   Sturtevant, Charles C. Gallaudet College, Some Aspects of Its Formation and Development. Master's thesis, Gallaudet College, 1943.

420   Tadie, Nancy B. A History of Drama at Gallaudet College: 1864 to 1969. Ph.D., New York University, 1979. 457p. UMI# 79-18869.

GEORGE WASHINGTON UNIVERSITY

421   Korcheck, Stephen J. A Historical Study of the Origin and Development of the Physical Education Major Field Program at the George Washington University. Ed.D., George Washington University, 1970. 104p. UMI# 70-24962.

422   Lawton, Willie O. A Historical Study of Selected Forces and Events Which Influenced the Founding, Growth and Development of the Tidewater Center of the George Washington University from 1952 to 1977. Ed.D., George Washington University, 1980. 201p. UMI# 81-06812.

423   Lobuts, John F., Jr. A Historical Study of the Establishment and Development of the College of General Studies of the George Washington University. Ed.D., George Washington University, 1970. 220p. UMI# 70-19729.

424   Manning, Randolph. The Establishment and Development of the Higher Education Degree Programs in the School of Education, George Washington University, and a Follow-Up of the First Graduates, June, 1969 - September, 1973. Ed.D., George Washington University, 1974. 193p. UMI# 75-12620.

GEORGETOWN UNIVERSITY

425   Chamberlain, Lawrence C. Georgetown University Library, 1789-1937. Master's thesis, Catholic University of America, 1962. 104p.

426   Gillis, Herbert R. The History, Theory and Practice of Speech Education at Georgetown, 1789 to 1890, First Jesuit College in the United States. Ph.D., Western Reserve University, 1958. 172p.

427   Gorka, Ronald R. Establishing Catholic Collegiate Education in America: Georgetown College, 1784-1832. Ph.D., Harvard University, 1964.

HOWARD UNIVERSITY

428   Alexander, Jo H. The History of Music Instruction at Howard University from the Beginning to 1942. Master's thesis, Catholic University of America, 1973. 115p.

429   Cheek, William F., III. Forgotten Prophet: The Life of John Mercer Langston. Ph.D., University of Virginia, 1961. 405p. UMI# 61-04534. [dean of law, Howard University, 1869-1876].

430   Davis, Brenda L. H. The Origin and Growth of Three Nursing Programs at Howard University, 1893-1973. Ed.D., Columbia University, 1976. 186p. UMI# 77-32022.

431   Duncan, Anne M. History of Howard University Library, 1867-1929. Master's thesis, Catholic University of America, 1951. 97p.

432   Harris, Janette H. Charles Harris Wesley, Educator and Historian, 1891-1947. Ph.D., Howard University, 1975. 256p. UMI# 8227395. [professor of history, 1913-1937; dean of graduate school, 1938-1942, Howard University].

433   Matthews, Lamoyne M. Portrait of a Dean: A Biography of Inabel Burns Lindsay, First Dean of the Howard University School of Social Work. Ph.D., University of Maryland, 1976. 262p. UMI# 77-10287.

434   McKnight, Arnold W. Academic Achievement of Selected Athletes and Selected Non-Athletes at Howard University. Ed.D., American University, 1972. 125p. UMI# 72-30100.

435   Melchor, Beulah H. A History of the Title to the Campus of Howard University, 1651-1885. Master's thesis, Howard University, 1943.

LIBRARY OF CONGRESS

436   Bartis, Peter T. A History of the Archive of Folk Song at the Library of Congress: The First Fifty Years. Ph.D., University of Pennsylvania, 1982. 342p. UMI# 82-17081.

437   Cole, John Y. Ainsworth Spofford and the 'National Library.' Ph.D., George Washington University, 1971. 170p. UMI# 72-8994. [Librarian of Congress, 1864-1897].

438   Elson, Beverly L. The Library of Congress: A Merger of American Functionalism and Cosmopolitan Eclecticism. Ph.D., University of Maryland, 1981. 448p. UMI# 8213807.

439   Krieg, Cynthia J. Herbert Putnam's Philosophy of Librarianship. Master's thesis, Long Island University, 1971. [Librarian of Congress, 1899-1939].

MINER TEACHERS' COLLEGE

440   Hatter, Henrietta R. History of Miner Teachers' College. Master's thesis, Howard University, 1939.

SMITHSONIAN INSTITUTION

441 Cohen, Marilyn S. American Civilization in Three Dimensions: The Evolution of the Museum of History and Technology of the Smithsonian Institution. Ph.D., George Washington University, 1980. 357p. UMI# 8101476.

442 King, JoAnn. Howard I. Chapelle: Maritime Scholar and His Contribution to Maritime Preservation. Ph.D., George Washington University, 1985. 274p.

443 Weiner, Charles I. Joseph Henry's Lectures on Natural Philosophy: Teaching and Research in Physics, 1832-1847. Ph.D., Case Western Reserve University, 1965. 302p. UMI# 65-13806. [professor of natural history, Princeton University, 1832-1846; first secretary and director, Smithsonian Institution, 1846-1878].

TRINITY COLLLEGE

444 Beach, Sister Francis Mary. A History of the Library of Trinity College, Washington, D.C. Master's thesis, Catholic University of America, 1951. 76p.

445 Hilliard, Annie P. An Investigation of Selected Events and Forces that Contributed to the Growth and Development of Trinity College, Washington, D.C. from 1897 to 1982. Ed.D., George Washington University, 1984. 276p. UMI# 8421999.

FLORIDA

GENERAL STUDIES

446   Aronofsky, David J. A History of Legislative Influence on the State University System of Florida, 1961-1974 with Special Reference to Republican Legislators: Volume I, Chapters I-VIII. Volume II, Appendices. Ph.D., Florida State University, 1975. 570p. UMI# 76-16512.

447   Goulding, Robert L. The Development of Teacher Training in Florida. Ph.D., George Peabody College for Teachers, 1934.

448   Hale, Morris S., Jr. A History of Florida Junior Colleges. Ed.D., George Peabody College for Teachers, 1966. 1,296p. UMI# 66-11228.

449   Hiett, Joseph H. The Florida State Wide Governing Board for Higher Education, 1905-1969: A Study of the Personal Characteristics of the Members and Selected Trends in the History of the Board. Ph.D., Florida State University, 1971. 187p. UMI# 72-13517.

450   Keck, Judith D. A Historical Review of the Organization and Development of Teacher Education in the State of Florida: A Case Study. Ph.D., University of Florida, 1985. 316p. UMI# 8606722.

451   Lanier, Raphael O. The History of Negro Education in Florida. Master's thesis, Stanford University, 1928.

452   Moon, Clyde L. The Development of Higher Education for Negroes in the State of Florida. Master's thesis, University of Florida, 1941.

453   Muscatell, Toni G.P. An Historical Analysis of Instructional Television in Public Higher Learning in the State of Florida. Ed.D., Florida-Atlantic University, 1973. 258p. UMI# 74-11604.

454   Paylor, Mary M. A History of Nursing Education in Florida from 1893 to 1970. Ph.D., Florida State University, 1975. 194p. UMI# 75-21427.

455   Rhodes, Francis A. The Legal Development of State Supported Higher Education in Florida. Ph.D., University of Florida, 1949. 146p.

456   Sanders, Marlin C. Trends in Teacher Certification in Florida, 1936-1961. Ed.D., Florida State University, 1963. UMI# 61-03646.

457   Smith, Walter L. A Study of the Black Public Junior Colleges in Florida: 1957-1966. Ph.D., Florida State University, 1974. 252p. UMI# 75-15509.

458   Tyree, Lawrence W. The History and Cooperative Relationships of a Community College and an Upper Level University. Ed.D., Indiana University, 1972. 237p. UMI# 73-10875.

459   Yarish, La Vera M. Twenty Years of Developmental Education in Florida Community Colleges (1957-1977). Ed.D., Florida State University, 1977. 116p. UMI# 7926841.

BETHUNE COOKMAN COLLEGE

460   Roane, Florence L. A Cultural History of Professional Teacher Preparation at Bethune Cookman College. Ed.D., Boston University, 1965. 309p. UMI# 66-00803.

FLORIDA AGRICULTURAL AND MECHANICAL UNIVERSITY

461   Griffin, Robert P. History and Development of Athletics at Florida Agricultural and Mechanical College. Master's thesis, Ohio State University, 1946.

462   Holland, Antonio F. Nathan B. Young and the Development of Black Higher Education. Ph.D., University of Missouri-Columbia, 1984. 357p. UMI# 8425629. [president, Florida Agricultural & Mechanical University, 1901-1922; Lincoln University, 1923-1927, 1929-1931].

FLORIDA SOUTHERN COLLEGE

463   Horwitz, Hattie S. The West Campus at Florida Southern College, Lakeland, Florida, and Its Builders. Master's thesis, University of Miami, 1977.

FLORIDA STATE UNIVERSITY

464   Carter, Gayvon D. A History of the Physical Education Program at Florida State University, 1901-1978. Ph.D., Florida State University, 1980. 330p. UMI# 81-00636.

465   Ellingsworth, June E. A History of Speech Education at Florida State University. Master's thesis, Florida State University, 1955.

466   Ellis, Leslie E. The Early History of a University Related, Regional Theatre: A Study of the Asolo Theatre, the Asolo Theatre Festival and the Asolo State Theatre through 1966 (Italy, Florida). Ph.D., Florida State University, 1982. 355p. UMI# 83-08669.

467   Fulton, Martha W. Hartley D. Price: His Contributions to Physical Education and Gymnastics. Ph.D., Florida State University, 1981. 188p. UMI# 8125769. [professor of physical education and gymnastics coach, Florida State University, 1948-1971].

468   Hewick, Laurence F. Mode L. Stone: Portrait of an Educational Leader. Ph.D., Florida State University, 1979. 121p. UMI# 8006273. [professor of school administration and dean, Florida State University, 1946-1973].

469   Kalb, John M. The Florida State University System, 1959-1974: A History through Student Distribution. Ph.D., Florida State University, 1978. 217p. UMI# 79-17049.

470   Kievit, KarenAnn. Growth, Change, and Economies of Scale, the Florida State University, 1963-64 through 1972-73. Ph.D., Florida State University, 1975. 267p. UMI# 75-26788.

471   Long, Curtiss M. A History of the Male Varsity Track and Field Program at Florida State University from 1948-1974. Ph.D., Florida State University, 1976. 577p. UMI# 77-13330.

472   Palcic, James L. The History of the Black Student Union at Florida State University, 1968-1978. Ph.D., Florida State University, 1979. 376p. UMI# 79-26796.

473   Price, Paula. History of Debate at F.S.U. Master's thesis, Florida State University, 1967.

474   Swingle, Marilyn R. A History of the Florida State University School of Music. Ph.D., Florida State University, 1973. 207p. UMI# 74-09500.

475   Thomas, Richard K. A History of General Education at the Florida State University in National Perspective, 1935-1969. Ph.D., Florida State University, 1970. 191p. UMI# 71-07118.

476   Usher, Mildred M. A History of Women's Collegiate Athletics at Florida State University from 1905-1972. Ph.D., Florida State University, 1980. 328p. UMI# 80-21109.

FLORIDA, UNIVERSITY OF

477   Adams, Kathryn B. The Growth and Development of the University of Florida Libraries, 1940-1958. Master's thesis, Catholic University of America, 1959.

478   Burrows, Edward L. Commercial Radio at the University of Florida: WRUF—An Historical Overview. Master's thesis, University of Florida, 1975.

479   Hansen, Jessie. Kimball Wiles' Contribution to Curriculum and Instruction: An Analysis within an Historical Context. Ph.D., University of Texas, 1971. 243p. UMI# 72-15,770. [professor of education, University of Florida, 1950-1968; dean, 1964-1968].

480   Kobasky, Michael G. A History of the General Extension Division of Florida at the University of Florida, 1919-1961. Ph.D., Florida State University, 1971. 275p. UMI# 72-18604.

481   McBride, Sara A. Forensic Activities at the University of Florida, 1905-1932: With Special Attention to Literary Society. Master's thesis, University of Florida, 1949.

482   Proctor, Samuel. The University of Florida: Its Early Years, 1853-1906. Ph.D., University of Florida, 1958. 574p. UMI# 58-01538.

INDIAN RIVER JUNIOR COMMUNITY COLLEGE

483   Lunceford, Charles R. The Historical Development of Indian River Junior Community College, 1960-1978. Ed.D., Florida-Atlantic University, 1980. 264p. UMI# 80-20455.

MIAMI-DADE JUNIOR COLLEGE

484   Cohen, Arthur M. Miami-Dade Junior College: A Study in Racial Integration. Ph.D., Florida State University, 1964. 135p. UMI# 64-10584.

MIAMI, UNIVERSITY OF

485   Husselbee, Margaret V. History of the University of Miami Libraries, 1928-1960. Master's thesis, University of North Carolina, 1962.

486   Marble, Robert F. A History of Veterans' Enrollment and an Examination of Undergradu-

ate Curriculum and Instruction at the University of Miami from 1940 through 1960. Doctor of Arts, University of Miami, 1974. 171p. UMI# 75-12877.

487   Sevick, Charles V. A History and Evaluation of the Cuban Teacher Retraining Program of the University of Miami, 1963-1973. Ph.D., University of Miami, 1974. 127p. UMI# 74-23415.

ROLLINS COLLEGE

488   Rider, Manning C. A Brief History of Rollins College, with Special Reference to the Curriculum. Master's thesis, Stetson University, 1937.

SOUTH FLORIDA, UNIVERSITY OF

489   Mix, Mary D. New College of Teachers College: A History, 1932-1939. Ph.D., Columbia University, 1968. 464p. UMI# 69-03085.

490   Reed, Donald E. Changes in a Small Liberal Arts College Following Its Merger with a Large State University: A Case Study of the New College Merger with the University of South Florida in July of 1975. Ph.D., Florida State University, 1978. 131p. UMI# 7909792.

ST. PETERSBURG JUNIOR COLLEGE

491   Lively, Roger M. An Historical-Descriptive Study of the Use of TV at St. Petersburg Junior College, St. Petersburg, Florida. Master's thesis, Indiana University, 1965.

ST. PETERSBURG, UNIVERSITY OF

492   Steinger, Charles S. Government Policy and the University of St. Petersburg, 1819-1849. Ph.D., Ohio State University, 1971. 230p. UMI# 71-27569.

GEORGIA

GENERAL STUDIES

493   Baker, Elaine. The Quest for Professional Licensure: A Case Study of the Social Work Profession in Georgia, 1970-1980. D.P.A., University of Georgia, 1986. 200p. UMI# 8613475.

494   Broughton, James H. A Historical Study of Selected Aspects of the Equalization of Educational Opportunity in Georgia, 1937-1968. Ed.D., University of Georgia, 1969. 477p. UMI# 70-10163.

495   Colston, James A. Higher Education in Georgia from 1932 to 1949 with Specific Reference to Higher Education for the Negro. Ph.D., New York University, 1950. 235p. UMI# 00-02177.

496   Cook, James F. Politics and Education in the Talmadge Era: The Controversy Over the University System of Georgia, 1941-42. Ph.D., University of Georgia, 1972. 336p. UMI# 72- 34057.

497   Finklea, J.J. The Historical Development of the Curricula of the Junior Colleges in Georgia. Master's thesis, Duke University, 1939. 43p.

498   Gibson, J.C. An Examination of Speech Teaching in Selected Georgia Educational Institutions, 1732-1900. Ed.D., University of Georgia, 1971. 203p. UMI# 72-02485.

499   Gignilliat, Elizabeth L. A History of the Development of Public Junior Colleges in Georgia. Master's thesis, Emory University, 1961.

500   Granade, Charles J. A Study of the Public Junior College Movement in Georgia with Emphasis on Trends. Ed.D., Alabama Polytechnic Institute, 1958. 421p. UMI# 58-05983.

501   Gurr, Charles S. Social Leadership and the Medical Profession in Antebellum Georgia. Ph.D., University of Georgia, 1973. 290p. UMI# 73-3189.

502   Hamilton, Zona. The Development of Higher Education for Women in Georgia. Master's thesis, Brown University, 1927.

503   Herndon, Mike E. History of the Junior Colleges in Georgia. Master's thesis, Mercer University, 1936. 87p.

504   Hynds, Ernest C., Jr. Ante-Bellum Athens and Clark County, Georgia. Ph.D., University of Georgia, 1961. 424p. UMI# 61-03831.

505   Ingram, I.S. The History and Significance of the A. and M. Schools in Georgia. Master's thesis, Emory University, 1933.

506   Levy, John W. Relationship Between Social Change and Curricular Trends in Georgia's

Four-Year State Colleges—1948 to 1968. Ed.D., University of Georgia, 1970. 269p. UMI# 71-13080.

507   Lide, Anne. Five Georgia Colleges from 1850 to 1875. Master's thesis, Emory University, 1957.

508   McCaul, Robert L., Jr. A Documentary History of Education in Colonial Georgia. Ph.D., University of Chicago, 1954.

509   Pullum, Fred D. Professional Preparation in Physical Education at Historically Black Institutions in Georgia. Ed.D., University of Georgia, 1974. 262p. UMI# 75-08197.

510   Rashid-Farokhi, Helen E. A Study of the Effect of State Financial Aid on the Private Colleges and Universities in the State of Georgia, 1972-1977. Ph.D., University of Georgia, 1978.

511   Rose, Richard M. For Our Mutual Benefit: Antebellum Georgia College Student Organizations. Ed.D., University of Georgia, 1984. 199p. UMI# 8504633.

512   Satterfield, Virginia. The History of College Libraries in Georgia as Interpreted from the Study of Seven Selected Libraries. Master's thesis, Columbia University, 1936. 49p.

513   Shehee, Blanche A. The Movement for and Establishment of a State College for Women in Georgia. Master's thesis, University of North Carolina, 1953.

514   Sherard, Catherine. The Development of Secondary, Industrial, and Higher Education of the Negro in Georgia. Master's thesis, University of North Carolina, 1930.

515   Styons, Robert B. The Junior College Act of 1958: A Study of Public Junior College Governance in Georgia. Ph.D., Georgia State University, 1983. 163p. UMI# 8317521.

ALBANY STATE COLLEGE

516   Harper, Hoyt H. A History of Albany State College. Master's thesis, Atlanta University, 1951.

517   Ramsey, Berkley C. The Public Black College in Georgia: A History of Albany State College, 1903-1965. Ph.D., Florida State University, 1973. 311p. UMI# 73-31528.

ANDREW COLLEGE

518   Engram, Irbi D. A History of Andrew College. Master's thesis, Emory University, 1939.

ANDREW FEMALE COLLEGE

519   Smith, Boyce O. A History of the Andrew Female College. Master's thesis, University of Texas, 1930.

ATLANTA UNIVERSITY

520   Adams, Eva D. Negro Social Life as Reflected by the Lives of the Students of Atlanta University, 1870-1900. Master's thesis, Atlanta University, 1968.

521   Heyliger, E.E. A Study of the Development of the Atlanta University School of Social Work, 1929-1942. Master's thesis, Atlanta University, 1943.

522   Summersette, John F. The Structure of Atlanta University Center. Ph.D., Stanford University, 1952.

523   Warren, Nagueyalti. The Contributions of W.E.B. DuBois to Afro-American Studies in Higher Education. Ph.D., University of Mississippi, 1984. 225p. UMI# 8502624. [professor of history and economics, Atlanta University, 1897-1910; professor of sociology, 1932-1944].

524   Williams, Hobie L. The Impact of the Atlanta University Exhibition of Black Arts (1942-1969) on Black and Non Black People. Ed.D., University of Pittsburgh, 1973. 144p. UMI# 73-29374.

BOWDON COLLEGE

525   Caswell, Render R. The History of Bowdon College. Master's thesis, University of Georgia, 1952.

CLARK COLLEGE

526   McPheeters, Alphonso A. The Origin and Development of Clark University and Gammon Theological Seminary, 1869-1944. Ph.D., University of Cincinnati, 1944. 67p.

EMMANUEL COLLEGE

527   Synan, Harold V. The Background and Founding of Emmanuel College. Master's thesis, University of Georgia, 1964.

EMORY UNIVERSITY

528   Bullock, Henry M. A History of Emory College, 1834-1915. Ph.D., Yale University, 1932.

529   Mann, Harold W. The Life and Times of Atticus Greene Haygood. Ph.D., Duke University, 1962. 444p. UMI# 63-03600. [president, Emory University, 1875-1884].

FLOYD JUNIOR COLLEGE

530   Borchardt, Lovie M. The Forces Leading to the Establishment and Evolution of a Selected Junior College in the State of Georgia, 1940-1980. Ph.D., University of South Carolina, 1980. 93p. UMI# 81-14325.

GAMMON THEOLOGICAL SEMINARY

531   Taylor, Prince A., Jr. A History of Gammon Theological Seminary. Ed.D., New York University, 1948. 169p. UMI# 00-01155.

GEORGIA COLLEGE

532   Curl, Lottie M. History of the Georgia State College for Women. Master's thesis, George Peabody College for Teachers, 1931.

GEORGIA SOUTHERN COLLEGE

533   Christie, Dudley B. A History of Georgia Teachers College. Master's thesis, University of Georgia, 1940.

GEORGIA, UNIVERSITY OF

534   Abney, George M. Forty Years of Communications Education at the Oldest Chartered State University (1915-1955). Master's thesis, University of Georgia, 1959.

535   Bonniwell, Hilton T. A Historical Analysis of Non-Credit Adult Education Program Development at the University of Georgia, 1804-1968. Ed.D., University of Georgia, 1969. 432p. UMI# 70-01142.

536   Burks, John B. The College of Education, University of Georgia, and the Development of Teacher Education, 1908-1958. Ed.D., University of Georgia, 1958. 277p. UMI# 58-05978.

537   Cantrell, Loula N. The Growth and Development of the Atlanta Division, University of Georgia, 1912-1952. Master's thesis, Emory University, 1953.

538   Gould, Florine R. The History of Student Counseling at the University of Georgia, 1900-1948. Master's thesis, University of Georgia, 1948.

539   Greer, Martha J. Martha Ella Lunday Soule: Her Career and Contributions to Health, Physical, and Recreation Education. Ed.D., University of Georgia, 1972. 305p. UMI# 73-5702. [University of Georgia, 1925-1960].

540   Hayn, Lloyd F. The Oldest Continuous State University in the United States. Master's thesis, Boston University, 1939.

541   Hiestand, Dwight W. History of Growth of Graduate Instruction at the University of Georgia. Master's thesis, University of Georgia, 1936.

542   Hilton, Thomas B. A Historical Analysis of Non-Credit Adult Education Program Development at the University of Georgia, 1904-1968. Ed.D., University of Georgia, 1979. 432p. UMI# 70-1142.

543   La Boone, Elizabeth. History of the University of Georgia Library. Master's thesis, University of Georgia, 1954.

544   Mathis, Gerald R. Walter B. Hill: Chancellor, the University of Georgia, 1899-1905. Ph.D., University of Georgia, 1967. 390p. UMI# 67-16,233.

545   Maxwell, Bernice J. An Historical Survey of the Non-Professional Theatrical Activities at the University of Georgia from 1785 through 1955. Master's thesis, University of Georgia, 1959.

546   McNeil, James H. Psychological Education at the University of Georgia. Ed.D., University of Georgia, 1972. 303p. UMI# 73-05741.

547   Ragsdale, Annie L. History of Coeducation in the University of Georgia, 1918-1945. Master's thesis, University of Georgia, 1948.

548   Silverman, Peter H. Horace T. Ward vs. Board of Regents of the University System of Georgia: A Study in Segregation and Desegregation. Master's thesis, Emory University, 1970.

GORDON MILITARY COLLEGE

549   Morgan, Charles C. History of Gordon Military College. Master's thesis, Birmingham-Southern College, 1958.

INTERDENOMINATIONAL THEOLOGICAL CENTER

550   Bronson, Oswald P. The Origin and Significance of the Interdenominational Theological Center. Ph.D., Northwestern University, 1965. 217p. UMI# 66-2687.

LA GRANGE COLLEGE

551   Birdsong, Irene B. The History of La Grange College. Master's thesis, University of Georgia, 1955.

MOREHOUSE COLLEGE

552   Irons, Ococie J. Morehouse Graduates Who Have Earned Doctorates. Master's thesis, Atlanta University, 1960.

MORRIS BROWN COLLEGE

553   Rothman, Norman C. Curriculum Formation in a Black College: A Study of Morris Brown College, 1881-1980. Ph.D., Georgia State University College of Education, 1981. 254p. UMI# 81-20117.

PAINE COLLEGE

554   Clary, George E., Jr. The Founding of Paine College: A Unique Venture in Inter-Racial Cooperation in the New South, 1882-1903. Ed.D., University of Georgia, 1965. 152p. UMI# 65-10286.

555   Johnson, Alandus C. The Growth of Paine College: A Successful Interracial Venture, 1903-1946. Ph.D., University of Georgia, 1970. 423p. UMI# 71-03747.

PIEDMONT COLLEGE

556   Lovett, Warren P. A History of Piedmont College. Master's thesis, University of Georgia, 1943.

557   Rountree, George W. Piedmont College: Its History, Resources, and Programs. Ed.D., University of Georgia, 1965. 170p. UMI# 66-02499.

SAVANNAH STATE COLLEGE

558   Patton, June O. Major Richard Robert Wright, Sr., and Black Higher Education in Georgia, 1880-1920. Ph.D., University of Chicago, 1980. [president, Savannah State College, 1891-1921].

SHORTER COLLEGE

559   Sheppard, Lydia D. The History of Shorter College. Master's thesis, Emory University, 1941.

SPELMAN COLLEGE

560   Vanlandingham, Karen E. In Pursuit of a Changing Dream: Spelman College Students and the Civil Rights Movement, 1955-1962. Master's thesis, Emory University, 1985.

TRUETT MCCONNELL JUNIOR COLLEGE

561   Holcomb, Jack B. A History of Truett-McConnell Junior College. Master's thesis, University of Georgia, 1958.

WESLEYAN COLLEGE

562   Curry, Betty L. Wesleyan College, 1836-1886: The First Half Century of America's Oldest College for Women. Master's thesis, Emory University, 1962.

563   Miller, Margaret. Founding and Early History of Wesleyan College. Master's thesis, University of Georgia, 1935.

564   Rees, Frances. A History of Wesleyan Female College from 1836 to 1874. Master's thesis, Emory University, 1936. 145p.

YOUNG HARRIS COLLEGE

565   Andress, Robert P. Young Harris College, Its Development, Resources, and Program. Ph.D., Columbia University, 1960.

566   Brogdon, Joseph M. A History of Young L.G. Harris College. Master's thesis, University of Georgia, 1938.

HAWAII

CHURCH COLLEGE OF HAWAII

567 Olson, Ralph D. History of the Church College of Hawaii, 1955-1960. Master's thesis, Utah State University, 1961.

HAWAII, UNIVERSITY OF

568 Fujimoto, Sumie. A History of the Speech Training Program of the University of Hawaii to 1948. Master's thesis, University of Hawaii, 1949.

569 Kittelson, David. The History of the College of Hawaii. Master's thesis, University of Hawaii, 1966.

IDAHO

GENERAL STUDIES

570   Shinn, Marion L. History of Vocational Education in Idaho. Ed.D., University of Idaho, 1972. 365p. UMI# 72-30520.

571   Truby, Roy E. A History of the Idaho Education Association. Ed.D., University of Idaho, 1969. 260p. UMI# 70-10690.

572   Young, Virgil M. The Development of Education in Idaho Territory: 1863-1890. Ed.D., University of Idaho, 1968. 287p. UMI# 68-17008.

BOISE STATE UNIVERSITY

573   Oliver, Henry L. Boise State University, the First Fifty Years: 1932-1982. Ph.D., Washington State University, 1983. 164p. UMI# 8315565.

IDAHO STATE UNIVERSITY

574   Dilweg, Joan K. A History of Drama: Idaho State University 1901-1960. Ph.D., Brigham Young University, 1981. UMI# 82-06693.

IDAHO, UNIVERSITY OF

575   Hart, Claude. A Handbook of the History of the Department of Men's Physical Education and Athletics of the University of Idaho. Master's thesis, University of Idaho, 1941.

576   Rhodes, Jess D. The Transition of the University of Idaho from Pre University to a University Organization: A Preliminary Survey of the First Quarter Century, 1889-1913. Master's thesis, University of Idaho, 1952.

577   Ryan, Michael G. The Historic Origins of the University of Idaho, with Special Reference to More Remote Origins as the Morrill Act, the Educational Philosophy Underlying It, the Land Grant Ordinances, and the Existence of Public Domain. Master's thesis, University of Idaho, 1939.

RICKS COLLEGE

578   Anderson, John M. The Development of a Community Music Program through the Cooperation of Ricks College and the People of Upper Snake River Valley, Idaho. Ph.D., Columbia University Teachers College, 1953.

579   Nielson, Dean C. The History of Intercollegiate Basketball, Football and Wrestling at Ricks College. Master's thesis, Brigham Young University, 1968.

580   Roundy, Jerry C. Ricks College: A Struggle for Survival. Ph.D., Brigham Young University, 1975. 364p. UMI# 76-13578.

ILLINOIS

GENERAL STUDIES

581   Askew, Thomas A., Jr. The Liberal Arts College Encounters Intellectual Change: A Comparative Study of Education at Knox and Wheaton Colleges, 1837-1925. Ph.D., Northwestern University, 1969. 316p. UMI# 70-00004.

582   Birney, Jane D. The Development of Departments of Education in the Catholic Universities and Colleges in Chicago, 1910-1958. Ph.D., Loyola University of Chicago, 1961.

583   Brown, Donald R. The Educational Contributions of Jonathan Baldwin Turner. Master's thesis, University of Illinois, 1954. [professor, Illinois College; founder, University of Illinois].

584   Chase, William G. Implications of Federal Legislation for 1958 through 1968 for Expansion and Improvement of Public Junior Colleges in Illinois. Ed.D., Illinois State University, 1968. 167p. UMI# 70-01458.

585   Gwaltney, John W. The Illinois Community College Board: Its Origins and Development, 1965-1978. Ph.D., Southern Illinois University at Carbondale, 1981. 260p. UMI# 82-15807.

586   Hamilton, Hallie J. The Role of the Weekly Press in the Proliferation of Colleges in Illinois, 1830-1860. Ed.D., Indiana University, 1968. 208p. UMI# 69-06737.

587   Hancock, Judith A. Jonathan Baldwin Turner (1805-1899): A Study of an Educational Reformer. Ph.D., University of Washington, 1971. 355p. UMI# 71-24040. [professor, Illinois College; founder, University of Illinois].

588   Hardin, Thomas L. A History of the Community Junior College in Illinois: 1901-1972. Ph.D., University of Illinois at Urbana-Champaign, 1975. 339p. UMI# 76-06779.

589   Harrison, Rodman P. The History and Development of the Illinois Association for Professional Preparation in Health, Physical Education, and Recreation. Ph.D., University of Illinois at Urbana-Champaign, 1971. 298p. UMI# 72-06946.

590   Hollatz, Edwin A. The Development of Literary Societies in Selected Illinois Colleges in the 19th Century, and Their Role in Speech Training. Ph.D., Northwestern University, 1965. 294p. UMI# 66-02712.

591   Johnson, Daniel T. Puritan Power in Illinois Higher Education Prior to 1870. Ph.D., University of Wisconsin, 1974. 234p. UMI# 74-30109.

592   Kaiser, Gertrude E. A History of the Illinois Home Economics Program of the Cooperative Extension Service. Ph.D., University of Chicago, 1969.

593   Lantz, Charles P. A History of the Illinois Intercollegiate Athletic Conference. Master's thesis, Pennsylvania State College, 1936.

594   McKenna, Jon F. Disputed Destiny: The Political and Intellectual Origins of Public-Supported Higher Education in Illinois. Ph.D., University of Illinois, 1973. 244p. UMI# 74-12106.

595   Mees, Carl F. The Historical Development of the Cooperative Agricultural Extension Service in Cook County, Illinois. Ph.D., University of Chicago, 1960.

596   Meisterheim, Matthew J. A History of the Public Junior College in Illinois, 1900-1965. Ed.D., Northern Illinois University, 1974. 199p. UMI# 74-11742.

597   Miller, Enid. Development of Intercollegiate Debating in the United States, Including a Specific Study of Northwestern and Chicago Universities. Master's thesis, Northwestern University, 1926.

598   Orr, John C. A Study of the Administration in Illinois of Title V, NDEA, from 1959 through 1967. Ph.D., Northwestern University, 1968. 209p. UMI# 69-01904.

599   Paul, Norma A. Catholic Schools and the Religious Teaching Orders in the State of Illinois from 1834 to 1939. Ph.D., Loyola University of Chicago, 1940. 526p.

600   Randolph, Victor R. An Historical Study of Certification Laws in Illinois. Ph.D., George Peabody College for Teachers, 1943.

601   Sanders, James W. The Education of Chicago Catholics: An Urban History. Ph.D., University of Chicago, 1971.

602   Smith, Melvin. The Legal Development of the Illinois Public Junior College, 1901-1968. Ed.D., Indiana University, 1970. 112p. UMI# 70-11674.

603   Stahl, Wayne K. The Illinois Board of Higher Education: A History of the Development of Its Statutory Responsibilities from 1961 through 1976. Ph.D., Southern Illinois University at Carbondale, 1979. 664p. UMI# 80-04098.

604   Tift, Thomas N. Theatre Education in the Illinois Public Community College System, 1976-77: A Comprehensive Survey. Ph.D., University of Illinois at Urbana-Champaign, 1979. 162p. UMI# 80-04288.

605   Tostberg, Robert E. Educational Ferment in Chicago 1883-1904. Ph.D., University of Wisconsin, 1960. 284p. UMI# 60- 05798.

606   Trimpe, Dale W. The History of Illinois Equalization Aid. Ed.D., University of Illinois at Urbana-Champaign, 1973. 141p. UMI# 74-12286.

607   Wemple, Quincy A. Some Pioneers in Higher Education in Illinois: Their Work and Influence. Master's thesis, University of Illinois, 1933.

608   Wickiser, Ralph L. The Development of a Public Education Policy in Illinois, 1818-1868. Ph.D., George Peabody College for Teachers, 1939.

609   Wyneland, John L. An Historical Study of the Junior College Movement in Illinois. Master's thesis, Northern Illinois University, 1966.

AUGUSTANA COLLEGE

610   Albrecht, Esther A. Gustav Andreen and the Growth of Augustana College. Master's thesis, University of Illinois, 1950. [president, 1901-1935].

611   Ander, Oscar F. The Career and Influence of T.N. Hasselquist, a Swedish-American Clergyman, Journalist, and Educator. Ph.D., University of Illinois, 1931. 260p. [president, Augustana College, 1863-1891].

612   Erpestad, Emil. Augustana College: A Venture in Christian Education. Ph.D., Vanderbilt University, 1957.

613   Johnson, Elinor C. A History of the Theological Book Collection in the Library of Augustana College and Theological Seminary. Master's thesis, University of Chicago, 1957. 122p.

BELLEVILLE JUNIOR COLLEGE

614   Cox, Marvin L. A Study of the Development and History of Belleville Junior College. 1946-1966. Ph.D., Saint Louis University, 1980. 112p. UMI# 81-00484.

615   Richards, Timothy J. The History and Development and Growth of Adult and Continuing Education at Belleville Area College: 1970 to 1980. Ph.D., Southern Illinois University at Carbondale, 1982. 123p. UMI# 82-21959.

BETHANY BIBLICAL SEMINARY

616   Heckman, Marlin L. A History of the Library of Bethany Biblical Seminary, Chicago, Illinois. Master's thesis, University of Chicago, 1963. 112p.

BRADLEY UNIVERSITY

617   Carter, Asa. History of Bradley Polytechnic Institute as a Junior College. Master's thesis, University of Chicago, 1930.

618   Hammer, Gerald K. Charles Alpheus Bennett, Dean of Manual Arts. Ph.D., University of California-Los Angeles, 1962. [Bradley University, 1897-1919].

CARL SANDBURG COLLEGE

619   Bonner, Harold G. The Founding of Carl Sandburg College. Master's thesis, Illinois State University, 1972.

CHICAGO LUTHERAN THEOLOGICAL SEMINARY

620   Lundean, Joel W. History of the Library of the Chicago Lutheran Theological Seminary of Maywood, Illinois. Master's thesis, University of Chicago, 1967. 210p.

CHICAGO STATE UNIVERSITY

621   Riley, Mary A. A History of the Chicago Normal School. Master's thesis, University of Chicago, 1914.

622   Swanson, Phyllis R. A Historical Study of the Professional Preparation Program in Elementary Physical Education at Chicago State University. Ed.D., University of Southern Mississippi, 1973. 203p. UMI# 74-03961.

CHICAGO, UNIVERSITY OF

623   Ansbro, James B. Albion Woodbury Small and Education. Ph.D., Loyola University, 1978. 216p. UMI# 7807060. [dean, University of Chicago, 1904-1924].

624   Archer, H. Richard. Some Aspects of the Acquisition Program at the University of Chicago: 1892-1928. Ph.D., University of Chicago, 1955. 930p.

625   Arthur, Thomas H. A History of the University of Chicago's Court Theatre: 1955-1964. Master's thesis, Indiana University, 1968.

626   Beck, Kenneth N. The American Institute of Sacred Literature: A Historical Analysis of an Adult Education Institution. Ph.D., University of Chicago, 1968.

627   Blake, Lincoln C. The Concept and Development of Science at the University of Chicago, 1890-1905. Ph.D., University of Chicago, 1967.

628   Boycheff, Kooman. Intercollegiate Athletics and Physical Education at the University of Chicago, 1892-1952. Ph.D., University of Michigan, 1954. 122p. UMI# 00-07611.

629   Cole, Brian A. (Robert) Hutchins and His Critics, 1936-1953. Ph.D., University of Maryland, 1976. 192p. UMI# 77-09498. [president and chancellor, University of Chicago, 1929-1951].

630   Conger, George R., III. Leonard V. Koos: His Contribution to American Education During Half a Century. Ed.D., Florida State University, 1968. 194p. UMI# 67-11288. [professor of education, University of Chicago, 1929-1946].

631   Dark, Harris J. The Life and Work of Herbert Ellsworth Slaught. Ph.D., George Peabody College for Teachers, 1948. [professor of mathematics, University of Chicago, 1892-1931].

632   Dell, George W. An Intensive Rhetorical Analysis of Selected Speeches of Robert Maynard Hutchins: 1940-1955. Ph.D., University of Southern California, 1960. 592p. UMI# 60-2069. [president and chancellor, University of Chicago, 1929-1951].

633   Diner, Steven J. A City and Its University: Chicago Professors and Elite Reform, 1892-1919. Ph.D., University of Chicago, 1972. 314p.

634   Ellsworth, Frank L. Developments in American Legal Education at the Turn of tʰ   ᒎentury: The Founding of the University of Chicago Law School. Ph.D., University of Cnicago, 1976.

635   Engle, Gale W. William Rainey Harper's Conceptions of the Structuring of the Functions Performed by Educational Institutions. Ph.D., Stanford University, 1955. 239p. UMI# 00-10369. [president, University of Chicago, 1891-1906].

636   Farr, Cleburne L. A Rhetorical Analysis of Selected Addresses by Robert Maynard Hutch-

ins. Ph.D., University of Iowa, 1959. 354p. UMI# 59-5708. [president and chancellor, University of Chicago, 1929-1951].

637   Fay, Maureen A. Origins and Early Development of the University of Chicago Extension Division, 1892-1911. Ph.D., University of Chicago, 1976.

638   Featherstone, J.M. Human Ecology and Sociology: The Development of Human Ecology in the Department of Sociology at the University of Chicago, 1914-1939. Master's thesis, Durham University, 1974.

639   Gould, Joseph E. William Rainey Harper and the University of Chicago. Ph.D., Syracuse University, 1951. [president, 1891-1906].

640   Griffiths, Nellie L. A History of the Organization of the Laboratory School of the University of Chicago. Master's thesis, University of Chicago, 1927. 199p.

641   Gustafson, David. The Origin and Establishment of the University High School of the University of Chicago. Master's thesis, University of Chicago, 1927. 134p.

642   Hoffman, Lars. William Rainey Harper and the Chicago Fellowship. Ph.D., University of Iowa, 1978. 327p. UMI# 79-12856. [president, University of Chicago, 1891-1906].

643   Humphreys, Joseph A. Changes in Certain Aspects of the College of the University of Chicago Following the Inauguration of the New Plan (1931). Ph.D., University of Chicago, 1935.

644   Jay, Charles D. The Doctoral Program of George S. Counts at the University of Chicago (1913-1916): An Intellectual History. Ph.D., Southern Illinois University at Carbondale, 1982. 722p. UMI# 82-29283. [professor of education, Columbia University Teachers College, 1927-1956].

645   Kromenaker, Joseph G. The Philosophy of Education of Robert M. Hutchins: Its Development and Change. Ph.D., Saint Louis University, 1973. 192p. UMI# 74-24106. [president and chancellor, University of Chicago, 1929-1951].

646   Laska, Vera. The Foreign Student: With Special Reference to the University of Chicago. Ph.D., University of Chicago, 1960.

647   Lester, Robin D. The Rise, Decline, and Fall of Intercollegiate Football at the University of Chicago, 1890-1940. Ph.D., University of Chicago, 1974.

648   Mavrogenes, Nancy A. William Scott Gray: Leader of Teachers and Shaper of American Reading Instruction. Ph.D., University of Chicago, 1985. [professor of education and dean, University of Chicago, 1914-1960].

649   McMullen, Charles H. The Administration of the University of Chicago Libraries, 1892-1928. Ph.D., University of Chicago, 1950. 298p.

650   Moore, Hastings. The Chicago School of Religious Empiricists: A Case Study Concerning Values in Higher Education. Ed.D., University of Colorado, 1962. 410p. UMI# 63-2004.

651   O'Shea, Joseph A. An Inquiry into the Development of the University of Chicago Evaluation Movement. Ph.D., University of Illinois, 1979. 275p. UMI# 8004245.

652   Patterson, Robert M. The Development of Academic Sociology at the University of Chicago, 1892-1920. Ph.D., Vanderbilt University, 1973. 290p. UMI# 74-01353.

653   Ravitch, Harold. Robert Maynard Hutchins: Philosopher of Education. Ph.D., University of Southern California, 1980. [president and chancellor, University of Chicago, 1929-1951].

654   Richardson, John V., Jr. The Spirit of Inquiry in Library Science: The Graduate Library School in Chicago, 1921-1951. Ph.D., Indiana University, 1978. 437p. UMI# 79-00419.

655   Rumjahn, Miriam C. A Chronicle of the Professional Activities of Ralph W. Tyler: An Oral History. Ed.D., Pepperdine University, 1984. 342p. UMI# 8418598. [professor and dean, University of Chicago, 1938-1953].

656   Schlichting, Harry F. The Nature and Extent of Educational Research in the Laboratory Schools of the University of Chicago, 1903-28. Ph.D., University of Chicago, 1953.

657   Stein, Lloyd E. Hutchins of Chicago: Philosopher- Administrator. Ed.D., University of Massachusetts, 1971. 295p. UMI# 71-25082. [president and chancellor, University of Chicago, 1929-1951].

658   Stone, Marie K. Ralph W. Tyler's Principles of Curriculum, Instruction and Evaluation: Past Influences and Present Effects. Ph.D., University of Chicago, 1985. 488p. UMI# 8506400. [professor and dean, University of Chicago, 1938-1953].

659   Stumpf, Wippert A. A Comparative Study of Certain Aspects of the Old and the New Plan at the University of Chicago. Ph.D., University of Chicago, 1942. 269p.

660   Ware, Lowry P. The Academic Career of William E. Dodd. Ph.D., University of South Carolina, 1956. 342p. UMI# 00-20267. [professor of history, University of Chicago].

661   White, Woodie T. The Study of Education at the University of Chicago, 1892-1958. Ph.D., University of Chicago, 1977.

662   Wurseter, Stephen H. The 'Modernism' of Shailer Mathews: A Study in American Religious Progressivism, 1894-1924. Ph.D., University of Iowa, 1972. 410p. UMI# 72-17,622. [dean, University of Chicago].

663   Zunzer, Robert F. Robert Maynard Hutchins' Conceptions of the Functions and Structures of Higher Education. Ph.D., Stanford University, 1952. [president and chancellor, University of Chicago, 1929-1951].

COLLEGE OF ST. FRANCIS

664   Lane, John J. An Examination of the Process of Merger of Lewis College in the College of St. Francis, Joliet, Illinois. Ph.D., University of Wisconsin, 1971. 88p. UMI# 72-02642.

665   Sterling, Jo Ann J. The College of St. Francis: An Examination of Institutional Response to Societal Influence from 1925 to 1980. Ed.D., Northern Illinois University, 1984. 308p. UMI# 8421289.

EASTERN ILLINOIS UNIVERSITY

666   Jacobs, Virgil M. The History of Basketball at Eastern Illinois University. Master's thesis, Eastern Illinois University, 1959. 124p.

667   Justis, Joel A. The History of Intercollegiate Track and Field at Eastern Illinois University, from 1912-1960. Master's thesis, Eastern Illinois University, 1967.

668   Kirby, Ronald F. History of Baseball at Eastern Illinois University. Master's thesis, Eastern Illinois University, 1963. 174p.

669   Lackey, Sue A. The History of Music at Eastern Illinois University, 1899-1963. Master's thesis, Eastern Illinois University, 1967. 80p.

ELMHURST COLLEGE

670   Denman, William F. Elmhurst: Developmental Study of a Church-Related College. Ph.D., Syracuse University, 1966. 768p. UMI# 67-07067.

GEM CITY BUSINESS COLLEGE

671   Brown, Robert O. A History of the Gem City Business College. Master's thesis, Northeast Missouri State Teachers College, 1959.

GREENVILLE COLLEGE

672   Jordahl, Donald C. Greenville College—The Antecedents: A History of Almira College. Ph.D., Southern Illinois University, 1974. 259p. UMI# 75-00122.

673   Miller, Donald G. A Historical Sketch of Greenville College, with a Special Reference to the Curriculum. Master's thesis, New York University, 1934.

674   Tade, Wilma J.D. A History of the Music Department of Greenville College. Master's thesis, Indiana State Teachers College, 1949. 36p.

ILLINOIS STATE UNIVERSITY

675   Carpenter, Barbara L. A History of Theater at Illinois State Normal University, 1857-1959. Master's thesis, Illinois State University, 1964.

676   Garrett, Donald E. A History of the Intercollegiate Athletic Program at Illinois State Normal University. Master's thesis, Illinois State University, 1959. 56p.

677   Hurst, Homer. Illinois State Normal University and the Public Normal School Movement. Ph.D., George Peabody College for Teachers, 1947. 278p.

678   Loomis, Burt W. The Educational Influence of Richard Edwards. Ph.D., George Peabody College for Teachers, 1932. 213p. [president, Illinois State University, 1862-1876].

679   Mowder, Barbara J. The History of Forensic Activity at Illinois State Normal University. Master's thesis, Illinois State University, 1960.

ILLINOIS, UNIVERSITY OF

680   Barber, William J. George Huff: A Short Biography. Master's thesis, University of Illinois, 1951. 89p. [director of physical education, University of Illinois, 1895-1936].

681   Bole, Ronald E. An Economic Analysis of the Factors Influencing Football Attendance at the University of Illinois, 1926-1968. Ph.D., University of Illinois at Urbana-Champaign, 1970. 136p. UMI# 70-20929.

682   Demartini, Joseph R. Student Protest During Two Periods in the History of the University of Illinois, 1867-1894 and 1929-1942. Ph.D., University of Illinois, 1974. 547p. UMI# 75-00292.

683   Fletcher, Robert C. The Development of Intercollegiate Tennis and Golf at the University of Illinois. Master's thesis, University of Illinois, 1959. 176p.

684   Gregory, Earle S. Mark H. Hindsley: The Illinois Years. Ed.D., University of Illinois at Urbana-Champaign, 1982. 326p. UMI# 8218477. [director of bands, University of Illinois, 1948-1970].

685   Grisso, Karl M. David Kinley, 1861-1944: The Career of the Fifth President of the University of Illinois. Ph.D., University of Illinois, 1980. 717p. UMI# 81-08525. [president, 1920-1930].

686   Grotzinger, Laurel A. The Power and the Dignity: Librarianship and Katharine Sharp. Ph.D., University of Illinois, 1964. 375p. UMI# 65-00821. [professor of library economy, head librarian, and library school director, University of Illinois, 1897-1907].

687   Haycock, Mervyn B. A History of Intercollegiate Basketball at the University of Illinois. Master's thesis, University of Illinois, 1958. 182p.

688   Homrighous, Mary E. A History of Non-Professional Theatrical Production at the University of Illinois from Its Beginning to 1923. Master's thesis, University of Illinois, 1949.

689   Jackson, Richard K. The Development and History of Intercollegiate Gymnastics at the University of Illinois, 1898-1960. Master's thesis, University of Illinois, 1960. 97p.

690   Johnson, Henry C., Jr. The Preparation of Teachers as a University Function: The Case of the University of Illinois. Ph.D., University of Illinois at Urbana-Champaign, 1970. 565p. UMI# 71-05137.

691   Johnson, Ronald M. Captain of Education: An Intellectual Biography of Andrew S. Draper, 1848-1913. Ph.D., University of Illinois at Urbana-Champaign, 1970. 260p. UMI# 70-20989. [president, University of Illinois, 1894-1904].

692   Kersey, Harry A., Jr. John Milton Gregory as a Midwestern Educator 1852-1880. Ph.D., University of Illinois at Urbana-Champaign, 1965. 473p. UMI# 66-04215. [president, University of Illinois, 1868-1880].

693   Lester, Paul F. The Development of Music at the University of Illinois and a History of the School of Music. Master's thesis, University of Illinois, 1943. 134p.

694   McCarthy, Robert E. The Development of Intercollegiate Fencing at the University of Illinois. Master's thesis, University of Illinois, 1960. 76p.

695   Patrick, Harold L. A History of Male Undergraduate Swimming at the University of Illinois. Master's thesis, University of Illinois, 1958.

696   Pullen, Carol F. A History of Intercollegiate Football at the University of Illinois. Master's thesis, University of Illinois, 1957.

697   Ratcliffe, Thomas E., Jr. Development of the Buildings, Policy, Collections of the University of Illinois Library in Urbana, 1895-1940. Master's thesis, University of Illinois, 1949. 111p.

698   Renner, William F. Perspectives of Decision: An Organizational History of the University High School of the University of Illinois. Ed.D., University of Illinois at Urbana-Champaign, 1981. 756p. UMI# 81-14469.

699   Rodnitzky, Jerome L. A History of Public Relations at the University of Illinois, 1904-1930. Ph.D., University of Illinois, 1967. 344p. UMI# 68-01841.

700   Scheinman, Muriel. Art Collecting at the University of Illinois: A History and Catalogue. Ph.D., University of Illinois at Urbana-Champaign, 1981. 592p. UMI# 81-14475.

701   Suen, Ming T. Robert Bingham Downs and Academic Librarianship. Master's thesis, Southern Connecticut State College, 1967. 75p. [director of libraries, University of Illinois, 1943-1971].

702   Swanson, Richardson A. Edmund J. James, 1855-1925; A 'Conservative Progressive' in American Higher Education. Ph.D., University of Illinois, 1966. 342p. UMI# 67-06749. [professor of finance, University of Pennsylvania, 1883-1895; president, Northwestern University, 1902-1904; president, University of Illinois, 1904-1920].

703   Weatherford, Terry L. A History of the Intra-Mural Sports Program at the University of Illinois—1903-1965. Master's thesis, University of Illinois, 1966.

704   Wilcox, Lucile E. History of the University of Illinois Library, 1868-1897. Master's thesis, University of Illinois, 1931. 77p.

705   Wilson, Robert A. A History of the Administration of Intercollegiate Athletics at the University of Illinois. Master's thesis, University of Illinois, 1948.

706   Wing, Roger L. The Development of Intercollegiate Track and Field at the University of Illinois. Master's thesis, University of Illinois, 1959. 193p.

707   Wolf, Donald L. A History of Intercollegiate Baseball at the University of Illinois. Master's thesis, University of Illinois, 1958.

708   Yenawine, Wayne S. The Influence of Scholars on Research Library Development at the University of Illinois. Ph.D., University of Illinois, 1955. 294p. UMI# 55-1114.

ILLINOIS WESLEYAN UNIVERSITY

709   Allan, Henry C. History of the Non-residential Degree Program at Illinois Wesleyan Uni-

versity, 1873-1910: A Study of a Pioneer External Degree Program in the United States. Ph.D., University of Chicago, 1984.

710   Bridges, Dennis L. The History of Basketball at Illinois Wesleyan University: A Compilation of the History of the Sport of Basketball at Illinois Wesleyan University from 1910-1965. Master's thesis, Illinois State University, 1965.

JOHN A. LOGAN COLLEGE

711   Hill, Jack D. Critical Decisions in the Organization and Development of John A. Logan College: A Historical Analysis of the Years 1965 through 1972. Ph.D., Southern Illinois University at Carbondale, 1978. 379p. UMI# 78-17525.

KASKASKIA COLLEGE

712   Pedtke, Dorothy A. H. A History of Kaskaskia College. Ph.D., Southern Illinois University at Carbondale, 1979. 154p. UMI# 80-04079.

KNOX COLLEGE

713   Plath, Paul J. The Secularization of Knox College. Master's thesis, University of Illinois, 1977.

LOYOLA UNIVERSITY OF CHICAGO

714   Riccio, Gregory J. The History of Loyola University of Chicago's Rome Center of Liberal Arts, 1962-1977. Ph.D., Loyola University of Chicago, 1978. 161p. UMI# 78-15878.

MCKENDREE COLLEGE

715   Rawlings, Wyatt. Development of the Curriculum at McKendree College. Master's thesis, Saint Louis University, 1933.

716   Weil, Oscar A., Jr. Origin and Establishment of McKendree College, 1828-1841. Master's thesis, Washington University, 1961.

MONTICELLO SEMINARY

717   Peterson, Charles E., Jr. Theron Baldwin and Higher Education in the Old Northwest. Ph.D., Johns Hopkins University, 1961. [principal, Monticello Seminary, 1838-1843].

MOODY BIBLE INSTITUTE

718   Getz, Gene A. A History of Moody Bible Institute and Its Contributions to Evangelical Education. Ph.D., New York University, 1968. 606p. UMI# 68-11791.

719   Wells, Donald A. D.L. Moody and His Schools: An Historical Analysis of an Educational Ministry. Ph.D., Boston University, 1972. 440p. UMI# 72-25,350.

MUNDELEIN COLLEGE FOR WOMEN

720   Chambers, Carole Z. The Presidential Years of Sister Ann Ida Gannon, BVM, Mundelein College, 1957-1975. Ph.D., Loyola University of Chicago, 1978. 188p. UMI# 78-07064.

NORTHEASTERN ILLINOIS UNIVERSITY

721   George, Melvin R. Northeastern Illinois University: The History of a Comprehensive State University. Ph.D., University of Chicago, 1979.

722   Torres, Maximino D. An Attempt to Provide Higher Educational Opportunity to Hispanics: The Evolution of Proyecto Pa'lante at Northeastern Illinois University—1971-1976. Ed.D., Loyola University of Chicago, 1983. 409p. UMI# 83-11684.

723   Wadsworth, Emily C. Programmatic Change in Higher Education: A Study of the History and Functioning of the Center for Program Development at Northeastern Illinois University, Chicago, Illinois. Ph.D., Northwestern University, 1982. 334p. UMI# 82-26038.

NORTHERN ILLINOIS UNIVERSITY

724   Marsh, Joseph T. A History of Teacher Education at Northern Illinois University: An Example of the Development of Teacher Preparatory Institutions from Normal Schools to State Universities in the United States. Ed.D., Indiana University, 1969. 261p. UMI# 71-11347.

725   Ottoson, Ronald. Historical Survey of Athletic Participation at Northern Illinois University. Master's thesis, Northern Illinois University, 1960.

726   Stomfay-Stitz, Aline M. Northern Illinois University Peace Education: Historical Perspectives, 1828-1983. Ed.D., Northern Illinois University, 1984. 300p. UMI# 8421290.

727   Tyler, Kenneth D. The Educational Life and Work of Charles A. McMurry: 1872-1929. Ed.D., Northern Illinois University, 1982. 259p. UMI# 8220330. [professor of education, Northern Illinois University, 1899-1915].

728   Waldorf, James A. A Study of the Doctor of Education Degree in Educational Administration at Northern Illinois University. Ed.D., Northern Illinois University, 1985. 231p. UMI# 8604350.

729   Walker, Mary M.J. The Reading and Study Skills Program at Northern Illinois University, 1963-1976. Ed.D., Northern Illinois University, 1980. 133p. UMI# 8020783.

NORTHWESTERN UNIVERSITY

730   Bauer, Otto F. A Century of Debating at Northwestern University, 1855-1955. Master's thesis, Northwestern University, 1955.

731   Guffin, Jan A. Winifred Ward: A Critical Biography. Ph.D., Duke University, 1976. 265p. UMI# 76-18954. [professor of speech education, Northwestern University, 1920-1950].

732   Hakkio, Joan S. A Comparison of 1958 and 1970 Women Student Leaders at Northwestern University: Their Characteristics, Self-Concepts, and Attitudes Toward the University. Ph.D., Northwestern University, 1972. 218p. UMI# 72-32449.

733   Hoadley, Grace. Significant Chapters in the History of Northwestern University, 1905-1923. Master's thesis, Northwestern University, 1923.

734   Kennel, Pauline G. Peter Christian Lutkin—Northwestern University's First Dean of Music. Ph.D., Northwestern University, 1981. 372p. UMI# 81-24921. [dean, 1897-1928].

735   Sedlak, Michael W. The Emergence and Development of Collegiate Business Education in the United States, 1881-1974: Northwestern University as a Case Study. Ph.D., Northwestern University, 1977. 479p. UMI# 78-05326.

736   Thornburgh, Daniel E. Contributions of Curtis D. MacDougall to Journalism Education. Ed.D., Indiana University, 1980. 321p. UMI# 8103404. [professor of journalism, Northwestern University, 1942-1971].

PRINCIPIA COLLEGE

737   Craig, Robert M. Maybeck at Principia: A Study of an Architect-Client Relationship. Ph.D., Cornell University, 1973. 787p. UMI# 74-6397. [instructor of architecture, University of California, 1894-1900; designed Principia College].

ROCKFORD COLLEGE

738   Cederborg, Hazel P. History of Rockford College. Master's thesis, Wellesley College, 1926.

739   Townsend, Lucy F. Anna Peck Sill and the Rise of Women's Collegiate Curriculum. Ph.D., Loyola University of Chicago, 1985. 316p. UMI# 8517377. [president, Rockford College, 1849-1884].

ROOSEVELT UNIVERSITY

740   Lelon, Thomas C. The Emergence of Roosevelt College of Chicago: A Search for an Ideal. Ph.D., University of Chicago, 1973. 525p.

741   Perlman, Daniel H. Faculty Trusteeship: Concept and Experience, a History of the Governance of Roosevelt University. Ph.D., University of Chicago, 1971. 316p. UMI# 72-03372.

SHIMER COLLEGE

742   Moorhead, Patrick H. The Shimer College Presidency: 1930 to 1980. Ed.D., Loyola University of Chicago, 1983. 248p. UMI# 8314083.

SOUTHEASTERN ILLINOIS COLLEGE

743   Szymczak, Donald R. Origin and Development of Southeastern Illinois College, 1960-1976. Ph.D., Southern Illinois University at Carbondale, 1977. 252p. UMI# 77-24041.

SOUTHERN ILLINOIS UNIVERSITY

744   Bortz, Jeanne M. A Study of University Level Prisoner Education in Correctional Institutions Served by Southern Illinois University at Carbondale from 1956 to 1975. Ph.D., Southern Illinois University, 1981. 118p. UMI# 8206445.

745   Canfield, Muriel N. The Latin American Institute at Southern Illinois University at Carbon-

dale, 1958-1973. Ph.D., Southern Illinois University at Carbondale, 1984. 202p. UMI# 8510004.

746 Covington, Patricia B. A History of the School of Art at Southern Illinois University at Carbondale 1869-1980. Ph.D., Southern Illinois University at Carbondale, 1981. 286p. UMI# 82-06449.

747 Fadil, Virginia A. The Board of Trustees: Lay Governance at Southern Illinois University— The Developmental Years 1949-1964. Ph.D., Southern Illinois University at Carbondale, 1976. 266p. UMI# 76-28736.

748 Gray, Charles E. Student Financial Support at Southern Illinois University at Carbondale: 1874-1974. Ph.D., Southern Illinois University, 1976. 383p. UMI# 76-28,741.

749 Kurtz, John L. The Development of Radio and Television at Southern Illinois University. Ph.D., Southern Illinois University, 1973. 496p. UMI# 74-06224.

750 Lagow, Larry D. A History of the Center for Vietnamese Studies at Southern Illinois University, 1969-1976. Ph.D., Southern Illinois University at Carbondale, 1978. 669p. UMI# 78-17533.

751 Metzger, John. John Page Wham: His Role as Trustee of Southern Illinois University, 1949-1965. Ph.D., Southern Illinois University, 1982. 200p. UMI# 82-21947.

752 Pierson, Charles L. A History of the Southern Illinois University School of Music, 1874-1970. Ph.D., Southern Illinois University, 1971. 400p. UMI# 72-10284.

753 Stracka, Daniel. International Education at Southern Illinois University at Carbondale, 1954-1974. Ph.D., Southern Illinois University, 1976. 234p. UMI# 76-28776.

754 Traxler, Joseph M. The Contributions of Delyte W. Morris to Southern Illinois University. Ph.D., Southern Illinois University, 1971. 184p. UMI# 72-05400. [president, 1948-1970].

SOUTHERN ILLINOIS UNIVERSITY, EDWARDSVILLE

755 Wadell, Keith A. The Establishment of Southern Illinois University at Edwardsville. Ph.D., Southern Illinois University at Carbondale, 1983. 645p. UMI# 8326574.

SPRINGFIELD COLLEGE

756 Trares, Thomas F. Ecumenical Actions: A History of Springfield College in Illinois, 1929-1969. Ph.D., Saint Louis University, 1972. 87p. UMI# 74-04585.

TRINITY JUNIOR COLLEGE

757 Wiebe, Jeffrey J. Trinity Junior College: Its History, Development and Institutional Mission. Ph.D., University of North Dakota, 1970. 176p. UMI# 72-16375.

WABASH VALLEY COLLEGE

758 Gillespie, James R. The Development of Wabash Valley College: 1960-1969. Ph.D., Southern Illinois University at Carbondale, 1985. 296p. UMI# 8526676.

WHEATON COLLEGE

759   Dattoli, Randall T. The Wheaton Graduate School (1936-1971): Its History and Contributions. Ph.D., Loyola University of Chicago, 1981. 200p. UMI# 81-09936.

WINSTON CHURCHILL COLLEGE

760   Schindbeck, David J. The Formation and Development of Winston Churchill College. Master's thesis, Illinois State University, 1969.

INDIANA

GENERAL STUDIES

761 Blackburn, James C. The Role of the Church-Related College in Higher Education: An Analysis of Four Evangelical Christian Colleges in Central Indiana. Ph.D., Miami University, 1979. 199p. UMI# 7920296.

762 Brayton, James H. Development of Medical Education in Indiana. Master's thesis, Indiana University, 1929. 164p.

763 Heller, Herbert L. Negro Education in Indiana from 1816 to 1869. Ph.D., Indiana University, 1952.

764 Jeffery, Eber W. History of Private Normal Schools in Indiana. Ph.D., New York University, 1932. 225p. UMI# 72-33579.

765 Morgan, Clarence M. The Development of Teacher Training in Indiana Prior to 1900. Ph.D., Indiana University, 1936. 532p.

766 Parker, Paul E. The Administration of Privately Controlled Colleges and Universities in Indiana. Ph.D., University of Arizona, 1949. 315p.

767 Perkins, Richard W. A History of College Entrance Requirements in Indiana. Master's thesis, Indiana State Teachers College, 1947. 57p.

768 Rahe, Herbert E. The History of Speech Education in Ten Indiana Colleges. Ph.D., University of Wisconsin, 1940. 239p.

769 Scheibner, Helen L. A History of the Evolution of Health Education as a Specialized Area of Professional Education in Indiana Colleges and Universities, 1816-1973. Doctor of Health Science, Indiana University, 1974. 140p. UMI# 74-24516.

770 Sherwood, Philip K. A Historical Study of the Associated Colleges of Indiana. Ed.D., Indiana University, 1973. 250p. UMI# 74-02705.

771 Smith, Paul R.G. The History of Corporate Financial Assistance to Member Institutions of the Associated Colleges of Indiana, 1948-1967. Ph.D., University of Notre Dame, 1968. 258p. UMI# 69-04082.

772 Thompson, Jay C., Jr. A History of the Servicemen's Readjustment Act and Its Effect Upon Education in Indiana. Ed.D., Ball State University, 1969. 262p. UMI# 70-6660.

773 Winston, Chauncey G. The Contributions of Indianians to the Work of the North Central Association of Colleges and Secondary Schools, 1895-1951. Ed.D., Indiana University, 1951. 436p.

774 Woodburn, James A. Higher Education in Indiana. Ph.D., Johns Hopkins University, 1890. 200p.

ANDERSON COLLEGE

775   Campbell, Marie K. A Historical Study of Anderson College, 1911 through 1930. Master's thesis, Clemson Agricultural College, 1961.

BALL STATE UNIVERSITY

776   Gray, Marvin R. The History and Philosophy of Intercollegiate Athletics for Men at Ball State University. Doctor of Physical Education, Indiana University, 1968. 180p. UMI# 69-13886.

777   Holmes, Marilou J. A History of Professional Nursing Education in Middletown, 1906-1968. Ed.D., Ball State University, 1983. 528p. UMI# 84-01298.

778   Thompson, Wade H., Jr. Historical Development of Student Personnel Services Administration at Ball State University, 1918-1968. Ed.D., Indiana University, 1971. 278p. UMI# 71-17889.

BETHEL COLLEGE

779   Beutler, Albert J. The Founding and History of Bethel College of Indiana. Ph.D., Michigan State University, 1970. 207p. UMI# 70-20436.

BUTLER UNIVERSITY

780   Fields, Thomas B. A History of Butler University, Indianapolis, Indiana. Master's thesis, Indiana University, 1928. 158p.

CANTERBURY COLLEGE

781   Beeler, Kent D. Canterbury College, 1946-1951: Its Decline and Demise. Ed.D., Indiana University, 1969. 234p. UMI# 70-23357.

CENTRAL NORMAL COLLEGE

782   Parr, James H. A History of Central Normal College. Master's thesis, Indiana University, 1927. 76p.

783   Unruh, Alice E. The Story of the Central Normal College. Master's thesis, Ft. Hays Kansas State College, 1953.

DEPAUW UNIVERSITY

784   Appleman, Mary J.N. History of the DePauw University Speech Department. Master's thesis, DePauw University, 1957.

785   Clithero, Edith P. History of Dramatic Activity at DePauw University. Master's thesis, DePauw University, 1957.

786   Kellog, John A. An Evaluation of the First Education Laboratory at DePauw University. Master's thesis, DePauw University, 1969.

EARLHAM COLLEGE

787   Stanley, Ellen L. The Earlham College Library; A History of Its Relation to the College, 1847-1947. Master's thesis, University of Illinois, 1947. 79p.

FRANKLIN COLLEGE OF INDIANA

788   Bukalski, Peter J. The Franklin College Liberal Studies Program: An Historical Study of the Process of Academic Policy Formation. Ph.D., Ohio State University, 1975. 256p. UMI# 76-03393.

INDIANA DENTAL COLLEGE

789   Carr, Jack D. History of Indiana Dental College, 1879-1925. Master's thesis, Butler University, 1957.

INDIANA STATE UNIVERSITY

790   Allen, Max P. History of the Indiana State Teachers College. Master's thesis, Indiana State Teachers College, 1931. 125p.

791   Coffey, Thomas J. The Emerging University: A Case Study of Organizational Change. Ph.D., University of Chicago, 1978.

792   Dean, Mark E. A History of Intercollegiate Athletics at Indiana State Teachers College from 1870 to 1940. Ph.D., Indiana University, 1956. 171p.

793   Henley, Emily A. The History and Development of the Teaching of Dramatics at Indiana State Teachers College from 1891 to 1937. Master's thesis, Indiana State Teachers College, 1949. 63p.

794   Morgan, Ruth H. History of the Radio Division of Indiana State Teachers College. Master's thesis, Indiana State Teachers College, 1951.

INDIANA UNIVERSITY

795   Baker, Michael R. A History of the Bureau of Studies in Adult Education at Indiana University. Master's thesis, Indiana University, 1966. 110p.

796   Baxter, Cynthia L. Indiana University, 1917-1929. Master's thesis, Indiana University, 1953. 180p.

797   Brown, F. Barry. Mirror for Instructional Systems Technology: An Historical Survey of Doctoral Dissertations at Indiana University, 1948-1976. Ed.D., Indiana University, 1979. 494p. UMI# 80-03813.

798   Buis, Almon R. The History and Work of the Extension Division of Indiana University. Master's thesis, Indiana University, 1927. 153p.

799   Cook, Anne W. A History of the Indiana University Audio-Visual Center: 1913-1975. Ph.D., Indiana University, 1980. 334p. UMI# 80-16402.

800   Cope, Garrett. History of the Origin and Development of Theatre Arts at Indiana University. Master's thesis, Indiana University, 1951.

801   Darby, MacArthur. The Origin and Development of the Campus Ombudsman Service at Indiana University, Bloomington. Ed.D., Indiana University, 1977. 125p. UMI# 77-27023.

802   Deputy, Manfred W. The Philosophical Ideas and Related Achievements of William Lowe Bryan. Ph.D., Indiana University, 1947. 231p. [professor of philosophy, 1885-1902; president, 1902-1937, Indiana University].

803   Elmes, Robert J. Henry Lester Smith, Dean, School of Education, Indiana University, 1916-1946. Ed.D., Indiana University, 1969. 209p. UMI# 70-11686.

804   Gaylord, Mark S. Edwin Sutherland and the Origins of Differential Association Theory. Ph.D., University of Missouri-Columbia, 1984. 294p. UMI# 8512212. [professor of sociology, Indiana University, 1935-1949].

805   Gering, William M. David Starr Jordan, Spokesman for Higher Education in Indiana. Ph.D., Indiana University, 1963. 197p. UMI# 64-05452. [president, Indiana University, 1885-1891].

806   Hofmann, Kurt O. The Relationship Between Indiana University Bloomington and the Campus Ministry from 1937 to 1972. Ed.D., Indiana University, 1972. 145p. UMI# 73-10771.

807   Jones, James H. The Origins of the Institute for Sex Research: A History. Ph.D., Indiana University, 1973. 311p. UMI# 73-12,333.

808   Lowell, Mildred H. Indiana University Libraries, 1829-1942. Ph.D., University of Chicago, 1957. 453p.

809   MacKay, Vera A. Intercultural Education: An Historical Narrative and the Role of the Indiana University. Ed.D., Indiana University, 1954. 286p. UMI# 00-08932.

810   Matthews, Alfred T. The Evolution of Student Participation in Policy Formation at Indiana University. Ph.D., Indiana University, 1967. 287p. UMI# 68-07252.

811   Moffatt, Georgabell H. A History of the Indiana University Auditorium and the Cultural Tastes of the Community as Reflected by the Attendance at Auditorium Events from 1941-1952. Master's thesis, Indiana University, 1953.

812   Nelson, Dorwin R. A History of Literary Societies at Indiana University. Master's thesis, Indiana University, 1965.

813   Rothenberger, Katharine. An Historical Study of the Position of Dean of Women at Indiana University. Master's thesis, Indiana University, 1942.

814   Swadener, Marc. National Science Foundation Summer Institute in Mathematics at Indiana University, 1957 through 1969. Ed.D., Indiana University, 1970. 133p. UMI# 70-25219.

815   Warriner, David R. The Veterans of World War II at Indiana University, 1944-1951. Ph.D., Indiana University, 1978. 284p. UMI# 78-13197.

INDIANA VOCATIONAL TECHNICAL COLLEGE

816   Martin, Robert E. Development of a Master Plan for the Indiana Vocational Technical College, 1973-1983. Ed.D., Indiana University, 1973. 422p. UMI# 74-02687.

MARIAN COLLEGE

817   Whalen, Mary G. Marian College, Indianapolis, Indiana: The First Quarter Century, 1937-1962. Ed.D., University of Cincinnati, 1966. 246p. UMI# 66-11507.

NOTRE DAME, UNIVERSITY OF

818   Arthur, David J. The University of Notre Dame, 1919-1933: An Administrative History. Ph.D., University of Michigan, 1973. 452p. UMI# 74-15660.

819   Jones, Thomas P. The Development of the Office of Prefect of Religion at the University of Notre Dame from 1842 to 1952. Ph.D., Catholic University of America, 1960.

820   Lenoue, Bernard J. The Historical Development of the Curriculum of the University of Notre Dame. Master's thesis, University of Notre Dame, 1933.

821   Schlaver, David E. The Notre Dame Ethos. Student Life in a Catholic Residential University (Volumes I and II). Ph.D., University of Michigan, 1979. 478p. UMI# 7925221.

822   Wack, John T. The University of Notre Dame Du Lac Foundation, 1842-1857. Ph.D., University of Notre Dame, 1967. 378p. UMI# 67-13606.

823   Weber, Ralph E. The Life of Reverend John A Zahm, C.S.C.: American Catholic Apologist and Educator. Ph.D., University of Notre Dame, 1956. 522p. UMI# 00-16546. [president, board of trustees, University of Notre Dame].

OAKLAND CITY COLLEGE

824   Robinson, Ivor J. A History of Oakland City College. Master's thesis, Indiana University, 1930. 130p.

825   Shirley, Betty L. History of Oakland City College. Master's thesis, Indiana State Teachers College, 1958.

PURDUE UNIVERSITY

826   Anderson, Kenneth C. Biography of Emerson White. Ph.D., Case Western Reserve University, 1952. 199p. [president, Purdue University, 1876-1883].

827   Burrin, Frank K. Edward Charles Elliott, Educator. Ph.D., Purdue University, 1956. 296p. UMI# 00-16453. [president, Purdue University, 1922-1945].

828   Johnson, Helen R. A History of Purdue University's Nursing Education Programs. Ed.D., Indiana University, 1975. 195p. UMI# 76-06277.

829   Runda, Robert L. History and Development of Theater at Purdue University. Master's thesis, Purdue University, 1963.

SAINT MARY-OF-THE-WOODS COLLEGE

830   O'Neill, Sister Margaret A. A History of Saint Mary-of-the-Woods College. Master's thesis, Indiana State Teachers College, 1941. 196p.

ST. FRANCIS COLLEGE

831   Scheetz, Mary J. Service through Scholarship: A History of St. Francis College. Ph.D., University of Michigan, 1970. 278p. UMI# 71-15293.

ST. MARY'S COLLEGE

832   Klein, Mary E. Sister M. Madelena Wolfe, C.S.C., St. Mary's College, Notre Dame, Indiana: A Study of Presidential Leadership, 1934-1961. Ph.D., Kent State University, 1983. 220p. UMI# 8406139.

TEACHERS COLLEGE OF INDIANAPOLIS

833   Hollingsworth, Virginia N. The History of the Teachers College of Indianapolis. Master's thesis, Butler University, 1946.

UNION CHRISTIAN COLLEGE

834   Conlin, James W. A History of Union Christian College, 1859-1924. Master's thesis, Indiana University, 1931. 178p.

VALPARAISO UNIVERSITY

835   Bigelow, Cecil L. A History of Valparaiso University, 1873-1925. Master's thesis, University of Chicago, 1937. 67p.

VINCENNES UNIVERSITY

836   Burnett, Howard R. A History of Vincennes University. Master's thesis, Indiana University, 1936. 294p.

WABASH COLLEGE

837   Sherockman, Andrew A. Caleb Mills, Pioneer Educator in Indiana. Ph.D., University of Pittsburgh, 1955. 313p. UMI# 00-15107. [professor of Greek language and literature and principal, Wabash College, 1833-1879].

IOWA

GENERAL STUDIES

838   Darling, Elmer C. Curricular Trends in Higher Education in Iowa Since 1900. Ph.D., University of Iowa, 1936.

839   Engel, Robert E. Non-Sectarianism and the Relationship of the Methodist Church in Iowa to Upper Iowa College and Iowa Wesleyan College. Ph.D., University of Iowa, 1969. 462p. UMI# 69-21688.

840   Hoffman, Warren F. Standards for the Establishment of Public Junior Colleges in Iowa as Determined by the Implications of an Historical Survey and Other Criteria. Ed.D., University of Colorado, 1963. 407p. UMI# 64-01924.

841   Johnson, Max R. A History of the Public Two-Year College Movement in Iowa, 1918-1965 (Volumes I and II). Ed.D., University of Northern Colorado, 1967. 887p. UMI# 68-00430.

842   Lowery, Paul J. A History of the First Fifteen Years of Community Colleges in Iowa, 1965-1980. Ph.D., Iowa State University, 1982. 244p. UMI# 8224229.

843   Smola, Bonnie K. A Study of the Development of Diploma and Baccalaureate Degree Nursing Programs in Iowa from 1907-1978. Ph.D., Iowa State University, 1980. 365p. UMI# 81-06057.

844   Story, Donna K. A Study of Practical and Associate Degree Nursing Education in Iowa from 1918 to 1978. Ph.D., Iowa State University, 1980. 311p. UMI# 81-06061.

CENTRAL UNIVERSITY OF IOWA

845   Cook, Thomas H. A History of Music at Central College During the Nineteenth Century. Doctor of Arts, University of Northern Colorado, 1983. 258p. UMI# 8408145.

DRAKE UNIVERSITY

846   Jones, Nathen E. Music at Drake University, 1881-1931. Ed.D., University of Michigan, 1964. 157p. UMI# 65-5326.

847   Kaley, Jack. A History of Intercollegiate Football at Drake University. Master's thesis, Drake University, 1956.

848   Slavens, Thomas P. A History of the Drake University Libraries. Master's thesis, University of Minnesota, 1962. 128p.

GRACELAND COLLEGE

849   Benson, Robert J. The Development of Music at Graceland College from 1895 to 1945. Ph.D., Chicago Musical College, 1955.

GRINNELL COLLEGE

850   Beatty, Shelton L. A Curricular History of Grinnell College, 1848-1931. Ph.D., Stanford University, 1955. 533p. UMI# 00-15357.

851   Coleman, John P. In Pursuit of Harmony: A Study of the Thought of Jesse Macy. Ph.D., University of Iowa, 1968. 248p. UMI# 68-16792. [professor of history and political science, Grinnell College, 1883-1912].

IOWA STATE UNIVERSITY

852   Collins, Robert M. History of Agronomy at the Iowa State College. Ph.D., Iowa State University, 1954.

853   Lee, James L. A Century of Military Training at Iowa State University, 1870-1970. Ph.D., Iowa State University, 1972. 480p. UMI# 72-26926.

854   Lokensgard, Erik. Formative Influences of Engineering Extension on Industrial Education at Iowa State College. Ph.D., Iowa State University, 1986. 422p. UMI# 8615066.

855   Spratt, Bessie W. Development of the Home Economics Curriculum of Iowa State College from 1923 to 1953. Master's thesis, Iowa State College, 1953.

856   Weller, L. David, Jr. A History of Undergraduate Teacher Education Programs at Iowa State University, 1869-1968. Ph.D., Iowa State University, 1975. 484p. UMI# 76-09207.

IOWA, UNIVERSITY OF

857   Barrett, Norbert C. History of the State University of Iowa: The College of Engineering. Ph.D., University of Iowa, 1945. 217p.

858   Bass, Jack E. The History of the State University of Iowa: The Extension Division. Master's thesis, University of Iowa, 1943.

859   Bates, Katherine V. History of the State University of Iowa: Aspects of the Physical Plant. Master's thesis, University of Iowa, 1946.

860   Bontekoe, Cornelius. Development of the Social Studies in the State University of Iowa: 1856-1906. Master's thesis, University of Iowa, 1936.

861   Carstensen, Vernon R. The State University of Iowa: The Collegiate Department from the Beginning to 1878. Ph.D., University of Iowa, 1936.

862   Conklin, Mary W. The History of the State University of Iowa: Thomas Houston MacBride. Master's thesis, University of Iowa, 1945. [professor and president, 1878-1916].

863   Cowperthwaite, Lowery L. A History of Intercollegiate Forensics at the State University of Iowa, 1874-1946. Master's thesis, University of Iowa, 1946.

864   Crary, Ryland W. History of the State University of Iowa. Ph.D., University of Iowa, 1946. 229p.

865   Cretzmeyer, Jane. History of the State University of Iowa: Foreign Languages Since 1900. Master's thesis, University of Iowa, 1944.

866   Culver, Daniel. A History of the University of Iowa Symphony Orchestra. Doctor of Musical Arts, University of Iowa, 1978.

867   Curtis, Orville B. The History of the State University of Iowa: The College of Commerce. Master's thesis, University of Iowa, 1945.

868   Davies, Frederick G. History of the State University of Iowa: The College of Liberal Arts, 1911-1934. Ph.D., University of Iowa, 1948.

869   Doty, Franklin A. History of the State University of Iowa: The College of Liberal Arts, 1900-1916. Ph.D., University of Iowa, 1947. 231p.

870   Fogdall, Vergil S. History of the State University of Iowa: The Governing Boards, 1847-1947. Ph.D., University of Iowa, 1948.

871   Gilson, James E. Changing Student Lifestyle at the University of Iowa, 1880-1900. Ph.D., University of Iowa, 1980. 396p. UMI# 80-22025.

872   Ginter, Eloise T. History of the State University of Iowa: Faculty Participation in Administrative Functions. Master's thesis, University of Iowa, 1946.

873   Hott, Leland E. The History of the State University of Iowa: Development of History and the Social Sciences, 1906-1946. Master's thesis, University of Iowa, 1947.

874   Howard, Donald F. History of the State University of Iowa: The Graduate College. Ph.D., University of Iowa, 1947. 231p.

875   Jackson, Harry D. University High School—The University of Iowa: A Task-Oriented Study of the First Fifty Years. Ph.D., University of Iowa, 1968. 191p. UMI# 68-10663.

876   Johnson, Ellen E. A History of the State University of Iowa: The Administration of President MacLean. Master's thesis, University of Iowa, 1946. [George E. MacLean, president, 1899-1911].

877   Johnson, Lauren T. History of the State University of Iowa: Musical Activity, 1916-1944. Master's thesis, University of Iowa, 1944.

878   Jones, Lewis L. Carl Emil Seashore: Dean of Graduate College of the University of Iowa, 1908 to 1936, Dean Pro Tempore, 1942 to 1946: A Study of His Ideas on Graduate Education. Ph.D., University of Iowa, 1978. 239p. UMI# 79-02915.

879   Kohler, Francis J. History of the State University of Iowa: Scientific Expeditions' Collections, and the Museum of Natural History. Master's thesis, University of Iowa, 1944.

880   Lang, William C. History of the State University of Iowa: The Collegiate Department from 1879 to 1900. Ph.D., University of Iowa, 1942. 146p.

881   McMaster, Robert K. A History of the Department of Philosophy at the State University of Iowa from Jared Stone to Herbert Martin. Ph.D., University of Iowa, 1979. 343p. UMI# 79-24504.

882   Meinhard, Robert W. History of the State University of Iowa: Physical Education and Athletics for Men. Master's thesis, University of Iowa, 1947.

883   Miller, Blanche. The History of the State University of Iowa: Physical Education for Women. Master's thesis, University of Iowa, 1943.

884   Nuss, Elizabeth F. History of the State University of Iowa: The Iowa Lakeside Laboratory. Master's thesis, University of Iowa, 1946.

885   Peterson, Elof R. History of State University of Iowa: The Problem of Finance, 1847-1900. Master's thesis, University of Iowa, 1944.

886   Rachut, Marie P. History of the State University of Iowa: The WSUI Radio Station. Master's thesis, University of Iowa, 1946.

887   Sadler, Esther A. History of the State University of Iowa: Co-Education. Master's thesis, University of Iowa, 1942.

888   Stinehart, James S. History of the State University of Iowa: Musical Activity to 1915. Master's thesis, University of Iowa, 1941.

889   Throne, Mildred. The History of the State University of Iowa: The University Libraries. Master's thesis, University of Iowa, 1943.

890   Wangberg, Martha I. History of the State University of Iowa: Languages and Literature to 1900. Master's thesis, University of Iowa, 1944.

891   Weidenbach, Amelia R. History of the University of Iowa: The College of Dentistry. Master's thesis, University of Iowa, 1944.

892   Westerberg, Virginia M. A History of the University Elementary School, State University of Iowa, 1915-1958. Ph.D., University of Iowa, 1959. 400p. UMI# 59-03824.

893   Wine, Margaret A.M. A Narrative History of the University High School, University of Iowa, 1916-1972. Ph.D., University of Iowa, 1979. 380p. UMI# 79-24543.

894   Yearnd, Moretta A. History of the State University of Iowa: The Experimental High School Since 1930. Master's thesis, University of Iowa, 1943.

JOHN FLETCHER COLLEGE

895   Dewey, Clifford S. The History of John Fletcher College with Special Reference to Its Religious Tradition. Master's thesis, University of Iowa, 1940.

MORNINGSIDE COLLEGE

896   Waage, James. A History of Speech Education at Morningside College, 1894-1963. Master's thesis, University of South Dakota, 1965.

NORTHERN IOWA, UNIVERSITY OF

897   Molen, Clarence T., Jr. The Evolution of a State Normal School into a Teachers College:

The University of Northern Iowa, 1876-1916. Ph.D., University of Iowa, 1974. 426p. UMI# 75-13797.

NORTHWESTERN COLLEGE

898   Hubers, Dale. A History of the Northwestern Classical Academy 1882-1957. Master's thesis, University of South Dakota, 1957.

PARSONS COLLEGE

899   Buell, Harold L. Parsons College: A Decade of Transition. Ph.D., Florida State University, 1966. 221p. UMI# 67-06462.

WILLIAM PENN COLLEGE

900   Moore, George H. A History of the Curriculum and Instruction of William Penn College, 1873-1954. Ph.D., University of Iowa, 1954. 232p. UMI# 00-10231.

KANSAS

GENERAL STUDIES

901   Buckner, Reginald T. A History of Music Education in the Black Community of Kansas City, Kansas, 1905-1954. Ph.D., University of Minnesota, 1974. 347p. UMI# 75-00157.

902   Conard, Erik P. A History of Kansas' Closed Colleges. Ph.D., University of Oklahoma, 1970. 219p. UMI# 71-01483.

903   Hanson, C. Norman. The Associated Colleges of Central Kansas, 1965-1985: A Case Study. Ph.D. University of Kansas, 1986. 246p. UMI# 8619904

904   Hollingsworth, Leon. Mennonite Education in Kansas, 1925- 1950. Master's thesis, Kansas State Teachers College (Emporia), 1951.

905   Maul, Ray C. The Certification of Teachers in Kansas. Ed.D., New York University, 1937. 219p. UMI# 73-03298.

906   Merwin, Bruce W. The Development of Collegiate Education in Kansas with Particular Emphasis on the Curriculum. Ph.D., University of Kansas, 1928.

907   Nenninger, Timothy K. The Fort Leavenworth Schools: Post Graduate Military Education and Professionalization in the United States Army, 1880-1920. Ph.D., University of Wisconsin, 1974. 391p. UMI# 74-18946.

908   Sloan, James C. A Historical Study of the Ghost Colleges of Kansas. Master's thesis, Kansas State Teachers College (Emporia), 1948.

909   Stone, Helen W. The History of Music Education in Kansas Community Junior College, 1917-1965. Ph.D., University of Kansas, 1981. 195p. UMI# 8128738.

910   Ward, Earl R. History of the Private Normal Schools in Kansas. Master's thesis, Kansas State Teachers College (Emporia), 1939.

911   Wiebe, David U. The Mennonite Institutions of Higher Learning in Kansas, with Special Reference to Their Educational Investments and Educational Contributions. Master's thesis, University of Kansas, 1927.

ARKANSAS CITY JUNIOR COLLEGE

912   Kahler, Arthur D. A History of Football and Basketball at Arkansas City Junior College, Arkansas City, Kansas, 1922-1952. Master's thesis, Kansas State Teachers College (Emporia), 1956.

BENEDICTINE COLLEGE

913   Moeder, Monica (Sister). History of St. Benedict's College. Master's thesis, University of Wichita, 1931.

BETHANY COLLEGE

914   Rasmussen, E. Keith. A History of Intercollegiate Athletics at Bethany College, Lindsborg, Kansas. Master's thesis, Kansas State University, 1966.

BETHEL COLLEGE

915   Buhr, Gerhard R. History of Intercollegiate Athletics at Bethel College. Master's thesis, Kansas State Teachers College (Emporia), 1962.

COLLEGE OF EMPORIA

916   Wierwillie, Donald E. Reviving a College from Bankruptcy: The Changing of the College of Emporia to the Way College of Emporia. Ed.D., University of Kansas, 1979. 159p. UMI# 78-09443.

EMPORIA STATE UNIVERSITY

917   Bodnarchuck, Steve. A Statistical Summary of Men's Intercollegiate Athletics at the College of Emporia from 1900 to the Fall of 1954. Master's thesis, Kansas State Teachers College (Emporia), 1956.

918   Fish, Everett D., and Kayser, Kathryn E. An Outline of the History of the Kansas State Teachers College of Emporia, 1865-1934. Master's thesis, Kansas State Teachers College (Emporia), 1936.

919   Matheny, Dave. History of the Development and Growth of the Department of Speech, Kansas State Teachers College, Emporia. Master's thesis, Kansas State Teachers College (Emporia), 1957.

920   Stephens, Harold H. Library of Kansas State Teachers College of Emporia, 1865-1930. Master's thesis, Kansas State Teachers College (Emporia), 1935.

921   Taylor, Bernard A. History of Athletics at Kansas State Teachers College, Emporia, Kansas. Master's thesis, Kansas State Teachers College (Emporia), 1947.

922   Williams, Marjorie G. The William Allen White Memorial Library of Kansas State Teachers College, Emporia. Master's thesis, Kansas State Teachers College (Emporia), 1959.

FORT HAYS STATE UNIVERSITY

923   Dickey, Otis. A History of the Fort Hays Kansas State College. Master's thesis, Fort Hays Kansas State College, 1942.

924   Heil, Eleanor L. An Historical Study of Teacher Education at Fort Hays Kansas State College, 1902-1964. Master's thesis, Fort Hays Kansas State College, 1964.

KANSAS, UNIVERSITY OF

925   Bell, Robert G. James C. Malin: A Study in American Historiography. Ph.D., University of California-Los Angeles, 1968. 176p. UMI# 69-03901. [professor of history, University of Kansas, 1921-1963].

926   Campbell, Larry L. A History of Football at the University of Kansas, 1889-1920. Master's thesis, University of Kansas, 1966. 90p.

927   Dalke, Jacob J. A History of Music Education at the University of Kansas from 1936-1947. Master's thesis, University of Kansas, 1980. 78p.

928   Dalzell, Arthur H. The First Fifty Years of Track Athletics at the University of Kansas. Master's thesis, University of Kansas, 1964.

929   Dewar, John D. The Life and Professional Contributions of James Naismith. Ed.D., Florida State University, 1965. 168p. UMI# 65-15453. [physical director, University of Kansas].

930   Eiland, Dianna K. A History of the University of Kansas Band from 1878 to 1934. Master's thesis, University of Kansas, 1984.

931   Fisher, Michael P. The Turbulent Years: The University of Kansas, 1960-1975: A History. Ph.D., University of Kansas, 1979. 270p. UMI# 79-25868.

932   Hicks, Wreatha. The First Seventy-Five Years of Forensic Activities of the University of Kansas (1867-1942). Master's thesis, University of Kansas, 1962.

933   Johnson, Ronald E. Student Unrest and the Kansas Press: Editorial Reactions to Violence in Lawrence and the University of Kansas in 1970. Master's thesis, University of Kansas at Lawrence, 1983.

934   Kirchoff, Kim A. A History of Music Education at the University of Kansas from 1866-1936. Master's thesis, University of Kansas, 1976. 133p.

935   LaBan, Frank K. A History of Theater Activities at the University of Kansas. Master's thesis, University of Kansas, 1960.

936   Laughlin, Lynn A. The Development of Music Therapy Program at the University of Kansas from Its Inception through 1971. Master's thesis, University of Kansas, 1975. 81p.

937   Turk-Roge, Janet L.C. A History of the Fine Arts School at the University of Kansas. Master's thesis, University of Kansas, 1941. 230p.

KANSAS WESLEYAN

938   Mann, Gordon C. An Outline History and Source Book of the Kansas Wesleyan University. Master's thesis, Kansas State Teachers College (Emporia), 1940.

MCPHERSON COLLLEGE

939   Kolzow, Virden J. An Outline History and Source Book of McPherson College. Master's thesis, Kansas State Teachers College (Emporia), 1940.

PITTSBURG STATE UNIVERSITY

940   Milner, Orlin. The Historical Development of Basketball at Kansas State College of Pittsburg. Master's thesis, Kansas State College of Pittsburg, 1967.

941   Stryker, Mabel K. A History of Kansas State Teachers College, Pittsburg, Kansas, 1903-1939. Master's thesis, Stanford University, 1939.

942   Wallis, Judith M. A History of the Theater at Kansas State Teachers College, Pittsburg, 1941-1946. Master's thesis, Kansas State College of Pittsburg, 1965.

SOUTHWESTERN COLLEGE

943   Callison, Norman. A History of the Department of Speech and Dramatics at Southwestern College in Winfield, Kansas. Master's thesis, Kansas State Teachers College (Emporia), 1967.

944   Kahler, Conrad A. History of Men's Intercollegiate Athletics at Southwestern College, Winfield, Kansas, from 1900 to 1950. Master's thesis, Kansas State Teachers College (Emporia), 1951.

STERLING COLLEGE

945   Dobbin, Paul R. A Study of Sterling College, with Special Reference to Its Educational Investments and Educational Contributions. Master's thesis, University of Kansas, 1932.

TABOR COLLEGE

946   Farquhar, Catherine B. History of Tabor College. Master's thesis, University of Iowa, 1941.

947   Schmidt, William. A History of Tabor College. Master's thesis, Wichita State University, 1961.

WESTERN UNIVERSITY

948   Smith, Thaddeus T. Western University: A Ghost College in Kansas. Master's thesis, Kansas State Teachers College (Emporia), 1967.

KENTUCKY

GENERAL STUDIES

949   Alston, Jerry G. The Role of the State Legislature in Public Higher Education in Kentucky, 1950-1968. Ph.D., Southern Illinois University, 1970. 167p. UMI# 71-02362.

950   Barkovich, Frank S. The Kentucky Council on Public Higher Education. Master's thesis, University of Louisville, 1970.

951   Bond, James A. Negro Education in Kentucky. Master's thesis, University of Cincinnati, 1930.

952   Chelf, Carl P. A Selective View of the Politics of Higher Education in Kentucky and the Role of H. H. Cherry, Educator-Politician. Ph.D., University of Nebraska-Lincoln, 1968. 280p. UMI# 68-18011.

953   Cole, Cathy L. A Historical Perspective of the Kentucky Council on Higher Education. Ph.D., Southern Illinois University at Carbondale, 1983. 361p. UMI# 8326521.

954   Doran, Adron. The Work of the Council on Public Higher Education in Kentucky. Ed.D., University of Kentucky, 1950. 180p. UMI# 25,017.

955   Godbey, Edsel T. Early Kentucky Governors and Education. Ph.D., University of Kentucky, 1959.

956   Howard, Boyd D. The Origins of Higher Education in the State of Kentucky. Ph.D., University of Cincinnati, 1940. 132p.

957   Lewis, Alvin F. History of Higher Education in Kentucky. Ph.D., Johns Hopkins University, 1899. 350p.

958   Reynolds, Margaret M. The History of Catholic Higher Education in Kentucky. Master's thesis, University of Kentucky, 1927.

959   Smith, Dolores F. Medical Education in Kentucky: A Study of Professional Medical Education in Kentucky from 1817-1920. Educational Specialist, University of Louisville, 1976. UMI# 13-9209.

960   Smith, Travis E. The Rise of Teacher Training in Kentucky. Ph.D., George Peabody College for Teachers, 1932. 191p.

961   Stanley, Larry D. The Historical Development of the Two-Year Colleges in Kentucky, 1903-1964. Ph.D., University of Kentucky, 1974. 236p. UMI# 75-05856.

ASBURY COLLEGE

962   McKee, Earl S. The Early History of Asbury College (1890-1910). Master's thesis, University of Kentucky, 1926.

963   Steinhauser, Richard G. A History of the Teacher Education Program at Asbury College from 1890 to 1962. Ph.D., Southern Illinois University at Carbondale, 1963. 168p. UMI# 64-04483.

BEREA COLLEGE

964   Durham, James G. A History of Berea College. Master's thesis, University of Kentucky, 1942.

965   Jones, Flora M. John G. Fee and Berea College. Master's thesis, Western Kentucky State College, 1934. [founder, 1855].

BETHEL COLLEGE

966   Haynes, William H. History of Bethel College, Russellville, Kentucky. Master's thesis, University of Kentucky, 1941.

BOWLING GREEN BUSINESS UNIVERSITY

967   Patterson, Charles E. A History of the Bowling Green Business University. Master's thesis, University of Kentucky, 1937. 48p.

DANVILLE THEOLOGICAL SEMINARY

968   Vaughn, William H. Robert Jefferson Breckinridge as an Educational Administrator. Ph.D., George Peabody College for Teachers, 1937. [professor, Danville Theological Seminary, 1851-1869].

EASTERN KENTUCKY UNIVERSITY

969   Hibbard, Janet G. Eastern Kentucky University, 1906-1960: Administrative Problems. Ed.D., Indiana University, 1973. 164p. UMI# 74-02668.

GEORGETOWN COLLEGE

970   Daley, John M. Georgetown College: The First Fifty Years. Ph.D., Georgetown University, 1953.

971   Dickey, Rex H. Basil Manly, II: Educator and Apostle of Southern Rights. Master's thesis, Auburn University, 1967. [president, Georgetown College, 1871-1877].

972   Huddle, Orlando E. A History of Georgetown College. Master's thesis, University of Kentucky, 1930.

KENTUCKY SOUTHERN COLLEGE

973   Hurtt, Steven T. The Closing of a College: An Analysis. Ed.D., Indiana University, 1977. 149p. UMI# 77-27,001.

KENTUCKY STATE UNIVERSITY

974   Edwards, Austin, Jr. History of the Kentucky State Industrial College for Negroes. Master's thesis, Indiana State Teachers College, 1936. 121p.

975   Hill, Helen C. Kentucky State College: Its Transition and Future. Ph.D., Southern Illinois University, 1971. 152p. UMI# 72-10256.

KENTUCKY, UNIVERSITY OF

976   Feinstein, Milton D. The History and Development of Football at the University of Kentucky, 1877-1920. Master's thesis, University of Kentucky, 1941.

977   Payne, Mary E. Florence Offutt Stout, Teacher of Physical Education for Forty Years at the University of Kentucky. Master's thesis, University of Kentucky, 1941.

978   Pyles, Henry M. The Life and Work of John Bryan Bowman. Ph.D., University of Kentucky, 1945. 219p. [trustee, University of Kentucky, 1865-1878].

LOUISVILLE MUNICIPAL COLLEGE

979   Collins, Wellyn F. Louisville Municipal College: A Study of the College Founded for Negroes in Louisville, Kentucky. Master's thesis, University of Louisville, 1976. 51p.

LOUISVILLE, UNIVERSITY OF

980   Bruner, Joyce E. The History of the University of Louisville Libraries. Master's thesis, University of North Carolina, 1953. 143p.

981   Conroy, Katherine. George Colvin. Master's thesis, University of Kentucky, 1934. [president, University of Louisville].

982   Cox, Dwayne D. A History of the University of Louisville. Ph.D., University of Kentucky, 1984. 226p. UMI# 8428410.

983   Coyte, Donna E. A History of the University of Louisville School of Law Library, 1846-1966. Master's thesis, University of North Carolina, 1968. 103p.

984   Hudson, James B., III. The History of Louisville Municipal College: Events Leading to the Desegregation of the University of Louisville. Ed.D., University of Kentucky, 1981. 142p. UMI# 81-29745.

985   Money, Mary G. A History of the Louisville Conservatory of Music at the University of Louisville: 1907-1935. Master's thesis, University of Louisville, 1976. 129p. UMI# 13-09727.

986   Nonacs, Merija. The Kornhauser Memorial Medical Library: Its History and Development. Master's thesis, University of Texas, 1966. 64p.

MOREHEAD STATE UNIVERSITY

987   Higginbotham, William J. The Development of the Morehead State University Alumni Association. Master's thesis, Morehead State University, 1967.

988   Nelson, Amy G. A Historical Study of Rural School Affiliation with the Morehead State Normal School, Later the Morehead State Teachers College, 1917-1951. Master's thesis, Morehead State College, 1968.

989   Rose, Harry E. The Historical Development of a State College: Morehead, Kentucky State College, 1887-1964. Ed.D., University of Cincinnati, 1965. 560p. UMI# 66-00708.

MURRAY STATE UNIVERSITY

990   Jeffrey, Buron. Origin and Development of Murray State Teachers College. Master's thesis, University of Kentucky, 1936.

991   Reichmuth, Roger E. Price Doyle, 1896-1967: His Life and Work in Music Education. Ed.D., University of Illinois, 1977. 456p. UMI# 7804123. [director of fine arts, Murray State University, 1930-1967].

OGDEN COLLEGE

992   Johnson, Jesse B. The History of Ogden College. Master's thesis, George Peabody College for Teachers, 1929. 148p.

SOUTHERN BAPTIST THEOLOGICAL SEMINARY

993   Barron, James R. The Contributions of John A. Broadus to Southern Baptists. Doctor of Theology, Southern Baptist Theological Seminary, 1972. 264p. UMI# 72-30,185. [president, Southern Baptist Theological Seminary].

994   Combs, Kermit S., Jr. The Course of Religious Education at the Southern Baptist Theological Seminary, 1902-1953: A Historical Study. Ed.D., Southern Baptist Theological Seminary, 1978. 349p. UMI# 78-14243.

995   Finley, John M. Edwin Charles Dargan: Baptist Denominationalist in a Changing South. Ph.D., Southern Baptist Theological Seminary, 1984. 227p. UMI# 8411014. [professor, Southern Baptist Theological Seminary, 1892-1907].

ST. JOSEPH'S COLLEGE

996   Bishop, Raymond J. St. Joseph's College, Bardstown, Kentucky, 1848-1868. Master's thesis, Saint Louis University, 1935. 86p.

SUE BENNETT COLLEGE

997   Jones, Cloyde C. A History of Sue Bennett College. Master's thesis, University of Kentucky, 1940.

THOMAS MORE COLLEGE

998   Hanna, Thomas H. The History and Status of Villa Madonna College, 1921-1961. Ed.D., University of Cincinnati, 1962. 497p. UMI# 63-01787.

999   Murphy, Jean M. Analysis of the Curriculum of Thomas More College: An Historical Perspective. Ph.D., Fordham University, 1984. 387p. UMI# 8423129.

TRANSYLVANIA UNIVERSITY

1000   Baker, Henry G. Transylvania: A History of the Pioneer University of the West, 1780-1865. Ph.D., University of Cincinnati, 1949. 368p.

1001   Edwards, Dorothy L. A History of Transylvania College from 1865 to 1940. Master's thesis, University of Kentucky, 1939. 148p.

1002   Greenfield, Esther. Reverend James Moore. Master's thesis, University of Kentucky, 1932. [acting president and professor, Transylvania University, 1799-1804].

1003   Judd, Ronnie D. The Educational Contributions of Horace Holley. Ph.D., George Peabody College for Teachers, 1936. 125p. [president, Transylvania University, 1818-1827].

1004   Lunger, H.J. A Catalogue of Unbound Documents of Transylvania University, 1783-1853. Master's thesis, Transylvania University, 1911.

1005   Scott, Ellen. The History and Influence of the Old Library of Transylvania University. Master's thesis, University of Kentucky, 1929. 60p.

UNION COLLEGE

1006   Hembree, Sillous G. A History of Union College. Master's thesis, University of Kentucky, 1938. 240p.

WESTERN KENTUCKY UNIVERSITY

1007   Cornette, James P. A History of the Western Kentucky State Teachers College. Ph.D., George Peabody College for Teachers, 1939.

LOUISIANA

GENERAL STUDIES

1008   Alexis, Roselle N. A Description and Analysis of the Perceived Impact of the Academic Governance Structure of Higher Education in the State of Louisiana After the Adoption of the Constitution of 1974. Ph.D., University of New Orleans, 1985. 201p. UMI# 8516301.

1009   Beasley, Leon O. A History of Education in Louisiana During the Reconstruction Period, 1862-1877. Ph.D., Louisiana State University, 1957. 328p. UMI# 00-21981.

1010   Butler, Daniel L., Jr. A History of the Certified Public Accounting Profession in Louisiana. Ph.D., Louisiana State University, 1976. 143p. UMI# 76-25,254.

1011   Garrett, John L., Jr. A Study of the Status and the Employment Histories of White College Graduates Certified as Science Teachers in Louisiana (1947-1956). Ph.D., Louisiana State University, 1959. 159p. UMI# 59-01532.

1012   Jones, John A. The Development of the Professional Education of White Teachers in Louisiana. Ph.D., Louisiana State University, 1948.

1013   Lynn, Louis A.A. A History of Teachers' Institutes of Louisiana, 1870-1921. Ph.D., Louisiana State University, 1961. 165p. UMI# 61-05148.

1014   Marshall, David C. A History of the Higher Education of Negroes in the State of Louisiana. Ph.D., Louisiana State University, 1956. 223p. UMI# 00-17447.

1015   Roy, Victor L. The History, Development and Present Status of the Curricula in the Teacher-Training Institutions of Louisiana. Master's thesis, Tulane University, 1925. 67p.

1016   Varnado, Otto S. A History of the Early Institutions of Higher Learning in Louisiana. Master's thesis, Louisiana State University, 1927.

1017   Wilson, Robert, Jr. A History of Theatrical Activities of the Four Negro Colleges in Louisiana from Their Beginnings through the 1966-67 School Year. Master's thesis, Louisiana State University, 1969.

CENTENARY COLLEGE OF LOUISIANA

1018   Bryson, Helen R. A History of Centenary College. Master's thesis, Louisiana State University, 1941.

GRAMBLING STATE UNIVERSITY

1019   Gallot, Mildred B. Grambling State University: A History, 1901-1977. Ed.D., Louisiana State University, 1982. 199p. UMI# 82-16836.

1020   Wade, Louise H. The History of the Development and Growth of the Speech and Drama Department at Grambling College. Master's thesis, Northeast Louisiana University, 1971.

JEFFERSON COLLEGE

1021   Niehaus, Earl F. Jefferson College in St. James Parrish, Louisiana: 1830-1875. Master's thesis, Tulane University, 1954. 118p.

LOUISIANA COLLEGE

1022   Kappel, Vernon E. Louis Dufau's Louisiana College. Master's thesis, Tulane University, 1949. 110p.

1023   Salley, Charles L. An Historical Survey of the Curriculum of Louisiana College (1906-1983). Ed.D., George Peabody College for Teachers of Vanderbilt University, 1985. 221p. UMI# 8517431.

LOUISIANA STATE UNIVERSITY

1024   Becnel, Joseph R. The History of the Military Establishment of Louisiana State University. Master's thesis, Louisiana State University, 1953.

1025   Brown, Harry W. A History of the Junior Division of Louisiana State University, 1933 to 1953. Master's thesis, Louisiana State University, 1953.

1026   Cutrer, Thomas W. 'My Boys at LSU': Cleanth Brooks, Robert Penn Warren and the Baton Rouge Literary Community, 1934-1942. Ph.D., University of Texas, 1980.

1027   Huff, Mary B. Legal History of the Louisiana State University and Agricultural and Mechanical College. Master's thesis, Louisiana State University, 1935.

1028   Lathrop, Ruth H. A History of Speech Education at Louisiana State University, 1860-1928. Master's thesis, Louisiana State University, 1949.

1029   Lopiccolo, John. A History of Summer Activities of the Speech Department of Louisiana State University: 1928-1963. Master's thesis, Louisiana State University, 1964.

1030   Mackey, James A. A History of the Louisiana State University Laboratory School, 1915-1965. Ed.D., Louisiana State University, 1971. 277p. UMI# 72-17786.

1031   Melebeck, Claude B., Jr. The History of the Speech Department at Louisiana State University, 1928-1950. Master's thesis, Louisiana State University, 1958.

1032   Peterson, Howard W. The Growth and Development of the Air Force Reserve Officers' Training Corps at Louisiana State University. Master's thesis, Louisiana State University, 1954.

1033   Powell, John B., III. A History of Louisiana State University Division of Continuing Education, 1924-1973. Ed.D., Louisiana State University, 1977. 148p. UMI# 78-07554.

1034   Reed, Germaine M. David Boyd, Southern Educator (Volumes I and II). Ph.D., Louisiana State University, 1970. 712p. UMI# 71-12431. [president, Louisiana State University, 1865-1880, 1884-1886].

1035   Roberts, Charlie W., Jr. The History of the Louisiana State University School of Music. Ed.D., Louisiana State University, 1968. 195p. UMI# 68-16326.

1036   Rouleau, Christine R. The Historical Development of Intramural Recreational Sports at Louisiana State University. Master's thesis, Louisiana State University, 1984.

1037   Tewell, Fred. A History of Intercollegiate Debating in the State Collegiate Institution of Louisiana. Master's thesis, Louisiana State University, 1949.

1038   Williams, Brenda G. A History of the Louisiana State University School of Music (1955-1979). (Volumes I and II). Ph.D., Louisiana State University, 1983. 527p. UMI# 8409600.

LOUISIANA TECH UNIVERSITY

1039   Thomas, George W. Development of the Program of Speech at the Louisiana Polytechnique Institute, Ruston, Louisiana, from 1927 to 1959. Master's thesis, Louisiana State University, 1959.

MEDICAL COLLEGE OF LOUISIANA

1040   Heintzen, Harry L. John Leonard Riddell: A Study of His Reading. Master's thesis, Tulane University, 1951. 85p. [professor of chemistry, Medical College of Louisiana, 1836-1865].

NORTHWESTERN STATE UNIVERSITY OF LOUISIANA

1041   Pettiss, John O. Development of the Louisiana State Normal College, 1884-1927. Master's thesis, Louisiana State University, 1927.

1042   Towry, Inez C. A History of the Growth and Development of Business Education at Northwestern State University of Louisiana, 1930-1970. Master's thesis, Northwestern State University, 1976.

OUR LADY OF HOLY CROSS COLLEGE

1043   Morrison, Betty L. A History of Our Lady of Holy Cross College, New Orleans, Louisiana. Ph.D., Louisiana State University, 1976. 183p. UMI# 76-25276.

SILLIMAN COLLEGE

1044   Harris, John F. A History of Silliman College. Master's thesis, Louisiana State University, 1942.

SOUTHEASTERN LOUISIANA COLLEGE

1045   Ancelet, Leroy. A History of Southeastern Louisiana College. Ph.D., Louisiana State University, 1971. 150p. UMI# 72-03455.

SOUTHERN UNIVERSITY AND AGRICULTURAL & MECHANICAL COLLEGE

1046   Lane, Ulysses S. The History of Southern University, 1879-1960. Ed.D., Utah State University, 1970. 189p. UMI# 71-19131.

1047   Perkins, Iris J. Felton Grandison Clark, Louisiana Educator. Ph.D., Louisiana State University, 1976. 98p. UMI# 77-10,391. [president, Southern University and Agricultural & Mechanical College, 1938-1970].

SOUTHWESTERN LOUISIANA, UNIVERSITY OF

1048   Galliano, Vernon F. An Occupational Study of the College of Agriculture Graduates of Southwestern Louisiana Institute, 1938-1958. Ph.D., Louisiana State University, 1960. 224p. UMI# 60-01465.

1049   Knighten, Loma. A History of the Library of Southwestern Louisiana Institute, 1900-1948. Master's thesis, Columbia University, 1949. 97p.

TULANE UNIVERSITY

1050   Fouche, James F. The Tulane University Graduate School of Business Administration: An Oral-Institutional History. Ph.D., University of Florida, 1978. 228p. UMI# 79-07742.

1051   Warner, Frank L. A History of the Tulane University Theatre, 1937-1967. Ph.D., Tulane University, 1968. 266p. UMI# 68-15280.

MAINE

GENERAL STUDIES

1052   Godfrey, Noel D. Some Phases of Collegiate and University Education in Maine, Historically Studied. Ph.D., New York University, 1931. 196p. UMI# 72-19968.

1053   Mayo, Helen N. A History of the Development of Teacher Training and Teacher Certification in the State of Maine. Master's thesis, University of Maine, 1936.

1054   Rush, N. Orwin. The History of College Libraries in Maine. Master's thesis, Columbia University, 1945.

1055   Sammis, George F., Jr. A History of the Maine Normal Schools. Ph.D., University of Connecticut, 1970. 305p. UMI# 71-16035.

BOWDOIN COLLEGE

1056   Michener, Roger E. The Bowdoin College Library: From Its Beginning to the Present Day. Master's thesis, University of Chicago, 1972.

1057   Swiss, Deborah J. The Evolution of a Small College Presidency: Bowdoin College 1885-1978. Ed.D., Harvard University, 1982. 143p. UMI# 8223234.

1058   Williamson, Phyllis M.D. A History of Speech Education at Bowdoin College. Master's thesis, Louisiana State University, 1953.

MAINE, UNIVERSITY OF

1059   Ladd, Robert M. The University of Maine in Augusta: Its Origins and an Evaluation of the Open Door Admissions Policy. Ed.D., University of Virginia, 1968. 80p. UMI# 68-18216.

1060   Rowe, Elizabeth. A History of Speech Education at the University of Maine—1868 to 1940. Master's thesis, University of Maine, 1952.

MAINE, UNIVERSITY OF (PORTLAND-GORHAM)

1061   Morton, Albert R. A History of Gorham State Teachers College. Master's thesis, University of Maine, 1947.

MARYLAND

GENERAL STUDIES

1062   Bloom, Raymond. History of Jewish Education in Baltimore During the Nineteenth and Twentieth Centuries. Ph.D., Dropsie University, 1972.

1063   Cain, Mary C. The Historical Development of State Normal Schools for White Teachers in Maryland. Ph.D., Columbia University, 1941. 184p.

1064   Chandlee, Elmer K. A History of the Maryland State Normal Schools for White Students. Master's thesis, University of Maryland, 1935.

1065   Gipe, Florence M. The Development of Nursing Education in Maryland. Ph.D., University of Maryland, 1952.

1066   McCarthy, Harry B. A History of Dental Education in Maryland. Master's thesis, University of Maryland, 1948.

1067   McNeill, Clayton. An Analysis of the Role of Gubernational Commissions, 1864-1980 and the State Board of Higher Education, 1976-1980 in Maryland. Ed.D., Temple University, 1986. 198p. UMI# 8611897.

1068   Pesci, Frank B. The Junior College Movement in Maryland: 1939-1962. Ph.D., Catholic University of America, 1963. 97p. UMI# 63-07982.

1069   Randolph, Stephen P. Emigration, Alteration, Confirmation: James Franck in Baltimore, 1935-1938. Master's thesis, Johns Hopkins University, 1975. [professor, University of Chicago, 1938-1949].

1070   Smith, James S. Development of Community Colleges in Maryland. Master's thesis, Alfred University, 1968.

1071   Steiner, Bernard C. The History of University Education in Maryland. Ph.D., Johns Hopkins University, 1891.

ANNE ARUNDEL COMMUNITY COLLEGE

1072   Likins, Jeanne M. A Stepping Stone: The History of Anne Arundel Community College. Ph.D., American University, 1981. 568p. UMI# 82-09080.

BALTIMORE CITY COLLEGE

1073   Hlubb, Julius G. An Analysis of Student Enrollment at the Baltimore City College, 1954-1965. Ph.D., George Washington University, 1965.

BALTIMORE JUNIOR COLLEGE

1074   Fields, Ralph R. A Case Study of Major Educational Changes in a Two-Year College: The

Democratization of Baltimore Junior College, 1947-1970. Ed.D., Columbia University, 1971. 348p. UMI# 72-17210.

1075   Whitney, Herbert C. The Origin and Development of the Baltimore Junior College. Master's thesis, University of Maryland, 1949.

BOWIE STATE COLLEGE

1076   Chapman, Oscar J. A Brief History of the Bowie Normal School for Colored Students. Master's thesis, University of Michigan, 1936.

1077   Hatcher, Cleophus C. An Historical Study of the Integration of Students and Faculty at Bowie State College. Ed.D., George Washington University, 1977. 196p. UMI# 77-20070.

1078   Jones Anglin, I. Patricia. Bowie State College: From a Private Normal School to a Multi-Purpose State College. Ph.D., University of Pittsburgh, 1983. 214p. UMI# 83-27710.

1079   Tipton, Elizabeth H. A Descriptive Analysis of Selected Forces and Events Which Influenced the Founding, Growth, and Development of Bowie State College from 1865 to 1975. Ed.D., George Washington University, 1976. 266p. UMI# 76-23561.

CHARLES COUNTY COMMUNITY COLLEGE

1080   Larkin, Charles W., Jr. Charles County Community College: The History of the First Twenty Years 1958-1978. Ed.D., George Washington University, 1982. 181p. UMI# 82-16986.

COLLEGE OF NOTRE DAME OF MARYLAND

1081   Nichols, Mary E. Historical Survey of the Library of the College of Notre Dame of Maryland. Master's thesis, Catholic University of America, 1957. 83p.

COLUMBIA UNION COLLEGE

1082   Griswold, Ardyce M. A History of the Columbia Union College Library, Takoma Park, Maryland 1904-1954. Master's thesis, Catholic University of America, 1964. 96p.

EDEN THEOLOGICAL SEMINARY

1083   Brueggemann, Walter A. Ethos and Ecumenism: The History of Eden Theological Seminary, 1925-1970. Ph.D., Saint Louis University, 1974. 290p. UMI# 74-24051.

GOUCHER COLLEGE

1084   Kirby, Madge B. A History of the Goucher College Library, Baltimore, Maryland, 1885-1949. Master's thesis, Catholic University of America, 1952.

JOHNS HOPKINS UNIVERSITY

1085   Benson, Keith R. William Keith Brooks (1848-1908): A Case Study in Morphology and the Development of American Biology. Ph.D., Oregon State University, 1979. 363p. UMI# 7922369.

1086   Birnbaum, Lucille T. Behaviorism: John Broadus Watson and American Social Thought, 1912-1933. Ph.D., University of California-Berkeley, 1964. 415p. UMI# 64-12,964. [professor of psychology, Johns Hopkins University, 1908-1920].

1087   Buckley, Kerry W. Behaviorism and the Professionalization of American Psychology: A Study of John Broadus Watson, 1878-1958. Ph.D., University of Massachusetts, 1982. 320p. UMI# 8210301. [professor of psychology, Johns Hopkins University, 1908-1920].

1088   Conner, George. Basil Lannear Gildersleeve, Scholar and Humanist, 1881-1924. Ph.D., University of Wisconsin, 1960. 264p. UMI# 60-03184. [professor of Greek, Johns Hopkins University, 1876-1915].

1089   Cordasco, Francesco M. The Role of Daniel Coit Gilman in American Graduate Education. Ed.D., New York University, 1959. 293p. UMI# 59-01934. [president, Johns Hopkins University, 1875-1901].

1090   Eichlin, Arthur S. An Historical Analysis of the Fellowships Program at the Johns Hopkins University, 1876-1889: Daniel Gilman's Unique Contribution. Ph.D., Loyola University of Chicago, 1976. 182p. UMI# 76-24439. [president, 1875-1901].

1091   Eschenbacher, Herman F., Jr. History at the Johns Hopkins University, 1876-1901: A Study in Early Graduate Education in History. Master's thesis, Brown University, 1952.

1092   Flood, Gerald J. Herbert Baxter Adams and the Study of Education. Ph.D., Johns Hopkins University, 1970. 270p. UMI# 72-28,955. [professor, Johns Hopkins University, 1876-1901].

1093   Gass, W. Conard. Herbert Baxter Adams and the Development of Historical Instruction in American Colleges and Universities. Ed.D., Duke University, 1963. 265p. UMI# 64-02825. [professor, Johns Hopkins University, 1876-1901].

1094   Hawkins, Hugh D. The Birth of a University: A History of the Johns Hopkins University from the Death of the Founder to the End of the First Year of Academic Work, 1873-1877. Ph.D., Johns Hopkins University, 1954.

1095   Koudelka, Janet B. A History of the Johns Hopkins Medical Libraries, 1889-1935. Master's thesis, Catholic University of America, 1963. 96p.

1096   Saunders, Bruce D. Herbert Baxter Adams and the Development of American Higher Education, 1876-1901. Ph.D., University of Texas at Austin, 1975. 303p. UMI# 75-16736. [professor, of history and political science, Johns Hopkins University, 1876-1901].

LOYOLA COLLEGE

1097   Thompson, Sister Mary M. The Brief History of Mt. St. Agnes College, 1890-1958. Master's thesis, Loyola College, 1959.

MARYLAND, UNIVERSITY OF

1098   Bair, Martha A. A History of Physical Education at the University of Maryland to 1949. Master's thesis, University of Maryland, 1967.

1099   Clutter, Bill G. A History of the University of Maryland College of Special and Continuation

Studies (University College): The Development of a World-Wide Education Program, 1947-1956. Ph.D., American University, 1984. 425p. UMI# 8505762.

1100   Higgins, William B. The University of Maryland and Its Relation as a Training Institution to Maryland Rural Life, 1920-1936. Master's thesis, University of Maryland, 1937.

1101   Matejski, Myrtle P. The Influence of Selected External Forces on Medical Education at the University of Maryland School of Medicine, 1910-1950. Ph.D., University of Maryland, 1977. 199p. UMI# 77-28747.

1102   Wilson, Wilbert R. An Historical Analysis of Events and Issues Which Have Led to the Growth and Development of the University of Maryland Eastern Shore from 1886-1975. Ed.D., George Washington University, 1976. 195p. UMI# 77-02966.

1103   Worthington, Leland G. Forces Leading to the Establishment of the Maryland Agricultural College. Master's thesis, University of Maryland, 1933.

MORGAN STATE UNIVERSITY

1104   Brodsky, Paul L. Radical Factors in the Administration of Morgan State College, 1937-1961. Ph.D., University of Maryland, 1976. 239p. UMI# 77-10,269.

1105   Owings, Vivian B. A History of the Library of Morgan State College from 1867 to 1939. Master's thesis, Catholic University of America, 1952. 32p.

PEABODY CONSERVATORY OF MUSIC

1106   Robinson, Ray E. A History of the Peabody Conservatory of Music. Doctor of Music Education, Indiana University, 1969. 704p. UMI# 70-01693.

PRINCE GEORGE'S COMMUNITY COLLEGE

1107   Rennie, Thomas P. A Historical Study of the Establishment and Development of Prince George's Community College, 1958-1973. Ed.D., George Washington University, 1974. 234p. UMI# 75-25394.

ST. JOHN'S COLLEGE

1108   Klein, Sarah J. The History and Present Status of the Library of St. John's College, Annapolis. Master's thesis, Catholic University of America, 1952. 53p.

ST. JOSEPH'S COLLEGE

1109   Crumlish, Sister John Mary. The History of St. Joseph's College, Emmitsburg, Maryland, 1809-1902. Master's thesis, Catholic University of America, 1948.

ST. MARY'S COLLEGE

1110   Kartendick, James J. The History of St. Mary's College, Baltimore, 1799-1852. Master's thesis, Catholic University of America, 1942.

1111   Ruane, Joseph W. The Founding of Saint Mary's College, Baltimore, 1799-1812. Master's thesis, Catholic University of America, 1933.

TOWSON STATE UNIVERSITY

1112   Miller, Lloyd D. A Historical Study of the Art Education Curriculum at the Maryland State Normal School from 1866 to 1909. Ed.D., Columbia University, 1970. 354p. UMI# 70-18,144.

UNITED STATES NAVAL ACADEMY

1113   Hart, Casper P. Founding of the United States Naval Academy. Master's thesis, Columbia University, 1938.

1114   Luckett, George R. A History of the United States Naval Academy Library, 1845-1907. Master's thesis, Catholic University of America, 1951. 39p.

1115   Sheppard, Charles P. An Analysis of Curriculum Changes at the United States Naval Academy During the Period 1959 through 1974. Ed.D., George Washington University, 1974. 520p. UMI# 75-12623.

UNITED STATES NAVAL INSTITUTE

1116   Heitzmann, William R. The United States Naval Institute's Contribution to the In-Service Education of Naval Officers, 1873-1973. Ph.D., University of Delaware, 1974. 254p. UMI# 74-26,105.

WESTERN MARYLAND COLLEGE

1117   Hoff, Alethea. A History of the Library of Western Maryland College. Master's thesis, Drexel Institute of Technology, 1954. 49p.

1118   Newcomer, Joe C. The Founding and Early History of Western Maryland College. Master's thesis, University of Maryland, 1941.

1119   Storm, Harrie P. A History of the Graduate Program at Western Maryland College. Master's thesis, Western Maryland College, 1972.

WOODSTOCK COLLEGE

1120   Greer, James J. A History of the Library of Woodstock College of Baltimore County, Maryland, from 1869 to 1957. Master's thesis, Drexel Institute of Technology, 1957. 84p.

1121   Ryan, Edmund G. The Early Years of Woodstock College in Maryland, 1869-1890: The First Jesuit Seminary in North America. Master's thesis, Catholic University of America, 1962.

1122   Ryan, Edmund G. An Academic History of Woodstock College in Maryland (1869-1944): The First Jesuit Seminary in North America. Ph.D., Catholic University of America, 1964. 269p. UMI# 64-07474.

MASSACHUSETTS

GENERAL STUDIES

1123   Beaulac, Ernest J., Jr. The Development of Community Colleges in Massachusetts with Implications for the Secondary Schools. Ph.D., University of Connecticut, 1967. 343p. UMI# 68-01315.

1124   Boyle, Thomas J. State Leadership in Massachusetts Public Education, 1780-1860. Ph.D., University of Connecticut, 1963. 171p. UMI# 64-03519.

1125   Dooher, Philip M. Higher Education and the Veterans: An Historical Study of Change in a Select Number of Massachusetts Colleges and Universities: 1944-1949. Ph.D., Boston College, 1980. UMI# 80-17833.

1126   Dunlea, Thomas A. Agricultural Education in Massachusetts, 1792-1867. Ph.D., University of Chicago, 1953.

1127   Eckert, Richard S. 'The Gentlemen of the Profession': The Emergence of Lawyers in Massachusetts, 1630-1810. Ph.D., University of Southern California, 1981.

1128   Gawalt, Gerard W. Massachusetts Lawyers: A Historical Analysis of the Process of Professionalization, 1760-1840. Ph.D., Clark University, 1969. 327p. UMI# 70-00197.

1129   Gould, David A. Policy and Pedagogues: School Reform and Teacher Professionalization in Massachusetts, 1840-1920. Ph.D., Brandeis University, 1977. 604p. UMI# 77-13372.

1130   Hansen, Lorentz I. The History and Educational Philosophy of the Early Massachusetts Academies. Ph.D., Boston University, 1934.

1131   Lunbeck, Elizabeth. Psychiatry in the Age of Reform: Doctors, Social Workers and Patients at the Boston Psychopathic Hospital, 1900-1925. Ph.D., Harvard University, 1984. 300p. UMI# 8503552.

1132   Malloy, Thomas A., Jr. A Historical Study of the Development of Social Science Programs of Elementary School Teacher Training Curricula in Massachusetts State Normal Schools and Teachers Colleges. Ed.D., University of Virginia, 1959. 250p. UMI# 59-06750.

1133   Mangun, Vernon L. The American Normal School: Its Rise and Development in Massachusetts. Ph.D., Columbia University, 1928. 443p.

1134   Manzer, Edna L. Woman's Doctors: The Development of Obstetrics and Gynecology in Boston, 1860-1930. Ph.D., Indiana University, 1979. 441p. UMI# 8008225.

1135   Marvelli, Alan L. An Historical Examination and Organizational Analysis of the Smith College-Clarke School for the Deaf Graduate Teacher Education Program. Ed.D., University of Massachusetts, 1974. 225p. UMI# 74-15029.

1136   McKirdy, Charles R. Lawyers in Crisis: The Massachusetts Legal Profession, 1760-1790. Ph.D., Northwestern University, 1969. 279p. UMI# 70-00117.

1137   Salwak, Stanley F. Some Factors Significant in the Establishment of Public Junior Colleges in the United States (1940-1951) with Special Reference to Massachusetts. Ed.D., Pennsylvania State University, 1953. 511p. UMI# 00-07370.

1138   Scott, William J. A History of the Massachusetts Community Colleges, 1960-1980: A Comparison of Occupational Education Policy and Practice. Ed.D., Boston College, 1983. 179p. UMI# 8314871.

1139   Stone, Bruce W. The Role of Learned Societies in the Growth of Scientific Boston, 1780-1848. Ph.D., Boston University, 1974. UMI# 74-20,405.

1140   Walsh, Mary R. Sexual Barriers in the Medical Profession: A Case Study of Boston Women Physicians, 1835-1973. Ph.D., Boston University, 1974.

AMHERST COLLEGE

1141   Engley, Donald B. The Emergence of the Amherst College Library, 1821-1911. Master's thesis, University of Chicago, 1947. 155p.

1142   Green, James M. Alexander Meiklejohn—Innovator in Undergraduate Education. Ph.D., University of Michigan, 1970. 411p. UMI# 71-04614. [president, Amherst College, 1912-1923].

1143   Le Duc, Thomas H.A. Piety and Intellect: The Relations of Religion and Learning at Amherst College, 1865-1912. Ph.D., Yale University, 1943.

1144   Perry, Eugene H. Alexander Meiklejohn and the Organic Theory of Democracy. Ph.D., Syracuse University, 1969. 312p. UMI# 70-12,800. [president, Amherst College, 1912-1923].

1145   Racz, Ernest B. Meiklejohn. Ed.D., Coumbia University Teachers College, 1979. 205p. UMI# 8105909. [president, Amherst College, 1912-1923].

1146   Samec, Charles E. A History of the Amherst Project: Revising the Teaching of American History, 1959 to 1972. Ph.D., Loyola University of Chicago, 1976. 141p. UMI# 76-24457.

1147   Welch, Joseph E. Edward Hitchcock, M.D.: Founder of Physical Education in the College Curriculum. Ed.D., George Peabody College for Teachers, 1962. 327p. UMI# 62-05688. [president, Amherst College, 1845-1855].

ANDOVER NEWTON THEOLOGICAL SCHOOL

1148   Harker, John S. The Life and Contributions of Calvin Ellis Stowe. Ph.D., University of Pittsburgh, 1951. 134p. [professor of sacred literature, Andover Theological Seminary, 1852-1864].

BOSTON COLLEGE

1149   Dunigan, David R. A History of Boston College. Ph.D., Fordham University, 1945. 411p.

1150   Higgins, Loretta P. The Development of Coeducation at Boston College. Ed.D., Boston College, 1986. 245p. UMI# 8616100.

BOSTON CONSERVATORY OF MUSIC

1151   McGrath, Robert M. A History of the Boston Conservatory of Music. Master's thesis, Catholic University of America, 1968. 47p.

BOSTON MUSEUM SCHOOL

1152   Sheehan, Roberta A. Boston Museum School, a Centennial History, 1876-1976. Ph.D., Boston College, 1983. 250p. UMI# 8327793.

BOSTON UNIVERSITY

1153   Gresham, Charles R. Walter Scott Athearn, Pioneer in Religious Education. Ph.D., Southwestern Baptist Theological Seminary, 1959. [professor of religion and dean, Boston University, 1916-1929; president, Butler University, 1931-1934].

1154   Kahn, Albert S. An Historical Perspective of Teacher Education at Boston University's School of Education, 1918-1962. Ed.D., Boston University, 1962. 349p. UMI# 62-05212.

1155   Mack, Henry W. Borden Parker Bowne as an Educational Philosopher. Ph.D., New York University, 1931. [professor of philosophy and dean, Boston University].

CLARK UNIVERSITY

1156   Rideout, Roger R. Granville Stanley Hall and Music Education: 1880-1924. Ed.D., University of Illinois at Urbana-Champaign, 1978. 154p. UMI# 7913588. [president and professor of psychology, Clark University, 1889-1919].

1157   Ross, Dorothy. G. Stanley Hall, 1844-1895: Aspects of Science and Culture in the Nineteenth Century. Ph.D., Columbia University, 1965. 530p. UMI# 68-08551. [president and professor of psychology, Clark University, 1889-1919].

COLLEGE OF THE HOLY CROSS

1158   Meagher, Walter J. History of the College of the Holy Cross, 1843-1901. Ph.D., Fordham University, 1944. 149p.

EMERSON COLLEGE

1159   Marderosian, Haig D. A Partial History of Debate at Emerson College. Master's thesis, Emerson College, 1957.

1160   O'Mara, Francis L., Jr. A Partial History of Emerson College, 1903-1920. Master's thesis, Emerson College, 1965.

1161   Woodnick, Michael L. A History of Emerson College During the Administration of Charles Wesley Emerson, 1880-1903. Master's thesis, Emerson College, 1965.

EMMANUEL COLLEGE

1162   Friel, Mary E. History of Emmanuel College 1919-1974. Ph.D., Boston College, 1980.
308p. UMI# 80-03731.

FISHER JUNIOR COLLEGE

1163   Fisher, Scott A. The Development and Recession of the Private Junior College Including
Fisher Junior College—A Case Study. Ed.D., Harvard University, 1983. 177p. UMI# 83-
21065.

HARVARD UNIVERSITY

1164   Anderson, Roy E. Contributions of Frederick G. Nichols to the Field of Business Education. Ed.D., Stanford University, 1963. 297p. UMI# 64-1571. [associate professor of business, Harvard University, 1922-1944].

1165   Barlow, Andrew L. Coordination and Control: The Rise of Harvard University, 1825-1910.
Ph.D., Harvard University, 1979. 464p. UMI# 7916362.

1166   Barney, Joseph A. The Educational Ideas of Irving Babbitt: Critical Humanism and American Higher Education. Ph.D., Loyola University of Chicago, 1974. 256p. UMI# 74-16934.
[professor of French literature, Harvard University].

1167   Berg, Walter L. Nathaniel Southgate Shaler: A Critical Study of an Earth Scientist. Ph.D.,
University of Washington, 1957. 371p. UMI# 22,159. [professor of paleontology, 1868-
1887; professor of zoology, 1888-1891; dean of Lawrence Scientific School, 1891-1906,
Harvard University].

1168   Boromé, Joseph A. The Life and Letters of Justin Winsor. Ph.D., Columbia University,
1950. 655p. UMI# 00-01834. [librarian, Harvard University, 1877-1897].

1169   Brown, Maurice F., Jr. Harvard Poetic Renaissance, 1885-1910. Ph.D., Harvard University, 1958.

1170   Church, Robert L. The Development of the Social Sciences as Academic Disciplines at
Harvard University, 1869-1900. Ph.D., Harvard University, 1966.

1171   Cohen, Paul E. Barrett Wendell: A Study in Harvard Culture. Ph.D., Northwestern University, 1974. 170p. UMI# 75-29790. [professor of English, 1890-1917].

1172   Curtis, William J. The History and Design of Le Corbusier's Carpenter Center for the
Visual Arts at Harvard University. Ph.D., Harvard University, 1975.

1173   Dunn, Edward T. Tutor Henry Flynt of Harvard College, 1675-1760. Ph.D., University of
Rochester, 1968. 505p. UMI# 70-02861. [tutor, 1699-1754].

1174   Ellis, Alan. An Historical Study of the General Education Program at Harvard College,
1946-1960. Master's thesis, Queens College, 1961.

1175   Fellows, Frederick H. J. H. Van Vleck: The Early Life and Work of a Mathematical Physicist. Ph.D., University of Minnesota, 1985. 419p. UMI# 8512070. [professor of physics,
Harvard University, 1935-1969].

1176   Field, Faye B. Influence of Charles William Eliot on Education. Master's thesis, Methodist University, 1939. [president, Harvard University, 1869-1909].

1177   Fisher, Raymond H. Charles W. Eliot's Views on College Education in the Light of Present Trends. Ph.D., University of Illinois, 1936. [president, Harvard University, 1869-1909].

1178   Flaherty, Terrance J. Charles W. Eliot and the Teaching of Composition. Ph.D., Northwestern University, 1978. 261p. UMI# 7907873. [president, Harvard University, 1869-1909].

1179   Foster, Margery S. Economic History of Harvard College in the Puritan Period (1636 to 1712). Ph.D., Radcliffe College, 1958.

1180   Fye, W. Bruce. Henry Pickering Bowditch: A Case Study of the Harvard Physiologist and His Impact on the Professionalization of Physiology in America. Master's thesis, Johns Hopkins University, 1978. [professor of physiology and dean of the medical school, 1871-1906].

1181   Golann, Ethel. The Reading of James Russell Lowell in the Harvard College Library. Master's thesis, Columbia University, 1934.

1182   Gruber, Christian P. The Education of Henry Thoreau: Harvard 1833-1837. Ph.D., Princeton University, 1953. 285p. UMI# 00-08077.

1183   Hartman, Paul T. Selected Student-Initiated Change at Harvard University, 1725-1925. Ph.D., Loyola University of Chicago, 1975. 206p. UMI# 75-22351.

1184   Hoffmann, John M. Commonwealth College: The Governance of Harvard in the Puritan Period. Ph.D., Harvard University, 1972.

1185   Howe, Daniel W. The Unitarian Conscience: Harvard Moral Philosophy and the Second Great Awakening (1805-67). Ph.D., University of California-Berkeley, 1967. 487p. UMI# 71-00872.

1186   Kaledin, Arthur D. The Mind of John Leverett. Ph.D., Harvard University, 1965. [president, Harvard University, 1708-1724].

1187   Kennedy, Steele M. Emerson's 'The American Scholar,' and the Other Harvard Phi Beta Kappa Operations. Ph.D., New York University, 1956. 750p. UMI# 00-17653.

1188   Koelsch, William A. The Enlargement of a World: Harvard Students and Geographical Experiences, 1840-1861. Ph.D., University of Chicago, 1966.

1189   Kohr, Russell V. Early History and Influence of Harvard College's Hollis Professorship of Divinity (the First Endowed Professorial Chair in America). Master's thesis, Western Michigan University, 1981. 114p. UMI# 13-17876.

1190   Krick, Gerald R. Harvard Volunteers: A History of Undergraduate Volunteer Social Service Work at Harvard. Ph.D., Boston University, 1970. 458p. UMI# 70-22431.

1191   Lipping, Alar. Charles W. Eliot's View on Education, Physical Education, and Intercollegiate Athletics. Ph.D., Ohio State University, 1980. 366p. UMI# 8100189. [president, Harvard University, 1869-1909].

1192   Lurie, Edward. Louis Agassiz and American Natural Science, 1846-1873. Ph.D., North-western University, 1956. 580p. UMI# 19,014. [professor of natural science, Harvard University, 1847-1855].

1193   MacDougall, James A. Abbott Lawrence Lowell, Educator and Innovator. Ph.D., New York University, 1980. 322p. UMI# 8027461. [president, Harvard University, 1909-1933].

1194   McCaughey, Robert A.P. Josiah Quincy, 1772-1864: The Last of the Boston Federalists. Ph.D., Harvard University, 1970. [president, Harvard University, 1829-1845].

1195   Moore, Kathryn S.M. Old Saints and Young Sinners: A Study of Student Discipline at Harvard College, 1636-1724. Ph.D., University of Wisconsin, 1972. 345p. UMI# 72-15372.

1196   Morris, Rita M. An Examination of Some Factors Related to the Rise and Decline of Geography as a Field of Study at Harvard, 1638-1948. Ph.D., Harvard University, 1962.

1197   Mosley, Calvin N. The Impact of the Merger of the Offices of Admissions and Financial Aids at Harvard and Radcliffe Colleges. Ed.D., Harvard University, 1981. 210p. UMI# 81-25489.

1198   Murdock, Mary E. Charles William Eliot, Crusader for the New Education. Ph.D., Brown University, 1962. 352p. UMI# 63-01044. [president, Harvard University, 1869-1909].

1199   Murphy, Mary E. The Harvard/Framingham Project: A Descriptive Case History of an Innovation in Higher Education. Ed.D., Harvard University, 1984. 162p. UMI# 8421219.

1200   Nelson, Clinton E. John Fiske's Harvard Lectures: A Case Study of Philosophical Lectures. Ph.D., University of Iowa, 1977. 268p. UMI# 77-21156. [professor of philosophy and history, 1869-1901].

1201   O'Connor, John A. Charles Eliot and American Education: An Historical Study. Ph.D., Loyola University of Chicago, 1970. [president, Harvard University, 1869-1909].

1202   Olsen, Richard A. Archibald Cary Coolidge and the Harvard University Library, 1910-1928. Master's thesis, Long Island University, 1967. [professor of history and director of libraries].

1203   Panchaud, Frances L. George Herbert Palmer. Ph.D., New York University, 1935. [professor of philosophy, Harvard University, 1872-1913].

1204   Powell, Arthur G. The Study of Education at Harvard, 1869- 1920. Ph.D., Harvard University, 1969.

1205   Price, Robert P. Academic Government at Harvard College, 1636-1723. Ph.D., University of Michigan, 1969. 315p. UMI# 70-14621.

1206   Ranson, Leonard B. The Vocational Basis for the Founding of Harvard College: An Alternative to Samuel Morison and Winthrop Hudson. Ph.D., University of Iowa, 1979. 177p. UMI# 79-24519.

1207   Ried, Paul E. The Philosophy of American Rhetoric as It Developed in the Boylston Chair of Rhetoric and Oratory at Harvard University. Ph.D., Ohio State University, 1959. 335p. UMI# 59-05869.

1208   Rogers, Clara L. Charles William Eliot's Contributions to Education. Master's thesis, University of Wisconsin, 1927. [president, Harvard University, 1869-1909].

1209   Salie, Robert D. The Harvard Annex Experiment in the Higher Education of Women: Separate But Equal? Ph.D., Emory University, 1976. 399p. UMI# 77-00979.

1210   Schwager, Sally. 'Harvard Women': A History of the Founding of Radcliffe College. Ed.D., Harvard University, 1982. 505p. UMI# 82-23230.

1211   Sexton, John E. Charles W. Eliot, Unitarian Exponent of the Doctrine of Tolerance in Religion. Ph.D., Fordham University, 1978. 347p. UMI# 78-14902. [president, Harvard University, 1869-1909].

1212   Sheehan, Patrick M. Harvard Alumni in Colonial America: Demographic, Theological, and Political Perspectives. Ph.D., Case Western Reserve University, 1972. 237p. UMI# 72-18736.

1213   Smith, Robert M. The American Business System and the Theory and Practice of Social Science: The Case of the Harvard Business School, 1925-1945. Ph.D., University of Maine, 1976. 288p. UMI# 77-08333.

1214   Swarz, Ilona P. A Historical Investigation of the Impact of World War II on Harvard Medical School—1938-1948. Ph.D., University of Connecticut, 1983. 523p. UMI# 8317731.

1215   Terrell, Darrell. History of the Dumbarton Oaks Research Library of Harvard University, 1940-1950. Master's thesis, Catholic University of America, 1954. 51p.

1216   Tuttle, William M., Jr. James B. Conant, Pressure Groups, and the National Defense, 1933-1945. Ph.D., University of Wisconsin, 1967. 427p. UMI# 70-03731. [president, Harvard University, 1933-1953].

1217   Walter, Maila L. K. Science and Cultural Crisis: An Intellectual Biography of Percy Williams Bridgman. Ph.D., Harvard University, 1985. 292p. UMI# 8602275. [professor of physics, Harvard University].

1218   Wang, Shu-ching Y. Harvard-Yenching Library; Harvard University, History and Development. Master's thesis, Southern Connecticut State College, 1967. 104p.

1219   Wert, Robert J. The Impact of Three Nineteenth Century Reorganizations Upon Harvard University. Ph.D., Stanford University, 1952.

1220   Wilder, Joan K. Charles William Eliot and American Education Reform, 1909-1926. Ph.D., University of Wisconsin, 1970. 332p. UMI# 70-13,946. [president, Harvard University, 1869-1909].

1221   Wkovich, Steven R. The Enigma of Productivity: Elton Mayo and the Origins of American Industrial Sociology. Ph.D., University of California-Irvine, 1984. 557p. UMI# 8502989. [professor of psychology, Harvard University, 1926-1947].

1222   Zaidenberg, Arthur. From Reforms to Professionalization: The Transition of Attitudes Toward Scientific Education in Harvard. Ph.D., University of California-Los Angeles, 1974. 231p. UMI# 75-05701.

MASSACHUSETTS INSTITUTE OF TECHNOLOGY

1223   Costantino, Nicholas V. Education in the Industrial Republic: An Interpretive Study of Francis Amasa Walker's Philosophy of Education. Ed.D., University of Florida, 1967. 303p. UMI# 68-12999. [president, Massachusetts Institute of Technology, 1881-1897].

1224   Tachikawa, Akira. The Two Sciences and Religion in Ante-Bellum New England: The Founding of the Museum of Comparative Zoology and the Massachusetts Institute of Technology. Ph.D., University of Wisconsin, 1978. 300p. UMI# 78-23089.

MASSACHUSETTS, UNIVERSITY OF

1225   Ball, Robert J. Teaching Teachers in the Seventies: The Search for Meaning. The History of the Creation of the 1971-72 Master of Arts in Teaching Program at the University of Massachusetts. Ed.D., University of Massachusetts, 1974. 286p. UMI# 74-25818.

1226   Peirce, Henry B., Jr. A History of the Dramatic Activities at the University of Massachusetts to 1953. Master's thesis, University of Michigan, 1955.

MOUNT HOLYOKE COLLEGE

1227   Rota, Tiziana. Between 'True Women' and 'New Women': Mount Holyoke Students, 1837-1908. Ph.D., University of Massachusetts, 1983. 410p. UMI# 8310328.

1228   Shea, Charlotte K. Mount Holyoke College, 1875-1910: The Passing of the Old Order. Ph.D., Cornell University, 1983. 248p. UMI# 83-21820.

1229   Wagner, Hilda S. A History of Forms of Dramatic Expression in Mount Holyoke College, 1873-1950. Ph.D., Columbia University, 1953. 496p. UMI# 00-06731.

REGIS COLLEGE

1230   McCaughey-Oreszak, Leona D. Liberal and General Education: Regis College: 1927-1985. Ed.D., Boston College, 1986. 258p. UMI# 8616109.

SCHOOL FOR SOCIAL WORKERS

1231   Lunt, Sally H. The Professionalization of Social Work: The History of Education for Social Work, with Special Reference to the School for Social Workers (Boston, 1904). Ed.D., Harvard University, 1974. 211p. UMI# 75-04906.

SMITH COLLEGE

1232   Freedberg, Sharon. Bertha Capen Reynolds—A Woman Struggling in Her Times. Doctor of Social Work, Columbia University, 1984. 244p. UMI# 8427391. [associate director, Smith College School of Social Work].

1233   Peterson, Hazel C. Dorothy S. Ainsworth: Her Life, Professional Career and Contributions to Physical Education (Volumes I and II). Ph.D., Ohio State University, 1968. 485p. UMI# 68-15367. [director of physical education, Smith College, 1926-1960].

SOUTHEASTERN MASSACHUSETTS UNIVERSITY

1234   Cass, Walter J. A History of Southeastern Massachusetts Technological Institute in Cultural Perspective. Ed.D., Boston University, 1967. 273p. UMI# 69-07801.

SPRINGFIELD COLLEGE

1235   Runquist, Kenneth. An Historical Study of the Development of Teacher Preparation in Physical Education at Springfield College with Special Reference to the Curriculum. Ph.D., Columbia University, 1953.

1236   Seetharaman, Arumbavur N. Peter V. Karpovich, M.D.: His Life and Contributions to Physical Education. Ed.D., Boston University, 1972. 344p. UMI# 72-25,464. [professor, Springfield College, 1929-1969].

TUFTS UNIVERSITY

1237   Vincent, Audrey W. 'A Fair Chance for the Girls': A Case Study in the Function of Prestige in the Controversy Over Admission of Women to Tufts College, 1852-1912. Doctor of Ministry, Claremont Graduate School, 1985. 106p. UMI# 8516153.

WELLESLEY COLLEGE

1238   Palmieri, Patricia A. In Adamless Eden: A Social Portrait of the Academic Community at Wellesley College, 1875-1920. Ed.D., Harvard University, 1981. 660p. UMI# 81-25492.

1239   Summers, Victoria F. The Historical Development of the Undergraduate Program in Health and Physical Education at Wellesley College. Master's thesis, Wellesley College, 1939.

1240   Ware, Bettie A. A Historical Study of Dance at Wellesley College. Master's thesis, Wellesley College, 1949.

WESTFIELD STATE COLLEGE

1241   Fiorello, James R. General Education in the Preparation of Teachers at Westfield State College, 1839-1960. Ph.D., University of Connecticut, 1969. 462p. UMI# 70-01254.

WILLIAMS COLLEGE

1242   Jones, Robert A. Consciousness and Sociology: The Intuitionism of John Bascom, 1827-1911. Ph.D., University of Pennsylvania, 1969. 300p. UMI# 70-16167. [professor of philosophy, Williams College, 1850-1872].

1243   Marlin, Bernard. Charles Keller: A Study of the Development of His Educational Thought. Ph.D., University of Connecticut, 1980. 187p. UMI# 8103202. [professor of history, Williams College].

1244   Rudolph, Charles F., Jr. Mark Hopkins and the Log. Ph.D., Yale University, 1953. 323p. [president, Williams College, 1836-1872].

WOODS HOLE MARINE BIOLOGICAL LABORATORY

1245   Werdinger, Jeffrey. Embryology at Woods Hole: The Emergence of a New American Biology. Ph.D., Indiana University, 1980. 659p. UMI# 8029260.

MICHIGAN

GENERAL STUDIES

1246   Barnes, Richard A. The Development of Teacher Education in Michigan. Ph.D., University of Chicago, 1940. 190p.

1247   Bennett, Kenneth F. Historical Factors Affecting the Vocational-Technical Emphases of Michigan's Public Community Colleges. Ph.D., University of Michigan, 1984. 209p. UMI# 8412099.

1248   Brown, Seymour H. The Origin of Some Denominational Colleges in the State of Michigan. Master's thesis, University of Detroit, 1933.

1249   Cooper, Harold J., Jr. Analysis and Implications of Historical Events in the Development of the Michigan Intercollegiate Athletic Association. Master's thesis, Michigan State University, 1959. 134p.

1250   Dunbar, Willis F. The Influence of Protestant Denominations on Higher Education in Michigan, 1817-1900. Ph.D., University of Michigan, 1939.

1251   Faverman, Gerald A. Higher Education in Michigan, 1958 to 1970 (with) Volume 2 and 3: Interviews. Ph.D., Michigan State University, 1975. 1,125p. UMI# 75-27214.

1252   Follbaum, Terry D. An Historical Analysis of National Budgetary Trends, Circa 1920 to 1970 with Major Emphasis on Budgeting Trends for Higher Education, State of Michigan, 1970 to 1977. Ed.D., Wayne State University, 1980. 220p. UMI# 80-22812.

1253   Glazer, Stanford H. Development of Michigan College Counseling Programs— 1940-1950. Ed.D., Wayne State University, 1954. 160p. UMI# 00-10055.

1254   Green, Grace H. Michigan Public Junior Colleges: A Decade of Development, 1914-1923. Ph.D., University of Michigan, 1968. 176p. UMI# 68-13317.

1255   Grimes, John O. A History of the Academies of the State of Michigan Prior to 1872. Ph.D., University of Michigan, 1929.

1256   Harton, Helen L. An Historical, Analytical, and Interpretive Study of Educational Theater Programs in Michigan Protestant Church-Related Liberal Arts Colleges. Ph.D., Northwestern University, 1956. 271p. UMI# 00-19565.

1257   Hayes, Richard A., Jr. Selected Characteristics of Michigan Legislators Related to Financial Support of Institutions of Higher Education: 1919-1969. Ph.D., Wayne State University, 1971. 262p. UMI# 72-14,567.

1258   Heck, Glenn E. The Constitutional and Legal Development of the State Board of Education as the Central Education Agency in Michigan. Ph.D., Michigan State University, 1973. 302p. UMI# 74-13,901.

1259   Henning, Sister Gabrielle. A History of Changing Patterns of Objectives in Catholic Higher Education in Michigan. Ph.D., Michigan State University, 1969. 213p. UMI# 69-16143.

1260   Hogancamp, Richard L. The Historical Significance of the Michigan Tenure Decisions Since 1964. Ed.D., Wayne State University, 1971. 183p.

1261   Ivey, Nathan A. The Development and Role of Non-Public Higher Education in Michigan. Ed.D., Michigan State University, 1963. 135p. UMI# 64-07515.

1262   Katz, Lee P. Effect of Title-1 of the Higher Education Act of 1965 Upon the Community Service Programs of Selected Urban Universities in Michigan (1966-1972). Ph.D., University of Michigan, 1973. 202p. UMI# 74-15773.

1263   Large, Margaret S. Factors Influencing Health Education Programs in Three Michigan Colleges from 1850 to 1956. Ph.D., University of Michigan, 1963. 352p. UMI# 64-00845.

1264   Magnuson, Roger P. The Concern of Organized Business with Michigan Education, 1910 to 1940. Ph.D., University of Michigan, 1963. 177p. UMI# 64-06717.

1265   Maybee, Harper C. The Development of the Music Education Curriculum in the State Colleges of Education in Michigan. Master's thesis, University of Michigan, 1951.

1266   McMenemy, Agnes C. The History of Collective Bargaining in Professional Nursing in Michigan. Ed.D., Wayne State University, 1979. 161p. UMI# 79-21699.

1267   Mendola, James J., Jr. The Development of Independent Institutions of Higher Education Founded in Michigan During the Nineteenth Century. Ed.D., Wayne State University, 1979. 201p. UMI# 79-21700.

1268   Quick, Donald M. A Historical Study of the Campus Laboratory Schools in Four Teacher Education Institutions in Michigan. Ph.D., University of Michigan, 1970. 315p. UMI# 71-04712.

1269   Ringenberg, William C. The Protestant College on the Michigan Frontier. Ph.D., Michigan State University, 1970. 219p. UMI# 70-20522.

1270   Rodehorst, Wayne L. An Analysis of the Introduction of Vocational-Technical Education Programs in Michigan Community Colleges Established Before 1930. Ph.D., Michigan State University, 1964. 168p. UMI# 65-00722.

1271   Ross, Margery R. Influences Affecting the Development of Undergraduate Social Work Education in Seven Michigan Colleges from 1920 to 1955. Ph.D., University of Michigan, 1957. 300p. UMI# 58-01458.

1272   Schlafmann, Norman J. An Examination of the Influence of the State Legislature on the Educational Policies of the Constitutionally Incorporated Colleges and Universities of Michigan through Enactment of Public Acts from 1851 through 1970. Ph.D., Michigan State University, 1970. 224p. UMI# 71-18291.

1273   Sebaly, Avis L. Michigan State Normal Schools and Teachers Colleges in Transition, with Special Reference to Western Michigan College of Education. Ph.D., University of Michigan, 1950. 444p. UMI# 00-02003.

1274   Valade, William J.A. A Study of the Origin, Development, and Trends of Selected Community Colleges of Michigan. Ed.D., Wayne State University, 1956. 275p. UMI# 00-17168.

1275   Vanvalkenburgh, Lloyd L. The History of Oral Interpretation in Selected Michigan Universities. Ph.D., Wayne State University, 1973. 435p. UMI# 74-11174.

ALBION COLLEGE

1276   Killion, Mead W. A History of Spring Arbor Seminary and Junior College. Master's thesis, University of Michigan, 1941.

1277   Masteller, Larry T. The History and Development of Intercollegiate Football at Albion College. Master's thesis, University of Illinois, 1960. 85p.

1278   Reed, George R. The Contributions of Thomas Milton Carter to Teacher Education, Albion College, 1923-1962. Ed.D., Michigan State University, 1970. 198p. UMI# 71-18278.

1279   Sprankle, Dale R. A History of Athletics at Albion College. Master's thesis, University of Michigan, 1940. 130p.

ANDREWS UNIVERSITY

1280   Cadwallader, Edward M. Educational Principles in the Writings of Ellen G. White. Ph.D., University of Nebraska at Lincoln, 1949. 675p. [founder, Andrews University and Loma Linda University].

1281   Lindsay, Allan G. Goodloe Harper Bell: Pioneer Seventh-Day Adventist Christian Educator. Ed.D., Andrews University, 1982. 472p. UMI# 8320337. [professor, Andrews University, 1872-1882].

CENTRAL MICHIGAN UNIVERSITY

1282   Bush, Joan D. The History of Dramatic Activities at Central Michigan College of Education from 1892 to 1950. Master's thesis, Michigan State College, 1951.

DETROIT, UNIVERSITY OF

1283   Anderson, James A. The History of "TV College" at the University of Detroit. Master's thesis, University of Michigan, 1962.

FLINT JUNIOR COLLEGE

1284   Prahl, Marie R. Case Study of the Development of a Junior College into a Community College. Ph.D., University of Michigan, 1966. 406p. UMI# 66-14572.

GRAND RAPIDS JUNIOR COLLEGE

1285   Riekse, Robert J. Analysis of Selected Significant Historical Factors in the History of the Pioneer Junior Colleges in Michigan: Grand Rapids Junior College (1914-1962). Ed.D., Michigan State University, 1964. 214p. UMI# 65-06120.

GRAND VALLEY STATE COLLEGE

1286   Swets, Marinus M. A Study of the Establishment of Grand Valley State College. Ph.D., Michigan State University, 1963. 380p. UMI# 64-00966.

HOPE COLLEGE

1287   Shackson, Marian. A History of Hope College. Master's thesis, Western Michigan University, 1942.

1288   Stegenga, Preston J. Hope College in Dutch-American Life, 1851-1951. Ph.D., University of Michigan, 1952. 374p. UMI# 00-03806.

1289   Seaton, Leslie T. The Rationale for Higher Education in the Reformed Church in America, with Particular Reference to Hope College and Its Relationships with New Brunswick and Western Theological Seminaries. Ed.D., Columbia University Teachers College, 1985. 157p. UMI# 8602070.

JACKSON COMMUNITY COLLEGE

1290   Pappas, Richard J. Access to Learning at Jackson Community College (1928-1978). Ph.D., University of Michigan, 1984. 267p. UMI# 8412078.

KALAMAZOO COLLEGE

1291   Barnard, Chester S. A History of Intercollegiate Athletics in Kalamazoo College. Master's thesis, West Virginia University, 1940. 106p.

LANSING COMMUNITY COLLEGE

1292   Randall, Joyce L. A Study of the Emergence and Development of an Associate Degree Nursing Program at Lansing Community College. Ph.D., Michigan State University, 1969. 146p. UMI# 69-16176.

MADONNA COLLEGE

1293   Kujawa, Rose Marie. Madonna College: Its History of Higher Education 1937-1977. Ph.D., Wayne State University, 1979. 289p. UMI# 79-21683.

MICHIGAN STATE UNIVERSITY

1294   Bryson, Norris C. The Response of the Cooperative Extension Service to the Great Depression in Michigan, 1929-38. Ph.D., Michigan State University, 1979. 170p. UMI# 8013705.

1295   Butt, William G. The History of Dramatic Activities at Michigan State College to 1937. Master's thesis, Michigan State College, 1947.

1296   Cullen, Maurice R. The Presidency of Jonathan LeMoyne Snyder at Michigan Agricultural College, 1896-1915. Ph.D., University of Michigan, 1966. 195p. UMI# 66-14110.

1297   Culpepper, Marilyn M. A History of Radio Broadcasting at Michigan State College from August 1922 to January 1954. Ph.D., University of Michigan, 1956. 162p. UMI# 00-21168.

1298   Dawson, Eugene D. The Rise and Development of Farmers' Institutes in Michigan in Relationship to Michigan Agricultural Colleges from 1876 to 1889. Ph.D., Michigan State University, 1974. 199p. UMI# 75-07149.

1299   Eklund, Lowell R. A Century of Service: An Historical Analysis of the Service Function of a State University. Doctor of Public Administration, Syracuse University, 1956. 549p. UMI# 00-18017.

1300   Gillette, Donald R. The Historical and Philosophical Development of Tuition Fees in United States Colleges and Universities and Attitudes of Michigan State University Parents Toward Fees. Ph.D., Michigan State University, 1968. 187p. UMI# 69-11098.

1301   Hughes, Thomas. A Study of the Forensic Activities at Michigan State College from 1857-1937. Master's thesis, Michigan State University, 1952.

1302   Kamins, Robert W. The History of Radio Broadcasting and Radio Education at Michigan State College, 1917-1947. Master's thesis, Michigan State University, 1947.

1303   Lezotte, Ruth A. A History and Contemporary Analysis of the Implementation of Credit by Examination at the Undergraduate Level at Michigan State University. Ph.D., Michigan State University, 1975. 126p. UMI# 76-05596.

1304   Smith, Faye E. Educational Television Broadcasting at Michigan State University: An Historical Analysis of the Impact of Operational Conditions on Programming, 1954-1974. Ph.D., Michigan State University, 1976. 382p. UMI# 76-27150.

1305   Stevens, Glenn R. An Assessment of an Experimental Venture in Liberal Education at Michigan State University. Ph.D., Michigan State University, 1971. 191p. UMI# 71-31314.

1306   Webster, Randolph W. The Development of the Dean of Students Office at Michigan State University. Ph.D., Michigan State University, 1972. 367p. UMI# 72-30063.

1307   Welch, Myron D. The Life and Work of Leonard Falcone with Emphasis on His Years as Director of Bands at Michigan State University, 1927 to 1967. Ed.D., University of Illinois, 1973. 314p. UMI# 74-12,287.

1308   White, Katherine E. Student Activism at Michigan State University During the Decade of the 1960's. Ph.D., Michigan State University, 1972. 448p. UMI# 72-30067.

1309   Wiegandt, Don B. A History of Sports Broadcasting at Michigan State University, 1922-1959. Master's thesis, Michigan State University, 1961.

1310   Winston, Eric V.A. Black Student Activism at Michigan State University, September, 1967 to June 30, 1972: The University's Response. Ph.D., Michigan State University, 1973. 214p. UMI# 73-20,424.

MICHIGAN, UNIVERSITY OF

1311   Armstrong, Robert A. A Descriptive History of Scenic Design in Speech Department Productions at the University of Michigan from 1928-1953. Master's thesis, University of Michigan, 1955.

1312   Behee, John R. Fielding H. Yost's Legacy to the University of Michigan. Ph.D., University of Michigan, 1970. 287p. UMI# 70-21,617. [director of athletics and football coach, 1901-1927].

1313   Bidlack, Russell E. The University of Michigan General Library: A History of Its Beginnings, 1837-1852. Ph.D., University of Michigan, 1954. 663p. UMI# 00-08274.

1314   Campbell, Sharon A.C. A History of the Development of the Flint and Dearborn Branches of the University of Michigan. Ph.D., University of Michigan, 1973. 336p. UMI# 74-03591.

1315   Carlson, William S. Scientific Report of the Fourth University of Michigan Greenland Expedition (1930-1931). Ph.D., University of Michigan, 1938.

1316   Chapel, Robert C. The University of Michigan Professional Theatre Program, 1961-1973. Ph.D., University of Michigan, 1974. 563p. UMI# 75-00654.

1317   Creutz, Alan. From College Teacher to University Scholar: The Evolution and Professionalization of Academics at the University of Michigan, 1841-1900. (Volumes I-II). Ph.D., University of Michigan, 1981. 538p. UMI# 81-16219.

1318   Damm, Helmut H. The University of Michigan from 1850 to 1917 as a Leading Center of German Influences During the Nation's Economic Take-Off. Ph.D., University of Michigan, 1970. 259p. UMI# 70-21639.

1319   Dawson, Edward B. The History of Curricular Expansion in the College of Literature, Science and Arts at the University of Michigan, 1840-1930. Master's thesis, University of Michigan, 1933.

1320   Drachler, Norman. The Influence of Sectarianism, Non- Sectarianism, and Secularism Upon the Public Schools of Detroit and the University of Michigan, 1837-1900. Ph.D., University of Michigan, 1948. 174p. UMI# 00-02398.

1321   Ellis, Elizabeth. A History of Play Production at the University of Michigan from 1915-1926. Master's thesis, University of Michigan, 1955.

1322   Esch, Marvin L. Students Speaking at the University of Michigan, 1841-1884. Ph.D., University of Michigan, 1959. 250p. UMI# 59-03923.

1323   Fallon, Jerome A. The Influence of the Summer School Movement on the State of Michigan, 1874-1931, with Special Reference to the University of Michigan. Ph.D., University of Michigan, 1960. 312p. UMI# 60-06865.

1324   Goddard, Aylene D. A Study of the Niles Branch of the University of Michigan, 1838-1841. Master's thesis, Western Michigan University, 1959.

1325   Hanson, Merle J. David Earl Mattern: A Biography. Ph.D., University of Michigan, 1974. 262p. UMI# 75-10,181. [professor of music, University of Michigan].

1326   Haushatter, William R. The Programming of Platform Artists at the University of Michigan, 1912-1961. Ph.D., University of Michigan, 1969. 273p. UMI# 70-04100.

1327   Johnson, Ruth M. A Brief History of Physical Education for Women at the University of Michigan. Master's thesis, University of Michigan, 1944.

1328   Jones, Alan H. Philanthropic Foundations and the University of Michigan, 1922-1965. Ph.D., University of Michigan, 1971. 236p. UMI# 72-14905.

1329   Karr, Joan M. The Department of Postgraduate Medicine: A History and Interpretation of Its Development. Ph.D., University of Michigan, 1979. 379p. UMI# 79-16742.

1330   Kittell, Janet R. A History of Intercollegiate Athletic Administration at the University of Michigan. Ph.D., University of Michigan, 1984. 220p. UMI# 8502856.

1331   Laird, David B., Jr. The Regents of the University of Michigan and the Legislature of the State, 1920-1950. Ph.D., University of Michigan, 1972. 225p. UMI# 72-29126.

1332   Liu, Yung-Szi. The Academic Achievement of Chinese Graduate Students at the University of Michigan (1907-1950). Ph.D., University of Michigan, 1956. 181p. UMI# 00-18620.

1333   Maxwell, Margaret N.F. Anatomy of a Book Collector: William L. Clements and the Clements Library. Ph.D., University of Michigan, 1971. 429p. UMI# 72-4931. [regent, University of Michigan, 1909-1933].

1334   Meredith, Cameron W. An Account of Changes in the School of Education at the University of Michigan During the Period 1921-1949. Ph.D., University of Michigan, 1951. 282p. UMI# 00-02432.

1335   Noffsinger, Mark G. The Evolution of Student Rights at the University of Michigan. Ph.D., University of Michigan, 1964. 257p. UMI# 65-05357.

1336   Nyikos, Michael S. A History of the Relationship Between Athletic Administration and Faculty Governance at the University of Michigan, 1945-1968. Ph.D., University of Michigan, 1970. 211p. UMI# 71-15252.

1337   Perry, Charles M. Tappan's Contribution to American Philosophy and Culture. Ph.D., University of Michigan, 1911. [president, University of Michigan, 1852-1863].

1338   Pollock, Edward W. Television Broadcasting at the University of Michigan, 1950-1963. Ph.D., University of Michigan, 1966. 341p. UMI# 67-08329.

1339   Saunders, Robert C. The Life and Professional Contributions of Matthew Mann II to Competitive Swimming in the United States. Ph.D., Ohio State University, 1980. 614p. UMI# 8015923. [swimming coach, University of Michigan, 1925-1954].

1340   Savage, Willinda H. The Evolution of John Dewey's Philosophy of Experimentalism as Developed at the University of Michigan. Ed.D., University of Michigan, 1950. 317p. UMI# 00-01999.

1341   Schrader, Shirley L. A History of the University Musical Society of Ann Arbor, Michigan: 1879-1892. (Volumes I and II). Ph.D., University of Michigan, 1968. 286p. UMI# 69-12234.

1342   Shennon, Ella W. The Life and Professional Contributions of Elmer Dayton Mitchell to American Physical Education and Sport. Ph.D., Ohio State University, 1975. 297p. UMI# 76-3550. [professor and chairman of physical education, University of Michigan, 1917-1958].

1343   Smith, Anthony R. College Town Radicals: The Case of the Ann Arbor Human Rights Party. Ph.D., University of Illinois at Urbana-Champaign, 1980. 265p. UMI# 81-08665.

1344   Snyder, Sam R. Academic Freedom at the University of Michigan: The Michigan Case. Ph.D., University of Michigan, 1970. 167p. UMI# 71-15312.

1345   Sparks, Claud G. William Warner Bishop. Ph.D., University of Michigan, 1967. 677p. UMI# 68-7732. [librarian, University of Michigan, 1915-1941].

1346   Stegath, William B. Radio Broadcasting at the University of Michigan, 1922-1958. Ph.D., University of Michigan, 1961. 387p. UMI# 61-02799.

1347   Taylor, William W. The Ann Arbor Drama Season: An Historical Study. Ph.D., University of Michigan, 1967. 385p. UMI# 68-7742.

1348   Tootle, Randolph F. A Historical Case Study of the Development of the Community Policy Board of the Urban Program in Education at the University of Michigan Beginning June, 1969, to March, 1971. Ph.D., University of Michigan, 1975. 130p. UMI# 75-29335.

1349   Van de Water, Peter E. 'Peace Maker': President Alexander G. Ruthven of Michigan and His Relationship to His Faculty, Students and Regents. Ph.D., University of Michigan, 1970. 231p. UMI# 71-4756. [president, 1929-1951].

1350   VanEyck, Daniel K. President Clarence Cook Little and the University of Michigan. Ph.D., University of Michigan, 1965. 238p. UMI# 66-06723. [president, 1925-1929].

1351   Wilbee, Victor R. The Religious Dimensions of Three Presidencies in a State University: Presidents Tappan, Haven, and Angell at the University of Michigan. Ph.D., University of Michigan, 1967. 244p. UMI# 67-17858.

1352   Wilson, Lois M. Henry P. Tappan's Conceptions of the Structuring of University Functions. Ph.D., Stanford University, 1954. 192p. UMI# 00-08226. [president, University of Michigan, 1852-1863].

OAKLAND COMMUNITY COLLEGE

1353   Manilla, Sunday J. A History of Oakland Community College with Emphasis on Multi-Campus Administration, Systems Approach to Instruction and the 'Educational Sciences.' Ed.D., Wayne State University, 1971. 497p. UMI# 72-14596.

OAKLAND UNIVERSITY

1354   Kanter, David R. The Academy Approach to the Teaching of Acting in a Liberal Arts University Setting: An Examination of the History, Philosophy and Practical Results for Students of the Meadow Brook Academy at Oakland University from Its Inception to Date. Ph.D., University of Minnesota, 1976. 203p. UMI# 77-12823.

1355   Stoutenburg, Herbert N., Jr. Oakland University, Its First Four Years: An Historical Analysis of Its Development and Its Administrative Policies. Ed.D., Michigan State University, 1968. 245p. UMI# 69-05964.

SHAW COLLEGE AT DETROIT

1356   Ingram, Anthony. The Institutional Impact of the Financial Crisis in Higher Education: A Case Study of Shaw College at Detroit. Ph.D., University of Michigan, 1979. 324p. UMI# 7916734.

WAYNE COUNTY COMMUNITY COLLEGE

1357   Strobel, Eugene C., Jr. Wayne County Community College: A History of Its Antecedents, Establishment, and Early Development in the Metropolitan Detroit Setting. Ph.D., Wayne State University, 1975. 613p. UMI# 76-11008.

WAYNE STATE UNIVERSITY

1358   Bellefleur, John R. Higher Education for the Many: The Realization and Abridgment of Extended Educational Access, in Detroit and at Wayne University, 1917-1961. Ph.D., University of Michigan, 1981. 513p. UMI# 81-16198.

1359   Green, Clarence D. Collective Bargaining and Power at Wayne State University from 1969 to 1976. Ph.D., Wayne State University, 1978. 229p. UMI# 7908914.

1360   Irwin, James R. Wayne University: A History. Ed.D., Wayne State University, 1952. 497p. UMI# 00-04307.

1361   Ritzenhein, Donald. A History of the Forensic Program at Wayne State University. Master's thesis, Wayne State University, 1980.

MINNESOTA

GENERAL STUDIES

1362   Christenson, Richard D. Minnesota Higher Education Coordinating Commission—Seven Years of Cooperative Effort. Ed.D., University of North Dakota, 1973. 175p. UMI# 74-14,897.

1363   Lindberg, Paul M. The Academies and Colleges of the Augustana Synod in Minnesota. Ph.D., University of Nebraska-Lincoln, 1946. 228p.

1364   Loso, Idelia. Community Services in Minnesota Junior Colleges, 1914-1964. Ph.D., University of Minnesota, 1971. 204p. UMI# 71-28257.

1365   Luetmer, Nora. The History of Catholic Education in the Present Diocese of St. Cloud, Minnesota, 1855-1965. Ph.D., University of Minnesota, 1970. 561p. UMI# 71-03335.

1366   Meyer, Roy F. A History of the Separate, Two-Year Public and Private Junior Colleges of Minnesota, 1905-1955. Ph.D., University of Minnesota, 1956. 585p. UMI# 00-20559.

1367   Prochnow, Larry A. The Story of Science in Minnesota's Denominational Colleges, 1850-1910. Master's thesis, University of Minnesota, 1970.

1368   Wood, Chester W. An Historical Study of Early Minnesota Academics. Ph.D., Stanford University, 1947. 416p.

BEMIDJI STATE UNIVERSITY

1369   Lee, Arthur O., Jr. A History of Bemidji State College, 1913- 1937. Ph.D., University of North Dakota, 1968. 312p. UMI# 69-08557.

COLLEGE OF ST. THOMAS

1370   Fortin, Charles C. A History of the St. Thomas College Library. Master's thesis, University of Minnesota, 1951. 187p.

GUSTAVUS ADOLPHUS COLLEGE

1371   Miller, Virginia P. A History of the Library of Gustavus Adolphus College, St. Peter, Minnesota. Master's thesis, University of Minnesota, 1961. 192p.

1372   Skoog, Rodney A. The Development of Intercollegiate Athletics at Gustavus Adolphus College, 1863-1943. Master's thesis, Mankato State College, 1964.

MANKATO STATE UNIVERSITY

1373   Fuchs, Kenneth D. The History of Intercollegiate Wrestling at Mankato State College. Master's thesis, Mankato State College, 1967.

1374   Giebel, Arlyn J. Development of Mankato Normal School from 1877-1890. Master's thesis, Minnesota State College, 1957.

1375   Grev, Julian R. Mankato State College, 1890-1900. Master's thesis, Mankato State College, 1964.

1376   Larson, Sexton. The Organization and Early Development of Mankato State Normal School. Master's thesis, Mankato State College, 1954.

1377   Mead, George W. The History of Intercollegiate Athletics at Mankato State College. Master's thesis, Mankato State College, 1966.

MINNESOTA, UNIVERSITY OF

1378   Althouse, Ronald C. The Intellectual Career of F. Stuart Chapin: An Examination of the Development and Contributions of a Pluralistic Behaviorist. Ph.D., University of Minnesota, 1964. 428p. UMI# 65-15,228. [professor of psychology, University of Minnesota].

1379   Borehardt, Donald D. The History of the Theatre at the University of Minnesota. Master's thesis, University of Minnesota, 1958.

1380   Dawald, Victor F. The Social Philosophy of Lotus Delta Coffman. Ph.D., University of Wisconsin, 1951. [president, University of Minnesota, 1920-1938].

1381   Engel, John W. Changing Attitudes Toward the Dual Work/Home Role of Women: University of Minnesota Freshmen, 1959-1974. Ph.D., University of Minnesota, 1978. 210p. UMI# 78-23900.

1382   Gee, Robert. The History of the Theatre at the University of Minnesota from Its Beginning to 1947. Master's thesis, University of Minnesota, 1949.

1383   Genaway, David C. Quasi-Departmental Libraries: Their Origin, Function and Relationship to the University of Minnesota Twin Cities Campus. Ph.D., University of Minnesota, 1975. 234p. UMI# 76-14890.

1384   Grabow, Wesley, J.F. The Development of Audio-Visual Education Program at the University of Minnesota. Ph.D., University of Minnesota, 1970. 821p. UMI# 70-27195.

1385   Graybeal, Susan E. Physical Education for Women in the University of Minnesota. Master's thesis, University of Minnesota, 1932.

1386   Heiss, George D. Edgar Bruce Wesley and the Social Studies. Ed.D., Rutgers University, 1967. 327p. UMI# 67-14,426. [professor of social studies, University of Minnesota, 1930-1951).

1387   Huntzicker, William E. The Political Ecology of an Academic Institution (Volumes I and II). Ph.D., University of Minnesota, 1978. 513p. UMI# 7813409.

1388   McCulley, Kathleen M. Dr. Errett Weir McDiarmed's Application of His Philosophy of Library Administration in the University of Minnesota Library, 1943-1951. Master's thesis, University of North Carolina, 1963. 84p. [director of libraries].

1389   McGrath, Gary L. The Establishment and Early Development of the University of Minnesota. Ed.D., Indiana University, 1974. 150p. UMI# 75-05566.

1390   Roberts, Norene A.D. An Early Political and Administrative History of the University of Minnesota, 1851-84. Ph.D., University of Minnesota, 1978. 561p. UMI# 79-12069.

1391   Wangensteen, Margaret R. The Historical Development of the Speaker Policy at the University of Minnesota. Master's thesis, University of Minnesota, 1967.

1392   Wiberg, Charles E. A History of the University of Minnesota Chapter of the American Association of University Professors, 1916-1960. Ph.D., University of Minnesota, 1964. 650p. UMI# 65-15322.

1393   Youngquist, Bernard E. A Critical Study and Analysis of the University of Minnesota Schools of Agriculture. Ph.D., University of Minnesota, 1958. 337p. UMI# 59-01310.

MINNESOTA, UNIVERSITY OF (MORRIS)

1394   Munson, Corliss D. A Description of the Changing Profile of the University of Minnesota, Morris 1960-65. Master's thesis, University of Minnesota, 1966.

SAINT MARY'S COLLEGE

1395   Haugh, Joyce E. History and Development of an Early Childhood Education Program for Undergraduate Students at Saint Mary's College in Winoa, Minnesota. Master's thesis, University of Wisconsin-Lacrosse, 1985.

ST. CLOUD STATE UNIVERSITY

1396   Erickson, George O. The Historical Development of the Social Science Program at St. Cloud State College, 1929-1959. Master's thesis, St. Cloud State College, 1959.

ST. JOHN'S UNIVERSITY

1397   Roloff, Ronald W. St. John's University Library: A Historical Evaluation. Master's thesis, University of Minnesota, 1953.

ST. OLAF COLLEGE

1398   Kelsey, Roger R. Fram! Fram! Christmenn, Crossmenn: The St. Olaf College Program, 1912-1952. Ph.D., George Peabody College for Teachers, 1954.

MISSISSIPPI

GENERAL STUDIES

1399 Bowen, Erie J. Affirmative Action Employment Programs in Mississippi Public Universities: 1972-1979. Ed.D., University of Mississippi, 1981. 173p. UMI# 8207667.

1400 Bridgforth, Lucie R. Medical Education in Mississippi. Ph.D., Memphis State University, 1982. 407p. UMI# 82-27403.

1401 Brown, Margaret. Graduate Programs in Mississippi to 1900. Master's thesis, University of Mississippi, 1968.

1402 Campbell, Leslie C. History of Pharmacy in Mississippi. Ph.D., University of Mississippi, 1967. 193p. UMI# 67-13,773.

1403 Causey, Patricia D.A.A History of Reading Programs in Mississippi's Public Junior Colleges. Ed.D., University of Mississippi,1985. 339p. UMI# 8603315.

1404 Daniel, Helen T. History of the American Association of University Women in Mississippi. Master's thesis, Mississippi College, 1955.

1405 DiMichele, Charles C. The History of the Roman Catholic Educational System in Mississippi. Ed.D., Mississippi State University, 1973. 217p. UMI# 74-02915.

1406 Lucas, Aubrey K. The Mississippi Legislature and Mississippi Public Higher Education: 1890-1960. Ph.D., Florida State University, 1966. 303p. UMI# 67-00336.

1407 Mathis, Emily D. An Historical Study of Curricular Changes in Selected Public Junior Colleges in Mississippi. Ed.D., University of Tennessee, 1971. 126p. UMI# 72-15537.

1408 Stark, Cruce. A Study of the Mississippi System of Public Junior Colleges. Ph.D., University of Houston, 1954.

1409 Stark, Grace W. Beginnings of Teacher Training in Mississippi. Ph.D., George Peabody College for Teachers, 1946. 229p.

1410 Vujnovich, Miles M. Ray S. Musgrave: A Biography of a Dedicated Educator. Ph.D., University of Southern Mississippi, 1976. 249p. UMI# 77-05978. [head of psychology department, University of Southern Mississippi, 1956-1975].

ALCORN STATE UNIVERSITY

1411 Buckles, Eddie. A History of Physical Education and Athletics at Alcorn Agricultural and Mechanical College. Ph.D., Ohio State University, 1972. 238p. UMI# 72-26984.

1412 Smith, Jay T., Sr. Origin and Development of Industrial Education at Alcorn Agricultural and Mechanical College. Ed.D., University of Missouri-Columbia, 1971. 176p. UMI# 72-10564.

BELHAVEN COLLEGE

1413   Gordon, James F., Jr. A History of Belhaven College, Jackson, Mississippi, 1894 to 1981. Ph.D., University of Mississippi, 1982. 298p. UMI# 82-17295.

BLUE MOUNTAIN COLLEGE

1414   Tyler, Frances L. Blue Mountain College Under the Administration of Lawrence Tyndale Lowrey, 1925-1960. Ph.D., University of Mississippi, 1974. 192p. UMI# 75-10688.

CLARKE MEMORIAL COLLEGE

1415   Gallaspy, Harold T. Fifty Years of Curriculum Development in Clarke Memorial College, 1908-1958. Doctor of Religious Education, New Orleans Baptist Theological Seminary, 1961. 191p.

1416   Reynolds, Thomas U. A History of Clarke Memorial College. Master's thesis, Texas Christian University, 1952.

COPIAH LINCOLN AGRICULTURAL HIGH SCHOOL
AND JUNIOR COLLEGE

1417   Donnan, Annette W. A Study of the History of Copiah-Lincoln Agricultural High School and Junior College, from 1914 to May 31, 1976. Ed.D., University of Southern Mississippi, 1977. 241p. UMI# 77-22866.

GULF PARK COLLEGE FOR WOMEN

1418   Elias, Louis, Jr. A History of Gulf Park College for Women, 1917-1971. Ed.D., University of Mississippi, 1981. 151p. UMI# 82-07668.

JACKSON STATE UNIVERSITY

1419   Burns, Ralph E. A History of the Department of Health, Physical Education, and Recreation at Jackson State University, Jackson, Mississippi, from 1877 to 1973. Ed.D., East Texas State University, 1976. 274p. UMI# 77-00475.

1420   Nash, Evelyn M. The Predominantly Black College: Changing the Role, Meeting the Challenge in Higher Education. Ph.D., University of Kansas, 1981. 171p. UMI# 8218807.

1421   Spofford, Timothy J. Lynch Street: The Story of Mississippi's Kent State—The May 1970 Slayings at Jackson State College. Doctor of Arts, State University of New York at Albany, 1984. 450p. UMI# 8414616.

JEFFERSON COLLEGE

1422   Fowler, William B. History of Jefferson College of Washington, Mississippi, Prior to the War for Southern Independence. Master's thesis, Louisiana State University, 1937.

JONES COUNTY JUNIOR COLLEGE

1423   Tisdale, Thomas T. From Agricultural High School to Comprehensive Junior College:

Jones County Junior College, 1910 to 1970. Ed.D., University of Southern Mississippi, 1972. 176p. UMI# 73-05589.

MISSISSIPPI COLLEGE

1424   Hicks, Billy R. Richard Aubrey McLemore and Mississippi College: A Study in Educational Leadership. Ph.D., University of Mississippi, 1983. 172p. UMI# 8323338. [president, 1957-1968].

MISSISSIPPI STATE UNIVERSITY

1425   Hattaway, Herman M. Stephen Dill Lee: A Biography. Ph.D., Louisiana State University, 1969. 389p. UMI# 70-00244. [president, Mississippi State University, 1880-1889].

MISSISSIPPI, UNIVERSITY OF

1426   Fisher, William B. Contributions to Academic Medicine by Medical Certificate, M.D., and Ph.D. Degree Graduates of the University of Mississippi, 1903-1976. Ph.D., University of Mississippi, 1976. 251p. UMI# 77-01408.

1427   Graham, Hardy P. Bilbo and the University of Mississippi, 1928-1932. Master's thesis, University of Mississippi, 1965. [governor of Mississippi].

1428   Hooker, Grover C. The Origin and History of the University of Mississippi. Ph.D., University of Mississippi, 1931.

1429   Measells, Dewitt T., Jr. History of the Expansion of the University of Mississippi, 1848-1947. Master's thesis, University of Mississippi, 1947.

1430   Nichols, Mary E. Early Development of the University of Mississippi Library. Master's thesis, University of Mississippi, 1957.

1431   Read, James C. The Williams Chancellorship at the University of Mississippi, 1946-68. Ed.D., University of Mississippi, 1978. 340p. UMI# 78-24061.

1432   Shackelford, Walter M. A History of Teacher Education at the University of Mississippi. Ph.D., University of Mississippi, 1959.

MISSISSIPPI VALLEY STATE UNIVERSITY

1433   Baker, Clemon. A Historical Investigation of the Goal Evolution of Mississippi Valley State University, 1946-1976. Ph.D., Southern Illinois University at Carbondale, 1977. 177p. UMI# 77-16610.

1434   Tinsley, Sammy J. A History of Mississippi Valley State College. Ph.D., University of Mississippi, 1972. 293p. UMI# 73-01295.

OAKLAND COLLEGE

1435   Bruss, Melvin. The History of Oakland College (Mississippi), 1830-1871. Master's thesis, Louisiana State University, 1966.

OKOLONA COLLEGE

1436   Stewart, Richard A. The History and Educational Programs of Okolona College, Okolona, Mississippi. Master's thesis, Tennessee A&I State University, 1962.

SOUTHERN MISSISSIPPI, UNIVERSITY OF

1437   Bacon, John P., Jr. A History of Intercollegiate Athletics at the University of Southern Mississippi, 1912-1949. Master's thesis, University of Southern Mississippi, 1967.

1438   Fagerberg, Seigfred W. A History of the Intercollegiate Athletic Program at the University of Southern Mississippi, 1949-1969. Ed.D., University of Southern Mississippi, 1970. 480p. UMI# 71-13570.

TOUGALOO COLLEGE

1439   Campbell, Clarice T. The Formative Years of Tougaloo College. Master's thesis, University of Mississippi, 1967.

1440   Campbell, Clarice T. History of Tougaloo College. Ph.D., University of Mississippi, 1970. 410p. UMI# 70-16392.

UTICA JUNIOR COLLEGE

1441   Washington, Walter. Utica Junior College, 1903-1957: A Half Century of Education for Negroes. Ed.D., University of Southern Mississippi, 1970. 202p. UMI# 71-05402.

WHITWORTH COLLEGE FOR WOMEN

1442   Rice, Kathleen G. A History of Whitworth College for Women. Ph.D., University of Mississippi, 1985. 145p. UMI# 8603326.

MISSOURI

GENERAL STUDIES

1443   Benton, Edwin J. A History of Public Education in Missouri, 1760-1964. Ph.D., Saint Louis University, 1965. 126p. UMI# 65-14633.

1444   Beshara, Anthony W. An Educational History of the County Junior College District. Ph.D., Saint Louis University, 1972. 364p. UMI# 74-04478.

1445   Dallinger, Carl A. History of Speech Training at William Jewell College and Park College, 1850-1940. Ph.D., University of Iowa, 1952. 844p. UMI# 67-08894.

1446   DeWoody, George M. Development of the Educational Provisions of the Missouri Constitution of 1945. Ph.D., University of Missouri, 1949. 274p.

1447   Edwards, Ralph. A History of Dental Education in Kansas City, Missouri. Master's thesis, University of Kansas City, 1947.

1448   Freund, Emma J. The History of Medical Social Work in St. Louis (1928-1944). Master's thesis, Washington University, 1945.

1449   Gersman, Elinor M. Education in St. Louis, 1880-1900: A Case Study of Schools in Society. Ph.D., Washington University, 1969. 399p. UMI# 70-10952.

1450   Glauert, Ralph E. Education and Society in Anti-Bellum Missouri. Ph.D., University of Missouri-Columbia, 1973. 267p. UMI# 74-18534.

1451   Grimes, Lloyd. The Development of Constitutional and Statutory Provisions for Education in Missouri Since 1874. Ph.D., University of Missouri, 1944. 490p.

1452   Henderson, Thomas A. The Development of Statewide Coordination of Higher Education in the State of Missouri. Ph.D., Southern Illinois University, 1976. 368p. UMI# 77-16623.

1453   Imhoff, Myrtle M.A. The Improvement of Teacher Qualifications in the State of Missouri—1839-1946. Ph.D., Washington University, 1952.

1454   Koch, Sister Madeline M. Growth and Development of Catholic Higher Education and Secondary Schools Conducted by the Sisters of Loretto in Missouri, 1823-1952. Master's thesis, Catholic University of America, 1957.

1455   Lubeck, Dennis R. University City: A Suburban Community's Response to Civil Rights, 1959-1970. Ph.D., Saint Louis University, 1978. 892p. UMI# 79-23839.

1456   Mann, George L. The Historical Development of Public Education in St. Louis, Missouri, for Negroes. Ph.D., Indiana University, 1949. 189p.

1457   McMurdock, Bertha J. The Development of Higher Education for Negroes in Missouri. Master's thesis, Howard University, 1939.

1458   McMurtry, George W. A History of the Teachers' Colleges of Missouri. Master's thesis, University of Chicago, 1926.

1459   Mileham, Hazel B. The Junior College Movement in Missouri. Ph.D., Yale University, 1934.

1460   Phillips, Claude A. The Origin and Development of Agencies for the Training of Teachers in the State of Missouri. Ph.D., George Peabody College for Teachers, 1920.

1461   Sawyer, Robert M. The Gaines Case: Its Background and Influence on the University of Missouri and Lincoln University 1936-1950. Ph.D., University of Missouri, 1966. 376p. UMI# 66-09000.

1462   Shankland, Wilbur M. Medical Education in St. Louis, 1836-1861. Ph.D., Washington University, 1953. 323p.

1463   Spainhower, James I. Missouri Politics and State Aid to Private Higher Education. Ph.D., University of Missouri-Columbia, 1971. 451p. UMI# 71-22944.

1464   Stein, David T. The Evolution of Policy Development for Programs of Higher Education in the Lutheran Church Missouri Synod and Its Relationship to Internal and External Governance 1944-1975. Ph.D., Saint Louis University, 1979. 375p. UMI# 79-23683.

1465   Wadsworth, L.E. A History of Junior Colleges in Missouri Since 1930. Master's thesis, University of Missouri, 1937. 163p.

1466   Wheadon, Rosetta F.D. An Historical Review of One Community's Efforts to Establish a Junior College. Ph.D., Saint Louis University, 1968. 136p. UMI# 69-16054.

1467   Young, Jerry G. A History of Athletics in the Missouri Inter Collegiate Athletic Association. Master's thesis, Northeast Missouri State Teachers College, 1954.

CENTRAL METHODIST COLLEGE

1468   Hinton, William H. A History of Howard Payne College with Emphasis on the Life and Administration of Thomas H. Taylor. Ph.D., University of Texas at Austin, 1957. [president, Central Methodist College].

1469   Hitt, Bowling M. History of Howard Payne College. Master's thesis, Sul Ross State College, 1951.

CENTRAL MISSOURI STATE UNIVERSITY

1470   Allen, Patricia A. George W. Diemer: Selected Aspects of His Presidency at Central Missouri State College, 1937-1956. Ph.D., Southern Illinois University at Carbondale, 1983. 309p. UMI# 83-26504.

1471   Dunnington, Nellie B. A History of the Development of Speech as an Academic Discipline in the State College of Missouri. Master's thesis, Central Missouri State College, 1964.

1472   Lane, Robert W. A History of Theater at Central Missouri State College from 1905 to 1942. Master's thesis, Central Missouri State College, 1969.

CHRISTIAN BROTHERS COLLEGE

1473   Archambeault, Brother Henry E. The History and Educational Program of Christian Brothers' College, St. Louis, Missouri. Master's thesis, Saint Louis University, 1947.

COLUMBIA COLLEGE

1474   Hughes, M.K. A History of Christian College, 1851-1900. Master's thesis, University of Missouri, 1944.

CONCORDIA SEMINARY

1475   Suelflow, Roy A. The History of Concordia Seminary, St. Louis, 1839-1865. Master's thesis, Washington University, 1946.

COTTEY COLLEGE

1476   Rhodes, Mary. Dried Flowers: The History of Women's Culture at Cottey College, 1884-1965. Ph.D., Ohio State University, 1981. 223p. UMI# 81-29081.

DRURY COLLEGE

1477   Pope, Richard M. Drury College: An Interpretation. Ph.D., University of Chicago, 1955. 105p.

HARRIS-STOWE STATE COLLEGE

1478   Davis, Julian. Harris Teachers' College and Stowe Teachers' College Growth and Development. Master's thesis, University of Iowa, 1941.

1479   Patterson, Richard H. Harris Teachers College, 1904-1966. Ph.D., Saint Louis University, 1972. 173p. UMI# 72-23994.

1480   Rosskopf, Lea A. Curriculum Development at Harris Teachers' College of Saint Louis, Missouri: 1857-1949. Master's thesis, Saint Louis University, 1950.

LINCOLN UNIVERSITY

1481   Houser, Steven D. O. Anderson Fuller, the First Black Doctor of Philosophy of Music in America, and His Development of the Music Education Curriculum at Lincoln University. Ph.D., University of Missouri, 1982. 151p. UMI# 8310400. [chairman of fine arts and music, 1942-1974].

LUTHERAN MEDICAL CENTER SCHOOL OF NURSING

1482   Von Conrad, Georgia B. The First Eighty Years: The History of Lutheran Medical Center School of Nursing, 1898-1978. Ph.D., Saint Louis University, 1980. 172p. UMI# 8207448.

MARILLAC COLLEGE

1483   Monahan, Danno R. Educating Women Religious: The History of Marillac College, 1955-1969. Ph.D., Saint Louis University, 1972. 127p. UMI# 72-31474.

MISSOURI, UNIVERSITY OF

1484   Adams, Helen B. Walter Williams: Spokesman for Journalism and Spokesman for the University of Missouri. Ph.D., University of Missouri, 1969. 337p. UMI# 70-6553. [dean of journalism, 1908-1931; president, 1931-1934].

1485   Eikelmann, Kenneth P. A History of Educational Television at the University of Missouri. Master's thesis, University of Missouri, 1960.

1486   Freeman, William W. The Life and Educational Contributions of John Rufi (University of Missouri, 1928-1962). Ed.D., University of Missouri, 1977. 387p. UMI# 7814115. [professor of education].

1487   Hejkal, Otto C. The Life and Work of Robert W. Selvidge. Ed.D., University of Missouri, 1950. 396p.

1488   Hoyer, Mina. The History of Automation in the University of Missouri Library, 1947-1963. Master's thesis, Indiana University, 1965.

1489   King, John L. Neil C. Aslin—Educator. Ed.D., University of Missouri, 1979. 388p. UMI# 8024368. [professor of education, University of Missouri-Columbia].

1490   Lynn, Harlan C. An Oral History of Extension Radio in Missouri. Ph.D., University of Missouri-Columbia, 1983. 226p. UMI# 8412789.

1491   Stefanov, Jan J. The Training of Teachers at the University of Missouri Until 1930: A History. Ph.D., University of MissouriColumbia, 1972. 307p. UMI# 73-07093.

1492   Stewart, Ralph E. Origin and Development of Intramural Sports for Men at the University of Missouri. Ed.D., University of Missouri, 1964. 232p. UMI# 64-13308.

MISSOURI VALLEY COLLEGE

1493   Parsons, Nellie F. The History of Missouri Valley College. Master's thesis, University of Missouri, 1940.

MOBERLY AREA JUNIOR COLLEGE

1494   Ricker, Paul A. A History of the Growth and Development of Moberly Area Junior College 1926-1984. Ed.D., University of Missouri-Columbia, 1984. 157p. UMI# 8500559.

NAZARENE THEOLOGICAL SEMINARY

1495   Miller, William C. The Governance of Theological Education: A Case Study of Nazarene Theological Seminary, 1945-1976. Ph.D., Kent State University, 1983. 273p. UMI# 8321152.

NORTHEAST MISSOURI STATE UNIVERSITY

1496   Bagley, Ronald E. A History of the Industrial Arts Department at the Northeast Missouri State Teachers College. Master's thesis, Northeast Missouri State Teachers College, 1960.

NORTHWEST MISSOURI STATE UNIVERSITY

1497   DelPizzo, Ferdinand. The Contributions of John R. Kirk to Teacher-Education. Ph.D., Washington University, 1955. 178p. UMI# 00-12795. [president, Northwest Missouri State University, 1899-1925].

1498   Workman, George L. A History of Intramural Athletics, Northwest Missouri State Teachers' College, Kirksville, Missouri. Master's thesis, Northwest Missouri State Teachers' College, 1955.

ROCKHURST COLLEGE

1499   Owens, Hugh M., S.J. History of Rockhurst College (Kansas City)—The First Quarter-Century (1914-1939). Master's thesis, Saint Louis University, 1953.

RUSKIN COLLEGE

1500   Owen, Helen R. Ruskin College, 1900-1963 Master's thesis, Northeast Missouri State University, 1971. 48p.

SAINT LOUIS UNIVERSITY

1501   Kenney, Daniel J., S.J. History of the Saint Louis University Graduate School, 1834-1900. Master's thesis, Saint Louis University, 1957.

1502   Labaj, Joseph J., S.J. The Development of the Department of Education at Saint Louis University, 1900-1942. Master's thesis, Saint Louis University, 1952.

SOUTHEAST MISSOURI STATE UNIVERSITY

1503   Page, John C. A History of Men's Physical Education at Southeast Missouri State College. Master's thesis, Southeast Missouri State College, 1971.

1504   Turlington, Terry T. A Historical Study of Intercollegiate Basketball at Southeast Missouri State College. Master's thesis, Southeast Missouri State College, 1970.

SOUTHWEST BAPTIST COLLEGE

1505   Mahan, L.D.J. A History of Southwest Baptist College, 1878-1946. Master's thesis, University of Missouri, 1948.

SOUTHWEST MISSOURI STATE UNIVERSITY

1506   Westphaf, Leonard W. The History of Forensics at Southwest Missouri State, 1906-1971. Master's thesis, Southwest Missouri State University, 1972.

ST. FRANCIS XAVIER COLLEGE

1507   Kramer, Urban J. History of St. Francis Xavier (College) Church, St. Louis, Missouri, 1837-1943. Master's thesis, Saint Louis University, 1944.

STEPHENS COLLEGE

1508   Ankrum, Ward E. The Implementation of Educational Philosophy and a Program of Educational Research in the Curricular Growth of Stephens College. Ed.D., University of Missouri-Columbia, 1951. 439p. UMI# 00-02670.

THREE RIVERS COMMUNITY COLLEGE

1509   Burke, Thomas R. Three Rivers Community College: The Formative Years, 1966-1979. Ph.D., University of Mississippi, 1981. 225p. UMI# 81-28091.

WASHINGTON UNIVERSITY

1510   Craig, James T. Origin and History of the Collegiate Department of Washington University, 1853-1870. Master's thesis, Washington University, 1941.

1511   Fowler, Queen E.D. Educating Adults: A History of University College at Washington University, Saint Louis: Its Purposes and Implications for the Future, 1908-1970. Ph.D., Saint Louis University, 1974. 178p. UMI# 75-26252.

1512   Hayes, Donn W. A History of Smith Academy of Washington University. Ph.D., Washington University, 1950. 117p.

1513   Held, Lois C. History of the College of Washington University. Master's thesis, Washington University, 1941.

1514   Jerzewiak, R.M. History of the O'Fallon Polytechnique Institute, 1855-1868: The Practical Department of Washington University. Master's thesis, Washington University, 1940.

1515   Keck, George R. Pre-1875 American Imprint Sheet Music in the Ernst C. Krohn Special Collections, Gaylord Music Library, Washington University, St. Louis, Missouri: A Catalog and Descriptive Study. Ph.D., University of Iowa, 1982. 973p. UMI# 82-22245.

1516   Parle, Grace. History of the Missouri Dental College (The Dental Department of Washington University, 1892-1901), 1866-1901. Master's thesis, Washington University, 1942.

1517   Williams, Cartus R. History of the Law Department of Washington University (the St. Louis Law School) 1867-1900. Master's thesis, Washington University, 1942.

1518   Worner, Lloyd E. The Public Career of Herbert Spencer Hadley. Ph.D., University of Missouri-Columbia, 1946. 367p. UMI# 00-00928. [chancellor, Washington University].

WESTERN COLLEGE

1519   Harding, Alfred D. Western College (1880-1893), LaBelle, Missouri: A Chapter in Northeast Missouri Educational History. Master's thesis, Northeast Missouri State Teachers' College, 1960.

MONTANA

GENERAL STUDIES

1520   Chenette, Edward B. The Montana State Board of Education: A Study of Higher Education in Conflict, 1884-1959. Ed.D., University of Montana, 1972. 507p. UMI# 73-11,310.

COLLEGE OF GREAT FALLS

1521   Cronin, Kathleen J. An Historical Perspective of the College of Great Falls. Ed.D., Boston University School of Education, 1974. 393p. UMI# 74-14230.

MONTANA STATE UNIVERSITY

1522   McAlduff, William H. A History of the Health, Physical Education, and Recreation Department at Montana State University, 1893-1979. Master's thesis, Montana State University, 1980.

MONTANA, UNIVERSITY OF

1523   Brennan, Joseph W. Development of the School of Education, Montana State University, 1895-1950. Master's thesis, Montana State University, 1953.

1524   Buysse, JoAnn. An Historical Analysis of Women's Athletics at Montana State University from 1893 to 1979. Master's thesis, Montana State University, 1980.

1525   Cowan, John R., Jr. A History of the School of Music, Montana State University (1895-1952). Master's thesis, Montana State University, 1952.

NORTHERN MONTANA COLLEGE

1526   Caskey, Gerald C. A History of Northern Montana College to 1951. Master's thesis, University of North Dakota, 1953.

WESTERN MONTANA COLLEGE

1527   Pyeatt, Margaret F. A Historical Study of the Growth of Montana State Normal College, 1914 through 1941. Master's thesis, Western Montana College, 1965.

1528   Spiegle, Edward F. Historical Study of the Formation and Early Growth of Western Montana College of Education. Master's thesis, Western Montana College, 1952.

NEBRASKA

GENERAL STUDIES

1529   Easton, Theodore A. The Development of Community Colleges in Nebraska. Ed.D., University of Colorado, 1973. 217p. UMI# 74-12367.

1530   Hickman, Glen E. The History of Teacher Education In Nebraska. Ph.D., University of Oregon, 1948.

1531   Horton, Agnes. Federal Land Grants Relating to Higher Education in Nebraska: Their Acquisition and Disposition. Ph.D., University of Denver, 1957.

1532   Hughes, Kathryn H. History of the Public Junior Colleges of Nebraska. Master's thesis, University of Nebraska, 1942.

1533   Hutches, George E. History of Union College and College View. Master's thesis, University of Nebraska, 1936.

1534   Korsgaard, Ross P. A History of Federal Aid to Education in Nebraska. Ed.D., University of Nebraska-Lincoln, 1963. 182p. UMI# 64-00228.

1535   Weyer, Frank E. Presbyterian Colleges and Academies in Nebraska. Ph.D., University of Nebraska, 1941. 259p.

1536   Williams, John R. Nebraska Governors and Education—1905-1915 and 1955-1965. Ed.D., University of Nebraska, 1970. 255p. UMI# 71-9594.

CHADRON STATE COLLEGE

1537   Coats, Kenneth W. A History of the Department of Speech at Chadron State College, 1911-1965. Master's thesis, University of Nebraska, 1967.

CONCORDIA TEACHERS COLLEGE

1538   Freitag, Alfred J. A History of Concordia Teachers College, 1864-1964. Ed.D., University of Southern California, 1965. 561p. UMI# 65-08909.

1539   Simon, Martin P. A History of Concordia Teachers College, Seward, Nebraska. Ph.D., University of Oregon, 1953. 323p.

COTNER UNIVERSITY

1540   Moomaw, Leon A. History of Cotner University. Master's thesis, University of Nebraska, 1916.

CREIGHTON UNIVERSITY

1541   Kirby, Maurice W. History of Creighton University, 1878-1926. Master's thesis, University of Nebraska, 1954.

1542   Vosper, James M. A History of Selected Factors in the Development of Creighton University. Ph.D., University of Nebraska-Lincoln, 1976. 278p. UMI# 77-00955.

HASTINGS COLLEGE

1543   Thurber, John H. History of Speech at Hastings College. Master's thesis, University of Nebraska, 1957.

KEARNEY STATE COLLEGE

1544   Bjorklun, John. History of Speech Education at Kearney State Teachers College. Master's thesis, University of Nebraska, 1964.

NEBRASKA, UNIVERSITY OF

1545   Bergquist, David H. The Latin School and the Emergence of a State University in Nebraska: A History of Preparatory Education at the University of Nebraska, 1871-1897. Ed.D., University of Nebraska-Lincoln, 1973. 223p. UMI# 74-00629.

1546   Biehn, Albert L. The Development of the University of Nebraska, 1871-1900. Master's thesis, University of Nebraska, 1934.

1547   Faulkner, Charles M. A History of the ROTC at the University of Nebraska, 1947-1957. Master's thesis, University of Nebraska, 1958.

1548   Gappa, LaVon M. Chancellor James Hulme Canfield: His Impact on the University of Nebraska, 1891-1895. Ph.D., University of Nebraska-Lincoln, 1985. 289p. UMI# 8521454.

1549   Hannah, James J. The Ideas and Plans in the Founding of the University of Nebraska 1869-1875. Master's thesis, University of Nebraska, 1951.

1550   Hughes, Elsie L. A History and Analysis of the University of Nebraska Speech Clinic. Master's thesis, University of Nebraska, 1952.

1551   Lee, Robert E. A History of Radio Broadcasting at the University of Nebraska. Master's thesis, University of Nebraska, 1952.

1552   McSweeney, John P. The Chancellorship of Reuben G. Gustavson at the University of Nebraska, 1946-1953. Ph.D., University of Nebraska, 1971. 198p. UMI# 72-03971.

1553   Murray, Floyd B. A History of Summer Sessions at the University of Nebraska. Master's thesis, University of Nebraska, 1942.

1554   Novotny, Marianne K. H. The Clare McPhee Laboratory School: A Historical Description of Functions, 1965-1974. Ed.D., University of Nebraska-Lincoln, 1974. 97p. UMI# 75-03431.

1555   Olson, Donald O. Debating at the University of Nebraska. Master's thesis, University of Wisconsin, 1947.

1556   Parks, Walter W. A History of Teacher Placement at the University of Nebraska. Ed.D., University of Nebraska, 1964. 161p. UMI# 64-12240.

1557   Ritchie, Linda C.S. History of the University of Nebraska Summer Sessions: 1891-1915. Ed.D., University of Nebraska, 1980. 142p. UMI# 81-14593.

1558   Rockwell, Leroy. The Origin and Development of Educational Television at the University of Nebraska to 1961. Master's thesis, University of Nebraska, 1961.

1559   Stiver, Harry E., Jr. A History of the Theater of the University of Nebraska (1900-1950). Master's thesis, University of Nebraska, 1952.

1560   Van Arsdall, James E. The Stated and Operative Objectives of the University of Nebraska Extension High School Program, 1929-1975. Ed.D., University of Nebraska, 1977. 205p. UMI# 77-23165.

1561   Walsh, Thomas R. Charles E. Bessey: Land Grant College Professor. Ph.D., University of Nebraska, 1972. 245p. UMI# 72-31882. [professor of botany, dean, and chancellor, University of Nebraska, 1884-1915; professor of botany, Iowa State University, 1870-1884].

NEBRASKA, UNIVERSITY OF (OMAHA)

1562   Camden, Lillian H. The Early History of the University of Omaha. Master's thesis, University of Omaha, 1951.

1563   Weintraub, Arnold. A History of Speech Education at Omaha University. Master's thesis, University of Nebraska, 1966.

NEBRASKA WESLEYAN UNIVERSITY

1564   Danskin, Warren L. A History of the School of Expression and Oratory at Nebraska Wesleyan University. Master's thesis, University of Nebraska, 1962.

1565   Winship, Frank L. Early History of Nebraska Wesleyan University. Master's thesis, University of Nebraska, 1930.

PERU STATE COLLEGE

1566   Lyon, Mona L. An Academic History of Peru State Teachers College. Master's thesis, George Peabody College for Teachers, 1936. 50p.

YORK COLLEGE

1567   Holm, Myron L. Teacher Training in York College, 1938-1949. Master's thesis, University of Nebraska, 1949.

1568   Larsen, Dale R. A History of York College. Ed.D., University of Nebraska, 1966. 221p. UMI# 67-03435.

NEVADA

GENERAL STUDIES

1569   Caserta, John A. A History of the Community College Movement in Nevada, 1967-1977. Ed.D., University of Nevada-Reno, 1979. 205p. UMI# 80-11911.

1570   Middlebrooks, Deloris J. A History of the Associate Degree Nursing Program in Nevada, 1963-1983. Ed.D., University of Nevada-Las Vegas, 1985. 136p. UMI# 8606975.

NEVADA, UNIVERSITY OF

1571   Russell, Tom S. A History of the University of Nevada ROTC and Its Distinguished Military Graduates. Master's thesis, University of Nevada-Reno, 1969.

NEW HAMPSHIRE

BELKNAP COLLEGE

1572 Rice, Abbott E. The Revolutionary Process at Belknap College: A Historical Study in Campus Governance. Ed.D., Boston University School of Education, 1978. 222p. UMI# 78-19775.

DARTMOUTH COLLEGE

1573 Campbell, Bruce A. Law and Experience in the Early Republic: The Evolution of the Dartmouth College Doctrine, 1780-1819. Ph.D., Michigan State University, 1973. 420p. UMI# 73-20320.

1574 Filkins, James H. An Analysis of the Dartmouth College Case with Respect to Its Impact upon the Evolution of Higher Education. Ph.D., North Texas State University, 1973. 171p. UMI# 74-14817.

1575 McKnight, Richard P. The Trustees of Dartmouth College, 1769-1800. Master's thesis, University of Wyoming, 1983.

1576 Stites, Francis N. The Dartmouth College Case, 1819. Ph.D., Indiana University, 1968. 227p. UMI# 69-04811.

1577 Tobias, Marilyn I. Old Dartmouth on Trial: The Transformation of the Academic Community in Nineteenth-Century America. Ph.D., New York University, 1977. 367p. UMI# 78-03036.

FRANKLIN PIERCE COLLEGE

1578 Dipietro, Frank S. Franklin Pierce College: A Case Study. Ed.D., Boston University, 1971. 260p. UMI# 71-26695.

RIVIER COLLEGE

1579 Cormier, Sister Marie C. A Brief History of Rivier College, 1933-1953. Master's thesis, Rivier College, 1955.

NEW JERSEY

GENERAL STUDIES

1580   Burr, Nelson R. History of Education in New Jersey. Ph.D., Princeton University, 1934.

1581   Consalus, Charles E. The History of Legal Education in New Jersey. Ed.D., Columbia University Teachers College, 1979. 563p. UMI# 79-23578.

1582   Damico, Claude S. The Emergence of Lay Members on Boards of Trustees of Roman Catholic Colleges of New Jersey. Ed.D., Rutgers University, 1978. 134p. UMI# 78-10223.

1583   Karlen, Janice M. Collective Bargaining and Tenure in Higher Education in New Jersey, 1970-1980. Ed.D., Seton-Hall University, 1984. 187p. UMI# 8601775.

1584   Manzo, Elizabeth. The Development of Teacher Education in New Jersey from the Colonial Period through the National Period. Master's thesis, Jersey City State College, 1967.

1585   Morgenroth, George W. An Historical Study of the Origin and Growth of the Essex County, New Jersey, Vocational Schools: A Study of the Relationships Between the Socio-Economic Conditions in a Community and a System of County Vocational Schools with Especial Emphasis on an Adjusted Program of Vocational Education. Ph.D., New York University, 1955. 271p. UMI# 00-15573.

1586   Rockwell, Jean A. History of Evening Business Education in the Four-Year Colleges and Universities of New Jersey. Ph.D., New York University, 1970. 257p. UMI# 70-26441.

1587   Sahm, Jay H. The Development of College-Based Adult Education Resource Centers in the State of New Jersey: 1965 to 1982. Ed.D., Rutgers University, 1983. 218p. UMI# 8325912.

1588   Shannon, Edith R. The Professional Education of Teachers in New Jersey: History of Its Origin and Development. Ph.D., New York University, 1932. 453p. UMI# 72-33737.

1589   Silver, George. A History and Analysis of the Duties, Functions and Professional Status of State College Business Managers in New Jersey. Ed.D., Temple University, 1964. 233p. UMI# 64-13694.

ALMA WHITE COLLEGE

1590   Lawrence, Evan J. Alma White College: A History of Its Relationship to the Development of the 'Pillar of Fire.' Ed.D., Columbia University, 1966. 152p. UMI# 66-10301.

BETH MEDRASH GOVOHO

1591   Lewitter, Sidney R. A School for Scholars, the Beth Medrash Govoho, the Rabbi Aaron Kotler Jewish Institute of Higher Learning in Lakewood, New Jersey: A Study of the Development and Theory of One Aspect of Jewish Higher Education in America. Ed.D., Rutgers University, 1981. 162p. UMI# 81-20836.

ESSEX COUNTY COLLEGE

1592   Jackson, Edison O. Essex County College: Dynamics of Governance. The Decision-Making Process of a Public Education Institution. Ph.D., Rutgers University, 1983. 163p. UMI# 8410990.

EVELYN COLLEGE FOR WOMEN

1593   Healy, Frances P. A History of Evelyn College for Women, Princeton, New Jersey, 1887 to 1897. Ph.D., Ohio State University, 1967. 207p. UMI# 68-02999.

JERSEY CITY STATE COLLEGE

1594   Sherman, John. The Origin and Development of Jersey City State College, 1927-1962. Ed.D., New York University, 1968. 338p. UMI# 68-11821.

KEAN COLLEGE OF NEW JERSEY

1595   Leonard, Janet G. History of the Curriculum of Newark State College, 1855-1934. Ed.D., Rutgers University, 1971. 486p. UMI# 72-16089.

MONTCLAIR STATE COLLEGE

1596   Davis, Earl C. The Origin and Development of the New Jersey State Teachers College at Montclair, 1908-1951. Ph.D., New York University, 1954. 235p. UMI# 00-10626.

1597   Goodman, Michael. An Evaluative Survey of the Student Personnel Program at the Jersey State Teachers College at Montclair, 1908-1954. Ed.D., New York University, 1957. 483p. UMI# 58-00631.

1598   Leef, Audrey J.V. An Historical Study of the Influence of the Mathematics Department of Montclair State College on the Teaching of Mathematics, 1927-1972, in the Context of the Changes in Mathematics Education During this Period. Ed.D., Rutgers University, 1976. 198p. UMI# 76-27333.

NEW BRUNSWICK THEOLOGICAL SEMINARY

1599   Bruins, Elton J. The New Brunswick Theological Seminary, 1884-1959. Ph.D., New York University, 1962. 234p. UMI# 63-5341.

NEWARK, UNIVERSITY OF

1600   Bennett, Hugh F. A History of the University of Newark, 1908-1946. Ph.D., New York University, 1956. 262p. UMI# 00-17634.

PRINCETON THEOLOGICAL SEMINARY

1601   Calhoun, David B. The Last Command: Princeton Theological Seminary and Missions (1812-1862). Ph.D., Princeton Theological Seminary, 1983. 546p. UMI# 8320287.

1602   Clutter, Ronald T. The Reorientation of Princeton Theological Seminary, 1900-1929. Ph.D., Dallas Theological Seminary, 1982. 252p. UMI# 8323133.

1603   Haines, George L. Princeton Theological Seminary, 1925-1960. Ph.D., New York University, 1966. 263p. UMI# 67-00113.

1604   Scovel, Raleigh D. Orthodoxy at Princeton: A Social and Intellectual History of Princeton Theological Seminary, 1812-1860. Ph.D., University of California-Berkeley, 1970. 358p. UMI# 71-09920.

PRINCETON UNIVERSITY

1605   Bailey, Kenneth M. Woodrow Wilson: The Educator Speaking. Ph.D., University of Iowa, 1970. 381p. UMI# 70-15577. [president, Princeton University, 1902-1910].

1606   Berberian, Kevork. Princeton University Library, 1746-1860. Master's thesis, Jersey City State College, 1976. 84p.

1607   Bradbury, Miles L. Adventure in Persuasion: John Witherspoon, Samuel Stanhope Smith, and Ashbel Green. Ph.D., Harvard University, 1967.

1608   Come, Donald R. The Influence of Princeton on Higher Education in the South Before 1825. Master's thesis, Duke University, 1943.

1609   Demerly, John A. Woodrow Wilson—Educator. Ph.D., State University of New York at Buffalo, 1957. [president, Princeton University, 1902-1910].

1610   Guder, Darrell L. The Story of Belles Lettres at Princeton: An Historical Investigation of the Expansion and Secularization of Curriculum of English and Letters. Ph.D., University of Hamburg, 1964.

1611   Mulder, John M. The Gospel of Order: Woodrow Wilson and the Development of His Religious, Political, and Educational Thought, 1856-1910. Ph.D., Princeton University, 1974. 440p. UMI# 74-17480. [president, Princeton University, 1902-1910].

1612   Rich, George E. John Witherspoon: His Scottish Intellectual Background. Doctor of Social Science, Syracuse University, 1964. 212p. UMI# 65-03433. [president, Princeton University, 1768-1794].

1613   Shereshewsky, Murray S. Academy Keeping and the Great Awakening: The Presbyterian Academies, College of New Jersey, and Revivalism, 1727-1768. Ph.D., New York University, 1980. 304p. UMI# 81-10685.

1614   Stavish, Emanuel. An Evaluation of the Educational Philosophy of Woodrow Wilson. Master's thesis, City College of New York, 1933. [president, Princeton University, 1902-1910].

RIDER COLLEGE

1615   Brower, Walter A., Jr. Rider College: The First One Hundred Years. Ed.D., Temple University, 1965. 280p. UMI# 66-00641.

RUTGERS UNIVERSITY

1616   Boelhauwer, Douglas. The History and Development of Football at Rutgers University. Master's thesis, University of Illinois, 1964.

1617   Dee, Frank P. A History of the Extension Division, Rutgers: The State University, 1891-1965. Ed.D., Rutgers University, 1966. 257p. UMI# 67-06399.

1618   Dwyer, Richard E. An Examination of the Development of Labor Studies at Rutgers University, 1931-1974: A Study in Union University Cooperation. Ed.D., Rutgers University, 1975. 339p. UMI# 76-1110.

1619   Geller, Marjorie A. Development of Education at Rutgers University, 1969-1981: A Descriptive Case Study. Ed.D., Rutgers University, 1984. 178p. UMI# 8424044.

1620   Rosenthal, Michael L. The Founding of the Office of the Dean of the Faculty. Undergraduate Life at the College of New Jersey. Ed.D., Rutgers University, 1974. 385p. UMI# 74-27341.

1621   Sidar, Jean W. George Hammell Cook, a Life in Agriculture and Geology: 1818-1889. Ph.D., Rutgers University, 1979. [professor of chemistry and natural science, Rutgers University, 1853-1889].

1622   Sperduto, Frank V. A History of Rutgers Preparatory School. Ed.D., Rutgers University, 1965. 280p. UMI# 66-6783.

1623   Vittum, Henry E. The Development of the Curriculum of Rutgers College of Rutgers, the State University, 1862-1958. Ph.D., New York University, 1962. 242p. UMI# 62-05356.

SETON HALL UNIVERSITY

1624   Kennelly, Edward F. A Historical Study of Seton Hall College. Ph.D., New York University, 1944. 246p. UMI# 73-08627.

TRENTON STATE COLLEGE

1625   Franz, Evelyn B. Trends in the Preparation of Teachers for the Elementary Schools at the New Jersey State Teachers College at Trenton, 1855-1956. Ed.D., Rutgers University, 1958. 462p. UMI# 58-05725.

1626   Fromm, Glenn E. A History of the New Jersey State Teachers College at Trenton, 1855-1950. Ed.D., New York University, 1951. 526p. UMI# 00-02507.

1627   Graham, Blanche E.O. History and Evaluation of the Health and Physical Education Program: New Jersey State Teachers College at Trenton. Ed.D., Temple University, 1954. 235p. UMI# 00-12869.

VINELAND TRAINING SCHOOL

1628   McCaffrey, Katherine R. Founders of the Training School at Vineland, New Jersey: S. Olin Garrison, Alexander Johnson, Edward R. Johnstone. Ed.D., Columbia University Teachers College, 1965. 337p. UMI# 65-14974.

WESTMINSTER CHOIR COLLEGE

1629   Page, Patricia A. The Westminster Choir College. Master's thesis, Union Theological Seminary, 1953.

1630   Schisler, Charles H. A History of Westminster's Choir College, 1926-1973. Ph.D., Indiana University, 1976. 566p. UMI# 77-10948.

NEW MEXICO

GENERAL STUDIES

1631   Gunn, Virgil R. A History of Higher Education in New Mexico. Master's thesis, University of Chicago, 1927.

1632   Haas, Francis. Education in New Mexico: A Study of the Development of Education in a Changing Social Order. Ph.D., University of Chicago, 1955. 105p.

1633   Meador, William R. A Historical Survey of Baptist-Sponsored Higher Education in New Mexico. Master's thesis, Eastern New Mexico University, 1959.

1634   Reed, Deward H. The History of Teachers Colleges in New Mexico. Ph.D., George Peabody College for Teachers, 1948.

1635   Tipps, Garland E. A Half-Century of Graduate Education in New Mexico. Ed.D., George Peabody College for Teachers, 1965. 277p. UMI# 66-04431.

EASTERN NEW MEXICO UNIVERSITY

1636   Mann, Aubrey E. The History and Development of Eastern New Mexico University. Ed.D., University of Northern Colorado, 1959. 233p. UMI# 59-06004.

NEW MEXICO HIGHLANDS UNIVERSITY

1637   Price, Hugh. A History of the New Mexico Normal University, 1893-1931. Master's thesis, New Mexico Highlands University, 1932.

1638   Valenzuela, Harvey. Student Protest Outcomes: Case Study and the Effect for Institutional Change of the Student Protest Movement at New Mexico Highlands University, 1971-1981. Ph.D., University of Washington, 1984.

NEW MEXICO MILITARY INSTITUTE

1639   Jackman, Eugene T. The New Mexico Military Institute, 1891- 1966: A Critical History. Ph.D., University of Mississippi, 1967. 525p. UMI# 67-07996.

NEW MEXICO STATE UNIVERSITY

1640   Bandy, Cheryl N.L. The First Fifty Years of the New Mexico State University Library, 1889-1939. Master's thesis, University of Oklahoma, 1971.

NEW MEXICO, UNIVERSITY OF

1641   Barney, Robert K. Turmoil and Triumph—A Narrative History of Intercollegiate Athletics at the University of New Mexico and Its Implication in the Social History of Albuquerque— 1889-1950. Ph.D., University of New Mexico, 1968. 548p. UMI# 69-09277.

1642   Caton, W. Barnie. A Study of the Extension Division of the University of New Mexico, with Emphasis on the Period, 1928-1938. Master's thesis, University of New Mexico, 1939.

1643   Lazzell, Carleen C. Academic Architecture and Changing Values in New Mexico: Hodgin Hall 1889-1909. Master's thesis, University of New Mexico, 1984.

1644   Lincoln, Winfred J. Admission Practices and the Success of Specially Admitted Students at the University of New Mexico and Selected State Colleges in New Mexico, 1935-1955. Ed.D., University of Southern California, 1959. 349p. UMI# 59-01852.

1645   Pugh, David W. A Study in Literary, Social, and University History: The Life and Often Hard Times of the 'New Mexico Quarterly,' 1931-1969. Ph.D., University of New Mexico, 1975. 325p. UMI# 76-07974.

1646   Reeve, Frank D. History of the University of New Mexico. Master's thesis, University of New Mexico, 1928.

WESTERN NEW MEXICO UNIVERSITY

1647   Overturf, Donald S. The History of New Mexico Western College. Ph.D., University of Nebraska-Lincoln, 1960. 770p. UMI# 60-05577.

NEW YORK

GENERAL STUDIES

1648 Aiken, John R. Utopianism and the Emergence of the Colonial Legal Profession: New York 1664-1710. A Test Case. Ph.D., University of Rochester, 1967. 313p. UMI# 67-08943.

1649 Allen, Harlan B. Origin, Development and Evaluation of the General Policies and Practices Governing Teacher Certification in New York State. Ph.D., New York University, 1939. 267p. UMI# 73-02999.

1650 Arone, Frank T. An Historical Investigation of the Contribution of the New York State Teachers Association to the Professionalization of Teachers (1904-1965). Ed.D., New York University, 1967. 355p. UMI# 67-11136.

1651 Bogart, Ruth E. College Library Development in New York State During the 19th Century. Master's thesis, Columbia University, 1948. 155p.

1652 Brier, Ellen M. Bridging the Academic Preparation Gap at Vassar College and Cornell University, 1865-1890. Ed.D., Columbia University, 1983. 148p. UMI# 8322180.

1653 Canuteson, Richard L. A Historical Study of Some Effects of Dual Control in the New York State Educational System, 1854-1904. Ph.D., Michigan State University, 1950. 432p. UMI# 00-01917.

1654 Conway, G. Allan. Columbia and New York Universities Consolidation: A Study in Urban Social Consciousness. Ph.D., New York University, 1974. 262p. UMI# 75-8537.

1655 Doran, Kenneth T. New York, New Yorkers, and the Two-Year College Movement: A History of the Debate Over Structure in Higher Education. Ed.D., Syracuse University, 1961. 578p. UMI# 62-01098.

1656 Egan, Margaret L. The Taylor Law: A Legislative History (New York). Ed.D., Harvard University, 1982. 203p. UMI# 82-23204.

1657 Entin, Nathaniel A. The Jewish Education Committee of New York, 1939-1965. Ph.D., Dropsie University, 1972.

1658 Eskow, Seymour. The Search for the Public Two-Year College in New York: A Study of the Forms and Forces Shaping the New York State Institutes of Applied Arts and Sciences, 1946-. Ph.D., Syracuse University, 1965. 728p. UMI# 66-06200.

1659 Falk, Gerhard. The Immigration of the European Professors and Intellectuals to the United States and Particularly the Niagara Frontier During the Nazi Era, 1933-1941. Ed.D., State University of New York at Buffalo, 1970. 301p. UMI# 70-10306.

1660 Fitzelle, Albert E. Origin and Development of the Normal School System of New York State. Ph.D., New York University, 1928. 180p. UMI# 72-33545.

1661   French, William M. Teacher Training in New York, 1834-1934. Ph.D., Yale University, 1934.

1662   Goodhartz, Abraham S. The Control of Free Higher Education in New York City. Ph.D., New York University, 1951. 193p. UMI# 00-02762.

1663   Harris, Jonathan. The Rise of Medical Science in New York, 1720-1870. Ph.D., New York University, 1971. 451p. UMI# 72-24,742.

1664   Hartstein, Jacob I. State Regulatory and Supervisory Control of Higher Education in New York from Its Beginning through the Civil War. Ph.D., New York University, 1945. 224p.

1665   Hedbavy, Leopold. Some Leisure-Time Organizations in New York City, 1830-1870: Clubs, Lyceums, and Libraries. Master's thesis, New York University, 1952.

1666   Henery, Clive. The Development and Status of Undergraduate Music Education Curricula in the State of New York. Doctor of Music Education, Indiana University, 1981. 314p. UMI# 82-11745.

1667   Jolt, Harvey A. The Optometric Center of New York, Its History, Organization, Development—A Case Study of the Impact of a Leadership Role and Analysis of Its Effects Upon a Segment of the Health Community. Ph.D., New York University, 1973. 695p. UMI# 74-13341.

1668   Klein, Christa R. The Jesuits and Catholic Boyhood in Nineteenth-Century New York City: A Study of St. John's College and the College of St. Francis Xavier, 1846-1912. Ph.D., University of Pennsylvania, 1976. 410p. UMI# 77-10180.

1669   Kniker, Charles R. The Chautauqua Literary and Scientific Circle, 1878-1914: An Historical Interpretation of an Educational Piety in Industrial America. Ed.D., Columbia University, 1969. 419p. UMI# 71-14328.

1670   Kun, Cecilia R. A Study of the Teaching of Russian in Selected Schools and Colleges of the Niagara Frontier from 1957 to the Present. Ed.D., State University of New York at Buffalo, 1970. 232p. UMI# 70-10307.

1671   Mallon, Arthur. The Development of the Municipal Teacher-Training Colleges in New York City. Ph.D., New York University, 1935. 211p. UMI# 73-03284.

1672   Maloney, Edward F. A Study of the Religious Orientation of Catholic Colleges and Universities in New York State from 1962 to 1972. Ph.D., New York University, 1974. 179p. UMI# 74-17148.

1673   Mattice, Howard L. The Growth and Development of Roman Catholic Education in New York City: 1842-1875. Ed.D., New York University, 1979. 261p. UMI# 79-11276.

1674   Miller, Richard V. The New York State Teachers Association, the Empire State Federation of Teachers, and State Educational Legislation 1949-1963. Ph.D., New York University, 1967. 169p. UMI# 68-04786.

1675   Mosher, Bryan J. A Century of Financial Aid by the State of New York to Students in Higher Education. Ph.D., Syracuse University, 1967. 130p. UMI# 68-5481.

1676   Neumann, Florence M. Access to Free Public Higher Education in New York City: 1847-1961. Ph.D., City University of New York, 1984. 408p. UMI# 8409411.

1677   Scudiere, Paul J. A Historical Survey of State Financial Support of Private Higher Education in New York. Ed.D., State University of New York at Albany, 1975. 118p. UMI# 75-25782.

1678   Trusz, Andrew R. The Activities of Governmental Education Bodies in Refining the Role of Post-Secondary Education Since 1945: A Comparative Case Study of New York and the Province of Ontario, 1945-1972. Ed.D., State University of New York at Buffalo, 1977. 402p. UMI# 7813994.

1679   Williams, Samuel A. The Growth of Physical Education in the State Teachers Colleges of New York in Relation to Certain Socio-Economic Factors. Ph.D., New York University, 1950. 365p. UMI# 00-01938.

ADELPHI UNIVERSITY

1680   Rosenberg, Helen. A History of the Department of Speech and Dramatic Art of the Adelphi University: 1935-1965. Master's thesis, Adelphi University, 1968.

ALBANY (UNIVERSITY), STATE UNIVERSITY OF NEW YORK

1681   Martin, David W. The Liberal Arts in the Curricula for the Preparation of Teachers at the State University of New York at Albany, 1844-1966. Ph.D., University of Connecticut, 1967. 270p. UMI# 68-1376.

AUBURN COMMUNITY COLLEGE, STATE UNIVERSITY OF NEW YORK

1682   Skinner, Albert T. A History of Auburn Community College During Its Founding Period, 1953-1959. Ph.D., Syracuse University, 1961. 540p. UMI# 62-01122.

BANK STREET COLLEGE OF EDUCATION

1683   Matthews, Emily P. Lucy Sprague Mitchell: A Deweyan Educator. Ed.D., Rutgers University, 1979. 209p. UMI# 7917913. [founder and president, Bank Street College of Education].

BROCKPORT (COLLEGE), STATE UNIVERSITY OF NEW YORK

1684   Butler, M. Alene. A History of the Brockport Collegiate Institute, 1836-1867. Master's thesis, University of Rochester, 1939.

BROOKLYN COLLEGE, CITY UNIVERSITY OF NEW YORK

1685   Sussman, Diane. History of the Brooklyn (N.Y.) College Library from 1930 to 1966. Master's thesis, Long Island University, 1967.

BUFFALO (COLLEGE), STATE UNIVERSITY OF NEW YORK

1686   Grant, Margaret A. The Preparation of Homemaking Teachers: Ten Years of Experience at the New York State College for Teachers, Buffalo, New York. Ph.D., State University of New York at Buffalo, 1953.

BUFFALO (UNIVERSITY), STATE UNIVERSITY OF NEW YORK

1687   Blau, Guitta D. Theory and Practice in Education: A Biography of Adelle Land (1901-1969). Ph.D., State University of New York at Buffalo, 1976. 302p. UMI# 77-3513. [professor of education, State University of New York at Buffalo].

1688   Collins, Charles R.J. The Herbartian Teachers College, University of Buffalo School of Pedagogy, 1895-1898. Ed.D., State University of New York at Buffalo, 1969. 101p. UMI# 69-15185.

1689   Crone, Douglas C. An Historical Study of the Growth and Devlopment of the Educational and Administrative Ideas of Samuel Paul Capen, 1902 to 1950. Ed.D., State University of New York at Buffalo, 1968. 153p. UMI# 68-12448. [chancellor, State University of New York at Buffalo, 1922-1950].

1690   Parsons, Jerry L. The Feinberg Law: A Case History of the Challenge at the State University of New York at Buffalo, 1963-1967. Ph.D., State University of New York at Buffalo, 1970. 332p. UMI# 71-07206.

1691   Roberts, Francis X. The Growth and Development of the Libraries in the University of Buffalo, 1846-1960. Ph.D., State University of New York at Buffalo, 1986. 476p. UMI# 8609148.

1692   Summer, Pepi. The Career Pattern of Women Graduates of the University of Buffalo Medical, Dental and Law Schools Between 1895 and 1915. Ph.D., State University of New York at Buffalo, 1980. UMI# 81-14722.

BUFFALO FINE ARTS ACADEMY

1693   Lehmann, Joyce W. The 'Albright Art School' of the Buffalo Fine Arts Academy: 1887-1954. Ph.D., State University of New York at Buffalo, 1984. 232p. UMI# 8410569.

CANISIUS COLLEGE

1694   McGowan, James E. The History of Sports at Canisius College. Master's thesis, Canisius College, 1954.

CITY UNIVERSITY OF NEW YORK

1695   Aquino-Bermudez, Frederico. Growth and Development of Puerto Rican Studies Departments: A Case Study of Two Departments at the City University of New York. Ed.D., University of Massachusetts, 1975. 388p. UMI# 75-16,534.

1696   Bergenthal, Hugo. The History of the German Language and Literature in the Curriculum of the College of the City of New York. Master's thesis, City College of New York, 1936.

1697   Blume, Eli. The History of Romance Languages in the Curriculum of the College of the City of New York. Master's thesis, City College of New York, 1934.

1698   Brown, Nathan. The Growth and Development of the Department of History in the College of the City of New York, 1847-1934. Master's thesis, City College of New York, 1935. 220p.

1699   Feinstein, Irving N. The Growth and Development of the Study of the English Language and Literature in the College of the City of New York, 1847-1934. Master's thesis, City College of New York, 1934.

1700   Gordon, Sheila C. The Transformation of the City University of New York, 1945-1970. Ph.D., Columbia University, 1975. 322p. UMI# 77-27856.

1701   Grayson, Gerald H. Professors Unite: A History of the Legislative Conference of City University of New York, 1938-1971. Ph.D., New York University, 1973. 489p. UMI# 74-12841.

1702   Hochman, Fred. The History of Art in the Curriculum of the College of the City of New York. Master's thesis, City College of New York, 1934.

1703   Klotzburger, Katherine M. Politics in Higher Education: The Issue of the Status of Women at the City University of New York, 1971-1973. Ph.D., New York University, 1976. 584p. UMI# 77-05419.

1704   McGurk, Josephine H. The History of the Department and School of Education of the College of the City of New York, 1906-1934. Master's thesis, City College of New York, 1934.

1705   Millamed, Israel S. The Origin and Development of Political Science in the Curriculum of the College of the City of New York. Master's thesis, City College of New York, 1933.

1706   Rosenthal, Irving. A History of Student Publications at the College of the City of New York. Master's thesis, City College of New York, 1934.

1707   Rudy, S. Willis. The College of the City of New York: A History, 1847-1947. Ph.D., Columbia University, 1950. 492p.

1708   Stallman, Abraham M. The History of Geology in the Curriculum of the College of the City of New York. Master's thesis, City College of New York, 1933.

1709   Startz, Milton. The Growth and Development of the Department of Economics at the College of the City of New York. Master's thesis, City College of New York, 1940.

1710   Stewart, Nathaniel J. A History of the Library of the College of the City of New York. Master's thesis, College of the City of New York, 1936.

1711   Warren, Constancia. Open Admissions at City College: The Implementation of an Egalitarian Reform in a Meritocratic Institution. Ph.D., Columbia University, 1984. 276p. UMI# 8427493.

COBLESKILL (COLLEGE), STATE UNIVERSITY OF NEW YORK

1712   Long, Douglas E. A Case Study of the Environment and Administrative Structural Adaptation of a College: From 1970 to 1980. Ed.D., State University of New York at Albany, 1984. 190p. UMI# 8503668.

COLGATE UNIVERSITY

1713   Burdick, Alger E. The Contributions of Albert Perry Brigham to Geographic Education. Ph.D., George Peabody College for Teachers, 1951. [professor of geology, Colgate University].

1714   Williams, Howard D. The History of Colgate University to 1869. Ph.D., Harvard University, 1949. 171p.

COLLEGE OF INSURANCE

1715   Leonard, A. Leslie. Establishing a Professional Institution of Higher Education: The College of Insurance. Ed.D., Columbia University, 1966. 304p. UMI# 66-08221.

COLLEGE OF ST. ROSE

1716   Soulier, Sister Catherine F. The College of St. Rose, 1920-1950. Master's thesis, College of St. Rose, 1952.

COLUMBIA UNIVERSITY

1717   Adamsons, Hannelore M. The Columbia Crisis of 1968: The Role of the Faculty. Ph.D., Columbia University, 1975. 276p. UMI# 75-27,376.

1718   Averette, George, Jr. A History of the Department of Health Education and Physical Education, Teachers College, Columbia University. Ph.D., Columbia University, 1953.

1719   Baker, Susan S. Out of the Engagement. Richard Hofstadter: The Genesis of a Historian. Ph.D., Case Western Reserve University, 1982. 415p. UMI# 8314579. [professor of history, Columbia University, 1946-1970].

1720   Bates, Mary D. Columbia's Bards: A Study of American Verse from 1783 through 1799. Ph.D., Brown University, 1954. 421p. UMI# 00-09805.

1721   Bromberg, Ailene J. Columbia University, Early Years as Revealed by a Study of the Columbiad. Master's thesis, Portland University, 1959.

1722   Cajoleas, Louis P. The Academic Record, Professional Development, and Return Adjustment of Doctoral Students from Other Lands: A Study of Teachers College Alumni, 1946-1955. Ph.D., Columbia University, 1958. 295p. UMI# 58-02611.

1723   Carron, Blossom R. Seth Low Junior College of Columbia University: A Case Study of an Abortive Experiment. Ed.D., Columbia University Teachers College, 1979. 268p. UMI# 8006794.

1724   Christy, Teresa E. A History of the Division of Nursing Education of Teachers College, Columbia University, 1899-1947. Ed.D., Columbia University, 1968. 229p. UMI# 70-12511.

1725   Chute, William J. The Life of Frederick A.P. Barnard to His Election as President of Columbia College in 1864. Ph.D., Columbia University, 1951. 355p. UMI# 00-08631. [president, Columbia University, 1864-1889].

1726   Doyle, Joseph. George E. Woodberry. Ph.D., Columbia University, 1952. 738p. UMI# 00-04565. [professor of comparative literature, Columbia University, 1891-1904].

1727   Drost, Walter H. Social Efficiency and the Curriculum: The Professional Career of David Snedden. Ph.D., University of Wisconsin, 1965. 515p. UMI# 65-10,600. [professor of education, Columbia University Teachers College, 1905-1909, 1916-1935].

1728   Ferrell, Hanson D. Samuel Johnson, American Educator (1696-1772). Master's thesis, Tulane University, 1940. [president, Columbia University, 1754-1763].

1729   Foster, Elaine E. A Great School of Fine Arts in New York City: A Study of the Development of Art in the Regular Undergraduate Curriculum of Columbia College and University, Including Affiliations with the National Academy of Design and the Metropolitan Museum of Art, 1860-1914. Ed.D., Columbia University, 1970. 215p. UMI# 72-08821.

1730   Gallagher, Carol T. A Scottish Contribution to American Higher Education: The Saint Andrew's Society of New York, 1756-1806, and the Founding of King's College. Ph.D., University of Kentucky, 1984. 159p. UMI# 8510728.

1731   Grant, William H. The Development of Student Government: A History of the Board of Student Representatives of Columbia University, 1892-1925. Ed.D., Columbia University, 1964. 125p. UMI# 65-06167.

1732   Hendricks, Luther V. James Harvey Robinson, Teacher of History. Ph.D., Columbia University, 1947. 120p. [Columbia University, 1895-1919].

1733   Holton, John T. The Educational Thought of Jacques Barzun: Its Historical Foundation and Significance for Teacher Education. Ph.D., Ohio State University, 1980. 227p. UMI# 8100168. [professor of history, Columbia University].

1734   Hoth, William E. The Development of a Communications Skill Course: A History of the Undergraduate Program at Teachers College, Columbia University. Ph.D., Columbia University Teachers College, 1955. 105p.

1735   Hoxie, Ralph G. John W. Burgess, American Scholar—Book I: The Founding of the Faculty of Political Science. Ph.D., Columbia University, 1950. 413p. UMI# 00-02345. [graduate dean, Columbia University, 1890-1912].

1736   Hughes, Arthur J. Carlton J. H. Hayes: Teacher and Historian. Ph.D., Columbia University, 1970. 372p. UMI# 72-33,426. [professor of history, Columbia University, 1907-1950].

1737   Humphrey, David C. King's College in the City of New York, 1754-1776. Ph.D., Northwestern University, 1968. 669p. UMI# 69-01852.

1738   Jaquith, L. Paul. The University Seminars at Columbia University: A Living Monument to Frank Tannenbaum. Ed.D., Columbia University, 1973. 155p. UMI# 73-19,348. [professor of Latin American history].

1739   Jones, Ruth. A History of the Library of Teachers College, Columbia University, 1887-1952. Master's thesis, Drexel Institute of Technology, 1953.

1740   Josephson, Harold. James Thomson Shotwell: Historian as Activist. Ph.D., University of

Wisconsin, 1968. 507p. UMI# 69-22,407. [professor of history, Columbia University, 1900-1942].

1741   Kao, Lin-Ying. Academic and Professional Attainments of Native Chinese Students Graduating from Teachers College, Columbia University, 1909-1950. Ph.D., Columbia University, 1952.

1742   Keating, James M. Seth Low and the Development of Columbia University, 1889-1901. Ed.D., Columbia University, 1973. 308p. UMI# 73-24072. [president, 1890-1901].

1743   Koch, Ruth M. The Professional Education of Student Personnel Workers in Higher Education at Teachers College, Columbia University, 1913-1938. Ed.D., Columbia University, 1966. 210p. UMI# 67-02815.

1744   Kurland, Gerald. Seth Low: A Study in the Progressive Mind. Ph.D., City University of New York, 1968. 461p. UMI# 68-15,937. [president, Columbia University, 1890-1901].

1745   Larson, Robert L. Charles Frederick Chandler, His Life and Work. Ph.D., Columbia University, 1950. 411p. [professor of chemistry and dean, Columbia University, 1864-1897].

1746   Lawton, Edward M., Jr. Columbia College and the New York State Legislature, 1784-1820. Master's thesis, Columbia University, 1950.

1747   Lee, William R. Education through Music: The Life and Work of Charles Hubert Farnsworth (1859-1947). Doctor of Musical Arts, University of Kentucky, 1982. 265p. UMI# 8307271. [director of music and speech, Columbia University Teachers College, 1901-1926].

1748   Linderman, Winifred B. History of the Columbia University Library, 1876-1926. Ph.D., Columbia University, 1959. 619p. UMI# 59-02859.

1749   Lord-Wood, June. Musical Americana in the Hunt-Berol Collection at the Columbia University Libraries. Doctor of Musical Arts, Columbia University, 1975. 390p.

1750   MacEachen, John. The Humanities in Columbia College, 1900-1960: An Analysis of Trends in Humanistic Studies in the Undergraduate Curriculum of Columbia College. Ph.D., New York University, 1960. 222p. UMI# 60-03752.

1751   Marley, Owen G. Thomas Henry Briggs: Philosopher and Educator. Ed.D., University of Massachusetts, 1974. 278p. UMI# 74-25,850. [professor of education, Columbia University Teachers College, 1912-1942].

1752   McGinnis, Robert S., Jr. A Model for Theological Education in Eighteenth Century America: Samuel Johnson, D.D., of King's College. Doctor of Divinity, Vanderbilt University Divinity School, 1971. 169p. UMI# 71-26146. [president, 1754-1763].

1753   McGrath, Gerard M. Collegiality at Columbia: The Origin, Development, and Utility of Two Faculty Clubs. Ed.D., Columbia University Teachers College, 1984. 411p. UMI# 84-03274.

1754   Moak, Franklin E. The Development of the International Teaching Service Bureau at Teachers College, Columbia University. Ph.D., Columbia University, 1956.

1755   Mock-Morgan, Mavera E. A Historical Study of the Theories and Methodology of Arthur Wesley Dow and Their Contribution to Teacher-Training in Art Education. Ph.D., University of Maryland, 1976. 322p. UMI# 77-09514. [professor of fine arts, Columbia University Teachers College, 1904-1922].

1756   Moore, David W. Liberalism and Liberal Education at Columbia University: The Columbia Careers of Jacques Barzun, Lionel Trilling, Richard Hofstadter, Daniel Bell, and C. Wright Mills. Ph.D., University of Maryland, 1978. 456p. UMI# 79-15794.

1757   Murray, Catherine A. Student Life at King's College and Early Columbia College in the City of New York—1754-1820. Master's thesis, Columbia University, 1943.

1758   Olsen, Richard N. Howard A. Murphy, Theorist and Teacher: His Influence on the Teaching of Basic Music Theory in American Colleges and Universities from 1940 to 1973. Ed.D., University of Illinois at Urbana-Champaign, 1973. 248p. UMI# 74-12278. [professor of music, Columbia University Teachers College, 1927-1961].

1759   Osysko, Edmund. Florian Znaniecki, Educator and Humanistic Sociologist. Ed.D., Columbia University Teachers College, 1982. 346p. UMI# 8223161. [visiting professor of sociology, Columbia University, 1931-1938].

1760   Randolph, Scott K. An Analysis of the Committee on the Role of Education in American History and Lawrence Cremin's Revisionist View of the Nature of American Education. Ed.D., Rutgers University, 1976. 181p. UMI# 77-13,286. [professor of education and president of Columbia University Teachers College].

1761   Reed, Larry W. The History of the Department of Music and Music Education Teachers College, Columbia University—The Early Years: 1887-1939 (New York). Ed.D., Columbia University Teachers College, 1982. 190p. UMI# 83-13396.

1762   Reid, John Y. The Public Career of Earl James McGrath: Vindicating Education for Holistic Man. Ph.D., University of Arizona, 1978. 324p. UMI# 78-13589. [professor of education, director of Institute of Higher Education, Columbia University Teachers College, 1956-1968].

1763   Roach, Helen P. History of Speech Education at Columbia College, 1754-1940. Ph.D., Columbia University, 1951. 134p.

1764   Rohfeld, Rae W. James Harvey Robinson and the New History. Ph.D., Case Western University, 1965. 287p. UMI# 66-5209. [professor of history, Columbia University, 1895-1919].

1765   Sahraie, Hashem; Sahraie, Janet. Educational Development in Afghanistan: History of the Teachers College, Columbia University Assistance Program, 1954-1971. Ed.D., Columbia University Teachers College, 1975. 543p. UMI# 75-13909.

1766   Schmunk, Paul L. Charles Austin Beard: A Free Spirit, 1874-1919. Ph.D., University of New Mexico, 1958. 454p. UMI# 58-1,500. [professor of politics, Columbia University, 1907-1917].

1767   Senkier, Robert J. The Development of a New Master of Business Administration Curriculum in the Columbia University Graduate School of Business—A Case History. Ph.D., Columbia University, 1961.

1768   Sheridan, Phyllis B. The Research Bureau in a University Context: A Case History of a Marginal Institution. Ed.D., Columbia University Teachers College, 1979. 191p. UMI# 79-23621.

1769   Smith, Raymond E. Educating for American Liberties: The Civil Liberties Educational Foundation, the National Assembly for Teaching the Principles of the Bill of Rights, and the Center for Research and Education in American Liberties, 1956-1970. Ed.D., Columbia University Teachers College, 1980. 687p. UMI# 8022162.

1770   Sokal, Michael M. The Education and Psychological Career of James McKeen Cattell, 1860-1904. Ph.D., Case Western Reserve University, 1972. 683p. UMI# 73-06341. [head of psychology department, Columbia University, 1891-1917].

1771   Stranges, John B. James T. Shotwell: The Ascendancy, 1874- 1919. Ph.D., Columbia University, 1970. 441p. UMI# 73-26,455. [professor of history, Columbia University, 1900-1942].

1772   Summerscales, William. Academic Affirmation and Dissent: Columbia's Response to the Crisis of World War I. Ph.D., Columbia University, 1969. 298p. UMI# 71-23630.

1773   Thomas, Milton H. The Gibbs Affair at Columbia in 1854. Master's thesis, Columbia University, 1942. [Wolcott Gibbs, professor of science, Harvard University, 1863-1887].

1774   Toepfer, Kenneth H. James Earl Russell and the Rise of Teachers College, 1897-1915. Ph.D., Columbia University, 1966. 433p. UMI# 67-00843. [professor of psychology and education and dean, Columbia University Teachers College, 1897-1927].

1775   Tutt, Celestine C. Library Service to the Columbia University School of Social Work, 1898-1979. Doctor of Library Service, Columbia University, 1983. 401p. UMI# 8406559.

1776   Waddell, John N. The Career of Isadore G. Mudge: A Chapter in the History of Reference Librarianship. Doctor of Library Service, Columbia University, 1973. 354p. UMI# 73-29,871. [reference librarian and professor, Columbia University, 1911-1941].

1777   Waldron, Calvin H. The Development of a Department of Education at the King's College, Briarcliff Manor, New York. Ph.D., University of Pennsylvania, 1958.

1778   Walker, Franklin T. William Peterfield Trent—A Critical Biography. Ph.D., George Peabody College for Teachers, 1944. 142p. [professor of English literature, Barnard College, 1900-1929].

1779   Walter, Judith M. Perceptions of Leadership Roles: Women in Barnard College, 1889-1939. Ph.D., Yeshiva University, 1984. 286p. UMI# 8502737.

1780   Whistler, Harvey S. The Life and Work of Theodore Thomas. Ph.D., Ohio State University, 1942. 249p. [professor of obstetrics and gynecology, College of Physicians and Surgeons, Columbia University].

1781   Whittemore, Richard F. Nicholas Murray Butler and Public Education, 1862-1911. Ph.D., Columbia University, 1962. 270p. UMI# 62-2877. [president, Columbia University, 1901-1945].

1782   Willson, John P. Carlton J.H. Hayes in Spain, 1942-1945. Ph.D., Syracuse University, 1969. 324p. UMI# 70-01983. [professor of history, Columbia University, 1907-1950].

1783   Winckler, Paul A. Charles Clarence Williamson (1877-1965): His Professional Life and Work in Librarianship and Library Education in the United States. Ph.D., New York University, 1968. 594p. UMI# 69-11,776. [director of libraries and the school of library service, Columbia University, 1926-1943].

1784   Winters, Elmer A. Harold Rugg and Education for Social Reconstruction. Ph.D., University of Wisconsin, 1968. 275p. UMI# 68-9151. [professor of education, Columbia University Teachers College, 1920-1951].

1785   Wygant, Foster L. A History of the Department of Fine and Industrial Arts of Teachers College, Columbia University. Ph.D., Columbia University, 1960.

1786   Ziegenfuss, George. Intercollegiate Athletics at Columbia University. Ph.D., Columbia University, 1951.

COOPER UNION

1787   Krasnick, Phyllis D. Peter Cooper and the Cooper Union for the Advancement of Science and Art. Ph.D., New York University, 1985. 229p. UMI# 8603884.

CORNELL UNIVERSITY

1788   Allen, Judith C. The History of Cornell University—New York Hospital School of Nursing, 1942-1979. Ed.D., Columbia University Teachers College, 1982. 241p. UMI# 82-15715.

1789   Altschuler, Glenn C. Progress and Public Service: A Life of Andrew D. White. Ph.D., Cornell University, 1976. 550p. UMI# 77-5715. [president, Cornell University, 1865-1885].

1790   Bierds, Betty K. Daniel Willard Fiske: His Professional Career and Its Influence on the Growth of the Cornell University Libraries. Master's thesis, Long Island University, 1966. [professor of North European languages and chief librarian, 1868-1881].

1791   Carron, Malcolm T. The Origin and Nature of the Contract Colleges of Cornell University: A Study of a Cooperative Educational Venture Between a State and a Private University. Ph.D., University of Michigan, 1956. 183p. UMI# 00-21157.

1792   Colman, Gould P. A History of Agricultural Education at Cornell University. Ph.D., Cornell University, 1962. 636p. UMI# 62-024666.

1793   Hotchkins, Eugene, III. Jacob Gould Schurman and the Cornell Tradition: A Study of Jacob Gould Schurman, Scholar and Educator, and His Administration of Cornell University, 1892-1920. Ph.D., Cornell University, 1960. 374p. UMI# 60-02084. [president, 1895-1914].

1794   LaBud, Verona. Liberty Hyde Bailey: His Impact on Science Education. Ph.D., Syracuse University, 1963. 224p. UMI# 64-5666. [dean of agriculture, Cornell University, 1903-1913].

1795   Marciano, John D. An Analysis of the Students for a Democratic Society (SDS) at Cornell University. Ed.D., State University of New York at Buffalo, 1969. 193p. UMI# 69-19032.

1796   Peterson, Karl G. Andrew Dickson White's Educational Principles: Their Sources, Development, Consequence. Ph.D., Stanford University, 1950. 117p. [president, Cornell University, 1865-1885].

1797   Piper, Emilie S. An Historical Study of Willard Straight Hall, the Student Union at Cornell University. Master's thesis, Cornell University, 1954.

1798   Rogers, Walter P. Andrew D. White and the Transition Period in American Higher Education. Ph.D., Cornell University, 1935. [president, Cornell University, 1865-1885].

1799   Stambaugh, Ben F., Jr. The Development of Post-Graduate Studies at Cornell: The First Forty Years, 1868-1908. Ph.D., Cornell University, 1965. 349p. UMI# 66-00048.

1800   Zimmerman, William D. Andrew D. White and the Role of the University Concerning Student Life. Ph.D., Cornell University, 1959. 176p. UMI# 59-06129. [president, Cornell University, 1865-1885].

CORTLAND (COLLEGE), STATE UNIVERSITY OF NEW YORK

1801   Brush, Carey W. The Cortland Normal School Response to Changing Needs and Professional Standards, 1866-1942. Ph.D., Columbia University, 1961. 382p. UMI# 62-01914.

1802   Gonino, Vincent J. The History and Development of Huntington Memorial Outdoor Education Center, Raquette Lake, New York, State University of New York College at Cortland. Ph.D., Ohio State University, 1972. 292p. UMI# 73-18896.

ELMIRA COLLEGE

1803   Meltzer, Gilbert W. Beginnings of Elmira College, 1851-1868. Master's thesis, University of Rochester, 1941.

EMPIRE STATE COLLEGE, STATE UNIVERSITY OF NEW YORK

1804   MacKenzie, Blair L. Empire State College: A Non-Traditional Approach to Higher Education in the State of New York. Ed.D., State University of New York at Albany, 1972. 222p. UMI# 73-19688.

EMPIRE STATE FM SCHOOL OF THE AIR

1805   Truscott, Natalie A. The Empire State FM School of the Air, 1947-1957: A Historical Account of the Origin, Growth, and Development of the Empire State FM School of the Air. Ed.D., State University of New York at Buffalo, 1959. 332p. UMI# 59-01739.

FORDHAM UNIVERSITY

1806   Curley, Thomas E., Jr. Robert I. Gannon, President of Fordham University 1936-49: A Jesuit Educator. Ph.D., New York University, 1974. 237p. UMI# 74-17136.

FREDONIA (COLLEGE), STATE UNIVERSITY OF NEW YORK

1807   Bancroft, B. Richard. The Historical Development of the Music Department of the State University College at Fredonia, New York. Ed.D., New York University, 1972. 373p. UMI# 72-26,628.

1808   Ohles, John F. The Historical Development of State University of New York College at Fredonia as Representative of the Evolution of Teacher Education in the State University of New York. Ed.D., State University of New York at Buffalo, 1964. 448p. UMI# 64-13671.

GENESEE COMMUNITY COLLEGE

1809   Peters, David E. The Founding of Genesee Community College: A Case Study. Ph.D., State University of New York at Buffalo, 1969. 266p. UMI# 69-20541.

GENESEO (COLLEGE), STATE UNIVERSITY OF NEW YORK

1810   Barraco, Anthony M. The Wadsworth Family of Geneseo, New York. A Study of Their Activities Which Relate to Public Education in New York State and to the State University College of New York at Geneseo. Ed.D., State University of New York at Buffalo, 1967. 257p. UMI# 67-11519.

HAMILTON COLLEGE

1811   Allan, John M. The Library of Hamilton College, Clinton, New York from January, 1763 to January, 1963: The Development of an American Liberal Arts College. Thesis, Library Association [United Kingdom], 1968.

1812   Caldwell, Brenda S. W. H. Cowley: A Life in Higher Education. Ph.D., University of Oklahoma, 1983. 323p. UMI# 8314759. [president, Hamilton College].

HARTWICK COLLEGE

1813   Gibbon, Peter H. Hartwick: Portrait of An Independent School. Ph.D., Columbia University, 1980. 251p. UMI# 8222390.

1814   Schmitthenner, John W. The Origin and Educational Contribution of Hartwick Seminary. Ph.D., New York University, 1934.

HOFSTRA UNIVERSITY

1815   Palais, Elliott S. A Study of the Founding and Development of Student Government at Hofstra College. Ed.D., New York University, 1965. 467p. UMI# 65-07311.

1816   Ross, Norma. History of the Hofstra University Library, 1935-1970. Master's thesis, Long Island University, 1971.

1817   Schoen, Walter T.J. Educational Experimentation: A Study Focused on the New College at Hofstra University. Ph.D., New York University, 1964. 247p. UMI# 65-00983.

HOUGHTON COLLEGE

1818   Shea, Whitney J. Houghton College and the Community. Ph.D., Columbia University Teachers College, 1953.

HUNTER COLLEGE, CITY UNIVERSITY OF NEW YORK

1819   Burns, Mae A. An Historical Background and Philosophical Criticism of the Curriculum of

Hunter College of the College of the City of New York from 1870 to 1938. Ph.D., Fordham University, 1938.

JAMESTOWN COMMUNITY COLLEGE

1820   Schlifke, William H. The Beginnings of the Jamestown Community College, Jamestown, New York. Master's thesis, State University of New York at Buffalo, 1953.

JUILLIARD SCHOOL

1821   Hayes, Marie T. The History of the Juilliard School from Its Inception to 1973. Master's thesis, Catholic University of America, 1974. 216p.

LONG ISLAND UNIVERSITY

1822   Gatner, Elliott S.M. Long Island: The History of a Relevant and Responsive University, 1926-1968. Ed.D., Columbia University, 1975. 732p. UMI# 75-13,887.

MANHATTAN COLLEGE

1823   Berrian, George R. Manhattan College: Tradition vs. Transition—A Case Study. Ed.D., Columbia University, 1975. 211p. UMI# 76-7769.

MANHATTANVILLE COLLEGE

1824   Kato, Mother Ayako. A History of Brady Memorial Library, Manhattanville College of the Sacred Heart; Purchase, New York, 1841-1957. Master's thesis, Catholic University of America, 1959. 143p.

MARYMOUNT MANHATTAN COLLEGE

1825   Doran, Micheileen J. A History of Marymount College, Tarrytown. Ed.D., Columbia University Teachers College, 1979. 393p. UMI# 80-06802.

NEW PALTZ (COLLEGE), STATE UNIVERSITY OF NEW YORK

1826   Campbell, Loren D. The Development of a Major Department of Health and Physical Education for Men and Women at the State Teachers College, New Paltz, New York. Ph.D., University of Nebraska-Lincoln, 1952.

1827   Klotzberger, Edward L. The Growth and Development of State Teachers College, New Paltz, State University of New York with Implications of Education in the State of New York. Ph.D., University of Connecticut, 1958. 310p. UMI# 58-03925.

NEW YORK ACADEMY OF MEDICINE

1828   Wortman, Leonore. A Study of the Library of the New York Academy of Medicine, 1847-1968. Master's thesis, Long Island University, 1969.

NEW YORK-HISTORICAL SOCIETY

1829   Smit, Pamela R. The New York-Historical Society Library: A History, 1804-1978. Doctor of Library Service, Columbia University, 1979. 235p. UMI# 16448.

NEW YORK UNIVERSITY

1830   Alfonso, Robert J. Ernest O. Melby: Evangelist for Education. Ph.D., Michigan State University, 1963. 328p. UMI# 63-614. [dean, school of education, New York University, 1945-1956].

1831   Boudreau, Allan. The Growth and Development of the Urban University Research Library Resources at the Washington Square Center of New York University. Ph.D., New York University, 1973. 286p. UMI# 73-19409.

1832   Coleman, Robert M. A History and Evaluation of the New York University Workshop—Field Study in Puerto Rican Education and Culture (1948-1967). Ed.D., New York University, 1969. 309p. UMI# 70-00756.

1833   Freidus, Anne. A History of the Division of General Education, New York University, 1934-1959. Ed.D., New York University, 1963. 214p. UMI# 64-00279.

1834   Hug, Elsie A. The Origin and Development of the Teacher Education Unit at New York University, 1890-1938. Ph.D., New York University, 1963. 309p. UMI# 64-06556.

1835   Lebowitz, Carl F. An Historical Study of the School of Retailing, New York University, 1919-1963. Ph.D., New York University, 1966. 273p. UMI# 67-00117.

OCTAVO SCHOOL OF MUSICAL ART

1836   Greene, Mary H. An Historical Study of the Octavo School of Musical Art, Albany, New York. Master's thesis, Catholic University of America, 1969. 106p.

OLD WESTBURY (COLLEGE), STATE UNIVERSITY OF NEW YORK

1837   Gray, George T. The Experimental College at Old Westbury, 1966-1971: A Case Study. Ed.D., Indiana University, 1973. 398p. UMI# 74-02661.

PACKARD JUNIOR COLLEGE

1838   Cahalan, Thomas L. Silas Sadler Packard, Pioneer in American Business Education. Ph.D., New York University, 1955. 355p. UMI# 00-13599. [founder, Packard Junior College, 1858].

PARSONS SCHOOL OF DESIGN

1839   Jones, Marjorie F. A History of the Parsons School of Design, 1896-1966. Ph.D., New York University, 1968. 465p. UMI# 69-11755.

1840   Levy, David C. An Historical Study of Parsons School of Design and Its Merger/Affiliation with the New School for Social Research. Ph.D., New York University, 1979. 395p. UMI# 8010195.

PEOPLE'S COLLEGE

1841   Lang, Daniel W. The People's College: An Experiment in Nineteenth Century Higher Education. Ph.D., University of Toronto, 1976.

PEOPLE'S INSTITUTE

1842   Fisher, Robert B. The People's Institute of New York City, 1897-1934: Culture, Progressive Democracy, and the People. Ph.D., New York University, 1974. 471p. UMI# 74-18156.

PINESVILLE (COLLEGE), STATE UNIVERSITY OF NEW YORK

1843   Schaffer, Edward W. Small Town State College in Transition. Ph.D., New School for Social Research, 1973. 183p.

PLATTSBURGH (COLLEGE), STATE UNIVERSITY OF NEW YORK

1844   Diebolt, Alfred L. Economic and Social Practices in Clinton County as Related to the Problems of the State Normal School in Plattsburgh, New York. Ph.D., New York University, 1939.

POTSDAM (COLLEGE), STATE UNIVERSITY OF NEW YORK

1845   Claudson, William D. The History of the Crane Department of Music, the State University of New York, College at Potsdam, 1884-1964. Ph.D., Northwestern University, 1965. 520p. UMI# 66-2690.

RAND SCHOOL OF SOCIAL SCIENCE

1846   Cornell, Frederic. A History of the Rand School of Social Science—1906-1956. Ed.D., Columbia University Teachers College, 1976. 271p. UMI# 7812007.

1847   Schwartz, Rachel C. The Rand School of Social Science, 1906-1924: A Study of Worker Education in the Socialist Era. Ph.D., State University of New York at Buffalo, 1984. 179p. UMI# 8411487.

RENSSELAER POLYTECHNIC INSTITUTE

1848   McAllister, Ethel M. Amos Eaton, Scientist and Educator. Ph.D., University of Pennsylvania, 1940. 239p. [professor, Rensselaer Polytechnic Institute, 1824-1842].

ROCHESTER THEOLOGICAL SEMINARY

1849   Moore, LeRoy, Jr. The Rise of American Religious Liberalism at the Rochester Theological Seminary, 1872-1928. Ph.D., Claremont Graduate School and University Center, 1966. 329p. UMI# 67-9520.

ROCHESTER, UNIVERSITY OF

1850   Parkman, Aubrey L. David Jayne Hill. Ph.D., University of Rochester, 1961. [president, University of Rochester, 1892-1897].

SCHENECTADY (COLLEGE), STATE UNIVERSITY OF NEW YORK

1851   Chestnut, Erma R. The Involvement and Influence of Voluntary Community Organizations in the Development of a Community College: The Schenectady Community College. Ed.D., State University of New York at Albany, 1973. 402p. UMI# 73-24352.

SIENA COLLEGE

1852   Mooney, Donald J. A History of Siena College from the Beginning to July, 1943. Master's thesis, Siena College, 1945.

SKIDMORE COLLEGE

1853   Hoffman, Allan M. History of an Idea: Skidmore College 1903-1925. Ed.D., Columbia University Teachers College, 1976. 267p. UMI# 77-06714.

ST. BONAVENTURE UNIVERSITY

1854   Angelo, Mark V. The History of St. Bonaventure University. Ph.D., Fordham University, 1958.

1855   Hayes, J. Metzger. A Study of the St. Bonaventure University Armory Reserve Officers Training Corps Program. Master's thesis, St. Bonaventure University, 1976.

ST. JOHN'S UNIVERSITY

1856   Morris, Barbara L. The Defense of a Catholic University: The 1965 Crisis at St. John's. Ed.D., Columbia University, 1977. 326p. UMI# 7804463.

STATE UNIVERSITY OF NEW YORK

1857   Dean, Larrie J. The Development of Policy for the Centralized Administration of the Overseas Academic Programs in the State University of New York: A History. Ph.D., Syracuse University, 1974. 202p. UMI# 75-13973.

1858   Fitzgerald, Pauline J. The State University of New York and Community Colleges from 1948-1973. Ed.D., Boston University School of Education, 1973. 200p. UMI# 74-20429.

1859   Greene, Robert J. The Growth of Radio in the State University of New York. Ph.D., Syracuse University, 1970. 191p. UMI# 71-10922.

1860   Holmes, Keith D. Frank Pierrepont Graves—His Influence upon American Education. Ph.D., Cornell University, 1952. [president, State University of New York, 1921-1940].

1861   Keenan, Hubert J. A View from the Tower: An Investigation of the Writings of John Huston Finley on the School and Higher Education from 1921 to 1940. Ph.D., New York University, 1970. 332p. UMI# 70-21135. [president, State University of New York, 1913-1921].

1862   Reilly, William J. Perceptions of the Origin, Development and Future of Student Personnel Services in the Community Colleges of the State University of New York. Ph.D., St. John's University, 1970. 242p. UMI# 70-25609.

1863   Sherwood, Sidney. The University of the State of New York: Origin, History and Present Organization. Ph.D., Johns Hopkins University, 1891. 100p.

1864   Wallace, Jeffry J. Historical Development of the Educational Opportunity Programs in the State University of New York. Ph.D., State University of New York at Buffalo, 1980. 531p. UMI# 81-04251.

SYRACUSE UNIVERSITY

1865   Cable, Jane T. The Beginnings of Speech at Syracuse University, with Particular Emphasis on the Contributions of Loche Richardson. Master's thesis, Syracuse University, 1967.

1866   Charvat, Arthur. A History of the Syracuse University History Department, 1871-1922. Ph.D., Syracuse University, 1957. 204p. UMI# 00-20816.

1867   Cole, Edgar B. The College of Fine Arts of Syracuse University, 1894-1922. Ph.D., Syracuse University, 1957. 154p.

1868   Craven, Clifford J. Why We Withdrew: An Investigation Into the Reasons Male Students Left Syracuse University During the Year 1948 and Into Their Attitude Toward the Institution. Ph.D., Syracuse University, 1951.

1869   Field, Earle. The New York State College of Forestry at Syracuse University: The History, Founding, and Early Growth, 1911-1922. Ph.D., Syracuse University, 1954.

1870   Guion, Harvey M. Analysis of the Development of the Syracuse Repertory Theatre. Master's thesis, Syracuse University, 1967.

1871   Lamb, Wallace E. George Washington Gale, Theologian and Educator. Ph.D., Syracuse University, 1949. [professor of philosophy and trustee, Syracuse University, 1837-1861].

1872   Parry, Alicia H. The Growth of the Syracuse University Library During Chancellor Day's Administration, 1894-1922. Master's thesis, Syracuse University, 1952.

1873   Seward, Doris M. A Historical Study of the Women's Residence Program at Syracuse University. Ph.D., Syracuse University, 1953. 323p.

1874   Stankiewicz, Mary Ann. Art Teacher Preparation at Syracuse University, the First Century. Ph.D., Ohio State University, 1979. 291p. UMI# 8001836.

1875   Wells, Margaret C. History and Evaluation of the Graduate Course for Women in Student Personnel Administration at Syracuse University. Ph.D., Syracuse University, 1950. 117p.

UNION COLLEGE

1876   Axen, Richard F. History and Analysis of a Liberal Arts College Curriculum: Four Perspectives of Union College. Ph.D., University of California-Los Angeles, 1952.

UNION SCHOOL OF RELIGION

1877   Parker, Harris H. Theory and Practice in Religious Education: A Case Study of the Union School of Religion, 1910-1929. Ed.D., Columbia University, 1966. 372p. UMI# 67-9452.

UNION THEOLOGICAL SEMINARY

1878   Slavens, Thomas P. The Library of Union Theological Seminary in the City of New York, 1836 to the Present. Ph.D., University of Michigan, 1965. 358p. UMI# 66-06705.

UNITED STATES MERCHANT MARINE ACADEMY

1879   Ferris, Charles W., Jr. The Development and Evaluation of the Department of History and Languages at the United States Merchant Marine Academy, Kings Point, New York. Ph.D., Columbia University, 1961.

UNITED STATES MILITARY ACADEMY

1880   Avaiolo, Frank J. West Point and the Presidency. Ph.D., St. John's University, 1961.

1881   Denton, Edgar, III. The Formative Years of the United States Military Academy, 1775-1833. Ph.D., Syracuse University, 1964. 307p. UMI# 65-01551.

1882   Dillard, Walter S. The United States Military Academy, 1865-1900, the Uncertain Years. Ph.D., University of Washington, 1972. 418p. UMI# 72-28589.

1883   Forman, Sidney. West Point: A History of the United States Military Academy. Ph.D., Columbia University, 1949.

1884   Godson, William F. H. The History of West Point, 1852-1902. Ph.D., Temple University, 1934.

1885   Griess, Thomas E. Dennis Hart Mahan: West Point Professor and Advocate of Military Professionalism, 1830-1871. Ph.D., Duke University, 1969. 397p. UMI# 69-16754.

1886   Harris, Theodore D. Henry Ossian Flipper: The First Negro Graduate of West Point. Ph.D., University of Minnesota, 1971. 174p. UMI# 72-14436.

1887   Kershner, James W. Sylvanus Thayer: A Bibliography. Ph.D., University of West Virginia, 1976. 426p. UMI# 77-12,314. [superintendent, United States Military Academy, 1817-1833].

1888   McMasters, Richard K. The Contribution of West Point to American Education. Master's thesis, Texas Western College, 1952.

1889   Molloy, Peter M. Technical Education and the Young Republic: West Point as America's Ecole Polytechnique, 1802-1833. Ph.D., Brown University, 1975. 497p. UMI# 76-15673.

1890   Morrison, James L., Jr. The United States Military Academy, 1833-1866: Years of Progress and Turmoil. Ph.D., Columbia University, 1970. 337p. UMI# 71-06230.

1891   Nye, Roger H. The United States Military Academy in an Era of Educational Reform, 1900-1925. Ph.D., Columbia University, 1968. 418p. UMI# 68-12943.

1892   Paciorek, Loretta A. The History of the United States Military Academy Library at West Point, New York. Master's thesis, Long Island University, 1968.

1893   Richards, John D. A History of Organization, Development, and Administration of the Cadet Counseling Center, United States Military Academy (1802-1980). Ed.D., University of Southern California, 1980.

1894   Webb, Lester A. Captain Alden Partidge, Cadet, Professor, and Superintendent United

States Military Academy,1806-1818. Master's thesis, University of North Carolina, 1957. 157p.

1895   Winton, George P., Jr. Ante-Bellum Military Instruction of West Point Officers, and Its Influence Upon Confederate Military Organization and Operations. Ph.D., University of South Carolina, 1972. 271p. UMI# 72-25930.

1896   Zuersher, Dorothy J.S. Benjamin Franklin, Jonathan Williams, and the United States Military Academy. Ed.D., University of North Carolina at Greensboro, 1974. 148p. UMI# 74-17969.

UPSTATE MEDICAL CENTER, STATE UNIVERSITY OF NEW YORK

1897   Stritter, Frank T. The Evolution of a Curriculum Medical Education at Syracuse, New York, 1872-1967. Ph.D., Syracuse University, 1968. 287p. UMI# 69-08653.

VASSAR COLLEGE

1898   Clement, Stephen M., III. Aspects of Student Religion at Vassar College, 1861-1914. Ed.D., Harvard University, 1977. 293p. UMI# 77-32060.

1899   Herman, Debra. College and After: The Vassar Experiment in Women's Education, 1861-1924. Ph.D., Stanford University, 1979. 365p. UMI# 79-17241.

1900   Imberman, Angela T. The History of Vassar College Library, 1861-1968. Ph.D., University of Chicago, 1970.

1901   Keller, Dorothy J. Maria Mitchell, an Early Woman Academician. Ed.D., University of Rochester, 1975. 163p. UMI# 75-15237. [professor of astronomy, Vassar College, 1865-1888].

1902   Priestley, Alice E.A. Maria Mitchell, as an Educator. Ph.D., New York University, 1947. 75p. UMI# 939. [professor of astronomy, Vassar College, 1865-1888].

WAGNER COLLEGE

1903   Oh, Song J. A Study of the Edwin Markham Collection of the Horrman Library of Wagner College, Staten Island, New York, 1940-1969. Master's thesis, Long Island University, 1969.

1904   Rowen, William A. The Emerging Identity of Wagner College. Ed.D., Indiana University, 1972. 124p. UMI# 73-10862.

WELLS COLLEGE

1905   McKean, John R.O. Wells College Student Life, 1868-1936. Ed.D., Cornell University, 1961. 261p. UMI# 61-06845.

1906   Russ, Anne J. Higher Education for Women: Intent, Reality, and Outcomes, Wells College, 1868-1913. Ph.D., Cornell University, 1980. 138p. UMI# 80-15732.

YESHIVA UNIVERSITY

1907   Klaperman, Gilbert. The Beginnings of Yeshiva University: The First Jewish University in America. Doctor of Hebrew Literature, Yeshiva University, 1955. 397p. UMI# 58-01825.

NORTH CAROLINA

GENERAL STUDIES

1908   Allen, John B., III. Developments in Teacher Education in North Carolina, 1941-1974.
        Ph.D., University of North Carolina, 1983. 266p. UMI# 8316573.

1909   Allen, Madeline M. An Historical Study of Moravian Education in North Carolina—The
        Evolution and Practice of the Moravian Concept of Education as It Applied to Women.
        Ph.D., Florida State University, 1971. 223p. UMI# 72-10014.

1910   Barrier, Lynn P. A History of Industrial Arts Education in North Carolina, 1919-1977.
        Ed.D., North Carolina State University at Raleigh, 1977. 263p. UMI# 78-11574.

1911   Boggs, Wade H., III. State Supported Higher Education for Blacks in North Carolina,
        1877-1945. Ph.D., Duke University, 1972. 310p. UMI# 73-22976.

1912   Clement, Rufus E. A History of Negro Education in North Carolina, 1865-1928. Ph.D.,
        Northwestern University, 1930.

1913   Donnelly, John F. A History of the National Youth Administration in the Schools and
        Colleges of North Carolina. Master's thesis, University of North Carolina, 1942. 124p.

1914   Emmeson, Fred B. History of the North Carolina State Intercollegiate Athletic Conference.
        Master's thesis, University of North Carolina, 1948.

1915   Henderson, Dale E. A Study of Opinions Concerning the Integration of Black History into
        the History or Social Science Curricula in the University System of North Carolina. Ed.D.,
        George Washington University, 1983. 165p. UMI# 8324479.

1916   Ingram, Margaret H. Development of Higher Education for White Women in North Caro-
        lina Prior to 1875. Ed.D., University of North Carolina, 1961. 285p. UMI# 62-03129.

1917   Lochra, Albert P. The North Carolina Community College System: Its Inception—Its
        Growth—Its Legal Framework. Ed.D., University of North Carolina at Greensboro, 1978.
        224p. UMI# 78-24894.

1918   McIntyre, Dorothy P. State Aid To Private Higher Education in North Carolina: A Historical
        Description. Ed.D., Virginia Polytechnic Institute and State University, 1982. 227p. UMI#
        8220662.

1919   Pope, Christie F. Preparation for Pedestals: North Carolina Antebellum Female Seminar-
        ies. Ph.D., University of Chicago, 1977.

1920   Pope, Louis B. The Historical Growth and Development of the North Carolina Guidance
        Movement. Ph.D., University of North Carolina, 1958. 452p. UMI# 58-05962.

1921   Rowe, Roy H., Jr. Educational Policy-Makers in the North Carolina General Assembly,
        1933-1974. Ed.D., Duke University, 1975. 210p. UMI# 75-29531.

1922   Segner, Kenyon B., II. A History of the Community College Movement in North Carolina, 1927-1963. Ed.D., University of North Carolina, 1966. 165p. UMI# 67-05364.

1923   Smith, Charles L. The History of Education in North Carolina. Ph.D., Johns Hopkins University, 1889. 180p.

1924   Teele, Arthur E. Education of the Negro in North Carolina, 1862-1872. Ph.D., Cornell University, 1954.

1925   Warlick, Kenneth R. Practical Education and the Negro College in North Carolina, 1800-1930. Ph.D., University of North Carolina, 1980. 467p. UMI# 80-22522.

1926   Westin, Richard B. The State and Segregated Schools: Negro Public Education in North Carolina, 1863-1923. Ph.D., Duke University, 1966. 512p. UMI# 67-06117.

1927   Young, Wade P. A History of Agricultural Education in North Carolina. Ph.D., University of North Carolina, 1934.

BLACK MOUNTAIN COLLEGE

1928   Garren, Charles M. The Educational Program at Black Mountain College, 1933-1943. Ph.D., University of North Carolina, 1980. 261p. UMI# 80-22455.

CLAREMONT COLLEGE

1929   Harris, James B. A History of Claremont College. Master's thesis, Appalachian State Teachers College, 1956.

CONCORDIA COLLEGE

1930   Voigt, Harry R. The History of Concordia College of Conover, North Carolina. Master's thesis, Appalachian State Teachers College, 1951.

DUKE UNIVERSITY

1931   Brandstadter, Dianne P. Developing the Coordinate College for Women at Duke University: The Career of Alice Mary Baldwin, 1924-1947. Ph.D., Duke University, 1977. 174p. UMI# 77-21863. [dean of women, professor of history].

1932   Chaffin, Nora C. Trinity College, 1839-1892: The Beginnings of Duke University. Ph.D., Duke University, 1943.

1933   Gifford, James F., Jr. A History of Medicine at Duke University. Volume I: Origins and Growth, 1865-1941. Ph.D., Duke University, 1970. 330p. UMI# 70-23397.

1934   Porter, Earl W. A History of Trinity College 1892-1924: Foundations of Duke University. Ph.D., Duke University, 1961. 410p. UMI# 63-02042.

1935   Ross, Andrea L. A History of the Duke University Press and Its Three Humanities Journals: *American Literature*, the *Hispanic American Historical Review*, and the *South Atlantic Quarterly*. Master's thesis, University of North Carolina, 1967. 182p.

EAST CAROLINA UNIVERSITY

1936   Wrenn, Jack. A History of Intercollegiate Football at East Carolina University from 1932 through 1975. Master's thesis, East Carolina University, 1976. 275p.

ELON COLLEGE

1937   Perkins, Theodore E. The History of Elon College Library, 1890-1957. Master's thesis, University of North Carolina, 1962. 148p.

1938   Tolley, Jerry R. The History of Intercollegiate Athletics for Men at Elon College. Ed.D., University of North Carolina at Greensboro, 1982. 382p. UMI# 82-18679.

FAYETTEVILLE STATE UNIVERSITY

1939   Murphy, Ella L. Origin and Development of Fayetteville State Teachers College, 1867-1959, a Chapter in the History of the Education of Negroes in North Carolina (Parts I-V). Ph.D., New York University, 1960. 371p. UMI# 61-00341.

GUILFORD COLLEGE

1940   Farrow, Mildred H. The History of Guilford College Library, 1837-1955. Master's thesis, University of North Carolina, 1959.

JOHNSON C. SMITH UNIVERSITY

1941   Battle, Margaret E. A History of the Carnegie Library at Johnson C. Smith University. Master's thesis, University of North Carolina, 1960. 55p.

1942   George, Arthur A. The History of Johnson C. Smith University, 1867 to the Present. Ed.D., New York University, 1954. 352p. UMI# 00-10661.

LINWOOD COLLEGE

1943   Davenport, Harold D. A History of Linwood College. Master's thesis, Appalachian State Teachers College, 1960.

LIVINGSTONE COLLEGE

1944   Davis, Lenwood G. A History of Livingstone College, 1879-1957. Doctor of Arts, Carnegie-Mellon University, 1979. 323p. UMI# 79-19137.

LOUISBURG COLLEGE

1945   Russell, Miriam L. A History of Louisburg College, 1787-1958. Master's thesis, Appalachian State Teachers College, 1959.

MARS HILL COLLEGE

1946   Carter, E.J. A History of Mars Hill College. Master's thesis, University of North Carolina, 1939.

MITCHELL COLLEGE

1947   Mize, Richard L. The History of Mitchell College. Master's thesis, Appalachian State Teachers College, 1954.

NORTH CAROLINA AGRICULTURAL & TECHNICAL STATE UNIVERSITY

1948   Pearsall, Thelma F. History of the North Carolina Agricultural and Technical College Library. Master's thesis, Western Reserve University, 1955. 48p.

NORTH CAROLINA STATE UNIVERSITY

1949   Allen, Christopher. The Land Grant Act of 1862 and Practical Education in North Carolina; The Founding of North Carolina College of Agriculture and Mechanic Arts. Master's thesis, North Carolina State University at Raleigh, 1984. 108p.

1950   Fearing, Bertie E. A History of the Department of Adult and Community College Education at North Carolina State University: A Need, a Response, and a Model. Ed.D., North Carolina State University at Raleigh, 1978. 184p. UMI# 78-20027.

1951   Fritz, John E. An Analysis of Ten Years of Doctoral Research in the Department of Adult and Community College Education—North Carolina State University. Ed.D., North Carolina State University, 1977. 173p.

NORTH CAROLINA, UNIVERSITY OF

1952   Beebe, George A. 150 Years of History in the University of North Carolina, 1795-1945. Master's thesis, University of North Carolina, 1946. 201p.

1953   Brabham, Robert F., Jr. Search for a Purpose: The University of North Carolina, 1875-1891. Master's thesis, University of North Carolina at Chapel Hill, 1977. 96p.

1954   Brandis, Martha M. History of the University of North Carolina Magazine, 1844-1948. Master's thesis, University of North Carolina, 1964. 89p.

1955   Cheek, Neal K. An Historical Study of the Administrative Actions in the Racial Desegregation of the University of North Carolina at Chapel Hill, 1930-1955. Ph.D., University of North Carolina, 1973. 235p. UMI# 74-05905.

1956   Clymer, Benjamin F., Jr. The History of the Division of Health Affairs Library of the University of North Carolina. Master's thesis, University of North Carolina, 1959. 118p.

1957   Cranford, Janet P. The Documents Collection of the University of North Carolina Library from Its Beginning through 1963. Master's thesis, University of North Carolina, 1965. 47p.

1958   Daniel, Carolyn A. David Lowry Swain. Ph.D., University of North Carolina, 1955. 367p. [president, University of North Carolina, 1835-1868].

1959   Diaz, Albert J. A History of the Latin American Collection of the University of North Carolina Library. Master's thesis, University of North Carolina, 1956. 83p.

1960   Eaton, Joan D. A History and Evaluation of the Hanes Collection in the Louis R. Wilson

Library, University of North Carolina. Master's thesis, University of North Carolina, 1957. 115p.

1961   Enger, William R. Samuel Eusebius McCorkle: North Carolina Educator. Ed.D., Oklahoma State University, 1973. 312p. UMI# 74-8004. [founding trustee, University of North Carolina].

1962   Gatewood, Willard B., Jr. Eugene Clyde Brooks: Educator and Public Servant. Ph.D., Duke University, 1957. [president, North Carolina State College of Agriculture and Engineering, 1923-1931].

1963   Hall, Peter W. The Fraternity Advisor at the University of North Carolina at Chapel Hill, 1964-1974. Master's thesis, University of North Carolina, 1975. 62p.

1964   Heindel, Sally W. A History of the Institute of Government Library of the University of North Carolina. Master's thesis, University of North Carolina, 1965.

1965   Holder, Elizabeth J. A History of the Library of the Woman's College of the University of North Carolina, 1892-1945. Master's thesis, University of North Carolina, 1955.

1966   List, Barbara T. The Friends of the University of North Carolina Library, 1932-1962. Master's thesis, University of North Carolina, 1965. 65p.

1967   Martus, Charles T. The History of Varsity Track and Field at the University of North Carolina. Master's thesis, University of North Carolina, 1951.

1968   Mitchell, Joseph T. Black Music in the University System of North Carolina: 1960-1974. Ed.D., University of North Carolina, 1975. 193p. UMI# 75-23148.

1969   Moore, Gay G. The Southern Historical Collection in the Louis Round Wilson Library of the University of North Carolina from the Beginning of the Collection through 1948. Master's thesis, University of North Carolina, 1958. 83p.

1970   Robinson, Blackwell P. William Richardson Davie: Soldier, Statesman, and University Founder. Ph.D., University of North Carolina, 1953. 318p. [University of North Carolina].

1971   Scott, Tom. A History of Inter-Collegiate Athletics at the University of North Carolina. Ph.D., Columbia University, 1955. 279p.

1972   Thorpe, Judith L. A Study of the Peace Movement at the University of North Carolina at Chapel Hill Viewed within the Context of the Nation 1964-1971. Master's thesis, University of North Carolina, 1972.

1973   Wing, Mary J. A History of the School of Library Science of the University of North Carolina: The First Twenty-Five Years. Master's thesis, University of North Carolina, 1958.

NORTH CAROLINA, UNIVERSITY OF (BOONE)

1974   Foxx, Virginia A. Watauga College: The Residential College at Appalachian State University. Ed.D., University of North Carolina at Greensboro, 1985. 152p. UMI# 8520594.

NORTH CAROLINA, UNIVERSITY OF (CHARLOTTE)

1975   Tarlton, Shirley M. The Development of the Library of Charlotte College, 1946 - July 1, 1965. Master's thesis, University of North Carolina, 1966. 72p.

NORTH CAROLINA, UNIVERSITY OF (GREENSBORO)

1976   Bowles, Elizabeth A. The University of North Carolina at Greensboro, 1892-1931. Ed.D., University of North Carolina at Chapel Hill, 1965. 288p. UMI# 65-14315.

1977   Watson, Jan C. Ethel Loroline Martus Lawther: Her Contributions to Physical Education. Ed.D., University of North Carolina at Greensboro, 1980. 327p. UMI# 8021788. [chairperson and dean of health, recreation and physical education, University of North Carolina at Greensboro].

QUEENS COLLEGE

1978   Hoyle, Hughes B., Jr. The Early History of Queens College to 1872. Ph.D., University of North Carolina, 1963. 319p. UMI# 64-09415.

1979   Tyran, Cynthia J. The Response of Queens College to the Women's Movement. Ph.D., Duke University, 1981. 206p. UMI# 8127138.

RICHMOND HILL LAW SCHOOL

1980   Wooten, Samuel R. A History of the Richmond Hill Law School. Master's thesis, Appalachian State Teachers College, 1964.

SHAW UNIVERSITY

1981   Jenkins, Clara Barnes. An Historical Study of Shaw University, 1865-1963. Ed.D., University of Pittsburgh, 1965. 153p.

1982   Jowers, Jonnie. The History of Athletics for Men at Shaw University. Master's thesis, North Carolina College, 1958.

ST. ANDREWS PRESBYTERIAN COLLEGE

1983   Bracey, William R. A History of Flora MacDonald College. Master's thesis, Appalachian State Teachers College, 1962.

1984   Decker, Rodger W. Founding St. Andrews Presbyterian College: A Case Study of Presbyterian Higher Education in North Carolina. Ed.D., Columbia University, 1968. 133p. UMI# 69-08069.

ST. AUGUSTINE'S COLLEGE

1985   Chadwick, James C. A History of Men's Intercollegiate Athletics at St. Augustine's College. Master's thesis, North Carolina College, 1964.

WAKE FOREST UNIVERSITY

1986   Bean, Sandra K. The Wake Forest University Golf Program, 1933-1976. Master's thesis, Wake Forest University, 1977. 106p.

1987   Nicholson, James M., Jr. A History of the Wake Forest College Library, 1878-1946. Master's thesis, University of North Carolina, 1954.

NORTH DAKOTA

GENERAL STUDIES

1988   Cook, Elsie J. Higher Education in North Dakota. Master's thesis, University of Colorado, 1936.

1989   Heine, Clarence J. A Study of the Decisions Made by the North Dakota Board of Higher Education from 1939 to 1969. Ph.D., University of Michigan, 1970. 244p. UMI# 70-21682.

1990   Olson, Gordon B. The Status of Four-Year State Institutions of Higher Learning in North Dakota. Ph.D., University of North Dakota, 1953. 323p.

MAYVILLE STATE COLLEGE

1991   McMullen, Harvey M. A Study to Identify the Role of Mayville State College and How It Serves the State and People of North Dakota. Ed.D., University of North Dakota, 1965. 150p. UMI# 66-02182.

NORTH DAKOTA, UNIVERSITY OF

1992   Lofthus, Richard R. A History of Lutheran Campus Ministry at the University of North Dakota Since 1942. Master's thesis, University of North Dakota, 1985.

VALLEY CITY STATE COLLEGE

1993   Hanna, Glenn A. History of the Valley City State Teachers College. Master's thesis, University of North Dakota, 1951.

1994   Hennessey, Daniel L. History of the Valley City State College, 1890-1970. Master's thesis, University of North Dakota, 1972.

OHIO

GENERAL STUDIES

1995   Barber, Richard E. Comparison of the History of the Departments of Music at the University of Toledo, Findlay College, and Bowling Green State University. Ph.D., University of Michigan, 1976. 155p. UMI# 76-27442.

1996   Barnett, Clarence R. College Athletics and Physical Education in Ohio During the Depression. Ph.D., Ohio State University, 1972. 312p. UMI# 73-01932.

1997   Beauregard, Erving E. History of Academic Freedom in Ohio: Case Studies 1808-1975. Ph.D., Union Graduate School (Ohio), 1976. 424p. UMI# 77-13830.

1998   Bosse, Richard C. Origins of Lutheran Higher Education in Ohio. Ph.D., Ohio State University, 1969. 434p. UMI# 70-06729.

1999   Briggs, Harry H. History of Teacher Training in Ohio Colleges and Universities. Ph.D., Case Western Reserve University, 1955.

2000   Cable, Nancy J. The Search for Mission in Ohio Liberal Arts Colleges: Denison, Kenyon, Marietta, Oberlin, 1870-1914. Ph.D., University of Virginia, 1984. 373p. UMI# 8424870.

2001   Cangi, Ellen C. Principles Before Practice: The Reform of Medical Education in Cincinnati Before and After the Flexner Report, 1870-1930. Ph.D., University of Cincinnati, 1983. 394p. UMI# 83-28295.

2002   Dandalides, Des A. The Origin, Development, and Present Status of Community Services in Ohio's Community Colleges. Ph.D., Kent State University, 1980. 184p. UMI# 8024591.

2003   Hathaway, Stephen C., Jr. A History and Description of Collegiate Carrier-Current Broadcasting in Ohio. Ph.D., University of Michigan, 1959. 201p. UMI# 59-02129.

2004   Heinrichs, Mary Ann. The Initiation and Development of Instruction in American Literature During the Nineteenth-Century in Five Ohio Colleges Established Before 1860. Ph.D., University of Toledo, 1973. 232p. UMI# 74-16921.

2005   Horner, John E. The Development of Corporate Giving to Private Higher Education, with Special Reference to the Rise and Growth of State and Regional College Foundations Including the Ohio Foundation of Independent Colleges. Ph.D., Ohio State University, 1955. 270p. UMI# 00-16078.

2006   Hummel, Dean L. Guidance in Ohio, Its Historical Development. Ph.D., Ohio State University, 1960. 343p. UMI# 61-00915.

2007   Kearney, June F. The History of Women's Intercollegiate Athletics in Ohio, 1945-1972. Ph.D., Ohio State University, 1973. 173p. UMI# 74-03218.

2008   Kinnison, William A. The Impact of the Morrill Act on Higher Education in Ohio. Ph.D., Ohio State University, 1967. 369p. UMI# 68-03005.

2009   Leahy, John F., Jr. The Development of a State Wide Plan for Establishing Community Colleges in Ohio. Ph.D., Ohio State University, 1953. 323p.

2010   Light, John J. The Development of Technical Institutes in Ohio. Ph.D., Ohio State University, 1973. 326p. UMI# 73-26860.

2011   Michael, Robert L. A History of Growth and Development of Football in Ohio Colleges. Master's thesis, Ohio State University, 1951.

2012   Navarre, Jane P. The Female Teacher: The Beginnings of Teaching as a 'Women's Profession'. Ph.D., Bowling Green State University, 1977. 273p. UMI# 78-05370. [Lake Erie College; Western College for Women].

2013   Rainsburger, Richard A. Sources of Current Operating Income in Ohio's Colleges Before 1960. Ph.D., University of Toledo, 1977. 235p. UMI# 77-380.

2014   Rogers, William F. The Historical Development of the Ohio Council for Education. Ph.D., Ohio State University, 1969. 226p. UMI# 70-06865.

2015   Scully, James A. A Biography of William Holmes McGuffey. Ed.D., University of Cincinnati, 1967. 189p. UMI# 68-2018. [professor of ancient languages and philosophy, Miami University, 1826-1836; president, Ohio University, 1836-1843].

2016   Strimer, Robert M. The Interrelation of Success or Failure in Athletics and Certain Dynamics of Growth and Development in Selected Colleges and Universities in the State of Ohio. Ph.D., Ohio State University, 1963. 203p. UMI# 64-06967.

2017   Wall, William L. The History of Inter-Collegiate Soccer in Ohio. Master's thesis, Ohio State University, 1956.

2018   Williams, Glenn D. The Community College in Ohio. Ph.D., Ohio State University, 1960. 236p. UMI# 60-06420.

2019   Wilson, Marlene. The History of Developmental Education in Public Higher Education Institutions in Ohio: The First Decade, 1968-78. Ph.D., Kent State University, 1980. 426p. UMI# 80-24609.

2020   Wims, Lu D. A History of the Administration of Intercollegiate Athletics in the Ohio Athletic Conference. Ph.D., Ohio State University, 1970. 221p. UMI# 71-18107.

2021   Young, William L. The Junior College Movement in Relation to Higher Education in Ohio. Ph.D., Ohio State University, 1930.

2022   Zam, Gerard A. The Competition Over the Morrill Land Grant Funds in Ohio, 1862-1870. Ph.D., Ohio State University, 1985. 406p. UMI# 852685.

AKRON, UNIVERSITY OF

2023   Clinefelter, Ruth W. A History of Bierce Library of the University of Akron. Master's thesis, Kent State University, 1956. 200p.

ANTIOCH COLLEGE

2024   Hubbell, George A. Horace Mann in Ohio: A Study of the Application of His Public School Ideals to College Administration. Ph.D., Columbia University, 1902. 71p. [president, Antioch College, 1853-1859].

2025   Meyers, Judith K. A History of the Antioch College Library, 1850-1929. Master's thesis, Kent State University, 1963.

2026   Nethers, John L. Simeon D. Fess: Educator and Politician (Volumes I and II). Ph.D., Ohio State University, 1964. 613p. UMI# 65-3894. [president and professor of history, Antioch College, 1907-1917].

2027   Newman, George C. The Morgan Years: Politics of Innovative Change, Antioch College in the 1920's. Ph.D., University of Michigan, 1978. 270p. UMI# 79-07146. [Arthur E. Morgan, president, 1920-1933].

2028   Vallance, Harvard F. A History of Antioch College. Ph.D., Ohio State University, 1937.

ASHLAND COLLEGE

2029   Dickerson, Kay W. The Development of Speech Education at Ashland College from 1900 to 1963. Master's thesis, Kent State University, 1964.

2030   Wilgus, Billy E. The History and Development of Intercollegiate Athletics at Ashland College, 1878-1959. Master's thesis, Ohio State University, 1960. 95p.

ATHENAEUM OF OHIO

2031   Miller, Francis J. A History of the Athenaeum of Ohio, 1829-1960. Ed.D., University of Cincinnati, 1964. 468p. UMI# 64-11973.

2032   Schnapp, Mary M., Sr. The History and Development of the Diocesan Teachers College of the Athenaeum of Ohio. Master's thesis, University of Cincinnati, 1942.

BALDWIN-WALLACE COLLEGE

2033   Barnett, Mildred F. A History of the Baldwin-Wallace College Library, 1913-1964. Master's thesis, Kent State University, 1967. 159p.

2034   Campbell, William J., Jr. A History of the Conservatory of Music, Baldwin-Wallace College, 1913-1970. Ed.D., University of Michigan, 1971. 236p. UMI# 71-23,682.

BOWLING GREEN STATE UNIVERSITY

2035   Ehrenfried, Michael. The History of Basketball at Bowling Green State University. Master's thesis, Bowling Green State University, 1976.

2036   Emmanuel, Narbeth. A Historical Study of Soccer at Bowling Green State University from a Club Level through the Intercollegiate Level. Master's thesis, Bowling Green State University, 1976.

2037   McFall, Kenneth. From Normal College to State University—the Development of Bowling Green State University. Ph.D., Case Western Reserve University, 1947. 258p.

2038   Picklesimer, Dorman, Jr. The History of Forensics at Bowling Green State University. Master's thesis, Bowling Green State University, 1965.

2039   Wright, Jerry J. The History of Intercollegiate Baseball at Bowling Green State University. Master's thesis, Bowling Green State University, 1977.

CASE WESTERN RESERVE UNIVERSITY

2040   Bobinski, George S. A Brief History of the Libraries of Western Reserve University, 1826-1952. Master's thesis, Western Reserve University, 1952.

2041   Bunge, Helen L. Changing the Basic Curriculum at the Frances Payne Bolton School of Nursing of Western Reserve University. Ph.D., Columbia University, 1950.

2042   Holmgren, Daniel M. Edward Webster Bemis and Municipal Reform. Ph.D., Case Western Reserve University, 1964. [professor of economics, Case Western Reserve University, 1892-1895].

2043   Richardson, Cora E. Alice Sarah Tyler: A Biographical Study. Master's thesis, Western Reserve University, 1951. 43p. [dean, School of Library Science, Case Western Reserve University, 1913-1929].

2044   Ruderman, Laurie P. Jesse Shera: A Bio-Bibliography. Master's thesis, Kent State University, 1968. 84p. [dean, School of Library Science, Case Western Reserve University, 1952-1970].

2045   Williams, Howard R. Edward Williams Morley. Ph.D., Case Western Reserve University, 1942. 401p. [professor of chemistry, Case Western Reserve University, 1869-1906].

CEDARVILLE COLLEGE

2046   McDonald, Cleveland. The History of Cedarville College. Ph.D., Ohio State University, 1966. 235p. UMI# 66-15114.

CENTRAL STATE UNIVERSITY

2047   Goggins, Lathardus. The Evolution of Central State College Under Dr. Charles H. Wesley from 1942-1965: An Historical Analysis (Ohio). Ed.D., University of Akron, 1983. 217p. UMI# 83-14386. [president].

CINCINNATI CONSERVATORY OF MUSIC

2048   Lewis, John, Jr. An Historical Study of the Origin and Development of the Cincinnati Conservatory of Music. Ph.D., University of Cincinnati, 1943. 413p.

CINCINNATI, UNIVERSITY OF

2049   Coleman, Paul E. Important Educational Achievements of the Cooperative Commercial Curriculum at University of Cincinnati. Ph.D., New York University, 1934.

2050   Hamel, Dana B. A History of the Ohio Mechanics Institute, Cincinnati, Ohio. Ed.D., University of Cincinnati, 1962. 173p. UMI# 63-01789.

2051   Nester, William R., Jr. The Development of the Student Personnel Program at the University of Cincinnati. Ed.D., University of Cincinnati, 1965. 269p. UMI# 66-706.

2052   Schmiel, Eugene D. The Career of Jacob Dolson Cox, 1828-1900: Soldier, Scholar, Statesman. Ph.D., Ohio State University, 1969. 534p. UMI# 70-14,094. [dean, Cincinnati Law School, 1881-1897; president, University of Cincinnati, 1885].

2053   Schwarberg, W.D. A History of Physical Education at the University of Cincinnati. Ph.D., Columbia University, 1957.

2054   Souder, Marian J. The College-Conservatory of Music of Cincinnati, 1955-1962: A History. Master's thesis, University of Cincinnati, 1970. 147p.

2055   Woofter, James A. The Historical Development of the Organization and Administration of a Municipal University. Ph.D., University of Cincinnati, 1937. 359p.

CLEVELAND COLLEGE

2056   Dorrance, David B. Cleveland College: Genesis, Ethos, Exodus. Ph.D., Case Western Reserve University, 1977. 195p. UMI# 770983.

COLLEGE OF MUSIC OF CINCINNATI

2057   Orlando, Vincent A. An Historical Study of the Origin and Development of the College of Music of Cincinnati. Ph.D., University of Cincinnati, 1946. 280p.

COLLEGE OF WOOSTER

2058   Pinkard, Elfred A. The College of Wooster: Case Study of an Institution's Response to the Presence of Black Students, 1970-1980. Ed.D., Harvard University, 1983. 220p. UMI# 8320186.

CUYAHOGA COMMUNITY COLLEGE

2059   Gilbride, M. James. The Coming of the Community College to Ohio: The Enabling Legislation and the Founding of Cuyahoga Community College, 1946-1963. Ph.D., Kent State University, 1979. 406p. UMI# 80-07303.

DAYTON, UNIVERSITY OF

2060   Mathews, Brother S.G. Marian Library of the University of Dayton: Origin and Development. Master's thesis, Western Reserve University, 1952.

DENISON UNIVERSITY

2061   Jenkins, Sidney. The History of Physical Education and Athletics for Men at Denison University. Master's thesis, Ohio State University, 1937.

EDGECLIFF COLLEGE

2062   Dooley, Mary E., Sr. Founding and Early Growth of Our Lady of Cincinnati College. Master's thesis, University of Cincinnati, 1942.

HIRAM COLLEGE

2063   Matthews, Herbert C. An Historical Study of the Development of Health and Physical Education at Hiram College (1850-1937). Master's thesis, Ohio State University, 1937.

2064   Saviers, Samuel H. The Literary Societies and Their Libraries at Hiram College. Master's thesis, Kent State University, 1958. 277p.

2065   Stein, John H. The Development of the Hiram College Library from the Literary Societies Which Formed Its Nucleus. Master's thesis, Kent State University, 1950. 105p.

KENT STATE UNIVERSITY

2066   Jackson, Miriam R. We Shall Not Be Moved: A Study of the May 4th Coalition and the Kent State University Gymnasium Controversy of 1977. Ph.D., Purdue University, 1982. 425p. UMI# 82-25724.

2067   Kegley, Charles F. The Response of Groups to the Events of May 1-4, 1970 at Kent State University. Ph.D., University of Pittsburgh, 1974. 331p. UMI# 75-13197.

2068   Ross, James A. The History of Broadcasting at Kent State University. Master's thesis, Kent State University, 1951.

2069   Summers, Kurt. A Study of Decisions Made by the Board of Trustees of Kent State University from 1968 through 1977. Ph.D., Kent State University, 1978. 143p. UMI# 79-12528.

MIAMI UNIVERSITY

2070   Allen, Marshall. Analysis and Description of the Growth and Development of Broadcasting at Miami University Since 1955. Master's thesis, Miami University, 1961.

2071   Church, Martha F. Student Life at Miami University in World War II. Master's thesis, Miami University, 1947. 273p.

2072   Cole, Mary A. The Development of Closed-Circuit Television at Miami University. Master's thesis, Miami University, 1957.

2073   David, Virgil E. The Literary Societies of 'Old Miami' from 1825-1873. Master's thesis, Miami University, 1950. 307p.

2074   Kinzig, Elizabeth S. The History and Development of Physical Education and Athletics at Miami University. Master's thesis, Ohio State University, 1945. 108p.

2075   Lewis, Linda A. A History of Radio Broadcasting at Miami University. Master's thesis, Miami University, 1955.

2076   Meinert, Charles W. American College Life and the Influence of the Korean War As Seen in Student Life at Miami University, 1949-1953. Master's thesis, Miami University, 1954. 180p.

2077   Moore, Albert A. The Development of Intercollegiate Athletics at Miami University, Oxford, Ohio. Master's thesis, Miami University, 1949. 94p.

2078   Rice, P. Jeannine. The Development of an Active Speech Program at Miami University, 1900-1940. Master's thesis, Miami University, 1967.

2079   Robb, Dale W. Religion in the History of Miami University, 1809-1932. Master's thesis, Miami University, 1954. 381p.

2080   Rodabaugh, James H. A History of Miami University from Its Origin to 1845. Master's thesis, Miami University, 1933. 216p.

2081   Rodabaugh, James H. History of Miami University from Its Origin to 1885. Ph.D., Ohio State University, 1937.

2082   Thompson, Bertha B. The History of Miami University from 1873 to 1900. Master's thesis, Miami University, 1954. 381p.

2083   Twohy, David W. Harvey C. Minnich: An Historical Study of the Man and His Work as Influences on the Teacher Training Unit of Miami University. Ph.D., Miami University, 1979. 298p. UMI# 80-01431. [professor and dean, 1903-1931].

2084   Vogt, Peter J. Guy Potter Benton—His Effect on Miami University. Master's thesis, Miami University, 1956. 165p. [president, 1902-1911; president, University of Vermont, 1911-1919].

2085   Wilson, Douglas. A History of the Miami Alumni Association. Master's thesis, Miami University, 1969. 109p.

2086   Wood, Joyce L. An Historical and Contemporary Chronicle of Women Faculty and/or Administrators at Miami University, 1902 through 1971. Ph.D., Miami University, 1975. 479p. UMI# 75-21690.

MOUNT UNION COLLEGE

2087   Harper, John R. A History of Mount Union College Library. Master's thesis, Kent State University, 1968. 134p.

2088   Wright, R.D. An Historical Study of the Development of Health and Physical Education at Mount Union College. Master's thesis, Ohio State University, 1934.

MUSKINGUM COLLEGE

2089   Bright, John H. Historical Development of Present-Day Problems of Muskingum College. Ph.D., University of Cincinnati, 1951.

2090   Cook, Elizabeth S. A History of Women's Physical Education at Muskingum College, 1893-1962. Master's thesis, Miami University, 1969.

2091   Mariner, P.M. A History of Health and Physical Education at Muskingum College. Master's thesis, Ohio State University, 1937.

2092   McCracken, Charles W. Developments in the Coordination of the Muskingum College Personnel Services During the Period from 1939 to 1950. Ph.D., Ohio State University, 1951. 134p.

2093   Musser, Adah. A History of the Muskingum College Library. Master's thesis, Kent State University, 1964.

NATIONAL NORMAL UNIVERSITY

2094   Heery, Chester R. The Development and the Educational Contributions of the National Normal University, Lebonon, Ohio. Master's thesis, University of Cincinnati, 1938.

NORTH CENTRAL TECHNICAL COLLEGE

2095   Sliney, Bruce M. The History of North Central Technical College: 1961-1981. Ed.D., University of Akron, 1983. 411p. UMI# 8314837.

OBERLIN COLLEGE

2096   Barnard, Virgil J. The Conscience of a College: A Study of Oberlin, 1866-1902. Ph.D., University of Chicago, 1964.

2097   Ellsworth, Clayton S. Oberlin and the Anti-Slavery Movement up to the Civil War. Ph.D., Cornell University, 1930. 211p. UMI# 00-00618.

2098   Fletcher, Juanita D. Against the Consensus: Oberlin College and the Education of American Negroes, 1835-1865. Ph.D., American University, 1974. 321p. UMI# 74-20887.

2099   Fletcher, Robert S. Oberlin College, 1833-1866. Ph.D., Harvard University, 1939.

2100   Keefe, Robert J. Physical Education at Oberlin College. Ph.D., Columbia University, 1953.

2101   Kinsey, Dan C. Health Activities at Oberlin and Other Ohio Colleges to 1850. Ph.D., University of Michigan, 1962. 226p. UMI# 63-00380.

2102   Kinsey, Daniel C. History of Physical Education in Oberlin College, 1833-1890. Master's thesis, Oberlin College, 1935.

2103   Larson, Arlin. A College's Purposes: The Idea of Education at Oberlin College. Doctor of Ministry, University of Chicago, 1976.

2104   Lendrim, Frank T. Music for Every Child. The Story of Karl Wilson Gehrkens. Ph.D., University of Michigan, 1962. 339p. UMI# 62-02761. [school of music department head, Oberlin College Conservatory of Music, 1907-1942].

2105   Luker, Richard M. The Western Reserve and a Legacy for Higher Education: Faculty Self-Governance at Oberlin College Under the Finney Compact, 1834-1846. Ed.D., University of Akron, 1985. 451p. UMI# 85-14701.

2106   Rogers, Walter P. A College Education a Hundred Years Ago. Master's thesis, Oberlin College, 1932.

2107   Rohrer, Daniel. Young Ladies' Literary Society of Oberlin College, 1835-1860. Master's thesis, University of Wisconsin, 1969.

2108   Rosell, Garth M. Charles Grandison Finney and the Rise of the Benevolence Empire. Ph.D., University of Minnesota, 1971. 263p. UMI# 72-14448. [president and professor of theology, Oberlin College, 1851-1866].

2109   Shults, Fredrick D. The History and Philosophy of Athletics for Men at Oberlin College. Doctor of Physical Education, Indiana University, 1967. 379p. UMI# 67-09460.

2110   Skyrm, Richard D. Oberlin Conservatory: A Century of Musical Growth and Influence. Doctor of Music Arts, University of Southern California, 1962. 420p. UMI# 62-3747.

2111   Tong, Curtis W. John Herbert Nichols, Doctor of Medicine: A Life of Leadership in Physical Education and Athletics. Ph.D., Ohio State University, 1968. 249p. UMI# 68-12881. [director of intramurals and athletic director, Oberlin College, 1928-1955].

2112   Tucker, Jennie S. Oberlin College Library, 1833-1885. Master's thesis, Western Reserve University, 1953.

2113   Tucker, John M. Librarianship as a Community Service: Azariah Smith Root at Oberlin College. Ph.D., University of Illinois at Urbana-Champaign, 1983. 231p. UMI# 8410061.

OHIO NORTHERN UNIVERSITY

2114   Molitor, Clarence W. A History of Physical Education at Ohio Northern University. Master's thesis, Ohio State University, 1955.

2115   Rogers, James T. A History of Ohio Northern University. Master's thesis, Ohio State University, 1933.

OHIO STATE UNIVERSITY

2116   Alcott, Pouneh M. Women at the Ohio State University in the First Four Decades, 1873-1912. Ph.D., Ohio State University, 1979. 235p. UMI# 80-01681.

2117   Batchellor, Robert W. The Development of the General Chemistry Program at the Ohio State University. Ph.D., Ohio State University, 1973. 290p. UMI# 74-03116.

2118   Block, Robert F. The Life of Lynn W. St. John and His Contributions to the Ohio State University and to Intercollegiate Athletics. Ph.D., Ohio State University, 1969. 338p. UMI# 69-04848. [athletic director and chairman of physical education, 1912-1947].

2119   Bowman, Georgiana H. Developmental Services and Cultural Programming for Black Students at the Ohio State University: 1968-1975. Ph.D., Ohio State University, 1976. 248p. UMI# 77-02355.

2120   Brannan, Joyce H. A History of Health Education at the Ohio State University, 1872-1981. (Volumes I and II) Ph.D., Ohio State University, 1981. 592p. UMI# 82-07159.

2121   Bullough, Robert V., Jr. Harold B. Alberty and Boyd H. Bode: Pioneers in Curriculum Theory. Ph.D., Ohio State University, 1976. 264p. UMI# 77-2359.

2122   Coyer, William J. The History of Baseball at Ohio State University. Master's thesis, Ohio State University, 1948.

2123   Daniels, Mary A. The Historical Transition of Women's Sports at the Ohio State University, 1885-1975 and Its Impact on the National Women's Intercollegiate Setting During That Period. Ph.D., Ohio State University, 1977. 410p. UMI# 77-24616.

2124   DiBiasio, Daniel A. Making the Most of Program Review: A Study of the Origins, Operations, and Outcomes of Program Review at the Ohio State University. Ph.D., Ohio State University, 1982. 238p. UMI# 82-22077.

2125   Ezell, Ernest B., Jr. Industrial Technology Education at the Ohio State University: Its Origin, Development, Leaders, and Influence Through the Warner Era. Ph.D., Ohio State University, 1982. 262p. UMI# 82-22082.

2126   Fry, James W. A History of the Ohio State University Library, 1913-1928. Master's thesis, Ohio State University, 1971.

2127   Furuichi, Suguru. A Comparative Study of the Intercollegiate Athletic Programs Between Two Selected Universities (Ohio State and Waseda) in the United States and Japan. Ph.D., Ohio State University, 1980. 156p. UMI# 8015876.

2128   Grady, Marilyn. The History of the Twilight School of Ohio State University: A Study in Leadership. Ph.D., Ohio State University, 1980. 207p. UMI# 81-07332.

2129   Green, Philip F. The History and Development of Men's Intramural Sports at the Ohio State University. Master's thesis, Ohio State University, 1957.

2130   Hayes, Walter S., Jr. Rutherford B. Hayes and His Connection with the Ohio State University. Master's thesis, Ohio State University, 1962.

2131   Heddesheimer, Walter J. The Study and Teaching of History in the United States Prior to 1940 with a Special Reference to the Ohio State University. Ph.D., Ohio State University, 1974. 351p. UMI# 75-11357.

2132   Hefflinger, Clifford C. History of Football at Ohio State University. Master's thesis, Ohio State University, 1948.

2133   Hotchkiss, William P., Jr. The Life and Professional Contributions of Michael Peppe to Physical Education and Aquatics. Ph.D., Ohio State University, 1971. 334p. UMI# 72-15224. [physical education instructor and swim coach, Ohio State University, 1927-1963].

2134   Irwin, William A. A Study of the Historical Development of On-Campus Housing at the Ohio State University. Ph.D., Ohio State University, 1977. 288p. UMI# 77-17100.

2135   Jacobs, G.G. A History and Evaluation of Physical Education for Women at the Ohio State University. Master's thesis, Ohio State University, 1938.

2136   Kovacic, Charles R. A History of Intercollegiate Athletics at the Ohio State University. Ph.D., Columbia University, 1953. 224p.

2137   Kyle, Judy M. A History of the Ohio State University Department of Speech. Master's thesis, Ohio State University, 1964.

2138   Madden, Richard H. Radio at the Ohio State University, 1910-1956. Master's thesis, Ohio State University, 1968.

2139   Martinelli, Fred M. A Brief History of Subsidization and a Followup Study Comparing Grant-in-Aid and Non Grant-in-Aid Athletics at the Ohio State University, 1957-1962. Ph.D., Ohio State University, 1968. 187p. UMI# 69-11671.

2140   Miller, Sandra K. Student Life at Ohio State University from the End of World War I to the Late 1930's. Master's thesis, Ohio State University, 1968.

2141   Newcomb, Joan I. The Historical Development of the Student Assistant Program at the Ohio State University. Master's thesis, Ohio State University, 1964.

2142   Ortiz, Hewtan S. A History of Basketball at Ohio State University. Master's thesis, Ohio State University, 1947.

2143   Pritchard, Pamela. The Negro Experience at the Ohio State University in the First Sixty-Five Years, 1873-1938: With Special Emphasis on Negroes in the College of Education. Ph.D., Ohio State University, 1982. 352p. UMI# 83-00328.

2144   Ramsey, Harold E. A History of Track Athletics at Ohio State University. Master's thesis, Ohio State University, 1951.

2145   Rosenstock, Sheldon A. The Educational Contributions of W(errett) W(allace) Charters. Ph.D., Ohio State University, 1984. 366p. UMI# 8410422. [director of research bureau, Ohio State University, 1928-1947].

2146   Russell, John C. Werrett Wallace Charters, Sr. (1875-1952): His Life, Career and Influence Upon Pharmaceutical Education. Ph.D., Loyola University of Chicago, 1981. 267p. UMI# 8109965. [director of research bureau, Ohio State University, 1928-1947].

2147   Ryan, John E. The History of Competitive Swimming at Ohio State University. Master's thesis, Ohio State University, 1951.

2148   Sabock, Ralph J. A History of Physical Education at the Ohio State University—Men and Women's Divisions, 1898-1969. Ph.D., Ohio State University, 1969. 483p. UMI# 70-06868.

2149   Skipper, James E. The Ohio State University Library, 1873-1913. Ph.D., University of Michigan, 1960. 330p. UMI# 60-6937.

2150   Vollmar, William J. The Issue of Compulsory Military Training at the Ohio State University, 1913-1973. Ph.D., Ohio State University, 1976. 480p. UMI# 76-18054.

OHIO UNIVERSITY

2151   Brady, William H. A History of Theatre at Ohio University, 1804-1920. Master's thesis, Ohio University, 1955.

2152   Bringer, Howard L. The History of Intercollegiate Football at Ohio University. Master's thesis, Ohio State University, 1950.

2153   Briscoe, Adelaide M. A History of Theatre at Ohio University (1920-1957). Master's thesis, Ohio University, 1959.

2154   Frey, Robert W. Major Motivating Factors and Events that Contributed to the Development of the College of Education of Ohio University. Ph.D., Ohio University, 1985. 436p. UMI# 8603300.

2155   Gordon, Eleanor W. The History and Development of Physical Education for Women at Ohio University. Master's thesis, Ohio State University, 1941.

2156   Stentz, Oren W. Evolution of Residence Hall Administration at Ohio University, 1883-1969. Ph.D., Ohio University, 1975. 183p. UMI# 76-08896.

2157   Sutton, William S. The Evolution of Black Studies Movement with Specific Reference to the Establishment of the Black Studies Institute at Ohio University. Ph.D., Ohio University, 1972. 342p. UMI# 72-26375.

2158   White, Jacqueline A. An Historical Study of the Forensic Program at Ohio University from 1812 to 1860. Master's thesis, Ohio University, 1969.

OHIO WESLEYAN UNIVERSITY

2159   Detrick, Raymond O. The History of Physical Education at Ohio Wesleyan University. Master's thesis, Ohio State University, 1937.

2160   Irwin, Maurine. History of the Ohio Wesleyan University Library, 1844-1940. Master's thesis, University of California-Berkeley, 1941. 263p.

OTTERBEIN COLLEGE

2161   Bartlett, Willard W. A Historical Study of Otterbein College at Westerville in the State of Ohio. Ph.D., Ohio State University, 1934.

2162   Dodrill, Charles W. History of Speech and Theatre at Otterbein College, 1847-1950. Ph.D., Ohio State University, 1965. 202p. UMI# 66-06243.

2163   Vermilya, Nancy C. A History of the Otterbein College Library. Master's thesis, Western Reserve University, 1955.

RIO GRANDE COLLEGE

2164   Evans, Benjamin R. A History of Rio Grande College. Master's thesis, Ohio State University, 1939.

SHAWNEE COLLEGE

2165   Idisi, C. Onokata. Shawnee College: An Analysis of the Organization and Establishment of a Post-Secondary Institution. Ph.D., Southern Illinois University at Carbondale, 1979. 224p. UMI# 8004052.

TOLEDO, UNIVERSITY OF

2166   Hickerson, Frank R. The History of the University of Toledo. Ph.D., University of Cincinnati, 1941. 596p. UMI# 00-00425.

2167   Klein, Melvyn S. The University of Toledo: Influential Factors in the Conversion from Municipal to State Status. Ed.D., Pennsylvania State University, 1971. 188p. UMI# 72-19333.

2168   Lee, Charles M. College of Education Doctoral Programs at the University of Toledo, 1960-1971. Ph.D., University of Toledo, 1973. 166p. UMI# 73-19534.

URSULINE COLLEGE

2169   Silva, Sister Frances C. A History of the Ursuline College Library, Cleveland, Ohio, 1922-1957. Master's thesis, Western Reserve University, 1958. 49p.

WESTERN LITERARY INSTITUTE

2170   Rich, Thomas R. The Western Literary Institute and College of Professional Teachers and the Common Movement in the West, 1830-1840. Ed.D., Northern Illinois University, 1973. 210p. UMI# 73-27606.

2171   Schweikert, Roman J. The Western Literary Institute and College of Professional Teachers: An Instrument in the Creation of a Profession (1831-1845). Ed.D., University of Cincinnati, 1971. 167p. UMI# 72-4313.

WILBERFORCE UNIVERSITY

2172   McGinnis, Frederick A. A History of Wilberforce University. Ph.D., University of Cincinnati, 1940. 132p.

XAVIER UNIVERSITY

2173   McNulty, Helen P. One Hundred and Ten Years of Education at Xavier. Ph.D., Fordham University, 1958.

YOUNGSTOWN STATE UNIVERSITY

2174   Jones, Marilyn. A Historical Study of Varsity Football at Youngstown College. Master's thesis, Ohio University, 1956. 192p.

2175   Schink, Ronald J. A History of the Youngstown University and Its Library. Master's thesis, Western Reserve University, 1956. 65p.

OKLAHOMA

GENERAL STUDIES

2176   Bennett, H.G. The Development of Higher Education in Oklahoma. Master's thesis, University of Oklahoma, 1924.

2177   Brewer, Wallace. History of Advanced Church Education in Oklahoma. Ph.D., University of Oklahoma, 1945. 217p.

2178   Brock, Raymond T. The Rise of Christian Higher Education in Oklahoma. Master's thesis, University of Tulsa, 1953.

2179   Cayton, Leonard B. A History of Black Public Education in Oklahoma. Ed.D., University of Oklahoma, 1976. 177p. UMI# 77-32851.

2180   Davison, Oscar W. History of Education in Oklahoma, 1907-1947. Ph.D., University of Oklahoma, 1949. 117p.

2181   Duke, Lila K.W. The Origin and Development of the First Higher Education Center in Oklahoma. Ed.D., Oklahoma State University, 1984. 169p. UMI# 8504347.

2182   Dunlap, E.T. The History of Legal Controls of Public Higher Education in Oklahoma. Ph.D., Oklahoma State University, 1957.

2183   Faust, Hugh G. The Development of Higher Education in Oklahoma. Master's thesis, University of Chicago, 1927.

2184   Frazier, Joseph M. Two Suburban Colleges: An Historical Analysis Using Factors Influencing Growth and Development. Ed.D., Oklahoma State University, 1984. 134p. UMI# 8427661.

2185   Harris, Emily F. Historical Development of Professional Laboratory Experiences for Elementary Teachers Provided by Seventeen Oklahoma Colleges. Ed.D., Oklahoma State University, 1961. 150p. UMI# 62-01600.

2186   Hoig, Stanley W. A History of the Development of Institutions of Higher Education in Oklahoma. Ph.D., University of Oklahoma, 1971. 395p. UMI# 71-27617.

2187   Jackson, Joe C. The History of Education in Eastern Oklahoma from 1898 to 1915. Ph.D., University of Oklahoma, 1950. 117p.

2188   Nunn, E.S. A History of Education in Oklahoma Territory. Ph.D., University of Oklahoma, 1941. 381p.

2189   Nutter, Larry W. A History of Junior Colleges in Oklahoma. Ph.D., University of Oklahoma, 1974. 118p. UMI# 75-06544.

2190   Shaw, Otto E. Development of the State Supported Junior College in Oklahoma. Master's thesis, Oklahoma State University, 1933.

2191   Strong, Evelyn R. Historical Development of the Oklahoma Association of Negro Teachers: A Study in Social Change, 1893-1958. Ph.D., University of Oklahoma, 1961. 306p. UMI# 61-05206.

2192   Timmons, David R. Development of Post-Secondary Two-Year Educational Service Areas for Oklahoma. Ph.D., University of Oklahoma, 1975. 78p. UMI# 75-21199.

2193   Wilkins, Orin L. The Development of the Private Church-Related Junior Colleges in Oklahoma. Ed.D., Oklahoma State University, 1979. 207p. UMI# 79-28243.

2194   Wright, Clare B. A History of Financial Support of Public Education in Oklahoma from 1907 to 1961. Ed.D., Oklahoma State University, 1963. 179p. UMI# 64-08961.

BACONE COLLEGE

2195   Bode, Coeryne. The Origin and Development of Bacone College. Master's thesis, University of Tulsa, 1957. 127p.

BETHANY NAZARENE COLLEGE

2196   Cantrell, Roy H. The History of Bethany Nazarene College. Ph.D., Southwestern Baptist Theological Seminary, 1956.

2197   McConnell, Leona B. A History of the Town and College of Bethany, Oklahoma. Master's thesis, University of Oklahoma, 1935.

FLAMING RAINBOW UNIVERSITY

2198   Kolhoff, Kathleen E. Flaming Rainbow: From a Sioux Vision to a Cherokee Reality. A Descriptive Study of the Development of an American Indian Institution of Higher Education. Ph.D., Union for Experimenting Colleges and Universities, 1979. 232p. UMI# 80-06731.

LANGSTON UNIVERSITY

2199   Anderson, Edison H., Sr. The Historical Development of Music in the Negro Secondary Schools of Oklahoma and at Langston University. Ph.D., University of Iowa, 1957. 348p. UMI# 00-20916.

NORTHEASTERN OKLAHOMA UNIVERSITY

2200   Caywood, Elzie R. A History of Northeastern State College. Master's thesis, University of Oklahoma, 1950.

NORTHWESTERN OKLAHOMA STATE UNIVERSITY

2201   Bridgewater, Herbert G. A History of Physical Education at Northwestern State College, Oklahoma, 1897 to 1965. Master's thesis, University of New Mexico, 1966.

2202   Brown, Lawrence S. A History of Speech Education at Northwestern State Teachers College. Master's thesis, South Dakota University, 1951.

2203   Carmichael, Yvonne C. A Historical Review of Physical Education and Athletics at Northwestern Oklahoma State University (1897-1982). Ed.D., Oklahoma State University, 1982. 114p. UMI# 8300143.

OKLAHOMA BAPTIST UNIVERSITY

2204   Bruster, Bill G. A History of Oklahoma Baptist University with Special Reference to the Contribution of John Wesley Raley. Ph.D., Southwest Baptist Theological Seminary, 1972. [president and chancellor, 1934-1968].

OKLAHOMA CITY UNIVERSITY

2205   McCoy, Connie M. The Educational Thought of the Presidents and Chancellors of Oklahoma City University. Ph.D., University of Oklahoma, 1976. 177p. UMI# 77-01836.

OKLAHOMA PRESBYTERIAN COLLEGE

2206   Semple, Anne R. The Origin and Development of the Oklahoma Presbyterian College. Ph.D., Oklahoma Agricultural & Mechanical College, 1955.

OKLAHOMA STATE UNIVERSITY

2207   Anderson, Melvin S. History of Wrestling at Agricultural and Mechanical: Brief Biography of E.C. Gallager. Master's thesis, Oklahoma Agricultural and Mechanical College, 1938. 51p.

2208   Gill, Jerry L. Oklahoma State University and the Great Adventure in International Education, 1951-1976. Ph.D., Oklahoma State University, 1976. 228p. UMI# 78-01255.

2209   Holmberg, Sharon M. Valerie Colvin: Pioneer Physical Educator in Oklahoma. Ed.D., Oklahoma State University, 1978. 172p. UMI# 7903681. [teacher, Oklahoma State University].

2210   McFarland, William E. A History of Student Financial Assistance Programs at Oklahoma State University, 1891-1978, with an Emphasis on the Creation and Administration of the Lew Wentz Foundation. Ph.D., Oklahoma State University, 1979. 200p. UMI# 79-28219.

2211   Rulon, Philip R. The Founding of the Oklahoma Agricultural and Mechanical College, 1890-1908. Ed.D., Oklahoma State University, 1968. 317p. UMI# 69-14324.

OKLAHOMA, UNIVERSITY OF

2212   Dellasega, Charles J. The Development and Present Status of Education for Business at the University of Oklahoma. Ph.D., University of Oklahoma, 1953. 323p.

2213   Evans, Samuel W. An Evalution of the Oklahoma Statutory Requirement in American History at the University of Oklahoma, 1945-1955. Ed.D., University of Oklahoma, 1957. 153p. UMI# 00-24418.

2214   Kassen, Tex. History and Development of Physical Education in Intramurals for Men in the University of Oklahoma. Master's thesis, University of Oklahoma, 1940.

188   Oklahoma

2215   Koch, Konrad K., Jr. An Administrative History of the Academic Divisions of the University of Oklahoma. Master's thesis, University of Oklahoma, 1950.

2216   Kohlenberg, Randy B. Harrison Kerr: Portrait of a Twentieth-Century American Composer. Ph.D., University of Oklahoma, 1978. 241p. UMI# 7921242. [professor and dean of fine arts, University of Oklahoma, 1949-1968].

2217   McBride, Jack E. The History and Development of Faculty Controls of Intercollegiate Athletics at Oklahoma University. Ph.D., University of Oklahoma, 1965. 150p. UMI# 65-09792.

2218   Morrissey, Robert S. David Ross Boyd and the University of Oklahoma: An Analysis of the Educational Contributions of the First President. Ed.D., University of Oklahoma, 1973. 277p. UMI# 74-06975. [president, 1892-1908].

2219   Penney, Grace J. A History of the Extension Division of the University of Oklahoma, 1892-1952. Master's thesis, University of Oklahoma, 1953.

2220   Weidman, John M. A History of the University of Oklahoma. Master's thesis, University of Oklahoma, 1928.

2221   Wood, Edwin K. The University of Oklahoma in the World War. Master's thesis, University of Oklahoma, 1923.

OLD WILLIE HALSELL COLLEGE

2222   George, Leonard F. The Origin, Development, Discontinuation and Influence on Oklahoma Education of the 'Old Willie Halsell College,' Craig County, Vinita, Indian Territory. Master's thesis, Oklahoma Agricultural and Mechanical College, 1939.

SEMINOLE JUNIOR COLLEGE

2223   Tanner, Louis E. An Analysis of the Emergence of a Community College: Factors Related to the Development of Seminole Junior College. Ed.D., University of Oklahoma, 1977. 177p. UMI# 77-21415.

SOUTHWESTERN OKLAHOMA STATE UNIVERSITY

2224   Fiegel, Melvin F. A History of Southwestern State College, 1903-1953. Ed.D., Oklahoma State University, 1968. 272p. UMI# 69-14245.

2225   Woodruff, Joe H. History of the Theatrical Activity at Southwestern State College, Weatherford, Oklahoma. Master's thesis, Southern Methodist University, 1952.

TULSA, UNIVERSITY OF

2226   Delfraisse, Betty D. The History of the University of Tulsa. Master's thesis, University of Texas, 1929.

2227   Logsdon, Guy W. The University of Tulsa: A History from 1882 to 1972. Ed.D., University of Oklahoma, 1975. 381p. UMI# 36-15814.

OREGON

GENERAL STUDIES

2228 Almack, John C. History of Oregon Normal Schools. Master's thesis, University of Oregon, 1920.

2229 Boufford, Marjorie J. A History of Nursing in Oregon. Master's thesis, Oregon State College, 1951.

2230 Cunningham, J. David. The Zorn-MacPherson Initiative Petition, 1932: A Study of the Development of Higher Education in Oregon. Ph.D., University of Oregon, 1983. 454p. UMI# 83-15741.

2231 Lane, Marilyn A. College Closure: A Comparative Study of Six Oregon Colleges, 1842-1930. Ph.D., University of Oregon, 1984. 141p. UMI# 8502004.

2232 Large, Larry D. The Impact of State Assistance on Oregon's Private Colleges and Universities. Ph.D., University of Oregon, 1974. 161p. UMI# 75-12545.

2233 Meinert, James D. A History of the Oregon State Scholarship Commission. Ph.D., University of Oregon, 1974. 127p. UMI# 75-04516.

2234 Murray, Neil D. A Comparative Historical Study of Student Protest at the University of Oregon and Oregon State University During the Sixties. Ph.D., University of Oregon, 1971. 196p. UMI# 72-08579.

2235 Nickerson, Francis B. A History of the High School-College Relations Committee in Oregon. Ed.D., University of Oregon, 1959. 288p. UMI# 59-04319.

2236 Sampson, Bill A. A History of Secondary Teacher Training in Oregon. Ph.D., University of Oregon, 1950. 117p.

2237 Santee, Joseph F. The History and Status of Public Elementary Teacher Training in Oregon. Ph.D., University of Washington, 1939.

2238 Savage, Nancy. A Historical Survey and Comparative Analysis of Speech and Drama at the University of Portland and Lewis and Clark College. Master's thesis, University of Portland, 1965.

2239 Schulz, John A. Historical Development in Centralizing Control of Higher Education in Oregon. Ph.D., University of Southern California, 1950. 117p.

LINFIELD COLLEGE

2240 Butcher, Paul A. Linfield College Tournament of Champions: History and Analysis. Master's thesis, University of Hawaii, 1968.

METHODIST UNIVERSITY OF PORTLAND

2241   McIntire, George R. History of the Methodist University of Portland, 1891-1900. Master's thesis, University of Oregon, 1922.

MOUNT ANGEL SEMINARY

2242   Hodes, Ursala. Mount Angel, Oregon, 1848-1921. Master's thesis, University of Oregon, 1932.

NORTHWEST CHRISTIAN COLLEGE

2243   Goodrich, Martha H. A History of Northwest Christian College. Master's thesis, University of Oregon, 1949.

OREGON STATE UNIVERSITY

2244   Bowman, Vernon L. A Historical Study of Business Education and Secretarial Science at Oregon State University. Ed.D., Oregon State University, 1974. 163p. UMI# 73-32750.

2245   Valenti, Paul B. History of Basketball at Oregon State College from 1928 through 1949. Master's thesis, Oregon State College, 1957.

2246   Van Loan, Lillian S. Historical Perspective of Oregon State College. Ed.D., Oregon State University, 1959. 389p. UMI# 59-03417.

OREGON, UNIVERSITY OF

2247   Carroll, Margaret M. A History of the Evolution and Early Development of the School of Physical Education at the University of Oregon 1894-1937. Ed.D., University of Oregon, 1975. 381p. UMI# 76-05147.

2248   Colvin, Lloyd W. A History of the School of Education at the University of Oregon. Ed.D., University of Oregon, 1964. 447p. UMI# 65-02461.

2249   Cunliffe, William E. A History of the Reserve Officers' Training Corps at the University of Oregon, 1919 to 1969. Ph.D., University of Oregon, 1970. 238p. UMI# 70-15311.

2250   Fisk, Gertrude M. A Case Study of Grace Graham Vacation College, University of Oregon. Ph.D., University of Oregon, 1980. 220p. UMI# 8109676.

2251   Freeman, William H. A Biographical Study of William Jay Bowerman. Ph.D., University of Oregon, 1972. 164p. UMI# 73-13,735. [football and track coach, University of Oregon].

2252   Mills, Thomas J. Historical Study of the Dean of Men and the Major Issues They Faced at the University of Oregon, 1920-1968. Ph.D., University of Oregon, 1974. 217p. UMI# 74-26550.

2253   Porter, James L. The First Fifty Years of Track and Field Athletics at the University of Oregon. Master's thesis, University of Oregon, 1955. 77p.

2254   Santee, J.F. University of Oregon: Admission Standards, 1876 to 1927. Master's thesis, University of Oregon, 1927.

2255   Warren, E.N. The Development of Football at the University of Oregon. Master's thesis, University of Oregon, 1937.

2256   White, Irle E. The Development of Educational Theatre at the University Level as Exemplified by the Dramatic Activity at the University of Oregon, 1876-1962. Master's thesis, University of Oregon, 1962.

PACIFIC UNIVERSITY

2257   Long, Watt A. A History of Pacific University. Master's thesis, University of Oregon, 1933.

PHILOMATH COLLEGE

2258   Springer, Clair G. A History of Philomath College. Master's thesis, University of Oregon, 1929.

PORTLAND STATE UNIVERSITY

2259   Richardson, John A. The Evolution of a University: A Case Study of an Organization and Its Environment. Ph.D., Stanford University, 1975. 459p. UMI# 75-13584.

WESTERN OREGON STATE COLLEGE

2260   North, Richard B. Early History of Oregon College of Education from its Beginnings to 1911. Master's thesis, Oregon College of Education, 1960.

WILLAMETTE UNIVERSITY

2261   Neiger, Helen M. A History of the Curriculum and Academic Requirements of Willamette University, 1853-1940. Master's thesis, Willamette University, 1941.

PENNSYLVANIA

GENERAL STUDIES

2262   Andruss, Harvey A. The Development of Pennsylvania State Teachers Colleges as Institutions of Higher Education (1927-1948). Ed.D., Pennsylvania State University, 1949. 201p. UMI# 00-01440.

2263   Babb, Wylie S. Legal Bases, Regulations and Procedures for the Chartering and Approval of Private, Nonprofit Degree-Granting Colleges, Universities and Seminaries in Pennsylvania. Ph.D., University of Pittsburgh, 1979. 172p. UMI# 8004786.

2264   Bell, Whitfield J., Jr. Science and Humanity in Philadelphia, 1775-1790. Ph.D., University of Pennsylvania, 1947. 323p. UMI# 00-02499.

2265   Bonar, James A. Benjamin Rush and the Theory and Practice of Republican Education in Pennsylvania. Ph.D., Johns Hopkins University, 1965. 269p. UMI# 65-06876. [professor of medicine, University of Pennsylvania, 1769-1813].

2266   Bonder, James B. The Growth and Development of the State Teachers Colleges of Pennsylvania. Ed.D., Temple University, 1952. 546p. UMI# 67-06223.

2267   Broomall, Lawrence W. Will Grant Chambers: His Contributions to Teacher Education in the Commonwealth of Pennsylvania, 1909-1937. Ed.D., Pennsylvania State University, 1966. 216p. UMI# 67-05899. [professor of education and dean, University of Pittsburgh and Pennsylvania State University, 1909-1937].

2268   Buell, Harold E. The Development of Higher Education Under the Methodist-Episcopal Church in the Pittsburgh Area. Ph.D., University of Pittsburgh, 1950. 117p.

2269   Cornell, William A. The Historical Development of the Patterns of Appropriations for Institutions of Higher Education by the General Assembly of the Commonwealth of Pennsylvania to 1960. Ed.D., State University of New York at Buffalo, 1963. 379p. UMI# 63-06708.

2270   Fleischer, Robert D. The Development of the Relationships of Legal Fiscal Control to the Extent of State Aid for Higher Education as Applied to Pennsylvania, 1921-1953. Ed.D., University of Pittsburgh, 1954. 191p. UMI# 00-08891.

2271   Fruechtel, Warren B. Relation of the State to Higher Education in Pennsylvania, 1776-1874. Ph.D., University of Pittsburgh, 1965. 422p. UMI# 65-12937.

2272   Getts, Paul R. A History of Education in Indiana, Pennsylvania. Ed.D., Pennsylvania State University, 1965. 327p. UMI# 65-14754.

2273   Graver, Lee A. A History of the First Pennsylvania State Normal School. Ph.D., Rutgers University, 1954.

2274   Hall, Allan W. A History of the Pennsylvania State Athletic Conference: An Analysis of

Selected Critical Issues and Incidents. Ed.D., University of Akron, 1984. 264p. UMI# 8400815.

2275   Halttunen, William R. Evolution of the Curriculum for the Preparation of Secondary School Teachers in Pennsylvania State Normal Schools and Teachers Colleges. Ed.D., University of Pennsylvania, 1969. 344p. UMI# 69-21,632.

2276   Huggins, Elizabeth. History of the Normal School in Philadelphia. Master's thesis, Temple University, 1934. 154p.

2277   Irby, Jon E. Branch Campuses of Pennsylvania's State Colleges and Universities—Past, Present, and Future. Ed.D., Pennsylvania State University, 1973. 202p. UMI# 73-24012.

2278   Issel, William H. Schools for a Modern Age: Educational Reform in Pennsylvania in the Progressive Era. Ph.D., University of Pennsylvania, 1969. 297p. UMI# 70-16164.

2279   Kepner, Charles W. The Contributions Early Presbyterian Leaders Made in the Development of the Educational Institutions in Western Pennsylvania Prior to 1850. Ph.D., University of Pittsburgh, 1942. 249p.

2280   Leslie, William B. A Comparative Study of Four Middle Atlantic Colleges 1870-1915: Bucknell University, Franklin and Marshall College, Princeton University, and Swarthmore College. Ph.D., Johns Hopkins University, 1971. 282p. UMI# 71-21027.

2281   Liebenau, Jonathan M. Medical Science and Medical Industry, 1890-1929: A Study of Pharmaceutical Manufacturing in Philadelphia. Ph.D., University of Pennsylvania, 1981. 498p. UMI# 8207994.

2282   Lozo, John P. A Brief History of Pennsylvania Colleges and Universities. Master's thesis, Pennsylvania State College, 1925.

2283   McCadden, Joseph J. Education in Pennsylvania, 1801-1935, and Its Debts to Roberts Vaux. Ph.D., Columbia University, 1937. 373p.

2284   Mezoff, Earl R. The Growth and Direction of the Curriculum in Selected Pennsylvania Liberal Arts Colleges Between 1954 and 1960. Ed.D., Pennsylvania State University, 1965. 142p. UMI# 65-14773.

2285   Mulka, John S. Student Pressures and Institutional Responses in Selected Colleges in Pennsylvania: A History. Ed.D., Pennsylvania State University, 1976. 331p. UMI# 77-09710.

2286   O'Hara, Leo J. An Emerging Profession: Philadelphia Medicine 1860-1900. Ph.D., University of Pennsylvania, 1976. 410p. UMI# 77-10201.

2287   Pinkston, Esther K. State Support of Black Institutions of Higher Learning in Pennsylvania: A Case Study of Lincoln University and Cheyney State College. Ed.D., Rutgers University, 1983. 179p. UMI# 8325899.

2288   Quatroche, John R. Efforts of the State Toward Centralization of Higher Educational Policy in Pennsylvania Since 1963. Ph.D., University of Pittsburgh, 1975. 142p. UMI# 75-22462.

2289   Rauch, Julia B. Unfriendly Visitors: The Emergence of Scientific Philanthropy in Philadelphia, 1878-1880. Ph.D., Bryn Mawr College, 1974. 362p. UMI# 75-15941.

2290   Sack, Saul. A History of Higher Education in Pennsylvania. Ph.D., University of Pennsylvania, 1959. 1,197p. UMI# 59-02266.

2291   Shaffer, Lowell D. A Comparison and Interpretation of the Historical Development of the University of Pittsburgh at Johnstown and the Altoona Campus of Pennsylvania State University. Ph.D., University of Pittsburgh, 1982. 311p. UMI# 83-12539.

2292   Stout, Loreen W. A Legislative History and Analysis of Act 188 of 1982 Establishing the State System of Higher Education in Pennsylvania. Ed.D., Lehigh University, 1983. 217p. UMI# 83-29480.

2293   Tiger, Dennis D. Business Degree Programs in Pennsylvania Colleges and Universities. Ed.D., University of Pittsburgh, 1965. 364p. UMI# 66-10092.

2294   Woomer, Dale W. The Growth and Development of Business Education in Three Pennsylvania State Owned Institutions of Higher Learning. Ed.D., Pennsylvania State University, 1970. 299p. UMI# 71-06375.

ALLEGHENY COLLEGE

2295   Smith, Dorothy J. The Early History of the Library of Allegheny College, Meadville, Pennsylvania. Master's thesis, Western Reserve University, 1953.

BLOOMSBURG UNIVERSITY OF PENNSYLVANIA

2296   Edwards, Charles S. The Contributions of David Jewett Waller, Jr., to Educational Administration in Pennsylvania. Ed.D., Pennsylvania State University, 1965. 215p. UMI# 66-04798. [principal, Bloomsburg University of Pennsylvania, 1877-1890, 1906-1920].

BRYN MAWR COLLEGE

2297   Briscoe, Virginia W. Bryn Mawr College Traditions: Women's Rituals as Expressive Behavior. Ph.D., University of Pennsylvania, 1981. 1,027p. UMI# 81-17762.

2298   Maddalena, Lucille A. The Goals of Bryn Mawr Summer School for Women Workers Established During Its First Five Years. Ed.D., Rutgers University, 1978. 367p. UMI# 79-14122.

BUCKNELL UNIVERSITY

2299   McFarland, M.M. History of the Development of Bucknell University Library, Lewisburg, Pennsylvania. Master's thesis, Drexel Institute of Technology, 1955.

2300   Nichols, Scott G. Volunteerism in Higher Education: A History of Bucknell University Alumni. Ed.D., University of Pennsylvania, 1977. 386p. UMI# 77-24168.

CALIFORNIA UNIVERSITY OF PENNSYLVANIA

2301   Bakewell, Arthur L. The History of Industrial Education at California State College, California, Pennsylvania. Master's thesis, California State College, 1972.

2302   Neill, Henry R. The History of Health and Physical Education at California State Teachers College. Master's thesis, University of Pittsburgh, 1933.

2303   Serinko, Regis J. California State College of Pennsylvania: From Private Normal College to Multi-Purpose Public Institution. Ph.D., University of Pittsburgh, 1974. 557p. UMI# 74-21675.

CARNEGIE MELLON UNIVERSITY

2304   Johnston, Judy A. A History of the One Year Experience of TTT (Trainer of Teacher Trainers) in English at Carnegie-Mellon University. Doctor of Arts, Carnegie-Mellon University, 1972. 203p. UMI# 73-00238.

CHESTNUT HILL COLLEGE

2305   Kraft, Sister M.I. A History of the Library of Chestnut Hill College: Philadelphia, Pennsylvania, 1890-1965. Master's thesis, Catholic University of America, 1967. 100p.

CHEYNEY UNIVERSITY OF PENNSYLVANIA

2306   Clark, Sulayman. The Educational Philosophy of Leslie Pickney Hill: A Profile in Black Educational Leadership, 1904-1951. Ed.D., Harvard University, 1984. UMI# 8421176. [president, Cheyney University of Pennsylvania, 1930-1951].

2307   Conyers, Charline F.H. A History of the Cheyney State Teachers College, 1837-1951. Ed.D., New York University, 1960. 389p. UMI# 60-03767.

2308   Fewell, Roberta J. Institutional Response to the Higher Education Act of 1965: A Case Study of Cheyney State College. Ph.D., University of Pittsburgh, 1979. 126p. UMI# 7924710.

COLLEGE MISERICORDIA

2309   Ference, Regina C. A History of College Misericordia. Master's thesis, University of Scranton, 1964.

DUQUESNE UNIVERSITY

2310   Clees, William J. Duquesne University: Its Years of Struggle, Sacrifice and Service. Ed.D., University of Pittsburgh, 1970. 204p. UMI# 70-20323.

2311   Gimper, Eileen R. The School of Nursing of Duquesne University: 1937-1979. Ph.D., University of Pittsburgh, 1983. 223p. UMI# 83-27724.

2312   Hanley, Francis X. Duquesne University: Evolution from College to University, Administration of Martin A. Hehir, C.S.SP., 1899-1931. Ph.D., University of Pittsburgh, 1979. 351p. UMI# 80-04808.

2313   Kupersanin, Michael. Intercollegiate Athletics at Duquesne University in Historical Perspective. Ph.D., University of Pittsburgh, 1980. 162p. UMI# 80-18314.

EASTERN BAPTIST THEOLOGICAL SEMINARY

2314   McTaggart, John B. The History of the Eastern Baptist Theological Seminary Library, 1925-1953. Master's thesis, Drexel Institute of Technology, 1954. 63p.

EDINBORO UNIVERSITY OF PENNSYLVANIA

2315   Neel, George W. A History of the State Teachers College at Edinboro, Pennsylvania. Ph.D., Rutgers University, 1950. 117p.

FRANKLIN AND MARSHALL COLLEGE

2316   Taylor, Charles W. A History of Intercollegiate Athletics at Franklin and Marshall College. Master's thesis, University of Maryland, 1962. 341p.

FRANKLIN INSTITUTE

2317   Elliott, Arlene A. The Development of the Mechanics' Institute and Their Influence Upon the Field of Engineering: Pennsylvania, A Case Study, 1824-1860. Ph.D., University of Southern California, 1972. 342p. UMI# 72-26,011.

2318   Sinclair, Joseph B. 'Science with Practice; Practice with Science'; A History of the Franklin Institute, 1824-1837. Ph.D., Case Institute of Technology, 1966. 245p. UMI# 67-11,569.

GENEVA COLLEGE

2319   Churovia, Robert M. An Intercollegiate Athletic History: The Geneva Story. Ph.D., University of Pittsburgh, 1978. 126p. UMI# 78-16782.

2320   Galbreath, Clarence R. A Christian College in Contemporary America: Geneva College, 1956-1976. Ph.D., University of Pittsburgh, 1981. 121p. UMI# 8213145.

GRATZ COLLEGE

2321   King, Diane. A History of Gratz College, 1893-1928. Ph.D., Dropsie University, 1979.

GROVE CITY COLLEGE

2322   Bartok, Leslie A. Grove City College and the United States Government Since 1977: A Case Study of Autonomy vs. Authority. Ph.D., University of Pittsburgh, 1983. 78p. UMI# 8327689.

2323   Dayton, David M. Building 'Mid the Pines: An Historical Study of Grove City College. Ph.D., University of Pittsburgh, 1971. 440p. UMI# 72-07867.

2324   Dietrich, Marietta. The History of Grove City College. Master's thesis, University of Pittsburgh, 1933.

HAGERSTOWN JUNIOR COLLEGE

2325   Alford, Stanley C. The Historical Development of Hagerstown Junior College: 1946 to 1975. Ed.D., George Washington University, 1976. 238p. UMI# 76-23540.

HERSHEY JUNIOR COLLEGE

2326   Klotz, Richard R. The Hershey Junior College, Hershey, Pennsylvania, 1938-1965. Ed.D., Pennsylvania State University, 1970. 406p. UMI# 71-21764.

HOLY FAMILY COLLEGE

2327   Valentine, Sister M. Holy Family College Library: The First Decade. Master's thesis, Marywood College, 1956. 36p.

INDIANA UNIVERSITY OF PENNSYLVANIA

2328   Merryman, John E., Sr. Indiana University of Pennsylvania: From Private Normal School to Public University, 1871-1968. Ph.D., University of Pittsburgh, 1972. 506p. UMI# 73-01676.

2329   Sims, Edward R. The History of the Music Department of the Indiana University of Pennsylvania and Its Contributions to Music Education. Ed.D., University of Michigan, 1968. 263p. UMI# 69-12018.

JUNIATA COLLEGE

2330   Messina, Salvatore M. Martin Grove Brumbaugh, Educator. Ph.D., University of Pennsylvania, 1965. 479p. UMI# 66-285. [president, Juniata College, 1895-1906, 1924-1930].

KUTZTOWN UNIVERSITY

2331   Myers, Clara A. History of the State Teachers' College, Kutztown, Pa. Master's thesis, Temple University, 1934. 154p.

LA SALLE COLLEGE

2332   Richardson, Ellen R. The La Salle College Library, Philadelphia, 1930-1953. Master's thesis, Drexel Institute of Technology, 1953. 43p.

LAFAYETTE COLLEGE

2333   Wagner, Lloyd F. A Descriptive History of the Library Facilities of Lafayette College, Easton, Pennsylvania, 1826-1941. Master's thesis, Catholic University of America, 1951.

LEBANON VALLEY COLLEGE

2334   Fisher, Paul G. Music: A Dominant Force in the First Century of Lebanon Valley College. Ed.D., University of Michigan, 1969. 251p. UMI# 70-4023.

LINCOLN UNIVERSITY

2335   Bethel, Leonard L. The Role of Lincoln University (Pennsylvania) in the Education of African Leadership: 1854-1970. Ed.D., Rutgers University, 1975. 391p. UMI# 76-1101.

LOCK HAVEN UNIVERSITY OF PENNSYLVANIA

2336   Wisor, Harold C. A History of Teacher Education at Lock Haven State College, Lock

Haven, Pennsylvania, 1870-1960. Ed.D., Pennsylvania State University, 1966. 334p. UMI# 67-05983.

LUTHERAN THEOLOGICAL SEMINARY

2337   Williams, C.W. History of the Krauth Memorial Library and Staff of the Lutheran Theological Seminary, at Philadelphia, from 1864 to 1951. Master's thesis, Drexel Institute of Technology, 1952.

LUZERNE COUNTY COMMUNITY COLLEGE

2338   Martin, John P. The Establishment of Luzerne County Community College: A Case Study. Ed.D., Pennsylvania State University, 1972. 257p. UMI# 73-14020.

MADISON COLLEGE

2339   Sandborn, William C. The History of Madison College. Ph.D., George Peabody College for Teachers, 1954.

MARYWOOD COLLEGE

2340   Turnbach, Catherine R. The Origin, Growth, and Development of Mary Wood College, 1919-1953. Master's thesis, Marywood College, 1954.

MEDICAL COLLEGE OF PENNSYLVANIA

2341   Foster, Pauline P. Ann Preston, M.D. (1813-1872): A Biography. The Struggle to Obtain Training and Acceptance for Women Physicians in Mid-Nineteenth Century America. Ph.D., University of Pennsylvania, 1984. 489p. UMI# 8417297. [professor of physiology and hygiene, Medical College of Pennsylvania].

MILLERSVILLE UNIVERSITY OF PENNSYLVANIA

2342   Bair, Lawrence. The Life and Educational Labors of James Pyle Wickersham, 1825-1891. Ph.D., University of Pittsburgh, 1939. [president, Millersville University of Pennsylvania, 1856-1866].

2343   Harrold, Kenneth R. Burl Neff Osburn: A Biographical Study of Selected Aspects of His Life and a Discussion of His Philosophy and Contributions to Industrial Arts. Ed.D., University of Maryland, 1978. 257p. UMI# 7917374. [director of industrial arts, Millersville University of Pennsylvania].

OLD JEFFERSON COLLEGE

2344   Hobbs, Jane E. Old Jefferson College. Master's thesis, University of Pittsburgh, 1929.

PENNSYLVANIA ACADEMY OF THE FINE ARTS

2345   Onorato, Ronald J. The Pennsylvania Academy of the Fine Arts and the Development of an Academic Curriculum in the Nineteenth Century. Ph.D., Brown University, 1977. 253p. UMI# 77-32,617.

2346   Schreiber, Lee L. The Philadelphia Elite in the Development of the Pennsylvania Academy of Fine Arts, 1805-1842. Ph.D., Temple University, 1977. 485p. UMI# 77-21841.

PENNSYLVANIA STATE UNIVERSITY

2347   Adams, David H. The History of Intercollegiate Wrestling at Pennsylvania State University from 1942 through 1957. Master's thesis, Pennsylvania State University, 1958. 62p.

2348   Booher, Dennis A. Joseph Vincent Paterno, Football Coach: His Involvement with the Pennsylvania State University and American Intercollegiate Football. Ph.D., Pennsylvania State University, 1985. 290p. UMI# 8606299.

2349   Brown, Harry N. An Historical Analysis of Intercollegiate Soccer at the Pennsylvania State College. Master's thesis, Pennsylvania State College, 1941.

2350   Davidson, Edgar O. Philosophical Emphasis in the Development of Graduate Professional Education at the Pennsylvania State College with Reference to Other Collegiate Programs. Ed.D., Pennsylvania State University, 1953. 200p. UMI# 00-07352.

2351   Edwards, Earle L. A History of Pennsylvania State College Program of Football. Master's thesis, Pennsylvania State College, 1939. 100p.

2352   Gross, Elmer A. The History of Basketball at Pennsylvania State College. Master's thesis, Pennsylvania State University, 1958. 182p.

2353   Hartman, Van A. A History of Intercollegiate Track and Field Athletics at the Pennsylvania State College. Master's thesis, Pennsylvania State College, 1946.

2354   Marlow, T. Stuart. An Historical Analysis of Intercollegiate Baseball at Pennsylvania State College. Master's thesis, Pennsylvania State University, 1942. 90p.

2355   McGovern, Sister Mary V. Federal State Relations with Emphasis on the Evolution of Federal Aid in Support of the Agricultural State College in Pennsylvania. Master's thesis, Temple University, 1941.

2356   Michener, A.O. Thomas Henry Burrowes, LL.D., Champion of the Common Schools of Pennsylvania. Master's thesis, Temple University, 1932. [president, Pennsylvania State University, until 1871].

2357   Reed, Neville F. The Contributions of the Pennsylvania State College to Education Under the Morrill Act of 1862 and Subsequent Legislation. Master's thesis, Temple University, 1928.

2358   Speidel, Charles M. The History of Wrestling at Pennsylvania State College. Master's thesis, Pennsylvania State College, 1941. 73p.

2359   Stark, Lois. The Role of the University Administration in the Development of Physical Education and Athletics at the Pennsylvania State University, 1855-1930. Master's thesis, Pennsylvania State University, 1970.

2360   Stine, George F. Male Undergraduate Student Life and Services at the Pennsylvania State University: 1850-1965. Ph.D., Pennsylvania State University, 1966. 367p. UMI# 67-05975.

2361   Valla, Joseph P. The History of Boxing at Pennsylvania State College. Master's thesis, Pennsylvania State University, 1947.

2362   Venuto, Louis J. Dean Edward Steidle's Contributions to the Growth of the College of Mineral Industries at the Pennsylvania State University: A Case Study. Ed.D., Pennsylvania State University, 1965. 166p. UMI# 66-04868. [dean, 1928-1953].

2363   Wentz, Richard E. The Role of Evangelical Protestantism in the Formative Years of the Pennsylvania State University. Ph.D., George Washington University, 1971. 185p. UMI# 71-19633.

2364   Wray, Mary E. The History of the Required Program of Health and Physical Education for Women at Pennsylvania State College. Master's thesis, Pennsylvania State College, 1945.

PENNSYLVANIA, UNIVERSITY OF

2365   Byrnes, Don R. The Pre-Revolutionary Career of Provost William Smith, 1751-1780. Ph.D., Tulane University, 1969. 280p. UMI# 70-06384. [provost, University of Pennsylvania, 1755-1779].

2366   Earnshaw, Jeannine. A History of the Henry Lea Library at the University of Pennsylvania. Master's thesis, Drexel Institute of Technology, 1955. 41p.

2367   Ebersole, Mark C. A History of the Christian Association of the University of Pennsylvania. Ph.D., Columbia University, 1952. 208p. UMI# 00-04176.

2368   Freund, Clare E. The Library of the College of Physicians of Philadelphia. Master's thesis, Drexel Institute of Technology, 1951. 58p.

2369   Gordon, Ann D. The College of Philadelphia, 1749-1779: Impact of an Institution. Ph.D., University of Wisconsin-Madison, 1975. 342p. UMI# 76-10660.

2370   Hires, William L. Josiah Harmar Penniman, Educator, 1868-1941. Ph.D., University of Pennsylvania, 1972. 267p. UMI# 72-25,587. [provost and president, University of Pennsylvania, 1920-1941].

2371   Hunter, Adelaide M. R. Tait McKenzie: Pioneer in Physical Education. Ph.D., Columbia University, 1950. [professor of physical education, University of Pennsylvania, 1904-1931].

2372   McColl, M.C. Evans Dental Library, University of Pennsylvania: History and Service. Master's thesis, Drexel Institute of Technology, 1955.

2373   McHugh, Thomas F. Thomas Woody: Teacher, Scholar, Humanist. Ph.D., University of Pennsylvania, 1973. 343p. UMI# 74-14,103. [professor, University of Pennsylvania].

2374   Meyerend, Maude H. A History and Survey of the Fine Arts Library of the University of Pennsylvania from Its Founding to 1953. Master's thesis, Drexel Institute of Technology, 1955. 92p.

2375   Peters, William R. The Contributions of William Smith, 1727-1803, to the Development of

Higher Education in the United States. Ph.D., University of Michigan, 1968. 291p. UMI# 69-02368. [provost, University of Pennsylvania, 1755-1779, 1789-1791].

2376   Sheehan, Michael T. The Annenberg Center: A History of Its Early Years, 1965-1972. Ph.D., University of Pennsylvania, 1974. 172p. UMI# 74-22,905.

2377   Simson, Sharon J.P. Metamorphoses of an Organization: The Graduate School of Medicine and the Graduate Hospital of the University of Pennsylvania. Ph.D., University of Pennsylvania, 1973. UMI# 74-02462.

2378   Smith, Terry W. 'Exercises' Presented During the Commencements of the College of Philadelphia and Other Colonial Colleges. Ph.D., University of Pennsylvania, 1962. 277p. UMI# 62-4341.

2379   Turner, William L. The College, Academy, and Charitable School of Philadelphia: The Development of a Colonial Institution of Learning, 1740-1779. Ph.D., University of Pennsylvania, 1952.

PHILADELPHIA ACADEMY OF NATURAL SCIENCES

2380   Porter, Charlotte M. The Excursive Naturalists or the Development of American Taxonomy at the Philadelphia Academy of Natural Sciences, 1812-1842. Ph.D., Harvard University, 1976.

PHILADELPHIA COLLEGE OF PHARMACY

2381   Higby, Gregory J. William Procter, Jr. (1817-1874) and His Contribution to American Pharmacy. Ph.D., University of Wisconsin-Madison, 1984. 409p. UMI# 8422694. [professor, Philadelphia College of Pharmacy, 1846-1866].

PHILADELPHIA COLLEGE OF TEXTILES AND SCIENCE

2382   Ward, Arthur. The Philadelphia College of Textiles and Science. Master's thesis, University of Pennsylvania, 1963.

PHILADELPHIA SCHOOL OF PEDAGOGY

2383   Kralovec, Dalibor W. A History of the Philadelphia School of Pedagogy. Master's thesis, Temple University, 1937.

PITTSBURGH, UNIVERSITY OF

2384   Baynham, Edward G. The Founding of the University of Pittsburgh. Master's thesis, University of Pittsburgh, 1935.

2385   Blockstein, Zaga. Graduate School of Public Health, University of Pittsburgh, 1948-1973. Ph.D., University of Pittsburgh, 1974. 369p. UMI# 75-51114.

2386   Brown, Martha A. Development of the Evening School and the Downtown Division at the University of Pittsburgh. Master's thesis, University of Pittsburgh, 1933.

2387   Hartzog, Julia A. History of the Preparation of Teachers and Other Specialists in Education of Exceptional Persons in the School of Education at the University of Pittsburgh. Ph.D., University of Pittsburgh, 1976. 304p. UMI# 76-19911.

2388   Herdlein, Richard J., III. A History of the Role of the Chief Student Affairs Officer at the University of Pittsburgh, 1919-1980. Ph.D., University of Pittsburgh, 1985. 271p. UMI# 8524085

2389   Herron, John B. History of the School of Education, University of Pittsburgh, 1953-1972. Ph.D., University of Pittsburgh, 1974. 202p. UMI# 75-05134.

2390   Holmes, Ralph H. The University of Pittsburgh's Trees Hall-Community Leisure-Learn Program. Ph.D., University of Pittsburgh, 1983. 205p. UMI# 8327735.

2391   Lowenstein, Arlene J. The Falk Clinic at the University of Pittsburgh: 1931-1983. Ph.D., University of Pittsburgh, 1985. 287p. UMI# 8517976.

2392   Maszkiewicz, Ruth A. The Presbyterian Hospital of Pittsburgh: From Its Founding to Affiliation with the University of Pittsburgh. Ph.D., University of Pittsburgh, 1977. 154p. UMI# 78-01814.

2393   McFadden, Daniel H. The Commonwealth and the University: A Descriptive Study of the University of Pittsburgh as a State Related University, 1972. Ph.D., University of Pittsburgh, 1973. 181p. UMI# 74-01535.

2394   Neff, William B. History of the School of Education, University of Pittsburgh, 1910-1950. Ph.D., University of Pittsburgh, 1974. 302p. UMI# 75-04080.

2395   Noroian, Elizabeth L. The School of Nursing of the University of Pittsburgh: 1939-1973. Ph.D., University of Pittsburgh, 1980. 452p. UMI# 80-28120.

2396   Schachner, Marcia K. Western Psychiatric Institute and Clinic of the University of Pittsburgh: Its Years of Research, Teaching, and Service. Ph.D., University of Pittsburgh, 1984. 527p. UMI# 85-11020.

2397   Suhrie, Eleanor B. Evidences of the Influence of Ruth Perkes Kuehn on Nursing and Nursing Education. Ph.D., University of Pittsburgh, 1975. 241p. UMI# 76-00375. [dean of nursing, University of Pittsburgh, 1939-1961].

POINT PARK COLLEGE

2398   Bern, Paula R. Point Park College: A History. Ph.D., University of Pittsburgh, 1980. 463p. UMI# 80-18287.

SETON HILL COLLEGE

2399   Troutman, R. Dwight. Hazard Yet Forward: A History of Seton Hill College. Ph.D., University of Pittsburgh, 1978. 323p. UMI# 78-16819.

SHIPPENSBURG UNIVERSITY OF PENNSYLVANIA

2400   Hubley, John E. A History of the Cumberland Valley State Normal School and the State Teachers College, Shippensburg, Pennsylvania. Ed.D., Pennsylvania State University, 1963. 275p. UMI# 63-06299.

SLIPPERY ROCK UNIVERSITY

2401   Watson, Robert J. Slippery Rock's Journey from Normal School to Multi-Purpose State College. Ph.D., University of Pittsburgh, 1979. 210p. UMI# 79-24745.

SWARTHMORE COLLEGE

2402   Babbidge, Homer D., Jr. Swarthmore College in the Nineteenth Century: A Quaker Experience in Education. Ph.D., Yale University, 1953. 323p.

2403   Enion, Ruth C. The Intellectual Incubation of a Quaker College, 1869-1903. Master's thesis, Swarthmore College, 1944.

TEMPLE UNIVERSITY

2404   Nelson, Clyde K. The Social Ideas of Russell H. Conwell. Ph.D., University of Pennsylvania, 1968. 458p. UMI# 69-00151. [founder and president, Temple University].

2405   Sevy, Barbara. Temple University School of Medicine Library, 1910-1954. Master's thesis, Drexel Institute of Technology, 1955. 61p.

2406   Zimring, Fred R. Academic Freedom and the Cold War: The Dismissal of Barrows Dunham from Temple University, a Case Study. Ed.D., Columbia University Teachers College, 1981. 440p. UMI# 82-07351. [professor and chairman of philosophy].

THOMAS JEFFERSON UNIVERSITY

2407   Cunning, Ellen T. A History of Jefferson Medical College Library, 1898-1973. Master's thesis, Drexel Institute of Technology, 1954. 36p.

UNITED STATES ARMY WAR COLLEGE

2408   Ball, Harry P. A History of the U.S. Army War College: 1901-1940. Ph.D., University of Virginia, 1983. 454p. UMI# 8419904.

2409   Whitson, William W. The Role of the United States Army War College in the Preparation of Officers for National Security Policy Formulation. Ph.D., Tufts University, 1959.

URSINUS COLLEGE

2410   Osborne, John T. The Ursinus College Library 1869-1953. Master's thesis, Drexel Institute of Technology, 1954. 44p.

WASHINGTON AND JEFFERSON COLLEGE

2411   Caton, Lewis H., Jr. Washington and Jefferson College: In Pursuit of the Uncommon Man. Ph.D., University of Pittsburgh, 1972. 685p. UMI# 73-13286.

2412   Scarborough, David K. Intercollegiate Athletics at Washington and Jefferson College: The Building of a Tradition. Ph.D., University of Pittsburgh, 1979. 183p. UMI# 80-04833.

WEST CHESTER UNIVERSITY

2413   Dinniman, Andrew E. Academic Freedom at West Chester: The Controversy of 1927. Ed.D., Pennsylvania State University, 1978. 211p. UMI# 79-09058.

2414   Lee, Kathryn H. Westchester College: Its Formative Years, 1811-1871. Master's thesis, Westchester State College, 1965.

2415   Rentschler, David M. A History of the School of Music of West Chester College from Its Inception to 1967. Master's thesis, West Chester University, 1968.

WIDENER COLLEGE

2416   Moll, Clarence R. A History of Pennsylvania Military College, 1821-1954. Ph.D., New York University, 1955. 481p. UMI# 00-15572.

2417   Norton, John O. Widener College—Minimizing Conflict in Accomplishing Change. Ed.D., Columbia University, 1977. 207p. UMI# 77-14,745.

WILSON COLLEGE

2418   Klingerman, E.M. Wilson College Library, 1870-1950. Master's thesis, Drexel Institute of Technology, 1951.

PUERTO RICO

GENERAL STUDIES

2419   Benitez de Avila, Crucita. A Study of the Administrative Development of Higher Education in Puerto Rico from 1957 to 1973. Ed.D., Lehigh University, 1983. 364p. UMI# 8306366.

2420   Castro, Apolinario. Higher Education in Puerto Rico, 1898-1956. Ed.D., Lehigh University, 1975. 256p. UMI# 76-10,363.

2421   Falu-Pesante, Georgina. Higher Education Finances: Private Universities in Puerto Rico, 1969-1978. Ed.D., Columbia University Teachers College, 1983. 163p. UMI# 8424281.

2422   Lizardi, Marie M. Origins and Development of Social Work Education in Puerto Rico. Doctor of Social Work, Tulane University, 1983. 274p. UMI# 8406430.

2423   Petrovich, Janice R. The Expansion of Post-Secondary Schooling in Puerto Rico. Ed.D., University of Massachusetts, 1979. 219p. UMI# 8004974.

PUERTO RICO, UNIVERSITY OF

2424   Aponte-Hernandez, Rafael. The University of Puerto Rico: Foundations of the 1942 Reform. Ph.D., University of Texas, 1966. 267p. UMI# 66-14349.

2425   Baker, John H. The Relationship of Student Activism at the University of Puerto Rico to the Struggle for Independence in Puerto Rico, 1923-1971. Ph.D., Boston College, 1973. 250p. UMI# 73-21,722.

RHODE ISLAND

GENERAL STUDIES

2426   Revkin, Amelia S. The Rhode Island Board of Regents for Education, 1969-1981: A Historical Case Study of How a Governing Board Dealt with Access to Higher Education. Ed.D., Boston University, 1984. 257p. UMI# 8414727.

2427   Riccitelli, Santo J. The Rhode Island Junior College System: Its Role in Higher Education. Ph.D., Boston College, 1979. 123p. UMI# 7920450.

2428   Tolman, William H. The History of Higher Education in Rhode Island. Ph.D., Johns Hopkins University, 1891. 210p.

BROWN UNIVERSITY

2429   Brown, Dorothy O. Civil War Songs in the Harris Collection of American Poetry and Plays at Brown University. Master's thesis, Brown University, 1959. 192p.

2430   Crane, Theodore R. Francis Wayland and Brown University, 1796-1841. Ph.D., Harvard University, 1959. [president, 1827-1855].

2431   Desjarlais-Lueth, Christine. Brown University and Its Library: A Study of the Beginnings of an Academic Library. Ed.D., University of Illinois, 1985. 212p. UMI# 8521753.

2432   Hansen, James E., II. Gallant, Stalwart Bennie: Elisha Benjamin Andrews (1844-1917): An Educator's Odyssey. Ph.D., University of Denver, 1969. 411p. UMI# 69-22243. [professor of history and president, Brown University, 1883-1898].

2433   Laurent, David. Secular Music Published in America Before 1830 in the Harris Collection of American Poetry at Brown University. Master's thesis, Brown University, 1953.

2434   McGovern, James H. College Presidents and Community Leadership: Brown University, 1764-1897. Ph.D., Boston College, 1975. 334p. UMI# 75-21,287.

2435   Van Horn, Harold E. Humanist as Educator: The Public Life of Henry Merrit Wriston. Ph.D., University of Denver, 1968. 418p. UMI# 69-13666. [president, Brown University, 1937-1955].

2436   West, Earle H. The Life and Educational Contributions of Barnas Sears (Volumes 1 and 2). Ph.D., George Peabody College for Teachers, 1961. 664p. UMI# 61-05832. [president, Brown University, 1855-1867].

PROVIDENCE COLLEGE

2437   McCaffrey, Donna T. The Origins and Early History of Providence College through 1947. Ph.D., Providence College, 1985. 537p. UMI# 8503904.

RHODE ISLAND COLLEGE

2438   Carbone, Hector R. The History of the Rhode Island Institute of Instruction and the Rhode Island Normal School as Agencies and Institutions of Teacher Education, 1845-1920. Ph.D., University of Connecticut, 1971. 440p. UMI# 71-29849.

2439   Lavery, Thomas F. Factors Related to the Development of Curricula for the Preparation of Secondary School Teachers at Rhode Island College, 1952-1972. Ph.D., University of Connecticut, 1974. 355p. UMI# 74-07124.

RHODE ISLAND, UNIVERSITY OF

2440   Eschenbacher, Herman F., Jr. Rhode Island and Its Land Grant College, 1863-1914: A Case Study of the Establishment of a Morrill Act College in New England. Ph.D., Harvard University, 1963.

2441   Hackett, John R. A History of Extension Education at the University of Rhode Island. Master's thesis, Rhode Island College, 1951. 89p.

UNITED STATES NAVAL WAR COLLEGE

2442   Kennedy, Gerald J. United States Naval War College, 1919-1941: An Institutional Response to Naval Preparedness. Ph.D., University of Minnesota, 1975. 385p. UMI# 75-27163.

2443   Spector, Ronald H. Professors of War: The Naval War College and the Modern American Navy. Ph.D., Yale University, 1967. 334p. UMI# 68-06852.

2444   Vlahos, Michael E. The Blue Sword: The Naval War College, and the American Mission, 1919-1941. Ph.D., Tufts University, 1981.

SOUTH CAROLINA

GENERAL STUDIES

2445   Canady, Hoyt P., Jr. Gentlemen of the Bar: Lawyers in Colonial South Carolina. Ph.D., University of Tennessee, 1979. 461p. UMI# 8005377.

2446   Charles, Allan D. History of Dentistry in South Carolina. Ph.D., University of South Carolina, 1981. 226p. UMI# 81-23402.

2447   Elder, Fred K. Freedom in South Carolina as Shown by Church State Relationships in Higher Education in South Carolina. Ph.D., University of North Carolina, 1940. 239p.

2448   Fries, Walter G. Developments in the Certification of Teachers in South Carolina, 1925-1961. Ed.D., Florida State University, 1962. 137p. UMI# 63-01811.

2449   McCain, John W., Jr. Development of Financial Support for the University of South Carolina, the Citadel, Clemson College, and Winthrop College as Revealed in Legislative Action. Master's thesis, Duke University, 1932.

2450   Meriwether, Colyer. History of Higher Education in South Carolina, with a Sketch of the Free School System. Ph.D., Johns Hopkins University, 1893. 247p.

2451   Sanford, Paul L. The Origins and Development of Higher Education for Negroes in South Carolina to 1920. Ph.D., University of New Mexico, 1965. 184p. UMI# 66-04451.

2452   Yarborough, Legrand I. A History of the Early Teaching of Agriculture in South Carolina. Ed.D., University of Florida, 1956. 160p. UMI# 00-17560.

ANDERSON COLLEGE

2453   Lindsey, William H. A Study of Anderson College During the Administration of Dr. Annie D. Denmark. Master's thesis, Furman University, 1955.

BENEDICT COLLEGE

2454   Richardson, Frederick. A Power for Good in Society: The History of Benedict College. Ph.D., Florida State University, 1973. 275p. UMI# 74-18039.

CLIFFORD SEMINARY

2455   Bennett, Emerson S. A History of Clifford Seminary, Union, South Carolina. Master's thesis, University of South Carolina, 1931.

COKER COLLEGE

2456   Parrish, William S. A History of Coker College. Master's thesis, University of South Carolina, 1938. 122p.

COLUMBIA COLLEGE

2457   Winn, Evelyn B. A History of Columbia College, Columbia, South Carolina. Master's thesis, University of South Carolina, 1927.

ERSKINE COLLEGE

2458   Kennedy, Walter A., Jr. The History of Erskine College to Confederate War. Master's thesis, University of South Carolina, 1945.

2459   Lesesne, Joab M., Jr. A Hundred Years of Erskine College, 1839-1939. Ph.D., University of South Carolina, 1967. 318p. UMI# 68-03932.

FURMAN UNIVERSITY

2460   Kinlaw, Howard M. Richard Furman as a Leader in Baptist Higher Education. Ph.D., George Peabody College for Teachers, 1960. 228p. UMI# 60-05865. [founder, Furman University].

2461   Wilkinson, Carl W., III. The Life and Work of William Joseph McGlothlin. Ph.D., Southern Baptist Theological Seminary, 1981. 267p. UMI# 81-13636. [president, Furman University, 1919-1933].

GREENWOOD FEMALE COLLEGE

2462   Deutsch, Lucille S. The Giles Sisters' Contribution Toward Higher Education of Women in the South: 1874-1904. Ph.D., University of Pittsburgh, 1978. 95p. UMI# 79-17418.

LIMESTONE COLLEGE

2463   Taylor, Walter C. History of Limestone College. Master's thesis, University of South Carolina, 1934.

MORRIS COLLEGE

2464   Sims, Frank K. A Socio-Historical Study of Morris College, Sumter, South Carolina. Master's thesis, Tennessee Agricultural & Industrial State University, 1960.

NEWBERRY COLLEGE

2465   Bedenbaugh, Jefferson H. A History of Newberry College, Newberry, South Carolina. Master's thesis, University of South Carolina, 1930.

2466   Kaufmann, Christopher A. A History of the Curriculum of Newberry College. Master's thesis, University of South Carolina, 1954.

PENN SCHOOL

2467   Harris, Yvonne B. The History of the Penn School Under Its Founders at St. Helena Island, Frogmore, South Carolina, 1862-1908. Ph.D., American University, 1979. 177p. UMI# 80-00753.

SOUTH CAROLINA COLLEGE

2468   Gustafson, Robert K. A Study of the Life of James Woodrow Emphasizing His Theological and Scientific Views as They Relate to the Evolution Controversy. Ph.D., Union Theological Seminary in Virginia, 1964. 777p. UMI# 83-00756. [president and professor, South Carolina College, 1880-1897].

SOUTH CAROLINA, UNIVERSITY OF

2469   Giles, Dorcus O. Development of the School of Education, University of South Carolina, 1882-1930. Master's thesis, University of South Carolina, 1966.

2470   Green, Charles E. A History of the Development of the Entrance Requirements of the South Carolina College and the University of South Carolina. Master's thesis, University of South Carolina, 1929.

2471   Hollis, Daniel W. South Carolina College. Ph.D., Columbia University, 1953.

2472   Long, Howard O. A Biography of Professor William Knox Tate: Southern Educational Engineer. Ph.D., George Peabody College for Teachers, 1953. [professor of elementary education, University of South Carolina, 1910-1914].

2473   Malone, Dumas. The Public Life and Writings of Thomas Cooper, 1783-1839. Ph.D., Yale University, 1923. 432p. [president, University of South Carolina].

2474   Singleton, Edward M. A History of the Regional Campus System of the University of South Carolina. Ph.D., University of South Carolina, 1971. UMI# 71-28895.

2475   Wilson, Herman K., III. The University of South Carolina College of Education: The First Fifty Years, 1883-1930. Ph.D., University of South Carolina, 1981. 287p. UMI# 81-29486.

SPARTANBURG JUNIOR COLLEGE

2476   Shealy, Cyrus S. A History of Spartanburg Junior College. Master's thesis, University of South Carolina, 1965.

SUMMERLAND COLLEGE

2477   McKenzie, Pearle. A History of Summerland College. Master's thesis, University of South Carolina, 1929.

VOORHEES COLLEGE

2478   Jabs, Albert E. The Mission of Voorhees College: Its Roots and Its Future. Ed.D., University of South Carolina, 1983. 205p. UMI# 8409311.

WINTHROP COLLEGE

2479   Fleming, Rhonda K. A History of the Department of Physical Education at Winthrop College, 1886-1970. Master's thesis, University of North Carolina at Greensboro, 1974.

WOMAN'S COLLEGE OF DUE WEST

2480   Wingard, Kathleen M. History of the Woman's College of Due West, South Carolina. Master's thesis, University of South Carolina, 1928.

SOUTH DAKOTA

GENERAL STUDIES

2481 Belding, Lester C. A History and Survey of Physical Education and Athletics in the South Dakota Intercollegiate Athletic Conference. Master's thesis, University of Iowa, 1940.

2482 Haslem, Melvin. A Study of the Development of Teachers Colleges in South Dakota. Master's thesis, Colorado Agricultural College, 1933.

2483 Hermann, Robert L. A History of the Efforts by the South Dakota Higher Education Faculty Association to Become the Collective Bargaining Unit for State Institutions Under the Jurisdiction of the Regents of Education: 1969-1974. Ed.D., University of South Dakota, 1979. 317p. UMI# 79-19035.

2484 Woodburn, Ethelbert C. The History and Development of Teachers' Colleges in South Dakota. Master's thesis, University of Chicago, 1928.

AUGUSTANA COLLEGE

2485 Hanson, Richard S. Augustana College, Canton, South Dakota, 1884-1919. Master's thesis, University of South Dakota, 1939. 48p.

2486 Meyer, Edward L. A History of Speech Education at Augustana College, 1884-1954. Master's thesis, University of South Dakota, 1953.

DAKOTA STATE COLLEGE

2487 Stewart, Charles J. A History of Eastern South Dakota State Normal School. Master's thesis, University of South Dakota, 1938.

DAKOTA WESLEYAN UNIVERSITY

2488 Johnson, Halvin S. A History of the Department of Education of Dakota Wesleyan University. Master's thesis, University of South Dakota, 1957.

2489 Shilling, Katheryn T. The History of Dramatic Art at Dakota Wesleyan University. Master's thesis, University of South Dakota, 1957.

SIOUX FALLS COLLEGE

2490 Sampson, Harold P. The History of Speech Education at Sioux Falls College. Master's thesis, University of South Dakota, 1953.

SOUTH DAKOTA SCHOOL OF MINES AND TECHNOLOGY

2491 Hilbert, John E. History of Speech Education at the South Dakota School of Mines and Technology, 1887-1960. Master's thesis, University of South Dakota, 1960.

SOUTH DAKOTA STATE UNIVERSITY

2492   Sladek, Lyle V. The History of Speech Education at South Dakota State College, 1884-1948. Master's thesis, South Dakota University, 1949.

2493   Zahorsky, Arthur. A History of Intercollegiate Athletics at South Dakota State. Master's thesis, South Dakota State University, 1959. 91p.

SOUTH DAKOTA, UNIVERSITY OF

2494   Allen, Roger B. A History of Radio and Television at the State University of South Dakota, 1949-1956. Master's thesis, University of South Dakota, 1963.

2495   Blake, Roger O. Selected Implications for the University of South Dakota in Becoming a Tri-State Supported University. Ed.D., University of South Dakota, 1973. 161p. UMI# 74-04073.

2496   Collins, Betty J. History of Dramatic Art at the University of South Dakota from 1882-1947. Master's thesis, South Dakota University, 1948.

2497   Dalen, Adrian E. A History of KUSD, the University of South Dakota Radio Station. Master's thesis, University of South Dakota, 1949.

2498   Duerre, Chester W. The Development of Educational Television (ETV) and Its Growth at the University of South Dakota. Master's thesis, University of South Dakota, 1966.

2499   Haase, Richard T. The History of Intercollegiate Football, Basketball, Track and Baseball at the State University of South Dakota. Master's thesis, University of South Dakota, 1965.

2500   Truman, Margot. The History of Speech Education in the University of South Dakota, 1882-1942. Master's thesis, University of South Dakota, 1947.

SOUTH DAKOTA, UNIVERSITY OF (SPRINGFIELD)

2501   Olsen, Obed M. The History of Speech Education at Southern State Teachers College, 1879-1948. Master's thesis, South Dakota University, 1951.

WESSINGTON SPRINGS COLLEGE

2502   Waller, Fred. A History of Wessington Springs College. Master's thesis, University of South Dakota, 1935.

TENNESSEE

GENERAL STUDIES

2503   Carter, Carolyn J. The Major Issues in the Merger of the Public Black and White Universities in Nashville, Tennessee: Implications for Montgomery, Alabama. Ed.D., Wayne State University, 1982. 250p. UMI# 8216136.

2504   Clough, Dick B. A History of Teachers' Institutes in Tennessee, 1875-1915. Ed.D., Memphis State University, 1972. 259p. UMI# 73-10393.

2505   Crain, Charles R. Music Performance and Pedagogy in Nashville, Tennessee, 1818-1900. Ph.D., George Peabody College for Teachers, 1975. 314p. UMI# 75-22,257.

2506   Fleming, Cynthia G. The Development of Black Education in Tennessee, 1865-1920. Ph.D., Duke University, 1977. 226p. UMI# 7807595.

2507   Horton, Allison N. Origin and Development of the State College Movement in Tennessee. Ph.D., George Peabody College for Teachers, 1954.

2508   Humphreys, Cecil C. State Financial Support to Higher Education in Tennessee from 1930 to 1952. Ph.D., New York University, 1957. 373p. UMI# 58-00652.

2509   Hunter, Catherine H. A History of Higher Education in Franklin County, Tennessee. Master's thesis, University of Tennessee, 1940.

2510   Kennedy, Elizabeth C. The Development of Higher Education in Tennessee for Negroes, 1865-1900. Master's thesis, Fisk University, 1950.

2511   Laska, Lewis L. A History of Legal Education in Tennessee, 1770-1970. Ph.D., George Peabody College for Teachers, 1978. 818p. UMI# 79-02503.

2512   Lewis, Stanley J. The History and Contributions of the Private Secondary Schools and Colleges in the Chattanooga Area. Master's thesis, University of Virginia, 1951.

2513   Phelph, Margaret S. The University of Tennessee-Memphis State University Center for Advanced Graduate Study in Education and Duplication for the Continuing Education of Educational Leaders. Ed.D., University of Tennessee, 1975. 245p. UMI# 76-11,080.

2514   Rhoda, Richard G.A Study of Transition in the Governance Structure of Tennessee Higher Education. Ph.D., George Peabody College for Teachers, 1985. 179p. UMI# 8527866.

2515   Smith, Janet F. The History of Tennessee Community Colleges: 1957-1979. Ph.D., George Peabody College for Teachers, 1983. 300p. UMI# 83-19078.

2516   Ward, Richard H. The Development of Baptist Higher Education in Tennessee. Ph.D., George Peabody College for Teachers, 1954.

2517   Witherington, Henry C. A History of State Higher Education in Tennessee. Ph.D., University of Chicago, 1931. 271p.

AUSTIN PEAY STATE UNIVERSITY

2518   Condell, Robert. A History of Austin Peay State University. Master's thesis, University of Tennessee at Knoxville, 1971.

BETHEL COLLEGE

2519   Oliver, Mary C. History of Bethel College. Master's thesis, Murray State College, 1946.

BURRITT COLLEGE

2520   West, Francis M. Pioneer of the Cumberlands: A History of Burritt College, 1848-1938. Master's thesis, Tennessee Technological University, 1969.

CARSON-NEWMAN COLLEGE

2521   Hall, William F. History of Carson Newman College. Master's thesis, University of Tennessee, 1936.

2522   Jones, John C. The Origin and Development of Intercollegiate Athletics at Carson Newman College. Ed.D., University of Georgia, 1973. 295p. UMI# 73-31907.

CHRISTIAN BROTHERS COLLEGE

2523   Witt, Michael J. The Devolution of Christian Brothers College: 1900-1931. Ph.D., Saint Louis University, 1980. 270p. UMI# 81-01279.

CUMBERLAND FEMALE COLLEGE

2524   Nunley, Joe E. A History of the Cumberland Female College, McMinnville, Tennessee. Ed.D., University of Tennessee, 1965. 153p. UMI# 66-00186.

DAVID LIPSCOMB COLLEGE

2525   Neil, Robert G. The History of David Lipscomb College. Master's thesis, George Peabody College for Teachers, 1938. 107p.

FISK UNIVERSITY

2526   Atkins, Eliza. A History of Fisk University Library and Its Standing in Relation to the Libraries of Other Comparable Institutions. Master's thesis, University of California-Berkeley, 1936. 83p.

2527   Beamon, Harry. The Rise and Demise of Physical Education at Fisk University: A Historical Analysis. Ed.D., George Peabody College for Teachers, 1979. 158p. UMI# 81-05428.

GEORGE PEABODY COLLEGE FOR TEACHERS

2528   Baird, James O. The Life and Works of Charles Edgar Little. Ph.D., George Peabody

College for Teachers, 1949. [professor of classical languages, George Peabody College for Teachers].

2529   Beasley, Wallis. The Life and Educational Contributions of James D. Porter. Ph.D., George Peabody College for Teachers, 1949. 231p. [governor of Tennessee, 1875-1879; president, board of trustees, George Peabody College for Teachers].

2530   Cochrane, Robert M. Fletcher Bascom Dresslar: His Life and Works. Ed.D., George Peabody College for Teachers, 1955. 162p. UMI# 00-15463. [George Peabody College for Teachers, 1912-1930; University of California, 1897-1909].

2531   Cullum, Edward N. George Peabody College for Teachers, 1914-1937. Ed.D., George Peabody College for Teachers, 1963. 620p. UMI# 64-05069.

2532   Dillingham, George A., Jr. Peabody Normal College in Southern Education, 1875-1909. Ph.D., George Peabody College for Teachers, 1970. 227p. UMI# 70-23349.

2533   Duncan, Ruth B. A History of the George Peabody College Library, 1785-1910. Master's thesis, George Peabody College for Teachers, 1940.

2534   Evans, George K. The American Career of Michael J. Demiashkevich. Ph.D., George Peabody College for Teachers, 1959. 447p. UMI# 59-03494. [professor of education, George Peabody College for Teachers, 1929-1938].

2535   Hall, Ida J. A History of Cumberland College. Master's thesis, University of Tennessee, 1962.

2536   Hedges, William D. Doctoral Candidates at George Peabody College for Teachers from 1919-1950. Ed.D., George Peabody College for Teachers, 1958. 355p. UMI# 59-01104.

2537   Howell, Isabel. Montgomery Bell Academy: A Chapter in the History of the University of Nashville. Master's thesis, George Peabody College for Teachers, 1940.

2538   Kegley, Tracy M. The Peabody Scholarships, 1877-1899. Ph.D., George Peabody College for Teachers, 1949. 231p.

2539   Kelton, Allen. The University of Nashville, 1850-1875. Ph.D., George Peabody College for Teachers, 1969. 968p. UMI# 70-07634.

2540   Morgan, Kenimer H. The University of Nashville, 1825-1850. (Volumes One and Two). Ph.D., George Peabody College for Teachers, 1960. 883p. UMI# 60-02912.

2541   Parker, Franklin. George Peabody, Founder of Modern Philanthropy (Volumes One-Three). Ed.D., George Peabody College for Teachers, 1956. 1,239p. UMI# 19,758.

2542   Poret, George C. The Contributions of William Harold Payne to Public Education. Ph.D., George Peabody College for Teachers, 1930. 164p. [president, George Peabody College for Teachers, 1888-1901].

2543   Robert, Edward B. The Administration of the Peabody Education Fund from 1880 to 1905. Ph.D., George Peabody College for Teachers, 1936.

2544   Trice, Ethel P. The Influence of George Peabody College for Teachers on Physical

Education in Southern Colleges. Ed.D., George Peabody College for Teachers, 1961. 360p. UMI# 61-05831.

2545   Waffle, Eugene M. Eben Sperry Stearns: Pioneer in American Education. Ph.D., George Peabody College for Teachers, 1940. 163p. [chancellor, George Peabody College for Teachers, 1875-1887].

2546   Wills, Lynette A. H. Peabody Women Doctorates: 1961-1975. Ph.D., George Peabody College for Teachers, 1978. 230p. UMI# 7902516.

2547   Windrow, John E. The Life and Works of John Berrrian Lindsley. Ph.D., George Peabody College for Teachers, 1937. [chancellor, George Peabody College for Teachers, 1855-1870].

HIWASSEE COLLEGE

2548   Amburgey, James H. An Analysis of the Decision-Making Process for Historically Important Decisions Made at Hiwassee College, 1955-1970. Ed.D., University of Tennessee, 1973. 221p. UMI# 74-03792.

LAMBUTH COLLEGE

2549   Hinton, David E. Origin, Development and Aims of Lambuth College. Master's thesis, George Peabody College for Teachers, 1936.

LANE COLLEGE

2550   Adair, Thomas J. Bishop Isaac Lane, a Portrait: 1834-1914. Master's thesis, Tennessee State A&I University, 1956. [trustee, Lane College].

LEE COLLEGE

2551   Hughes, Ray H. The Transition of Church-Related Junior Colleges to Senior Colleges, with Implications for Lee College. Ed.D., University of Tennessee, 1966. 249p. UMI# 67-01368.

2552   Ray, Mauldin A. A Study of the History of Lee College, Cleveland, Tennessee. Ed.D., University of Houston, 1964. 242p. UMI# 64-10617.

2553   Stephens, Raphael W., III. A History of the Governance at Lee College: A Study in Pentecostal Higher Education. Ed.D., College of William & Mary, 1981. 161p. UMI# 82-06125.

LEMOYNE OWEN COLLEGE

2554   Qualls, J. Winfield. The Beginnings and Early History of the LeMoyne School at Memphis—1871-1874. Master's thesis, Memphis State University, 1952.

2555   Searcy, Sylvia C.L. Critical Decisions Affecting the 1968 Merger Between LeMoyne College and Owen College of Memphis, Tennessee. Ph.D., Southern Illinois University at Carbondale, 1981. 154p. UMI# 8206496.

MARSHALL COLLEGE

2556   Toole, Robert C. History of Marshall College, 1837 to 1915. Master's thesis, Marshall College, 1951.

MEMPHIS STATE UNIVERSITY

2557   Ford, Helen L. An Academic History of the State Teachers College, Memphis, Tennessee. Master's thesis, George Peabody College for Teachers, 1937. 89p.

2558   Stathis, John C. The Establishment and Early Development of the West Tennessee State Normal School 1909-1914. Master's thesis, Memphis State University, 1951.

2559   Wooten, Rebecca G. A History of Memphis State College. Master's thesis, University of Texas, 1942.

MIDDLE TENNESSEE STATE UNIVERSITY

2560   Pittard, Homer. Middle Tennessee State College: Its Historical Aspects and Its Relation to Significant Teacher Education Movements. Ed.D., George Peabody College for Teachers, 1957. 482p. UMI# 00-24484.

MILLIGAN COLLEGE

2561   Stout, Billy H. A History of Intercollegiate Athletics at Milligan College, 1887-1973. Ed.D., East Tennessee State University, 1974. 282p. UMI# 75-05008.

MORRISTOWN COLLEGE

2562   Hammond, Brenda H. A Historical Analysis of Selected Forces and Events Which Influenced the Founding, Growth, and Development of Morristown College, a Historically Black Two-Year College from 1881 to 1981. Ed.D., George Washington University, 1983. 374p. UMI# 8307884.

SOUTH, UNIVERSITY OF THE

2533   Finney, Raymond A. History of the Private Educational Institutions of Franklin County, Tennessee. Master's thesis, University of Tennessee, 1939.

2564   Keene, Charles J., Jr. Alexander Guerry: Educator. Ph.D., George Peabody College for Teachers, 1952. [president, University of the South].

TENNESSEE MEDICAL COLLEGE

2565   Orr, Billy M. A History of Tennessee Medical College, 1889-1914. Master's thesis, University of Tennessee, 1960.

TENNESSEE STATE UNIVERSITY

2566   Fancher, Evelyn P. Tennessee State University (1912-1974): A History of an Institution with Implications for the Future. Ph.D., George Peabody College for Teachers, 1975. 302p. UMI# 76-03721.

2567   Shannon, Samuel H. Agricultural and Industrial Education at Tennessee State University During the Normal School Phase, 1912-1922: A Case Study. Ph.D., George Peabody College for Teachers, 1974. 350p. UMI# 74-29,188.

2568   Simmons, Joseph D. A History of the Development of the Curriculum in Health, Physical Education and Recreation at the Tennessee A&I University, 1912-1953. Master's thesis, Tennessee Agricultural & Industrial University, 1955.

2569   Watkins, Mary B.S. Historical and Biographical Studies of Women Olympic Participants at Tennessee State University, 1948-1980: Implications and Recommendations for Program and Staff Development. Ed.D., George Peabody College for Teachers, 1980. 245p. UMI# 81-16085.

TENNESSEE, UNIVERSITY OF

2570   Arwood, Victor B. The History of Varsity Basketball at the University of Tennessee. Master's thesis, University of Tennessee, 1968.

2571   Davis, Betty. The Master's Program in Teacher Education at the University of Tennessee, 1909-1951. Master's thesis, University of Tennessee, 1953.

2572   Hornburckle, Adam R. Women's Sports and Physical Education at the University of Tennessee, 1899-1939. Master's thesis, University of Tennessee, 1984.

2573   Jarrell, John E. The History and Development of the Air Force Reserve Officers' Training Corps at the University of Tennessee. Master's thesis, University of Tennessee, 1956.

2574   Montgomery, James R. The University of Tennessee During the Administration of President Brown Ayres, 1904-1919. Master's thesis, University of Tennessee, 1956.

2575   Montgomery, James R. The University of Tennessee, 1887-1919. Ph.D., Columbia University, 1961. 375p. UMI# 62-00094.

2576   Petree, Colbert G. A Survey of the History of Music and Music Education at the University of Tennessee. Master's thesis, University of Tennessee at Knoxville, 1965.

TENNESSEE, UNIVERSITY OF (MARTIN)

2577   Inman, Elmer B. A History of the Development of the University of Tennessee, Martin Branch. Ed.D., University of Tennessee, 1960. 250p. UMI# 60-02497.

TREVECCA NAZARENE COLLEGE

2578   Cole, Harper L., Jr. A Study of the Governance Style of A.B. Mackey, President of Trevecca Nazarene College, 1936-1963. Ed.D., Oklahoma State University, 1978. 276p. UMI# 7903655.

2579   Downey, J. Paul. History of Trevecca Nazarene College. Master's thesis, University of Alabama, 1938.

TUSCULUM COLLEGE

2580   Bailey, Gilbert L. A History of Tusculum College, 1944-1964. Master's thesis, Tennessee State University, 1965.

WASHINGTON COLLEGE

2581   Carr, Howard E. Washington College: A Study of an Attempt to Provide Higher Education in Eastern Tennessee. Master's thesis, Duke University, 1935.

TEXAS

GENERAL STUDIES

2582   Ables, Luther R. Purposes of Texas Public Junior Colleges: An Historical Approach. Ph.D., University of Texas Austin, 1970. 195p. UMI# 71-11505.

2583   Aiken, Wreathy P. A Survey of the Social and Philosophical Factors Which Have Affected the Higher Education of White Women in Texas, 1825-1945. Ph.D., University of Texas at Austin, 1946. 399p.

2584   Alexander, George D. The Historical Development of State Aid in Texas, 1930-1968. Ph.D., East Texas State University, 1970. 165p. UMI# 71-00219.

2585   Allen, Ernest L. History of the Colleges in Bell County. Master's thesis, Southwest State Teachers College, 1957.

2586   Barnard, Hilliard. History of the Development of the Junior Colleges in Texas. Master's thesis, North Texas State Teachers College, 1936. 100p.

2587   Castleberry, Martha A.F. The History of the Teaching of Oral English in Texas Colleges. Master's thesis, University of Texas, 1933.

2588   Christopher, Nehemiah M. The History of Negro Public Education in Texas, 1865-1900. Ph.D., University of Pittsburgh, 1949.

2589   Comer, John R. The Origin and Development of the Junior College, with Special Reference to Texas. Master's thesis, University of Texas, 1927.

2590   Crossley, Samuel M. A Study of Methodist Higher Education in Texas. Ed.D., North Texas State University, 1983. 162p. UMI# 8404307.

2591   Crowder, Eleanor L.M. The Evolution of Diploma Curricula of Three Schools of Nursing in Texas: An Historical Treatment. Ph.D., University of Texas, 1979. 227p. UMI# 80-09845.

2592   Daley, Billy D. The Development of Public Junior College Financing in Texas. Ed.D., University of Texas, 1959. 172p. UMI# 59-2501.

2593   Dodson, Pat S. Development and Present Status of the Junior College in Texas. Master's thesis, Texas Christian University, 1931.

2594   Dyess, Stewart W. A History and Analysis of Library Formula Funding in Texas Public Higher Education. Ed.D., Texas Tech University, 1977. 99p. UMI# 77-25504.

2595   Ford, Hoyt. The Junior College Movement in Texas. Ph.D., University of Texas, 1940. 239p.

2596   Fouts, Theron J. The History and Influence of Football in Texas Colleges and Universities. Master's thesis, Southern Methodist University, 1927.

2597   Gibbons, Harold E. The Historical Development of the Dallas County Community College District: A Study of a Multi-College District. Ph.D., University of Oklahoma, 1975. 151p. UMI# 76-03079.

2598   Glick, Walter R. Hiram A. Boaz. Ph.D., University of Texas at Austin, 1949. [president, Texas Wesleyan College, 1902-1911; Texas Woman's University, 1913-1918].

2599   Harlan, William L. An Historical Study of the Trends Toward Collective Bargaining in Public Education in Texas. Ed.D., East Texas State University, 1978. 194p. UMI# 79-09656.

2600   Harrison, Ardie R. A History of the Association of Texas Colleges. Master's thesis, Baylor University, 1933.

2601   Hays, Charles D. Significant Elements Contributing to the Success and Failure of Six Junior Colleges in Texas. Ph.D., Texas A&M University, 1971. 176p. UMI# 72-05668.

2602   Heintze, Michael R. A History of the Black Private Colleges in Texas, 1865-1954. Ph.D., Texas Tech University, 1981. 344p. UMI# 8202071.

2603   Johnson, Roy J. Music Education in Texas Higher Institutions, 1840-1947. Ph.D., University of Texas at Austin, 1951.

2604   Jones, Lewis N. Ghost Colleges on the South Plains. Master's thesis, Texas Technological College, 1939.

2605   Laird, Ray A. The Development of the Junior College in Texas. Ph.D., University of Texas, 1952.

2606   Lanier, Raphael O. The History of Higher Education for Negroes in Texas, 1930-1955, with Particular Reference to Texas Southern University. Ed.D., New York University, 1957. 331p. UMI# 58-00634.

2607   Marcom, Robert. An Historical Assessment of Articulation Between Junior Colleges and Selected Upper Division Universities in Texas. Ph.D., University of Texas, 1976. 142p. UMI# 77-3948.

2608   McLeroy, Nellie M. A History of Texas Baptist Training Union Work from 1891 to 1950. Ph.D., Southwestern Baptist Theological Seminary, 1959.

2609   Miller, Frederick R. A History of the Development of the Theatre Programs in Selected Texas Junior Colleges. Ph.D., University of Texas at Austin, 1963. 138p. UMI# 64-06619.

2610   Moseley, Carolyn. Higher Education in Texas. Master's thesis, University of Texas, 1967.

2611   Mullins, Lula L. A History of the Methodist Junior Colleges in Texas. Master's thesis, University of Texas, 1937.

2612   Ortega-Wheless, Ludivina G. Growth Patterns of the Texas Coordinating Board for Higher Education: A Theoretical Analysis of Its Bureaucratic Nature. Ph.D., University of California-Berkeley, 1981. 184p. UMI# 82-00231.

2613   Parker, Edith H. History of Land Grants for Education in Texas. Ph.D., University of Texas at Austin, 1952.

2614   Patton, B. Development of the American Association of University Women in Texas. Master's thesis, Texas Technological College, 1941.

2615   Phelps, Ralph A., Jr. The Struggle for Public Higher Education for Negroes in Texas. Ph.D., Southwestern Baptist Theological Seminary, 1949.

2616   Pope, Emma. History of Nursing Education in Texas. Master's thesis, Southern Methodist University, 1937. 154p.

2617   Pruitt, Harvie M. A Study of the Speech Programs at the Colleges and Universities of Texas. Master's thesis, Texas Technological College, 1953.

2618   Randolph, William L. An Interpretive Analysis of the Political Process Involved in the Establishment and Development of the Dallas County Community College District: 1964-74. Ed.D., North Texas State University, 1974. 238p. UMI# 75-13680.

2619   Roark, Daniel B. The Junior College Movement in Texas. Master's thesis, Baylor University, 1926.

2620   Sewell, Tom S. An Analysis of the Public Junior College Movement in Texas, 1922-1973. Ed.D., University of Houston, 1975. 459p. UMI# 75-2947.

2621   Shelton, William E. A History of Public Education in Texas During the Reconstruction Period. Ph.D., University of Chicago, 1951.

2622   Shockley, Ethel V. The Junior College Movement in Texas. Master's thesis, Texas Christian University, 1928.

2623   Smith, Clustor Q. Senior Colleges and Universities in Texas, 1906-1936. Master's thesis, Southern Methodist University, 1939.

2624   Snowden, Gary L. An Historical Study of the Life and Times of R.E.B. Baylor: His Contributions to Texas and Texas Baptists. Ph.D., Southwestern Baptist Theological Seminary, 1986. 260p. UMI# 8614905. [chairman, board of trustees, Baylor University].

2625   Stevenson, William I. History of the Junior College Movement as Fostered by the Churches of Christ in Texas. Master's thesis, University of Texas, 1930.

2626   Taliaferro, William. A Historical Study of Campus Governance, Tenure and Salaries in Public Two-Year Colleges in Texas. Ed.D., University of Houston, 1979. 352p. UMI# 79-19393.

2627   Thompson, Lloyd K. The Origins and Development of Black Religious Colleges in East Texas. Ph.D., North Texas State University, 1976. 178p. UMI# 77-11122.

2628   Tompson, Horace R. Origin and Development of Teachers' Colleges of Texas. Master's thesis, New York University, 1929.

2629   Waddell, Frederick J. A Historical Review of the Coordination of Higher Education in Texas. Ed.D., North Texas State University, 1972. 195p. UMI# 73-02931.

2630   Warren, J.I. The Development and Present Status of the Municipal Junior College in Texas. Master's thesis, Texas Technological College, 1935. 115p.

2631   Webb, Russell F. History of Early Colleges of Callahan County, Texas. Master's thesis, Hardin-Simmons University, 1949.

2632   White, Michael A. History of Education in Texas, 1860-1884. Ed.D., Baylor University, 1969. 347p. UMI# 70-08023.

2633   Williams, David A. The History of Higher Education for Black Texans, 1872-1977. Ed.D., Baylor University, 1978. 192p. UMI# 78-22691.

2634   Winship, Frank L. The Development of Educational Theater in Texas. Ph.D., University of Texas, 1953. 323p.

2635   Wootton, Ralph T. Oscar Henry Cooper: Master Builder in Texas Education. Ed.D., University of Texas at Austin, 1959. 320p. UMI# 59-06739. [president, Hardin-Simmons University, 1902-1909].

2636   Younker, Donna L. Teacher Education in Texas, 1879-1919. Ph.D., University of Texas, 1964. 260p. UMI# 64-11,862.

ABILENE CHRISTIAN UNIVERSITY

2637   Banowski, William S. A Historical Study of Speechmaking at the Abilene Christian College Lectureship, 1918-1961. Ph.D., University of Southern California, 1963. 745p. UMI# 64-03091.

2638   Beck, Don E. A History of Speech Education at Abilene Christian College, 1906-1958. Master's thesis, Abilene Christian College, 1959.

2639   Cosgrove, Owen G. The Administration of Don Heath Morris at Abilene Christian College. Ph.D., North Texas State University, 1976. 273p. UMI# 76-29,130. [president and chancellor, 1940-1974].

2640   Craig, Earl L. The Development of Abilene Christian College. Master's thesis, West Texas State College, 1940.

2641   Hardcastle, Pat. A Homiletic Analysis of the Abilene Christian College Lectures on Preaching from 1951-1955. Master's thesis, Abilene Christian College, 1967.

AMARILLO COLLEGE

2642   Curl, Carroll A. The History of Amarillo College, 1929-1946. Master's thesis, West Texas State College, 1947.

ANGELO STATE UNIVERSITY

2643   Rawls, Ruth E. Angelo State College, 1926-1965. Master's thesis, Southwest Texas State College, 1969.

AUSTIN COLLEGE

2644   Wallace, Percival E. The History of Austin College. Master's thesis, University of Texas, 1924.

BAYLOR UNIVERSITY

2645   Adams, Charles S. Twentieth Century Baylor University Presidents and Christian Education: The Educational Philosophies of Samuel Palmer Brooks, Pat Morris Neff, and William Richardson White. Master's thesis, Baylor University, 1964.

2646   Amyett, Paddy D.W. A History of Literary Societies at Baylor University. Master's thesis, Baylor University, 1963.

2647   Bennett, Ray E. Pat M. Neff: His Denominational Leadership. Master's thesis, Baylor University, 1960. [president, Baylor University, 1932-1947].

2648   Dickinson, William C. Baylor University—A Century of Discipline, 1845-1947. Master's thesis, Baylor University, 1962.

2649   Duncan, Frances H. The Life and Times of R.E.B. Baylor, 1793-1846. Master's thesis, Baylor University, 1954. [chairman, board of trustees, Baylor University].

2650   Edwards, Margaret R. A Sketch of Baylor University. Master's thesis, Baylor University, 1920.

2651   Gambrell, Herbert P. The Early Baylor University (1841-1961). Master's thesis, Southern Methodist University, 1924.

2652   Gunn, Jack W. The Life of Rufus C. Burleson. Ph.D., University of Texas at Austin, 1951. 423p. [president, Baylor University, 1851-1897].

2653   Henderson, Robert L. The Baylor Administration of Pat M. Neff, 1939-1947. Master's thesis, Baylor University, 1960. [president, 1932-1947].

2654   Kulesz, John M., Jr. A History and Analysis of Radio Broadcasting at Baylor University - 1935-1968. Master's thesis, Baylor University, 1968.

2655   McCain, Clara E. Schools of Baylor University in Dallas. Master's thesis, Southern Methodist University, 1946.

2656   Miles, Dorothy W. A History of the School of Music of Baylor University. Master's thesis, Baylor University, 1950.

2657   Palmer, James F. Pat Morris Neff, President of Baylor University, 1932-1939. Master's thesis, Baylor University, 1961. [president, 1932-1947].

2658   Renberg, James B. Samuel Palmer Brooks: President of Baylor University, 1920-1931. Master's thesis, Baylor University, 1961. [president, 1902-1931].

2659   Rouse, Roscoe, Jr. A History of the Baylor University Library, 1845-1919. Ph.D., University of Michigan, 1962. 390p. UMI# 62-3257.

2660   Sinclair, Oran L. Samuel Palmer Brooks: President of Baylor University, 1902-1920. Master's thesis, Baylor University, 1961. [president, 1902-1931].

2661   White, Michael A. History of Baylor University, 1845-1861. Master's thesis, Baylor University, 1962.

2662   Williams, Earl F. History of Baylor University. Master's thesis, Baylor University, 1941.

BURLESON COLLEGE

2663   Smith, Jesse G. History of Burleson College, Greenville, Texas. Master's thesis, Southern Methodist University, 1931.

CARR-BURDETTE COLLEGE

2664   Schumacher, Billy G. A History of Carr-Burdette College. Master's thesis, Texas Christian University, 1951. 107p.

CLARENDON COLLEGE

2665   Talley, Kate. A History of Clarendon College. Master's thesis, West Texas State Teachers College, 1933.

CONCRETE COLLEGE

2666   Wildman, Edward L. Concrete College and its Founders. Master's thesis, Southwest Texas State Teachers College, 1944.

DALLAS COLLEGE

2667   Coad, Nola E. A History of Dallas College. Master's thesis, University of Oregon, 1930.

DALLAS THEOLOGICAL SEMINARY

2668   Renfer, Rudolf A. A History of Dallas Theological Seminary. Ph.D., University of Texas, 1959. 335p. UMI# 59-04736.

DANIEL BAKER COLLEGE

2669   Williams, Mima A. History of Daniel Baker College. Master's thesis, University of Texas, 1940.

EAST TEXAS BAPTIST COLLEGE

2670   Boyd, James H. History of the College of Marshall. Master's thesis, Baylor University, 1944.

EAST TEXAS STATE UNIVERSITY

2671   Franks, Marie S. A History of the Department of Health and Physical Education of East Texas State University from 1889 through 1969. Ph.D., East Texas State University, 1970. 320p. UMI# 71-08640.

2672   Hankins, Martha L. History of the East Texas State Teachers College. Master's thesis, University of Texas, 1937.

2673   McDowell, Henderson. A Study of the Development of East Texas State Teachers College as Reflected by the Reports of the College Registrar and the State Auditor for the Years 1935-1941. Master's thesis, East Texas State Teachers College, 1942.

2674   Riddle, Billy R. A Comparative Analysis of the Graduate Industry and Technology Program at East Texas State University. Ed.D., East Texas State University, 1973. 180p. UMI# 74-05773.

2675   Smith, Lewis I. A Survey of the History and Growth of the East Texas State Teachers College. Master's thesis, Southern Methodist University at Dallas, 1928.

2676   Westhaver, Steven J. A History of Drama at East Texas State University, 1889-1967. Master's thesis, East Texas State College, 1967.

EL PASO JUNIOR COLLEGE

2677   Agee, Forrest J. A History of El Paso Junior College, 1920-1927. Master's thesis, University of Texas, 1937.

FRANKLIN COLLEGE

2678   Glazener, S.M. The History of Franklin College, Pilot Point, Texas. Master's thesis, Southern Methodist University, 1932.

GONZALES COLLEGE

2679   Lacy, George R. A History of Gonzales College. Master's thesis, University of Texas, 1936. 133p.

GOODNIGHT COLLEGE

2680   Fanning, James D. The History of Goodnight College. Master's thesis, West Texas State University, 1967. 100p.

GRAYSON COLLEGE

2681   McMahon, Aileen. History of Grayson College. Master's thesis, Southern Methodist University, 1940.

HARDIN-SIMMONS UNIVERSITY

2682   Bentley, Anne. A Study of the History and Development of the Graduate Program at Hardin-Simmons University, Abilene, Texas. Master's thesis, Hardin-Simmons University, 1965.

2683   Jay, Ike W. History of Hardin-Simmons University, 1890-1940. Master's thesis, Texas Technological College, 1941.

2684   Maroscher, Albert C. A History of the Reserve Officers Training Corps at Hardin-Simmons University. Master's thesis, Hardin-Simmons University, 1967.

2685   Prescott, Thomas B. History of Simmons University. Master's thesis, University of Texas, 1930.

2686   Prescott, Thomas B. The History of Simmons University. Ph.D., Kansas City Baptist Theological Seminary, 1933. 126p.

2687   Richardson, Charles R. A History of the Landes Administration at Hardin-Simmons University. Master's thesis, Hardin-Simmons University, 1970. [James H. Landes, president, 1922-1966].

HILLSBORO JUNIOR COLLEGE

2688   Little, Faye M. History of Hillsboro (Texas) Junior College. Master's thesis, Baylor University, 1965.

HOUSTON, UNIVERSITY OF

2689   Bell, David P. An Analysis of Undergraduate Curricular Innovation at the University of Houston Central Campus Since 1960. Ed.D., Stanford University, 1977. 195p. UMI# 78-02263.

2690   Cochran, James C. The Municipal University as a Community Service Institution, Especially as Exemplified in the Aims, Organization and Growth of the University of Houston. Ph.D., University of Texas at Austin, 1950. 117p.

2691   McBride, James C. A History of Quantitative Components of Enrollment, Current Expenditures, and Revenue Sources in the University of Houston, 1948-1962. Ed.D., University of Houston, 1965. 160p. UMI# 65-13074.

2692   Mohr, Eleanor S. The History of the Houston Junior College. Master's thesis, University of Texas, 1936.

JARVIS CHRISTIAN COLLEGE

2693   Noe, Minnie A. History of Jarvis Christian College. Master's thesis, Texas Christian University, 1966. 107p.

KIDD-KEY COLLEGE

2694   Connelly, Annie L. History of Kidd-Key College, Sherman Grayson County, Texas. Master's thesis, Southern Methodist University, 1942.

KILGORE COLLEGE

2695   Martin, James L. A History of the Van Cliburn Auditorium, a Small Theatre with a Multiform Stage Constructed as a Portion of the Applied Arts Building at Kilgore College, Kilgore, Texas. Ph.D., University of California-Los Angeles, 1971. 142p. UMI# 72-09231.

LAMAR UNIVERSITY

2696   Hutchison, Earl E. History of Lamar Junior College. Master's thesis, Texas College of Arts and Industries, 1938.

2697   McLaughlin, Marvin L. Reflections of the Philosophy and Practices of Lamar State College of Technology as Shown through Its History. Ed.D., University of Houston, 1955. 294p. UMI# 00-12290.

2698   Welch, Joe B. A History of the Growth and Development of Lamar University from 1942 to 1973. Ed.D., McNeese State University, 1974. 217p. UMI# 74-29281.

LON MORRIS COLLEGE

2699   Archer, Will H. History of the Theatrical Activities at Lon Morris College, 1873-Present. Master's thesis, Southern Methodist University, 1955.

2700   Brown, David R. A Historical Survey of the Theatre Program at Lon Morris College from the School's Beginnings through 1979. Master's thesis, Baylor University, 1983.

2701   Jones, Glendell A. A History of Lon Morris College. Ph.D., North Texas State University, 1973. 359p. UMI# 73-23737.

2702   Strother, Martha D. The History of Lon Morris College. Master's thesis, Southern Methodist University, 1941.

MARY HARDIN-BAYLOR COLLEGE

2703   Walker, Thomas T. Mary Hardin-Baylor College, 1845-1937. Ed.D., George Peabody College for Teachers, 1962. 241p. UMI# 63-01901.

MCMURRY COLLEGE

2704   Humphrey, Joe C. The History of Intercollegiate Athletics at McMurry College (Abilene, Texas). Master's thesis, Hardin-Simmons University, 1967.

2705   Newman, V. A History of McMurry College, 1920-1936. Master's thesis, Texas Technological College, 1937.

MIDLAND COLLEGE

2706   Hickman, Lillian W. The History of Midland College. Master's thesis, University of Oregon, 1949.

2707   Schanke, Robert A. History of Speech and Drama at Midland College. Master's thesis, University of Nebraska, 1963.

NORTH TEXAS STATE UNIVERSITY

2708   Anderson, Julia M. The Development and Growth of Sport Activities for Women in the North Texas State Teachers College from 1908-1938. Master's thesis, North Texas State Teachers College, 1939.

2709   Atkins, Noble J. The Growth and Development of the Recreation Program of the North Texas State Teachers College from 1911 to 1939. Master's thesis, North Texas State Teachers College, 1939.

2710   Barber, Gerald J. The History of the Industrial Arts Department of North Texas State University from 1955 to 1975. Master's thesis, North Texas State University, 1977. 76p.

2711   Duncan, William N. The Student Use of English Examination at TexasNorth Texas State University: 1944-1976. Ed.D., North Texas State University, 1976. 307p. UMI# 77-11,102.

2712   Hall, Morris E. The Development of North Texas State College, 1890-1949. Ed.D., New York University, 1954. 277p. UMI# 00-09310.

2713   Higginbotham, Robert L. A History of North Texas State Teachers College. Master's thesis, North Texas State Teachers College, 1936.

2714   Johns, Lorenzo M. A Quarter of a Century of Health and Physical Education in North Texas State Teachers College. Master's thesis, North Texas State Teachers College, 1939.

2715   Martin, Doris M. A History of the North Texas State Teachers College Demonstration School. Master's thesis, North Texas State Teachers College, 1940.

2716   Miller, Robert W. The North Texas State University Jazz Degree: A History and a Study of Its Significance. Ph.D., Michigan State University, 1979. 277p. UMI# 8001565.

2717   Sandel, Mildred J. History of the Speech and Drama Department at North Texas State University as It Relates to General Trends in Speech Education, 1890-1970. Master's thesis, North Texas State University, 1971.

2718   Sisco, Sue L.P. The Development of the Health and Physical Education Curriculum in the North Texas State Teachers College from 1901 to 1939 with a Discussion of Certain Philosophies That Appear to Have Affected the Curriculum. Master's thesis, North Texas State Teachers College, 1939.

2719   Smith, J.W. A Survey of the Development and the Needs of the North Texas State Teacher's College, Denton, Texas. Master's thesis, Southern Methodist University, 1925.

2720   Taylor, Luciann W. Intercollegiate Athletics in North Texas State Teachers College from 1924-1925 through 1934-1935. Master's thesis, North Texas State Teachers College, 1936. 71p.

2721   Vick, Mildred W. The History of the Growth and Development of the Health Science Program of North Texas State Teachers College from November 1918 through August 1941. Master's thesis, North Texas State Teachers College, 1942.

PANOLA COLLEGE

2722   Pefley, Wallace B. The Evolution of Music Activities at Panola College, Carthage, Texas. Ph.D., Columbia University, 1959.

PARIS JUNIOR COLLEGE

2723   Newton, James H. History of the Paris Junior College. Master's thesis, Southern Methodist University, 1935. 93p.

PRAIRIE VIEW AGRICULTURAL & MECHANICAL UNIVERSITY

2724 Gee, Ruth E. The History and Development of the Prairie View Training School, 1916-1946. Master's thesis, Prairie View University, 1946.

2725 White, Annie Mae V. The Development of the Program of Studies of the Prairie View State Normal and Industrial College. Master's thesis, University of Texas, 1938.

RANGER JUNIOR COLLEGE

2726 Baskin, Henry L. History of the Ranger Junior College. Master's thesis, University of Texas, 1937.

RICE UNIVERSITY

2727 Fitts, Dora A. A History of Rice Institute. Master's thesis, Butler University, 1934.

RUSK BAPTIST COLLEGE

2728 Quillen, Herbert N. A History of the Rusk Baptist College from 1895 to 1928. Master's thesis, Stephen F. Austin State University, 1968.

2729 Whitehead, Marie H. A History of the Rusk Cherokeean, 1847-1973. Master's thesis, Stephen F. Austin State University, 1974.

SAM HOUSTON STATE UNIVERSITY

2730 Bunting, David E. A Documentary History of Sam Houston Normal Institute. Master's thesis, University of Texas, 1933.

2731 Smith, Willis L. The Development of Sam Houston State Teachers College. Master's thesis, Southern Methodist University, 1928.

SAN ANTONIO COLLEGE

2732 Pope, Wilbur A. A Study of the Growth and Development of San Antonio College. Master's thesis, Trinity University, 1953.

SAN ANTONIO JUNIOR COLLEGE

2733 Ralson, Hugh E. History of the San Antonio Junior College. Master's thesis, University of Texas, 1933.

SAN JACINTO COLLEGE

2734 England, Bobby L. The Legal Evolution of Public Junior College Financial Practices Featuring an Examination of the San Jacinto College Case. Ph.D., East Texas State University, 1968. 216p. UMI# 69-05426.

2735 Spencer, Thomas M., Jr. Population Characteristics in the Elections to Establish San Jacinto College. Ph.D., University of Texas at Austin, 1964. 208p. UMI# 64-11842.

SOUTHERN METHODIST UNIVERSITY

2736   Abbot, Billy M. A History of the Arden Club of Southern Methodist University From 1915 to 1942. Master's thesis, Southern Methodist University, 1951.

2737   Blair, John E. The Founding of Southern Methodist University. Master's thesis, Southern Methodist University, 1926.

2738   Craig, John D. Southern Methodist University Under the Leadership of Dr. Charles C. Selecman (1923-1925). Master's thesis, Southern Methodist University, 1965. [president, 1923-1938].

2739   Petit, Judith L. The Founding of Southern Methodist University, 1910-1916. Master's thesis, Southern Methodist University, 1965.

2740   Spalding, Sharon B. A Study of Contributions of Mary Lizzie McCord to Drama Education at Southern Methodist University. Ph.D., North Texas State University, 1976. 163p. UMI# 76-29,172. [professor of drama and speech, 1915-1945].

2741   Thomas, Mary M. Southern Methodist University: The First Twenty-Five Years, 1915-1940. Ph.D., Emory University, 1971. 373p. UMI# 71-27802.

2742   Williams, Sidney A. The Organization and Development of a Course in Economics as General Education at Southern Methodist University. Ph.D., University of Texas at Austin, 1954.

SOUTHWEST TEXAS JUNIOR COLLEGE

2743   Gray, Leona S. The History of Southwest Texas Junior College. Master's thesis, East Texas State College, 1962.

SOUTHWEST TEXAS STATE UNIVERSITY

2744   French, Roger F. A History of the Southwest Texas State Teachers College. Master's thesis, Southwest Texas State Teachers College, 1939.

2745   Wilson, Ben Jr. History of Teacher Education at Southwest Texas State University. Ed.D., Baylor University, 1977. 206p. UMI# 78-01561.

SOUTHWESTERN ASSEMBLIES OF GOD COLLEGE

2746   Farmer, Blake L. Southwestern Assemblies of God College: Founding, Growth and Development, 1927-1965. Ed.D., Baylor University, 1965. 169p. UMI# 65-15000.

SOUTHWESTERN BAPTIST THEOLOGICAL SEMINARY

2747   Churchill, Ralph D. The History and Development of Southwestern's School of Religious Education to 1956. Doctor of Religious Education, Southwestern Baptist Theological Seminary, 1956. 173p.

2748   Mathis, Robert R. A Descriptive Study of Joe Davis Heacock: Educator, Administrator, Churchman. Ed.D., Southwestern Baptist Theological Seminary, 1984. [professor and dean, Southwestern Baptist Theological Seminary, 1956-1973].

SOUTHWESTERN UNIVERSITY

2749   Jones, Ralph W. A History of Southwestern University, 1873-1949. Ph.D., University of Texas at Austin, 1960. 676p. UMI# 60-01983.

2750   Willbern, Glen D. A History of Southwestern University, Georgetown, Texas. Master's thesis, University of Texas at Austin, 1928. 195p.

ST. PHILIP'S COLLEGE

2751   Norris, Clarence W., Jr. St. Philip's College: A Case Study of a Historically Black Two-Year College. Ed.D., University of Southern California, 1975. 327p. UMI# 75-15558.

STEPHEN F. AUSTIN STATE UNIVERSITY

2752   Craddock, Bettye. The Golden Years: The First Half Century of Stephen F. Austin State University. Master's thesis, Stephen F. Austin State University, 1972.

2753   Waller, Charlie F. A History of Debate at Stephen F. Austin State College. Master's thesis, Stephen F. Austin State College, 1951.

SUL ROSS STATE UNIVERSITY

2754   Pollitt, Frank C. A History of Sul Ross State Teachers College from 1917 to 1939. Master's thesis, Sul Ross State College, 1939.

TARLETON STATE UNIVERSITY

2755   Cockrell, Frank S. History of John Tarleton Agricultural College. Master's thesis, Southwest Texas State Teachers College, 1941.

2756   Grissom, Preston B. The Development of John Tarleton College. Master's thesis, West Texas State Teachers College, 1933.

TEMPLE JUNIOR COLLEGE

2757   Farrell, Harry C., Jr. Temple Junior College: Its Founding, Growth and Development, 1926-1964 (Volumes I and II). Ph.D., Colorado State University, 1964. 567p. UMI# 65-00227.

2758   Havekost, Irene. History of Temple Junior College. Master's thesis, Southwest Texas State Teachers College, 1943.

TEXAS ARTS & INDUSTRIAL UNIVERSITY

2759   Kellam, Nettie L. The History of the Texas College of Arts and Industries. Master's thesis, University of Texas, 1938.

2760   Lee, Joe B. A History of the Library of Texas College of Arts and Industries, 1925-1955. Master's thesis, University of Texas, 1958. 148p.

TEXAS ARTS & MECHANICAL UNIVERSITY

2761   Adams, John A. The History of the Association of Former Students of Texas A&M University, 1876-1976. Master's thesis, Texas A&M University, 1977.

2762   Parks, Deborah Z. The History of College Station, Texas, 1938-1982. Master's thesis, Texas A&M University, 1984.

2763   Roby, Lorene M. The History of Education and Psychology at Texas A&M University. Master's thesis, Texas Agricultural & Mechanical University, 1968.

2764   Schatte, Curtis E. Doctoral Programs at Texas A&M University, 1940-1968: An Appraisal by the Graduates. Ph.D., Texas Agricultural & Mechanical University, 1970. 392p. UMI# 70-16758.

2765   Tomlinson, Marie G. The State Agricultural and Mechanical College of Texas, 1871-1879. Master's thesis, Texas A&M University, 1977.

TEXAS CHRISTIAN UNIVERSITY

2766   Cognard, Anne M.M. An Historical Analysis of Rhetorical Practices at Texas Christian University. Master's thesis, Texas Christian University, 1970.

2767   Fleming, Yancy B. A History of the Department of Speech Communication at Texas Christian University, 1878-1972. Master's thesis, Texas Christian University, 1972. 141p.

2768   Mason, Frank M. The Beginnings of Texas Christian University. Master's thesis, Texas Christian University, 1930.

2769   Powell, Mae M. The History of Texas Christian University from 1895 to 1939. Master's thesis, Southern Methodist University, 1939.

TEXAS LUTHERAN COLLEGE

2770   Klags, Alfred D. A History of Texas Lutheran College, 1851-1951. Master's thesis, University of Texas at Austin, 1951.

2771   Moore, Elif A. The History of Clifton College. Master's thesis, University of Texas, 1927.

TEXAS PRESBYTERIAN COLLEGE

2772   Woodward, Mary T. History of Texas Presbyterian College, Milford, Texas. Master's thesis, Southern Methodist University, 1945.

TEXAS SOUTHERN UNIVERSITY

2773   Proctor, Mamie M. Historical Survey of the Law School Library of Texas Southern University, Houston, Texas. Master's thesis, Catholic University of America, 1966. 105p.

2774   Terry, William E. Origin and Development of Texas Southern University, Houston, Texas. Ed.D., University of Houston, 1968. 323p. UMI# 70-12861.

TEXAS TECHNOLOGICAL UNIVERSITY

2775   Dewese, James E. A History of Speech at Texas Technological College, 1925-1963. Master's thesis, Texas Technological College, 1963.

2776   Evans, Floyd C. A History of Varsity Basketball at Texas Technological College. Master's thesis, Texas Technological College, 1965. 56p.

2777   Fairey, Jerry. History of Track and Field at Texas Technological College. Master's thesis, Texas Technological College, 1965. 67p.

2778   Gibbs, Clifford L. The Establishment of Texas Technological College. Master's thesis, Texas Technological College, 1939.

2779   Jones, Doris E.G. Toward Reaching the First Class: Graduate Education at Texas Tech University, 1930 to 1980. Ed.D., Texas Tech University, 1983.

2780   Wilbanks, Floy F. The Life and Work of Dr. Bradford Knapp. Master's thesis, Texas Technological College, 1940. [president, Texas Tech University, 1932-1938].

TEXAS, UNIVERSITY OF

2781   Barnard, Helen D. Early History of Research in Texas Archaeology by the Department of Anthropology, and the History of the Anthropology Museum of the University of Texas. Master's thesis, University of Texas, 1939.

2782   Berry, Margaret C. Student Life and Customs, 1883-1933, at the University of Texas. Ed.D., Columbia University, 1965. 740p. UMI# 65-08834.

2783   Brewer, Tom B. A History of the Department of History at the University of Texas, 1883-1951. Master's thesis, University of Texas, 1957.

2784   Brown, Billye J. The Historical Development of the University of Texas System School of Nursing, 1890-1973. Ed.D., Baylor University, 1975. 462p. UMI# 75-27838.

2785   Cochrane, Mary A. The University of Texas Package Loan Library, 1914-1954. Master's thesis, University of Texas, 1956. 206p.

2786   Cox, Alice C. The Rainey Affair: A History of the Academic Freedom Controversy at the University of Texas, 1938-1946. Ph.D., University of Denver, 1970. 163p. UMI# 71-08770.

2787   Danna, Debra. A History and Participant Evaluation of the English Language and Orientation Program Conducted at the University of Texas. Master's thesis, University of Texas, 1980.

2788   Hayes, Arthur R. The Influence and Impact of Edwin DuBois Shurter on Speech Education in Texas. Ph.D., University of Texas, 1952. [professor of speech, University of Texas, 1899-1923].

2789   Mabry, Mary V. The School of Journalism of the University of Texas: Origins and Early Development. Master's thesis, University of Texas, 1965.

2790   Mayer, Gary H. Journalism at the University of Texas, 1927-1964. Master's thesis, University of Texas, 1965.

2791   Moloney, Louis C. A History of the University Library at the University of Texas, 1883-1934. Doctor of Library Service, Columbia University, 1970. 404p. UMI# 71-17525.

2792   Mullen, Kathryn R. A Study of the Evolution of the Philosophy of Student Housing at the University of Texas at Austin from 1883 to 1973. Ph.D., University of Texas at Austin, 1975. 122p. UMI# 75-16628.

2793   O'Neill, Norman W. The Role of the University of Texas in the Impeachment of James Ferguson, 1915-1917. Master's thesis, Southwest Texas State University, 1972. [governor of Texas].

2794   Payne, John W. David Franklin Houston: A Biography. Ph.D., University of Texas at Austin, 1953. 318p. [professor and dean, University of Texas, 1894-1902; president, 1905-1908].

2795   Pevey, Wayne. A History of the Department of Drama (the University of Texas). Ph.D., University of Texas, 1965.

2796   Rhodes, James L. The Life and Times of Frederick Eby. Ph.D., University of Texas, 1959. 308p. UMI# 59-04737. [professor of philosophy and history of education, University of Texas, 1909-1959].

2797   Scarborough, John A.L. The University of Texas and the Great War. Master's thesis, University of Texas, 1927.

2798   Sitter, Clara L. The History and Development of the Rare Books Collections of the University of Texas Based on Recollections of Miss Fannie Ratchford. Master's thesis, University of Texas, 1966. 116p.

2799   Willers, Jack C. The Philosophy of Education of Alexander Caswell Ellis. Ph.D., University of Texas, 1964. 352p. UMI# 65-4359. [professor of education, University of Texas, 1897-1926].

2800   Wolfe, Thomas H. Dimensions of a Prominent, American Graduate School: The Graduate School, the University of Texas, Austin, 1883-1969. Master's thesis, University of Texas, 1970.

TEXAS, UNIVERSITY OF (ARLINGTON)

2801   Furman, Necah F. Cast in a Long Shadow: A Study of the Import of Walter Prescott Webb on the University of Texas at Arlington, Including the Genesis, Background, and History of Dr. Walter Prescott Webb. Master's thesis, University of Texas at Arlington, 1972. [professor of history].

2802   Hudspeth, Junia E. The History of the North Texas Agricultural College. Master's thesis, Southern Methodist University, 1935. 172p.

TEXAS WESLEYAN COLLEGE

2803   Cox, John E. A Brief History of Texas Wesleyan College. Ed.D., University of Northern Colorado, 1953. 155p. UMI# 00-07437.

2804   Mathews, Ben A. A History of Polytechnic College, Fort Worth, Texas. Master's thesis, Southern Methodist University, 1930.

TEXAS WOMAN'S UNIVERSITY

2805   Balkus, Mary P. History and Development of the Modern Dance Group of the Texas Woman's University from 1936 through 1965: Its Scope of Influence and Contributions to the Understanding and Appreciation of Dance as a Contemporary Art Form. Master's thesis, Texas Woman's University, 1965.

2806   Holt, Mildred P. A History of the College of Industrial Arts. Master's thesis, University of Texas, 1926.

2807   Weeks, Sandra R. Anne Schley Duggan: Portrait of a Dance Educator. Ph.D., Texas Woman's University, 1980. 331p. UMI# 8025590. [Texas Woman's University].

TRINITY UNIVERSITY

2808   Hetherington, Martha A. Trinity University, 1939-1952: The Story of Relocation in San Antonio, Texas. Master's thesis, University of Texas, 1965.

2809   Mitchell, Yetta G. The History of Trinity University from 1869 to 1934. Master's thesis, Southern Methodist University, 1936.

TYLER JUNIOR COLLEGE

2810   Ballard, Robert M., Jr. Tyler Junior College: Its Founding, Growth and Development. Ph.D., East Texas State University, 1971. 192p. UMI# 72-22740.

2811   Sidnell, Robert G., Jr. The Influence of the Tyler Junior College on the Fine Arts Culture of Tyler, Texas. Ph.D., University of Texas at Austin, 1960. 280p. UMI# 60-06633.

WACO UNIVERSITY

2812   Guemple, John R. A History of Waco University. Master's thesis, Baylor University, 1964.

WESLEY COLLEGE

2813   Houser, J. H. The History of Wesley College, Greenville, Texas. Master's thesis, Southern Methodist University, 1939.

WEST TEXAS STATE UNIVERSITY

2814   Cleveland, Truman. A Historical Study of the West Texas State College. Master's thesis, West Texas State College, 1953.

2815   Craig, Richard H. The Development of West Texas State Teachers College, 1932-1945. Master's thesis, West Texas State College, 1947.

2816   Priest, Jimmie R. A History of the West Texas State University Music Department, 1917-1965. Master's thesis, West Texas State University, 1965.

2817   Rowan, Jonnie. A History of the West Texas State Teachers College. Master's thesis, West Texas State Teachers College, 1932.

UTAH

GENERAL STUDIES

2818   Barker, Lincoln. History of the State Junior Colleges of Utah. Ph.D., New York University, 1945. 378p.

2819   Bernhard, Randall L. Contemporary Musical Theatre: History and Development in the Major Colleges and Universities of Utah. Ph.D., Brigham Young University, 1979. 365p. UMI# 80-00096.

2820   Deboer, Ray L. Historical Study of Mormon Education and the Influence of Its Philosophy on Public Education in Utah. Ph.D., University of Denver, 1952.

2821   Foulger, James R. The Public Junior College—With Special Reference to the State of Utah. Ph.D., Harvard University, 1947. 436p.

2822   Grishman, Lee H. The Influence of Brigham Young on the Development of Education in Early Utah. Ed.D., Columbia University Teachers College, 1983. 182p. UMI# 8403259.

2823   Hair, Mary Jane S. History of the Efforts to Coordinate Higher Education in Utah. Ph.D., University of Utah, 1974. 422p. UMI# 75-00587.

2824   Noall, Sandra H. The History of Nursing Education in Utah. Ph.D., University of Utah, 1970.

BRIGHAM YOUNG UNIVERSITY

2825   Brooks, Ben H. A History of Brigham Young University Track and Field in State Divisions and Conference Contests. Master's thesis, Brigham Young University, 1959. 104p.

2826   Fugal, John P. University Wide Religious Objectives: Their History and Implementation at Brigham Young University. Doctor of Religious Education, Brigham Young University, 1967. 231p. UMI# 67-17217.

2827   Henson, Charles A. A History of the Theatre and Cinematic Arts Department: Brigham Young University 1920-1978. Ed.D., Brigham Young University, 1978. 443p. UMI# 80-27650.

2828   Kernan, John N. A History of Brigham Young University Men's Cross Country, and Track and Field, and an Evaluation of Program Success 1960-1980. Ed.D., Brigham Young University, 1984. 242p. UMI# 8412462.

2829   Kunz, Calvin S. A History of the Intern Doctoral Program of the College of Education at Brigham Young University. Ed.D., Brigham Young University, 1981. 142p. UMI# 81-29540.

2830   O'Brien, James P. The History of Intercollegiate Baseball at Brigham Young University. Master's thesis, Brigham Young University, 1961. 165p.

2831   Olauson, Clarence R. Dramatic Activities at the Brigham Young University from the Earliest Beginnings to the Present, 1849-1961. Master's thesis, University of Utah, 1963.

2832   Pease, Harold W. The History of the Alumni Association and Its Influence on the Development of Brigham Young University. Ph.D., Brigham Young University, 1974. 569p. UMI# 75-00545.

2833   Pinckney, George H., Jr. The History of Intercollegiate Football at Brigham Young University. Master's thesis, Brigham Young University, 1960.

2834   Rhoda, Leonard G. The Life and Professional Contributions of Milton F. Hartvigsen. Ed.D., Brigham Young University, 1979. 214p. UMI# 7925331. [dean of physical education, Brigham Young University].

2835   Rimington, David B. An Historical Appraisal of Educational Development Under Howard S. McDonald at Brigham Young University, 1945-1949. Ed.D., University of Southern California, 1982. [president].

2836   Robison, Richard W. Albert Miller, His Musical Achievements and Contributions to the Teaching of Music at Brigham Young University. Master's thesis, Brigham Young University, 1957. 38p.

2837   Smith, Keith L. An Historical Study of Adult Education Programs of the Brigham Young University from 1921 to 1966. Master's thesis, Brigham Young University, 1968.

2838   Smith, Keith L. A History of the Brigham Young University—The Early Years, 1875-1921. Ph.D., Brigham Young University, 1972. 281p. UMI# 72-23193.

2839   Struthers, Robert E. An Historical-Analytical Study of the Secondary Speech Program at Brigham Young University High School, 1936-1938. Ph.D., Ohio State University, 1970. 260p. UMI# 71-18091.

2840   Taylor, Ethelyn P. The Counseling Service at Brigham Young University: A Developmental History. Master's thesis, Stanford University, 1949.

2841   VanderGriend, Ward M. Alma Heaton: The Professor of Fun. Ed.D., Brigham Young University, 1981. 220p. UMI# 8128181. [teacher of dance and social recreation, Brigham Young University].

COLLEGE OF EASTERN UTAH

2842   Welch, Tony J. The History of Athletics at College of Eastern Utah. Master's thesis, Utah State University, 1967.

DIXIE COLLEGE

2843   Gregerson, Edna J. The Evolution of Dixie College as a Public Institution of Higher Education in Utah from 1871 to 1935. Ed.D., University of Nevada-Las Vegas, 1981. 431p. UMI# 82-29756.

MCCUNE SCHOOL OF MUSIC AND ART

2844   Schaefer, Donald G. Contributions of the McCune School of Music and Art to Music Education in Utah, 1917-1957. Master's thesis, Brigham Young University, 1962. 123p.

SNOW COLLEGE

2845   Findlay, Ross P. Snow College, Its Founding and Development, 1888-1932. Master's thesis, Utah State Agricultural College, 1952.

2846   Woodbury, Darwin S. The History of Athletics at Snow College. Master's thesis, University of Utah, 1960. 106p.

SOUTHERN UTAH STATE COLLEGE

2847   Sherratt, Gerald R. A History of the College of Southern Utah, 1897 to 1947. Master's thesis, Utah State University, 1954.

UTAH STATE UNIVERSITY

2848   Hart, Alfred B. The Evolution of the Curriculum of the Utah State Agricultural College. Master's thesis, Utah State Agricultural College, 1934.

2849   McCrary, Delwin W. The History of Intercollegiate Wrestling at Utah State University. Master's thesis, Utah State University, 1967.

2850   Tidwell, Frank R. A History of the Men's Physical Education Program at Utah State Agricultural College. Master's thesis, Utah State Agricultural College, 1955.

UTAH, UNIVERSITY OF

2851   Adair, Alice J.L. A Study of Women at the University of Utah from 1953 to 1964. Ph.D., University of Utah, 1980. 186p. UMI# 81-09566.

2852   Adix, Shauna M. Differential Treatment of Women at the University of Utah from 1850 to 1915. Ph.D., University of Utah, 1976. 192p. UMI# 77-10433.

2853   Christiansen, Grace V.T. An Appraisal of the Education Doctoral Program in Educational Administration of the University of Utah 1950-1974. Ph.D., University of Utah, 1975. 347p. UMI# 75-22,104.

2854   Engar, Keith M. History of Dramatics at the University of Utah from Beginnings Until June 1919. Master's thesis, University of Utah, 1948.

2855   Gannon, Russell J. History and Evaluation of the University of Utah, Campus Chapter of Phi Delta Kappa. Master's thesis, University of Utah, 1968.

2856   Hankin, John F. The History of College Wrestling at University of Utah. Master's thesis, University of Utah, 1965. 159p.

2857   Hess, Marvin G. An Historical Study of Physical Education for Men at the University of Utah. Master's thesis, University of Utah, 1955.

2858   Jeppson, Joseph H. The Secularization of the University of Utah to 1920. Ph.D., University of California-Berkeley, 1973. 357p. UMI# 73-19729.

2859   Lees, Sondra. A History of Dramatics at the University of Utah from September 1919. Master's thesis, University of Utah, 1959.

2860   Mouritsen, Russell H. A Study of Women at the University of Utah Between 1941 and 1953. Ph.D., University of Utah, 1980. 153p. UMI# 80-25606.

2861   Pugsley, Sharon G. The Board of Regents of the University of Utah, 1850-1920: Historical Development and Prosopography. Master's thesis, University of Utah, 1985.

2862   Sylvester, Blaine E. The History of Intercollegiate Baseball at the University of Utah. Master's thesis, University of Utah, 1965.

2863   Wilcox, Reba W. A Study of the Education of Women at the University of Utah, 1915-1916 to 1924-1925. Ph.D., University of Utah, 1979. 168p. UMI# 80-09806.

2864   Willey, Darrell S. A History of Teacher Training at the University of Utah. Ph.D., University of Utah, 1953. 323p.

WEBER STATE COLLEGE

2865   Overstreet, Earle L. The History of Athletics at Weber College. Master's thesis, University of Utah, 1964.

WESTMINSTER COLLEGE

2866   Buzza, David E. Contributions to a History of Utah's Westminster College. Master's thesis, University of Chicago, 1939.

VERMONT

BENNINGTON COLLEGE

2867   Cornehlsen, John H., Jr. The Development of the Junior Division of Bennington College. Ph.D., Stanford University, 1943.

2868   Flexner, Hans. Institutional Change at Bennington College: A Historical Analysis. Ph.D., Columbia University, 1969. 420p. UMI# 72-19058.

GREEN MOUNTAIN JUNIOR COLLEGE

2869   Reed, Lloyd D. Jesse Parker Bogue, Missionary for the Two-Year College. Ed.D., Michigan State University, 1965. 238p. UMI# 66-06162. [president, Green Mountain Junior College, 1931-1946].

MIDDLEBURY COLLEGE

2870   Stameshkin, David M. The Town's College: Middlebury College, 1800-1915. (Volumes I and II) Ph.D., University of Michigan, 1978. 690p. UMI# 78-13738.

NORWICH UNIVERSITY

2871   Grabowski, John. Alden Partridge and Military Education: 1818-1834. Master's thesis, University of Pittsburgh, 1973. [president, Norwich University, 1819-1843].

2872   Smith, Peter P. The Transformation of Norwich University: 1971-1981. Ed.D., Harvard University, 1983. 128p. UMI# 8405306.

VIRGINIA

GENERAL STUDIES

2873   Bacote, C.A. Higher Education in Virginia Between 1830 and 1860. Master's thesis, University of Chicago, 1929.

2874   Blume, Clarence J.M. The Growth and the Development of Sixteen Institutions of Higher Learning in the State of Virginia from 1910 to 1928. Master's thesis, University of Virginia, 1929.

2875   Bounds, Stuart M. Environmental and Political Correlates of Appropriations for Higher Education in Virginia, 1950-1972. Ed.D., College of William & Mary, 1974. 137p. UMI# 75-00540.

2876   Brown, Emma W. A Study of the Influence of the Philosophies of Accommodation and Protest of Five Colleges Established in Virginia for Negroes, 1865-1940. Ed.D., Columbia University, 1967. 193p. UMI# 67-16748.

2877   Capps, Marian P. The Virginia Out-of-State Graduate Aid Program, 1936-1950. Ph.D., Columbia University, 1954.

2878   Cato, William H. The Development of Higher Education for Women in Virginia. Ph.D., University of Virginia, 1941.

2879   Clayborne, William M. A History of the Teacher Education Programs in Five Negro Colleges of Virginia from 1876 to 1954. Ed.D., George Washington University, 1971. 174p. UMI# 71-22417.

2880   Cordaro, Russell T. The Community College Movement in Virginia. Master's thesis, Catholic University of America, 1968.

2881   Cristo, Anthony B. The Development of the Community College System in Virginia to 1972. Ph.D., Duke University, 1973. 417p. UMI# 74-07528.

2882   Emerson, Bruce. A History of the Relationships Between the State of Virginia and Its Public Normal Schools, 1869-1930. Ed.D., College of William & Mary, 1973. 201p. UMI# 74-00083.

2883   Ferree, A.W. The History of Higher Education for Women in Virginia. Master's thesis, University of North Carolina, 1934. 78p.

2884   Hornsby, Virginia R. The Higher Education of Virginia in Colonial Days. Master's thesis, College of William & Mary, 1936.

2885   Jeffrey, Gertrude E. An Evaluation of the Junior College Movement in Virginia. Master's thesis, University of Virginia, 1945.

2886   Kellogg, Richard A. State Controlled Higher Education in Virginia and the Budgeting

Process: 1950-1972: A Move Toward Formal Methods. Ed.D., College of William & Mary, 1974. 229p. UMI# 74-13180.

2887   Kiracofe, Edgar S. An Historical Study of Athletics and Physical Education in the Standard Four-Year Colleges of Virginia. Ph.D., University of Virginia, 1932. 90p.

2888   Maiden, Marvin. History of the Professional Training of Teachers in Virginia. Ph.D., University of Virginia, 1927.

2889   Medlin, Stuart B. The Founding of the Permanent Denominational Colleges in Virginia, 1776-1861. Ed.D., College of William & Mary, 1976. 143p. UMI# 76-11137.

2890   Pearce, Donald C. The Development of the Junior Colleges in Virginia. Ed.D., George Peabody College for Teachers, 1957. 378p. UMI# 00-24483.

2891   Reilly, Patricia M. A History of the Development of Baccalaureate Degrees in Music Education in Virginia Colleges. Ed.D., Indiana University, 1966. 252p. UMI# 66-12677.

2892   Rives, Ralph H. A History of Oratory in the Commonwealth of Virginia Prior to the War Between the States. Ed.D., University of Virginia, 1960. 344p. UMI# 60-04636.

2893   Smith, Aine P. A Study of Administrators' Perceptions of Change in Three Private Liberal Arts Women's Junior Colleges. Ed.D., College of William & Mary, 1978. 160p. UMI# 7904278.

2894   Smith, Alan M. Virginia Lawyers, 1680-1776: The Birth of an American Profession. Ph.D., Johns Hopkins University, 1967. 432p. UMI# 68-06578.

2895   Vaughan, George B. Broadening the Base of Higher Education in Virginia: Emergence of the Community College System. Ph.D., Florida State University, 1970. 205p. UMI# 72-31254.

2896   Woodburn, Robert O. An Historical Investigation of the Opposition to Jefferson's Educational Proposals in the Commonwealth of Virginia. Ph.D., American University, 1974. 231p. UMI# 75-11123.

AVERETT COLLEGE

2897   Davis, James A. Dr. Curtis V. Bishop: Focus on a Junior College Career. Ph.D., Florida State University, 1973. 319p. UMI# 73-30275. [professor of English, business manager, and president, Averett College].

2898   Gray, David W. A History of Averett College. Master's thesis, University of Richmond, 1961.

BRIDGEWATER COLLEGE

2899   Warden, James E. Bridgewater College, 1880-1972. Ed.D., University of Pittsburgh, 1973. 279p. UMI# 73-29370.

COLLEGE OF WILLIAM AND MARY

2900   Chapman, Anne W. Benjamin Stoddert Ewell: A Biography. Ph.D., College of William &

Mary, 1984. 342p. UMl# 8429747. [president, College of William & Mary, 1854-1861, 1865-1881].

2901   Denbo, Marilou. The Nineteenth-Century Presidents of the College of William and Mary. Ph.D., New York University, 1974. 223p. UMl# 74-24985.

2902   Dillard, Carra G. The Grammar School of the College of William & Mary, 1693-1888. Master's thesis, College of William & Mary, 1951.

2903   Fehr, Carl A. the Development of a Curriculum in Music for the College of William and Mary. Ph.D., Columbia University, 1951. 134p.

2904   Harrison, Margaret T. Commissary James Blair of Virginia: A Study in Personality and Power. Master's thesis, College of William & Mary, 1958. [president, College of William & Mary, 1693-1743].

2905   Hemphill, William E. George Wythe, the Colonial Briton: A Biographical Study of the Pre-Revolutionary Era in Virginia. Ph.D., University of Virginia, 1937. [professor of law, College of William & Mary, 1779-1790].

2906   Jennings, John M. The First Hundred Years of the Library of the College of William and Mary, 1693-1793. Master's thesis, American University, 1948.

2907   Mansfield, Stephen S. Thomas Roderick Dew: Defender of the Southern Faith. Ph.D., University of Virginia, 1968. 215p. UMl# 69-03976. [professor and president, College of William & Mary, 1827-1846].

2908   McNeer, James B. Political Factors Affecting the Establishment and Growth of Richard Bland College of the College of William and Mary 1958-1972. Ed.D., College of William & Mary, 1981.

2909   Mohler, Samuel R. Commissary James Blair: Churchman, Educator, and Politician of Colonial Virginia. Ph.D., University of Chicago, 1941. 389p. [president, College of William & Mary, 1693-1743].

2910   Motley, Daniel E. Life of Commissary James Blair, Founder of William and Mary College. Ph.D., Johns Hopkins University, 1899. [president, College of William & Mary, 1693-1743].

2911   Osborne, Ruby O. The College of William and Mary in Virginia, 1800-1827. Ed.D., College of William & Mary, 1981. 627p. UMl# 82-05153.

2912   Schoenberger, Karen C. The Development of the Image of a Selective Collegiate Public Institution and the Effects of that Image Upon Admissions: The Case of The College of William and Mary in Virginia, 1946-1980. Ed.D, College of William & Mary , 1984. 278p. UMl# 8604300.

2913   Smith, Russell T. Distinctive Traditions at The College of William and Mary and Their Influence on the Modernization of the College, 1865-1919. Ed.D., College of William & Mary, 1981. 245p. UMl# 85-00984.

2914   Wilbur, Barbara. The Influence of English and Scottish Universities on the Curriculum of the College of William & Mary. Master's thesis, College of William & Mary, 1957.

EMORY AND HENRY COLLEGE

2915   Orr, Helen A. The History of the Emory and Henry College Library, 1839-1954. Master's thesis, East Tennessee State College, 1954.

FERRUM COLLEGE

2916   Ayres, Ethel S. A History of Ferrum College: The First Fifty Years, 1913-1963. Master's thesis, Appalachian State Teachers College, 1963.

HAMPDEN-SYDNEY COLLEGE

2917   Carlson, Alden L. The Life and Educational Contributions of John Holt Rice. Ph.D., University of Virginia, 1954. 296p. UMI# 00-09637. [professor of theology, Hampden-Sydney College, 1824-1831].

2918   Overton, Edward F. A Study of the Life and Work of Joseph Dupuy Eggleston, Junior. Ph.D., University of Virginia, 1943. [president, Hampden-Sydney College, 1919-1939].

2919   Topping, Leonard W. A History of Hampden-Sydney College in Virginia, 1771-1883. Master's thesis, University of Richmond, 1950.

HAMPTON INSTITUTE

2920   Carson, Suzanne C. Samuel Chapman Armstrong, Missionary to the South. Ph.D., Johns Hopkins University, 1952. [president, Hampton Institute, 1868-1893].

2921   Hunter, Wilma K. Coming of Age: Hollis B. Frissell and the Emergence of Hampton Institute, 1893-1917. Ph.D., Indiana University, 1982. 357p. UMI# 8307980. [principal].

2922   Robinson, William H. The History of Hampton Institute, 1868-1949. Ph.D., New York University, 1954. 467p. UMI# 00-10646.

2923   Tingey, Joseph W. Indians and Blacks Together: An Experiment in Biracial Education at Hampton Institute (1878-1923). Ed.D., Columbia University Teachers College, 1978. 397p. UMI# 79-23636.

JAMES MADISON UNIVERSITY

2924   Frost, Gary J. The Building of an Academic Community: James Madison College. Ph.D., Michigan State University, 1971. 416p. UMI# 71-23186.

LONGWOOD COLLEGE

2925   Dalton, Thomas C. Institutional Changes in a State Teachers College: An Analysis of the Decision Making at Longwood College: 1946-1967. Ed.D., University of Virginia, 1976. 238p. UMI# 76-22,828.

2926   Fraser, Walter J., Jr. William Henry Ruffner: A Liberal in the Old and New South. Ph.D., University of Tennessee, 1970. 549p. UMI# 70-20304. [president, Longwood College, 1884-1887].

LYNCHBURG COLLEGE

2927   Wake, Orville W. A History of Lynchburg College, 1903-1953. Ph.D., University of Virginia, 1957. 375p. UMI# 00-22911.

MADISON COLLEGE

2928   Sonner, Ray V. Madison College: The Miller Years, 1949-1970. Ed.D., University of Virginia, 1974. 153p. UMI# 74-29,212.

MARION COLLEGE

2929   Hunter, Katrina. A History of Marion College, Marion, Virginia. Master's thesis, East Tennessee State University, 1969.

MARY WASHINGTON COLLEGE

2930   Carlson, Alden L. A History of Mary Washington College. Master's thesis, University of Virginia, 1948.

MARYMOUNT COLLEGE OF VIRGINIA

2931   Walsh, Walter. The Growth and Development of Marymount College, Arlington, Virginia, 1948-1965. Master's thesis, Catholic University of America, 1966.

OLD DOMINION UNIVERSITY

2932   Harris, Woodrow W. A History of the Division of Continuing Education at Old Dominion University, 1919-1970. Master's thesis, Old Dominion University, 1971.

PROTESTANT EPISCOPAL THEOLOGICAL SEMINARY

2933   Edsall, Margaret H. History of the Library of the Protestant Episcopal Theological Seminary in Virginia, 1823-1955. Master's thesis, Catholic University of America, 1955.

RANDOLPH MACON COLLEGE

2934   Becker, James M. Was Randolph-Macon Different? Revivalism, Sectionalism, and the Academic Tradition: The Methodist Mission in Higher Education, 1830-1880. Ph.D., University of North Carolina at Chapel Hill, 1980. 436p. UMI# 81-14788.

SAINT PAUL'S COLLEGE

2935   Thurman, Francis A. The History of Saint Paul's College in Lawrenceville, Virginia, 1888-1959. Ph.D., Howard University, 1978. 320p. UMI# 7917010.

SOUTHERN SEMINARY

2936   Kling, Frederick W. The History of Southern Seminary. Master's thesis, University of Virginia, 1937.

STONEWALL JACKSON COLLEGE

2937   Britt, Samuel S., Jr. A History of Stonewall Jackson College, 1868-1930. Master's thesis, University of Virginia, 1949.

UNION SEMINARY

2938   Overy, David H. Robert Lewis Dabney: Apostle of the Old South. Ph.D., University of Wisconsin, 1967. 338p. [professor of theology, Union Seminary].

VIRGINIA COMMONWEALTH UNIVERSITY

2939   Giunta, Mary A. A History of the Department of Legal Medicine at the Medical College of Virginia. Master's thesis, University of Richmond, 1966.

2940   Griggs, Walter S., Jr. The Influence of Accreditation on the Development of the Medical College of Virginia into an Institution with University Affiliation. Ed.D., College of William & Mary, 1979. 87p. UMI# 80-02567.

2941   Williams, Ann L. In Search of a Home: An Historical Analysis of the Major Factors Concerning the Location of Virginia Commonwealth University. Ed.D., College of William & Mary, 1985. 104p. UMI# 8608914.

VIRGINIA POLYTECHNIC INSTITUTE AND STATE UNIVERSITY

2942   Cochran, John P. The Virginia Agricultural and Mechanical College: The Formative Half Century, 1872-1919, of Virginia Polytechnic Institute. Ph.D., University of Alabama, 1961. 328p. UMI# 61-04234.

2943   Gaunt, Roger N. Three Perspectives on the Political History of Virginia's Veterinary School. Ph.D., University of Virginia, 1980. 393p. UMI# 81-02596.

VIRGINIA STATE UNIVERSITY

2944   Braxton, Harold E. A History of the General Education Program at Virginia State College Since 1950. Ed.D., University of Virginia, 1973. 121p. UMI# 73-32426.

2945   Norbrey, Grace V. H. A Study of the Development of the Land Grant Program at Virginia State University (1920-1980). Ed.D., George Washington University, 1983. 181p. UMI# 83-07891.

2946   Ryder, William H. Music at Virginia State College, 1883-1966. Ph.D., University of Michigan, 1970. 200p. UMI# 71-23,865.

VIRGINIA, UNIVERSITY OF

2947   Allen, Milton R. A History of the Young Men's Christian Association at the University of Virginia. Ph.D., University of Virginia, 1947. 183p.

2948   Barnhardt, Robert A. The Process of Undergraduate Curriculum Change at the School of Engineering and Applied Science, University of Virginia, 1940-1973. Ed.D., University of Virginia, 1974. 242p. UMI# 74-29213.

2949   Betts, Leonidas J., Jr. George Frederick Holmes: A Critical Biography of a Nineteenth Century Southern Educator. Ed.D., Duke University, 1966. 151p. UMI# 67-09740. [professor of history and literature, University of Virginia].

2950   Carey, Alma P. Thomas Jefferson's Ideal University: Dream and Actuality. Master's thesis, University of Texas, 1937.

2951   Fisher, Regina B. Co-Education at the University of Virginia, 1920-1940. Master's thesis, University of Virginia, 1942.

2952   Hellenbrand, Harold L. The Unfinished Revolution: Education and Community in the Thought of Thomas Jefferson (Volumes I and II). Ph.D., Stanford University, 1980. 624p. UMI# 8103519.

2953   Holmes, George B. The Life and Contributions of George Frederick Holmes, Scholar, Teacher and Writer (1820-1897). Master's thesis, Virginia Polytechnic Institute, 1957. [professor of history and literature, University of Virginia].

2954   Nolen, Claude B. An Appraisal of the Program Leading to the Doctor of Education Degree in Educational Administration and Supervision at the University of Virginia. Ed.D., University of Virginia, 1974. 213p. UMI# 75-02021.

2955   Pence, James W., Jr. A History and Evaluation of Student Public Speaking in the Literary Societies of the University of Virginia, 1825-1950. Master's thesis, University of Virginia, 1951.

2956   Reveley, David R. The Degree Requirements at the University of Virginia from 1825-1930. Master's thesis, University of Virginia, 1931.

2957   Rodgers, Elise A. The Foundation & Early History of the Medical School of the University of Virginia (to 1840). Master's thesis, University of Virginia, 1930.

2958   Rumbolz, Harry H. A Study of Thomas Jefferson and His Influence on Higher Education. Master's thesis, Stanford University, 1934.

2959   Shawen, Neil M. The Casting of a Lengthening Shadow: Thomas Jefferson's Role in Determining the Site of a State University in Virginia. Ed.D., George Washington University, 1980. 479p. UMI# 8017730.

2960   Tanner, Carol M. Joseph C. Cabell, 1778-1856. Ph.D., University of Virginia, 1948. [founder, University of Virginia].

2961   Wall, Charles C. Students and Student Life at the University of Virginia, 1825 to 1861. Ph.D., University of Virginia, 1978. 341p. UMI# 79-16286.

2962   Weakley, Margaret E. The Origin and History of the Medical Library of the University of Virginia School of Medicine, 1825-1962. Master's thesis, University of North Carolina, 1966. 117p.

2963   Wiley, Wayne H. Academic Freedom at the University of Virginia: The First Hundred Years—From Jefferson through Alderman. Ph.D., University of Virginia, 1973. 399p. UMI# 73-31174.

2964   Wilson, George P., Jr. A History of Speech Education at the University of Virginia, 1825-1953. Ph.D., Columbia University, 1958. 347p. UMI# 58-02720.

VIRGINIA UNION UNIVERSITY

2965   Taliaferro, Cecil R. Virginia Union University, the First One Hundred Years, 1865-1965. Ph.D., University of Pittsburgh, 1975. 144p. UMI# 75-22,468.

WASHINGTON AND LEE UNIVERSITY

2966   Britt, Samuel S., Jr. Henry Ruffner, 19th Century Educator. Ed.D., University of Arizona, 1962. 181p. UMI# 62-06573. [president, Washington and Lee University, 1836-1848].

2967   Miller, Richard. A History of Wrestling at Washington and Lee University and the Southern Conference Wrestling Tournament, 1921 to 1961. Master's thesis, Springfield College, 1961. 136p.

WESLEYAN FEMALE INSTITUTE

2968   Brown, Charles K. The Wesleyan Female Institute: A College for Young Women Under the Auspice of the Baltimore Conference, Methodist-Episcopal Church, Staunton, Virginia, 1846-1897. Master's thesis, University of Virginia, 1936.

WASHINGTON

GENERAL STUDIES

2969   Cosgriffe, Harry A. The Washington State Agricultural Extension Service, 1912-1961. Ph.D., University of Chicago, 1966.

2970   Crawford, Allan P. The Junior College Movement in Washington State from 1915 to 1955 with Proposals for Further Development. Ph.D., University of Denver, 1959.

2971   Cremer, Henry. The History of Teacher Training in the Public Higher Institutions of Washington. Ph.D., University of Washington, 1928.

2972   Hite, Floyd H. An Evaluation of Teacher Training Activities in Audiovisual Education in the State of Washington, 1937-1947. Ph.D., Washington State University, 1951.

2973   Lash, Frederick M. An Historical and Functional Study of Public Education in Seattle, Washington. Ph.D., University of Washington, 1934.

2974   Leister, Terry G. An Analysis of the Centralization of Community College Authority in Washington State from 1917-1973 Using Easton's Political Systems Framework. Ph.D., University of Washington, 1975. 265p. UMI# 76-17545.

2975   Nelson, Torlef. A History of the Washington State Permanent Common School Fund. Ph.D., University of Washington, 1953. 323p.

2976   Schlauch, Gustav H. A Study of Public Junior Colleges in Washington. Ph.D., University of Washington, 1932.

2977   Willoughby, Glenn E. Promises Vs. Performance: An Historical Analysis of the Pledge of Equal Educational Opportunity and Washington's Community Colleges. Ph.D., Washington State University, 1980. 355p. UMI# 80-15171.

EASTERN WASHINGTON UNIVERSITY

2978   Oliphant, James O. History of the State Normal School at Cheney. Master's thesis, University of Washington, 1924.

EVERGREEN STATE COLLEGE

2979   Stevens, William H., III. The Philosophical and Political Origins of the Evergreen State College (Washington). Ph.D., University of Washington, 1983. 392p. UMI# 83-26917.

NORTHWEST COLLEGE OF THE ASSEMBLIES OF GOD

2980   Williams, Mary M. The History of the Northwest College of the Assemblies of God, 1934-1966. Master's thesis, University of Washington, 1967.

PUGET SOUND, UNIVERSITY OF

2981   Matthews, Alfred W. History of the College of Puget Sound. Master's thesis, University of Washington, 1926.

2982   Mills, George H. Secularization at the University of Puget Sound. Ph.D., University of Washington, 1983. 407p. UMI# 8326893.

SEATTLE PACIFIC COLLEGE

2983   Hedges, Richard G. A Historical Study of Seattle Seminary and Seattle Pacific College, 1891-1920. Master's thesis, University of Washington, 1963.

SEATTLE UNIVERSITY

2984   Barker, Linda A.Leadership: Albert A. Lemieux and Seattle University.Ed.D., Seattle University, 1985. 216p. UMI# 8529786. [president, 1948-1965].

2985   Cronin, Timothy F. Seattle University: 1891-1966. Ed.D., Seattle University, 1982. 401p. UMI# 82-25162.

ST. MARTIN'S COLLEGE

2986   Curtis, Dunstan E.F. The Historical-Philosophical Bases for Teacher Education in a Benedictine College. Ph.D., Stanford University, 1960. 586p. UMI# 60-06725.

WASHINGTON STATE UNIVERSITY

2987   Adams, Sarah J. The Historic Role of the Liberal Arts at Washington State University. Master's thesis, University of Washington, 1963.

2988   Gorchels, Clarence C. A Land Grant University Library: The History of the Library of Washington State University, 1892-1946. Ph.D., Columbia University, 1971. 427p.

2989   Landrus, Wilfred M. An Historical Study of the Organization and Development of Student Personnel Services at the State College of Washington. Ed.D., State College of Washington, 1956. 313p. UMI# 20,482.

2990   Murdock, Patrick M. A Critical History of the College of Agriculture, State College of Washington, 1892-1916. Ph.D., Washington State University, 1955. 262p. UMI# 00-11848.

2991   Smith, Mazine H. The History of the Development of the Women's Physical Education Major Program at the State College of Washington, from Its Inception in 1919 to 1929. Master's thesis, State College of Washington, 1951.

WASHINGTON, UNIVERSITY OF

2992   Bennett, Marilyn D. The Glenn Hughes Years, 1927-1961; University of Washington School of Drama. Ph.D., University of Washington, 1982. 309p. UMI# 8304376.

2993   Cronk, Ernest L. A History of the Department of Physical and Health Education for Men at the University of Washington 1894-1956. Master's thesis, University of Washington, 1958.

2994   Hall, Helen L. Vernon Louis Parrington: The Genesis and Design of *Main Currents in American Thought*. Ph.D., Case Western Reserve University, 1979. 506p. UMI# 7924807. [professor of English, University of Washington].

2995   Hall, Margaret A. A History of Women Faculty at the University of Washington, 1896-1970. Ph.D., University of Washington, 1984. 360p. UMI# 8412393.

2996   Hedges, Richard G. A Study of Leftist Student Activists at the University of Washington. Ph.D., University of Washington, 1970. 119p. UMI# 71-00975.

2997   Hewitt, Lynn R. The History of Intercollegiate Football at the University of Washington from Its Origin through 1965. Master's thesis, University of Washington, 1968. 236p.

2998   Lawrence, Cora J. University Education for Nursing in Seattle 1912-1950: An Inside Story of the University of Washington School. Ph.D., University of Washington, 1972. 287p. UMI# 72-28622.

2999   Peterson, Daniel E. University of Washington, History, 1887-1902. Master's thesis, University of Washington, 1959.

3000   Potter, Jessica C. The History of the University of Washington Library. Master's thesis, University of Washington, 1954. 101p.

3001   Royster Horn, Juana R. The Academic and Extracurricular Undergraduate Experiences of Three Black Women at the University of Washington, 1935 to 1941. Ph.D., University of Washington, 1980. 274p. UMI# 80-26297.

3002   Rulifson, John R. Frederick Elmer Bolton: American Educator in the Pacific Northwest. Ph.D., University of Washington, 1967. 313p. UMI# 68-3878. [professor of education and dean, University of Washington, 1912-1928].

3003   Sanders, Jane A. Academic Freedom at the University of Washington During the Cold War Years: 1946-1964. Ph.D., University of Washington, 1976. 384p. UMI# 77-00617.

3004   Thornton, Thurle C., Jr. The History of Intercollegiate Swimming at the University of Washington through 1961. Master's thesis, University of Washington, 1962. 157p.

3005   Tobacco, Charles T. An Historical Study of Intercollegiate Track and Field at the University of Washington Prior to 1960. Master's thesis, University of Washington, 1961. 164p.

3006   Ulbrickson, Alvin E. The History of Intercollegiate Rowing at the University of Washington through 1963. Master's thesis, University of Washington, 1964.

3007   Walker, Phillip N. A History of Dramatics at the University of Washington from the Beginning to June 1919. Master's thesis, University of Washington, 1947.

3008   Warren, Shirley C. The History of the Undergraduate Teacher Education Program in Physical Education for Women at the University of Washington, 1920-1935. Master's thesis, University of Washington, 1968.

3009   Wilson, Henrietta. History, Development and Present Status of the General Studies Division of the University of Washington. Master's thesis, University of Washington, 1949.

WESTERN WASHINGTON UNIVERSITY

3010   Dreves, Vivian E. Head, Heart and Hand: A Study of Bellingham State Normal School, 1899-1909. Master's thesis, Western Washington University, 1983.

WHITMAN COLLEGE

3011   Minnick, Walter C. The Effect of Inflation on the Endowment of Whitman College: 1940-1963. Master's thesis, Whitman College, 1964.

3012   Wilkinson, Jean L. The Development of Whitman College Curriculum, 1882-1959. Master's thesis, Whitman College, 1959.

WEST VIRGINIA

GENERAL STUDIES

3013   Harris, Virgie. Library Development in Five Denominational Colleges in West Virginia. Master's thesis, Western Reserve University, 1952. 106p.

3014   Jackameit, William P. The Political, Social, and Economic Factors in the Shaping of the Structure of Public Higher Education in West Virginia: A History, 1863-1969. Ed.D., College of William & Mary, 1973. 211p. UMI# 74-00085.

3015   Machesney, John D. The Development of Higher Education Governance and Coordination in West Virginia. Ed.D., University of West Virginia, 1972. 137p. UMI# 72-26850.

3016   McGinnis, Howard J. A History of Teacher Training in West Virginia. Master's thesis, University of Chicago, 1924.

3017   Sheets, Norman L. The Development and Application of Evaluative Criteria for Undergraduate Professional Preparation in Physical Education in Institutions of Higher Learning in the State of West Virginia. Ph.D., West Virginia University, 1959.

BLUEFIELD STATE COLLEGE

3018   Garrett, R.T. A Study of the Transition of Bluefield State College from a Black Teacher Preparation College to a Predominantly White Liberal Arts College. Ed.D., Rutgers University, 1979. 111p. UMI# 80-00853.

CONCORD COLLEGE

3019   Sizemore, Virginia L. A History of Concord College. Master's thesis, Marshall University, 1950.

FAIRMONT STATE COLLEGE

3020   Powell, Ruth A. A History of the Fairmont State College Library, 1867-1967. Master's thesis, Kent State University, 1967. 149p.

GLENVILLE STATE COLLEGE

3021   Amos, Autumn. A History of Robert F. Kidd Library. Master's thesis, Western Reserve University, 1953. 45p.

MARSHALL UNIVERSITY

3022   Clark, Robert R. The History of Music at Marshall University, Huntington, West Virginia: 1837-1970. Ph.D., University of Michigan, 1972. 233p. UMI# 73-11,076.

3023   Gullickson, Richard A. The Contributions of Otta A. Swede Gullickson to Marshall University, 1930-1963. Master's thesis, Marshall University, 1982.

3024   Roop, Jeane. History of Speech Education at Marshall University. Master's thesis, Marshall University, 1968.

MORRIS HARVEY COLLEGE

3025   Coburn, Frances G. An Historical Study of the Growth of Morris Harvey College from 1888-1952. Master's thesis, Marshall College, 1953.

SHEPHERD COLLEGE

3026   Slonaker, Arthur G. A History of Shepherd College, Shepherdstown, West Virginia. Ed.D., University of Virginia, 1958. 293p. UMI# 58-05556.

WEST VIRGINIA STATE COLLEGE

3027   Kalme, Albert P. Racial Desegregation and Integration in American Education: The Case History of West Virginia State College, 1891-1973. Ph.D., University of Ottawa-(Canada), 1977.

3028   Wilson, Ella M. An Historical Study of Desegregation at West Virginia State College, 1954-1973: An Application of a Theory of Mandated Academic Change. Ph.D., Kent State University, 1985. 338p. UMI# 8609189.

WEST VIRGINIA UNIVERSITY

3029   Billups, Helen K. A History of Physical Education for Women in West Virginia University. Master's thesis, West Virginia University, 1940.

3030   Colebank, Albert D. History of Intercollegiate Basketball in the United States with Special Reference to West Virginia University. Master's thesis, West Virginia University, 1939. 111p.

3031   Munn, Robert F. West Virginia University Library, 1867-1917. Ph.D., University of Michigan, 1962. 260p. UMI# 62-02770.

3032   Schwartzwalder, Wayne W. A History of Intercollegiate Football at West Virginia University. Master's thesis, West Virginia University, 1940. 161p.

3033   Williamson, Graydon G. A Historical Analysis of the West Virginia College of Graduate Studies from 1958 to 1976: The Study of Organizational Birth, Growth, and Development. Ed.D., West Virginia University, 1981. 267p. UMI# 81-18403.

WISCONSIN

GENERAL STUDIES

3034   Bailey, Richard P. The Wisconsin State Colleges, 1875-1955, with Respect to the Function of Preparing Secondary School Teachers. Ph.D., University of Wisconsin, 1959. 344p. UMI# 59-05745.

3035   Gearity, James L. The First Brain Trust: Academics, Reform, and the Wisconsin Idea. Ph.D., University of Minnesota, 1979. 355p. UMI# 79-26127.

3036   Herrmann, William H. The Rise of the Public Normal School System in Wisconsin. Ph.D., University of Wisconsin, 1953. 627p. UMI# 72-24046.

3037   Kelly, Gale L. The Politics of Higher Educational Coordination in Wisconsin, 1956-1969. Ph.D., University of Wisconsin, 1972. 433p. UMI# 72-24887.

3038   McIntyre, Calvin M. The Influence and Influence Strategies of the Wisconsin Student Association on University Policy-Making, 1938-1970. Ph.D., University of Wisconsin, 1972. 426p. UMI# 72-29505.

3039   Pollak, Peter G. Socialism and Social Science in the Formation of the American University: The Intercollegiate Socialist Society and the Case of Wisconsin. Ph.D., State University of New York at Albany, 1977. UMI# 78-05711.

3040   Reed, Lawrence L. The Development of the Manuscript Collections at the State Historical Society of Wisconsin through 1969. Ph.D., University of Wisconsin, 1983. 312p. UMI# 8315022.

3041   Smith, Ronald A. From Normal School to State University: A History of the Wisconsin State University Conference. Ph.D., University of Wisconsin, 1969. 486p. UMI# 69-22482.

3042   Ulrich, Robert J. The Bennett Law of 1889: Education and Politics in Wisconsin. Ph.D., University of Wisconsin, 1965. 580p. UMI# 65-10672.

CARDINAL STRITCH COLLEGE

3043   Flahive, Robert F. Cardinal Stritch College: Yesterday, Today and Tomorrow. Ed.D., Marquette University, 1973. 397p. UMI# 73-27502.

CARROLL COLLEGE

3044   Krueger, Hanna E. History of the Carroll College Library. Master's thesis, University of Chicago, 1943. 164p.

3045   Pelton, Carol N. A Chronicle of Carroll College. Master's thesis, Marquette University, 1940.

LAWRENCE UNIVERSITY

3046   Busch, Stephen E. A History of the Lawrence Conservatory of Music. Ed.D., University of Michigan, 1961. 211p. UMI# 61-1727.

3047   Lau, Estelle P.O. Ellen C. Sabin, President of Milwaukee-Downer College, 1895-1921: Proponent of Higher Education for Women. Ph.D., Marquette University, 1976. 142p. UMI# 76-21752.

MARQUETTE UNIVERSITY

3048   Gawrysiak, Kenneth J. The Administration of Albert C. Fox, S.J.: A Portrait of Educational Leadership at Marquette University, 1922-1928. Ed.D., Marquette University, 1973. 192p. UMI# 74-18228.

3049   Mitchem, Arnold L. Marquette University's Educational Opportunity Program: A Case Study of a Compensatory Education Program in Higher Education, 1968-1981. Ph.D., Marquette University, 1981. 144p. UMI# 8307068.

3050   Ross, Raymond S. Preliminary Research Toward a History of Intercollegiate Debating at Marquette University. Master's thesis, Marquette University, 1951.

MILTON COLLEGE

3051   Smith, Gregory L. Milton College: An Evaluative Case Study in Decline. Ph.D., University of Wisconsin at Madison, 1985. 276p. UMI# 8513482.

WISCONSIN, UNIVERSITY OF

3052   Andrews, Cheryl A. The Audiovisual Center Phenomenon: An Historical Survey of the Forces Influencing the Foundation and Development of One Audiovisual Center. Ph.D., University of Wisconsin, 1979. 147p. UMI# 80-07538.

3053   Beardsley, Edward H. Portrait of a Scientist: The Professional Career of Harry Luman Russell. Ph.D., University of Wisconsin, 1966. 558p. UMI# 66-09886. [dean of agriculture, director of the Wisconsin Experiment Station, University of Wisconsin, 1907-1931].

3054   Beilke, Reuben. Student Political Action at the University of Wisconsin, 1930-1940. Master's thesis, University of Wisconsin, 1951.

3055   Buchanan, Marjorie H. Mission and Merger: Legislative Mandate and Institutional Response—A Case History of the University of Wisconsin System. Ph.D., University of Chicago, 1977.

3056   Carothers, Otto M., Jr. The Merger of the University of Wisconsin with the Wisconsin State Universities System. Ed.D., Indiana University, 1974. 297p. UMI# 75-05602.

3057   Cook, John F. A History of Liberal Education at the University of Wisconsin, 1862-1918. Ph.D., University of Wisconsin, 1970. 439p. UMI# 70-22044.

3058   Fenster, Valmai R. The University of Wisconsin Library School: A History, 1895-1921. Ph.D., University of Wisconsin-Madison, 1977. 687p. UMI# 77-19758.

3059   Graham, Robert H. Graduate Student Discontentment, Political Activism and Academic Reform: A Study of the University of Wisconsin, 1966-1970. Ph.D., University of Wisconsin, 1972. 265p. UMI# 72-31531.

3060   Hustvedt, Lloyd M. Pioneer Scholar: A Biography of Rasmus Bjorn Anderson. Ph.D., University of Wisconsin, 1962. 506p. UMI# 62-03889. [professor of Scandinavian languages and literature, University of Wisconsin, 1875-1883].

3061   Johnson, William R. The University of Wisconsin Law School: 1868-1930. Ph.D., University of Wisconsin, 1972. 403p. UMI# 73-2546.

3062   Klopf, Gordon J. A History of Speech Training at the University of Wisconsin from 1851 to 1941. Master's thesis, University of Wisconsin, 1941.

3063   Knauf, Vincent H. The History of Literary Societies at the University of Wisconsin. Master's thesis, University of Wisconsin, 1948.

3064   Larsen, Lawrence H. Glenn Frank: The Boy Wonder from Missouri. Ph.D., University of Wisconsin, 1962. 267p. UMI# 63-00665. [president, University of Wisconsin, 1925-1937].

3065   Lowell, Maurice W. The Persuasive Techniques of Glenn Frank. Master's thesis, University of Wisconsin, 1933. [president, University of Wisconsin, 1925-1937].

3066   Macy, William K. A Study of the University of Wisconsin Summer Music Clinic. Ph.D., University of Wisconsin, 1957. 288p. UMI# 57-3686.

3067   Mailer, Julia H. Dramatics as Fostered by Dramatic Clubs: An Historical Study Based on Student Dramatic Activities at the University of Wisconsin from 1891 to 1944. Master's thesis, University of Wisconsin, 1944.

3068   McMurray, Howard J. Some Influences of the University of Wisconsin on the State Government of Wisconsin: An Inquiry into the Effect of Inter-Institutional Relations on Policy, Administration, and Personnel. Ph.D., University of Wisconsin, 1940. 226p.

3069   Penn, John S. The Origin and Development of Radio Broadcasting at the University of Wisconsin to 1940. Ph.D., University of Wisconsin, 1959. 505p.

3070   Pittet, Marcel. Carl Russell Fish: An Essay on His Life and Writings. Master's thesis, University of Wisconsin, 1953. [professor of history, University of Wisconsin].

3071   Rader, Benjamin G. The Professor as a Reformer: Richard T. Ely, 1854-1943. Ph.D., University of Maryland, 1964. 260p. UMI# 65-00620. [head of political economy department, University of Wisconsin, 1892-1925].

3072   Rosentreter, Frederick M. The Boundaries of the Campus: A History of the Extension Division of the University of Wisconsin. Ph.D., University of Wisconsin, 1954.

3073   Ross, Donald K. W.G. Bleyer and the Development of Journalism Education. Master's thesis, University of Wisconsin, 1952. [professor of journalism, University of Wisconsin].

3074   Semmes, David H. A History of the Haresfoot Club of the University of Wisconsin. Master's thesis, University of Wisconsin, 1964.

3075   Sklar, Bernard. Faculty Culture and Community Conflict: A Historical, Political and Socio-logical Analysis of the October 18, 1967 Dow Demonstration at the University of Wiscon-sin. Ph.D., University of Chicago, 1970.

3076   Smith, Michael D. The Development of Positions Taken by the Faculty Regarding Intercol-legiate Athletics at the University of Wisconsin, 1873-1925. Master's thesis, University of Wisconsin, 1967.

3077   Titowsky, Bernard. The Growth of Historical Studies at the University of Wisconsin, 1876-1910: A Study in Historiography. Master's thesis, University of Wisconsin, 1949.

3078   Tufano, Alfred G. Michael Vincent O'Shea and the Professionalization of Teacher Educa-tion. Ph.D., University of Wisconsin, 1975. 304p. UMI# 75-28031. [professor of education, University of Wisconsin, 1897-1932].

3079   Vance, Maurice M. Charles Richard Van Hise: A Biography. Ph.D., University of Wiscon-sin, 1960. 318p. [president, University of Wisconsin, 1903-1918].

3080   Wallace, Sylvia F. Charles Kenneth Leith, Scientific Adviser. Ph.D., University of Wiscon-sin, 1966. 465p. UMI# 66-09981. [professor of geology, University of Wisconsin, 1902-1945].

3081   Wallenfeldt, Evert C. A State University President and the Social Psychology of Meeting Legislative and Gubernatorial Opposition: A Case Study of the Manner in which Charles Richard Van Hise Met Opposition in Wisconsin in 1915. Ed.D., Indiana University, 1962. 213p. UMI# 63-02620. [president, 1903-1918].

3082   Weinberg, Julius. Edward Alsworth Ross: An Intellectual Biography. Ph.D., University of Michigan, 1963. 389p. UMI# 64-08223. [professor of sociology, University of Wisconsin, 1906-1937].

3083   Zimmerman, Norman A. A Triumph for Orthodoxy: The University of Wisconsin During World War I. Ph.D., University of Minnesota, 1971. 243p. UMI# 72-00384.

WISCONSIN, UNIVERSITY OF (LACROSSE)

3084   Fogle, Rick A. The Historical Development of the Student Centers Committee at the University of Wisconsin-Lacrosse. Master's thesis, University of Wisconsin-LaCrosse, 1983.

3085   Knutson, Keith A. A History of the Office of Extension Education at the University of Wisconsin. Lacrosse, 1974-1982. Master's thesis, University of Wisconsin-LaCrosse, 1985.

WISCONSIN, UNIVERSITY OF (OSHKOSH)

3086   Hubbard, Corinne. History of Wisconsin State College, Oshkosh, Library, September, 1871-August, 1943. Master's thesis, Drexel Institute of Technology, 1954. 69p.

3087   Schwartfeger, Sylvia. The History of Educational Materials Center at the University of Wisconsin-Oshkosh. Master's thesis, University of Wisconsin-Oshkosh, 1981.

WYOMING

CASPER COLLEGE

3088   McCollom, Stewart F. A History of Casper College with Special References to Selected Historical Aspects of the Junior College Movement in the United States and Wyoming. Ph.D., University of Wyoming, 1965.

SHERIDAN COLLEGE

3089   Cavanna, Robert C. A History of Sheridan College, 1948-1973. Ed.D., University of Wyoming, 1977. 323p. UMI# 78-00166.

WYOMING, UNIVERSITY OF

3090   Hill, Daniel N. Everett F. Shelton: Teacher, Coach, Commissioner. Ed.D., Brigham Young University, 1978. 135p. UMI# 7813822. [University of Wyoming, 1939-1959].

3091   Woodward, George R. History of the College of Education, University of Wyoming, 1887-1945. Ed.D., University of Wyoming, 1971. 161p. UMI# 72-13056.

PART TWO

TOPICAL STUDIES

ACADEMIC FREEDOM

3092   Aby, Stephen H. The Political Economy of Academic Freedom. Ph.D., State University of New York at Buffalo, 1979. 312p. UMI# 7921843.

3093   Anderson, Stanley D., Jr. An Analysis of the Meaning of Academic Freedom in American Higher Education, 1860-1920. Ph.D., University of Minnesota, 1980. 297p. UMI# 81-02063.

3094   Deering, Thomas E. Academic Freedom: Issues and Controversies, 1963-1985. Ph.D., University of Missouri at Columbia, 1985. 249p. UMI# 8611731.

3095   Harris, Benedict O. A Review of Some Aspects of Academic Freedom in Colleges and Universities in the Perspective of the 1915 Declaration of the American Association of University Professors. Ph.D., State University of New York at Buffalo, 1978. 110p. UMI# 78-10627.

3096   Hartsell, Lee E. An Analysis of Judicial Decisions Regarding Academic Freedom in Public and Private Elementary and Secondary Schools and the Institutions of Higher Education, 1960-1975. Ed.D., Auburn University, 1977. 154p. UMI# 77-24,497.

3097   Holbrook, Sandra L.R. Faculty Academic Freedom and the Federal Appellate Courts: Legal Dimensions of a Professional Concept. Ph.D., University of Minnesota, 1984. 220p. UMI# 8503068.

3098   Lucas, Christopher J. American Conceptions of Academic Freedom in the Twentieth Century. Ph.D., Ohio State University, 1967. 409p. UMI# 67-16303.

3099   McDougall, Daniel J. McCarthyism and Academia: Senator Joe McCarthy's Political Investigations of Educators, 1950-54. Ph.D., Loyola University of Chicago, 1977. 372p. UMI# 77-22346.

3100   Metzger, Loya F. Professors in Trouble: A Quantitative Analysis of Academic Freedom and Tenure Cases (1913-1957). Ph.D., Columbia University, 1978. 427p. UMI# 7819393.

3101   Morgan, Alda C.M. Academic Freedom in Higher Education: An Historical and Theological Examination of Its Place and Function in the Light of Five Cases. Ph.D., Graduate Theological Union, 1984. 698p. UMI# 8418051.

3102   Nass, Deanna R. The Image of Academic Freedom Conveyed by Select Scholarly Journals of the McCarthy Era (Volumes I and II). Ph.D., Columbia University, 1979. 455p. UMI# 80-09359.

3103　　Nelson, Karen C. Historical Origins of the Linkage of Academic Freedom and Faculty Tenure. Ph.D., University of Denver, 1984. 172p. UMI# 8500215.

3104　　Ogilvie, Charles F. Academic Freedom in the Colleges of Three Major Southern Denominations, 1865-1965. Ph.D., University of South Carolina, 1966. 261p. UMI# 66-13387.

3105　　Quenzel, Carrol. Academic Freedom in Southern Colleges and Universities. Master's thesis, University of West Virginia, 1933.

3106　　Rolnick, Stanley R. The Development of the Idea of Academic Freedom in American Higher Education, 1870-1920. Ph.D., University of Wisconsin, 1952.

3107　　Sanders, Gabe. Selected Aspects of Academic Freedom in American Colleges and Universities (1918-1951). Ph.D., Columbia University, 1953.

3108　　Schaehrer, Peter C. McCarthyism and Academic Freedom: Three Case Studies. Ed.D., Columbia University, 1974. 314p. UMI# 74-23,532.

3109　　Schwegler, John S. Academic Freedom and the Disclaimer Affidavit of the National Defense Education Act: The Response of Higher Education. Ed.D., Columbia University Teachers College, 1982. 148p. UMI# 8215757.

3110　　Sutton, Robert B. European and American Backgrounds of the Concept of Academic Freedom, 1500-1914. Ph.D., University of Missouri at Columbia, 1950. 337p. UMI# 00-01802.

ACCREDITATION

3111　　Cable, David B. The Development of the Accrediting Function of the American Association of Theological Schools, 1918-1938. Ph.D., University of Pittsburgh, 1970. 194p. UMI# 71-16181.

3112　　Cocking, Herbert. Bible College Accreditation by the North Central Association: 1970-1980. Ph.D., University of Michigan, 1982. 390p. UMI# 8304456.

3113　　Gengel, Kenneth O. A Study of the Evolution of College Accreditation Criteria in the North Central Association and Its Effect on Bible Colleges. Ph.D., University of Missouri-Kansas-City, 1969. 227p. UMI# 70-09860.

3114　　Harper, William S. G. A History of Criticisms of 'Extra-Legal' Accrediting of Higher Education in the United States from 1890 to 1970. Ed.D., University of Missouri-Columbia, 1972. 339p. UMI# 73-21430.

3115　　Hopkins, David R. The Development of the Six Regional Voluntary Accrediting Associations in American Higher Education: An Historical Analysis. Ed.D., University of Georgia, 1974. 251p. UMI# 75-02598.

3116　　Millman, Howard L. Accreditation of Teacher Education Institutions: An Historical and Case Study Perspective (Volumes I and II). Ed.D., University of Massachusetts, 1972. 671p. UMI# 73-05247.

3117　　Overby, George R. A Critical Review of Selected Issues Involved in the Establishment and Functioning of the National Council for Accreditation of Teacher Education from Its Origin through 1965. Ph.D., Florida State University, 1966. 258p. UMI# 67-00349.

3118   Robertson, Mary P.P. A Study of the Characteristics of Specialized Accreditation Evaluation Teams for Associate Degree Programs, 1970-1980. Ed.D., Rutgers University, 1983. 191p. UMI# 835908.

3119   Talbot, Gordon G. A Study of the Accrediting Association of Bible Colleges from 1947 through 1966. Ph.D., New York University, 1968. 290p. UMI# 69-11773.

3120   Wood, Thomas C. The Development of Accreditation of Recreation Programs in Higher Education, 1949-1982. Ph.D., Southern Illinois University at Carbondale, 1983. 237p. UMI# 8321476.

3121   Ziemba, Walter J. Changes in Policies and Procedures of the Accrediting Process of the Commission on Colleges and Universities of the North Central Association of Colleges and Secondary Schools, 1909-1958. Ph.D., University of Michigan, 1966. 390p. UMI# 67-01828.

ADMINISTRATION

3122   Barosko, Samuel, Jr. Business Values and Practices in Education, a Historical Perspective and Conceptual Analysis of the Accountability Movement and Its Relationship to the Efficiency Era. Ph.D., University of Wisconsin, 1972. 177p. UMI# 72-23297.

3123   Beach, Mark B. Professors, Presidents, and Trustees: A Study of University Governance, 1825-1918. Ph.D., University of Wisconsin, 1966. 354p. UMI# 66-01262.

3124   Born, William M. The Historical Development of Governing Boards of State Universities in the United States: An Analysis of Some Trends and Portents. Ph.D., Michigan State University, 1974. 205p. UMI# 74-27390.

3125   Brown, Alice W. Growth in Administration: A Longitudinal Study of Administration in Four Regional Universities. Ed.D., University of Kentucky, 1979. 345p. UMI# 80-11114.

3126   Clements, Patricia L. A Content Analysis of Time Magazine's Posture on Administrative Policies in Higher Education, 1923-1973. Ph.D., Florida State University, 1975. 102p. UMI# 75-17927.

3127   Corson, Louis D. University Problems as Described in the Personal Correspondence Among D.C. Gilman, A.D. White and C.W. Eliot. Ph.D., Stanford University, 1951.

3128   Danilov, Victor J. The Western Regional Education Compact. Ed.D., University of Colorado, 1964. 469p. UMI# 65-4237.

3129   Edelson, Ivan J. The Historical Development of the Cluster College Concept and Its Present Implementation. Ed.D., State University of New York at Albany, 1973. 239p. UMI# 74-00777.

3130   Ford, Frederick R. The Growth of Supporting Operations within a University Organization: A Historical Study. Ph.D., Purdue University, 1963. 215p. UMI# 64-05726.

3131   Healey, Rose M. Trustees and College Failure: The Role of Governing Boards in Privately

Controlled College Terminations. Ph.D., University of Toledo, 1977. 267p. UMI# 77-23666.

3132   Howard, Sherwin W. Prelude to Merger: An Historical Case Study of Trustee Decision-Making Leading to the Merger of a Small College. Ph.D., University of Wisconsin, 1980. 263p. UMI# 81-02204.

3133   Khan, Muhammad. A Study of the Activities of the Council for Administrative Leadership in Relation to Professionalism in Educational Administration: 1956-1969. Ed.D., State University of New York at Albany, 1970. 237p. UMI# 70-25441.

3134   Klepper, William M., II. An Investigation of the Historical and Philosophical Development of the Management by Objectives Principle of Administration in Higher Education. Ph.D., Saint Louis University, 1975. 115p. UMI# 75-26273.

3135   Lefebvre, Jeanne M. Toward Credible Authority: Selected National Efforts to Renew Academic Governance Structures Between 1964 and 1974. Ph.D., Georgetown University, 1978. 324p. UMI# 7909317.

3136   Lykes, Richard W. A History of the Division of Higher Education, United States Office of Education, from Its Creation in 1911 Until the Establishment of the Department of Health, Education, and Welfare in 1953. Ph.D., American University, 1960. 477p. UMI# 60-03027.

3137   McGrath, Earl J. The Evolution of Administrative Offices in Institutions of Higher Education from 1860 to 1933. Ph.D., University of Chicago, 1936. 132p.

3138   Munford, James K. Committees in Higher Education: A Study of the Evolution and Function of Faculty Administrative Committees in Thirty-Eight American Colleges and Universities, 1870-1915. Ph.D., Stanford University, 1949.

3139   Owen, Stephen P. The Impact of University Expansion on the Evolution of the Chief Campus Executive's Office in Public Universities. Ph.D., University of Wisconsin, 1977. 154p. UMI# 77-14355.

3140   Page, Barbara A.S. Crisis Management in American Higher Education, 1960 to 1980. Ph.D., New School for Social Research, 1979. 706p. UMI# 81-03452.

3141   Rabe, William F. The Evolution of Government and Administration of Higher Education. Ph.D., Stanford University, 1947. 416p.

3142   Richards, Robert O., Jr. The Growth of Administration within Universities. Ph.D., Michigan State University, 1970. 169p. UMI# 70-20520.

3143   Shapiro, Ira G. A History of the Professionalization of Recreation Administration from 1930 to 1970. Ph.D., University of North Carolina, 1970. 301p. UMI# 71-11746.

3144   Williams, Omer S. Democracy in Educational Administration. Ph.D., Northwestern University, 1940. 239p.

3145   Zwerman, Gilda N. The Organization of Industry and the Organization of Academe: A Study of Managerial Ideology in the American University, 1880-1980. Ph.D., New York University, 1982. 386p. UMI# 82-14856.

ADMISSIONS

3146   Bath, Joseph R. An Historical Survey of College Admission Practices in Baccalaureate Degree Granting Colleges in America, 1636-1876. Ph.D., Boston College, 1966.

3147   Broome, Edwin C. Historical and Critical Discussion of College Admission Requirements. Ph.D., Columbia University, 1902. 157p.

3148   Casale, John F. Development of College Admission Practices from 1890 to 1958. Master's thesis, Catholic University of America, 1961.

3149   Cheuvront, Harold R. The Evolution from Elitism to Egalitarianism and Its Effects on Undergraduate Higher Education. Ph.D., University of Northern Colorado, 1975. 236p. UMI# 76-00188.

3150   Elwell, Donald B. A History of the Advanced Placement Program of the College Entrance Examination Board to 1965. Ed.D., Columbia University, 1967. 332p. UMI# 67-16755.

3151   Gibson, J'nelle S. The Eight Year Study: A Limited View of College Admission Reform. Ph.D., University of Michigan, 1974. 261p. UMI# 75-10,176.

3152   Gould, Robert C. An Historical Survey of Admissions Practices in Baccalaureate Degree Granting Colleges of the United States from 1915 to 1940. Ph.D., Boston College, 1967.

3153   Hays, Edna. College Entrance Requirements in English: Their Effects on the High Schools: An Historical Survey. Ph.D., Columbia University, 1937. 141p.

3154   Malick, Herbert. An Historical Study of Admission Practices in Four-Year Undergraduate Colleges of the United States, 1870-1915. Ph.D., Boston College, 1966.

3155   McKown, Harry C. The Trend of College Entrance Requirements, 1913-1922. Ph.D., Columbia University, 1925. 172p.

3156   Synnott, Marcia G. A Social History of Admissions Policies at Harvard, Yale, and Princeton, 1900-1930. Ph.D., University of Massachusetts, 1974. 791p. UMI# 74-25906.

3157   Wechsler, Harold S. The Selective Function of American College Admissions Policies, 1870-1970. Ph.D., Columbia University, 1974. 481p. UMI# 75-07546.

ADULT EDUCATION

3158   Allen, Lawrence A. The Growth of Professionalism in the Adult Educational Movement, 1928-1958: A Content Analysis of the Periodical Literature. Ph.D., University of Chicago, 1962.

3159   Anania, Pasquale. Adult Age and the Educating of Adults in Colonial America. Ph.D., University of California-Berkeley, 1969. 467p. UMI# 70-06053.

3160   Hall, James C. A History of Special Baccalaureate Programs for Adults, 1945-1970. Ph.D., University of Chicago, 1976.

3161   Jacques, Joseph W. Recollections and Reflections of Professors of Adult Education: Early

Twentieth-Century Leaders and Pioneers in the Field. Ph.D., Florida State University, 1973. 286p. UMI# 73-31548.

3162   Portman, David N. The Origin and Development of Higher Adult Education in the United States. Ph.D., Syracuse University, 1972. 290p. UMI# 73-07760.

3163   Salyard, Ann B. The Educated American: A Study of Intellectual Development in Adulthood. Ed.D., University of California-Los Angeles, 1981. 474p. UMI# 82-06071.

3164   Shoemaker, Alice. Developments in the Field of Adult Education in the United States in the Second and Third Quarters of the Nineteenth Century. Ph.D., University of Wisconsin, 1931.

3165   Stubblefield, Harold W. Adult Education for Civic Participation: A Historical Analysis. Ed.D., University of Indiana, 1972. 205p. UMI# 73-10,788.

3166   White, Estelle E. Professionalization Process in Adult Education, USA, 1953-1969. Ed.D., North Carolina State University at Raleigh, 1970. 216p. UMI# 71-19937.

AGRICULTURAL EDUCATION

3167   Deatherage, J. Dal. History of Federal Participation in Vocational Education in Agriculture. Ph.D., Washington State University, 1950. 117p.

3168   Kennedy, Harold W. Objectives of Agricultural Education, Historical and Present Status. Ph.D., Ohio State University, 1940. 239p.

3169   Kirkendall, Richard S. The New Deal Professors and the Politics of Agriculture. Ph.D., University of Wisconsin, 1958. 430p. UMI# 58-02564.

3170   Lang, Charles L. A Historical Review of the Forces that Contributed to the Formation of the Cooperative Extension Service. Ed.D., Michigan State University, 1975. 203p. UMI# 76-12477.

3171   Mitchell, Theodore R. Oppositional Education in the Southern Farmers' Alliance: 1890-1900. Ph.D., Stanford University, 1983. 385p. UMI# 83-29754.

ALUMNI

3172   Blakely, Bernard E. Historical and Contemporaneous Predictors of Alumni Involvement. Ph.D., Purdue University, 1974. 267p. UMI# 75-10847.

3173   Hans, Patricia H. The Growth and Influence of the Alumni Movement on the Governance of Four Private Colleges: Williams, Union, Hamilton, and Amherst: 1821-1925. Ph.D., State University of New York at Buffalo, 1983. 220p. UMI# 83-25061.

3174   Kubik, Jan B. Migrational Patterns of College Students from Harvard, Princeton and Yale, 1915-1965, with Special Reference to the Out Migration of Students from the South. Ph.D., University of Illinois, 1978. 141p. UMI# 7913520.

3175   Maxwell, Howard B. The Formative Years of the University Alumni Movement as Illustrated by Studies of the University of Michigan and Columbia, Princeton, and Yale Universities, 1854-1918. Ph.D., University of Michigan, 1965. 436p. UMI# 65-10997.

ARCHITECTURE

3176   Bush-Brown, Albert. Image of a University: A Study of Architecture as an Expression of Education at Colleges and Universities in the United States Between 1800 and 1900. Ph.D., Princeton University, 1959. 519p. UMI# 59-05164.

3177   Tolles, Bryant F., Jr. College Architecture in Northern New England Before 1860: A Social and Cultural History. Ph.D., Boston University, 1970. 462p. UMI# 70-22390.

ASSOCIATIONS AND SOCIETIES

3178   Allen, George J., Jr. A History of the Commission on Colleges of the Southern Association of Colleges and Schools, 1949-1975. Ph.D., Georgia State University, 1978. 320p. UMI# 79-01820.

3179   Baum, Eugene L. History of the Commission on Relation of School and College of the Progressive Education Association, 1930-1942. Ph.D., Washington University, 1969. 323p. UMI# 69-22519.

3180   Bouseman, John. The Pulled-Away College: A Study of the Separation of Colleges from the Young Men's Christian Association. Ph.D., University of Chicago, 1970.

3181   Crawford, Esther K. History of the North Central Association of Colleges and Secondary Schools. Master's thesis, University of Chicago, 1930.

3182   Davis, Frank B. The Literary Societies of Selected State Universities of the Lower South. Ph.D., Louisiana State University, 1949. 449p.

3183   Grinnell, John E. The Rise of the North Central Association of Colleges and Secondary Schools. Ph.D., Stanford University, 1935.

3184   Harding, Thomas S. College Literary Societies: Their Contribution to Higher Education in the United States, 1815-1876. Ph.D., University of Chicago, 1957.

3185   Jackson, Isabel H. Nineteenth Century American Literary Societies. Master's thesis, University of California-Berkeley, 1934.

3186   Kerr, Kenneth M. An Analysis of the Cases Leading to Institutional Censure by the American Association of University Professors, 1940-1965. Ph.D., Indiana University, 1967. 236p. UMI# 68-2308.

3187   Layton, Donald B. The Education Commission of the States. Ph.D., University of Chicago, 1972.

3188   Maiden, Arthur L. Analysis of the Educational Studies Made Under the Auspices of the Association of American Universities for 1910 to 1931. Ph.D., American University, 1933.

3189   Mann, Lawrence R. The National Association of State Universities and Land Grant Colleges: A Political Interest Group and Its Congressional Relations, 1887-1958. Ph.D., University of Illinois at Urbana-Champaign, 1979.

3190   Naylor, Natalie A. Raising a Learned Ministry: The American Education Society, 1815-1860. Ed.D., Columbia University, 1971. 430p. UMI# 12,805.

3191   Partridge, Ronald R. A Study of the University Council for Educational Administration with Regard to Its Origin, Development, and Perceived Influence on Member Institutions. Ph.D., Ohio State University, 1971. 265p. UMI# 72-15270.

3192   Pugh, Darrell L. A History of the American Society for Public Administration: 1939-1979. Ph.D., University of Southern California, 1983.

3193   Simpson, Lowell. The Little Republics: Undergraduate Literary Societies at Columbia, Dartmouth, Princeton, and Yale, 1753-1865. Ed.D., Columbia University Teachers College, 1976. 194p. UMI# 76-17294.

3194   Solomon, Alan L. A Historical Study of the National Association for Music Therapy, 1960-1980. Ph.D., University of Kansas, 1985. 578p. UMI# 8529157.

3195   Williams, David. A Historical Study of the Involvement of the North Central Association with Higher Education in the United States. Ph.D., Wayne State University, 1972. 202p. UMI# 73-12619.

ATHLETICS

3196   Baptista, Robert C. A History of Intercollegiate Soccer in the United States of America. Doctor of Physical Education, Indiana University, 1962. 257p. UMI# 62-04117.

3197   Boerigter, Robert J. A History of the American College of Sports Medicine. Ph.D., University of Utah, 1978. 289p. UMI# 79-05074.

3198   Bowen, Keith A. A History of Intercollegiate Wrestling in the United States. Ph.D., Indiana University, 1952.

3199   Brooke, Jr., William O. Assessing the Impact of Title IX and Other Factors on Women's Intercollegiate Athletic Programs, 1972-1977. A National Study of Four-Year AIAW Institutions. Ed.D., Arizona State University, 1979. 154p. UMI# 7919171.

3200   Byrd, John W. The History of the Big Eight Conference. Ed.D., University of Alabama, 1970. 210p. UMI# 71-09064.

3201   Cobb, Justin L. The Evolution of the Rules of Intercollegiate Lacrosse. Master's thesis, Pennsylvania State University, 1952.

3202   Cochrane, Cornelius R., Jr. A Study of Intercollegiate Soccer Data in the United States from 1905 to 1961. Master's thesis, University of Maryland, 1962. 54p.

3203   Coe, George R. Amos Alonzo Stagg's Contribution to Athletics. Master's thesis, College of the Pacific, 1946. 47p. [football coach, University of Chicago, 1892-1932; and University of the Pacific, 1933-1946].

3204   Conant, Coit. The Evolution of Offensive Football in American Colleges (1800-1913). Master's thesis, University of Wisconsin, 1962.

3205   Corrie, Bruce A. A History of the Atlantic Coast Conference. Doctor of Physical Education, Indiana University, 1970. 406p. UMI# 70-23776.

3206   Cunningham, Lee C. A History of Southern Intercollegiate Gymnastic League from Its

Beginning in 1949 to Its Demise in 1977. Ph.D., Florida State University, 1980. 371p. UMI# 80-20330.

3207   Duval, Earl H., Jr. An Historical Analysis of the Central Intercollegiate Athletic Association and Its Influence on the Development of Black Intercollegiate Athletics: 1912-1984. Ph.D., Kent State University, 1985. 185p. UMI# 8604166.

3208   Earl, Charles D. The Academic Achievement of College Athletes and Non Athletes from Four Ethnic Groups. Ph.D., University of New Mexico, 1968. 93p. UMI# 69-09242.

3209   Flath, Arnold W. A History of Relations Between the National Collegiate Athletic Association and the Amateur Athletic Union of the United States (1905-1963). Ph.D., University of Michigan, 1963. 339p. UMI# 64-00812.

3210   Fleischer, Michael M. A History of the Eastern Collegiate Athletic Conference. Ph.D., Columbia University, 1960.

3211   Forbes, Theodore W. The National Collegiate Athletic Association Since 1942. Ph.D., Columbia University, 1955. 289p.

3212   Frindell, Harold M. The Origin and Development of the National Collegiate Athletic Association—A Force for Good in Intercollegiate Athletics. Master's thesis, New York University, 1938. 57p.

3213   Gay, Robert E. A History of the American Football Coaches Association. Ph.D., University of North Carolina at Chapel Hill, 1971. 183p. UMI# 72-10683.

3214   Green, Lawrence J. A Chronology of Changes in Collegiate Football Rules, 1873 to 1954. Ph.D., University of Iowa, 1955. 278p. UMI# 00-14111.

3215   Gruensfelder, Melvin. A History of the Origin and Development of the Southeastern Conference. Master's thesis, University of Illinois, 1964. 365p.

3216   Guynne, Albert C. History of Intercollegiate Wrestling in the United States. Master's thesis, West Virginia University, 1938. 41p.

3217   Hackney, Rufus R., Jr. The History of the Dixie Conference and a Comparative Study of the Athletic Departments of the Member Institutions. Ph.D., University of North Carolina at Chapel Hill, 1970. 311p. UMI# 71-11703.

3218   Hall, Sylvester R. The Evolution of Intramural Sports for Men in American Colleges and Universities. Master's thesis, Howard University, 1936.

3219   Harms, William B. An Analysis of the Major Issue Confronting the National Collegiate Athletic Association, 1973-1976. Ph.D., Kansas State University, 1977. 204p. UMI# 7800813.

3220   Hecker, Jack L. The Historical Development of Professional Football and Its Relation to Intercollegiate Athletics. Master's thesis, Bowling Green State University, 1958.

3221   Hodgdon, Paula D. An Investigation of the Development of Interscholastic and Intercollegiate Athletics for Girls and Women from 1917-1970. Ph.D., Springfield College, 1973.

3222   Hoover, Francis L. A History of the National Association of Intercollegiate Athletics. Ph.D., Indiana University, 1959.

3223   Hunt, Virginia. Governance of Women's Intercollegiate Athletics: An Historical Perspective. Ed.D., University of North Carolina at Greensboro, 1976. 331p. UMI# 76-24943.

3224   Ilowit, Roy. A History of Inter-Collegiate Lacrosse in the United States. Ed.D., Columbia University, 1957. 136p.

3225   Krankling, James D. History of the Zone Defense in Men's Intercollegiate Basketball. Master's thesis, University of Maryland, 1954.

3226   Land, Carroll B. A History of the National Association of Intercollegiate Athletics. Ph.D., University of Southern California, 1977.

3227   Lawrence, Paul R. The Intercollegiate Athletic Cartel: The Economics, History, Institutions, and Legal Arrangements of the National Collegiate Athletic Association. Ph.D., Virginia Polytechnic Institute, 1982. 572p. UMI# 8310725.

3228   Leslie, Mary E. Principles of Women's Intercollegiate Athletics. Ph.D., University of Southern California, 1979.

3229   Lewis, Guy M. The American Intercollegiate Football Spectacle, 1869-1917. Ph.D., University of Maryland, 1965. 318p. UMI# 65-04457.

3230   Lunsford, Walter C. A History of the Track and Field Athletics and the Improvements in the Events of the National Collegiate Athletic Association Meets. Master's thesis, University of Washington, 1946.

3231   Martin, John C. The History of Football in the Central Intercollegiate Athletic Association. Master's thesis, Springfield College, 1959. 108p.

3232   Martin, Thomas S. A Study of the Development of Colored Intercollegiate Athletic Associations. Master's thesis, University of Michigan, 1946. 123p.

3233   Mason, Robert L. A History of Wrestling in the Mountain State Athletic Conference. Master's thesis, University of Wyoming, 1956.

3234   McConnell, John J. A Chronology of Changes in Basketball Rules 1915-1916 to 1952-1953. Ph.D., University of Iowa, 1953. 180p. UMI# 00-06538.

3235   Mould, Michael W. A History of the Development of the National Junior College Athletic Association. Ph.D., Springfield College, 1971.

3236   Nader, Samuel J. Financing Intercollegiate Athletics in the Southeastern Conference 1970-1979. Ph.D., Louisiana State University, 1982. 181p. UMI# 8216861.

3237   Novolony, George. A Study of Changes in Intercollegiate Football Rules from 1911 through 1948 and Their Effect on the Game. Master's thesis, Ohio State University, 1949.

3238   Parker, Giles E. A History of the Rocky Mountain, Skyline, and Western Athletic Conferences: 1909-1976. Ed.D., Brigham Young University, 1976. 987p. UMI# 77-04845.

3239   Powell, John T. The Development and Influence of Faculty Representation in the Control of Inter-Collegiate Sport within the Conference of Faculty Representatives from Its Inception in January, 1895 to July, 1963. Ph.D., University of Illinois, 1964. 325p. UMI# 65-00884.

3240   Ramsay, John T., Jr. The Development of an Intercollegiate Athletic Program in a Liberal Arts College. Ph.D., University of Pennsylvania, 1964.

3241   Rhoads, Lester. A Study of Collegiate Sailing in the United States. Ph.D., Columbia University, 1967. 423p. UMI# 67-12,703.

3242   Rickenbach, Robert L. A History of the Evolution of the Rules of Intercollegiate Wrestling. Master's thesis, Springfield College, 1959. 158p.

3243   Robertson, David F. The History and Development of Men's Intercollegiate Swimming in the United States from 1897 to 1970. Ph.D., Ohio State University, 1977. 520p. UMI# 77-31961.

3244   Rodrigo, Arambawattage D. The History of Men's Intercollegiate Volleyball in the United States from 1895 to Present Day. Ph.D., Ohio State University, 1981. 220p. UMI# 8207250.

3245   Rothwell, William J. The Life of Victor Heyliger and His Contributions in the Establishment and Development of Intercollegiate Hockey in the United States. Ph.D., Ohio State University, 1977. 260p. UMI# 77-31,965. [hockey coach, University of Michigan, University of Illinois, and United States Air Force Academy].

3246   Runkle, Raymond J. The History of Intercollegiate Gymnastics in the United States. Ed.D., Columbia University, 1957. 231p.

3247   Rutherford, Joann K. Women's Intercollegiate Athletics in the United States: A Geographical Explanation, 1971-1977. Ed.D., Oklahoma State University, 1977. 178p. UMI# 7801326.

3248   Sack, Allen L. The Commercialization and Rationalization of Intercollegiate Football: A Comparative Analysis of the Development of Football at Yale and Harvard in the Latter Nineteenth Century. Ph.D., Pennsylvania State University, 1974. 197p. UMI# 75-19807.

3249   Sievers, Camille G. A History of the Women's Sports Teams in the Southeastern Conference through Records and Statistics of Competition 1973-82 (Volumes I and II). Ed.D., Temple University, 1984. 658p. UMI# 8419838.

3250   Soare, Warren G. A History from 1820 to 1890 of Two Theories of Physical Training: The Collegiate Gymnastics Movement and the Rise of Intercollegiate Athletic Teams at Amherst, Harvard, Princeton, and Yale. Ed.D., Columbia University Teachers College, 1979. 364p. UMI# 80-06859.

3251   Sparhawk, Ruth M. A Study of the Life and Contributions of Amos Alonzo Stagg to Intercollegiate Football. Ph.D., Springfield College, 1968. [football coach, University of Chicago, 1892-1932; and University of the Pacific, 1933-1946].

3252   Sponberg, Adryn L. The Evolution of Athlete Subsidization in the Intercollegiate Conference of Faculty Representatives (Big Ten). Ph.D., University of Michigan, 1969. 248p. UMI# 69-12241.

3253   Stagg, Paul. The Development of the National Collegiate Athletic Association in Relationship to Inter-Collegiate Athletics in the United States. Ph.D., New York University, 1947. 416p. UMI# 73-08784.

3254   Thomas, Dale O. Chronology of Changes in College Wrestling Rules, 1921 to 1956. Ph.D., University of Iowa, 1956. 135p. UMI# 17,151.

3255   Thompson, Kenneth D. The Decline of Intercollegiate Boxing. Master's thesis, Washington State University, 1963. 85p.

3256   Thurmond, Raymond C. The History of Sport and Physical Education as a Field of Study in Higher Education. Ed.D., University of Oklahoma, 1976. 550p. UMI# 77-01856.

3257   Torney, John A. A History of Competitive Rowing in Colleges and Universities of the United States of America. Ph.D., Columbia University, 1959. 628p.

3258   Tucker, Kenneth W. The Reform Movement in College Football, 1890-1910. Master's thesis, University of California-Los Angeles, 1973.

3259   Van Bibber, Edward C. The History and Development of Intercollegiate Eligibility Rules. Master's thesis, Purdue University, 1937. 85p.

3260   Veron, Gale. A Survey and Analysis of the National Collegiate Athletic Association Football Rule Changes from 1945 to 1954. Master's thesis, Wyoming University, 1955.

3261   Voltmer, Carl D. A Brief History of the Intercollegiate Conference of Faculty Representatives, with Special Consideration of Athletic Problems. Ph.D., Columbia University, 1935. 100p.

3262   Wang, Peter Y.K. A Comparative Analysis of the Scholastic Performance in Required General Education Courses of College Athletes, Subsequently Matriculating in Either Physical Education or Other Majors, and Non-Athlete Physical Education Majors. Ph.D., University of New Mexico, 1971. 92p. UMI# 72-04803.

3263   Westlake, Richard K. A History of the North Central Intercollegiate Athletic Conference. Master's thesis, University of North Dakota, 1963.

3264   Woerlin, George W. Intercollegiate Athletic Conferences: Their History and Significance. Master's thesis, Ohio State University, 1938.

3265   Wolf, Harold H. The History of Intercollegiate Baseball. Ed.D., Columbia University, 1962. 306p. UMI# 63-02300.

BLACK HIGHER EDUCATION

3266   Arce, Carlos H. Historical, Institutional, and Contextual Determinants of Black Enrollment in Predominantly White Colleges and Universities, 1946 to 1974. Ph.D., University of Michigan, 1976. 386p. UMI# 76-27437.

3267   Beall, Noble Y. The Northern Baptists and the Higher Education of Southern Negroes During 1865-75. Master's thesis, Emory University, 1944.

3268   Beasley, Thaddeus V. A Study of Faculty Development in Historically Black Public Colleges and Universities, 1968-1973. Ph.D., American University, 1979. 142p. UMI# 80-10689.

3269   Bowen, James S. Black Student Militance: Campus Unrest Among Black Students, 1968-1972. Ph.D., Columbia University, 1982. 683p. UMI# 84-27357.

3270   Brown, Genevieve S. An Analytical and Statistical Study of Higher Education for Negroes During the Period 1877-1900. Master's thesis, Howard University, 1950.

3271   Brown, Herman. Origin, Development and Contributions of Negro Colleges and Universities as Institutions of Higher Education in the United States, 1776-1890. Ph.D., Catholic University of America, 1972. 261p. UMI# 73-14323.

3272   Browning, Jane E.S. The Origins, Development and Desegregation of the Traditionally Black Public Colleges and Universities: 1837-1975. Ed.D., Harvard University, 1975. 273p. UMI# 76-10557.

3273   Bryant, Mynora J. A Historical Study of Factors That Have Contributed to and/or Influenced the Mortality of Negro Colleges and Universities, 1860-1980. Ed.D., George Washington University, 1982. 151p. UMI# 8216978.

3274   Burnett, Dorothy. Black Studies Departments and Afro-American Library Collections At Two Predominanetly White Universities: A Comparative Analysis. Ph.D., University of Pittsburgh, 1984. 14lp. UMI# 8600631.

3275   Butler, Addie L.J. The Distinctive Black College: Talladega, Tuskegee, and Morehouse. Ed.D., Columbia University Teachers College, 1976. 252p. UMI# 76-27699.

3276   Carroll, Evelyn C.J. Priorities in Philanthropic Support for Private Negro Colleges and Universities, 1930-1973. Ph.D., University of Michigan, 1982. 671p. UMI# 82-14970.

3277   Chait, Richard P. The Desegregation of Higher Education: A Legal History. Ph.D., University of Wisconsin, 1972. 316p. UMI# 73-09190.

3278   Chapman, Oscar J. A Historical Study of Negro Land Grant Colleges in Relationship with Their Social, Economic, Political, and Educational Backgrounds and a Program for Their Improvement. Ph.D., Ohio State University, 1940. 443p. UMI# 00-00325.

3279   Cheslik, Helen E. Effect of World War II Military Educational Training on Black Colleges. Ed.D., Wayne State University, 1980. 219p. UMI# 8022810.

3280   Cooper, Arnold. Five Black Educators: Founders of Schools in the South, 1881-1915. Ph.D., Iowa State University, 1983. 439p. UMI# 83-16146.

3281   Davis, Yvonne H. The Genesis, Development, and Impact of the United States Defense Department's Race Relations Institute 1940-1975. Ph.D., University of Pittsburgh, 1975. 114p. UMI# 76-05426.

3282   Dickerson, Milton O., Jr. The External Administration of Negro Land Grant Colleges and

Universities from 1890 to 1920. Ph.D., Catholic University of America, 1975. 134p. UMI# 75-16829.

3283   Franklin, Bernard W. Deeds and Dreams: The Extra-Curriculum in Selected Afro-American Colleges 1915-1930. Ed.D., Columbia University Teachers College, 1983. 208p. UMI# 83-22200.

3284   Glotzer, Richard S. Higher Education in the American South, 1660-1984: Class and Race in Institutional Development. Ph.D., University of Wisconsin-Madison, 1984. 480p. UMI# 8417950.

3285   Goodwin, Louis C. A Historical Study of Accreditation in Negro Public and Private Colleges, 1927-1952, with Special Reference to Colleges in the Southern Association. Ph.D., New York University, 1956. 328p. UMI# 00-19989.

3286   Griffin, Paul R. Black Founders of Reconstruction Era Methodist Colleges: Daniel A. Payne, Joseph C. Price, and Isaac Lane, 1863-1840. Ph.D., Emory University, 1983. 300p. UMI# 8316279.

3287   Grossley, Richard S. The Public Relations Program of the Negro Land Grant College: Determination of Factors and Trends in the Recent Development of the Public Relations Program of the Negro Land Grant Colleges. Ed.D., New York University, 1943. 216p. UMI# 73-008576.

3288   Hardin, Willie. An Analysis of Growth Patterns in Select Black Land Grant College and University Libraries; Five Case Studies. Doctor of Arts, Simmons College, 1979.

3289   High, Juanita J. Black Colleges as Social Intervention: The Development of Higher Education within the African Methodist Episcopal Church. Ed.D., Rutgers University, 1978. 251p. UMI# 78-10230.

3290   Holman, Forest H.C., Jr. A History of Selected Critical Factors and Barriers in the Development of Black Higher Education. Ph.D., Michigan State University, 1975. 324p. UMI# 75-20847.

3291   Holmes, Dwight O.W. The Evolution of the Negro College. Ph.D., Columbia University, 1935.

3292   Howard, Michael E. The Social Scientists, the Courts, and 'The School Segregation Cases': A Historical Review. Ph.D., Stanford University, 1972. 204p. UMI# 73-04517.

3293   Jackson, Prince A. The Negro Land Grant College of the United States: A Study of Developments in Administration, Faculty, and Curriculum from 1940 to 1965. Ph.D., Boston College, 1966.

3294   Johnson, Adolph, Jr. A History and Interpretation of the William Edward Burghardt DuBois-Booker Taliaferro Washington Higher Educational Controversy. Ph.D., University of Southern California, 1976.

3295   Johnson, Lillian P. A Study of Articles of Negro Colleges and Universities in Selected Magazines from 1950 to 1975. Ph.D., Florida State University, 1982. 185p. UMI# 8217969.

3296   Kelly, Samuel E. A Model for Emerging Black Studies Programs; An Analysis of Selected Black Studies Programs Viewed in Historical Perspective. Ph.D., University of Washington, 1971. 217p. UMI# 72-15109.

3297   Lang, William L. Black Bootstraps: The Abolitionist Educators: Ideology and the Education of the Northern Free Negro, 1828-1860. Ph.D., University of Delaware, 1974. 256p. UMI# 74-27858.

3298   Lewis, Elmer C. A History of Secondary and Higher Education in Negro Schools Related to the Disciples of Christ. Ph.D., University of Pittsburgh, 1957. 215p. UMI# 00-22853.

3299   Little, Monroe H., Jr. The Black Student at the Black College, 1880-1964. Ph.D., Princeton University, 1977. 264p. UMI# 78-00286.

3300   MacLeish, Marlene Y. Medical Education in Black Colleges and Universities in the United States of America: An Analysis of the Emergence of Black Medical Schools Between 1867 and 1976. Ed.D., Harvard University, 1978. 264p. UMI# 79-09888.

3301   Maskin, Melvin R. Black Education and the New Deal: The Urban Experience. Ph.D., New York University, 1973. 373p. UMI# 73-19948.

3302   McBride, Ullysses. A Survey of Black Studies Offerings in Traditionally Black Institutions of Higher Education Between 1960-73. Ed.D., Auburn University, 1974. 132p. UMI# 75-12492.

3303   McCarthy, John R. The Slavery Issue in Selected Colleges and Universities in Illinois, Ohio, Kentucky and Indiana, 1840-1860. Ph.D., Florida State University, 1974. 205p. UMI# 75-12656.

3304   McCarthy, Joseph J. History of Black Catholic Education, 1871-1971. Ph.D., Loyola University of Chicago, 1973. 206p. UMI# 73-23150.

3305   McCoy, Walter J. The Black College: An Analysis of Recurring Themes in the Literature on the Black Colleges. Ph.D., University of Pittsburgh, 1973. 238p. UMI# 74-14966.

3306   McGee, Leo. Adult Education for the Black Man in America, 1860-1880: An Historical Study of the Types. Ph.D., Ohio State University, 1972. 245p. UMI# 72-27066.

3307   McMillan, Joseph T. The Development of Higher Education for Blacks During the Late Nineteenth Century: A Study of the African Methodist Episcopal Church; Wilberforce University; The American Missionary Association; Hampton Institute; and Fisk University. Ed.D., Columbia University Teachers College, 1986. 535p. UMI# 8612271.

3308   McMillan, William A. The Evolution of Curriculum Patterns in Six Senior Negro Colleges of the Methodist Church from 1900 to 1950. Ph.D., University of Michigan, 1957. 192p. UMI# 58-00956.

3309   Mitchell, Reavis L., Jr. Blacks in American History Textbooks: A Study of Selected Themes in Post-1900 College Level Surveys. Doctor of Arts, Middle Tennessee State University, 1983. 182p. UMI# 84-04787.

3310   Moten, Sarah E.P. Growth Patterns of Predominantly Black Four Year Higher Education

Institutions During the Period 1966-1976, with Projections About Their Future. Ed.D., Atlanta University, 1979. UMI# 79-21222.

3311   Nicholas, Freddie W. The Black Land Grant Colleges: An Assessment of the Major Changes Between 1965-66 and 1970-71. Ed.D., University of Virginia, 1973. 215p. UMI# 73-31149.

3312   Owens, Robert L., II. Financial Assistance for Negro College Students in America: A Social Historical Interpretation of the Philosophy of Negro Higher Education. Ph.D., University of Iowa, 1953. 227p. UMI# 00-06548.

3313   Patterson, Joseph N. A Study of the History of the Contribution of the American Missionary Association to the Higher Education of the Negro with Special Reference to Five Selected Colleges Founded by the Association, 1865-1900. Ed.D., Cornell University, 1956. 346p. UMI# 00-20423.

3314   Payne, Joseph A. An Analysis of the Role of the Association of Colleges and Secondary Schools for Negroes from 1934 to 1954. Ed.D., Indiana University, 1957. 239p. UMI# 00-24836.

3315   Pfanner, Daniel J. The Thought of Negro Educators in Negro Higher Education, 1900-1950. Ph.D., Columbia University, 1958.

3316   Pierro, Armstead A. A History of Professional Preparation for Physical Education in Some Selected Negro Colleges and Universities, 1924-1958. Ph.D., University of Michigan, 1962. 357p. UMI# 63-00429.

3317   Preer, Jean L. Law and Social Policy: Desegregation in Public Higher Education (Volumes I and II). Ph.D., George Washington University, 1980. 595p. UMI# 80-23864.

3318   Robinson, Omelia T. Contributions of Black American Academic Women to American Higher Education. Ph.D., Wayne State University, 1978. 247p. UMI# 7816079.

3319   Robinson, Walter G., Jr. Blacks in Higher Education in the United States Before 1865. Ph.D., Southern Illinois University, 1976. 220p. UMI# 76-28773.

3320   Rosenbaum, Judy J. Black Education in Three Northern Cities in the Early Twentieth Century. Ph.D., University of Illinois at Urbana-Champaign, 1974. 262p. UMI# 75-11741.

3321   Sandle, Floyd L. A History of the Development of Educational Theatre in Negro Colleges and Universities, 1911-1959. Ph.D., Louisiana State University, 1959. 310p. UMI# 59-03486.

3322   Scott, Gregory M. Faculty Unionization at a Black Public College: A Case Study in the Evolution of Academic Governance. Ed.D., Rutgers University, 1983. 312p. UMI# 83-25914.

3323   Shepherd, Robert E. A Study of National Fellows in Predominantly Black Public Colleges, 1968-72. Ph.D., Southern Illinois University, 1978. 135p.

3324   Smith, Lamar. A Study of the Historical Development of Selected Black College and University Bands as a Curricular and Aesthetic Entity, 1867-1975. Ph.D., Kansas State University, 1976. 497p. UMI# 76-30024.

3325   Stallings, Charles W. Some Aspects of the Evolution of Negro Colleges in America as Depicted by the Execution of a Mural. Ed.D., Pennsylvania State University, 1954. 133p. UMI# 00-11767.

3326   Sullivan, John E. A Historical Investigation of the Negro Land Grant Colleges from 1890 to 1964. Ph.D., Loyola University of Chicago, 1969.

3327   Tata, Samba S. A Study of the Occupational Origins and Career Patterns of Presidents of Black Colleges and Universities in the United States. Ed.D., University of Cincinnati, 1980. 165p. UMI# 80-29704.

3328   Taylor, Cyrus B. Mechanic Arts Programs in Land Grant Colleges Established for Negroes: A Study of the Types and Status of the Programs Operating and An Analysis of Selected Factors that Influenced the Development of these Programs. Ph.D., University of Minnesota, 1955. 477p. UMI# 00-15964.

3329   Thomas, Gregory. Historical Survey of Black Education as a Means of Black Liberation, 1875-1969. Ph.D., Ohio State University, 1971. 171p. UMI# 72-04669.

3330   Thompkins, Robert E. A History of Religious Education Among Negroes in the Presbyterian Church in the United States of America. Ph.D., University of Pittsburgh, 1951. 134p.

3331   Thornton, David H. Establishment of Land Grant Colleges for Negroes. Master's thesis, University of Wisconsin, 1936.

3332   Trueheart, William E. The Consequences of Federal and State Resource Allocation and Development Policies for Traditionally Black Land Grant Institutions: 1862-1954. Ed.D., Harvard University, 1979. 306p. UMI# 80-12324.

3333   Waters, Rudolph E. A Profile of Presidents of Historically Black Colleges and Universities. Ph.D., Kansas State University, 1977. 223p. UMI# 77-26065.

3334   Welch, Eloise T. The Background and Development of the American Missionary Association's Decision to Educate Freedmen in the South, with Subsequent Repercussions for Higher Education. Ph.D., Bryn Mawr College, 1976. 205p. UMI# 77-6542.

3335   White, Clarence, Jr. Doctor Martin Luther King, Jr.'s Contributions to Education as a Black Leader (1929-1968). Ed.D., Loyola University of Chicago, 1974. 224p. UMI# 74-23079.

3336   White, Katherine H. Black Colleges Since 1954 Brown vs. Board of Education. Ph.D., University of Pittsburgh, 1983. 165p. UMI# 8327708.

3337   Williams, Lea E. The United Negro College Fund: Its Growth and Development. Ed.D., Columbia University Teachers College, 1978. 166p. UMI# 78-10907.

3338   Wilson, George D. Developments in Negro Colleges During the Twenty Year Period, 1914-1915 to 1933-1934. Ph.D., Ohio State University, 1935.

3339   Wright, Chester W. A History of the Black Land Grant Colleges 1890-1916. Ph.D., American University, 1981. 203p. UMI# 81-25432.

3340   Yerby, Frank G. The Little Theater in the Negro College. Master's thesis, Fisk University, 1938.

BROADCASTING

3341   Akin, Lew. A History of Campus-Limited Radio in the United States of America From 1936 Through 1962. Master's thesis, University of Denver, 1964.

3342   Berkman, Dave I. The Undergraduate Curriculum in Broadcasting: Its History and Current Status. Ed.D., New York University, 1963. 245p. UMI# 64-06523.

3343   Curry, Myron M. A History and Description of College-Wired Radio Systems in the United States. Master's thesis, University of Wisconsin, 1948.

3344   McReynolds, Billy. An Analysis of the Radio Curricula in a Selected Group of Colleges and Universities from 1935 to 1945. Master's thesis, University of Florida, 1947.

3345   Nakireru, Alexander O. The Development of Instructional Television in American Higher Education: A Historical Analysis. Ph.D., Ohio University, 1985. 460p. UMI# 8603303.

3346   Neville, John P. The Development and Educational Significance of the Intercollegiate Broadcasting System. Master's thesis, Ohio State University, 1942.

3347   Phillips, Robert L. A History of W I L L with Special Attention to the Development of Program Areas. Master's thesis, University of Illinois, 1954.

BUSINESS AND EDUCATION

3348   Keenan, James P., III. The Public Educational Thought of Selected American Big Business Leaders, 1860-1917. Ed.D., Columbia University, 1972. 549p. UMI# 72-23702.

3349   Metzger, Walter P. College Professors and Big Business Men: A Study of American Ideologies, 1880-1915. Ph.D., University of Iowa, 1950. 404p.

BUSINESS EDUCATION

3350   Carrington, Max R. History and Contributions of the National Business Education Association, Divisions and Sub-Divisions. Ph.D., Colorado State University, 1967.

3351   Czarniewicz, Casimir M. Historical Survey of the Subject Matter Content of the General Marketing Course, 1900-1959. Ed.D., Syracuse University, 1969. 252p. UMI# 69-08658.

3352   Dykman, Dorothy J. A History of Business Education from 1917 to 1967 as Observed by Selected Leaders (Volumes I and II). Ed.D., University of Northern Colorado, 1969. 449p. UMI# 70-07178.

3353   Fisher, Berenice M. Industrial Education in the United States: An Historical Study of Ideas and Institutions. Ph.D., University of California-Berkeley, 1965. 328p. UMI# 66-03586.

3354   Gurnick, Stanley I. A Comprehensive Analysis, Classification, and Synthesis of Research Findings on Business Teacher Education, 1956-1963. Ph.D., Indiana University, 1974. 573p. UMI# 75-9018.

3355   Hebron, Arthur E. Education for Business in Liberal Arts Colleges. Ph.D., University of Missouri, 1973. 124p. UMI# 74-9942.

3356   Kaufman, Arnold. Graduate Accounting Education from 1926-1955. Ph.D., New York University, 1958. 208p. UMI# 58-7620.

3357   Lee, Dorothy E. Changing Objectives in Business Education on the Collegiate Level in the United States from 1899 to 1954. Ph.D., New York University, 1957. 268p. UMI# 00-21711.

3358   Milligram, Emerson N. The Development of Business Communications Textbooks Designed for American Undergraduate Schools. Ph.D., University of Pittsburgh, 1973. 201p. UMI# 74-1534.

3359   Miranti, Paul J., Jr. From Conflict to Consensus: The American Institute of Accountants and the Professionalization of Public Accountancy, 1886-1940. Ph.D., Johns Hopkins University, 1985. 410p. UMI# 8518514.

3360   Smith, Jessie M. Development of Business Teacher Education in the United States, 1893-1950. Ph.D., Columbia University, 1954. UMI# 00-08834.

3361   Sobolik, Gayle A. A History of Business Letter-Writing Theory as Revealed in an Interpretative Analysis of American Collegiate Business Communication Textbooks, 1915-1967. Ph.D., University of North Dakota, 1970. 534p. UMI# 71-15676.

3362   Stillwell, Hamilton. A Historical and Comparative Study of Four State Supported Institutes of Industrial and Labor Relations. Ed.D., New York University, 1957. 627p. UMI# 00-22736.

3363   Weiss, Janice H. Educating for Clerical Work: A History of Commercial Education in the United States Since 1850. Ed.D., Harvard University, 1978. 301p. UMI# 78-23695.

3364   Zaheer, Mohammad. The Development of Two-Year Post-Secondary Education for Business in the Southern New England States, 1950-1970. Ph.D., University of Connecticut, 1973. 331p. UMI# 74-07135.

CATHOLIC HIGHER EDUCATION

3365   Baer, Campion R. The Development of Accreditation in American Catholic Seminaries, 1890-1961. Ph.D., University of Notre Dame, 1963. 367p. UMI# 63-07322.

3366   Bernad, Miguel A. The Faculty of Arts in the Jesuit Colleges in the Eastern Part of the United States: Theory and Practice (1782-1923). Ph.D., Yale University, 1951. 483p. UMI# 8507574.

3367   Bouey, Sister Mary C. The Sisters of Mercy in American Higher Education. Ph.D., Catholic University of America, 1962. 195p. UMI# 64-00347.

3368   Bowler, Mary M. A History of Catholic Colleges for Women in the United States of America. Ph.D., Catholic University of America, 1933. 145p.

3369   Buttell, Mary F. A History of Catholic Colleges for Women in the United States of America. Ph.D., Catholic University of America, 1934.

3370   Casey, John J. A Historical Study of a Recent Model of Pre-Professional Catholic Clerical Education in the United States. Ph.D., University of Chicago, 1971.

282   Catholic Higher Education

3371   Cassidy, Francis P. Catholic College Foundations and Development in the United States (1677-1850). Ph.D., Catholic University of America, 1924.

3372   Connolly, Mary K. The Anomaly of Catholic Higher Education for Women. Ed.D., Columbia University, 1976. 269p. UMI# 76-17,277.

3373   Dixon, Henry W. An Historical Survey of Jesuit Higher Education in the United States with Particular Reference to the Objectives of Education. Ed.D., Arizona State University, 1974. 196p. UMI# 74-19,282.

3374   Erbacher, Sebastian A. Catholic Higher Education for Men in the United States, 1850-1866. Ph.D., Catholic University of America, 1931. 143p.

3375   Erbacher, Sebastian A. Catholic Colleges for Boys in the United States, 1850-1866. Master's thesis, Catholic University of America, 1929.

3376   Evans, John W. The Newman Movement: A Social and Intellectual History of Roman Catholics in American Higher Education, 1883-1969. Ph.D., University of Minnesota, 1970. 897p. UMI# 71-08145.

3377   Fehlig, Mary B. The Emerging Role of the Catholic Two-Year Commuter College. Ph.D., Saint Louis University, 1968. 203p. UMI# 69-00340.

3378   Gallagher, James P. The Effect of Selected Variables on the Financial Development of Jesuit Institutions of Higher Education in America. Ph.D., Catholic University of America, 1975. 150p. UMI# 76-23581.

3379   Galvin, James M. Secularizing Trends in Roman Catholic Colleges and Universities, 1960-1970. Ed.D., Indiana University, 1971. 124p. UMI# 72-01545.

3380   Hynes, Eleanor M. Some Issues in Catholic Social Work Education: 1910-1950. Ph.D., Tulane University, 1971. 174p. UMI# 72-14,192.

3381   Kearney, Anna R. James A. Burns, C.S.C.—Educator. Ph.D., University of Notre Dame, 1975. 216p. UMI# 75-19,940. [president, University of Notre Dame, 1919-1922].

3382   LaMagdeleine, Donald R. The Changing American Catholic University. Ph.D., Loyola University of Chicago, 1984. 244p. UMI# 8407146.

3383   Linehan, Joseph A. The History of the Augustinians in the Middle West as a Teaching Order. Ph.D., Loyola University of Chicago, 1965.

3384   McCarren, Edgar P. The Origin and Early Years of the National Catholic Educational Association. Ph.D., Catholic University of America, 1966. 360p. UMI# 67-01259.

3385   Meighan, Cecilia. Nativism and Catholic Higher Education, 1840-1860. Ed.D., Columbia University, 1972. 138p. UMI# 72-30340.

3386   Murphy, Kathleen M. A Study of the History and Development of the Functions of the Office of Dean of Women in Catholic Higher Education Since 1927. Master's thesis, Catholic University of America, 1956.

3387   Noone, Bernard J. A Critical Analysis of the American Catholic Response to Higher

Education as Reflected in Selected Catholic Periodicals—1870 to 1908. Ph.D., Drew University, 1976. 457p. UMI# 76-26250.

3388   O'Brien, John J. A History of Catholic Education in the Mississippi Valley, 1704-1866. Ph.D., Saint Louis University, 1951. 134p.

3389   Plough, James H. Catholic Colleges and the Catholic Educational Association: The Foundation and Early Years of the CEA, 1899-1919. Ph.D., University of Notre Dame, 1967. 566p. UMI# 67-13602.

3390   Rosinski, Bernard J. Roman Catholic Seminary Survival (1968-1983): A Multivariate Statistical Analysis of the Cara Seminary Directories. Ed.D., Ball State University, 1985. 361p. UMI# 8518672.

3391   Sawers, William K. Changes in Jesuit Higher Education and the Influence of Teilhard de Chardin. Ed.D., University of Southern California, 1973. 147p. UMI# 73-31386.

3392   Tremonti, Joseph B. The Status of Catholic Junior Colleges in the United States. Ph.D., Temple University, 1950. 117p.

3393   Vollmar, Edward R. History of the Jesuit Colleges of New Mexico and Colorado, 1867-1919. Master's thesis, Saint Louis University, 1939. 168p.

3394   Wilson, M. Debora. Benedictine Higher Education and the Development of American Higher Education. Ph.D., University of Michigan, 1969. 353p. UMI# 69-18,138.

3395   Woerman, Melodie B. Within the Ivy Walls: A History of the Sisters of Bethany. Master's thesis, University of Kansas, 1983.

CHURCH AND STATE

3396   Barry, James C. A Historical Study of Religion in Higher Tax-Supported Education. Ph.D., Southern Baptist Theological Seminary, 1953. 323p.

3397   Blanton, Harry A. The Entanglement Theory: Its Development and Some Implications for Future Aid to Church-Related Higher Education. Ph.D., Saint Louis University, 1976. 160p. UMI# 77-12079.

3398   Bolick, Ernest B., Jr. A Historical Account of the Controversy Over State Support of Church-Related Higher Education in the Fifty States. Ed.D., University of North Carolina at Greensboro, 1978. 420p. UMI# 78-24293.

3399   Brill, Earl H. Religion and the Rise of the University: A Study of the Secularization of American Higher Education, 1870-1910. Ph.D., American University, 1969. 636p. UMI# 70-15693.

3400   Hale, Toby A. Three Processes by Which Religious Studies Have Developed in Public Universities. Ed.D., Indiana University, 1972. 242p. UMI# 73-06982.

3401   Lang, Martin A. Religion in the Undergraduate Curriculum of the American State University: An Historical Study. Ph.D., Catholic University of America, 1964. 399p. UMI# 65-05558.

3402   Lawn, Evan. Fundamental Differences Between the Philosophies of Public and Parochial Education: A Socio-Historical Study. Ph.D., University of Connecticut, 1959. 393p. UMI# 61-05405.

3403   Loveless, William A. Federal Aid and the Church-Operated College: A Case Study. Ed.D., University of Maryland, 1964. 242p. UMI# 65-00629.

3404   McNeely, Richard I. The Widmar (1981) Decision and the Status of Religious Liberty on the Public College and University Campus: Antecedents, Effects, and Prospects. Ph.D., University of Southern California, 1986.

3405   Whitehead, John S. The Separation of College and State: The Transformation of Columbia, Dartmouth, Harvard, and Yale from Quasi-Public to Private Institutions, 1776-1876. Ph.D., Yale University, 1971. 317p. UMI# 72-17197.

COLONIAL HIGHER EDUCATION

3406   Erenberg, Phyllis V. Change and Continuity: Values in American Higher Education, 1750-1800. Ph.D., University of Michigan, 1974. 302p. UMI# 75-00681.

3407   Fink, Jerome S. The Purposes of the American Colonial Colleges. Ed.D., Stanford University, 1958. 224p. UMI# 58-01272.

3408   Lang, Elizabeth H. Colonial Colleges and Politics: Yale, King's College, and the College of Philadelphia, 1740-1764. Ph.D., Cornell University, 1976. 356p. UMI# 77-20002.

3409   Masson, Margaret W. The Premises and Purposes of Higher Education in American Society, 1745-1770. Ph.D., University of Washington, 1971. 295p. UMI# 72-15121.

3410   Mathews, Alice E. Pre College Education in the Southern Colonies. Ph.D., University of California-Berkeley, 1968. 410p. UMI# 69-10348.

3411   Robson, David W. Higher Education in the Emerging American Republic, 1750-1800. Ph.D., Yale University, 1974. 325p. UMI# 74-24564.

3412   Schieb, Gwendolyn P. Colonial Colleges. Master's thesis, University of Buffalo, 1928.

3413   Schneider, Donald O. Education in Colonial American Colleges, 1750-1770, in the Occupation and Political Offices of Their Alumni. Ph.D., George Peabody College for Teachers, 1965. 254p. UMI# 66-10705.

3414   Smith, Willard W. The Relations of College and State in Colonial America. Ph.D., Columbia University, 1950. 177p. UMI# 00-01654.

3415   Stoeckel, Althea L. Politics and Administration in the American Colonial Colleges. Ph.D., University of Illinois at Urbana-Champaign, 1958. 176p. UMI# 59-00586.

3416   Wilson, S.K. American Colonial Colleges. Ph.D., Cambridge University, 1925.

3417   Wright, Irvin L. Piety, Politics, and Profit: American Indian Missions in the Colonial Colleges. Ed.D., Montana State University, 1985. 215p. UMI# 8607966.

3418   Yazawa, Melvin M. The Forming of a Republican Identity: Politics and Education in Revolutionary America. Ph.D., Johns Hopkins University, 1977.

COMMUNITY COLLEGES

3419   Adams, Dennis P. The American Junior/Community College Historical Roots, Contemporary Trends, and Implications for Growth. Ed.D., University of Northern Colorado, 1979. 130p. UMI# 80-04432.

3420   Aldridge, Jack H. A Comparative Study of Ideas and Theories Concerning Junior Colleges: 1900-1935 and 1945-1960. Ph.D., Stanford University, 1967. 302p. UMI# 68-08382.

3421   Anderson, Albert T. An Appraisal of the *Junior College Journal*, 1946-1953. Ph.D., Columbia University, 1954.

3422   Bibus, Connie M. The Development of the Junior College and the Cult of Efficiency. Ed.D., Texas Tech University, 1982. 162p. UMI# 8221970.

3423   Bremer, Fred H. Philanthropic Support for Public Junior Colleges. Ph.D., University of Texas at Austin, 1965. 259p. UMI# 65-08029.

3424   Brick, Michael. The American Association of Junior Colleges: Forum and Focus for the Junior College Movement. Ph.D., Columbia University, 1963. 331p. UMI# 65-07438.

3425   Clifton, Nancy P. Professionalization in Community College Education: 1975-1982. Ed.D., North Carolina State University at Raleigh, 1985. 168p. UMI# 8518231.

3426   Diener, Thomas J. Federal Interest in the Junior College: A Study of the United States Office of Education. Ph.D., Columbia University, 1968. 205p. UMI# 69-09185.

3427   Edwards, Kenneth L. The Emerging Role of the Junior College in Comprehensive Planning for Higher Education. Ph.D., Southern Illinois University, 1966. 302p. UMI# 67-03154.

3428   Edwards, Nancy J. The Public Community College in America: Its History, Present Condition, and Future Outlook with Special Reference to Finance. Ph.D., Claremont Graduate School, 1982. 198p. UMI# 82-06203.

3429   Elkins, Floyd S. Philanthropic Support of Private Junior Colleges in the United States. Ph.D., University of Texas at Austin, 1965. 324p. UMI# 65-08040.

3430   Foss, Robert N. A Historical Overview of Voluntary State Junior College Associations Existing in the United States as of August 1969. Ed.D., Florida State University, 1970. 172p. UMI# 71-13496.

3431   Gacek, Edward J. Private Junior College Legislation in the United States. Ph.D., University of Connecticut, 1958. 316p. UMI# 58-03915.

3432   Gallagher, Edward A. From Tappan to Lange: Evolution of the Public Junior College Idea. Ph.D., University of Michigan, 1968. 259p. UMI# 69-02319. [Henry Tappan—president, University of Michigan, 1852-1863; Alexis F. Lange—dean, University of California School of Education, 1913-1924].

3433   Garza, George J. Trends in the Development of Private Junior Colleges in Arkansas, Louisiana, Oklahoma, and Texas, 1900-1953. Ph.D., University of Texas, 1954.

3434   Goodwin, Gregory L. The Historical Development of the Community Junior College Ideology: An Analysis and Interpretation of the Writings of Selected Community Junior College National Leaders from 1890 to 1970. Ph.D., University of Illinois at Urbana-Champaign, 1971. 314p. UMI# 72-12178.

3435   Grady, Eugene J. The Community College Movement in the United States. Ph.D., University of Southern California, 1949.

3436   Gray, A.A. The Junior College. Master's thesis, University of California-Berkeley, 1915.

3437   Hardy, John B. The Junior College. Master's thesis, Southern Methodist University, 1939.

3438   Horn, Jefferson L. William Rainey Harper and Alexis Frederick Lange, Productive Pioneers in the Junior College Movement. Ph.D., University of Texas, 1952. [William R. Harper—president University of Chicago, 1891-1906; Alexis F. Lange—dean, University of California School of Education, 1913-1924].

3439   Houghton, Alcina B. A Survey of the History of the Junior College. Master's thesis, New York University, 1933.

3440   Hutchinson, Allen C. The Development of the Controls of Public Junior Colleges. Ph.D., University of Texas at Austin, 1951.

3441   Jackson, Edward D., Jr. The American Association of University Professors and Community/Junior Colleges. Ph.D., Florida State University, 1974. 227p. UMI# 75-8048.

3442   Littlefied, Henry W. Factors Influencing Growth of Junior College Movement. Ph.D., Yale University, 1940. 239p.

3443   Maclaren, Sharon A. Dialectical Materialism as an Explanatory Mechanism for the Community Junior College Movement in the United States, 1950-1965. Ph.D., Wayne State University, 1970. 392p. UMI# 71-17283.

3444   Martin, Robert G. The Quest for a Just Society 1914-1945: A History Curriculum for Community College Students. Doctor of Arts, Carnegie-Mellon University, 1980. 733p. UMI# 80-23837.

3445   McKinney, Robert Q. An Analysis of Factors Affecting the Legal Status of the Community Junior College in the Pacific Northwest, 1939-1965. Ph.D., Washington State University, 1968. 357p. UMI# 68-15789.

3446   Mealy, Franklin R. A Historical and Evaluative Study of the Midwest Community College Leadership Program with Suggested Guidelines for Future Directions. Ph.D., University of Michigan, 1968. 291p. UMI# 69-12182.

3447   Messersmith, Lloyd E. The Impact of Specialized Accreditation on the Community College. Ed.D., University of California-Berkeley, 1967. 236p. UMI# 68-10271.

3448   Norris, Larry B. Professionalization in Community College Education, 1952-1974. Ed.D., North Carolina State University at Raleigh, 1976. 166p. UMI# 76-28504.

3449   Oakley, Jesse R. The Origins and Development of the Public Junior College Movement, 1850-1921. Ed.D., University of North Carolina at Greensboro, 1979. 239p. UMI# 79-22417.

3450   Palinchak, Robert S. The Evolution of the Community College. Ph.D., Syracuse University, 1972. 516p. UMI# 73-07756.

3451   Porter, George H. A Comparative Analysis of the Origin of Community Colleges and Program Emphasis. Ed.D., North Carolina State University at Raleigh, 1973. 103p. UMI# 73-29570.

3452   Reid, Hubert D. Phenomena Affecting the Community Junior College in the United States: 1960-1975. Ph.D., Wayne State University, 1978. 854p. UMI# 7816075.

3453   Robinson, Joseph. The Development of a Community College as a Reflection of Selected Social, Economic, and Political Characteristics of the Community. Ed.D., New York University, 1972. 110p. UMI# 73-08207.

3454   Rutledge, Lawrence A. A History of the American Association of Junior Colleges, 1920-50. Ph.D., University of Texas, 1952.

3455   Salisbury, Harland R. The Development of the Community Junior Colleges' Image in the United States from 1937 to 1967. Ed.D., Washington State University, 1969. 213p. UMI# 70-01076.

3456   Smeby, Myrtle V. A Study of the Junior College Movement. Master's thesis, North Dakota Agricultural College, 1927.

3457   Smolich, Robert S. An Analysis of Influences Affecting the Origin and Early Development of Three Mid-Western Public Junior Colleges—Joliet, Goshen, and Crane. Ed.D., University of Texas at Austin, 1967. 291p. UMI# 68-04241.

3458   Storey, Bertha M. An Historical Study of the Junior College and Its Development as Part of Our Educational System. Master's thesis, Niagara University, 1953.

3459   Struthers, Frederick R. The Development of Community Junior College Legislation in the United States to 1961. Ph.D., University of Texas at Austin, 1963. 308p. UMI# 64-06634.

3460   Sturgeon, Angie H. The Junior College—Its History and Place in the Scheme of American Education. Master's thesis, Smith College, 1923.

3461   Syme, Eric D. A History of the Southwestern Junior College, 1894-1958. Master's thesis, American University, 1959.

3462   Temple, Ronald J. A History of the Emergence of the Urban Two-Year College and Leadership's Perception of Its Current and Future Move into High Technology Education. Ph.D., University of Cincinnati, 1985. 195p. UMI# 8512640.

3463   Thompson, John F. The Junior College Movement in New England. Master's thesis, Boston University, 1938. 113p.

3464   Wolf, Hugh A. The Courts and the Community Junior Colleges. Ed.D., Indiana University, 1971. 242p. UMI# 72-01531.

3465   Wright, Richard G. Professionalization of Administrators: Developments in the Community College Field, 1917-1975. Ed.D., Columbia University Teachers College, 1976. 201p. UMI# 76-21042.

COURTS

3466   Binder, John J. The Impact of Dixon v. Alabama Upon Student Discipline in Higher Education. Ph.D., Kent State University, 1972. 175p. UMI# 72-31,590.

3467   Brockmeyer, Marta A. The Warren Court First Amendment Decisions: Freedom of Expression Redefined for Students Enrolled in Public Institutions of Higher Education. Ph.D., Saint Louis University, 1982. 350p. UMI# 8325336.

3468   Davidson, Phillip L. The Warren Court and Its Impact on the Fourteenth Amendment Rights of College and University Students. Ph.D., George Peabody College for Teachers, 1981. 72p. UMI# 81-21545.

3469   Decker, James T. Historical Evolution of the Fourteenth Amendment Due Process of Law as it Relates to Students in Private Educational Institutions. Ph.D., University of Minnesota, 1976. 161p. UMI# 76-27884.

3470   Ferguson, Paul W. The Evolution of the Fourteenth Amendment to Its Present Position of Authority Over Disciplinary Proceedings in Higher Education. Ed.D., University of Maryland, 1971. 484p. UMI# 72-01636.

3471   Iovacchini, Eric V. A Study of Academic Due Process in Public Higher Education Subsequent to Dixon v. Alabama State Board of Education, through 1977. Ph.D., University of Wyoming, 1978. 81p. UMI# 7818937.

3472   Lain, Gayle R. The Evolving Concept of Legal Relationship Between Students and Public Institutions of Higher Education. Ed.D., University of Wyoming, 1979. 111p. UMI# 80-18011.

3473   Lorensen, Frederick H. The Evolution and Implications of Tilton v. Richardson: The First United States Supreme Court Test of the Constitutionality of Federal Grants to Religious-Affiliated Colleges and Universities. Ph.D., University of Connecticut, 1979. 351p. UMI# 80-03749.

3474   Metzger, Jerome C. Litigation, 1960-1970, Involving Students and Higher Education Institutions. Ed.D., Indiana University, 1971. 325p. UMI# 71-24,557.

3475   Myricks, Noel. Changing Practices and Concepts in Due-Process of Law in Public Institutions of Higher Education as It Relates to Non-Tenured Faculty, 1950-1973. Ed.D., American University, 1974. 263p. UMI# 75-11120.

3476   O'Brien, Kenneth B., Jr. The Supreme Court and Education. Ph.D., Stanford University, 1956. 329p. UMI# 00177732.

CURRICULUM

3477   Acosta, Harold. Undergraduate Curriculum Trends in Sixteen Private Liberal Arts Colleges Over a Period of Twenty-Five Years: 1953-1978. Ph.D., Michigan State University, 1980. 212p. UMI# 81-06348.

3478   Allen, Edward L. Time and the Baccalaureate: An Analysis of the Three-Year Undergradu-
        ate Degree Concept in the American College and University. Ph.D., University of Illinois at
        Urbana-Champaign, 1973. 286p. UMI# 74-11932.

3479   Altman, Robert A. A Study of the Establishment of Upper Division Colleges in the United
        States. Ph.D., Columbia University, 1969. 322p. UMI# 72-19,043.

3480   Angell, Charles E. A Study of the Origin and Development of the 4-1-4 Undergraduate
        College Program with Special Considerations for the Interim Term. Ed.D., University of
        Arkansas, 1969. 348p. UMI# 70-00377.

3481   Barbeau, Joseph E. The Historical Development of Cooperative Education in American
        Higher Education. Ed.D., Boston University, 1973. 231p. UMI# 73-23533.

3482   Butts, R. Freeman. The Development of the Principle of Election of Studies in American
        Colleges and Universities. Ph.D., University of Wisconsin, 1935.

3483   Carlson, Bryan E. A Functional Analysis of Three Private Junior College Curricula in Histori-
        cal Perspective to Determine Their Legitimacy for Present Curricular Policy. Ed.D., Boston
        University, 1971. 386p. UMI# 71-26679.

3484   Chadwick, Ronald P. A Descriptive Study of the Historical Development of 4-1-4 Calendar
        Organization and Its Related Administrative and Curricular-Instructional Innovation. Ph.D.,
        University of Missouri-Kansas City, 1974. 254p. UMI# 74-23781.

3485   Craine, M.K. Changes in the American College Curriculum Between 1825-1850. Master's
        thesis, University of Illinois, 1931.

3486   Delaney, Peter H., II. Changing America and the College Curriculum, 1865-1900. Master's
        thesis, Columbia University, 1939.

3487   DeViney, Charles E. The Development of the Curriculum in American Colleges from 1824
        to 1900. Master's thesis, University of Texas, 1928. 97p.

3488   Dickerman, Watson B. The Historical Development of the Summer Session in Higher
        Institutions in the United States. Ph.D., University of Chicago, 1945. 342p.

3489   Edwards, Harry E. Trends in the Development of the College Curriculum within the Area
        of the North Central Association from 1830 to 1930. Ph.D., Indiana University, 1934.

3490   Faurer, Judson C. The Granting of Academic Degrees by Federal Institutions: A History,
        1775-1964. Ph.D., University of Denver, 1974. 368p. UMI# 75-01324.

3491   Fought, Carol A. The Historical Development of Continuing Education for Women in the
        United States, Economic, Social and Psychological Implications. Ph.D., Ohio State Uni-
        versity, 1966. 413p. UMI# 67-02444.

3492   Fraley, Angela E. Core Curriculum: An Epic in the History of Educational Reform. Ed.D.,
        Columbia University Teachers College, 1977. 243p. UMI# 78-04457.

3493   Fuller, Lawrence B. Education for Leadership: The Emergence of the College Preparatory
        School. Ph.D., Johns Hopkins University, 1974. 465p. UMI# 74-27,910.

3494   Furtado, Lorraine T. An Interpretive History of Distributive Education, 1936-1972, as Seen
        by Selected Leaders. (Volumes I and II). Ph.D., Michigan State University, 1973. 1,272p.
        UMI# 73-29700.

3495   Gerrity, Thomas W. College-Sponsored Correspondence Instruction in the United States:
        A Comparative History of Its Origins (1873-1915) and Its Recent Developments (1960-
        1975). Ed.D., Columbia University Teachers College, 1976. 214p. UMI# 76-17282.

3496   Goldman, David I. The History of Tutorial Instruction in the Colleges and Universities of
        the United States. Ph.D., New York University, 1949. 136p. UMI# 73-08567.

3497   Gray, Gordon W. Origin and Development of the College or University Reading Clinic in
        the United States. Ed.D., University of Tennessee, 1967. 303p. UMI# 68-09801.

3498   Gwynn, John M. Changes in the Curriculum of the American College, 1890-1934. Ph.D.,
        Yale University, 1935.

3499   Howard, Virginia P. H. Developments in Instruction in Selected Four-Year College Read-
        ing Improvement Programs Throughout the United States, 1950-1974. Ed.D., George
        Washington University, 1975. 244p. UMI# 75-25,387.

3500   Iverson, Maurice T. A Historical and Structural Survey of Audio-Visual Techniques in
        Education, 1900-1950. Ph.D., University of Iowa, 1953. 350p. UMI# 00-05478.

3501   Jessup, Michael H. An Historical Analysis of the Development of Selected Areas of
        University Extension Programs in the United States, 1900-1956, as Related in Profes-
        sional Literature. Ed.D., George Washington University, 1967. 189p. UMI# 67-15933.

3502   Jordan, Kathryn S.N. Articulation of American Higher Education: Selected Nineteenth
        Century Approaches to Bisection. Ph.D., University of Iowa, 1974. 173p. UMI# 74-21,911.

3503   Kalapos, Stephen A., Jr. An Historical Study of Curriculum Development for American
        Public Education by National and Regional Organizations, 1892-1965. Ed.D., Temple
        University, 1968. 300p. UMI# 69-14092.

3504   Kelly, Edward J. An Historical Analysis of the Development of the Use of Collateral
        Reading from 1900 to 1950. Ph.D., University of Iowa, 1953. 341p. UMI# 00-05479.

3505   Kline, William A. The 'Amherst Project': A Case Study of a Federally-Sponsored Curricu-
        lum Development Project. Ph.D., Stanford University, 1974. 292p. UMI# 74-13649.

3506   Leedy, Paul D. A History of the Origin and Development of Instruction in Reading Im-
        provement at the College Level. Ph.D., New York University, 1958. 508p. UMI# 59-01016.

3507   Lunsford, Andrea A. An Historical, Descriptive, and Evaluative Study of Remedial English
        in American Colleges and Universities. Ph.D., Ohio State University, 1977. 354p. UMI#
        77-24660.

3508   Matheson, Robert G. A Quarter Century of Curriculum Patterns in Southern Presbyterian
        Colleges. Ph.D., George Peabody College for Teachers, 1953.

3509   May, Russell A. A History of the Association of University Summer Sessions: Fifty Years
        of Progress. Ed.D., Indiana University, 1971. 209p. UMI# 71-17875.

3510   McMahon, Ernest E. The Emerging Evening College: A Study of Faculty Organization and Academic Control in Ten Eastern University Evening Colleges. Ph.D., Columbia University, 1959. 516p. UMI# 59-02862.

3511   McVey, William E. University Extension in the United States. Master's thesis, University of Chicago, 1919.

3512   Neeley, William G., III. An Analysis of Curricular Change at Four-Year United Methodist Church Related Colleges, 1970-1979. Ed.D., University of Georgia, 1985. 133p. UMI# 8519646.

3513   Payton, Philip W. Undergraduate Specialization or Majoring in American Colleges and Universities. Ed.D., Stanford University, 1959. 602p. UMI# 59-6875.

3514   Phillips, Richard C. An Historical Study of the Concept Curriculum. Ph.D., Northwestern University, 1962. 155p. UMI# 63-01335.

3515   Reid, Robert H. Degree Mills in the United States. Ph.D., Columbia University, 1963. 441p. UMI# 64-7155.

3516   Rickman, Claude R. Trends in Provisions for Gifted Students in American Colleges and Universities, 1920-1955. Ph.D., University of North Carolina, 1957.

3517   Romer, Robert D. A Historical Study of the Controversy Regarding the Use of Phonics in Teaching Reading. Ed.D., University of California-Los Angeles, 1971. 447p. UMI# 72-02896.

3518   Schleich, Miriam. The Evolution of a College Reading Program. Ph.D., Columbia University, 1959.

3519   Smawley, Robert B. Changes in Purposes and Programs of Colleges in the Southern Appalachian Region, 1933-1958. Master's thesis, University of Tennessee, 1960.

3520   Smith, Nila B. A Historical Analysis of American Reading Instruction. Ph.D., Columbia University, 1935.

3521   Stack, Elizabeth C. The Philosophical and Psychological Antecedents of the Core Curriculum in Educational Theory, 1800-1918. Ph.D., University of North Carolina, 1960. 327p. UMI# 60-04869.

3522   Stein, Charles W. An Historical Survey of Independent Study Plans in American Colleges with Specific Reference to the Development of Honors Programs. Ph.D., State University of New York at Buffalo, 1954.

3523   Temin, Charlotte B. A Study of the Growth and Development of College-Age Volunteers in a Supervised Companion-Tutoring Program. Ed.D., Harvard University, 1980. 362p. UMI# 81-00366.

3524   Thompson, Mary M. A Survey of Problems Impeding the Growth of Independent Study in Institutions of Higher Education in the United States. Ph.D., Michigan State University, 1971. 131p. UMI# 71-31324.

3525   Winters, Marilyn B. The Course of Study in American Education: Past, Present and Future. Ph.D., Claremont Graduate School, 1984. 242p. UMI# 83-28283.

3526   Wisneski, Carl A. A Contribution Toward the Professionalization of the Media Field through the Development of a Media Doctoral Program Model. Ed.D., Temple University, 1974. 129p. UMI# 75-28150.

3527   Woytanowitz, George M. 'To Train Good Citizens': The Early Years of University Extension in the United States, 1885-1915. Ph.D., Johns Hopkins University, 1970. 358p. UMI# 71-16756.

DEANS

3528   Bailey, Walter R. The Changing Role of the Dean of Men in American Higher Education: An Analysis of Influencing Factors. Ph.D., Ohio State University, 1968. 289p. UMI# 69-04837.

3529   Findlay, James F. The Origin and Development of the Work of the Dean of Men in Higher Education. Ph.D., New York University, 1938. 252p. UMI# 73-03127.

3530   Holmes, Lulu H. A History of the Position of Dean of Women in a Selected Group of Coeducational Colleges and Universities in the United States. Ph.D., Columbia University, 1939. 141p.

3531   Kletzly, Brother Paul F. A Study of the History and Development of the Office of the Dean of Men in Catholic Men's Colleges and Universities. Master's thesis, Catholic University of America, 1950.

3532   MacMitchell, T. Leslie. A Study of the Evolution and Present Functions of the Dean of Students in Selected Colleges of the College Entrance Examination Board. Ed.D., New York University, 1963. 187p. UMI# 64-06535.

3533   Sayre, Mildred B. Half a Century: An Historical Analysis of the National Association of Deans of Women, 1900-1950. Ph.D., Columbia University, 1951. 134p.

3534   Spencer, Louise W. Eleven Years of Change in the Role of Dean of Women in Colleges, Universities, and Teachers Colleges. Ph.D., Columbia University, 1952.

3535   Steph, Harlan J. The Dean of Men's Office—Its Development and Current Trends. Ph.D., University of Colorado, 1949. 197p.

EUROPEAN INFLUENCE

3536   Bigham, Wanda D. The Germanic Impact on the American Professor in the Late Nineteenth Century. Ed.D., University of Kentucky, 1978. 127p. UMI# 78-24379.

3537   Carrigg, Anne T. The English Contribution to Higher Educational Reform in the Post Civil War Period. Ph.D., Boston College, 1971. 521p. UMI# 71-19791.

3538   Herbst, Jergen F. H. Nineteenth Century German Scholarship in America: A Study of Five German-Trained Social Scientists. Ph.D., Harvard University, 1958.

3539   Hodgman, Robert S. Shaping the Idea of the University: An Historical Analysis of the

Origins and Development of the University Idea in European and American Thought. Ph.D., University of Southern California, 1964. 396p. UMI# 64-09619.

3540   Reeves, Dorothy E. British Commentary on American Culture and Higher Education, 1814-1914. Ed.D., George Peabody College for Teachers, 1974. 848p. UMI# 74-29151.

EXAMINATIONS

3541   Armstrong, Ross O., Jr. An Historical and Empirical Study of the Methods of Developing Expected Achievement Scores. Ph.D., University of Iowa, 1962. 317p. UMI# 63-00898.

3542   Crotty, Daniel L., Jr. An Historical Study of Examinations and Grading Policies in Selected American Undergraduate Colleges Based on the Scholarly Literature of the Period from 1900 to 1940. Ph.D., Boston College, 1969. 315p. UMI# 70-03370.

3543   Ruger, Marcus C., Jr. A History of the American College Testing Program (1959-1974). Ed.D., University of Northern Colorado, 1975. 163p. UMI# 76-00222.

3544   Sesney, John W. The Development of Teaching Proficiency Tests at the University Level. Ph.D., University of Utah, 1972. 251p. UMI# 73-01601.

3545   Shoen, Harriet H. The History Examinations of the College Entrance Examination Board, 1901-1933. Ph.D., Columbia University, 1945. 117p.

FACULTY

3546   Adkins, Roma L. Faculty Development Among Organized Faculties in U.S. Colleges and Universities, 1972-1982. Ed.D., West Virginia University, 1983. 288p. UMI# 84-07828.

3547   Ancell, Mary K.Z. Academic Tenure and the Courts: An Historical and Legal Analysis of the Concept of Academic Tenure in the United States Higher Education. Ph.D., Stanford University, 1978. 174p. UMI# 79-05812.

3548   Bowman, Claude C. The College Professor in America: A Study of Attitudes Expressed in the General Magazines, 1890-1936. Ph.D., University of Pennsylvania, 1937.

3549   Brown, Margaret J. Gender, Patriotism and the Academic's Role in Post-Industrial America: An Interpretation. Ph.D., University of Toronto, 1984.

3550   Calvert, Stanton C. An Analysis of the Historical Development and Legal Basis of the Professional Rights of Faculty in American Higher Education. Ph.D., University of Texas at Austin, 1975. 209p. UMI# 75-16651.

3551   Carrell, William D. Social, Political, and Religious Involvements of American College Professors, 1750-1800. Ph.D., George Peabody College for Teachers, 1968. 194p. UMI# 68-16341.

3552   Covert, James R. The Academic Profession: A Critical Analysis. Ph.D., Michigan State University, 1972. 200p. UMI# 73-05352.

3553   Farley, Delbert R. The Image of the College Professor as Disclosed in General Magazines, 1938-1963. Ph.D., Florida State University, 1964. 100p. UMI# 64-10577.

3554   Farmer, Donna J. Immorality and the Public College Teacher: A Historical and Legal Analysis. Ed.D., University of Southern California, 1982.

3555   Ferguson, John A.M. The Development of Academic Tenure in American Higher Education, 1870-1915: Judicialization as a Response to a Changing Academic Environment. Ph.D., University of Michigan, 1976. 280p. UMI# 77-07913.

3556   Finkelstein, Martin J. Three Decades of Research on American Academics: A Descriptive Portrait and Synthesis of Findings. Ph.D., State University of New York at Buffalo, 1978. 446p. UMI# 7817031.

3557   Furstenberg, Barbara J. The Emergence of Drama in the Curriculum: A Study of Contrasting Images of the University Professor. Ph.D., University of Wisconsin, 1968. 240p. UMI# 69-00914.

3558   Hakanson, Eugene E. The College Professor, 1946-1965, as Revealed by an Analysis of Selected Magazine Articles. Ed.D., Indiana University, 1967. 137p. UMI# 67-16403.

3559   Hall, Clifton L. Some Historical Considerations of the Status of the Teacher. Ph.D., University of North Carolina at Chapel-Hill, 1950. 117p.

3560   Howell, Sarah H.M. Scholars of the Urban-Industrial Frontier, 1880-1889. Ph.D., Vanderbilt University, 1970. 374p. UMI# 70-24-872.

3561   Hunter, Deborah E. Factors Associated with the Publication Productivity of Prolific Higher Education Scholars. Ph.D., Indiana University, 1985. 431p. UMI# 8525364.

3562   Jennings, Lawrence C. The Image of the Professor from Carlyle to Snow. Ed.D., University of Oklahoma, 1971. 188p. UMI# 71-26554.

3563   Kennedy, Sister M. St. Mel. The Changing Academic Characteristics of the Nineteenth Century American College Teacher. Ph.D., Saint Louis University, 1961. 318p. UMI# 61-06476.

3564   Meckler, Alan M. Scholarly Micropublishing in America, 1938-1979. Ph.D., Columbia University, 1980. 237p. UMI# 8222447.

3565   Orr, Kenneth B. The Impact of the Depression Years, 1929-1939, on Faculty in American Colleges and Universities. Ph.D., University of Michigan, 1978. 418p. UMI# 78-13714.

3566   Palmer, Barbara H. Lace Bonnets and Academic Gowns: Faculty Development in Four Women's Colleges, 1875-1915. Ph.D., Boston College, 1980. 356p. UMI# 80-26752.

3567   Peach, Larry D. De Facto Academic Tenure: A Synthesis of Federal Appellate Case Law Since Sinderman. Ph.D., Kent State University, 1980. 146p. UMI# 8112890.

3568   Price, Rebecca R. An Historical Analysis of the Concepts of Teacher in America Between the 1850s, 1930s, and 1960s as Portrayed in the Writings of the Times. Ph.D., Miami University, 1974. 194p. UMI# 75-14317.

3569   Reinert, Paul C. Faculty Tenure in Colleges and Universities from 1900 to 1940. Ph.D., University of Chicago, 1944. 150p.

3570   Schufletowski, Frank W. The Development of the College Professor's Image in the United States from 1946-1964. Ph.D., Washington State University, 1966. 261p. UMI# 66-07251.

3571   Stevenson, Perry L. A Historical Study of the Methods of Teaching as Used by Eminent University and College Teachers. Ph.D., New York University, 1932. 185p. UMI# 72-33762.

3572   Watson, Rollin J. The Priestly Professors: The Mind of a Generation of University Men of Letters. Ph.D., University of Maryland, 1975. 416p. UMI# 76-18843.

FEDERAL AID

3573   Alterman, Richard C. Manpower Policy and Individual Need in the Development of Federal Aid to College Students. Ph.D., University of Michigan, 1973. 203p. UMI# 74-15,657.

3574   Arora, Sudesh. An Historical Study of the Impact of Political, Social, and Economic Factors on Federal Funding of Higher Education During 1946-1980. Ph.D., Wayne State University, 1983. 299p. UMI# 8315571.

3575   Beck, Harry L. The History and Development of the Federal College Work-Study Program. Ed.D., University of Kentucky, 1975. 249p. UMI# 76-06122.

3576   Bloom, Samuel B. The Servicemen's Readjustment Act of 1944: A Case Study of Federal Aid to Higher Education, 1944-1954. Ph.D., University of California-Berkeley, 1963. 328p. UMI# 64-05196.

3577   Brock, Stephen C. A Comparative Study of Federal Aid to Higher Education: The Higher Education Act of 1965 and Project Upward Bound. Ph.D., Cornell University, 1968. 121p. UMI# 69-07278.

3578   Bryce, Robert C. The Technical and Vocational Training Assistance Act of 1961-1967, an Historical Survey and Documentary Analysis. Ph.D., University of Alberta-(Canada), 1971.

3579   Carroll, James D. The Implications of President Johnson's Memoranda of September 13 and 14, 1965, for the Funding of Academic Research by Federal Agencies: A Study of Federal University Research Policies. Ph.D., Syracuse University, 1967. 546p. UMI# 68-07050.

3580   Chaudry, Muhammad A. The Higher Education Act of 1965: An Historical Case Study. Ed.D., Oklahoma State University, 1981. 190p. UMI# 81-23829.

3581   Citron, Henry. The Study of the Arguments of Interest Groups Which Opposed Federal Aid to Education from 1949-1965. Ph.D., New York University, 1977. 253p. UMI# 77-20739.

3582   Cook, Wayne S. Precedents for Federal Action in Higher Education: 1862-1950. Ph.D., State University of New York at Buffalo, 1983. 230p. UMI# 8528245.

3583   Crowley, John C. The Federal College Work-Study Program, University Policy-Making and the Graduate Student. Ph.D., Syracuse University, 1977. 432p. UMI# 77-30719.

3584   Gale, Barbara R. The National Defense Student Loan Program: Its History, Significance, and Problems. Ed.D., George Washington University, 1974. 315p. UMI# 74-23489.

3585   Gayton, Carver C. Federal Funding and Its Impact on the University. Ph.D., University of Washington, 1976. 207p. UMI# 77-18,348.

3586   Hansen, Janet S. The Politics of Federal Scholarships: A Case Study of the Development of General Grant Assistance for Undergraduates. Ph.D., Princeton University, 1977. 257p. UMI# 77-16891.

3587   Kidd, Charles V. American Universities and Federal Research Funds. Ph.D., Harvard University, 1957.

3588   Larson, Gary O. The Reluctant Patron: The United States Government and the Arts, 1943-1965. Ph.D., University of Minnesota, 1981. 511p. UMI# 8211498.

3589   Lyon, Bruce W. The Federal Government and College Students During the Great Depression; A Study of the College Student Aid Programs of the Federal Emergency Relief Administration and the National Youth Administration. Ph.D., Ohio State University, 1969. 151p. UMI# 69-22170.

3590   Mackaye, Ruth C. Federal Relations to the Field of Higher Education. Ph.D., New York University, 1944. 120p. UMI# 693.

3591   McCann, Maurice J. The Truman Administration and Education. Ph.D., Southern Illinois University, 1976. 287p. UMI# 7813560.

3592   Mosch, Theodore R. The G.I. Bill: A Precedent in Educational and Social Policy in the United States. Ph.D., University of Oklahoma, 1970. 481p. UMI# 70-22999.

3593   Rainsford, George N. Federal Assistance to Higher Education in the Nineteenth Century. Ph.D., Stanford University, 1968. 224p. UMI# 68-11339.

3594   Ross, Naomi V. Congresswomen Edith Green on Federal Aid to Schools and Colleges. Ed.D., Pennsylvania State University, 1980. 319p. UMI# 8024488.

3595   Schott, Charles J. The Development of a Program of Federal Aid to Education During the New Deal Era, 1933-1945, with Special Emphasis on the Role of the President. Doctor of Social Science, Syracuse University, 1967. 375p. UMI# 68-05491.

3596   Smith, Gilbert E., III. The Limits of Reform: Politics and Federal Aid to Education, 1937-1950. Ph.D., Columbia University, 1975. 442p. UMI# 75-25,722.

3597   Weaver, Samuel H. The Truman Administration and Federal Aid to Education. Ph.D., American University, 1972. 359p. UMI# 72-30117.

3598   Young, James N. Title I of the Higher Education Act of 1965. Public Law 80-329 (1919-1969): A Chronological Review. Ed.D., George Washington University, 1971. UMI# 71-22429.

FICTION, HIGHER EDUCATION IN

3599   Ainsworth, Charles P. Academia in Recent American Fiction: An Exploration of Main Themes in Novels Related to Higher Education, 1961-1971. Ed.D., University of Kentucky, 1973. 342p. UMI# 74-19607.

3600   Belok, Michael V. The College Professor in the Novel, 1940-1957. Ph.D., University of Southern California, 1958. 306p. UMI# 59-00863.

3601   Brandom, Martha E. Adult Developmental Stages in Female Professors as Portrayed in Novels (1940-1981). Ed.D., University of Arkansas, 1984. 306p. UMI# 8426129.

3602   Cameron, Alex J. The Image of the Physician in the American Novel 1859-1973. Ph.D., University of Notre Dame, 1973. 185p. UMI# 73-12,077.

3603   Campbell, Andrew M. Geology in Modern Poetry. Ph.D., University of Kentucky, 1985. 168p. UMI# 8523908.

3604   Caram, Richard G. The Secular Priests: A Study of the College Professor as Hero in Selected American Fiction (1955-1977). Ph.D., Saint Louis University, 1980. 522p. UMI# 81-20599.

3605   Catenacci, Edward N. The Academic Novel: Symbolic Action as Revealed Attitude Toward Academia. Ph.D., Southern Illinois University, 1974. 178p. UMI# 75-00104.

3606   Click, Donald W. The Image of Higher Education in American Novels, 1920-1966. Ed.D., University of Southern California, 1970. 208p. UMI# 70-16858.

3607   Colozzi, John J. Educational Values as Reflected in Some Best-Selling American Fiction, 1895-1916. Ed.D., George Peabody College for Teachers, 1976. 141p. UMI# 76-21,620.

3608   Ezor, Edwin L. The Image of the Teacher in the American Academic Novel, 1900-1960. Ph.D., New York University, 1969. 524p. UMI# 70-15959.

3609   Finn, Thomas. College Teaching as Portrayed in the American College Novel, 1962-1972. Ph.D., University of California-Berkeley, 1979. 232p. UMI# 80-14675.

3610   Gober, Ruth B. The American Novelist Interprets the Student of Higher Education. Ed.D., University of Oklahoma, 1956. 212p. UMI# 16,973.

3611   Hendrickson, Bobby G. A Portrait of College Professors in the Novels of the 1960s. Ed.D., University of Arkansas, 1976. 443p. UMI# 76-26362.

3612   Hirsch, David H. The Intellectual in the American Novel, 1792-1860: A Study in the Search for Reality and Form. Ph.D., Ohio State University, 1961. 291p. UMI# 62-02140.

3613   Jacobs, Rita D. Individuals and Institutions: The American Academic Novel 1960-1970. Ph.D., University of Pennsylvania, 1974. 188p. UMI# 75-02743.

3614   Johnson, Clarence S. The Teacher in the American Novel, 1900-1950: A Study of the Teacher as Seen by the Novelist. Ed.D., Rutgers University, 1966. 204p. UMI# 67-06400.

3615   Kane, Patricia L. Legal Fictions: The Lawyer in the American Novel. Ph.D., University of Minnesota, 1961. 285p. UMI# 61-04600.

3616   King, James B. The Persona of the College Professor in the American Novel, 1828-1968. Ph.D., University of Michigan, 1970. 303p. UMI# 71-04652.

3617   Kissiah, Herman C. The College Student in the American Novel, 1930-1939 and 1964-1967. Ph.D., Michigan State University, 1969. 174p. UMI# 70-15066.

3618   Lauffer, Carolyn. The Satiric Treatment of College Teaching in the Novel, 1960-1972. Ph.D., Duke University, 1977. 239p. UMI# 78-07811.

3619   Lee, Robert C. Portrayal of the College in Modern American Novels, 1932-1942. Ph.D., George Peabody College for Teachers, 1944. 142p.

3620   Lisherness, Nancy L. The American College Novel: A Microcosm of Female Academia. Ph.D., Arizona State University, 1985. 292p. UMI# 8513585.

3621   Loberger, Gordon J. The Portrayal of the University Professor in the American Short Story, 1940-1959. Ed.D., Ball State University, 1973. 245p. UMI# 74-03464.

3622   Lyons, John O. The Novel of Academic Life in America. Ph.D., University of Florida, 1960. 374p. UMI# 60-05139.

3623   Moore, Irene. The Tradition of the College in the American Novel, 1895-1937. Master's thesis, University of Texas, 1940.

3624   Narel, Ronald A. Characteristics of College Students in Contemporary American Novels, 1960-1965. Ph.D., Florida State University, 1968. 112p. UMI# 68-16,380.

3625   Nichols, Edward L. The Image of the College Professor as a Protagonist in Selected American Novels from 1945 through 1965. Ed.D., University of Tulsa, 1970. 217p. UMI# 71-04450.

3626   Peo, John R. The Image of the University as Related in American University Novels, 1957-1963. Ed.D., State University of New York, 1968. 406p. UMI# 68-13,236.

3627   Scholz, Carol K. They Share the Suffering: The Psychoanalyst in American Fiction Between 1920 and 1940. Ph.D., University of Pennsylvania, 1977. 355p. UMI# 7730250.

3628   Schutter, Howard N. Academic Freedom and the American College Novel of the Nineteen Fifties. Ph.D., University of Michigan, 1966. 217p. UMI# 68-7765.

3629   Seaton, Chadwick L. The Image of College Life as Reflected in a Sampling of American Novels, 1950-1969. Ed.D., Indiana University, 1974. 218p. UMI# 75-05663.

3630   Smith, Charles R., Jr. The American Academic Novel, 1950-1960. Ph.D., Syracuse University, 1968. 203p. UMI# 69-07778.

3631   Staib, Mary P. The Academic Woman in the American College Novel. Ph.D., Arizona State University, 1975. 228p. UMI# 75-22562.

3632   Sundstrand, Lyndon D. The Academic Community as Reflected in Selected American Novels. Ph.D., University of Southern California, 1977.

3633   Turner, Theodore B., III. Mind Forged Manacles: Images of the University in American Fiction of the Nineteen-Sixties: A Study in Kesey, Mailer, Barth, Bellow, Nabokov, and Burroughs. Ph.D., University of Iowa, 1974. 254p. UMI# 75-01279.

3634   VanderMeer, Barbara G. The Academic Novel as a Resource in the Study of Higher Education. Ph.D., University of Alabama, 1982. 202p. UMI# 8224313.

3635   Webber, Robert S. Fictional and Poetic Perspectives on Higher Education: The Last Decade. Ph.D., State University of New York at Buffalo, 1975. 232p. UMI# 75-18,855.

3636   Yevish, Irving A. The Education of the Literary Artist in Modern Novels of College and University Life. Ph.D., Columbia University, 1965. 339p. UMI# 68-05663.

FINANCES

3637   Beck, Norman E. A History of Modern Student Financial Aids. Ph.D., Ball State University, 1971. 380p. UMI# 71-23025.

3638   Daniels, James E. An Inquiry into the History and Trends in Financing and Accounting for the Self-Liquidating Auxiliary Enterprises of Colleges and Universities. Ph.D., University of Arkansas, 1970. 251p. UMI# 70-26207.

3639   Desmond, Richard L. The Federal Tax History of Life Income Gifts to Higher Education. Ph.D., University of Michigan, 1965. 239p. UMI# 66-06593.

3640   Edwards, Marsha. The Relation of College Enrollment to Economic Depression in the United States, 1890-1930. Master's thesis, University of Minnesota, 1931.

3641   McClintock, David H. Relationships Between Growth and Financial Conditions Among Selected Private Liberal Arts Colleges. Ed.D., Indiana University, 1973. 124p. UMI# 73-10847.

3642   Morris, Stephen A. A History of the Midwest Association of Student Financial Aid Administrators. Ed.D., Indiana University, 1985. 208p. UMI# 8605817.

3643   Webb, David L. Farmers, Professors, and Money: Agriculture and the Battle for Managed Money, 1920-1941. Ph.D., University of Oklahoma, 1978. 466p. UMI# 78-24618.

FOREIGN HIGHER EDUCATION

3644   Bernert, Christopher J. Die WanderJahre: The Higher Education of American Students in German Universities, 1870-1914. Ph.D., State University of New York at Stony Brook, 1984. 321p. UMI# 85-13858.

3645   Brown, Cynthia S. The American Discovery of the German University: Four Students at Göttingen, 1815-1822. Ph.D., Johns Hopkins University, 1966.

3646   Greenwood, Keith M. Robert College: The American Founders. Ph.D., Johns Hopkins University, 1965. 328p. UMI# 65-06888.

3647   Guckert, John C. The Adaptation of Robert College to its Turkish Environment, 1900-1927. Ph.D., Ohio State University, 1968. 194p. UMI# 68-15328.

3648   Hayden, Dale L. A History of the External Degree in Britain and the United States. Ph.D., University of Alabama, 1979. 128p. UMI# 7915013.

3649   Louden, Lois M.R. A Comparison of the Development of the American Community Junior

College and the English Sixth Form College. Ph.D., University of North Carolina, 1974. 315p. UMI# 74-26906.

3650   Parker, Paul C. Change and Challenge in Caribbean Higher Education: The Development of the University of the West Indies and the University of Puerto Rico. Ph.D., Florida State University, 1971. 548p. UMI# 73-04209.

3651   Sproul, Christine. The American College for Girls, Cairo, Egypt: Its History and Influence on Egyptian Women. A Study of Selected Graduates. Ph.D., University of Utah, 1982. 209p. UMI# 82-21991.

3652   Weaver, Mary L. Policy and Its Consequences: Higher Education in the United States and Great Britain, 1957-1977. Ph.D., Cornell University, 1980. 516p. UMI# 80-20901.

3653   Wetzel, Charles J. The American Rescue of Refugee Scholars and Scientists from Europe, 1933-1945. Ph.D., University of Wisconsin, 1964. 446p. UMI# 64-3251.

FORENSICS

3654   Busch, Carliss T. Oral Interpretation in American Colleges and Universities from 1930-1965. Ph.D., University of Utah, 1966. 334p. UMI# 66-09875.

3655   Capp, Glenn R., Jr. History and Analysis of Intercollegiate Debating in America. Master's thesis, Baylor University, 1967.

3656   Ferris, Millicent M. The Pillsbury Oratorical Contest: A Study of Seventy-Five Years of College Oratory. Master's thesis, University of Minnesota, 1967.

3657   Guthrie, Warren A. The Development of Rhetorical Theory in America, 1635-1850. Ph.D., Northwestern University, 1940.

3658   Harrison, Carolyn P. American Intercollegiate Debate: A General Survey with Emphasis on Past and Present Controversies, 1892-1968. Master's thesis, Western Kentucky University, 1968.

3659   Jordan, Harold M. Rhetorical Education in American Colleges and Universities, 1850-1915. Ph.D., Northwestern University, 1952.

3660   Kitzhaber, Albert R. Rhetoric in American Colleges, 1850-1900. Ph.D., University of Washington, 1953. 382p. UMI# 00-05899.

3661   Laine, Joseph B. Rhetorical Theory in American Colleges and Universities, 1915-1954. Ph.D., Northwestern University, 1958. 535p. UMI# 59-00213.

3662   Manning, Robert N. An Historical Survey of Modern Rhetoric as Evidenced in Introductory Speech Textbooks from 1935 to 1965. Ph.D., Syracuse University, 1972. 189p. UMI# 73-20,103.

3663   Nabors, D.J., Jr. The Historical Development of Intercollegiate Forensic Activities, 1915-1956. Ed.D., University of Oklahoma, 1957. 227p. UMI# 00-24422.

3664   Perrin, Porter G. The Teaching of Rhetoric in the American Colleges Before 1750. Ph.D., University of Chicago, 1936.

3665   Thomas, Ota. The Theory and Practice of Disputation at Yale, Harvard, and Dartmouth from 1700 to 1800. Ph.D., University of Iowa, 1941.

3666   Veith, Donald P. An Historical Analysis of the Relations Between English and Speech Since 1910. Ph.D., Columbia University, 1953.

FOUNDATIONS

3667   Bell, Dorothy E. A Phoenix in Our Midst: The Carnegie Foundation for the Advancement of Teaching and Its Relationship to American Higher Education, (1950-1970). Ph.D., University of Illinois, 1972. 479p. UMI# 73-17,115.

3668   Blount, Lawanna M.L. Contributions of Selected Private Philanthropic Foundations for Higher Education Administration. 1966-1975. Ph.D., University of Wisconsin-Madison, 1978. 315p. UMI# 79-02388.

3669   Boom, Kathleen W. The Julius Rosenwald Fund's Aid to Education in the South. Ph.D., University of Chicago, 1950.

3670   Browning, Robert G. Ideology and Educational Philanthropy: An Historical Analysis. Ph.D., Ohio State University, 1979. 251p. UMI# 7915959.

3671   Bryan, Alison R. The Westminister Foundation: Its History, Program, and Goal, Particularly as Represented in Five University Centers. Doctor of Theological Studies, Temple University, 1954.

3672   Butler, John H. An Historical Account of the John F. Slater Fund and the Anna T. Jeans Foundation. Ed.D., University of California-Berkeley, 1932.

3673   Dane, John H. An Analysis of the Trends of Financial Support by Philanthropic Foundations to General Programs in United States Higher Education, 1955-1970. Ph.D., University of Pittsburgh, 1974. 195p. UMI# 74-21670.

3674   Fedje, Raymond N. The Wesley Foundation Idea: A Selective History. Ph.D., Boston University, 1964. 379p. UMI# 64-11,604.

3675   Fisher, Donald. The Impact of American Foundations on the Development of British University Education, 1900-1939. Ph.D., University of California-Berkeley, 1977. 803p. UMI# 77-31353.

3676   Johns, Robert. Ten Philanthropies to American Higher Education. A Study of the Philanthropists and Their Influence on the Beneficiaries. Ph.D., Stanford University, 1950.

3677   Kaplan, Anne C. The National Endowment for the Humanities: Private Men and Public Causes. Ph.D., Washington University, 1983. 623p. UMI# 8402203.

3678   Sears, Jesse B. Philanthropy in the History of American Higher Education. Ph.D., Columbia University Teachers College, 1919. 112p.

3679   Swanson, Jon W. University Foundations: Environmental Factors That Influence Their Establishment and Development. Ph.D., University of Michigan, 1981. 304p. UMI# 82-04771.

FRATERNITIES

3680   Cipic, Margaret S. A History of Gamma Chapter, Delta Pi Epsilon, 1940-1978. Ed.D., University of Pittsburgh, 1980. 181p. UMI# 80-18293.

3681   Dobrunz, Carol A. The History, Development, and Contributions of Delta Psi Kappa from 1916 to 1970. Ph.D., University of Oregon, 1973. 180p. UMI# 74-06821.

3682   Jones, Mary A. The Influence of the Woman's College Fraternity on Character Development. Ph.D., Yale University, 1935.

3683   Lapradd, Charles W. College Male Fraternities in Controversy, 1950-1965 as Reported in American Magazines. Ed.D., Florida State University, 1965. 121p. UMI# 66-05455.

3684   Lee, Julius W., Jr. The History of Phi Delta Kappa, 1906-1954. Ed.D., Indiana University, 1954. 271p. UMI# 00-11,199.

3685   Lourie, Stephen J. The Historical Development of the Relationship Between the Fraternity and the University in the United States. Master's thesis, University of Missouri-Columbia, 1971. 90p.

3686   Mondale, Clarence C. Gentleman of Letters in a Democracy: Phi Beta Kappa Orations, 1788-1865. Ph.D., University of Minnesota, 1960. 312p. UMI# 61-615.

3687   Siske, James H. The Development of the Guidance Concept in the College Social Fraternity. Ed.D., University of Virginia, 1956. 722p. UMI# 00-20351.

GENERAL EDUCATION

3688   Baker, James K. The Evolution of the Concept of General Education. Ph.D., Yale University, 1947. 258p.

3689   Chen, Victor W.K. The Professionalization of Social Inquiry and the Decline of General Education. Ph.D., University of California-Berkeley, 1983. 303p. UMI# 8328821.

3690   Koch, Gail A. The General Education Movement in American Higher Education: An Account and an Appraisal of Its Principles and Policies and Their Relation to Democratic Thought in Modern American Society. Ph.D., University of Minnesota, 1979. 313p. UMI# 8011837.

3691   La Fauci, Horatio M. A Study of the University General College Historical, Educational, and Sociological Factors in the Origin, Development, and Growth of a University's General Education Programs. Ph.D., Harvard University, 1957.

3692   LeBlanc, M. Elizabeth. The Concept of General Education in Colleges and Universities, 1945-1979. Ed.D., Rutgers University, 1980. 780p. UMI# 8023605.

3693   Miller, Gary E. The Meaning of General Education: The Development of the General Education Paradigm and Practices. Ed.D., Pennsylvania State University, 1985. 261p. UMI# 8526045.

3694   Nelson-Jones, Richard C. General Education in American Higher Education, 1955-56 to 1964-65. Ph.D., Stanford University, 1967. 253p. UMI# 67-17,469.

3695   Orth, Andrew P. The History of General Education as a Philosophical Development in American Higher Education. Ed.D., Pennsylvania State University, 1952. 233p. UMI# 00-04792.

GRADUATE EDUCATION

3696   Betters-Reed, Bonita L. A History and Analysis of Three Innovative Graduate Institutions: The Arthur D. Little Management Education Institute, the Massachusetts General Hospital Institute of Health Professions and the Wang Institute of Graduate Studies. Ph.D., Boston College, 1982. 324p. UMI# 8311098.

3697   Etheridge, Carroll D. The Influence of Science on the Development of the American Graduate School. Ed.D., University of Southern California, 1976.

3698   Horton, Byrne J. The Origin of the Graduate School and the Development of Its Administration. Ph.D., New York University, 1939. 238p. UMI# 73-03194.

3699   Hoskins, Glenister C. The Development of Graduate Instruction in the Upper Mississippi Valley Area, 1900-1945. Ph.D., University of Missouri, 1949. 386p. UMI# 00-01278.

3700   Huegel, Mary A. A Study of Ph.D. and Ed.D. Programs in Fourteen Graduate Schools of Arts and Sciences and Graduate Schools of Education: 1950-1984. Ph.D., Boston College, 1986. 200p. UMI# 8616103.

3701   Malone, Thomas L. A History of the Doctor of Philosophy Dissertation in the United States 1861-1930. Ph.D., Wayne State University, 1981. 166p. UMI# 81-17081.

3702   McPeake, Thomas E. The Development of the Doctor of Education Degree. Ph.D., New York University, 1957. 287p. UMI# 24,982.

3703   Messinger, Milton A. Historical Evolution of the Master of Arts Degree in the United States. Ph.D., University of Texas at Austin, 1969. 480p. UMI# 70-10836.

3704   Partridge, Arthur R. The Rise of the University School of Education as a Professional Institution. Ed.D., Stanford University, 1958. 408p. UMI# 58-01274.

3705   Puthoff, Martilu. The Doctoral Programs in Health, Physical Education and Recreation: A Historical Case Study. Doctor of Physical Education, Indiana University, 1969. 425p. UMI# 70-03405.

3706   Reagan, Gaylord B.L. The Emergence of the Graduate Fellow, 1865-1910: Changing Conceptions and Changing Roles. Ph.D., University of Oregon, 1978. UMI# 7814325.

3707   Reed, Glenn A. Crticisms of the American Graduate School, 1900-1945. Ph.D., Stanford University, 1951.

3708   Storr, Richard J. An Academic Overture: The American Graduate School of Arts and Sciences from Its Beginnings to 1865. Ph.D., Harvard University, 1949.

3709   Turrentine, Mrs. Richard J. History of the Requirements for a Master's Degree in American Colleges and Universities. Master's thesis, Southern Methodist University, 1926.

HEALTH SCIENCES

3710   Ainsworth, Dorothy S. The History of Physical Education in Colleges for Women as Illustrated by Barnard, Bryn Mawr, Elmira, Goucher, Mills, Mount Holyoke, Radcliffe, Rockford, Smith, Vassar, Wellesley, and Wells. Ph.D., Columbia University, 1930. 116p.

3711   Allemang, Margaret M. Nursing Education in the United States and Canada, 1873-1950: Leading Figures, Forces, Views on Education. Ph.D., University of Washington, 1974. 316p. UMI# 75-28,308.

3712   Armeny, Susan. Resolute Enthusiasts: The Effort to Professionalize American Nursing, 1880-1915. Ph.D., University of Missouri-Columbia, 1983. 675p. UMI# 8412757.

3713   Asan, Virginia M. Carl L. Anderson: Life and Contributions to Public Health and Health Education. Ed.D., Oregon State University, 1975. 166p. UMI# 75-4535. [head of health department, Oregon State University; chairman of physiology, public health, and hygiene, Utah State University].

3714   Ashley, Jo Ann. Hospital Sponsorship of Nursing Schools: Influence of Its Apprenticeship and Paternalism on Nursing Education in America, 1893-1948. Ed.D., Columbia University, 1972. 337p. UMI# 77-4181.

3715   Bandy, Susan J. The Historical Development of American Physical Education as a Disciplined Form of Scholarly Inquiry. Ph.D., Arizona State University, 1982. 251p. UMI# 82-02806.

3716   Barker, Ruel M. Biographies of Historical Leaders in Health, Physical Education and Recreation. Ed.D., Brigham Young University, 1971. 412p. UMI# 72-02565.

3717   Brown, Janie M. History of Masters Education in Nursing in the United States, 1945-1969. Ed.D., Columbia University Teachers College, 1979. 236p. UMI# 79-13184.

3718   Buerki, Robert A. Historical Development of Continuing Pharmaceutical Education in American Universities. Ph.D., Ohio State University, 1972. 542p. UMI# 73-01954.

3719   Buhler-Wilkerson, Karen A. False Dawn: The Rise and Decline of Public Health Nursing, 1900-1930. Ph.D., University of Pennsylvania, 1984. 342p. UMI# 8417273.

3720   Burn, Mary A. An Analysis of the 'American Journal of Nursing' as a Resource for the Self-Education of Nurses. Ed.D., Boston University, 1972. 197 p. UMI# 72-25422.

3721   Bussell, N.E. The History of Physical Education in Public Schools and Colleges of the United States. Master's thesis, University of Illinois, 1921.

3722   Bytheway, Ruth E. History and Development of the Nursing Service of the Veterans Administration Under the Direction of Mrs. Mary A. Hickey, 1919-1942. Ed.D., Columbia University, 1972. 144p. UMI# 73-02583.

3723   Cissell, William B. A History of the Organization and Development of the Society for Public Health Education Inc. Ph.D., Southern Illinois University at Carbondale, 1977. 363p. UMI# 77-16614.

3724   Clayton, Bonnie C.W. Historical Perspectives of Psychiatric Nursing in Higher Education, 1946 to 1975. Ph.D., University of Utah, 1976. 174p. UMI# 76-25845.

3725   Coffey, Margaret A. The Development of Professional Preparation in Physical Education for Women in the Colleges and Universities of the Northwest. Ph.D., University of Iowa, 1963. 242p. UMI# 63-04725.

3726   Cortes, Kathleen F. Democracy in the American Public Health Association: A Historical Analysis. Ph.D., Columbia University, 1976. 374p. UMI# 76-29041.

3727   Dickens, Marion R. The Influence of the Position of Women in the Society on the Development of Nursing as a Profession in America. Ph.D., University of New Mexico, 1977.

3728   Dunbar, Henry F. A Brief History of the College Physical Education Association. Ph.D., Columbia University, 1950. 231p. UMI# 00-01844.

3729   Dwyer, Kathleen M. A Study of the Impact of Funding on Growth and Development of Selected Schools and Colleges of Allied Health. Ph.D., Ohio State University, 1983. 185p. UMI# 84-03511.

3730   Fales, Martha J. H. History of Dental Hygiene Education in the United States, 1913 to 1975. Ph.D., University of Michigan, 1975. 371p. UMI# 75-29217.

3731   Felshin, Janet R. Changing Conceptions of Purpose in Physical Education in the United States from 1880 to 1930. Ph.D., University of California-Los Angeles, 1958.

3732   Fitzpatrick, Louise. The History of the National Organization for Public Health Nursing. Ph.D., Columbia University, 1972. 462p. UMI# 73-24,066.

3733   Foss, Jean L. A History of Professional Preparation in Physical Education for Women in the Teachers Colleges of Wisconsin, Illinois and Iowa. Ph.D., University of Iowa, 1966. 229p. UMI# 67-02614.

3734   Greene, Margaret D. The Growth of Physical Education for Women in the United States in the Early Nineteenth Century. Ph.D., University of California-Los Angeles, 1950.

3735   Gunnell, Reid J. Biographies of Historical Leaders in Physical Health and Recreation Education. Ed.D., Brigham Young University, 1973. 449p. UMI# 73-18227.

3736   Hamilton, Penny R. The Dental Hygienist: The First Half Century 1913 to 1963. Ph.D., University of Nebraska, 1981. 483p. UMI# 81-18160.

3737   Harden, Victoria A. Toward a National Institute of Health: The Development of Federal Bio-Medical Research Policy: 1900-1930. Ph.D., Emory University, 1983. 390p. UMI# 8328059.

3738   Haritos, Dolores J. The Evolution of Conceptual Framework as the Structural Design for Collegiate Nursing Programs 1842-1979. Ed.D., Boston College, 1980. 200p. UMI# 80-14943.

3739   Hess, Ford A. American Objectives of Physical Education from 1900-1957 Assessed in the Light of Certain Historical Events. Ed.D., New York University, 1959. 469p. UMI# 59-06221.

3740   Hiestand, Wanda C. Midwife to Nurse-Midwife: A History of the Development of Nurse-Midwifery Education in the Continental United States to 1965. Ed.D., Columbia University Teachers College, 1977. 306p. UMI# 78-12009.

3741   Hileman, Betty J. Emerging Patterns of Thought in Physical Education in the United States: 1956-1966. Ph.D., University of Southern California, 1967. 271p. UMI# 67-13,027.

3742   Huber-Paul, Frieda. History of the Administration in Schools of Nursing in the United States from 1800-1913. Master's thesis, Catholic University of America, 1942.

3743   Kersten, Evelyn S. Industrial Nursing from 1895 to 1942: Development of a Specialty. Ed.D., Columbia University Teachers College, 1985. 174p. UMI# 8525482.

3744   Krampitz, Sydney D. The Historical Development of Baccalaureate Nursing Education in the American University: 1899-1935. Ph.D., University of Chicago, 1978.

3745   Labecki, Geraldine. Baccalaureate Programs in Nursing in the Southern Region, 1925-1960. Ed.D., George Peabody College for Teachers, 1967. 149p. UMI# 67-14999.

3746   Lawson, Hal A. The Evolution of Elective Programs of Physical Education in American Universities. Ph.D., University of Michigan, 1969. 268p. UMI# 70-14577.

3747   Leaf, Carol A. History of the American Academy of Physical Education, 1950-1970. Ph.D., University of Utah, 1974. 413p. UMI# 74-29554.

3748   Martin, Margaret I. The History and Development of Physical Education in the Mennonite Colleges of the United States. Ed.D., George Peabody College for Teachers, 1962. 153p. UMI# 63-01885.

3749   Matassarin-Jacobs, Esther R. The Development of Professionalism: An Application to Nursing. Ph.D., Northwestern University, 1985. 200p. UMI# 8523559.

3750   Melosh, Barbara. 'Skilled Hands, Cool Heads and Warm Hearts': Nurses and Nursing, 1920-1960. Ph.D., Brown University, 1979. 357p. UMI# 8007047.

3751   Miller, Lucy H. Reformation and Resistance in American Nursing Education: Implications of Landmark Report Implementation. Ph.D., Vanderbilt University, 1984. 203p. UMI# 8417025.

3752   Nelson, Allen E. A Biographical Analysis of Historical Leaders in Health, Physical Education and Recreation. Ed.D., Brigham Young University, 1972. 491p. UMI# 72-9832.

3753   Parietti, Elizabeth S. Development of Doctoral Education for Nurses: An Historical Survey. Ed.D., Columbia University Teachers College, 1979. 231p. UMI# 80-06848.

3754   Pearson, Robert W. An Historical Analysis of Motivations and Contributions Attributed to Selected Medical Doctors in Physical Education. Ed.D., University of New Mexico, 1970. 259p. UMI# 71-09321.

3755   Peavy, Robert D. History of the American Academy of Physical Education, 1926-1950. Ph.D., University of Utah, 1973. 289p. UMI# 73-32485.

3756   Piemonte, Robert V. A History of the National League of Nursing Education 1912-1932:

Great Awakening in Nursing Education. Ed.D., Columbia University Teachers College, 1976. 177p. UMI# 76-17921.

3757   Pinkston, Dorothy. A History of Physical Therapy Education in the United States: An Analysis of the Development of the Curricula. Ph.D., Case Western Reserve University, 1978. 238p. UMI# 7816554.

3758   Pittman, Jacquelyn. The Development of Graduate Programs in Psychiatric Nursing, 1932-1968, and the Relationship to Congressional Legislation. Ed.D., Columbia University, 1974. 159p. UMI# 75-07848.

3759   Reverby, Susan M. The Nursing Disorder: A Critical History of the Hospital-Nursing Relationship, 1860-1945. Ph.D., Boston University, 1982. 539p. UMI# 8320028.

3760   Richardson, Janice K. A Study of the Forces and Influences Leading to the Development of Specialization in the Profession of Physical Therapy in the United States. Ph.D., University of Pittsburgh, 1983. 159p. UMI# 8411702.

3761   Rocker, Jack L. Major Themes of Undergraduate Professional Preparation in Physical Education from 1860 to 1962. Ph.D., University of Southern California, 1971. 235p. UMI# 72-17504.

3762   Schubert, Florence M. The Emergence of Preparation for Psychiatric Nursing in Professional Nursing Programs in the United States, 1873-1918. Ed.D., Columbia University, 1972. 165p. UMI# 73-2630.

3763   Sheahan, Dorothy A. The Social Origins of American Nursing and Its Movement into the University: A Microscopic Approach. Ph.D., New York University, 1979. 620p. UMI# 80-17528.

3764   Shields, Elizabeth A. A History of the United States Army Nurse Corps (Female): 1901-1907. Ed.D., Columbia University Teachers College, 1980. 242p. UMI# 81-11540.

3765   Sloan, Patricia E. A History of the Establishment and Early Development of Selected Nurse Training Schools for Afro-Americans, 1886-1906. Ed.D., Columbia University, 1978. 355p. UMI# 7909022.

3766   Smith, Nina B. The Women Who Went to the War: The Union Army Nurse in the Civil War. Ph.D., Northwestern University, 1981. 188p. UMI# 8125013.

3767   Sonnedecker, Glenn A. American Pharmaceutical Education Before 1900. Ph.D., University of Wisconsin, 1953. 323p.

3768   Thomson, Mary. Innovation in Nurse Education, a History of the Associate Degree Program 1940-1964—Champagne. Ph.D., University of Texas at Austin, 1981. 494p. UMI# 82-24153.

3769   Wacker, Hazel M. The History of the Private Single Purpose Institutions Which Prepared Teachers of Physical Education in the United States of America from 1861 to 1958; A Study of the Founding Progress, Current Status and Contributions to Physical Education of Twelve Single Purpose Schools (Books I-III). Ed.D., New York University, 1959. 576p. UMI# 59-06231.

3770   Washke, Paul R. The Development of the American Association for Health, Physical Education, and Recreation, and Its Relationship to Physical Education in the United States. Ph.D., New York University, 1943. 382p. UMI# 73-08817.

3771   Zeigler, Earle F. A History of Professional Preparation for Physical Education in the United States, 1861-1948. Ph.D., Yale University, 1951.

3772   Zingale, Donald P. A History of the Involvement of the American Presidency in School and College Physical Education and Sports During the Twentieth Century. Ph.D., Ohio State University, 1973. 237p. UMI# 73-18967.

HIGHER EDUCATION, GENERAL

3773   Alschuler, John H., Jr. The Historical Roots of Educational Innovation. Ed.D., University of Massachusetts, 1973. 141p. UMI# 73-31061.

3774   Angelo, Richard M. Unassigned Frequencies: Four Essays in the History of American Education. Ed.D., Temple University, 1979. 164p. UMI# 7909980.

3775   Asher, Helen D. The Growth of Colleges, 1850 to 1860, Particularly in the Northwest. Master's thesis, University of Wisconsin, 1926.

3776   Beard, Marshall R. The Collegiate System in the United States, 1870-1902. Ph.D., University of Wisconsin, 1930.

3777   Benjamin, Harold H. The Role of the Hypothesis in Selected Histories of American Education, 1912-1951. Ph.D., University of Michigan, 1955. 179p. UMI# 00-11242.

3778   Bjork, Richard E. The Changing Roles of American Universities in International Relations: A Study of Certain Perceptions of Universities' International Activities and the Impacts of Such Activities on Universities' Participation in International Relations. Ph.D., Michigan State University, 1961. 342p. UMI# 61-02677.

3779   Boram, William A. *The New York Times'* Editorial Stance on American Education, 1946-1961. Ph.D., University of Pittsburgh, 1963. 162p. UMI# 63-7790.

3780   Chambers, Stephen L. Guardian of a Free Society: The Educational Thought of Dwight David Eisenhower. Ph.D., Northern Arizona University, 1985. 333p. UMI# 8528064.

3781   Currie, Bruce F. Specialized Journalism for Professionals: The *Chronicle of Higher Education*. Ph.D., University of Michigan, 1973. 275p. UMI# 74-15,694.

3782   Davis, James M. Frontier and Religious Influences on Higher Education, 1796-1860. Ed.D., Northern Illinois University, 1975. 226p. UMI# 76-08909.

3783   Dennis, Philip M. Authority in Higher Education in the American Grain: An Autobiographical Portrait and an Intellectual Biography of George E. Axtell. Ph.D., United States International University, 1973. 236p. UMI# 73-22662. [professor of education, New York University, 1946-1959; Southern Illinois University, 1959-1974].

3784   Gardner, Frederick P. Institutional Histories: Their Contribution to Understanding the American College and University. Ed.D., State University of New York at Buffalo, 1976. 252p. UMI# 77-06137.

3785   Gray, Billy R. The Growth and Development of Midwestern Universities, 1922-1957. Master's thesis, University of Texas, 1960.

3786   Greenberg, Howard. The American College During the Revolutionary Era and the Early National Period: A Survey. Master's thesis, Brooklyn College, 1964.

3787   Ha, Inho. Historical Development of Specialization in American Higher Education. Ph.D., University of Pittsburgh, 1981.

3788   Halfond, Jay A. Between Two Cultures: The History of the Debates Surrounding the Organization of the American University. Ph.D., Boston College, 1981. 259p. UMI# 82-03941.

3789   Holtz, Harvey S. The Struggle for the University: Mass Higher Education and the Transformation of the Academic Profession. Ph.D., City University of New York, 1983. 223p. UMI# 8312351.

3790   Huehner, David R. Reform and the Pre-Civil War American College. Ph.D., University of Illinois, 1972. 378p. UMI# 73-09952.

3791   Jones, Bertis L. The History of Community Development in American Universities with Particular Reference to Four Selected Institutions. Ph.D., University of California-Los Angeles, 1962.

3792   Kent, Lori A. The Expansion of American Higher Education, 1880-1920: Status Maintenance for the Elite or Human Resource Development for the Country? Ph.D., University of Washington, 1984. 218p. UMI# 8419158.

3793   Knights, Paul A. The Responsibilities of Higher Education in America. Ph.D., University of Iowa, 1948.

3794   Knowles, Robert L. A Bibliographic Citation Analysis of Selected Higher Education Journal Literature. Ph.D., Florida State University, 1974. 86p. UMI# 74-18055.

3795   Kopecky, Paul J., Jr. The American Academy Movement and Its Influence on the Development of American Education, 1776 to 1860. Ed.D., University of Colorado, 1968. 333p. UMI# 68-14387.

3796   Levine, David O. The Functions of Higher Education in American Society Between World War I and World War II. Ph.D., Harvard University, 1981.

3797   Lottick, Kenneth V. A History of the Development of Education in the Western Reserve. Ph.D., Harvard University, 1951. 134p.

3798   Maxwell, Grace R. An Historical Survey and Analysis of the Annual National Conferences on Higher Education of the Association for Higher Education. Ph.D., Florida State University, 1964. 168p. UMI# 65-05593.

3799   McDannel, James H. The Council for the Advancement of Small Colleges, April, 1956 - June, 1980: A Developmental Study of Voluntary Educational Organization. Ph.D., Southern Illinois University, 1981. 553p. UMI# 22652.

3800   McKinney, Robert. The Public Interest, the Public College and the American Professoriat. Ed.D., Columbia University, 1973. 338p. UMI# 75-07845.

3801   Mondschein, Eric S. The United States Constitution and the Private College and University. Ed.D., University of Massachusetts, 1977. 240p. UMI# 77-08703.

3802   Nayebkhail, Mohammad Y. Higher Education and the National Government. Ed.D., Indiana University, 1976. 234p. UMI# 77-3357.

3803   Nelsen, Randle W. Growth of the Modern University and the Development of a Sociology of Higher Education in the United States. Ph.D., McMaster University, 1975.

3804   Newsome, George L., Jr. American University Patterns, 1776-1900. Ph.D., Yale University, 1956.

3805   Olcott, Ruth H. An Analysis of the Impact of Changing Times and an Expanding Nation Upon Five Selected Institutions of Higher Learning from 1869-1917. Ed.D., University of Houston, 1954. 275p. UMI# 00-08263.

3806   Ortenzio, Paul J. The Problem of Purpose in American Education: The Rise and Fall of the Educational Policies Commission (1935-1967). Ed.D., Rutgers University, 1977. 452p. UMI# 7804601.

3807   Person, Peter P. A History of Higher Education Among the Swedish Emigrants in America. Ph.D., Harvard University, 1950. 117p.

3808   Reitzer, Paul G. The Transformation of American Higher Education: A Study of Nineteenth Century Reformism. Ph.D., Florida State University, 1966. 237p. UMI# 67-00335.

3809   Richards, Alden LeG. The Secularization of the Academic World-View: The History of a Process and Its Consequences for the Study of Education. Ph.D., Brigham Young University, 1982. 375p. UMI# 8214776.

3810   Rincon, Frank L. Factors Related to the Founding and Development of Special Purpose Private Institutions of Higher Education. Ph.D., University of Arizona, 1982. 372p. UMI# 82-17465.

3811   Robertson, Neville L. Higher Education and Economic Growth: A Regional Study. Ed.D., Indiana University, 1968. 170p. UMI# 69-06767.

3812   Rogers, James F. Evolution of the Standard Four-Year College in America Since 1800. Ph.D., University of Texas at Austin, 1952.

3813   Runge, Janis M. Professional Educational Reform in Comparative Perspective (U.S.-Canada). Ph.D., University of Toronto, 1979.

3814   Sadnytzky, Nicholas O.O. A Statistical Theory of the Development of Mass Higher Education in the United States of America from 1633 through 1970. Ed.D., Columbia University Teachers College, 1979. 655p. UMI# 79-23616.

3815   Shoub, Ralph D. Social and Occupational Expectations: Women, Blacks, and Immigrants, 1890-1929. Ph.D., Arizona State University, 1981. 473p. UMI# 81-17186.

3816   Smith, Peggy C. Books Published in Higher Education: A Study of the Most Cited and Significant. Ph.D., University of Oklahoma, 1979. 144p. UMI# 7921265.

3817   Spence, Judson C., Sr. A Study of the Development of American Higher Education During the Period 1811-1849 as Reported by 'Niles' Weekly Register.' Ph.D., Florida State University, 1968. 246p. UMI# 69-13287.

3818   Stetar, Joseph M. Development of Southern Higher Education, 1865-1910: Selected Case Studies of Six Colleges. Ph.D., State University of New York at Buffalo, 1975. 208p. UMI# 75-18848.

3819   Tewksbury, Donald G. The Founding of American Colleges and Universities Before the Civil War, with Particular Reference to the Religious Influences Bearing Upon the College Movement. Ph.D., Columbia University Teachers College, 1932.

3820   Thelin, John R. The Collegiate Ideal and the Education of Elites in American Culture. Ph.D., University of California-Berkeley, 1972.

3821   Thompson, Jo Ann G. On the Idea of the University: An Analysis of Selected Themes Found in the Literature on Higher Education 1962-1972, with Special Reference to the Relationship of the Modern Themes to Those Found in Nineteenth Century English Thought. Ed.D., University of Kentucky, 1983. 290p. UMI# 8322724.

3822   Travers, Paul D. Interest in European Education and the Development of Comparative Education as a Subject of Study in American Universities and Colleges in the Nineteenth Century. Ed.D., George Peabody College for Teachers, 1967. 333p. UMI# 68-02885.

3823   Veysey, Laurence R. The Emergence of the American Universities 1865-1910: A Study in the Relations Between Ideals and Institutions. Ph.D., University of California-Berkeley, 1962.

3824   Wagner, Marta. The American Scholar in the Early National Period: The Changing Context of College Education, 1782-1837. Ph.D., Yale University, 1983. 314p. UMI# 8412443.

3825   Webster, David S. The Origins and Early History of Academic Quality Rankings of American Colleges, Universities, and Individual Departments, 1888-1925. Ph.D., University of California-Los Angeles, 1981. 362p. UMI# 82-01164.

3826   Whitmer, Edith F. Expression of Ideas on the Problem of Peace by Scholars in Higher Learning in the United States, 1915-1950. Ed.D., University of Missouri, 1954. 547p. UMI# 00-09202.

3827   Wilson, Ellen G. Higher Education in the Old South, Its Contribution to the Nation. Master's thesis, New York University, 1928.

3828   Wing, Lucy F. Northern Educators in the Colleges of the Lower South, 1800-1850. Master's thesis, Columbia University, 1943.

3829   Woelfel, Norman. A Critical Review of the Social Attitudes of Seventeen Leaders in American Education. Ph.D., Columbia University, 1933. 304p.

3830   Wyer, Jean C. Institutional Origin: Labor Market Signaling in Higher Education. Ed.D., College of William & Mary, 1980. 157p. UMI# 82-05606.

3831   Yakely, Leon. The Development of Higher Education in the Jacksonian Period, 1825-1840. Ph.D., University of Southern California, 1937.

3832   Zimmer, Agatho P. Changing Concepts of Higher Education in America Since 1700. Ph.D., Catholic University of America, 1939.

HUMANITIES

3833   Ackley, Bob G. A Comparative Study of Acting and Oral Interpretation Theory and Practice as Revealed in Selected American College Texts: 1900-1970. Ph.D., University of Southern California, 1973. 158p. UMI# 73-316.

3834   Aronson, Jack L. Classsical and Modern Foreign Languages in American Secondary Schools and Colleges—An Historical Analysis. Ed.D., Boston University, 1975. 171p. UMI# 75-12,224.

3835   Atwater, Elizabeth A. A History of Classical Scholarship in America. Ph.D., University of Pittsburgh, 1939.

3836   Barlow, Mark. An Analysis of Moral Philosophy and its Decline in Nineteenth Century American Colleges. Ed.D., Cornell University, 1962. 208p. UMI# 62-02522

3837   Basham, Rosemary. The Development of Music Curricula in American Colleges and Universities. Master's thesis, University of Louisville, 1971. 83p.

3838   Bird, Nancy K. The Conference on College Composition and Communication: A Historical Study of Its Continuing Education and Professionalization Activities, 1949-1975. Ed.D., Virginia Polytechnic Institute and State University, 1977. 250p. UMI# 7808114.

3839   Bushey, Richard J. Societal Influences on the Programs of Modern Dance in American Colleges and Universities: 1918-1945. Ph.D., University of Southern California, 1976.

3840   Cady, Henry L. Music in the Liberal Arts Colleges of Kansas and Missouri: An Investigation of Mutations in Philosophy from 1900 to 1960. Ph.D., University of Kansas, 1962. 302p. UMI# 63-799.

3841   Chappell, Diane L. The Selection of Emily Dickinson's Poems in College Textbook Anthologies, 1890-1976. Ph.D., University of Tennessee, 1979. 128p. UMI# 80-05379.

3842   Clark, John L. Dramatic Activity in the Colleges and Universities of the United States Prior to 1905. Ph.D., Stanford University, 1955. 222p. UMI# 00-15361.

3843   Cleary, Marie. Thomas Bulfinch, 'The Age of Fable,' and the Continuity of the Classics in American Education. Ed.D., University of Massachusetts, 1982. 206p. UMI# 82-29533.

3844   Clinger, Morris M. A History of Theater in Mormon Colleges and Universities. Ph.D., University of Minnesota, 1963. 461p. UMI# 63-07918.

3845   Cook, Bruce F. Twenty-Five Years of Music Competition Under University Interscholastic League Administration. Doctor of Musical Arts, University of Texas, 1975. 223p. UMI# 76-7986.

3846   Copenhaver, Harold L. An Historical Investigation of Music Education in the United States Air Force. Ed.D., American University, 1961. 191p. UMI# 61-03708.

3847   Damon, Ruth A. A Study of the Origin and Rise of Curricular Instruction in Dramatics in the Colleges and Universities of the United States. Ed.D., New York University, 1954. 311p. UMI# 00-08017.

3848   Darian, Steven G. A History of the Teaching of English as a Foreign Language in American Colleges and Universities, 1880-1965. Ph.D., New York University, 1968. 420p. UMI# 69-03165.

3849   Davidson, Levette J. A History of College English as a Requirement for the A.B. Degree in the United States. Ph.D., University of Michigan, 1922.

3850   Duffy, William E. An Historical and Philosophical Examination of Two Competing Views of Man and the State, Their Origins and Their Effect on American Education. Ph.D., Northwestern University, 1967. 182p. UMI# 67-15224.

3851   Engle, Gale W. The President's Moral Philosophy Course in the Early American College: Its Functions at Yale, Princeton, Brown. Master's thesis, Stanford University, 1949.

3852   Faulkner, Maurice E. The Roots of Music Education in American Colleges and Universities. Ph.D., Stanford University, 1956. 265p. UMI# 00-16022.

3853   Fisher, Philip A. Emerson's Vision in 'The American Scholar' as Recapitulated in the Inaugural Addresses of Andrew D. White and Charles W. Eliot. Ed.D., University of Southern California, 1978.

3854   Foster, Robert B. A History of the American Educational Theatre Association: The Formative Years. Ph.D., University of Oregon, 1983. 490p. UMI# 8315745.

3855   Fullbright, Wilbur D. The History and Development of the Master's Degree in Music in the United States. Ph.D., Boston University, 1960. 266p. UMI# 60-93448.

3856   Gardiner, Helen J. American Utopian Fiction, 1895-1910: The Influence of Science and Technology. Ph.D., University of Houston, 1978. 207p. UMI# 7910490.

3857   Geltner, Frank J., Jr. Standards and Accreditation for Theatre Arts Programs in American Higher Education: A History and Analysis. Ph.D., University of Oregon, 1980. 428p. UMI# 80-24854.

3858   Giles, Frederic P. Development of Art Courses in Southern Association State Teachers Colleges. Ph.D., George Peabody College for Teachers, 1942. 89p.

3859   Goodman, Alvin H. Development of the Symphony Orchestra in Higher Education. Ed.D., University of Southern California, 1960. 183p. UMI# 60-4480.

3860   Griffith, Betty R. Theoretical Foundations of Dance in Higher Education in the United States, 1933-1965. Ph.D., University of Southern California, 1975. 377p. UMI# 76-05243.

3861   Hamar, Clifford E. The Rise of Drama and Theatre in the American College Curriculum, 1900-1920. Ph.D., Stanford University, 1952.

3862   Harris, John M. The Pedagogical Development of College Harmony Textbooks in the United States. Doctor of Musical Arts, University of Texas at Austin, 1969. 259p. UMI# 70-10,741.

3863   Haynie, Jerry T. The Changing Role of the Band in American Colleges and Universities, 1900 to 1968. Ph.D., George Peabody College for Teachers, 1971. 338p. UMI# 71-26,211.

3864   Hendricks, Walter E. An Historical Analysis of Programs, Materials and Methods Used in Broadcasting Music Education Programs. Ph.D., Northwestern University, 1953. 323p.

3865   Hildebrand, Janet E. Methods of Teaching College German in the United States, 1753-1903: An Historical Study. Ph.D., University of Texas, 1977. 230p. UMI# 77-29,044.

3866   Hill, Melvin S. A History of Music Education in Seventh-Day Adventist Western Colleges. Doctor of Musical Arts, University of Southern California, 1959. 314p. UMI# 59-3520.

3867   Hubbard, Guy A. The Development of the Visual Arts in the Curriculums of American Colleges and Universities. Ph.D., Stanford University, 1963. 329p. UMI# 63-04607.

3868   Hutchcroft, John C. An Analysis of American College Level Sight Singing Materials Published Since 1960. Ph.D., Florida State University, 1985. 472p. UMI# 8517341.

3869   Jennings, Robert L. A Study of the Historical Development of Choral Ensembles in Selected Lutheran Liberal Arts Colleges in the United States. Ph.D., Michigan State University, 1969. 470p. UMI# 70-9567.

3870   Karier, Clarence J. The Neo-Humanist Protest in American Education, 1890-1930. Ph.D., University of Wisconsin, 1960. 307p. UMI# 60-3032.

3871   Kennedy, Arthur W. The Doctoral Degree in Music in Universities and Colleges of the United States. Ph.D., Northwestern University, 1955. 218p. UMI# 56-208.

3872   Lanphier, David N. A History of the American College Theatre Festival: 1963-1973. Ph.D., Florida State University, 1974. 308p. UMI# 75-08288.

3873   Lasko, Richard. A History of the College Band Directors National Association. Ed.D., University of Cincinnati, 1971. 266p. UMI# 72-02956.

3874   Lawrence, Robert R. A Desire to See: An Analysis of Popular Reading of College Students 1965-1975. Ed.D., Columbia University Teachers College, 1980. 550p. UMI# 8015080.

3875   Lewis, John S., Jr. The History of Instruction in American Literature in Colleges and Universities of the United States, 1827-1939. Ph.D., New York University, 1941. 402p. UMI# 00-00431.

3876   Maust, Earl M. The History and Development of Music in Mennonite-Controlled Liberal Arts Colleges in the United States. Ed.D., George Peabody College for Teachers, 1968. 313p. UMI# 69-13817.

3877   McCarrell, Lamar K. A Historical Review of the College Band Movement from 1875 to 1969. Ph.D., Florida State University, 1971. 330p. UMI# 72-10,037.

3878   Melendy, Earle R. The Development of Selected College and University Orchestras in the United States. Ed.D., University of Virginia, 1955. 516p. UMI# 56-1193.

3879   Meyer, Donald H. The American Moralists: Academic Moral Philosophy in the United States: 1835-1880. Ph.D., University of California-Berkeley, 1967. 454p. UMI# 68-00117.

3880   Molster, Jean L. Daniel Read and Higher Education in the Mississippi Valley, 1805-1878. Master's thesis, George Washington University, 1939. 94p. [professor of ancient languages, Ohio University, Indiana State University, University of Wisconsin].

3881   Mountney, Virginia R. The History of the Bachelor's Degree in the Field of Music in the United States. Ph.D., Boston University, 1961.

3882   Neve, Paul E. The Contribution of the Lutheran College Choirs to Music in America. Doctor of Sacred Music, Union Theological Seminary, 1967. 237p. UMI# 68-4875.

3883   O'Brien, Dorothy A. Theoretical Foundations of Dance in American Higher Education: 1885 to 1932. Ph.D., University of Southern California, 1966. 267p. UMI# 66-08794.

3884   Panzer, Vern A. Trends in the Articulation of English Between High Schools and Colleges, 1875-1958. Ed.D., University of Michigan, 1963. 233p. UMI# 64-06.

3885   Plugge, Domis E. History of Greek Play Production in American Colleges and Universities from 1881 to 1936. Ph.D., Columbia University, 1939. 175p.

3886   Radner, Sanford. An Historical Analysis of the Presidential Addresses of the National Council of Teachers of English, 1912-1955. Ph.D., Columbia University, 1958.

3887   Regier, Bernard W. The Development of Choral Music in Higher Education. Doctor of Musical Arts, University of Southern California, 1963. 58p. UMI# 63-5063.

3888   Saunders, Pearl I. Paradigmatic Transformations in College Freshman Composition Instruction from 1960-1980: A Historical Survey. Ph.D., Saint Louis University, 1983. 329p. UMI# 8418695.

3889   Simon, Henry W. The Reading of Shakespeare in American Schools and Colleges: An Historical Survey. Ph.D., Columbia University, 1932. 169p.

3890   Smith, Andrew W. Undergraduate Curriculums for Public School Music Teachers from 1920 to 1930. Ph.D., University of Michigan, 1970. 248p. UMI# 71-4732.

3891   Smith, Marjory A.I. Dramatic Activity Before 1800 in the Schools and Colleges of America. Master's thesis, Cornell University, 1948.

3892   Sollinger, Charles E. The Music Men and the Professors—A History of String Class Methods in the United States, 1800-1911. Ed.D., University of Michigan, 1970. 219p. UMI# 71-4549.

3893   Star, Bonnie S. The Evolution of the Foreign Language Methods Course from the Middle of the Nineteenth Century to the Present Time. Ed.D., State University of New York at Buffalo, 1968. 114p. UMI# 69-3884.

3894   Super, Sister Dolores. Musical Performance in American Higher Education: 1850 to 1951. Ed.D., University of Michigan, 1970. 186p. UMI# 71-15,068.

3895   Taub, Andrew. Laughing at the Law: An Examination of Legal Criticism in the Works of Selected American Humorists, 1780-1900. Ph.D., State University of New York at Stony Brook, 1979. 187p. UMI# 8007328.

3896   Texter, Merry E. A Historical and Analytical Investigation of the Beginning Band Method Book. Ph.D., Ohio State University, 1975. 235p. UMI# 75-26675.

3897   Thomas, Arnold R. The Development of Male Glee Clubs in American Colleges and Universities. Ed.D., Columbia University, 1962. 165p. UMI# 62-4924.

3898   Thomas, Katherine E. The Development of Comparative Literature as a Discipline in Selected American Universities. Ed.D., Pennsylvania State University, 1981. 266p. UMI# 82-05979.

3899   Umberson, George E. Development and Trends of Summer Music Camps for Junior and Senior High School Students in Selected Colleges and Universities in the Southwest. Ed.D., Colorado State College, 1967. 407p. UMI# 68-7160.

3900   Van Camp, Leonard W. The Development and Present Status of A Cappella Singing in United States Colleges and Universities. Doctor of Music Arts, University of Missouri at Kansas City, 1964. 343p. UMI# 67-10,110.

3901   Weintraub, Stanley A. A Comparison of Textbooks in Oral Interpretation of Literature, 1760-1952, with Reference to Principles and Methods. Ph.D., Columbia University, 1953. 368p. UMI# 6734.

3902   Wilson, Maureen P. Bilingualism as a Concern of Higher Education: A History of Changing Rationales. Ed.D., Columbia University Teachers College, 1985. 310p. UMI# 8602081.

3903   Young, James M. How Bright the Vision: Social and Educational Structures in Modern Utopian Literature. Ph.D., University of Minnesota, 1980. 146p. UMI# 8025529.

3904   Zielonka, Alfred W. The Modern Language Association of America, 1883-1960: An Historical Account of Selected Activities. Ed.D., State University of New York at Buffalo, 1964. 297p. UMI# 64-13673.

INTERCULTURAL EDUCATION

3905   Bailen, Frank G. Mutual Educational and Cultural Exchange Act of 1961: An Historical Analysis and Chronological Review, 1938-1964. Ed.D., Loyola University of Chicago, 1980. 207p. UMI# 8005355.

3906   Duffy, Christopher G. The Development of Non-Western Area Studies Programs at Selected Accredited Private Liberal Arts Colleges. Ed.D., Indiana University, 1970. 145p. UMI# 70-25187.

3907   King, Lovern C. Multicultural Education in U.S. Higher Education: 1970-1980. Ed.D., University of Washington, 1984. 290p. UMI# 8412400.

3908   Montalto, Nicholas V. The Forgotten Dream: A History of the Intercultural Education Movement, 1924-1941. Ph.D., University of Minnesota, 1977. 327p. UMI# 78-13436.

3909   Smedley, Margaret A. A History of the East West Cultural and Technical Interchange Center Between 1960 and 1966. Ph.D., Catholic University of America, 1970. 201p. UMI# 70-22694.

JEWISH HIGHER EDUCATION

3910   Greenwald, Eli B. Rabbinic Education in the United States, 1867-1939. Ph.D., Dropsie University, 1975.

3911   Loren, Morris J. Hebrew Higher Educational Institutions in the United States, 1830-1975. Ph.D., Wayne State University, 1976. 199p. UMI# 76-17327.

3912   Shapiro, Max A. An Historical Analysis and Evaluation of Jewish Religious Textbooks Published in the United States, 1817-1903. Ed.D., University of Cincinnati, 1960. 262p. UMI# 60-06159.

LAND-GRANT INSTITUTIONS

3913   Eddy, Edward D., Jr. The Development of the Land Grant Colleges: Their Programs and Philosophy. Ph.D., Cornell University, 1956. 672p. UMI# 00-18272.

3914   Fitzgerald, Peter H. Democracy, Utility, and Two Land-Grant Colleges in the Nineteenth Century: the Rhetoric and the Reality of Reform. Ph.D., Stanford University, 1972. 222p. UMI# 73-04.

3915   Foster, Parker V. The Land Grant Concept in Contemporary Society—Anachronism or Viable Entity? Ed.D., University of California-Los Angeles, 1972. 179p. UMI# 72-20,437.

3916   Harrison, Fred, Jr. The Projected Role of the Cooperative Extension Service in the States that Contain Both 1862 and 1890 Land Grant Institutions as Perceived by County Extension Agents, State Specialists and Administrators. Ph.D., Ohio State University, 1979. 359p. UMI# 8001742.

3917   Jensen, Axel C. A Study of the Educational Services of Justin Morrill. Master's thesis, Stanford University, 1936.

3918   Knight, George W. Landgrants for Education in the Northwest Territory. Ph.D., University of Michigan, 1884.

3919   Kuykendall, Dean W. The Land-Grant College: A Study in Transition. Ph.D., Harvard University, 1946. 229p.

3920   Merrill, George D. Land and Education: The Origin and History of Land Grants for the Support of Education. Ed.D., University of Southern California, 1965. 254p. UMI# 65-12262.

3921   Murphy, John P. Congress and the Colleges a Century Ago: A Political History of the First Morrill Act: Other Congressional Support for Educational Purposes, and the Political Climate of the United States as it Involved Education Prior to 1862. Ed.D., Indiana University, 1967. 207p. UMI# 67-16422.

3922   Pauli, Kenneth W. Evidence of Popular Support for the Land Grant College Act of 1862 as Revealed in Selected Speeches in New England, 1850-1860. Ph.D., Stanford University, 1960. 232p. UMI# 60-01370.

3923   Roeske, Clarence E. The Land Grant Philosophy: Historical Implications in Its Changing Definition through the American Experience. Ph.D., Ohio State University, 1973. 163p. UMI# 73-26899.

3924   Sawyer, William E. The Evolution of the Morrill Act of 1862. Ph.D., Boston University, 1948. 276p.

3925   Thompson, Willard C. The Philosophy and History of the Land Grant Colleges and Universities in the United States of America. Ph.D., New York University, 1934. 182p. UMI# 73-03455.

3926   Thurber, Evangeline. The Library of the Land Grant College, 1862-1900: A Preliminary Study. Master's thesis, Columbia University, 1928.

3927   Welch, Robert W. A Rhetorical Study of the Legislative Speaking of Congressman Justin Smith Morrill of Vermont in the U.S. House of Representatives on Selected Issues, 1855-1867. Ph.D., Pennsylvania State University, 1977. 374p. UMI# 7803378.

LEGISLATION

3928   Curry, Leonard P. The Thirty-Seventh Congress: Blueprint for Modern America. Ph.D., University of Kentucky, 1961. 365p. UMI# 69-18830.

3929   Dameron, Ronald F. An Historical Analysis of Legislators' Statements Made in Relation to Selected Federal Bills Regarding the Role of the Federal Government in Public Education. Ph.D., Claremont Graduate School, 1966. 253p. UMI# 67-09541.

3930   Fisher, Lois A. State Legislatures and the Autonomy of Colleges and Universities: A Comparative Study of Legislation in Four States, 1900-1979. Ph.D., University of Chicago, 1984.

3931   Richter, Suzanne L. An Analysis of Legal Provisions in Governance of Postsecondary Education in Fourteen Southern States 1970-1979. Ph.D., University of Florida, 1981. 327p. UMI# 8124453.

3932   Runkel, H. John. An Historical Study and Analysis: Public Law 874. Ed.D., University of Denver, 1969. 184p. UMI# 69-22245.

LIBERAL ARTS

3933   Farrell, Richard A. A History of Liberal Education and Liberalism: The Traditional Humanist in Conflict with the Liberal Ideologue. Ed.D., University of Massachusetts, 1986. 214p. UMI# 8612036.

3934   Haines, George, IV. Correlations in the Developments of Two Arts and Two Social Sciences, 1900-1940. Ph.D., University of Pennsylvania, 1942. 267p.

3935   Hange, Philip E. A Study of Trends in Subjects Required and Presented for College

Admission and Curricula Changes in Liberal Arts Colleges of the Northwest, 1915-1940. Ph.D., University of Washington, 1942. 100p.

3936   Hanks, Paul A. Changes and Trends in Private Liberal Arts Colleges, 1930-1966. Ed.D., University of Southern California, 1972. 231p. UMI# 72-17470.

3937   Harvey, John H. Innovation in Liberal Arts College Curriculum. Ph.D., Boston College, 1972. 195p. UMI# 72-22748.

3938   Heisler, Jules. A Model Provided to Explain the Factors Associated with the Demise of Independent Liberal Arts II Colleges Since 1970. Ph.D., University of Kentucky, 1982. 142p. UMI# 8215429.

3939   Kimball, Bruce A. A Historical and Typographical Analysis of Ideas of Liberal Education in America. Ed.D., Harvard University, 1981. 455p. UMI# 8416932.

3940   Lyons, Mack D. The Liberal Arts as Viewed by Faculty Members in Nine Professional Schools and Three Types of Universities 1958-1978. Ph.D., University of Alabama, 1978. 258p. UMI# 79-15015.

3941   McIvers, William D. An Analysis of Professional Educational Periodical Literature Relating to the Objectives of American Liberal Arts Education, 1920 to 1950. Ph.D., New York University, 1964. 216p. UMI# 64-08473.

3942   Richardson, Orvin T. Requirements for Bachelor's Degrees in Liberal Arts Colleges, 1890-1940. Ph.D., University of Chicago, 1947. 250p.

3943   Yin, Tsi-chieh L. An Evaluation of Undergraduate Liberal Arts Curriculum Changes of the 1960's. Ed.D., Indiana University, 1972. 148p. UMI# 73-7002.

LIBRARIES AND LIBRARIANS

3944   Boll, John J. Library Architecture 1800-1875; A Comparison of Theory and Buildings, with Emphasis on New England College Libraries. Ph.D., University of Illinois, 1961. 461p. UMI# 61-04263.

3945   Bradley, Carol J. The Genesis of American Music Librarianship, 1902-1942. (Volumes I and II) Ph.D., Florida State University, 1978. 839p. UMI# 7822150.

3946   Brough, Kenneth J. Evolving Conceptions of Library Service in Four American Universities: Chicago, Columbia, Harvard, and Yale, 1876-1946. Ph.D., Stanford University, 1949. 337p.

3947   Carrol, Carmal E. The Professionalization of Education for Librarianship, with Special Reference to the Years 1940-1960. Ph.D., University of California-Berkeley, 1969. 464p. UMI# 69-18,892.

3948   Church, Frances E. A Historical Survey of the Libraries in a Group of State Normal Schools Prior to 1900. Master's thesis, Columbia University, 1931.

3949   DePew, John N. Architectural, Cost, and Planning Trends in American Academic Library Buildings, 1950-1958. Master's thesis, Western Reserve University, 1960.

3950   Erickson, Ernest W. College and University Library Surveys, 1938-1952. Ph.D., University of Illinois, 1958. 459p. UMI# 58-05412.

3951   Gelfand, Morris A. A Historical Study of the Evaluation of Libraries in Higher Institutions by the Middle States Association of Colleges and Secondary Schools. Ph.D., New York University, 1960. 449p. UMI# 61-00324.

3952   Hale, Charles E. The Origin and Development of the Association of College and Research Libraries, 1889-1960. Ph.D., Indiana University, 1976. 294p. UMI# 77-10937.

3953   Janney, Ruthann G. Post-War Trends in the Planning and Construction of College and University Library Buildings in the United States, 1945-1953. Master's thesis, University of Illinois, 1954.

3954   Jarred, Ada D. Patterns of Growth in Academic Libraries of Four-Year, State Supported Institutions of Louisiana and South Carolina, 1960-1979: A Comparative Study. Ph.D., Texas Woman's University, 1985. 145p. UMI# 8608491.

3955   Johnson, Edward R. The Development of the Subject-Divisional Plan in American University Libraries. Ph.D., University of Wisconsin, 1974. 240p. UMI# 75-5936.

3956   Jones, Vance H. The Influence of the American College Fraternity on Chapter House Library Development. Master's thesis, Emory University, 1964.

3957   Kansfield, Norman J. The Origins of Protestant Theological Seminary Libraries in the United States. Master's thesis, University of Chicago, 1970.

3958   Kansfield, Norman J. 'Study the Most Approved Authors': The Role of the Seminary Library in Nineteenth Century American Protestant Ministerial Education. Ph.D., University of Chicago, 1981.

3959   Knoer, Sister Mary M.A. A Historical Survey of the Libraries of Certain Catholic Institutions of Learning in the United States. Master's thesis, University of Illinois, 1930. 114p.

3960   Kraske, Gary E. The American Library Association in the Emergence of U.S. Cultural Diplomacy, 1938-1949. Doctor of Library Service, Columbia University, 1983. 498p. UMI# 8311849.

3961   Kraus, Joe W. Book Collections of Five Colonial College Libraries; A Subject Analysis. Ph.D., University of Illinois at Urbana-Champaign, 1960. 312p. UMI# 60-01661.

3962   Lawrence, Marie K. Trends in Law School Librarianship, 1926-1946. Master's thesis, Columbia University, 1949.

3963   Lee, Michael M.S. Melvil Dewey (1851-1931): His Educational Contributions and Reforms. Ph.D., Loyola University, 1979. 309p. UMI# 7910342. [librarian and professor, Columbia University, 1883-1889].

3964   Lowell, Mildred H. College and University Library Consolidations. Master's thesis, University of Chicago, 1939. 179p.

3965   McGowan, Frank. The Association of Research Libraries, 1932-1962. Ph.D., University of Pittsburgh, 1972. 262p.

3966   Mehl, Warren R. The Role of the American Theological Library Association in American Protestant Theological Libraries and Librarianship, 1947-1970. Ph.D., Indiana University, 1973. 226p. UMI# 73-23026.

3967   Miller, Lawrence A. Changing Patterns of Circulation Services in University Libraries. Ph.D., Florida State University, 1971. 188p. UMI# 72-10058.

3968   Miller, Richard E., Jr. The Development of Reference Services in the American Liberal Arts College, 1876-1976. Ph.D., University of Minnesota, 1984. 218p. UMI# 8418515.

3969   Mirwis, Allan N. The Development of 16 MM Film Collections by Colleges and Universities in the United States. Ed.D., Indiana University, 1976. 127p. UMI# 77-03356.

3970   Molyneux, Robert E. An Examination of the Growth of Academic Libraries in the United States, 1972/73-1981/82. Ph.D., University of North Carolina, 1984. 317p. UMI# 8425504.

3971   Mullins, James L. A Study of Selected Factors Affecting Growth Rates in American Law School Libraries, 1932-1976. Ph.D., Indiana University, 1984. 100p. UMI# 8425079.

3972   Orr, Robert S. Financing and Philanthropy in the Building of Academic Libraries Constructed Between 1919 and 1958. Master's thesis, Western Reserve University, 1959. 87p.

3973   Parham, Paul M. Malcolm Glenn Wyer, Western Librarian: A Study in Leadership and Innovation. Ph.D., University of Denver, 1964. 428p. [librarian, University of Iowa, 1904-1913; University of Nebraska, 1913-1924; director of libraries, University of Denver].

3974   Perrins, Barbara C. Business and Industrial Reference Service by Academic Libraries, 1900-1965. Master's thesis, Southern Connecticut State College, 1967. 71p.

3975   Petersen, Vesta. The American Colonial Library Movement. Master's thesis, Columbia University, 1932.

3976   Powell, Benjamin E. The Development of Libraries in the Southern State Universities to 1920. Ph.D., University of Chicago, 1947. 233p.

3977   Radford, Neil A. The Carnegie Corporation and the Development of American College Libraries, 1928-1941. Ph.D., University of Chicago, 1972. 312p.

3978   Reynolds, Helen M. University Library Buildings in the United States, 1890-1939. Master's thesis, University of Illinois, 1946. 88p.

3979   Ruffin, Mary B. Some Developments Toward Modern Cataloging Practice in University Libraries as Exemplified in the Printed Book Catalogs of Harvard and Yale Before the Year 1776. Master's thesis, Columbia University, 1935.

3980   Salinas, Anna. John Edward Goodwin: University Librarian. Master's thesis, University of Texas, 1966. 68p. [director of libraries, University of Texas, 1912-1923; and University of California, Los Angeles, 1923-1944].

3981   Schley, Ruth. Cataloging in the Libraries of Princeton, Columbia, and the University of Pennsylvania Before 1876. Master's thesis, Columbia University, 1946.

3982   Scott, Richard P. A Survey of the Literature on the Financial Aspects of Libraries in Institutions of Higher Education in the United States, 1926-1956. Master's thesis, Catholic University of America, 1958.

3983   Seavey, Marceta J. A Proposal to Develop a Collection of Documents of American Higher Education. Ed.D., Stanford University, 1959. 334p. UMI# 59-3670.

3984   Shafer, Henry B. College Libraries in the United States from 1790-1830. Master's thesis, Columbia University, 1927.

3985   Shiflett, Orvin L. The Origins of American Academic Librarianship. Ph.D., Florida State University, 1979. 372p. UMI# 79-26818.

3986   Shores, Louis. Origins of the American College Library, 1638-1800. Ph.D., George Peabody College for Teachers, 1934.

3987   Smith, Jessie C. Patterns of Growth in Library Resources in Certain Land Grant Universities. Ph.D., University of Illinois at Urbana-Champaign, 1964. 227p. UMI# 65-00917.

3988   Storie, Catharine. What Contributions Did the American College Society Library Make to the History of the American College Library? Master's thesis, Columbia University, 1938. 116p.

3989   Strauss, Lovell H. The Liberal Arts College Library, 1929-1940: A Comparative Interpretation of Financial Statistics of Sixty-Eight Representative and Twenty Selected Liberal Arts College Libraries. Master's thesis, University of Chicago, 1942. 125p.

3990   Thomison, Dennis V. The History and Development of the American Library Association, 1876-1957. Ph.D., University of Southern California, 1973. 457p. UMI# 73-18846.

3991   Waldo, Michael J. A Comparative Analysis of Nineteenth-Century Academic and Literary Society Library Collections in the Midwest. Ph.D., Indiana University, 1985. 235p. UMI# 8527040.

3992   Wicker, William W. The Growth and Development of the Organizational Structures of University Libraries. Ph.D., Florida State University, 1977. 235p. UMI# 77-24823.

3993   Williams, Barbara J. A Study of Academic Library Relationships and Institutional Self-Study in Selected 1890 Land Grant Colleges and Universities. Ph.D., Rutgers University, 1980. 360p. UMI# 8105062.

3994   Zubatsky, David E. 'No Book Should be Out of Reach': The Role of the American Library Association in the Sharing of Resources for Research, 1922-1945. Ph.D., University of Illinois, 1982. 526p. UMI# 8218602.

MEDICAL EDUCATION

3995   Cohen, Marcine J. Medical Social Movements in the United States (1820-1982): The Case of Osteopathy. Ph.D., University of California-San Diego, 1983. 188p. UMI# 8319111.

3996   Hale, Nathan G., Jr. The Origins and Foundations of the Psychoanalytic Movement in

America, 1909-1914. Ph.D., University of California-Berkeley, 1965. 503p. UMI# 65-13501.

3997   Movrich, Ronald F. Before the Gates of Excellence: Abraham Flexner and Education, 1866-1918. Ph.D., University of California-Berkeley, 1981. 253p. UMI# 82-12047. [Carnegie Foundation, General Education Board, Institute for Advanced Studies].

3998   Norwood, William F. History of Medical Education in the United States Before the Civil War. Ph.D., University of Southern California, 1939.

3999   Riley, Mary L. The 'Family Physician': Health Advice and Domestic Medicine from the American Revolution to the Civil War. Ph.D., University of Chicago, 1985.

4000   Schnur, Sidney. A Genetic Study of Medical Education in the United States. Master's thesis, City College of New York, 1931.

4001   Smith, Dale C. The Emergence of Organized Clinical Instruction in the Nineteenth Century American Cities of Boston, New York and Philadelphia. Ph.D., University of Minnesota, 1979. 365p. UMI# 7926175.

4002   Wheatley, Steven C. The Politics of Philanthropic Management: Abraham Flexner and Medical Education. Ph.D., University of Chicago, 1982. [Carnegie Foundation, General Education Board, Institute for Advanced Studies].

MILITARY EDUCATION

4003   Berry, David C. Higher Education in the United States Army. Ed.D., University of Maryland, 1974. 337p. UMI# 75-18084.

4004   Cummings, Donald L. Army ROTC: A Study of the Army's Primary Officer Procurement Program, 1862-1977. Ph.D., University of California-Santa Barbara, 1982. 406p. UMI# 8310191.

4005   Easterling, Henry W., Jr. Nonmilitary Education in the United States Air Force with Emphasis on the Period 1945-1979. Ed.D., Indiana University, 1980. 210p. UMI# 8022694.

4006   Garber, Lee O. History and Present Status of Military Training in Land Grant Colleges. Master's thesis, University of Illinois, 1926.

4007   Hirshauer, Victor B. The History of the Army Reserve Officer's Training Corps, 1916-1973. Ph.D., Johns Hopkins University, 1975. 491p. UMI# 7821968.

4008   Johnson, Vernon E. Development of the National War College and Peer Institutions: A Comparative Study of the Growth and Interrelationship of U.S. Military Senior Service Colleges. Ed.D., College of William & Mary, 1982. 172p. UMI# 82-19047.

4009   Junod, Alfred E. An Historical Study of the Air Force Reserve Officers Training Corps. Ph.D., State University of New York at Buffalo, 1955. 105p.

4010   Kofmehl, William E., Jr. Non-Military Education and the United States Army: A History. Ph.D., University of Pittsburgh, 1973. 327p. UMI# 73-27,146.

4011   Kraus, John D., Jr. The Civilian Military Colleges in the Twentieth Century: Factors Influencing Their Survival. Ph.D., University of Iowa, 1978. 521p. UMI# 7902920.

4012   Nalley, Charles G., Jr. A Descriptive Study of the United States Army, Navy, and Air Force Academy Preparatory Schools. Ph.D., George Washington University, 1965.

4013   Rilling, Alexander W. The First Fifty Years of Graduate Education in the U.S. Navy, 1909-1959. Ph.D., University of Southern California, 1972. 404p. UMI# 73-00761.

4014   Schwartz, Rudolph. Non-Military Education in the United States Army and Air Force, 1900-1960. Ed.D., New York University, 1963. 279p. UMI# 64-6542.

4015   Shaughnessy, Thomas E. Beginnings of National Professional Military Education in America, 1775-1825. Ph.D., Johns Hopkins University, 1957.

4016   Stompler, Russell. The Origin and Growth of the Reserve Officers' Training Corps, 1916-1950. Master's thesis, University of Alabama, 1951.

4017   Webb, Lester A. The Origin of Military Schools in the United States Founded in the Nineteenth Century. Ph.D., University of North Carolina, 1958. 297p. UMI# 59-62.

NATIONAL UNIVERSITY

4018   Champlin, Carroll D. The Movement for a National University in the United States. Ph.D., University of Pittsburgh, 1925.

4019   Harrison, Marjorie D. A National University and the National Interest, 1870-1902. Ph.D., University of Kentucky, 1968. 292p. UMI# 69-18202.

4020   Harrison, Theta. The History of the Movement for a National University in the United States. Ph.D., Stanford University, 1931.

4021   Hill, James W. The Movement to Establish a National University Prior to 1860: A Documentary History. Master's thesis, University of North Carolina, 1946.

4022   Madsen, David L. History of an Idea: The University of the United States. Ph.D., University of Chicago, 1962.

4023   Woolums, Edward C. An Historical Study of Proposals in Favor of a National or a Federal System of Education. Ed.D., University of Colorado, 1966. 294p. UMI# 67-10022.

NATIVE AMERICANS

4024   Coates, Lawrence G. A History of Indian Education by the Mormons, 1830-1900. Ed.D., Ball State University, 1969. 373p. UMI# 70-05259.

4025   Haymond, Jack H. The American Indian and Higher Education: From the College for the Children of the Infidels (1619) to Navajo Community College (1969). Ph.D., Washington State University, 1982. 177p. UMI# 8301307.

4026   Morris, Harold W. A History of Indian Education in the United States. Ph.D., Oregon State University, 1954.

4027   Skelton, Robert H. A History of the Educational System of the Cherokee Nation, 1801-1910. Ed.D., University of Arkansas, 1970. 291p. UMI# 70-26233.

PHILOSOPHY OF EDUCATION

4028   Blinderman, Abraham. Upton Sinclair's Criticism of Higher Education in America: A Study of 'The Goose-Step', Its Sources, Critical History, and Relationship to Criticisms of Higher Education. Ph.D., New York University, 1963. 462p. UMI# 64-06547.

4029   Burton, C. Grant. A Historical Study of the Concept of the Individual and Society in Educational Philosophy. Ph.D., University of Southern California, 1954.

4030   Carey, John P. Influences on Thomas Jefferson's Theory and Practice of Higher Education. Ph.D., University of Michigan, 1969. 383p. UMI# 69-17976.

4031   Casteel, James D. Professors and Applied Ethics: Higher Education in a Revolutionary Era, 1750-1800. Ph.D., George Peabody College for Teachers, 1964. 320p. UMI# 65-03560.

4032   Content, Mary. The National Impact of the 'Wisconsin Idea': A Bibliographical Study. Master's thesis, George Washington University, 1964.

4033   Coughlan, Neil P. Dewey and the University. Ph.D., University of Wisconsin, 1970. 176p. UMI# 72-11234. [professor of philosophy, Columbia University, 1904-1930].

4034   Densford, John P. The Educational Philosophy of Thomas Jefferson. Ed.D., Oaklahoma State University, 1961. 202p. UMI# 62-01591.

4035   Donovan, Charles F. Education in American Social Thought, 1865-1900. Educational Ideas of Social Scientists and Social-Minded Clergymen. Ph.D., Yale University, 1948. 306p. UMI# 64-11368.

4036   Flicker, Bernard. Abraham Flexner's Educational Thought and Its Critical Appraisal. Ph.D., New York University, 1963. 276p. UMI# 62-244. [Carnegie Foundation, General Education Board, Institute for Advanced Studies].

4037   Frank, Thomas E. Conserving a Rational World: Theology, Ethics, and the Nineteenth Century American College Ideal. Ph.D., Emory University, 1981. 366p. UMI# 81-24260.

4038   Grauls, Paul A. A Historical Study: The Essentialist Committee for the Advancement of American Education. Ed.D., State University of New York at Albany, 1974. 400p. UMI# 75-05010.

4039   Grennan, Kevin F. Liberal Learning in American Higher Education. Ed.D., University of Massachusetts, 1981. 276p. UMI# 81-18001.

4040   Guyotte, Roland L., III. Liberal Education and the American Dream: Public Attitudes and the Emergence of Mass Higher Education, 1920-1952. Ph.D., Northwestern University, 1980. 356p. UMI# 80-26818.

4041   Hansen, Kenneth H. The Educational Philosophy of the Great Books Program. Ph.D., University of Missouri, 1949. 232p. UMI# 1369.

4042   Haran, William J. Admiral Hyman G. Rickover, USN: A Decade of Educational Criticism, 1955-1964. Ph.D., Loyola University of Chicago, 1982. 240p. UMI# 8219595.

4043   Harris, Michael R. American Critics of the Ideal of Operational Utility in Higher Education. Ph.D., Stanford University, 1966. 298p. UMI# 66-06350.

4044   Jarech, Leon N. Two Contrasting Views of the Uses of the University: Robert M. Hutchins and Clark Kerr. Ph.D., University of Illinois, 1978. 359p. UMI# 7913500. [Robert M. Hutchins—president and chancellor, University of Chicago, 1929-1951; Clak Kerr—president, University of California, 1958-1967].

4045   Jones, Richard B. Higher Learning for America: A Comparison of Abraham Flexner and Robert Maynard Hutchins and Their Views on Higher Education. Ph.D., Saint Louis University, 1978. 327p. UMI# 78-14586.

4046   Nostrand, Geraldine S. The Education of 'Man as Man' as a Continuous Theme in the History of Educational Theory: A Study of This Theme from Antiquity to the Present in the Educational Writing of Selected Scholars. Ed.D., Rutgers University New Brunswick, 1978. 135p. UMI# 78-20340.

4047   Parish, William A. The Educational Philosophy of Thorstein Veblen. Ed.D., University of Arkansas, 1973. 185p. UMI# 73-27,458. [professor of economics, University of Chicago, Stanford University, New School for Social Research].

4048   Peterson, Lawrence L. The Historical Development of the Problem-Solving Method in Education. Ph.D., University of Southern California, 1951. 134p.

4049   Wegener, Frank C. A Study of the Philosophical Beliefs of Leaders in American Education. Ph.D., University of Southern California, 1947. 416p.

4050   Young, Alfred. The Educational Philosophies of Booker T. Washington and Carter G. Woodson: A Liberating Praxis. Ph.D., Syracuse University, 1977. 189p. UMI# 78-13356. [Booker T. Washington—president Tuskegee Institute, 1881-1915; Carter G. Woodson—organizer, Association for the Study of Negro Life and History].

4051   Yulish, Stephen M. The Search for a Civic Religion: A History of the Character Education Movement in America, 1890-1935. Ph.D., University of Illinois, 1975. 292p. UMI# 76-07021.

POLITICS AND SOCIAL POLICY

4052   Adams, Stephanie M. The Creative Adjustment of Higher Education to Social and Philosophical Tensions in the United States, 1865-1915. Ed.D., University of Southern California, 1975.

4053   Agnew, Walker F. The Federal Government in Education from 1855 to 1900. Ph.D., University of Texas at Austin, 1949.

4054   Bargerstock, Charles T. An Historical-Legal Analysis of the Influences of Public Policy on Gifts from Individuals to Institutions of Higher Education. Ed.D., Lehigh University, 1982. 341p. UMI# 8207286.

4055   Briggs, Ernest E. The Educational Policies of Richard M. Nixon. Ed.D., Auburn University, 1973. UMI# 73-19,648.

4056   Clowse, Barbara B. Education as an Instrument of National Security: The Cold War Campaign to 'Beat the Russians' From Sputnik to the National Defense Education Act of 1958. Ph.D., University of North Carolina at Chapel-Hill, 1977. 281p. UMI# 78-07122.

4057   Karnoutsos, Carmela A. Harry W. Laidler and the Intercollegiate Socialist Society. Ph.D., New York University, 1974. 313p. UMI# 75-08549.

4058   Kerr-Tener, Janet C. From Truman to Johnson: Ad Hoc Policy Formulation in Higher Education. Ph.D., University of Virginia, 1985. 485p.

4059   King, Lauriston R. The Politics of Higher Education: The Washington Lobbyists. Ph.D., University of Connecticut, 1972. 504p. UMI# 72-32148.

4060   Lieuallen, Roy E. The Jeffersonian and Jacksonian Conceptions in Higher Education. Ed.D., Stanford University, 1955. 175p. UMI# 00-11160.

4061   Marden, David L. The Cold War and American Education (Volumes I and II). Ph.D., University of Kansas, 1975. 489p. UMI# 76-16749.

4062   Marotta, Gary M. Professors and Imperialism: A Study of the American Academic Community in the Great Debate, 1898-1902. Ph.D., New York University, 1973. 459p. UMI# 74-01928.

4063   Mathews, Forrest D. The Politics of Education in the Deep South: Georgia and Alabama, 1830-1860. Ph.D., Columbia University, 1965. 492p. UMI# 66-01714.

4064   Murphy, Donald J. Professors, Publicists and Pan Americanism, 1905-1917: A Study in the Origins of the Use of Experts in Shaping American Foreign Policy. Ph.D., University of Wisconsin, 1970. 516p. UMI# 70-24808.

4065   Shapiro, Harvey S. Education and Ideology: A Sociological Study of Educational Thought in the American Radical Movement, 1900-1925. Ed.D., Boston University, 1978. 314p. UMI# 7819781.

4066   Smith, Francis W. Moral Philosophers in Northern Society: Studies of Academic Men and Public Affairs, 1830-1860. Ph.D., Columbia University, 1955. 298p. UMI# 00-16297.

4067   Vaughn, William P. The Sectional Conflict in Southern Public Education: 1865-1876. Ph.D., Ohio State University, 1961. 315p. UMI# 61-05130.

PRESIDENTS

4068   Barr, Clifford V. Profiles of American College Presidents—1968 and 1980: A Comparison. Ph.D., Bowling Green State University, 1981. 166p. UMI# 8121513.

4069   Gordon, Joseph E. The University Presidents: A Study of Their Background and Educational Concerns in 1900 and 1950. Ph.D., University of Chicago, 1952.

4070   McGehee, Larry T. Changing Conceptions of American Higher Education, 1800-1860:

Ideas of Five Frontier Presidents on Transplanting and Transforming Collegiate Education. Ph.D., Yale University, 1969. UMI# 70-02767.

4071   McGinnis, Howard J. The State Teachers College President. Ph.D., George Peabody College for Teachers, 1932. 187p.

4072   Mohr, Joland E. Higher Education and the Development of Professionalism in Post-Civil War America: A Content Analysis of Inaugural Addresses Given by Selected Land Grant College and University Presidents, 1867-1911. (Volumes I and II). Ph.D., University of Minnesota, 1984. 422p. UMI# 8418518.

4073   Mwonyonyi, Isaya. Perceptions of Changes in Campus Governance During Their Tenure as Viewed by Former Presidents of Public Colleges and Universities, 1960-1976. Ph.D., Kent State University, 1982. 225p. UMI# 8311447.

4074   Schmidt, George P. The Old-Time College President. Ph.D., Columbia University, 1930. 245p.

PROFESSIONS

4075   Abbott, Andrew D. The Emergence of American Psychiatry, 1880-1930. Ph.D., University of Chicago, 1982.

4076   Ahern, John J. An Historical Study of the Professions and Professional Education in the United States. Ph.D., Loyola University of Chicago, 1971. 316p. UMI# 71-28111.

4077   Bailey, Percival R. Progressive Lawyers: A History of the National Lawyers Guild, 1936-1958. Ph.D., Rutgers University, 1979. 569p. UMI# 7916128.

4078   Brand, Barbara E. The Influence of Higher Education on Sex-Typing in Three Professions, 1870-1920: Librarianship, Social Work, and Public Health. Ph.D., University of Washington, 1978. 467p. UMI# 78-20705.

4079   Fetner, Gerald L. Counsel to the Situation: The Lawyer as Social Engineer, 1900-1945. Ph.D., Brown University, 1973. 303p. UMI# 81-23454.

4080   Foster, James C. Lawyers, Professionalization and Politics: Ideology and Organization in the American Bar, 1870-1920. Ph.D., University of Washington, 1976. 332p. UMI# 77-00570.

4081   Gevitz, Norman. The D.O.'s: A Social History of Osteopathic Medicine. Ph.D., University of Chicago, 1980.

4082   Good, Howard A. Acquainted with the Night: The Journalist in American Fiction, 1890-1930. Ph.D., University of Michigan, 1984. 285p. UMI# 8412147.

4083   Greene, Rebecca S. The Role of the Psychiatrist in World War II. Ph.D., Columbia University, 1977. 590p. UMI# 7924895.

4084   Heitman, Frederick R. State Licensure: The Professions of Speech Pathology and Audiology. Ph.D., University of Florida, 1980. 356p. UMI# 80-29064.

4085   Hobson, Wayne K. The American Legal Profession and the Organizational Society, 1890-1930. Ph.D., Stanford University, 1977. 476p. UMI# 77-25679.

4086   Kaufman, Martin. Homeopathy and the American Medical Profession, 1820-1960. Ph.D., Tulane University, 1969. 376p. UMI# 70-06403.

4087   Kett, Joseph F. Regulation of the Medical Profession in America, 1780-1860. Ph.D., Harvard University, 1964.

4088   Klegon, Douglas A. Lawyers and the Social Structure: An Historical Analysis of the Role of Professionalization Among Lawyers in the United States. Ph.D., University of Wisconsin, 1975. 212p. UMI# 75-26510.

4089   Larson, Magali S. The Development of Modern Professions: Monopolies of Competence and Bourgeois Ideology. Ph.D., University of California-Berkeley, 1974. 586p. UMI# 74-21709.

4090   Layton, Edwin T. The American Engineering Profession and the Idea of Social Responsibility. Ph.D., University of California-Los Angeles, 1957.

4091   Levy, Richard M. The Professionalization of American Architects and Civil Engineers, 1865-1917. Ph.D., University of California-Berkeley, 1980. 441p. UMI# 80-29465.

4092   Martin, Rochelle. The Difficult Path: Women in the Architecture Profession. Arch.D., University of Michigan, 1986. 173p. UMI# 8612453.

4093   Mattingly, Paul H. Professional Strategies and New England Educators, 1825-1860. Ph.D., University of Wisconsin, 1968. 283p. UMI# 69-00958.

4094   Noble, David F. Science and Technology in the Corporate Search for Order: American Engineers and Social Reform, 1900-1929. Ph.D., University of Rochester, 1974. 567p. UMI# 74-22617.

4095   Orbach, Noreen R.F. The Evolution of a Professional: The Case of Women in Dentistry. Ph.D., University of Illinois at Chicago Circle, 1977. 195p. UMI# 77-15332.

4096   Pernick, Martin S. A Calculus of Suffering: Pain, Anesthesia, and Utilitarian Professionalism in Nineteenth Century American Medicine. Ph.D., Columbia University, 1979. 560p. UMI# 81-25367.

4097   Peterson, Mildred J. Kinship, Status, and Social Mobility in the Mid-Victorian Medical Profession. Ph.D., University of California-Berkeley, 1972.

4098   Rothstein, William G. Engineers: Case and Theory in the Sociology of Professions. Ph.D., Cornell University, 1965. 543p. UMI# 65-6974.

4099   Schiller, Preston L. Marginality and Authority in Medicine: The Profession of Pathology. Ph.D., University of Chicago, 1976. 501p. UMI# 77-21034.

4100   Schudson, Michael S. Origins of the Ideal Objectivity in the Professions: Studies in the History of American Journalism and American Law 1830-1940. Ph.D., Harvard University, 1976. 391p. UMI# 77-19,138.

4101   Shafer, Henry B. The American Medical Profession, 1783 to 1850. Ph.D., Columbia University, 1937. 273p.

4102   Stooke, David E. The Portrait of the Physician in Selected Prose Fiction of Nineteenth Century American Authors. Ph.D., George Peabody College for Teachers, 1976. 151p. UMI# 77-3120.

4103   Tomlan, Michael A. Popular and Professional American Architectural Literature in the Late Nineteenth Century. Ph.D., Cornell University, 1983. 513p. UMI# 8322138.

4104   Weatherhead, Arthur C. The History of Collegiate Education in Architecture in the United States. Ph.D., Columbia University, 1942. 259p.

4105   Ziporyn, Terra D. The Popularization of Medicine: Medical Science in Popular American Magazines, 1870-1920. Ph.D., University of Chicago, 1985.

PROTESTANT HIGHER EDUCATION

4106   Andeen, Gustav K. Trends in the Development of the Program of Higher Education in the Augustana Lutheran Church. Ph.D., Columbia University, 1952. 270p. UMI# 00-04155.

4107   Anderson, Allen G. A Historical Survey of the Full-Time Institutes of Religion of the Church of Jesus Christ of Latter-Day Saints, 1926-1966. Ed.D., Brigham Young University, 1968. 593p. UMI# 68-13710.

4108   Ashcraft, Robert R. A Historical Study of Higher Education in the American Baptist Association. Ph.D., East Texas State University, 1968. 284p. UMI# 69-05421.

4109   Corvin, Raymond O. History of the Educational Institutions of the Pentecostal Holiness Church. Ph.D., Southern Baptist Theological Seminary, 1957.

4110   Dannelly, Clarence M. The Development of Collegiate Education in the Methodist Episcopal Church, South, 1846-1902. Ph.D., Yale University, 1933. 454p. UMI# 72-22304.

4111   Duvall, Sylvanus M. The Methodist Episcopal Church and Education up to 1869. Ph.D., Columbia University, 1928. 127p.

4112   Evans, Henry B. A History of Higher Education in the Cumberland Presbyterian Church. Ph.D., George Peabody College for Teachers, 1939.

4113   Garwood, Harry C. Religious Education in Southern Baptist Colleges and Universities Especially Since 1900. Ph.D., Yale University, 1934.

4114   Geiger, C. Harve. The Program of Higher Education of the Presbyterian Church in the United States of America; An Historical Analysis of Its Growth in the United States. Ph.D., Columbia University Teachers College, 1940. 238p.

4115   Grimes, Lewis H. Making Lay Leadership Effective: A Historical Study of Major Issues in the Use of Laymen by the Methodist Church, Especially for Its Educational Purposes. Ph.D., Columbia University, 1953.

4116   Hanle, Robert V. A History of Higher Education Among the German Baptist Brethren, 1708-1908. Ph.D., University of Pennsylvania, 1974. 345p. UMI# 75-14569.

4117   Harris, Daniel S., Jr. Activism and Adventist Higher Education. Ed.D., University of Southern California, 1974. 313p. UMI# 74-14444.

4118   Heisler, Daniel P. Higher Education Among the Society of Friends in the Mid-West During the Nineteenth Century. Master's thesis, Miami University, 1954.

4119   Henkel, Julia S. An Historical Study of the Educational Contributions of the Brethren of the Common Life. Ph.D., University of Pittsburgh, 1962. 301p. UMI# 63-02428.

4120   Howard, Ivan C. Controversies in Methodism Over Methods of Education of Ministers up to 1856. Ph.D., University of Iowa, 1965. 332p. UMI# 65-6692.

4121   Humphrey, Clyde W. History and Development of Graduate Programs in Church Management Sponsored by Selected Protestant Institutions of Higher Education, 1960-1969. Ed.D., American University, 1972. 224p. UMI# 73-16613.

4122   Jones, Lawrence N. The Inter-Varsity Christian Fellowship in the United States: A Study of Its History, Theology, and Relations with Other Groups. Ph.D., Yale University, 1961. 502p. UMI# 64-9660.

4123   Kelly, Carl R. The History of Religious Instruction in United Presbyterian Colleges. Ph.D., University of Pittsburgh, 1953. 323p.

4124   Keyser, Bernard D. A History of Baptist Higher Education in the South to 1865. Ph.D., Southern Baptist Theological Seminary, 1956.

4125   Lansman, Quentin C. An Historical Study of the Development of Higher Education and Related Theological and Educational Assumptions in the Evangelical United Brethren Church, 1800-1954. Ph.D., Northwestern University, 1969. 418p. UMI# 70-00102.

4126   Magruder, Edith M.C. A Historical Study of the Educational Agencies of the Southern Baptist Convention, 1845-1945. Ph.D., Columbia University, 1951. 161p.

4127   Martens, Alice. A Study of the History and Development of the Protestant Theological Seminary Library Movement in the United States. Master's thesis, Southern Connecticut State College, 1958. 73p.

4128   Massengale, Robert G. Collegiate Education in the Methodist Episcopal Church, South, 1902-1939. Ph.D., Yale University, 1950. 727p. UMI# 65-07555.

4129   McBride, Don W. The Development of Higher Education in the Church of Jesus Christ of Latter-Day Saints. Ph.D., Michigan State University, 1952. 524p. UMI# 00-04030.

4130   McCloy, Frank D. The Founding of Protestant Theological Seminaries in the United States, 1784-1840. Ph.D., Harvard University, 1960.

4131   Meservy, Royal R. A Historical Study of Changes in Policy of Higher Education in the Church of Jesus Christ of Latter Day Saints. Ed.D., University of California-Los Angeles, 1966. 546p. UMI# 66-09328.

4132   Mileham, Hazel B. History of Higher Education of the Methodist Church in the United States from 1820 to 1844. Master's thesis, University of Chicago, 1926.

4133   Miller, Guy H. A Contracting Community: American Presbyterians, Social Conflict, and Higher Education, 1730-1820 (Volumes I and II). Ph.D., University of Michigan, 1970. 562p. UMI# 71-15239.

4134   Moore, Ernest W. An Historical Study of Higher Education and the Church of the Nazarene, 1900-1965. Ph.D., University of Texas at Austin, 1965. 304p. UMI# 66-01946.

4135   Orsini, Joseph E. An Educational History of the Pentecostal Movement. Ed.D., Rutgers University, 1973. 132p. UMI# 73-32230.

4136   Peterson, Orville C. Early Methodist Education: The Conversion of American Methodism to Higher Education in the Period from 1816 to 1968. Master's thesis, Fresno State College, 1969.

4137   Philo, L.C. The Historical Development and Present Status of the Educational Institutions of the Church of the Nazarene. Ph.D., University of Oklahoma, 1958. 278p. UMI# 58-03877.

4138   Potts, David B. Baptist Colleges in the Development of American Society, 1812-1861. Ph.D., Harvard University, 1967.

4139   Roda, Alfonso P. Financing Seventh Day Adventist Institutions of Higher Education in the United States, 1959-60 through 1969-70. Ed.D., University of California-Los Angeles, 1972. 253p. UMI# 73-01726.

4140   Schoenhals, Lawrence R. Higher Education in the Free Methodist Church in the United States: 1860-1954. Ph.D., University of Washington, 1955. 515p. UMI# 00-13003.

4141   Smith, Willard G. The History of Church-Controlled Colleges in the Wesleyan Methodist Church. Ph.D., New York University, 1951. 433p. UMI# 73-08779.

4142   Spindle, Oran R. An Analysis of Higher Education in the Church of the Nazarene 1945-1978. Ed.D., Oklahoma State University, 1981. 415p. UMI# 82-03140.

4143   Taylor, Charles W. History of the Higher Educational Movement of the Wesleyan Methodist Church of America. Ph.D., Indiana University, 1959. 361p. UMI# 59-04043.

4144   Tiffin, Gerald C. The Interaction of the Bible College Movement and the Independent Disciples of Christ Denomination. Ph.D., Stanford University, 1968. 228p. UMI# 69-08283.

4145   Trapp, Leonard Y. The Methodist Periodical Press and Tax-Supported Education, 1900-1950. Ph.D., George Peabody College for Teachers, 1955. 253p. UMI# 00-15477.

4146   Trout, Douglas G. The Changing Character of Ten United Presbyterian Church-Related Colleges, 1914-1964. Ph.D., Michigan State University, 1965. 191p. UMI# 66-06177.

4147   Vandever, William T., Jr. An Educational History of the English and American Baptists in the Seventeenth and Eighteenth Centuries. Ph.D., University of Pennsylvania, 1974. 523p. UMI# 75-14633.

4148   Vaughan, John E. The Future and Growth and Development of Higher Education in the Reorganized Church of Jesus Christ of Latter Day Saints. Ed.D., New York University, 1960. 321p. UMI# 61-00382.

4149   Walter, Edwin C. A History of Seventh-Day Adventist Higher Education in the United States. Ed.D., University of California-Berkeley, 1966. 246p. UMI# 66-08255.

4150   Warford, Malcolm L. Piety, Politics, and Pedagogy: An Evangelical Protestant Tradition in Higher Education at Lane, Oberlin, and Berea, 1834-1904. Ed.D., Columbia University, 1973. 231p. UMI# 74-09654.

4151   Winkleman, Gerald G. Polemics, Prayers, and Professionalism: The American Protestant Theological Seminaries from 1784 to 1920. Ph.D., State University of New York at Buffalo, 1975. 412p. UMI# 76-09132.

4152   Yanagihara, Hikaru. Some Educational Attitudes of the Protestant Episcopal Church in America: A Historical Study of the Attitudes of the Church and Churchmen Toward the Founding and Maintaining of Colleges and Schools Under Their Influence Before 1900. Ph.D., Columbia University, 1958. 617p. UMI# 58-02721.

4153   Young, Matt N. History of the Organization and Development of Church of Christ Colleges. Ph.D., George Peabody College for Teachers, 1944. 142p.

PUBLIC RELATIONS

4154   Cook, Paul B. A Study of the Involvement of Academicians in Government Service from 1900 through the Early Years of the New Deal. Ed.D., University of Kentucky, 1972. 207p. UMI# 72-29266.

4155   Davidson, Robert C. The Growth and Development of Public Relations Programs in American Colleges and Universities. Ph.D., University of Southern California, 1958.

4156   Reinke, Earl F. College and University Publicity: A Study of Publicity as a Specialized Function within American Colleges and Universities, with Particular Consideration Given to the Developments in Theory and Practice from 1917 to 1936. Master's thesis, Northwestern University, 1937.

4157   Seller, M. Charles. The American College Public Relations Association: A Study of Its Development During the Period 1915 to 1950. Master's thesis, Pennsylvania State University, 1963.

RELIGION

4158   Bushko, Andrew A. Religious Revivals at American Colleges 1783-1860: An Exploratory Study. Ed.D., Columbia University, 1974. 251p. UMI# 75-06460.

4159   Calam, John H. Parsons and Pedagogues: The SPG Adventure in American Education. Ph.D., Columbia University, 1969. 395p. UMI# 69-15664.

4160   Deschamps, Nello E. The Secularization of American Higher Education: The Relationship Between Religion and the University as Perceived by Selected University Presidents, 1867-1913. Ph.D., University of Southern California, 1976.

4161   Hershey, C.B. The Church and Higher Education in the United States. Ed.D., Harvard University, 1923.

4162   Hovenkamp, Herbert J. Science and Religion in America, 1800-1860. Ph.D., University of Texas at Austin, 1976. 424p. UMI# 76-26640.

4163   Lacy, Edmund E. The Conflict in Thought Over the Role of Religion in American Higher Education, 1865-1910. Ph.D., University of Illinois, 1969. 349p. UMI# 69-15340.

4164   Morgan, William H. Student Religion During Fifty Years: Programs and Policies of the Intercollegiate Y.M.C.A. Ph.D., Columbia University, 1935.

4165   Reed, Myer S., Jr. Differentiation and Development in a Scientific Specialty: The Sociology of Religion in the United States from 1895-1970. Ph.D., Tulane University, 1975. 377p. UMI# 75-23,293.

4166   Schmotter, James W. Provincial Professionalism: The New England Ministry: 1692-1745. Ph.D., Northwestern University, 1973. 368p. UMI# 74-07814.

4167   Towler, Daniel L. The Secularization of Higher Education in the United States as Reflected in the Inaugural Addresses of Selected College and University Presidents, 1860-1972. Ed.D., University of Southern California, 1973. 302p. UMI# 73-30042.

RELIGIOUS COLLEGES

4168   Banzhof, Richard F. The Eight Colleges of the Evangelical and Reformed Church: A Study in Changing Religious Character. Ed.D., Columbia University, 1973. 692p. UMI# 73-19,341.

4169   Bauman, Harold E. The Believers: Church and the Church College. Ed.D., Columbia University, 1972. 248p. UMI# 72-19508.

4170   Boyer, Edward S. The Development of Religious Education in Higher Institutions with Special Reference to Schools of Religion at State Universities and Colleges. Ph.D., Northwestern University, 1926.

4171   Brock, Michael G. Religiously Affiliated Colleges in the Old Northwest, 1800-1861. Master's thesis, Illinois State University, 1966.

4172   Connors, Manning A., Jr. Curricular Changes and Innovation in Selected Church-Related Institutions of Higher Education, 1961-1970. Ph.D., Indiana University, 1971. 157p. UMI# 72-1539.

4173   Kincheloe, Joe L. The Antebellum Southern Evangelical and State Supported Colleges: A Comparative Study. Ed.D., University of Tennessee, 1980. 225p. UMI# 80-24917.

4174   Reed, Charles R. Image Alteration in a Mass Movement: A Rhetorical Analysis of the Role of the Log College in the Great Awakening. Ph.D., Ohio State University, 1972. 282p. UMI# 73-02103.

4175   Schmitz, Mary P. The Diocesan College. Ph.D., Catholic University of America, 1967. 148p. UMI# 67-15449.

4176   Schock, Eldon D. A Comparative Study of the History of Representative Denominational Colleges and Universities of the Northwest. Master's thesis, University of Idaho, 1932.

4177   Schwalm, Vernon F. The Historical Development of the Denominational Colleges of the Old Northwest to 1870. Ph.D., University of Chicago, 1926. 1,923p.

4178   Yeaney, Darrell W. The United Ministries in Higher Education: A Historical and Critical Appraisal (Volumes I and II). Ph.D., Boston University, 1975. 621p. UMI# 75-21020.

RESEARCH

4179   Anderson, Patricia W. The Finance of Research in Private Sector, 1966-1982. Ph.D., Claremont Graduate School, 1985. 611p. UMI# 8515187.

4180   Kruytbosch, Carlos E. The Organization of Research in the University: The Case of Research Personnel. Ph.D., University of California-Berkeley, 1970. 319p. UMI# 71-15815.

4181   Miller, Howard S. A Bounty for Research: A Philanthropic Support of Scientific Investigation in America: 1838-1902. Ph.D., University of Wisconsin, 1964. 388p. UMI# 64-13,905.

4182   Nozicka, George J. Distributional Analysis of Federally Funded Research and Development at Universities and Colleges (1973-1977). Ph.D., American University, 1979. 196p. UMI# 7924360.

4183   Swann, John P. The Emergence of Cooperative Research Between American Universities and the Pharmaceutical Industry, 1920-1940. Ph.D., University of Wisconsin-Madison, 1985. 439p. UMI# 8522537.

4184   Wheadon, William C. Identification and Evaluation of Certain Major Factors in Federal Sponsorship of Research Affecting Goals and Growth of Private Institutions of Higher Education. Ph.D., Syracuse University, 1967. 181p. UMI# 68-05496.

SCIENCES

4185   Bates, Ralph S. The Rise of Scientific Societies in the United States. Ph.D., Harvard University, 1938.

4186   Blunt, John. On the Growth of a Prescient Speculation: Galacial Geology in Nineteenth Century America.Ph.D., New York University, 1984. 402p. UMI# 8411394.

4187   Boekenkamp, Richard P. Geological Education in the United States During the Late Nineteenth Century. Ph.D., Ohio State University, 1974. 189p. UMI# 74-24,299.

4188   Borut, Michael. The Scientific American in Nineteenth Century America. Ph.D., New York University, 1977. 317p. UMI# 7808449.

4189   Braley, Ian. The Evolution of Humanistic-Social Courses for Undergraduate Engineers. Ph.D., Stanford University, 1961. 193p. UMI# 62-00289.

4190   Calvert, Monte A. The Professionalization of the American Mechanical Engineer, 1830-1910. Ph.D., University of Pittsburgh, 1965. 327p. UMI# 66-10053.

4191   Carroll, P. Thomas. Academic Chemistry in America, 1876-1976: Diversification, Growth, and Change. Ph.D., University of Pennsylvania, 1982. 569p. UMI# 8307294.

4192   Cathcart, Maude E. The Historical Development of the Teachings of Biology in the Carolinas. Ph.D., George Peabody College for Teachers, 1940. 163p.

4193   Christiansen, Persturla A. Theory and Practice in the Formative Years of American Mechanical Engineering Education: A Cultural and Historical Analysis. Ed.D., Boston University School of Education, 1975. 246p. UMI# 75-23520.

4194   Clarke, Adele E. Emergence of the Reproductive Research Enterprise: A Sociology of Biological, Medical and Agricultural Science in the United States, 1910-1940. Ph.D., University of California-San Francisco, 1985. 498p. UMI# 8608572.

4195   Cutler, Mary E. American Patterns in General Chemistry Texts, 1800-1850. Ph.D., Columbia University, 1962. 338p. UMI# 62-3830.

4196   Davies, Shannon M. American Physicists Abroad: Copenhagen, 1920-1940. Ph.D., University of Texas Austin, 1985. 300p. UMI# 8609491.

4197   deB. Beaver, Donald. The American Scientific Community, 1800-1860: A Statistical-Historical Study. Ph.D., Yale University, 1966. 386p. UMI# 67-7346.

4198   Del Giorno, Bette J. The Impact of Changing Scientific Knowledge on Science Education in the United States Since 1850. Ph.D., University of Connecticut, 1967. 402p. UMI# 68-1334.

4199   Ehrmann, Stephen C. Academic Adaptation: Historical Study of a Civil Engineering Department in a Research-Oriented University. Ph.D., Massachusetts Institute of Technology, 1978.

4200   Eldridge, Janice C. A Historical Study of the Relationship Between the Philosophy of John Dewey and the Early Progressive Colleges: An Investigation of the Role of Science. Ed.D., University of Massachusetts, 1981. 417p. UMI# 81-17989.

4201   Elliott, Clark A. The American Scientist, 1800-1863: His Origins, Career, and Interests. Ph.D., Case Western Reserve University, 1970. 383p. UMI# 71-01685.

4202   Ford, Charles E. Botany in the American College Curriculum, 1642-1914. Ed.D., Washington University, 1962. 370p. UMI# 62-02445.

4203   Gavurin, Lester L. Teachers of Mathematics in Liberal Arts Colleges of the U.S., 1888-1941. Ph.D., Columbia University, 1957. 298p. UMI# 00-21635.

4204   Gieryn, Thomas F. Patterns in the Selection of Problems for Scientific Research: American Astronomers, 1950-75. Ph.D., Columbia University, 1980. 312p. UMI# 80-16953.

4205   Glover, Thomas H. Development of the Biological Sciences in Teachers Colleges of the Middle West. Ph.D., George Peabody College for Teachers, 1941. 185p.

4206   Gough, Jerry B. The Foundations of Modern Chemistry: The Origin and Development of the Concept of the Gaseous State and Its Role in the Chemical Revolution of the Eighteenth Century. Ph.D., Cornell University, 1971. 222p. UMI# 71-27382.

4207   Grigsby, Donald L. Some Adverse Effects on Increased Federal Funding on Certain Basic

Conditions in Academic Scientific Research: An Exploratory Study, 1950-1970. Ph.D., University of Southern California, 1971. 206p. UMI# 72-21,674.

4208   Gross, Walter E. The American Philosophical Society and the Growth of Science in the United States, 1835-1850. Ph.D., University of Pennsylvania, 1970. 429p. UMI# 71-19,230.

4209   Guralnick, Stanley M. Science and the American College: 1828-1860. Ph.D., University of Pennsylvania, 1969. 365p. UMI# 69-21362.

4210   Hagen, Joel B. Experimental Taxonomy, 1930-1950: The Impact of Cytology, Ecology, and Genetics on Ideas of Biological Classification. Ph.D., Oregon State University, 1982. 233p. UMI# 8128569.

4211   Heywood, Charles W. Scientists and Society in the United States, 1900-1940: Changing Concepts of Social Responsibility. Ph.D., University of Pennsylvania, 1954. 198p. UMI# 00-08552.

4212   Hodes, Elizabeth. Precedents for Social Responsibility Among Scientists: The American Association of Scientific Workers and the Federation of American Scientists, 1938-1948. Ph.D., University of California-Santa Barbara, 1982. 358p. UMI# 8321523.

4213   Hollister, Paul L. Development of the Teaching of Introductory Biology in American Colleges. Ph.D., George Peabody College for Teachers, 1940. 163p.

4214   Jones, Kenneth M. Science, Scientists, and Americans: Images of Science and the Formation of Federal Science Policy, 1945-1950. Ph.D., Cornell University, 1975. 430p. UMI# 75-24202.

4215   Keeney, Elizabeth B. The Botanizers: Amateur Scientists in Nineteenth-Century America. Ph.D., University of Wisconsin-Madison, 1985. 237p. UMI# 8519769.

4216   Kevles, Daniel J. The Study of Physics in America, 1865-1916. Ph.D., Princeton University, 1964. 354p. UMI# 65-1697.

4217   Kohlstedt, Sally L.G. The Formation of the American Scientific Community: The Association for the Advancement of Science, 1848-1860. Ph.D., University of Illinois, 1972. 425p. UMI# 73-17,286.

4218   Kuslan, Louis. Science in Selected Normal Schools of the Nineteenth Century. Ph.D., Yale University, 1954.

4219   Kuznick, Peter J. Beyond the Laboratory: Scientists as Political Activists in 1930's America. Ph.D., Rutgers University, 1984. 630p. UMI# 8507120.

4220   Kwik, Robert J. The Function of Applied Science and the Mechanical Laboratory During the Period of Formation of the Profession of Mechanical Engineering, as Exemplified in the Career of Robert Henry Thurston, 1839-1903. Ph.D., University of Pennsylvania, 1974. 367p. UMI# 74-22867. [director, Sibley College, Cornell University, 1885-1903].

4221   LaFollette, Marcel E.C. Authority, Promise, and Expectation: The Images of Science and Scientists in American Popular Magazines, 1910-1955. Ph.D., Indiana University, 1979. 404p. UMI# 8000667.

4222   Mallonee, Richard C., II. An Historical Analysis of Major Issues and Problems in the Development of the Baccalaureate Degree in Engineering Technology. Ph.D., University of Washington, 1979. 310p. UMI# 80-13559.

4223   McCune, Robert P. Origins and Development of the National Science Foundations and Its Division of Social Sciences, 1945-1961. Ed.D., Ball State University, 1971. 312p. UMI# 71-23026.

4224   McGivern, James G. First One Hundred Years of Engineering Education in the United States (1807-1907). Ed.D., Washington State University, 1961. 269p. UMI# 60-05347.

4225   Merritt, Raymond H. Engineering and American Culture, 1850-1875. Ph.D., University of Minnesota, 1968. 296p. UMI# 68-17,697.

4226   Midgette, Nancy S. The Role of the State Academies of Science in the Emergence of the Scientific Profession in the South, 1883-1983. Ph.D., University of Georgia, 1984. 341p. UMI# 8421137.

4227   Milacek, Barbara R. The Microscope and Nineteenth Century Education. Ph.D., University of Oklahoma, 1966. 204p. UMI# 66-14,232.

4228   Millbrooke, Anne M. State Geological Surveys of the Nineteenth Century. Ph.D., University of Pennsylvania, 1961. 326p. UMI# 8208013.

4229   Mitchell, Merle. The Calculus Program in the Twentieth Century American College. Ph.D., George Peabody College for Teachers, 1958. 435p. UMI# 59-01110.

4230   Rand, Albert N. College Biology Teaching, 1918-1982: Objectives as Stated in Periodical Literature. Ed.D., East Texas State University, 1984. 286p. UMI# 8425054.

4231   Root-Bernstein, Robert S. The Ionists: Founding Physical Chemistry, 1872-1890. Ph.D., Princeton University, 1980. 667p. UMI# 81-01554.

4232   Rothenberg, Marc. The Educational and Intellectual Background of American Astronomers, 1825-1875. Ph.D., Bryn Mawr College, 1974. 281p. UMI# 75-08290.

4233   Rowan, Milton. Politics and Pure Research: The Origins of the National Science Foundation, 1942-1954. Ph.D., Miami University, 1985. 232p. UMI# 8526818.

4234   Sackmary, Benjamin D. The Sociology of Science: The Emergence and Development of a Sociological Specialty. Ph.D., University of Massachusetts, 1974. 448p. UMI# 75-06082.

4235   Schultz, Susan F. Thomas C. Chamberlin: An Intellectual Biography of a Geologist and Educator. Ph.D., University of Wisconsin, 1976. 468p. UMI# 76-20,921. [president, University of Wisconsin, 1887-1892; professor of geology, University of Chicago, 1892-1919].

4236   Servos, John W. Physical Chemistry in America, 1890-1933: Origins, Growth, and Definition. Ph.D., Johns Hopkins University, 1979. 552p. UMI# 79-14304.

4237   Shank, Russell. Physical Science and Engineering Societies in the United States as Publishers, 1939-1964. Doctor of Library Service, Columbia University, 1966. 447p. UMI# 67-5836.

4238   Shaw, Ralph R. Engineering Books Available in America Prior to 1830. Master's thesis, Columbia University, 1931.

4239   Singer, Claude C. The Analagous Science: Scientific History in America, 1880-1900. Ph.D., University of Washington, 1977. 261p. UMI# 78-14494.

4240   Smith, Herbert E. The Historical Development of Technical Education in the First Nine Colleges Founded in the United States, 1636 to 1862. Ph.D., New York University, 1940. 430p. UMI# 73-03423.

4241   Sorensen, Willis C. Brethren of the Net: American Entomology, 1840-1880. Ph.D., University of California-Davis, 1984. 432p. UMI# 8425021.

4242   Stachiw, Jaroslaw D. The Birth of a Profession: The Transition from Mechanic to Engineer. Ed.D., Pennsylvania State University, 1963. 393p. UMI# 64-05393.

4243   Staud, Margaret C. History of College Zoology Textbooks in the United States. Ph.D., Columbia University, 1967. 423p. UMI# 68-05628.

4244   Sturchio, Jeffrey L. Chemists and Industry in Modern America: Studies in the Historical Application of Science Indicators. Ph.D., University of Pennsylvania, 1981. 445p. UMI# 8127078.

4245   Talbott, Laurence F. The Development of Four-Year Programs Designated Industrial Technology by Colleges and Universities in the United States to 1971. Ed.D., Utah State University, 1973. 183p. UMI# 73-19282.

4246   Tilley, Winthrop. The Literature of Natural and Physical Science in the American Colonies from the Beginnings to 1765. Ph.D., Brown University, 1933.

4247   Tobey, Ronald C. The New Sciences and Democratic Society: The American Ideology of National Science, 1919-1930. Ph.D., Cornell University, 1969. 390p. UMI# 70-539.

4248   Tomikel, John. American Geological Education: 1954-1969. Ph.D., University of Pittsburgh, 1970. 157p. UMI# 70-20,331.

4249   Turner, Edna M. Education of Women for Engineering in the United States 1885-1952. Ph.D., New York University, 1954. 218p. UMI# 00-10651.

4250   Tuttle, John G. The Historical Development of Computer Capabilities Which Permitted the Use of the Computer as an Educational Medium in the United States from 1958 to 1968, with Implications of Trends. Ph.D., New York University, 1970. 506p. UMI# 70-26454.

4251   Van de Wetering, Maxine S. The New England Clergy and the Development of Scientific Professionalism. Ph.D., University of Washington, 1970. 237p. UMI# 71-08557.

4252   Veasey, Columbus, Jr. Analysis of Changes in the Federal Funding Trends to Higher Education for Basic Research in Space, Solar, and Nuclear Sciences Compared to Government and Industry, 1967-1985. Ph.D., University of Denver, 1985. 131p. UMI# 8524517.

4253   Volberg, Rachel A. Constraints and Commitments in the Development of American

Botany, 1880-1920. Ph.D., University of California-San Francisco, 1983. 323p. UMI# 8401311.

4254   Wanamaker, John F. A Survey of the Natural History of a College Campus as a Possible Means of Suggesting Its More Effective Educational Significance. Ph.D., Cornell University, 1951. 134p.

4255   Whittington, Russell, Jr. A Study of the Factors Conditioning College Mathematics, 1890-1945. Ph.D., University of North Carolina, 1967. 227p. UMI# 68-06779.

4256   Wilmarth, David L. A Study of the Origins and Development of Science Education in the Colleges of the 'Venerable Nine,' 1790-1860. Ph.D., Boston College, 1970. 487p. UMI# 70-24615.

4257   Zuckerman, Harriet A. Nobel Laureates in the United States: A Sociological Study of Scientific Collaboration. Ph.D., Columbia University, 1965. 469p. UMI# 68-5664.

SOCIAL SCIENCES

4258   Albrecht, Frank M., Jr. The New Psychology in America: 1880-1895. Ph.D., Johns Hopkins University, 1961.

4259   Auerbach, Eugene C. The Opposition to Schools of Education by Professors of the Liberal Arts: A Historical Analysis. Ph.D., University of Southern California, 1957.

4260   Auston, John T. Dimensions of Published Speech Research, 1915-1949. Ph.D., Cornell University, 1951. 215p.

4261   Baggett, Wallace E. Changes in Social Work Education During the Period from 1960 to 1975. Ph.D., Southern Illinois University, 1975. 117p. UMI# 76-13,217.

4262   Ballew, Laurie K. The Impact of the Veteran's Medical Care System on the Growth of Speech Pathology During the Years 1898-1983. Ed.D., George Peabody College for Teachers of Vanderbilt University, 1983. 124p. UMI# 8412718.

4263   Baritz, Loren. The Use of Social Science in American Industry, 1910-1955: A Historical Analysis. Ph.D., University of Wisconsin, 1956. 447p. UMI# 00-19068.

4264   Barrese, Edward F. The Historical Records Survey: A Nation Acts to Save Its Memory. Ph.D., George Washington University, 1980. 180p. UMI# 8023846.

4265   Best, John H. A History of the Development of the Concept of Citizenship Education in America, 1900 to 1950. Ph.D., University of North Carolina-Chapel Hill, 1960. 266p. UMI# 60-06975.

4266   Blakey, George T. Historians on the Homefront: Propagandists for the Great War. Ph.D., Indiana University, 1970. 242p. UMI# 70-14,957.

4267   Blostein, Stanley H. Specific Themes and Unresolved Issues in the Development of Education for Social Work Within Higher Education in the United States, 1893-1975. Ed.D., University of Kentucky, 1977. 184p. UMI# 7802434.

4268   Boozer, Howard R. The American Historical Association and the Schools, 1884-1956. Ph.D., Washington University, 1960. 455p. UMI# 60-04639.

4269   Bouchard, Louis M. An Historical Study of College History of Civilization Courses as Revealed by the Textbooks. Ph.D., George Peabody College for Teachers, 1960. 248p. UMI# 60-05860.

4270   Brandt, Gunther. The Origins of American Sociology: A Study in the Ideology of Social Science, 1865-1895. Ph.D., Princeton University, 1974. 118p. UMI# 75-20615.

4271   Breinan, Alexander. The Origin of Departments of Education in American Colleges and Universities. Master's thesis, City College of New York, 1933.

4272   Brown, JoAnne. The Semantics of Profession: Metaphor and Power in the History of Psychological Testing, 1890-1929. Ph.D., University of Wisconsin-Madison, 1985. 378p. UMI# 8601091.

4273   Burwell, Ronald J. Religion and the Social Sciences: A Study of Their Relationship as Set Forth in the Terry Lectures: 1924-1971. Ph.D., New York University, 1976. 258p. UMI# 76-19,015.

4274   Card, Brigham Y. American Educational Sociology from 1890 to 1950—A Sociological Analysis. Ph.D., Stanford University, 1959. 501p. UMI# 59-3687.

4275   Cina, Carol. Social Science for Whom? A Structural History of Social Psychology. Ph.D., State University of New York at Stony Brook, 1981. 425p. UMI# 81-19229.

4276   Clark, Florence E. The Development of a System of Education for Social Workers in the United States. Master's thesis, University of Chicago, 1936. 237p.

4277   Cook, H. Moreland. History of the History of Education as a Professional Study in the United States. Doctor of Pedagogy, New York University, 1916. 122p. UMI# 72-33508.

4278   Cooper, Brian L. The Objectives of Teaching Survey History Courses in American High Schools and Colleges: A Content Analysis of Articles from Selected Periodicals, 1939-1969. Ph.D., Ohio State University, 1971. 213p. UMI# 71-22459.

4279   Coulton, Thomas E. Trends in Speech Education in American Colleges, 1835-1935. Ph.D., New York University, 1936. 182p. UMI# 73-03085.

4280   Dean, Martha C. The Evolution of Experimental Operant Psychology: A Quantitative Analysis of 'Progress' in Behavioral Science. Ph.D., Syracuse University, 1981. 255p. UMI# 8123895.

4281   Dedman, W. Wayne. The Development of Historical Studies in American Colleges and Universities, 1865-1915. Ph.D., University of Rochester, 1952.

4282   Dobbertin, Gerald F. Statistics and Social Science: The Introduction of Inferential Statistics into Higher Education in America from 1890 to 1930. Ph.D., Michigan State University, 1981. 306p. UMI# 8126495.

4283   Dodge, Ellen E. A Study of the Articulation of American History Courses in High Schools and Colleges in the Twentieth Century. Ed.D., Columbia University Teachers College, 1979. 173p. UMI# 7923584.

4284   Doughty, Sylvia J.K. The German Science of Politics in the American University: Civil War to World War I. Ph.D., Johns Hopkins University, 1969. 295p. UMI# 73-12093.

4285   Ewing, John C. The Development and Current Status of Higher Education as a Field of Graduate Study and Research in American Universities. Ph.D., Florida State University, 1963. 141p. UMI# 64-7577.

4286   Falk, Ursula A. A History of the Development of the Discipline of Social Work in the United States. Ed.D., State University of New York at Buffalo, 1976. 178p. UMI# 77-06136.

4287   Feigenbaum, Carl E. American Educational Historiography, 1900-1920: Review and Synthesis. Ph.D., Cornell University, 1973. 386p. UMI# 73-16,109.

4288   Fleming, Daniel B., Jr. A Legislative History of Federally Supported Teacher Institutes in History and the Social Sciences. Ed.D., George Washington University, 1970. 112p. UMI# 70-20106.

4289   Flowers, Elsie A.M. Developments in Speech Pathology in America: 1925-1950. Ed.D., University of Virginia, 1965. 481p. UMI# 66-3143.

4290   Franck, Michel N. A Study of the Treatment of the Soviet Union in American College Textbooks of History. Ph.D., New York University, 1949. 562p. UMI# 73-08546.

4291   Franks, Peter E. A Social History of American Social Psychology up to the Second World War. Ph.D., State University of New York at Stony Brook, 1975. 311p. UMI# 75-25073.

4292   Fritz, Charles A. The Content of the Teaching of Speech in the American College Before 1850: With Special Reference to Its Influence on Current Theories. Ph.D., New York University, 1928. 143p. UMI# 72-33550.

4293   Frueh, Anna. The Scientific Trend in Speech Education. Master's thesis, Bradley University, 1951.

4294   Furner, Mary O. Advocacy and Objectivity: The Professionalization of Social Science 1865-1905. Ph.D., Northwestern University, 1972. 356p. UMI# 72-32437.

4295   Gampper, Mary M. Speculative 'Educational Psychology': A Study of Its Historical Development in the United States. Ph.D., Saint Louis University, 1963. 291p. UMI# 64-4225.

4296   Ginsberg, Alan H. The Historian as Lobbyist: J. Franklin Jameson and the Historical Activities of the Federal Government. Ph.D., Louisiana State University, 1973. 334p. UMI# 73-835. [professor of history, Brown University, 1888-1901; director of historical research, Carnegie Institution, 1905-1928].

4297   Gordon, Judith B. H. Ideology and the History of American Sociology. Ph.D., University of Michigan, 1970. 341p. UMI# 70-21668.

4298   Greenberg, Estelle F. Pioneers of Professional Social Work: A Case Study in Professionalization, 1908-1919. Ph.D., New York University, 1969. 323p. UMI# 70-03072.

4299   Grossman, David M. Professors and Public Service, 1885-1925: A Chapter in the Profes-
         sionalization of the Social Sciences. Ph.D., Washington University, 1973. 376p. UMI# 74-
         13775.

4300   Haddow, Anna. History of the Teaching of Political Science in the Colleges and Universi-
         ties of the United States, 1636-1916. Ph.D., George Washington University, 1937.

4301   Haskell, Thomas L. Safe Havens for Sound Opinion: The American Social Science Asso-
         ciation and the Professionalization of Social Thought in the United States, 1865-1909.
         Ph.D., Stanford University, 1973. 405p. UMI# 73-14903.

4302   Heiligmann, Katharine S. The Regional Course in Geography: Its Growth and Functions in
         American Higher Education. Ed.D., Oklahoma State University, 1976. 123p. UMI# 77-
         05093.

4303   Hibbitts, Wanda B. Faculty Salaries and Selected Academic Events, 1636-1975: An Appli-
         cation of Schumpeterian Economic Cycle Theory. Ph.D., Southern Illinois University at
         Carbondale, 1984. 152p. UMI# 8510026.

4304   Hile, Frederic W. An Historical-Critical Analysis of the Influences of Dominant Western
         Educational Philosophies on the Natural Versus Technical Problem in the Teaching of the
         Interpretative Speech Arts. Ed.D., University of Washington, 1955. 532p. UMI# 00-14251.

4305   Holstein, Edwin J. The Development of Thought Concerning Economics Instruction in
         American Engineering Colleges. Ph.D., New York University, 1957. 289p. UMI# 00-
         22727.

4306   Howard, Ronald L. A Social History of American Family Sociology, 1865-1970. Ph.D.,
         University of Missouri, 1975. 282p. UMI# 76-7506.

4307   Hubbell, Leigh G. The Development of University Departments of Education in Six States
         of the Middle West with Special Reference to Their Contributions to Secondary-School
         Progress. Ph.D., Catholic University of America, 1924. 125p.

4308   Irvine, Janice M. Disorders of Desire: The Professionalization of Sexology. Ph.D., Bran-
         deis University, 1984. 298p. UMI# 8420773.

4309   Jackson, Pauline F. The Development of Home Economics and Its Status in Twenty-Five
         Selected Colleges and Universities. Master's thesis, Harvard University, 1951.

4310   Jacobsen, Glenn M. Social Work in Rural Areas: The Resurgence of Interest within Social
         Work Education, 1969 to 1984. Ph.D., University of Iowa, 1984. 344p. UMI# 8428254.

4311   Jax, Judy A. A Comparative Analysis of the Meaning of Home Economics: The 1899-1908
         Lake Placid Conferences and Home Economics: A Definition. Ph.D., University of Minne-
         sota, 1981. 195p. UMI# 8125973.

4312   Jones, Horace R. The Development and Present Status of Beginning Speech Courses in
         the Colleges and Universities in the United States. Ph.D., Northwestern University, 1953.
         323p.

4313   Jones, Katharine G. The Views of Selected American Historians on Issues Bearing Upon
         the Teaching of History. Ph.D., Ohio State University, 1955. 284p. UMI# 00-14469.

4314   Keels, Oliver M. The Beginnings of Modern Curricula of History in American Colleges and Universities. Ph.D., Indiana University, 1984. 205p. UMI# 8406814.

4315   Kinzie, Glenn L. Historians and the Social Studies: A History and Interpretation of the Activities of the American Historical Association in the Secondary School Social Studies, 1884-1964. Ed.D., University of Nebraska, 1965. 204p. UMI# 66-2075.

4316   Kirby, Jack R. Evarts Boutell Greene, the Career of a Professional Historian. Ph.D., University of Illinois at Urbana-Champaign, 1969. 384p. UMI# 70-13378. [professor of history, Columbia University, 1923-1939].

4317   Lawrence, Irene J. A History of Educational Sociology in the United States. Ph.D., Stanford University, 1952.

4318   Leach, Eugene E. Concepts of Human Sociality in American Social Science and Social Philosophy, 1890-1915. Ph.D., Yale University, 1977. 597p. UMI# 7817598.

4319   Lefcourt, Robert. Democratic Influences on Legal Education from Colonial Times to the Civil War. Ph.D., Union for Experimenting Colleges and Universities, 1983. 223p. UMI# 8315760.

4320   Leighninger, Leslie H. The Development of Social Work as a Profession, 1930-1960. Doctor of Social Work, University of California-Berkeley, 1981. 377p. UMI# 8211838.

4321   Maloney, Sara E. The Development of Group Work Education in Schools of Social Work in the United States, 1919-1948. Ph.D., Case Western Reserve University, 1963.

4322   Marshall, Max L. Frank Luther Mott: Journalism Educator. Ph.D., University of Missouri, 1968. 684p. UMI# 69-3401. [dean of journalism, University of Missouri, 1942-1951; professor of English and journalism, University of Iowa, 1921-1942].

4323   Marshall, Philip C. The Social Ideas of American Historians, 1815-1865. Ph.D., Rutgers University, 1963. 468p. UMI# 64-1163.

4324   Mason, Peter W. The Humanistic Orientation in Twentieth-Century American Social Science. Ph.D., University of Minnesota, 1973. 299p. UMI# 73-25,695.

4325   McBride, Esther B. Protestant Contributions to American Social Work, 1870-1912. Ph.D., Tulane University, 1972. 599p. UMI# 72-24,414.

4326   McGlon, Charles A. Speech Education in Baptist Theological Seminaries in the United States, 1819-1943. Ph.D., Columbia University, 1951. 484p. UMI# 00-02837.

4327   McNeil, William K. A History of American Folklore Scholarship Before 1908. Ph.D., Indiana University, 1980. 992p. UMI# 80-29240.

4328   Means, Richard L. Protestantism in American Sociology 1930-1963: A Study of the Relations Between Theory, Research, and Historical Sociology. Ph.D., Cornell University, 1964. 387p. UMI# 64-8751.

4329   Melville, Keith E. Obstacles to Applied Social Research in Education: A Study of the National Institute of Education. Ph.D., Columbia University, 1984. 183p. UMI# 8413006.

4330   Napoli, Donald S. The Architects of Adjustment: The Practice and Professionalization of American Pyschology, 1920-1945. Ph.D., University of California-Davis, 1975. 361p. UMI# 76-14224.

4331   Numark, Eleanor J. Ethel Bowers, Dorothy Enderis and Eva Whiting White: A Historical Perspective of Their Contributions to the Professionalization of the Recreation Movement. Ed.D., New York University, 1979. 293p. UMI# 79-18880.

4332   O'Dell, DeForest. The History of Journalism Education in the United States. Ph.D., Columbia University, 1936. 117p.

4333   O'Donnell, John M. The Origins of Behaviorism: American Psychology, 1870-1920. Ph.D., University of Pennsylvania, 1979. 682p. UMI# 7828159.

4334   Ofiesh, Gabriel D. The History, Development, Present Status, and Purpose of the First Introductory Course in Psychology in American Undergraduate Education. Ed.D., University of Denver, 1959. 757p. UMI# 60-02669.

4335   Oziri, Ihemadubuinroya. The Relation of Cognitive, Technical, and Social Factors in the Growth or Decay of Comparative Sociology to the Possibility of a General Knowledge-Claim for Sociology as Science. Ph.D., Kent State University, 1984. 778p. UMI# 8508390.

4336   Palmquist, Eben O. A History of the American Historical Association's Commission of the Social Studies, 1926-1934. Ph.D., Loyola University of Chicago, 1981. 368p. UMI# 8109958.

4337   Pruitt, Franklin B. A Historical Study of the Teaching of History in American Colleges. Ed.D., Texas Technological University, 1978. 256p. UMI# 78-19897.

4338   Rediger, Joseph L. Social-Pyschological Factors Influencing Education: An Historical Study. Ph.D., Stanford University, 1944. 152p.

4339   Robarts, James R. The Rise of Educational Science in America. Ph.D., University of Illinois at Urbana-Champaign, 1963. 223p. UMI# 64-06137.

4340   Romney, Leonard S. History of Change: From Social Work Practice to Human Service Teaching. Ed.D., Yeshiva University, 1975. 291p. UMI# 75-20577.

4341   Rothberg, Morey D. Servant to History: A Study of John Franklin Jameson, 1859-1937. Ph.D., Brown University, 1983. 356p. UMI# 8228327. [professor of history, Brown University, 1888-1901; director of historical research, Carnegie Institution, 1905-1928].

4342   Rutkowski, Edward. A Study of the Various Viewpoints Expressed Concerning the Establishment of University Schools of Education During Their Formative Years 1890-1905. Ph.D., Michigan State University, 1963. 239p. UMI# 64-07539.

4343   Saunders, Harold H. The Group Concept in American Sociology and Political Science, 1883-1929. Ph.D., Yale University, 1956.

4344   Schaper, Florence W. The Rise and Development of Educational Sociology in the United States. Ph.D., New York University, 1932. 135p. UMI# 72-33727.

4345   Schrader, Alvin M. Toward a Theory of Library and Information Science. Ph.D., Indiana University, 1983. 1,016p. UMI# 8401534.

4346   Shields, JoAnn B. Sara Lowrey: Speech Teacher. Ph.D., Louisiana State University, 1985. 252p. UMI# 8610667.

4347   Shultz, Alva T. A Survey of the Pioneer Methods of Teaching Television Journalism in the Universities. Master's thesis, Ohio University, 1951.

4348   Smith, Mark C. Knowledge for What: Social Science and the Debate Over Its Role in 1930's America. Ph.D., University of Texas at Austin, 1980. 703p. UMI# 8128595.

4349   South, Oron P. Systematics in American Historiography Since 1900. Ph.D., Vanderbilt University, 1967. 173p. UMI# 68-5399.

4350   Stafford, Frances J. An Historical Examination of the Goals for History Instruction in Courses Required as Part of the General Education of Students in Post-Secondary Institutions. Ph.D., Florida State University, 1978. 191p. UMI# 78-15485.

4351   Super, Stacia I. Florence Hollis and the Development of Psychosocial Casework Theory: An Intellectual Biography 1927-1940. Doctor of Social Work, University of Illinois at Chicago Circle, 1980. 163p. UMI# 8023255. [professor of social work, Smith College and Case Western Reserve University].

4352   Tergerson, Charles J. The Growth and Development of the Education Program for Men in the Colleges and Universities of the United States of America. Master's thesis, North Texas State Teachers College, 1938.

4353   Torsey, Kathleen E. The Application of Tenets of Austin, Rush, and Curry by Writers of Representative Collegiate Speech Texts: 1925-1955. Ph.D., University of Florida, 1964. 267p. UMI# 64-11,547.

4354   Travis, William G. The Presbyterian Church in the United States of America and the Development of Sociology, 1870-1930. Ph.D., New York University, 1972. 342p. UMI# 72-31,138.

4355   Triebwasser, Marc A. American Government by the Book: The Rise (and Perhaps the Fall) of an 'Apolitical' Conceptualization of the Politics in Major College Level American Government Texts, 1900-1975. (Volumes I-IV) Ph.D., New York University, 1978. 1,521p. UMI# 78-24282.

4356   White, Maxwell O. A History of American Historical Periodicals to the Founding of the American Historical Review, 1741-1895. Ph.D., University of Iowa, 1947. 321p.

4357   Wills, Elbert V. The Early Development of the Teaching of Economic Theory in the United States. Ph.D., New York University, 1923. 212p. UMI# 72-33801.

4358   Wilson, Karl K. Historical Survey of the Religious Content of American Geography Textbooks from 1784 to 1895. Ph.D., University of Pittsburgh, 1951. 134p.

4359   Winn, Janet B. 'Sociology' as an Essentially Contested Concept. Ph.D., State University of New York at Albany, 1984. 208p. UMI# 8416991.

4360   Woo, Kun K. Learning Theory: Its Historical Development and Current Trends. Ph.D., University of Colorado, 1950.

4361   Zimbalist, Sidney E. Major Trends in Social Work Research: An Analysis of the Nature and Development of Research in Social Work, as Seen in the Periodical Literature, 1900-1950. Doctor of Social Work, Washington University, 1955. 245p. UMI# 12,817.

STATE AID AND COORDINATION

4362   Dees, Charles R., Jr. An Analysis of the Transition of Three Universities from Private to State Status. Ph.D., University of Pittsburgh, 1973. 184p. UMI# 73-29372.

4363   Giddens, Thomas R. A History of Selected Forms of State Aid to Private Institutions of Higher Education in the United States. Ph.D., Indiana University, 1969. 267p. UMI# 70-007448.

4364   Grafton, Carl T. The Coordination of State Universities in Indiana and Illinois. Ph.D., Purdue University, 1970. 285p. UMI# 70-18648.

4365   Lamb, Jane A. An Analysis of the Structure of 1985 State Budget Formulas for Public Higher Education with a Comparison of 1973, and 1985 Data. Ed.D., University of Tennessee, 1986. 629p. UMI# 8611608.

4366   Stephens, Cline B., Jr. A Descriptive Assessment of the States' Tax Support of Higher Education, 1960-1972. Ed.D., Illinois State University, 1974. 227p. UMI# 74,20,072.

4367   Toles, Caesar F. Regionalism in Southern Higher Education. Ph.D., University of Michigan, 1953. 213p. UMI# 00-05749.

STATE UNIVERSITY

4368   Foerster, Alma P. The State University in the Old South: A Study of Social and Intellectual Influences in State University Education. Ph.D., Duke University, 1939.

4369   Hicks, Fred W. Constitutional Independence and the State University. Ph.D., University of Michigan, 1963. 343p. UMI# 64-828.

4370   Michalik, Craig A. The Southern State University During the Progressive Era. Ph.D., University of Arkansas, 1978. 255p. UMI# 79-19251.

STUDENT ACTIVISM

4371   Bolinder, Calvin H. A Theoretical Analysis of Student Protest in Modern America (1960-1972). Ph.D., University of Wisconsin, 1973. 374p. UMI# 74-7458.

4372   Bowes, Harry P. University and College Student Rebellions in Retrospect and Sociological Implications. Ed.D., University of Colorado, 1964. 310p. UMI# 65-04177.

4373   Carson, Clayborne, Jr. Toward Freedom and Community : The Evolution of Ideas in the Student Nonviolent Coordinating Committee, 1960-1966. Ph.D., University of California-Los Angeles, 1975. 419p. UMI# 75-26953.

4374   Donnelly, Thomas H. Student Activists Seven Years Later: A Study of Change in Political Attitudes and Activity. Ph.D., New York University, 1978. 389p. UMI# 7912268.

4375   Eagan, Eileen M. The Student Peace Movement in the U.S., 1930-1941. Ph.D., Temple University, 1979. 345p. UMI# 7910045.

4376   Evans, Kenneth J., Jr. The Era of Student Unrest: Student Personnel. Professional Associations' Perceptions of Major Campus Changes Occurring Between 1964 and 1970. Ph.D., University of Pittsburgh, 1980. 352p. UMI# 8112671.

4377   Horn, Max. The Intercollegiate Socialist Society, 1905-1921: Origins of the Modern American Student Movement. Ph.D., Columbia University, 1975. 348p. UMI# 75-27426.

4378   Howison, David L. Attitudes Revealed by Student Newspaper Editorials at Five Liberal Arts Colleges, 1963 to 1973. Ed.D., Indiana University, 1977. 112p. UMI# 7801023.

4379   Malek-Madani, Firouz. American College Unrest from Colonial Times to 1976, in Relation to the Kondratieff Theory of Business Cycles. Ph.D., Southern Illinois University, 1977. 157p. UMI# 78-04289.

4380   Miller, Michael H. The American Student Movement of the Depression, 1931-1941: A Historical Analysis. Ph.D., Florida State University, 1981. 251p. UMI# 82-05733.

4381   Novak, Steven J. The Rights of Youth: The Impact of Student Revolt on American Higher Education, 1798-1815. Ph.D., University of California-Berkeley, 1974.

4382   Penrod, Michael R. Patterns of American Student Activism Since 1950: A Historical Analysis. Ph.D., Kansas State University, 1985. 264p. UMI# 8515966.

4383   Phelps, Marianne R. The Response of Higher Education to Student Activism, 1933-1938. Ph.D., George Washington University, 1980. 340p. UMI# 80-23863.

4384   Rappaport, Margaret M. Perspectives on University Student Activism in America, 1960-1970. Ph.D., University of Colorado, 1971. 347p. UMI# 71-25,867.

4385   Ritchie, Gladys W. The Rhetoric of American Students in Protest During the 1960s: A Study of Ends and Means. Ph.D., Temple University, 1973. 210p. UMI# 73-18,703.

4386   Rosenbrier, Gilbert M. An Historical Analysis of Student Unrest. Ed.D., Boston University, 1971. 332p. UMI# 71-26734.

4387   Schnell, Rudolph L. National Activist Student Organizations and American Higher Education, 1905-1944. Ph.D., University of Michigan, 1975. 263p. UMI# 76-09506.

4388   Schreiber, Stephen T. American College Student Riots and Disorders Between 1815 and the Civil War. Ed.D., Indiana University, 1979. 311p. UMI# 80-00649.

4389   Stevenson, William J. Radical Political Thought: SDS, 1960-68. Ph.D., Rutgers University, 1972. 261p. UMI# 72-27-595.

4390   Swisher, Randall S. Student Activists in the Seventies: The Public Interest Research Group Movement. Ph.D., George Washington University, 1978. 589p. UMI# 7903793.

STUDENT LIFE

4391   Allmendinger, David F., Jr. Indigent Students and Their Institutions, 1800-1860. Ph.D., University of Wisconsin, 1968. 288p. UMI# 68-15960.

4392   Burke, Colin B. The Quiet Influence: The American Colleges and Their Students, 1800-1860. Ph.D., Washington University, 1973. 388p. UMI# 74-13766.

4393   Byar, T. Madison. The Student Population in the Institutions of Higher Education in the Southern Appalachian Region, 1933-1958. Ed.D., University of Tennessee, 1950. 228p. UMI# 59-06972.

4394   Charles, Milton R. The Development of the Extracurriculum in Higher Education. Ph.D., Stanford University, 1953. 224p. UMI# 5376.

4395   Charlton, David H. Food for Thought: The Collegiate Way of Living. Ed.D., College of William & Mary, 1985. 232p. UMI# 8604297.

4396   Conrath, Richard C. In Loco Parentis: Recent Developments in This Legal Doctrine as Applied to the University Student Relationship in the United States of America, 1965-75. Ph.D., Kent State University, 1976. 202p. UMI# 77-7814.

4397   Davis, Mollie C. Quest for a New America: Ferment in Collegiate Culture, 1921-1929. Ph.D., University of Georgia, 1972. 382p. UMI# 72-34063.

4398   DeVine, Mary L.J. A Study of the Historical Development of Coeducation in American Higher Education. Ph.D., Boston College, 1966.

4399   Deyoung, Henry G. An Historical Review of Attorneys General's Opinions and an Analysis of Their Potential Value in Enforcing a Right to an Education for All Handicapped Students. Ph.D., University of Michigan, 1976. 126p. UMI# 77-07901.

4400   Dillon, Kristine E. The Rising Costs of Higher Education, 1946-1977. Ph.D., Claremont Graduate School, 1980. 165p. UMI# 80-15600.

4401   Fleming, George M. Historical Survey of the Educational Benefits Provided Veterans of World War II by the Servicemen's Readjustment Act of 1944. Ed.D., University of Houston, 1957. 181p. UMI# 00-21731.

4402   Frank, Frederick J. Student Life in Selected Colleges in the Early Nineteenth Century. Ph.D., University of Pittsburgh, 1975. 332p. UMI# 76-05438.

4403   Harcleroad, Fred F., Jr. Influence of Organized Student Opinion on American College Curricula: An Historical Survey. Ph.D., Stanford University, 1948.

4404   Harms, Herman E. A History of the Concept of In Loco Parentis in American Education. Ed.D., University of Florida, 1970. 174p. UMI# 71-00249.

4405   Hirschberger, Emma J. A Study of the Development of the In Loco Parentis Doctrine, Its Application and Emerging Trends. Ph.D., University of Pittsburgh, 1971. 284p. UMI# 72-07887.

4406   Ihle, Elizabeth L. The Development of Coeducation in Major Southern State Universities. Ed.D., University of Tennessee, 1976. 205p. UMI# 77-10776.

4407   Jankiewicz, Paul. Study of Disciplinary Practices in American Higher Education from 1636 to 1900. Ph.D., University of Connecticut, 1971. 250p. UMI# 71-29875.

4408   Janzen, Fred G. A Historical Study of the Campus Ombudsman in United States Higher Education. Ed.D., Texas Tech University, 1971. 265p. UMI# 71-25625.

4409   Lazar, Stephen H. The Role of the Federal Government in the Extent and Structure of American College and University Housing. Ed.D., Syracuse University, 1967. 246p. UMI# 68-05511.

4410   Lenn, Marjorie P. A Study of Residence Hall Development: Shifting Organizational Patterns and Roles of Residence Hall Staff from 1961 to 1976. Ed.D., University of Massachusetts, 1978. 173p. UMI# 78-18015.

4411   Li, Shu-Tang. Coeducation in American Colleges and Universities: An Historical, Psychological, and Sociological Study with Some Applications to China. Ph.D., New York University, 1928. 258p. UMI# 72-33615.

4412   Livingston, Inez B. Social, Economic, and Political Influences on the Development of Residence Halls for Women in Colleges and Universities in the United States. Ph.D., Ohio State University, 1966. 208p. UMI# 66-15107.

4413   Longenecker, Justin G. History of the University Book Store, 1900-1955. Doctor of Business Administration, University of Washington, 1976. 410p. UMI# 00-18502.

4414   Meredith, Thomas C. Migratory Trends of Students in Senior Colleges and Universities in the United States by States, 1949 through 1968. Ed.D., University of Mississippi, 1971. 162p. UMI# 72-3928.

4415   Moran, Kaye D. An Historical Development of the Doctrine Loco Parentis with Court Interpretations in the United States. Ph.D., University of Kansas, 1967. 115p. UMI# 68-00560.

4416   Reed, John D. Toward A Theory of the First Amendment for the College Press. Ph.D., Southern Illinois University at Carbondale, 1986. 287p. UMI# 8610587.

4417   Rees, Arland B. In Loco Parentis and Student Discipline in Private Higher Education. Ph.D., State University of New York at Buffalo, 1979. 211p. UMI# 7921894.

4418   Saslaw, Rita S. Student Societies: Nineteenth Century Establishment. Ph.D., Case Western Reserve University, 1971. 249p. UMI# 72-00101.

4419   Schlesinger, Sue H. Student Lobbies: A New Voice in the Politics of Higher Education. Ph.D., University of California-Los Angeles, 1979. 238p. UMI# 7926062.

4420   Schulken, Emma W. A History of Foreign Students in American Higher Education from Its Colonial Beginning to the Present: A Synthesis of the Major Forces Influencing Their Presence in American Higher Education. Ph.D., Florida State University, 1968. 262p. UMI# 72-21329.

4421   Schwerner, Stephen A. An Historical Study of the Changing Emphasis on Social, Political, and Educational Issues Since World War I in Undergraduate Newspapers at Four Eastern Colleges. Ed.D., New York University, 1970. 130p. UMI# 71-13622.

4422   Shay, John E., Jr. Residence Halls in the Age of the University: Their Development at Harvard and Michigan, 1850-1930. Ph.D., University of Michigan, 1966. 250p. UMI# 66-14594.

4423   Thackery, John. History and Social Significance of the College Yearbook. Master's thesis, Kansas State College, 1934.

4424   Wagoner, Jennings L., Jr. From 'In Loco Parentis' Toward 'Lernfreiheif': An Examination of the Attitudes of Four Early University Presidents Regarding Student Freedom and Character Development. Ph.D., Ohio State University, 1968. 324p. UMI# 69-04992.

4425   Zimmerman, Joan G. College Culture in the Mid-West, 1890-1930. Ph.D., University of Virginia, 1978. 275p. UMI# 79-16278.

STUDENT PERSONNEL SERVICES

4426   Barry, Ruth E. A History of the Guidance Personnel Movement in Education. Ph.D., Columbia University, 1956.

4427   Candon, Sarah A. The Evolution of Three Student Personnel Perspectives and Their Effect on Professional Preparation Programs. Ed.D., Columbia University Teachers College, 1981. 172p. UMI# 8122936.

4428   Conard, Wilbern E. A Study to Re-Examine the 1937 Student Personnel Point of View in Light of American Social and Education Change. Ph.D., Florida State University, 1981. 210p. UMI# 8125852.

4429   Dewey, Mary E. An Investigation of Holism in Student Personnel Work, with Special Emphasis on the Depression Year 1931-32. Ph.D., Syracuse University, 1967. 339p. UMI# 68-7054.

4430   Ewing, James W. An Historical Investigation of the Training Programs in Counseling and Psychotherapy in American Higher Education 1880-1941. Ph.D., Saint Louis University, 1972. 239p. UMI# 72-23924.

4431   Fley, Jo Ann. Discipline in Student Personnel Work: The Changing Views of Deans and Personnel Workers. Ed.D., Columbia University, 1963. 471p. UMI# 63-08157.

4432   Jenkins, Edwin G. History and Development of the Southern College Personnel Association as a Professional Organization, 1949-1972. Ed.D., Auburn University, 1974. 214p.

4433   Mendenhall, William R. A Case Study of the American College Personnel Association: Its Contributions to the Professionalization Process of Student Personnel Work. Ph.D., Florida State University, 1975. 148p. UMI# 75-26797.

4434   Nunn, Norman L. Student Personnel Work in American Higher Education: Its Evolution as an Organized Movement. Ph.D., Florida State University, 1964. 244p. UMI# 65-00333.

4435   Pitts, James H. The Historical and Philosophical Foundations of College Student Person-
        nel Work. Ph.D., University of Northern Colorado, 1969. 145p. UMI# 70-07154.

4436   Price, Robert M. A History of the American College Personnel Association. Ed.D., Indiana
        University, 1965. 171p. UMI# 65-14059.

4437   Purchard, Dora. Historical Backgrounds and Philosophy of Guidance. Ph.D., University of
        Pittsburgh, 1942. 249p.

4438   Robertson, Henry M. The Genesis and Development of Student Personnel Work in Ameri-
        can Higher Education. Ph.D., University of Minnesota, 1967. 217p. UMI# 68-1562.

4439   Stathis-Ochoa, Roberta A. The Development of American Higher Education in the West:
        The Role of the Western Personnel Organization, 1919-1964. Ph.D., Claremont Graduate
        School, 1985. 328p. UMI# 8517265.

4440   Taylor, George D. Changes in Student Personnel Organization Structures and Functions
        in Selected Universities from 1964-1974. Ed.D., Illinois State University, 1976. 89p. UMI#
        76-30362.

4441   Traylor, Judy A.G. An Historical Study of the National Association of Personnel Workers:
        An Examination of the Efforts of Blacks in the Formation and Development of Student
        Personnel Organizations. Ed.D., East Texas State University, 1983. 354p. UMI# 8319224.

4442   Triggs, Frances O. The Development of Student Personnel Service in Colleges and
        Universities. Master's thesis, University of Chicago, 1937. 84p.

4443   Wolf, Ruth B. A History of the Guidance Personnel Movement in Education. Ph.D., Co-
        lumbia University, 1956.

TEACHER EDUCATION

4444   Aaronson, Warren J. A History of Teacher Preparation Programs in Mental Retardation in
        America. ED.D, Boston University, 1967. 231p. UMI# 69-07792.

4445   Arundel, Edna. The Evolution of Human Geography in Teacher-Education. Ph.D., Yale
        University, 1942. 274p. UMI# 65-7554.

4446   Borrowman, Merle L. The Liberal and Technical in Teacher Education, an Historical
        Survey of American Thought. Ph.D., Columbia University, 1954.

4447   Burk, Harry L. Historical Background and Early Development of the Normal School.
        Master's thesis, Kansas State Teachers College, 1939. 114p.

4448   Carroll, Raymond A. Teacher Education: Trends in Concepts of the Professional Prepara-
        tion of Teachers, 1940-1968. Ph.D., Michigan State University, 1969. 327p. UMI# 69-
        20833.

4449   Carter, Karl C. A Historical Study of the Evolution of the Objectives of the National
        Science Foundation Teacher-Training Programs as Exemplified Specifically by the Aca-
        demic Year Institute Programs in Science. Ph.D., Michigan State University, 1970. 225p.
        UMI# 71-11800.

4450   Chiappetta, Michael. A History of the Relationship Between Collegiate Objectives and the Professional Preparation of Arts College Teachers in the United States. Ph.D., University of Michigan, 1950. 130p. UMI# 00-01953.

4451   Christensen, James W. An Historical and Descriptive Study of the Development of Teacher Selection and Teacher Education in the Department of Seminaries and Institutes of Religion in the Church of Jesus Christ of Latter-Day Saints. Ed.D., Utah State University, 1970. 200p. UMI# 70-10931.

4452   Clarke, Charles M. Philanthropic Foundations and Teacher Education in the South, 1867-1948. Ph.D., University of North Carolina at Chapel Hill, 1948.

4453   Colgrove, Pitt P. An Historical Study of Normal School Curricula to Determine the Function of These Institutions in Our Present Educational System. Doctor of Pedagogy, New York University, 1900. 59p. UMI# 72-33504.

4454   Coyner, Ruth E. The Professional Aspects of Teacher Education in American Universities During the Nineteenth Century. Ph.D., George Washington University, 1936.

4455   Daly, Richard F. Curriculum Innovations in the Collegiate Preparation of Elementary School Teachers, 1945-1957. Ed.D., University of Nebraska-Lincoln, 1971. 165p. UMI# 71-19479.

4456   Dryer, Linnie. The History of the Teaching of Education in Leading Universities and Colleges in the United States. Master's thesis, University of Texas, 1928.

4457   Ellis, Peter D. An Analysis of Six Major Reports on Teacher Education in the United States, with Special Reference to Their Recommendations for the Preservice Curriculum (1933-1983). Ph.D., Ohio State University, 1984. 332p. UMI# 8426382.

4458   Glovinsky, Arnold. Factors in the Development of Professional Education for Secondary School Teachers in the United States, 1870-1907. Ed.D., Wayne State University, 1961. 156p. UMI# 62-00908.

4459   Griffin, Kevin J. A History of Teacher Education in the Seven Colleges Conducted by the American Christian Brothers. Ph.D., Saint Louis University, 1976. 152p. UMI# 76-22542.

4460   Heflin, William H. The Historical Development of Training Programs for Secondary Public School Teachers of Modern Foreign Languages in the United States to 1940. Ph.D., Florida State University, 1971. 282p. UMI# 72-10,056.

4461   Hoover, Irene W. Historical and Theoretical Development of a Language Experience Approach to Teaching Reading in Selected Teacher Education Institutions. Ed.D., University of Arizona, 1971. 184p. UMI# 71-29511.

4462   Hough, John M. A Study of the Evolution of Five Current Issues in Teacher Education in the United States. Ed.D., University of North Carolina, 1966. 357p. UMI# 67-01000.

4463   Johanningmeier, Erwin V. A Study of William Chandler Bagley's Educational Doctrines and His Program for Teacher Preparation, 1895-1918. Ph.D., University of Illinois at Urbana-Champaign, 1967. 364p. UMI# 68-08123. [professor of education, Columbia University Teachers College, 1917-1940].

4464   Johnston, Ruth V. Trends in Secondary Education School Curriculum Concepts: Their Implications for the Teaching Function and Teacher Preparation (An Analysis of Selected Curriculum Guides and Courses of Study 1926-1950). Ph.D., University of Minnesota, 1952. 325p. UMI# 00-04336.

4465   Lane, Genevieve. Twentieth Century Trends in the Professional Preparation of Teachers of the Educable Mentally Retarded. Ph.D., Saint Louis University, 1972. 157p. UMI# 72-23963.

4466   Leach, Georgia B. Art Requirements in Teacher Training Programs of Southern Colleges Since 1900. Ph.D., University of Oklahoma, 1963. 160p. UMI# 63-00027.

4467   Lewis, William J. The Educational Speaking of Jabez L.M. Curry. Ph.D., University of Florida, 1955. 369p. UMI# 00-14319. [professor of philosophy and law, University of Richmond, 1868-1881].

4468   Lowman, Harmon L. The History of the Teacher-Training Institutions in the Gulf States. Ph.D., University of Chicago, 1930. 359p.

4469   Martin, Curtis A. A History of the Social Foundations of Teacher Education, 1930-1963. Ph.D., University of Washington, 1968. 329p. UMI# 69-07067.

4470   Marwah, Surinder K. The Professional Preparation and the Public Record of Teachers' College Faculty from 1895 to 1920. Master's thesis, University of Nebraska at Lincoln, 1969.

4471   McCleary, Iva D. A Study of Formal Projects to Improve College and University Teaching, 1956-1976. Ph.D., University of Utah, 1976. 198p. UMI# 77-9268.

4472   McDermott, Maria C. A History of Teacher Education in a Congregation of Religious Women: 1843-1964, Sisters of the Holy Cross. Ph.D., University of Notre Dame, 1964. 365p. UMI# 65-1133.

4473   Mosher, E.R. The Rise and Organization of State Teachers Colleges. Ed.D., Harvard University, 1924.

4474   Nawaz, Muhammad. Historical Development of Counselor Training in the United States of America (1919-1959) and Its Implications for Pakistan. Ph.D., Indiana University, 1964. 381p. UMI# 64-12065.

4475   Pangburn, Jessie M. The Evolution of the American Teachers College. Ph.D., Columbia University, 1932. 140p.

4476   Parker, Clara M. The Development of Teacher-Training Schools in the United States of America. Master's thesis, University of Texas, 1920.

4477   Peck, Richard C. Jabez Lamar Monroe Curry: Educational Crusader. Ph.D., George Peabody College for Teachers, 1943. [professor of philosophy and law, University of Richmond, 1868-1881].

4478   Reed, Marian E. The History of the Psychological Foundations of Teacher Education. Ph.D., Stanford University, 1957. 283p. UMI# 00-20465.

4479   Rhodes, Dent M. Professional Models for the American Teacher, 1815-1915. Ph.D., Ohio State University, 1965. 149p. UMI# 66-01819.

4480   Rice, Jessie P. J.L.M. Curry, Southerner, Statesman and Educator. Ph.D., Columbia University, 1950. 242p. UMI# [professor of philosophy and law, University of Richmond, 1868-1881].

4481   Roach, John K. Conflicting Viewpoints on Certain Issues in Education, 1933-1950: A Study of Twenty-Three Fundamental Issues in Education and of the Opinions of Sixty-One Leaders in General Teacher Education and Fifty Leaders in Business Teacher Education Regarding These Issues. Ed.D., New York University, 1954. 425p. UMI# 00-10678.

4482   Robinson, Chester H. The Work of Eight Major Educational Associations Toward the Improvement of College Teaching, 1920-1940. Ph.D., Stanford University, 1950. 117p.

4483   Roblee, Dana B. A Careerline Study of the Professorship in Teacher Education Institutions. Ph.D., George Washington University, 1957.

4484   Seamster, Frederick C. The Evolution of Teacher Education, 1890-1935. Ph.D., Yale University, 1938.

4485   Snarr, Otto W. The Education of Teachers in the Middle States: A Historical Study of the Professional Education of Public School Teachers as a State Function. Ph.D., University of Chicago, 1942. 269p.

4486   Sprague, Harry A. A Decade of Progress in the Preparation of Secondary School Teachers: A Study of Curriculum Requirements in 55 State Teachers Colleges in 1928 and 1938. Ph.D., Columbia University, 1940. 170p.

4487   Staton, Mary L. Trends in Teacher Certification in the South Since 1900. Ph.D., University of North Carolina, 1953. 323p.

4488   Stone, Charles A. The Teachers' Institute in American Education. Ph.D., Stanford University, 1951.

4489   Tatum, Beulah B. Teacher Training in the South, 1875-1900: State Training of White Elementary Teachers. Ph.D., Johns Hopkins University, 1943.

4490   Thomasson, Arnold L. A Half Century of Teacher Training in State Normal Schools and Teachers Colleges of the United States, 1890-1940. Ph.D., University of Illinois at Urbana-Champaign, 1943. 462p.

4491   Wilson, Ann E.J. Knowledge for Teachers: The National Teacher Examinations Program, 1940 to 1970. Ph.D., University of Wisconsin, 1984. 433p. UMI# 8414265.

4492   Wofford, Kate V. A History of the Status and Training of Elementary Rural Teachers of the United States, 1860-1930. Ph.D., Columbia University, 1936. 170p.

4493   Young, Burns B. The Rise and Development of Instructional Courses in Higher Education. Ph.D., Stanford University, 1952.

TEACHING, GENERAL

4494   Chisholm, Linda A. The Art of Undergraduate Teaching in the Age of the Emerging University. Ph.D., Columbia University, 1982. 624p. UMI# 8427368.

4495   Farmakis, George L. The Role of the American Teacher, an Historical View through Readings. Ph.D., Wayne State University, 1971. 661p. UMI# 72-14553.

4496   Hangartner, Carl A. Movements to Change American College Teaching, 1700-1830. Ph.D., Yale University, 1955. 394p. UMI# 65-07517.

4497   Robb, Mary M. Oral Interpretation of Literature in American Colleges and Universities: A Historical Study of Teaching Methods. Ph.D., Columbia University, 1942. 242p.

4498   Smallwood, Mary L. An Historical Study of Teaching and Grading Systems in Early American Universities: A Critical Study of the Original Records of Harvard, William & Mary, Yale, Mt. Holyoke, and Michigan from Their Founding to 1900. Ph.D., Yale University, 1934.

THEOLOGICAL EDUCATION

4499   Barrick, William E. Field Education in Protestant Theological Seminaries in the United States: An Interpretation of Major Trends, 1920-1970. Ed.D., Columbia University (Union Theological Seminary), 1975. 190p. UMI# 75-20186.

4500   Boon, Harold W. The Development of the Bible College or Institute in the United States and Canada Since 1880 and Its Relationship to the Field of Theological Education in America. Ed.D., New York University, 1950. 204p. UMI# 73-08441.

4501   Bostrom, Harvey R. Contributions to Higher Education by the Society for the Promotion of Collegiate and Theological Education at the West, 1843-1874. Ph.D., New York University, 1960. 260p. UMI# 60-03736.

4502   Brereton, Virginia L. Protestant Fundamentalist Bible Schools, 1882-1940. Ph.D., Columbia University, 1981. 470p. UMI# 83-27185.

4503   Brittain, Raymond F. The History of the Associate, Associate Reformed, and United Presbyterian Theological Seminaries in the United States. Ph.D., University of Pittsburgh, 1946. 399p.

4504   Kendall, Philip E. Intellectual Formation in the Major Seminary Curriculum Principles and Considerations, a Canonical Historical Study. Doctor of Canon Law, Catholic University of America, 1970. 900p. UMI# 70-23674.

4505   Moore, Ralph R. History of Baptist Theological Education in South Carolina and Georgia. Ph.D., Southwest Baptist Theological Seminary, 1949. 175p.

4506   Morris, William S. The Seminary Movement in the United States: Projects, Foundations, and Early Development, 1833-1866. Ph.D., Catholic University of America, 1932. 119p.

4507   Pease, Norval F. Charles E. Weniger's Theory of the Relationship of Speech and Homiletics as Revealed in His Teaching Procedures, His Writings, and His Public Addresses.

Ph.D., Michigan State University, 1964. 269p. UMI# 65-2047. [dean and professor of speech and homiletics, Pacific Union College and Andrews University].

4508   Robey, Margaret D. A History of the Southern Seminary and Junior College, 1937-1952. Master's thesis, University of Virginia, 1953.

4509   Winegarden, Neil A. A Historical Survey of Homiletical Education in the United States. Ph.D., Northern Baptist Theological Seminary, 1953. 323p.

UNIONS

4510   Altenbaugh, Richard J. Forming the Structure of a New Society Within the Shell of the Old: A Study of Three Labor Colleges and Their Contributions to the American Labor Movement. Ph.D., University of Pittsburgh, 1980. 396p. UMI# 8018284.

4511   Close, William E. An Historical Study of the American Federation of Labor - Congress of Industrial Organizations Involvement in Higher Education with an Emphasis on the Period 1960-1969. Ph.D., Catholic University of America, 1972. 173p. UMI# 72-26250.

4512   Collinwood, Dean W. Organizational Origins of the Faculty Unionism in American Higher Education. Ph.D., University of Chicago, 1979.

4513   Goulding, Joel A. The History of Unionism in American Higher Education. Ed.D., Wayne State University, 1970. 327p. UMI# 71-00409.

4514   Lester, Jeanette A. The American Federation of Teachers in Higher Education: A History of Union Organization of Faculty Members in Colleges and Universities, 1916-1966. Ed.D., University of Toledo, 1968. 375p. UMI# 69-03431.

4515   McCamey, Marion B. Unionism in Academia. Ed.D., University of Massachusetts, 1977. 156p. UMI# 77-22030.

4516   Newman, Christy M. A Legal History of Collective Bargaining in Private Higher Education. Ed.D., Boston College, 1984. 178p. UMI# 8416011.

4517   Watkins, Bari J. The Professors and the Unions: American Academic Social Theory and Labor Reform, 1883-1915. Ph.D., Yale University, 1976. 358p. UMI# 77-00407.

URBAN UNIVERSITY

4518   Ar-Rifai, Taleb D.E. The New University Environment: A 20th Century Urban Ideal. Ph.D., University of Pennsylvania, 1983. 223p. UMI# 8316080.

4519   Carey, James T. The Development of the University Evening School in Urban America: An Aspect of Institutionalization in Higher Education. Ph.D., University of Chicago, 1958. 172p.

4520   Hirsh, James B. The Response of Selected Urban Private Universities to the Forces of Economic Depression of the 1930s. Ph.D., University of Denver, 1976. 358p. UMI# 76-24,415.

4521   Kaluzynski, Thomas A. An Historical View of the Concept of the Urban University. Ph.D., University of Illinois at Urbana-Champaign, 1975. 283p. UMI# 75-24331.

4522   Shores, Louis S. A Survey of the Municipal University: Its Origin, Development and Present Status. Master's thesis, City College of New York, 1928.

WAR AND HIGHER EDUCATION

4523   Camfield, Thomas M. Psychologists at War: The History of American Psychology and the First World War. Ph.D., University of Texas, 1969. 344p. UMI# 70-10,766.

4524   Goode, James M. The Confederate University: The Forgotten Institution of the American Civil War. Master's thesis, University of Virginia, 1966.

4525   Gruber, Carol S. Mars and Minerva: World War I and the American Academic Man. Ph.D., Columbia University, 1968. 359p. UMI# 68-11715.

4526   Jaffe, Joseph L., Jr. Isolationism and Neutrality in Academe, 1938-1941. Ph.D., Case Western Reserve University, 1979. 426p. UMI# 79-09358.

4527   Jones, Daniel P. The Role of Chemists in Research on War Gases in the United States During World War I. Ph.D., University of Wisconsin, 1969. 279p. UMI# 69-22,406.

4528   Nicholas, William E., III. Academic Dissent in World War I, 1917-1918. Ph.D., Tulane University, 1970. 264p. UMI# 71-08076.

4529   Stillman, Rachel B. Education in the Confederate States of America, 1861-1865. Ph.D., University of Illinois at Urbana-Champaign, 1972. 485p. UMI# 72-19937.

WOMEN

4530   Antler, Joyce. The Educated Woman and Professionalization: The Struggle for a New Feminine Identity, 1890-1920. Ph.D., State University of New York at Stony Brook, 1977. 459p. UMI# 77-28,142.

4531   Belson, Beverly A. Journal of the National Association for Women Deans, Administrators, and Counselors: An Historical Analysis, 1938-1974. Ph.D., Michigan State University, 1974. 218p. UMI# 75-14698.

4532   Boehmer, Florence E. Vocational Continuity of College Women: A Study Based on Data Secured from 6466 Women Who Matriculated in Land Grant Colleges Between 1889 and 1922. Ph.D., Columbia University, 1932. 100p.

4533   Brown, Naomi B. The National Association of Women Deans and Counselors, 1951-1961. Ed.D., University of Denver, 1963. 520p. UMI# 64-04860.

4534   Carter, Susan B. Academic Women Revisited: An Empirical Study of Changing Patterns in Women's Employment as College and University Faculty, 1890-1963. Ph.D., Stanford University, 1981. 139p. UMI# 81-15779.

4535   Churgin, Jonah R. The Quiet Revolution: The New Woman and the Old Academic. Ed.D., Columbia University Teachers College, 1976. 371p. UMI# 77-06712.

4536   Conway, Jill K. The First Generation of American Women Graduates. Ph.D., Harvard University, 1969.

4537   Cookingham, Mary E. The Demographic and Labor Force Behavior of Women College Graduates, 1865 to 1965. Ph.D., University of California-Berkeley, 1980. 221p. UMI# 81-12999.

4538   Drachman, Virginia G. Women Doctors and the Women's Medical Movement: Feminism and Medicine 1850-1895. Ph.D., State University of New York at Buffalo, 1976. 250p. UMI# 77-03530.

4539   Edmund, Gertrude M. The Higher Education of Women in the United States up to 1870. Ph.D., New York University, 1919. 341p. UMI# 74-03384.

4540   Feldman, Rochelle C. The Institutionalization of the Women's Movement in American Higher Education. Ph.D., University of Connecticut, 1982. 267p. UMI# 8300128.

4541   Fitzpatrick, Ellen F. Academics and Activists: Women Social Scientists and the Impulse for Reform: 1892-1920. Ph.D., Brandeis University, 1981. 304p.

4542   Gordon, Lynn D. Women with Missions: Varieties of College Life in the Progressive Era. Ph.D., University of Chicago, 1980.

4543   Grieder, Freida A. American Women in the Professions: A Study of Trends, 1870-1940, and Their Implications for Counseling College Women. Ph.D., Stanford University, 1950. 117p.

4544   Hall, Barbara C. A Historical Study of the Early Development of Teacher Education for Women in Physical Education. Ph.D., Columbia University, 1952.

4545   Henderson, Janet K. Four Nineteenth Century Professional Women. Ed.D., Rutgers University, 1982. 315p. UMI# 8218323.

4546   Hickson, Shirley A. The Development of Higher Education for Women in the Antebellum South. Ph.D., University of South Carolina, 1985. 175p. UMI# 8528175.

4547   Horn, Marcia A. Ideas of the Founders of Early Colleges for Women on the Role of Women's Education in American Society. Ed.D., Rutgers University, 1977. 157p. UMI# 77-13465.

4548   Huffman, Mabel. The Advancement of American Women's Education in Relation to the Kondratieff Theory of Business Cycles. Ph.D., Southern Illinois University, 1976. 248p. UMI# 77-6227.

4549   Hummer, Patricia M. The Decade of Elusive Promise: Professional Women in the United States, 1920-1930. Ph.D., Duke University, 1976. 261p. UMI# 76-27977.

4550   Jennings, Robert B. A History of the Educational Activities of the Women's Educational and Industrial Union from 1877-1927. Ed.D., Boston College, 1978. 175p. UMI# 78-16105.

4551   Kilman, Gail A. Southern Collegiate Women: Higher Education at Wesleyan Female College and Randolph-Macon Woman's College. Ph.D., University of Delaware, 1984. 201p. UMI# 8420977.

4552   Kirkpatrick, Wyona J. The Emerging Role of Women in Institutions of Higher Education in the United States. Ed.D., University of Alabama, 1965. 214p. UMI# 65-8460.

4553   Lagemann, Ellen C. A Generation of Women: Studies in Educational Biography. Ph.D., Columbia University, 1978. 357p. UMI# 7819374.

4554   MacMillan, Genevieve. History of Higher Education of Women in the South. Master's thesis, University of North Carolina, 1923.

4555   Marsh, Josephine P. A Study of Selected Stated Objectives of American Higher Education of Women to 1940. Ph.D., Harvard University, 1959.

4556   Martin, Theodora P. Women's Study Clubs, 1860-1900: 'The Sound of Our Own Voices.' Ed.D., Harvard University, 1985. 308p. UMI# 8601983.

4557   McPherson, Linda M.G. A Historical Perspective of Career Patterns of Women in the Teaching Profession: 1900-1940. Ph.D., Illinois State University, 1981. 176p. UMI# 81-23327.

4558   Okin, Susan M. Women and Citizens: The Status of Women in the History of Political Philosophy. Ph.D., Harvard University, 1975.

4559   Olmstead, Madeline. The Higher Education of Women in the Nineteenth Century. Master's thesis, University of Idaho, 1936.

4560   Parker, Lockie. Factors in the Development of the Higher Education of Women in the United States. Master's thesis, New York University, 1932.

4561   Pollard, Lucille A. Women on College and University Faculties: A Historical Survey and a Study of Their Present Academic Status. Ed.D., University of Georgia, 1965. 346p. UMI# 66-02494.

4562   Rogers, Nancy L.D. The Development of Federal Policy for the Elimination of Discrimination in the Postsecondary Education of Women. Ph.D., University of Michigan, 1979. 168p. UMI# 7916802.

4563   Simeone, Angela M. Academic Women: The Progress of Two Decades. Ph.D., University of Pennsylvania, 1983. 539p. UMI# 8406719.

4564   Simmons, S.A. Ante-Bellum Columbia Female Colleges. Master's thesis, University of Missouri, 1945.

4565   Smith, Mildred P. Early History of Higher Education for Women in the Seaboard South. Master's thesis, Duke University, 1932.

4566   Strain, Sibyl M. An Exploratory Investigation of Women's Studies in Selected Institutions of Higher Education with Emphasis Upon the Historical Background of the Status of Women and the Special Needs of Women in Higher Education. Ph.D., University of Southern California, 1977.

4567   Strobel, Marian E. Ideology and Women's Higher Education, 1945-1960. Ph.D., Duke University, 1976. 291p. UMI# 76-09148.

4568   Waas, Lulu M. The Development of Higher Education for Women in the United States. Master's thesis, Oklahoma Agricultural & Mechanical College, 1937.

4569   Williams, Sallye L. The Development of Higher Education for Women in America. Master's thesis, Louisiana State University, 1929.

4570   Zschoche, Sue. Preserving Eden: Higher Education, Woman's Sphere, and the First Generation of College Women, 1870-1910. Ph.D., University of Kansas, 1984. 156p. UMI# 85-13786.

AUTHOR INDEX

[Numbers refer to entry numbers]

Aaronson, Warren J., 4444
Abbot, Billy M., 2736
Abbott, Andrew D., 4075
Ables, Luther R., 2582
Abney, George M., 534
Aby, Stephen H., 3092
Ackley, Bob G., 3833
Acosta, Harold, 3477
Adair, Alice J.L., 2851
Adair, Thomas J., 2550
Adams, Charles S., 2645
Adams, David H., 2347
Adams, Dennis P., 3419
Adams, Eva D., 520
Adams, Helen B., 1484
Adams, John A., 2761
Adams, Kathryn B., 477
Adams, Sarah J., 2987
Adams, Stephanie M., 4052
Adamsons, Hannelore M., 1717
Adix, Shauna M., 2852
Adkins, Roma L., 3546
Agee, Forrest J., 2677
Agnew, Walker F., 4053
Ahern, John J., 4076
Ahern, Patrick H., 408
Aiken, John R., 1648
Aiken, Wreathy P., 2583
Ainsworth, Charles P., 3599
Ainsworth, Dorothy S., 3710
Akin, Lew, 3341
Albrecht, Esther A., 610
Albrecht, Frank M., Jr., 4258
Alcott, Pouneh M., 2116
Alderson, Willis B., 83
Aldridge, Jack H., 3420
Alexander, George D., 2584
Alexander, Jo H., 428
Alexis, Roselle N., 1008
Alfonso, Robert J., 1830
Alford, Stanley C., 2325
Allan, Henry C., 709
Allan, John M., 1811
Allemang, Margaret M., 3711
Allen, Christopher, 1949
Allen, Edward L., 3478
Allen, Ernest L., 2585
Allen, George J., Jr., 3178
Allen, Harlan B., 1649

Allen, John B., III, 1908
Allen, Judith C., 1788
Allen, Lawrence A., 3158
Allen, Madeline M., 1909
Allen, Marshall, 2070
Allen, Max P., 790
Allen, Milton R., 2947
Allen, Patricia A., 1470
Allen, Roger B., 2494
Allmendinger, David F., Jr., 4391
Almack, John C., 2228
Alschuler, John H., Jr., 3773
Alston, Jerry G., 949
Altenbaugh, Richard J., 4510
Alterman, Richard C., 3573
Althouse, Ronald C., 1378
Altman, Robert A., 3479
Altschuler, Glenn C., 1789
Alverson, Roy T., 48
Amburgey, James H., 2548
Amos, Autumn, 3021
Amyett, Paddy D.W., 2646
Anania, Pasquale, 3159
Ancelet, Leroy, 1045
Ancell, Mary K.Z., 3547
Andeen, Gustav K., 4106
Ander, Oscar F., 611
Anderson, Albert T., 3421
Anderson, Allen G., 4107
Anderson, Edison H., Sr., 2199
Anderson, James A., 1283
Anderson, John M., 578
Anderson, Julia M., 2708
Anderson, Kenneth C., 826
Anderson, Melvin S., 2207
Anderson, Patricia W., 4179
Anderson, Roy E., 1164
Anderson, Stanley D., Jr., 3093
Anderson, William H., 301
Andress, Robert P., 565
Andrews, Cheryl A., 3052
Andruss, Harvey A., 2262
Angel, Donald E., 316
Angell, Charles E., 3480
Angelo, Mark V., 1854
Angelo, Richard M., 3774
Ankrum, Ward E., 1508
Ansbro, James B., 623
Antler, Joyce, 4530

Aponte-Hernandez, Rafael, 2424
Appleman, Mary J.N., 784
Aquino-Bermudez, Frederico, 1695
Ar-Rifai, Taleb D.E., 4518
Arce, Carlos H., 3266
Archambeault, Brother Henry E., 1473
Archer, H. Richard, 624
Archer, Will H., 2699
Armentrout, William W., 108
Armeny, Susan, 3712
Armistead, Timothy W., 154
Armstrong, Neal A., 64
Armstrong, Robert A., 1311
Armstrong, Ross O., Jr., 3541
Arone, Frank T., 1650
Aronofsky, David J., 446
Aronson, Jack L., 3834
Arora, Sudesh, 3574
Arrington, Michael E., 106
Arthur, David J., 818
Arthur, Thomas H., 625
Arundel, Edna., 4445
Arwood, Victor B., 2570
Asan, Virginia M., 3713
Ashcraft, Robert R., 4108
Asher, Helen D., 3775
Ashley, Jo Ann, 3714
Askew, Thomas A., Jr., 581
Atkins, Eliza, 2526
Atkins, Jerome A., 331
Atkins, Noble J., 2709
Atwater, Elizabeth A., 3835
Auerbach, Eugene C., 4259
Austin, Florence O., 155
Auston, John T., 4260
Avaiolo, Frank J., 1880
Averette, George, Jr., 1718
Averill, Donald C., 338
Axen, Richard F., 1876
Ayres, Ethel S., 2916

Babb, Wylie S., 2263
Babbidge, Homer D., Jr., 2402
Bacon, John P., Jr., 1437
Bacote, C.A., 2873
Baer, Campion R., 3365
Baggett, Wallace E., 4261
Bagley, Ronald E., 1496
Bailen, Frank G., 3905
Bailey, Gilbert L., 2580
Bailey, Kenneth M., 1605
Bailey, Percival R., 4077
Bailey, Richard P., 3034
Bailey, Walter R., 3528
Bair, Lawrence, 2342
Bair, Martha A., 1098
Baird, James O., 2528

Baker, Clemon, 1433
Baker, Elaine, 493
Baker, Henry G., 1000
Baker, James K., 3688
Baker, John H., 2425
Baker, Michael R., 795
Baker, Susan S., 1719
Bakewell, Arthur L., 2301
Balkus, Mary P., 2805
Ball, Harry P., 2408
Ball, Robert J., 1225
Ballard, Robert M., Jr., 2810
Ballew, Laurie K., 4262
Bancroft, B. Richard, 1807
Bandy, Cheryl N.L., 1640
Bandy, Susan J., 3715
Bannon, Michael F., 47
Banowski, William S., 2637
Banzhof, Richard F., 4168
Baptista, Robert C., 3196
Barbeau, Joseph E., 3481
Barber, Gerald J., 2710
Barber, Richard E., 1995
Barber, William J., 680
Barclay, Kenneth B., 339
Bargerstock, Charles T., 4054
Baritz, Loren, 4263
Barker, Lincoln, 2818
Barker, Linda A., 2984
Barker, Ruel M., 3716
Barkovich, Frank S., 950
Barlow, Andrew L., 1165
Barlow, Mark, 3836
Barnard, Chester S., 1291
Barnard, Helen D., 2781
Barnard, Hilliard., 2586
Barnard, Virgil J., 2096
Barnes, Richard A., 1246
Barnett, Clarence R., 1996
Barnett, Mildred F., 2033
Barney, Joseph A., 1166
Barney, Robert K., 1641
Barnhardt, Robert A., 2948
Barosko, Samuel, Jr., 3122
Barr, Clifford V., 4068
Barraco, Anthony M., 1810
Barrese, Edward F., 4264
Barrett, Norbert C., 857
Barrick, William E., 4499
Barrier, Lynn P., 1910
Barron, James R., 993
Barry, James C., 3396
Barry, John H., Jr., 72
Barry, Ruth E., 4426
Bartis, Peter T., 436
Bartlett, Willard W., 2161
Bartok, Leslie A., 2322
Basham, Robert H., 99
Basham, Rosemary, 3837

Baskin, Henry L., 2726
Bass, Jack E., 858
Batchellor, Robert W., 2117
Bates, Katherine V., 859
Bates, Mary D., 1720
Bates, Ralph S., 4185
Bath, Joseph R., 3146
Battle, Margaret E., 1941
Bauer, Otto F., 730
Bauersfield, Stephanie H., 400
Baughman, Robert T., 418
Baum, Eugene L., 3179
Bauman, Harold E., 4169
Baxter, Cynthia L., 796
Baynham, Edward G., 2384
Beach, Mark B., 3123
Beach, Sister Francis Mary, 444
Beall, Noble Y., 3267
Beamon, Harry., 2527
Bean, Sandra K., 1986
Beard, Marshall R., 3776
Beardsley, Edward H., 3053
Beasley, Joan H., 317
Beasley, Leon O., 1009
Beasley, Thaddeus V., 3268
Beasley, Wallis, 2529
Beatty, Shelton L., 850
Beaulac, Ernest J., Jr., 1123
Beauregard, Erving E., 1997
Beck, Don E., 2638
Beck, Harry L., 3575
Beck, Julian, 109
Beck, Kenneth N., 626
Beck, Norman E., 3637
Becker, James M., 2934
Becnel, Joseph R., 1024
Bedenbaugh, Jefferson H., 2465
Beebe, George A., 1952
Beeler, Kent D., 781
Behee, John R., 1312
Beilke, Reuben, 3054
Belding, Lester C., 2481
Bell, David P., 2689
Bell, Dorothy E., 3667
Bell, James R., 84
Bell, Robert G., 925
Bell, Whitfield J., Jr., 2264
Bellefleur, John R., 1358
Belok, Michael V., 3600
Belson, Beverly A., 4531
Benitez de Avila, Crucita, 2419
Benjamin, Harold H., 3777
Bennett, Emerson S., 2455
Bennett, H.G., 2176
Bennett, Henry W., 49
Bennett, Hugh F., 1600
Bennett, Kenneth F., 1247
Bennett, Marilyn D., 2992
Bennett, Ray E., 2647

Benson, Keith R., 1085
Benson, Robert J., 849
Bentley, Anne, 2682
Benton, Edwin J., 1443
Berberian, Kevork, 1606
Berg, Walter L., 1167
Bergenthal, Hugo, 1696
Bergquist, David H., 1545
Berkman, Dave I., 3342
Bern, Paula R., 2398
Bernad, Miguel A., 3366
Bernert, Christopher J., 3644
Bernhard, Randall L., 2819
Berrian, George R., 1823
Berry, David C., 4003
Berry, Margaret C., 2782
Beshara, Anthony W., 1444
Best, Betty J., 185
Best, John H., 4265
Bethel, Leonard L., 2335
Betters-Reed, Bonita L., 3696
Betts, Leonidas J., Jr., 2949
Beutler, Albert J., 779
Bibus, Connie M., 3422
Bidlack, Russell E., 1313
Biehn, Albert L., 1546
Bienvenu, Harold J., 276
Bierds, Betty K., 1790
Bigelow, Cecil L., 835
Bigham, Wanda D., 3536
Billups, Helen K., 3029
Binder, John J., 3466
Bird, Nancy K., 3838
Birdsong, Irene B., 551
Birnbaum, Lucille T., 1086
Birney, Jane D., 582
Bishop, Raymond J., 996
Bjork, Richard E., 3778
Bjorklun, John, 1544
Blackburn, James C., 761
Blackwell, Velma L., 50
Blair, John E., 2737
Blake, Lincoln C., 627
Blake, Roger O., 2495
Blakely, Bernard E., 3172
Blakey, George T., 4266
Blankfort, Joelle R., 365
Blanton, Harry A., 3397
Blau, Guitta D., 1687
Bledsoe, Bennie G., 102
Blinderman, Abraham, 4028
Block, Robert F., 2118
Blockstein, Zaga, 2385
Bloom, Raymond, 1062
Bloom, Samuel B., 3576
Blostein, Stanley H., 4267
Blount, Lawanna M.L., 3668
Blume, Clarence J.M., 2874
Blume, Eli, 1697

Blunt, John, 4186
Bobinski, George S., 2040
Bode, Coeryne, 2195
Bodnarchuck, Steve, 917
Boehmer, Florence E., 4532
Boekenkamp, Richard P., 4187
Boelhauwer, Douglas, 1616
Boerigter, Robert J., 3197
Bogart, Ruth E., 1651
Boggs, Wade H., III, 1911
Bohl, Jacqueline, 222
Bole, Ronald E., 681
Bolick, Ernest B., Jr., 3398
Bolinder, Calvin H., 4371
Boll, John J., 3944
Bomhoff, Carl B., 340
Bonar, James A., 2265
Bond, James A., 951
Bonder, James B., 2266
Bonner, Harold G., 619
Bonniwell, Hilton T., 535
Bontekoe, Cornelius, 860
Booher, Dennis A., 2348
Boom, Kathleen W., 3669
Boon, Harold W., 4500
Boothe, Bradlee J., 198
Boozer, Howard R., 4268
Boram, William A., 3779
Borchardt, Lovie M., 530
Borehardt, Donald D., 1379
Born, William M., 3124
Borome, Joseph A., 1168
Borrowman, Merle L., 4446
Bortz, Jeanne M., 744
Borut, Michael, 4188
Bosse, Richard C., 1998
Bostrom, Harvey R., 4501
Bosworth, Ruth, 352
Bouchard, Louis M., 4269
Boudreau, Allan, 1831
Bouey, Sister Mary C., 3367
Boufford, Marjorie J., 2229
Bounds, Stuart M., 2875
Bouseman, John, 3180
Bowen, Erie J., 1399
Bowen, James S., 3269
Bowen, Keith A., 3198
Bower, Donald G., 223
Bowes, Harry P., 4372
Bowler, Mary M., 3368
Bowles, Elizabeth A., 1976
Bowman, Claude C., 3548
Bowman, Georgiana H., 2119
Bowman, Vernon L., 2244
Boycheff, Kooman, 628
Boyd, James H., 2670
Boyer, Edward S., 4170
Boyle, Thomas J., 1124
Brabham, Robert F., Jr., 1953

Bracey, William R., 1983
Brackett, Charles H., 152
Bradbury, Miles L., 1607
Bradley, Adelbert E., 19
Bradley, Bertha J., 20
Bradley, Carol J., 3945
Brady, William H., 2151
Braley, Ian, 4189
Brand, Barbara E., 4078
Brandis, Martha M., 1954
Brandom, Martha E., 3601
Brandstadter, Dianne P., 1931
Brandt, Gunther, 4270
Brannan, Joyce H., 2120
Brasfield, Elizabeth B., 37
Braxton, Harold E., 2944
Brayton, James H., 762
Brazee, Annie L., 277
Brazil, Doris J., 51
Breinan, Alexander, 4271
Bremer, Fred H., 3423
Brennan, Joseph W., 1523
Brenner, Johanna, 110
Brereton, Virginia L., 4502
Brewer, Tom B., 2783
Brewer, Wallace, 2177
Brick, Michael, 3424
Brickley, Donald P., 249
Bridges, Dennis L., 710
Bridgewater, Herbert G., 2201
Bridgforth, Lucie R., 1400
Brier, David H., 308
Brier, Ellen M., 1652
Briggs, Ernest E., 4055
Briggs, Harry H., 1999
Bright, John H., 2089
Brill, Earl H., 3399
Bringer, Howard L., 2152
Briscoe, Adelaide M., 2153
Briscoe, Georgia K., 256
Briscoe, Virginia W., 2297
Britt, Samuel S., Jr., 2937, 2966
Brittain, Raymond F., 4503
Brock, Michael G., 4171
Brock, Raymond T., 2178
Brock, Stephen C., 3577
Brockmeyer, Marta A., 3467
Brodsky, Paul L., 1104
Brogdon, Joseph M., 566
Bromberg, Ailene J., 1721
Bronson, Oswald P., 550
Brooke, Jr., William O., 3199
Brooks, Ben H., 2825
Brooks, Robert E., 366
Brooks, Thomas E., 52
Broomall, Lawrence W., 2267
Broome, Edwin C., 3147
Brough, Kenneth J., 3946
Broughton, James H., 494

Brower, Walter A., Jr., 1615
Brown, Alice W., 3125
Brown, Billye J., 2784
Brown, Charles K., 2968
Brown, Cynthia S., 3645
Brown, David R., 2700
Brown, Donald R., 583
Brown, Dorothy O., 2429
Brown, Emma W., 2876
Brown, F. Barry, 797
Brown, Genevieve S., 3270
Brown, Harry N., 2349
Brown, Harry W., 1025
Brown, Herman, 3271
Brown, Janie M., 3717
Brown, JoAnne, 4272
Brown, Lawrence S., 2202
Brown, Margaret J., 3549
Brown, Margaret, 1401
Brown, Martha A., 2386
Brown, Maurice F., Jr., 1169
Brown, Naomi B., 4533
Brown, Nathan, 1698
Brown, Robert O., 671
Brown, Seymour H., 1248
Brown, Sherman L., 111
Browning, Jane E.S., 3272
Browning, Robert G., 3670
Brueggemann, Walter A., 1083
Bruins, Elton J., 1599
Brundin, Robert E., 112
Bruner, Joyce E., 980
Brush, Carey W., 1801
Bruss, Melvin, 1435
Bruster, Bill G., 2204
Bryan, Alison R., 3671
Bryant, Mynora J., 3273
Bryce, Robert C., 3578
Bryson, Helen R., 1018
Bryson, Norris C., 1294
Buchanan, Marjorie H., 3055
Buck, Janet C., 278
Buckles, Eddie, 1411
Buckley, Grace L., 306
Buckley, Kerry W., 1087
Buckner, Reginald T., 901
Budge, Orla C., 113
Buell, Harold E., 2268
Buell, Harold L., 899
Buerki, Robert A., 3718
Buhler-Wilkerson, Karen A., 3719
Buhr, Gerhard R., 915
Buis, Almon R., 798
Bukalski, Peter J., 788
Bullock, Henry M., 528
Bullough, Robert V., Jr., 2121
Bulpitt, Mildred B., 81
Bunge, Helen L., 2041
Bunting, David E., 2730

Burdick, Alger E., 1713
Burk, Harry L., 4447
Burke, Colin B., 4392
Burke, Thomas R., 1509
Burks, John B., 536
Burn, Mary A., 3720
Burnett, Dorothy, 3274
Burnett, Howard R., 836
Burns, Mae A., 1819
Burns, Ralph E., 1419
Burns, Robert E., 243
Burr, Nelson R., 1580
Burrin, Frank K., 827
Burrows, Edward L., 478
Burton, C. Grant, 4029
Burwell, Ronald J., 4273
Busch, Carliss T., 3654
Busch, Stephen E., 3046
Bush, Joan D., 1282
Bush-Brown, Albert, 3176
Bushey, Richard J., 3839
Bushko, Andrew A., 4158
Bussell, N.E., 3721
Butcher, Paul A., 2240
Butler, Addie L.J., 3275
Butler, Daniel L., Jr., 1010
Butler, John H., 3672
Butler, M. Alene, 1684
Butt, William G., 1295
Buttell, Mary F., 3369
Butts, R. Freeman, 3482
Buysse, JoAnn, 1524
Buzza, David E., 2866
Byar, T. Madison, 4393
Byrd, John W., 3200
Byrnes, Don R., 2365
Bytheway, Ruth E., 3722

Cable, David B., 3111
Cable, Jane T., 1865
Cable, Nancy J., 2000
Cadwallader, Edward M., 1280
Cady, Henry L., 3840
Cahalan, Thomas L., 1838
Cain, Mary C., 1063
Cajoleas, Louis P., 1722
Calam, John H., 4159
Caldwell, Brenda S., 1812
Calhoun, David B., 1601
Calkins, Keith D., 186
Callison, Norman, 943
Calvert, Monte A., 4190
Calvert, Stanton C., 3550
Camden, Lillian H., 1562
Cameron, Alex J., 3602
Camfield, Thomas M., 4523
Campbell, Andrew M., 3603

Campbell, Bruce A., 1573
Campbell, Clarice T., 1439-1440
Campbell, Kenneth, 409
Campbell, Larry L., 926
Campbell, Leslie C., 1402
Campbell, Loren D., 1826
Campbell, Marie K., 775
Campbell, Sharon A.C., 1314
Campbell, William J., Jr., 2034
Canady, Hoyt P., Jr., 2445
Candon, Sarah A., 4427
Canfield, Muriel N., 745
Cangi, Ellen C., 2001
Cantrell, Loula N., 537
Cantrell, Roy H., 2196
Canuteson, Richard L., 1653
Capp, Glenn R., Jr., 3655
Capps, Marian P., 2877
Caram, Richard G., 3604
Carbone, Hector R., 2438
Card, Brigham Y., 4274
Carey, Alma P., 2950
Carey, James T., 4519
Carey, John P., 4030
Carlson, Alden L., 2917, 2930
Carlson, Bryan E., 3483
Carlson, William S., 1315
Carmichael, Yvonne C., 2203
Carothers, Otto M., Jr., 3056
Carpenter, Barbara L., 675
Carr, Howard E., 2581
Carr, Jack D., 789
Carrell, William D., 3551
Carrigg, Anne T., 3537
Carrington, Max R., 3350
Carrol, Carmal E., 3947
Carroll, Evelyn C.J., 3276
Carroll, James D., 3579
Carroll, Margaret M., 2247
Carroll, P. Thomas, 4191
Carroll, Raymond A., 4448
Carron, Blossom R., 1723
Carron, Malcolm T., 1791
Carson, Clayborne, Jr., 4373
Carson, Suzanne C., 2920
Carstensen, Vernon R., 861
Carter, Asa, 617
Carter, Carolyn J., 2503
Carter, E.J., 1946
Carter, Gayvon D., 464
Carter, Karl C., 4449
Carter, Susan B., 4534
Casale, John F., 3148
Caserta, John A., 1569
Casey, John J., 3370
Cashel, Patricia M., 279
Caskey, Gerald C., 1526
Cass, Walter J., 1234
Cassidy, Francis P., 3371

Casteel, James D., 4031
Castleberry, Martha A.F., 2587
Castro, Apolinario, 2420
Caswell, Render R., 525
Catenacci, Edward N., 3605
Cates, David A., 199
Cathcart, Maude E., 4192
Cather, George D., 265
Catlin, Daniel, Jr., 367
Cato, William H., 2878
Caton, Lewis H., Jr., 2411
Caton, W. Barnie, 1642
Causey, Patricia D.A., 1403
Cavanna, Robert C., 3089
Caver, Joseph D., 18
Cayton, Leonard B., 2179
Caywood, Elzie R., 2200
Cederborg, Hazel P., 738
Chadwick, James C., 1985
Chadwick, Ronald P., 3484
Chaffin, Nora C., 1932
Chait, Richard P., 3277
Chamberlain, Lawrence C., 425
Chambers, Carole Z., 720
Chambers, Frederick, 96
Chambers, Stephen L., 3780
Champlin, Carroll D., 4018
Chandlee, Elmer K., 1064
Chapel, Robert C., 1316
Chapman, Anne W., 2900
Chapman, Oscar J., 1076, 3278
Chappell, Diane L., 3841
Charles, Allan D., 2446
Charles, Milton R., 4394
Charlton, David H., 4395
Charvat, Arthur, 1866
Chase, William G., 584
Chaudry, Muhammad A., 3580
Cheek, Neal K., 1955
Cheek, William F., III, 429
Cheeves, Lyndell D., 217
Chelf, Carl P., 952
Chen, Victor W.K., 3689
Chenette, Edward B., 1520
Cheslik, Helen E., 3279
Chestnut, Erma R., 1851
Cheuvront, Harold R., 3149
Chiappetta, Michael, 4450
Chisholm, Linda A., 4494
Christensen, James W., 4451
Christenson, Richard D., 1362
Christiansen, Grace V.T., 2853
Christiansen, Persturla A., 4193
Christie, Dudley B., 533
Christopher, Nehemiah M., 2588
Christy, Teresa E., 1724
Chu, Buoy-mun, 114
Church, Frances E., 3948
Church, Martha F., 2071

Church, Robert L., 1170
Churchill, Ralph D., 2747
Churgin, Jonah R., 4535
Churovia, Robert M., 2319
Chute, William J., 1725
Cina, Carol, 4275
Cipic, Margaret S., 3680
Cissell, William B., 3723
Citro, Joseph F., 53
Citron, Henry, 3581
Clancy, Lynn R., Jr., 115
Clark, Florence E., 4276
Clark, John L., 3842
Clark, Robert R., 3022
Clark, Sulayman, 2306
Clarke, Adele E., 4194
Clarke, Charles M., 4452
Clary, George E., Jr., 554
Claudson, William D., 1845
Clayborne, William M., 2879
Clayton, Bonnie C.W., 3724
Cleary, Marie, 3843
Clees, William J., 2310
Clem, Lawrence V., 54
Clement, Rufus E., 1912
Clement, Stephen M., III, 1898
Clements, Patricia L., 3126
Cleveland, Truman, 2814
Click, Donald W., 3606
Clifton, Nancy P., 3425
Clinefelter, Ruth W., 2023
Clinger, Morris M., 3844
Clithero, Edith P., 785
Close, William E., 4511
Clough, Dick B., 2504
Clover, Haworth A., 212
Clowse, Barbara B., 4056
Clutter, Bill G., 1099
Clutter, Ronald T., 1602
Clymer, Benjamin F., Jr., 1956
Coad, Nola E., 2667
Coates, Lawrence G., 4024
Coats, Kenneth W., 1537
Cobb, Justin L., 3201
Coburn, Frances G., 3025
Cochran, James C., 2690
Cochran, John P., 2942
Cochrane, Cornelius R., Jr., 3202
Cochrane, Mary A., 2785
Cochrane, Robert M., 2530
Cocking, Herbert, 3112
Cockrell, Frank S., 2755
Coe, George R., 3203
Coffey, Margaret A., 3725
Coffey, Thomas J., 791
Cognard, Anne M.M., 2766
Cohen, Arthur M., 484
Cohen, Marcine J., 3995
Cohen, Marilyn S., 441

Cohen, Paul E., 1171
Cole, Brian A., 629
Cole, Cathy L., 953
Cole, Edgar B., 1867
Cole, Harper L., Jr., 2578
Cole, John Y., 437
Cole, Mary A., 2072
Cole, Tommie J., 85
Colebank, Albert D., 3030
Coleman, John P., 851
Coleman, Paul E., 2049
Coleman, Robert M., 1832
Colgrove, Pitt P., 4453
Colla, Sister Maria B., 361
Collins, Betty J., 2496
Collins, Charles R.J., 1688
Collins, Robert M., 852
Collins, Wellyn F., 979
Collinwood, Dean W., 4512
Colman, Gould P., 1792
Colozzi, John J., 3607
Colston, James A., 495
Colucci, Nicholas D., Jr., 341
Colvin, Lloyd W., 2248
Combs, Kermit S., Jr., 994
Come, Donald R., 1608
Comer, John R., 2589
Comm, Walter, 116
Conant, Coit, 3204
Conard, Erik P., 902
Conard, Wilbern E., 4428
Condell, Robert, 2518
Conger, George R., III, 630
Conklin, Mary W., 862
Conlin, James W., 834
Conmy, Peter T., 156
Connelly, Annie L., 2694
Conner, George, 1088
Connolly, Mary K., 3372
Connor, Donald B., 318
Connors, Manning A., Jr., 4172
Conrath, Richard C., 4396
Conroy, Katherine, 981
Consalus, Charles E., 1581
Content, Mary, 4032
Conway, G. Allan, 1654
Conway, Jerry D., 255
Conway, Jill K., 4536
Conyers, Charline F.H., 2307
Cook, Anne W., 799
Cook, Bruce F., 3845
Cook, Elizabeth S., 2090
Cook, Elsie J., 1988
Cook, H. Moreland, 4277
Cook, James F., 496
Cook, John F., 3057
Cook, Paul B., 4154
Cook, Thomas H., 845
Cook, Wayne S., 3582

Cookingham, Mary E., 4537
Cooper, Arnold, 3280
Cooper, Brian L., 4278
Cooper, Harold J., Jr., 1249
Cooper, Winnie M., 244
Cope, Garrett, 800
Copenhaver, Harold L., 3846
Cordaro, Russell T., 2880
Cordasco, Francesco M., 1089
Cormier, Sister Marie C., 1579
Cornehlsen, John H., Jr., 2867
Cornell, Frederic, 1846
Cornell, Thomas D., 407
Cornell, William A., 2269
Cornette, James P., 1007
Corrie, Bruce A., 3205
Corson, Louis D., 3127
Cortes, Kathleen F., 3726
Corvin, Raymond O., 4109
Cosgriffe, Harry A., 2969
Cosgrove, Owen G., 2639
Costantino, Nicholas V., 1223
Coughlan, Neil P., 4033
Coulton, Thomas E., 4279
Covert, James R., 3552
Covington, Patricia B., 746
Cowan, John R., Jr., 1525
Cowperthwaite, Lowery L, 863
Cox, Alice C., 2786
Cox, Dwayne D., 982
Cox, James N., 224
Cox, John E., 2803
Cox, Marvin L, 614
Coyer, William J., 2122
Coyner, Ruth E., 4454
Coyte, Donna E., 983
Craddock, Bettye, 2752
Craig, Earl L., 2640
Craig, James T., 1510
Craig, John D., 2738
Craig, Richard H., 2815
Craig, Robert M., 737
Crain, Charles R., 2505
Craine, M.K., 3485
Crane, Theodore R., 2430
Cranford, Janet P., 1957
Crary, Ryland W., 864
Craven, Clifford J., 1868
Crawford, Allan P., 2970
Crawford, Esther K., 3181
Cremer, Henry, 2971
Cretzmeyer, Jane, 865
Creutz, Alan, 1317
Cristo, Anthony B., 2881
Crone, Douglas C., 1689
Cronin, Kathleen J., 1521
Cronin, Timothy F., 2985
Cronk, Ernest L, 2993
Crossley, Samuel M., 2590

Crotty, Daniel L., Jr., 3542
Crowder, Eleanor L.M., 2591
Crowley, John C., 3583
Crumlish, Sister John Mary, 1109
Cullen, Maurice R., 1296
Cullum, Edward N., 2531
Culpepper, Marilyn M., 1297
Culver, Daniel, 866
Cummings, Donald L, 4004
Cunliffe, William E., 2249
Cunning, Ellen T., 2407
Cunningham, J. David, 2230
Cunningham, Lee C., 3206
Curl, Carroll A., 2642
Curl, Lottie M., 532
Curley, Thomas E., Jr., 1806
Currie, Bruce F., 3781
Curry, Betty L., 562
Curry, Leonard P., 3928
Curry, Myron M., 3343
Curtis, Dunstan E.F., 2986
Curtis, Marcia, 368
Curtis, Orville B., 867
Curtis, William J., 1172
Cutler, Mary E., 4195
Cutrer, Thomas W., 1026
Czarniewicz, Casimir M., 3351

Dabney, Lillian G., 404
Daggy, Robert E., 369
Dalen, Adrian E., 2497
Daley, Billy D., 2592
Daley, John M., 970
Dalke, Jacob J., 927
Dallinger, Carl A., 1445
Dalton, Thomas C., 2925
Dalton, Ulysses G., III, 97
Daly, Richard F., 4455
Dalzell, Arthur H., 928
Dameron, Ronald F., 3929
Damico, Claude S., 1582
Damm, Helmut H., 1318
Damon, Ruth A., 3847
Dandalides, Des A., 2002
Dane, John H., 3673
Daniel, Carolyn A., 1958
Daniel, Helen T., 1404
Daniels, James E., 3638
Daniels, Mary A., 2123
Danielson, Melvin D., 207
Danilov, Victor J., 3128
Danna, Debra, 2787
Dannelly, Clarence M., 4110
Danskin, Warren L., 1564
Darby, MacArthur, 801
Darian, Steven G., 3848
Dark, Harris J., 631

Darling, Elmer C., 838
Dattoli, Randall T., 759
Davenport, Harold D., 1943
David, Virgil E., 2073
Davidson, Edgar O., 2350
Davidson, Levette J., 3849
Davidson, Phillip L., 3468
Davidson, Robert C., 4155
Davies, Frederick G., 868
Davies, Sarah M., 219
Davies, Shannon M., 4196
Davis, Betty, 2571
Davis, Brenda L.H., 430
Davis, Earl C., 1596
Davis, Frank B., 3182
Davis, James A., 2897
Davis, James M., 3782
Davis, Julian, 1478
Davis, Lenwood G., 1944
Davis, Mollie C., 4397
Davis, William E., 309
Davis, Yvonne H., 3281
Davison, Oscar W., 2180
Dawald, Victor F., 1380
Dawson, Edward B., 1319
Dawson, Eugene D., 1298
Day, Robert W., 1
Dayton, David M., 2323
De Loney, Willie L., 55
Dean, Larrie J., 1857
Dean, Mark E., 792
Dean, Martha C., 4280
Deatherage, J. Dal, 3167
deB. Beaver, Donald, 4197
Deboer, Ray L., 2820
Decker, James T., 3469
Decker, Rodger W., 1984
Dedman, W. Wayne, 4281
Dee, Frank P., 1617
Deering, Thomas E., 3094
Dees, Charles R., Jr., 4362
Delaney, Peter H., II, 3486
Delfraisse, Betty D., 2226
DelGiorno, Bette J., 4198
Dell, George W., 632
Dellasega, Charles J., 2212
DelPizzo, Ferdinand, 1497
Demartini, Joseph R., 682
Demerly, John A., 1609
Denbo, Marilou, 2901
Denbo, Philip G., 329
Denman, William F., 670
Dennis, Philip M., 3783
Densford, John P., 4034
Denton, Edgar, III, 1881
DePew, John N., 3949
Deputy, Manfred W., 802
Deschamps, Nello E., 4160
Desjarlais-Lueth, Christine, 2431

Desmond, Richard L., 3639
Detrick, Raymond O., 2159
Deutsch, Lucille S., 2462
DeVine, Mary L.J., 4398
DeViney, Charles E., 3487
Dewar, John D., 929
Dewese, James E., 2775
Dewey, Clifford S., 895
Dewey, Mary E., 4429
DeWoody, George M., 1446
Deyoung, Henry G., 4399
Dial, Henry C., 86
Diaz, Albert J., 1959
DiBiasio, Daniel A., 2124
Dickens, Marion R., 3727
Dickerman, Watson B., 3488
Dickerson, Kay W., 2029
Dickerson, Milton O., Jr., 3282
Dickey, Otis, 923
Dickey, Rex H., 971
Dickinson, Augustus C., 2
Dickinson, William C., 2648
Diebolt, Alfred L., 1844
Diederich, Alphonsus F., 117
Diener, Thomas J., 3426
Dietrich, Marietta, 2324
Dillard, Carra G., 2902
Dillard, Walter S., 1882
Dillingham, George A., Jr., 2532
Dillon, Kristine E., 4400
Dilweg, Joan K., 574
DiMichele, Charles C., 1405
Diner, Steven J., 633
Dinniman, Andrew E., 2413
Dipietro, Frank S., 1578
Dixon, Blaise P., 410
Dixon, Henry W., 3373
Dobbertin, Gerald F., 4282
Dobbin, Paul R., 945
Dobrunz, Carol A., 3681
Dodge, Ellen E., 4283
Dodge, Norman B., 315
Dodrill, Charles W., 2162
Dodson, Pat S., 2593
Donnan, Annette W., 1417
Donnelly, John F., 1913
Donnelly, Thomas H., 4374
Donovan, Charles F., 4035
Dooher, Philip M., 1125
Dooley, Mary E., Sr., 2062
Doran, Adron, 954
Doran, Kenneth T., 1655
Doran, Micheileen J., 1825
Dorrance, David B., 2056
Dotson, James R., 3
Doty, Franklin A., 869
Doughty, Sylvia J.K., 4284
Downey, J. Paul, 2579
Doyle, Joseph, 1726

Drachler, Norman, 1320
Drachman, Virginia G., 4538
Draper, Owen H., 4
Dreves, Vivian E., 3010
Drost, Walter H., 1727
Dryer, Linnie, 4456
Duerre, Chester W., 2498
Duffy, Christopher G., 3906
Duffy, William E., 3850
Duke, Lila K.W., 2181
Dunbar, Henry F., 3728
Dunbar, Willis F., 1250
Duncan, Anne M., 431
Duncan, Frances H., 2649
Duncan, Ruth B., 2533
Duncan, William N., 2711
Dunigan, David R., 1149
Dunlap, E.T., 2182
Dunlea, Thomas A., 1126
Dunleavy, Jeannette J., 319
Dunn, Edward T., 1173
Dunnington, Nellie B., 1471
Durham, James G., 964
Duval, Earl H., Jr., 3207
Duvall, Sylvanus M., 4111
Dwyer, Kathleen M., 3729
Dwyer, Richard E., 1618
Dyess, Stewart W., 2594
Dykman, Dorothy J., 3352

Eagan, Eileen M., 4375
Earl, Charles D., 3208
Earnshaw, Jeannine, 2366
Easterling, Henry W., Jr., 4005
Easton, Theodore A., 1529
Eaton, Joan D., 1960
Ebersole, Mark C., 2367
Eckert, Richard S., 1127
Eddy, Edward D., Jr., 3913
Edelson, Ivan J., 3129
Edmund, Gertrude M., 4539
Edsall, Margaret H., 2933
Edwards, Austin, Jr., 974
Edwards, Charles S., 2296
Edwards, Dorothy L., 1001
Edwards, Earle L., 2351
Edwards, Harry E., 3489
Edwards, Kenneth L, 3427
Edwards, Margaret R., 2650
Edwards, Marsha, 3640
Edwards, Nancy J., 3428
Edwards, Ralph, 1447
Egan, Margaret L., 1656
Ehrenfried, Michael, 2035
Ehrmann, Stephen C., 4199
Eichlin, Arthur S., 1090
Eikelmann, Kenneth P., 1485

Eiland, Dianna K., 930
Eklund, Lowell R., 1299
Elder, Fred K., 2447
Eldridge, Janice C., 4200
Elias, Louis, Jr., 1418
Elkins, Floyd S., 3429
Ellenwood, Theodore S., 259
Ellingsworth, June E., 465
Elliott, Arlene A., 2317
Elliott, Clark A., 4201
Ellis, Alan, 1174
Ellis, Elizabeth, 1321
Ellis, Leslie E., 466
Ellis, Peter D., 4457
Ellsworth, Clayton S., 2097
Ellsworth, Frank L., 634
Elmes, Robert J., 803
Elsea, Janet G., 157
Elson, Beverly L, 438
Elwell, Donald B., 3150
Emerson, Bruce, 2882
Emmanuel, Narbeth, 2036
Emmeson, Fred B., 1914
Engar, Keith M., 2854
Engel, John W., 1381
Engel, Robert E., 839
Enger, William R., 1961
England, Bobby L., 2734
Engle, Gale W., 635, 3851
Engley, Donald B., 1141
Engram, Irbi D., 518
Enion, Ruth C., 2403
Entin, Nathaniel A., 1657
Epler, Stephen M., 229
Epstein, Sandra P., 158
Epting, James B., 39
Erbacher, Sebastian A., 3374-3375
Erenberg, Phyllis V., 3406
Erickson, Ernest W., 3950
Erickson, George O., 1396
Erpestad, Emil, 612
Esch, Marvin L., 1322
Eschenbacher, Herman F., Jr., 1091, 2440
Eskow, Seymour, 1658
Etheridge, Carroll D., 3697
Evans, Benjamin R., 2164
Evans, Floyd C., 2776
Evans, George K., 2534
Evans, Henry B., 4112
Evans, James M., 254
Evans, John W., 3376
Evans, Kenneth J., Jr., 4376
Evans, Samuel W., 2213
Ewing, James W., 4430
Ewing, John C., 4285
Ezell, Ernest B., Jr., 2125
Ezor, Edwin L., 3608

Fadil, Virginia A., 747
Fagerberg, Seigfred W., 1438
Fairey, Jerry, 2777
Fales, Martha J.H., 3730
Falk, Gerhard, 1659
Falk, Ursula A., 4286
Fallon, Jerome A., 1323
Falu-Pesante, Georgina, 2421
Fancher, Evelyn P., 2566
Fanning, James D., 2680
Farley, Delbert R., 3553
Farmakis, George L., 4495
Farmer, Blake L., 2746
Farmer, Donna J., 3554
Farquhar, Catherine B., 946
Farr, Cleburne L., 636
Farrell, Harry C., Jr., 2757
Farrell, Richard A., 3933
Farrow, Mildred H., 1940
Faulkner, Charles M., 1547
Faulkner, Maurice E., 3852
Faurer, Judson C., 3490
Faust, Hugh G., 2183
Faverman, Gerald A., 1251
Fay, Maureen A., 637
Fearing, Bertie E., 1950
Featherstone, J.M., 638
Fedje, Raymond N., 3674
Feeler, William, 300
Fehlig, Mary B., 3377
Fehr, Carl A., 2903
Feigenbaum, Carl E., 4287
Feinstein, Irving N., 1699
Feinstein, Milton D., 976
Feldman, Rochelle C., 4540
Fellows, Frederick H., 1175
Felshin, Janet R., 3731
Fenster, Valmai R., 3058
Ference, Regina C., 2309
Ferguson, Janet S., 220
Ferguson, John A.M., 3555
Ferguson, Paul W., 3470
Ferree, A.W., 2883
Ferrell, Hanson D., 1728
Ferris, Charles W., Jr., 1879
Ferris, Millicent M., 3656
Fetner, Gerald L., 4079
Fewell, Roberta J., 2308
Fiegel, Melvin F., 2224
Field, Earle, 1869
Field, Faye B., 1176
Fields, Ralph R., 1074
Fields, Thomas B., 780
Filkins, James H., 1574
Fillinger, Louis C., 323
Findlay, James F., 3529
Findlay, Ross P., 2845

Fink, Jerome S., 3407
Finkelstein, Martin J., 3556
Finklea, J.J., 497
Finley, John M., 995
Finn, Thomas, 3609
Finney, Raymond A., 2563
Fiorello, James R., 1241
Fish, Everett D., and Kayser, Kathryn E., 918
Fisher, Berenice M., 3353
Fisher, Donald, 3675
Fisher, Lois A., 3930
Fisher, Michael P., 931
Fisher, Paul G., 2334
Fisher, Philip A., 3853
Fisher, Raymond H., 1177
Fisher, Regina B., 2951
Fisher, Robert B., 1842
Fisher, Scott A., 1163
Fisher, William B., 1426
Fisk, Gertrude M., 2250
Fiske, Emmett P., 159
Fitts, Dora A., 2727
Fitzelle, Albert E., 1660
Fitzgerald, Pauline J., 1858
Fitzgerald, Peter H., 3914
Fitzpatrick, Ellen F., 4541
Fitzpatrick, Louise, 3732
Flaherty, Mary B., 257
Flaherty, Terrance J., 1178
Flahive, Robert F., 3043
Flath, Arnold W., 3209
Fleischer, Michael M., 3210
Fleischer, Robert D., 2270
Fleming, Cynthia A., 2506
Fleming, Daniel B., Jr., 4288
Fleming, George M., 4401
Fleming, Rhonda K., 2479
Fleming, Yancy B., 2767
Fletcher, Juanita D., 2098
Fletcher, Robert C., 683
Fletcher, Robert S., 2099
Flexner, Hans, 2868
Fley, Jo Ann, 4431
Flicker, Bernard, 4036
Flood, Gerald J., 1092
Florell, David M., 230
Flowers, Elsie A.M., 4289
Foerster, Alma P., 4368
Fogarty, Gerald P., 411
Fogdall, Vergil S., 870
Fogle, Rick A., 3084
Foley, Patrick J., 160
Follbaum, Terry D., 1252
Forbes, Theodore W., 3211
Ford, Charles E., 4202
Ford, Frederick R., 3130
Ford, Helen L., 2557
Ford, Hoyt, 2595
Forman, Sidney, 1883

Forst, Arthur C., Jr., 359
Fortin, Charles C., 1370
Foss, Jean L., 3733
Foss, Robert N., 3430
Foster, Elaine E., 1729
Foster, James C., 4080
Foster, Margery S., 1179
Foster, Parker V., 3915
Foster, Pauline P., 2341
Foster, Robert B., 3854
Fouche, James F., 1050
Fought, Carol A., 3491
Foulger, James R., 2821
Fouts, Theron J., 2596
Fowler, Queen E.D., 1511
Fowler, William B., 1422
Fox, Frederick G., 118
Foxx, Virginia A., 1974
Fraley, Angela E., 3492
Franck, Michel N., 4290
Frank, Frederick J., 4402
Frank, Thomas E., 4037
Franklin, Bernard W., 3283
Franks, Marie S., 2671
Franks, Peter E., 4291
Franz, Evelyn B., 1625
Fraser, Walter J., Jr., 2926
Frazier, Joseph M., 2184
Frazier, Robert C., 73
Freedberg, Sharon, 1232
Freeman, David D., Jr., 5
Freeman, William H., 2251
Freeman, William W., 1486
Freidus, Anne, 1833
Freitag, Alfred J., 1538
French, Roger F., 2744
French, William M., 1661
Freund, Clare E., 2368
Freund, Emma J., 1448
Frey, Robert W., 2154
Friedman, Henry A., 260
Friel, Mary E., 1162
Fries, Walter G., 2448
Frindell, Harold M., 3212
Fritz, Charles A., 4292
Fritz, John E., 1951
Froehlich, Edna P., 119
Fromm, Glenn E., 1626
Frost, Gary J., 2924
Fruechtel, Warren B., 2271
Frueh, Anna, 4293
Fry, James W., 2126
Fuchs, Kenneth D., 1373
Fugal, John P., 2826
Fujimoto, Sumie, 568
Fullbright, Wilbur D., 3855
Fuller, Katherine B., 41
Fuller, Lawrence B., 3493
Fulton, Martha W., 467

Furman, Necah F., 2801
Furner, Mary O., 4294
Furstenberg, Barbara J., 3557
Furtado, Lorraine T., 3494
Furuichi, Suguru, 2127
Fye, W. Bruce, 1180

Gacek, Edward J., 3431
Galbreath, Clarence R., 2320
Gale, Barbara R., 3584
Gallagher, Carol T., 1730
Gallagher, Edward A., 3432
Gallagher, James P., 3378
Gallaspy, Harold T., 1415
Galliano, Vernon F., 1048
Gallot, Mildred B., 1019
Galvin, James M., 3379
Gambrell, Herbert P., 2651
Gampper, Mary M., 4295
Gannon, Russell J., 2855
Gappa, LaVon M., 1548
Garber, Lee O., 4006
Gardiner, Helen J., 3856
Gardner, David P., 161
Gardner, Frederick P., 3784
Garren, Charles M., 1928
Garrett, Donald E., 676
Garrett, John L., Jr., 1011
Garrett, R.T., 3018
Garwood, Harry C., 4113
Garza, George J., 3433
Gass, W. Conard, 1093
Gates, Charlynne M.L., 180
Gates, Samuel E., 266
Gatewood, Willard B., Jr., 1962
Gatner, Elliott S.M., 1822
Gault, Lon A., 120
Gaunt, Roger N., 2943
Gavurin, Lester L., 4203
Gawalt, Gerard W., 1128
Gawrysiak, Kenneth J., 3048
Gay, Leslie F., Jr., 267
Gay, Robert E., 3213
Gaylord, Mark S., 804
Gayton, Carver C., 3585
Gearity, James L., 3035
Gee, Robert, 1382
Gee, Ruth E., 2724
Geiger, C. Harve, 4114
Gelfand, Morris A., 3951
Geller, Marjorie A., 1619
Geltner, Frank J., Jr., 3857
Genaway, David C., 1383
Gengel, Kenneth O., 3113
George, Arthur A., 1942
George, Leonard F., 2222
George, Melvin R., 721

Gerber, Daniel R., 302
Gering, William M., 805
Gerrity, Thomas W., 3495
Gersman, Elinor M., 1449
Gerth, Donald R., 121
Getts, Paul R., 2272
Getz, Gene A., 718
Gevitz, Norman, 4081
Gibbon, Peter H., 1813
Gibbons, Harold E., 2597
Gibbs, Clifford L., 2778
Gibson, De Lois, 105
Gibson, J'nelle S., 3151
Gibson, J.C., 498
Giddens, Thomas R., 4363
Giebel, Arlyn J., 1374
Gieryn, Thomas F., 4204
Gifford, James F., Jr., 1933
Gignilliat, Elizabeth L, 499
Gilbride, M. James, 2059
Giles, Dorcus O., 2469
Giles, Frederic P., 3858
Gill, Jerry L., 2208
Gilleland, Diane S., 87
Gillespie, James R., 758
Gillette, Donald R., 1300
Gilliland, John H., 200
Gillis, Herbert R., 426
Gilson, James E., 871
Gimper, Eileen R., 2311
Ginsberg, Alan H., 4296
Ginter, Eloise T., 872
Gipe, Florence M., 1065
Giunta, Mary A., 2939
Gladen, Frank H., Jr., 65
Glauert, Ralph E., 1450
Glazener, S.M., 2678
Glazer, Stanford H., 1253
Glick, Walter R., 2598
Glotzer, Richard S., 3284
Glover, Thomas H., 4205
Glovinsky, Arnold, 4458
Glynn, John J.A., 412
Gober, Ruth B., 3610
Godbey, Edsel T., 955
Goddard, Aylene D., 1324
Godfrey, Noel D., 1052
Godson, William F.H., 1884
Goggins, Lathardus, 2047
Golann, Ethel, 1181
Goldberg, Barbara L.S., 63
Golden, Donna L, 201
Goldman, David I., 3496
Gonino, Vincent J., 1802
Good, Howard A., 4082
Goode, Elizabeth A., 370
Goode, James M., 4524
Goodhartz, Abraham S., 1662
Goodman, Alvin H., 3859

Goodman, Michael, 1597
Goodrich, Martha H., 2243
Goodwin, Gregory L., 3434
Goodwin, Louis C., 3285
Gorchels, Clarence C., 2988
Gordon, Ann D., 2369
Gordon, Eleanor W., 2155
Gordon, James F., Jr., 1413
Gordon, Joseph E., 4069
Gordon, Judith B.H., 4297
Gordon, Lynn D., 4542
Gordon, Sheila C., 1700
Gorka, Ronald R., 427
Gough, Jerry B., 4206
Gould, David A., 1129
Gould, Florine R., 538
Gould, Joseph E., 639
Gould, Robert C., 3152
Goulding, Joel A., 4513
Goulding, Robert L., 447
Grabow, Wesley, J.F., 1384
Grabowski, John, 2871
Grady, Eugene J., 3435
Grady, Marilyn, 2128
Grafton, Carl T., 4364
Graham, Blanche E.O., 1627
Graham, Hardy P., 1427
Graham, Robert H., 3059
Granade, Charles J., 500
Granade, Samuel R., 6
Grant, Margaret A., 1686
Grant, William H., 1731
Grauls, Paul A., 4038
Graver, Lee A., 2273
Gray, A.A., 3436
Gray, Billy R., 3785
Gray, Charles E., 748
Gray, David W., 2898
Gray, George T., 1837
Gray, Gordon W., 3497
Gray, Leona S., 2743
Gray, Marvin R., 776
Graybeal, Susan E., 1385
Grayson, Gerald H., 1701
Green, Charles E., 2470
Green, Clarence D., 1359
Green, Grace H., 1254
Green, James M., 1142
Green, Lawrence J., 3214
Green, Marvin, 88
Green, Philip F., 2129
Greenberg, Estelle F., 4298
Greenberg, Howard, 3786
Greene, Margaret D., 3734
Greene, Mary H., 1836
Greene, Rebecca S., 4083
Greene, Robert J., 1859
Greenfield, Esther, 1002
Greenwald, Eli B., 3910

Greenwood, Keith M., 3646
Greer, James J., 1120
Greer, Martha J., 539
Gregerson, Edna J., 2843
Gregory, Earle S., 684
Grennan, Kevin F., 4039
Gresham, Charles R., 1153
Grev, Julian R., 1375
Grieder, Freida A., 4543
Griess, Thomas E., 1885
Griffin, Kevin J., 4459
Griffin, Paul R., 3286
Griffin, Robert P., 461
Griffith, Betty R., 3860
Griffiths, Nellie L., 640
Griggs, Walter S., Jr., 2940
Grigsby, Donald L., 4207
Grimes, John O., 1255
Grimes, Lewis H., 4115
Grimes, Lloyd, 1451
Grinnell, John E., 3183
Grishman, Lee H., 2822
Grisso, Karl M., 685
Grissom, Preston B., 2756
Griswold, Ardyce M., 1082
Gross, Elmer A., 2352
Gross, Walter E., 4208
Grossley, Richard S., 3287
Grossman, David M., 4299
Grotzinger, Laurel A., 686
Gruber, Carol S., 4525
Gruber, Christian P., 1182
Gruensfelder, Melvin, 3215
Guckert, John C., 3647
Guder, Darrell L., 1610
Guemple, John R., 2812
Guffin, Jan A., 731
Guion, Harvey M., 1870
Gullickson, Richard A., 3023
Gunn, Jack W., 2652
Gunn, Virgil R., 1631
Gunnell, Reid J., 3735
Guralnick, Stanley M., 4209
Gurnick, Stanley I., 3354
Gurr, Charles S., 501
Gustafson, Alburn M., 66
Gustafson, David, 641
Gustafson, Robert K., 2468
Guthrie, Warren A., 3657
Guynne, Albert C., 3216
Guyotte, Roland L., III, 4040
Gwaltney, John W., 585
Gwynn, John M., 3498

Ha, Inho, 3787
Haas, Francis, 1632
Haase, Richard T., 2499

Hackett, John R., 2441
Hackney, Rufus R., Jr., 3217
Haddow, Anna, 4300
Hagen, Joel B., 4210
Haines, George L., 1603
Haines, George, IV, 3934
Hair, Mary Jane S., 2823
Hakanson, Eugene E., 3558
Hakkio, Joan S., 732
Hale, Charles E., 3952
Hale, Morris S., Jr., 448
Hale, Nathan G., Jr., 3996
Hale, Toby A., 3400
Halfond, Jay A., 3788
Hall, Allan W., 2274
Hall, Barbara C., 4544
Hall, Clifton L., 3559
Hall, Helen L., 2994
Hall, Ida J., 2535
Hall, James C., 3160
Hall, John G., 103
Hall, Julia A.O., 371
Hall, Margaret A., 2995
Hall, Morris E., 2712
Hall, Peter W., 1963
Hall, Reginald W., 27
Hall, Sylvester R., 3218
Hall, William F., 2521
Halm, Dennis R., 214
Halttunen, William R., 2275
Hamar, Clifford E., 3861
Hamel, Dana B., 2050
Hamilton, Hallie J., 586
Hamilton, Penny R., 3736
Hamilton, Zona, 502
Hammer, Gerald K., 618
Hammond, Brenda H., 2562
Hancock, Judith A., 587
Hangartner, Carl A., 4496
Hange, Philip E., 3935
Hankin, John F., 2856
Hankins, Martha L., 2672
Hanks, Paul A., 3936
Hanle, Robert V., 4116
Hanley, Francis X., 2312
Hanna, Glenn A., 1993
Hanna, Thomas H., 998
Hannah, James J., 1549
Hans, Patricia H., 3173
Hansbrough, Vivian M., 89
Hansen, James E., II, 2432
Hansen, Janet S., 3586
Hansen, Jessie, 479
Hansen, Kenneth H., 4041
Hansen, Lorentz I., 1130
Hanson, Merle J., 1325
Hanson, Norman C., 903
Hanson, Richard S., 2485
Haran, William J., 4042

Harcleroad, Fred F., Jr., 4403
Hardcastle, Pat, 2641
Harden, Victoria A., 3737
Hardin, Thomas L., 588
Hardin, Willie, 3288
Harding, Alfred D., 1519
Harding, Thomas S., 3184
Hardy, John B., 3437
Haritos, Dolores J., 3738
Harker, John S., 1148
Harkins, Richard H., 153
Harlan, William L., 2599
Harms, Herman E., 4404
Harms, William B., 3219
Harney, Paul J., 122
Harper, Hoyt H., 516
Harper, James C., 7
Harper, John R., 2087
Harper, William S.G., 3114
Harris, Benedict O., 3095
Harris, Daniel S., Jr., 4117
Harris, Emily F., 2185
Harris, James B., 1929
Harris, Janette H., 432
Harris, John F., 1044
Harris, John M., 3862
Harris, Jonathan, 1663
Harris, Michael R., 4043
Harris, Theodore D., 1886
Harris, Virgie, 3013
Harris, Woodrow W., 2932
Harris, Yvonne B., 2467
Harrison, Ardie R., 2600
Harrison, Carolyn P., 3658
Harrison, Fred, Jr., 3916
Harrison, Margaret T., 2904
Harrison, Marjorie D., 4019
Harrison, Rodman P., 589
Harrison, Theta, 4020
Harrold, Kenneth R., 2343
Hart, Alfred B., 2848
Hart, Casper P., 1113
Hart, Claude, 575
Hartman, Paul T., 1183
Hartman, Van A., 2353
Hartman, William F., 324
Harton, Helen L., 1256
Hartsell, Lee E., 3096
Hartstein, Jacob I., 1664
Hartzog, Julia A., 2387
Harvey, John H., 3937
Hashem, Erfan A., 268
Haskell, Thomas L., 4301
Haslem, Melvin, 2482
Hatcher, Cleophus C., 1077
Hathaway, Stephen C., Jr., 2003
Hattaway, Herman M., 1425
Hatter, Henrietta R., 440
Haugh, Joyce E., 1395

Haushatter, William R., 1326
Havekost, Irene, 2758
Havner, Carter S., 372
Hawkins, Hugh D., 1094
Haycock, Mervyn B., 687
Hayden, Dale L., 3648
Hayes, Arthur R., 2788
Hayes, Donn W., 1512
Hayes, J. Metzger, 1855
Hayes, Marie T., 1821
Hayes, Richard A., Jr., 1257
Hayes, Walter S., Jr., 2130
Haymond, Jack H., 4025
Hayn, Lloyd F., 540
Haynes, William H., 966
Haynie, Jerry T., 3863
Hays, Charles D., 2601
Hays, Edna, 3153
Healey, Rose M., 3131
Healy, Frances P., 1593
Hebron, Arthur E., 3355
Heck, Glenn E., 1258
Hecker, Jack L., 3220
Heckman, Marlin L., 616
Hedbavy, Leopold, 1665
Heddesheimer, Walter J., 2131
Hedges, Jack R., 123
Hedges, Richard G., 2983, 2996
Hedges, William D., 2536
Heery, Chester R., 2094
Hefflinger, Clifford C., 2132
Heflin, William H., 4460
Heikkinen, Karena D., 187
Heil, Eleanor L., 924
Heiligmann, Katharine S., 4302
Heindel, Sally W., 1964
Heine, Clarence J., 1989
Heinrichs, Mary Ann, 2004
Heintze, Michael R., 2602
Heintzen, Harry L., 1040
Heirich, Max A., 162
Heisler, Daniel P., 4118
Heisler, Jules, 3938
Heiss, George D., 1386
Heisser, Wilma A., 82
Heitman, Frederick R., 4084
Heitzmann, William R., 1116
Hejkal, Otto C., 1487
Hekymara, Kuregiy, 208
Held, Lois C., 1513
Hellenbrand, Harold L., 2952
Heller, Herbert L., 763
Hembree, Sillous G., 1006
Hemphill, William E., 2905
Henderson, Adin D., 280
Henderson, Dale E., 1915
Henderson, Janet K., 4545
Henderson, Robert L., 2653
Henderson, Thomas A., 1452

Hendricks, Luther V., 1732
Hendricks, Walter E., 3864
Hendrickson, Bobby G., 3611
Henery, Clive, 1666
Henkel, Julia S., 4119
Henley, Emily A., 793
Hennessey, Daniel L., 1994
Henning, Sister Gabrielle, 1259
Henson, Charles A., 2827
Herbst, Jergen F.H., 3538
Herdlein, Richard J., III, 2388
Herman, Debra, 1899
Hermann, Robert L., 2483
Herndon, Mike E., 503
Herrmann, William H., 3036
Herron, John B., 2389
Hershey, C.B., 4161
Hess, Ford A., 3739
Hess, Marvin G., 2857
Hetherington, Martha A., 2808
Hewick, Laurence F., 468
Hewitt, Lynn R., 2997
Heyliger, E.E., 521
Heywood, Charles W., 4211
Hibbard, Janet G., 969
Hibbitts, Wanda B., 4303
Hickerson, Frank R., 2166
Hickman, Glen E., 1530
Hickman, Lillian W., 2706
Hicks, Billy R., 1424
Hicks, Fred W., 4369
Hicks, Wreatha, 932
Hickson, Shirley A., 4546
Hiestand, Dwight W., 541
Hiestand, Wanda C., 3740
Hiett, Joseph H., 449
Higby, Gregory J., 2381
Higginbotham, Robert L., 2713
Higginbotham, William J., 987
Higgins, Loretta P., 1150
Higgins, William B., 1100
High, Juanita J., 3289
Hilbert, John E., 2491
Hildebrand, Janet E., 3865
Hile, Frederic W., 4304
Hileman, Betty J., 3741
Hill, Daniel N., 3090
Hill, Helen C., 975
Hill, Jack D., 711
Hill, James W., 4021
Hill, Melvin S., 3866
Hillegas, Lyle C., 299
Hilliard, Annie P., 445
Hilton, Thomas B., 542
Hinsdale, Rosejean C., 67
Hinsley, Curtis M., 405
Hinton, David E., 2549
Hinton, William H., 1468
Hires, William L., 2370

Hirsch, David H., 3612
Hirschberger, Emma J., 4405
Hirsh, James B., 4520
Hirshauer, Victor B., 4007
Hite, Floyd H., 2972
Hitt, Bowling M., 1469
Hlubb, Julius G., 1073
Hoadley, Grace, 733
Hobbs, Jane E., 2344
Hobson, Wayne K., 4085
Hochman, Fred, 1702
Hodes, Elizabeth, 4212
Hodes, Ursala, 2242
Hodgdon, Paula D., 3221
Hodgman, Robert S., 3539
Hoff, Alethea, 1117
Hoffman, Allan M., 1853
Hoffman, Lars, 642
Hoffman, Philip G., 246
Hoffman, Warren F., 840
Hoffmann, John M., 1184
Hofmann, Kurt O., 806
Hogan, Fred P., 193
Hogancamp, Richard L., 1260
Hogin, James E., 245
Hoig, Stanley W., 2186
Holbrook, Sandra L.R., 3097
Holcomb, Jack B., 561
Holden, Reuben A., IV, 373
Holder, Elizabeth J., 1965
Holland, Antonio F., 462
Holland, Ralph T., 320
Hollatz, Edwin A., 590
Hollingsworth, Leon, 904
Hollingsworth, Virginia N., 833
Hollis, Daniel W., 2471
Hollister, Paul L., 4213
Holm, Myron L., 1567
Holman, Forest H.C., Jr., 3290
Holmberg, Sharon M., 2209
Holmes, Dwight O.W., 3291
Holmes, George B., 2953
Holmes, Keith D., 1860
Holmes, Lulu H., 3530
Holmes, Marilou J., 777
Holmes, Ralph H., 2390
Holmgren, Daniel M., 2042
Holstein, Edwin J., 4305
Holt, Mildred P., 2806
Holton, John T., 1733
Holtz, Harvey S., 3789
Homesley, John F., 91
Homrighous, Mary E., 688
Hondrum, Jon O., 68
Hooker, Grover C., 1428
Hoole, Martha D., 21
Hoover, Francis L., 3222
Hoover, Irene W., 4461
Hopkins, David R., 3115

Horn, Jefferson L., 3438
Horn, Larry, 298
Horn, Marcia A., 4547
Horn, Max, 4377
Hornburckle, Adam R., 2572
Horner, John E., 2005
Hornsby, Virginia R., 2884
Horton, Agnes, 1531
Horton, Allison N., 2507
Horton, Byrne J., 3698
Horwitz, Hattie S., 463
Hoskins, Glenister C., 3699
Hotchkins, Eugene, III, 1793
Hotchkiss, William P., Jr., 2133
Hoth, William E., 1734
Hott, Leland E., 873
Hough, John M., 4462
Houghton, Alcina B., 3439
Houghton, Laura L., 281
House, Lloyd L., 78
Houser, J.H., 2813
Houser, Steven D., 1481
Hovee, Gene H., 374
Hovenkamp, Herbert J., 4162
Howard, Boyd D., 956
Howard, Donald F., 874
Howard, Ivan C., 4120
Howard, Michael E., 3292
Howard, Ronald L., 4306
Howard, Sherwin W., 3132
Howard, Virginia P.H., 3499
Howe, Catherine P., 296
Howe, Daniel W., 1185
Howell, Isabel, 2537
Howell, Sarah H.M., 3560
Howison, David L., 4378
Hoxie, Ralph G., 1735
Hoyer, Mina, 1488
Hoyle, Hughes B., Jr., 1978
Hronek, Pamela C., 74
Hubbard, Corinne, 3086
Hubbard, Guy A., 3867
Hubbell, George A., 2024
Hubbell, Leigh G., 4307
Huber-Paul, Frieda, 3742
Hubers, Dale, 898
Hubley, John E., 2400
Huddle, Orlando E., 972
Hudson, James B., III, 984
Hudspeth, Junia E., 2802
Huegel, Mary A., 3700
Huehner, David R., 3790
Huff, Mary B., 1027
Huffman, Harold T., Jr., 253
Huffman, Mabel, 4548
Hug, Elsie A., 1834
Huggins, Elizabeth, 2276
Hughes, Arthur J., 1736
Hughes, Elsie L., 1550

Hughes, Kathryn H., 1532
Hughes, M.K., 1474
Hughes, Ray H., 2551
Hughes, Thomas, 1301
Hummel, Dean L., 2006
Hummer, Patricia M., 4549
Humphrey, Clyde W., 4121
Humphrey, David C., 1737
Humphrey, Joe C., 2704
Humphreys, Cecil C., 2508
Humphreys, Joseph A., 643
Hungerford, Curtiss R., 269
Hunt, Virginia, 3223
Hunter, Adelaide M., 2371
Hunter, Catherine H., 2509
Hunter, Deborah E., 3561
Hunter, Katrina, 2929
Hunter, Wilma K., 2921
Huntley, Richard T., 231
Huntzicker, William E., 1387
Hurley, Rev. Mark J., 124
Hurst, Homer, 677
Hurtt, Steven T., 973
Husselbee, Margaret V., 485
Hustvedt, Lloyd M., 3060
Hutchcroft, John C., 3868
Hutches, George E., 1533
Hutchinson, Allen C., 3440
Hutchinson, Melvin T., 79
Hutchison, Earl E., 2696
Hynds, Ernest C., Jr., 504
Hynes, Eleanor M., 3380

Idisi, C. Onokata, 2165
Ihle, Elizabeth L., 4406
Ilowit, Roy, 3224
Imberman, Angela T., 1900
Imhoff, Myrtle M.A., 1453
Ingram, Anthony, 1356
Ingram, I.S., 505
Ingram, Margaret H., 1916
Inman, Elmer B., 2577
Iovacchini, Eric V., 3471
Irby, Jon E., 2277
Irons, Ococie J., 552
Irvine, Janice M., 4308
Irwin, James R., 1360
Irwin, Maurine, 2160
Irwin, William A., 2134
Isaac, Amos, 125
Isaacs, Michael, 216
Issel, William H., 2278
Iverson, Maurice T., 3500
Ivey, Nathan A., 1261

Jabs, Albert E., 2478
Jackameit, William P., 3014
Jackman, Eugene T., 1639
Jackson, Edison O., 1592
Jackson, Edward D., Jr., 3441
Jackson, George F., 126
Jackson, Harry D., 875
Jackson, Isabel H., 3185
Jackson, Joe C., 2187
Jackson, McArthur, 56
Jackson, Miriam R., 2066
Jackson, Pauline F., 4309
Jackson, Prince A., 3293
Jackson, Richard K., 689
Jacobs, G.G., 2135
Jacobs, Rita D., 3613
Jacobs, Virgil M., 666
Jacobsen, Glenn M., 4310
Jacques, Joseph W., 3161
Jacquot, Louis F., 61
Jaffe, Joseph L., Jr., 4526
James, W.T., 375
Jankiewicz, Paul, 4407
Janney, Ruthann G., 3953
Janzen, Fred G., 4408
Jaquith, L. Paul, 1738
Jarech, Leon N., 4044
Jarred, Ada D., 3954
Jarrell, John E., 2573
Jax, Judy A., 4311
Jay, Charles D., 644
Jay, Ike W., 2683
Jeffery, Eber W., 764
Jeffrey, Buron, 990
Jeffrey, Gertrude E., 2885
Jenke, James M., 77
Jenkins, Clara Barnes, 1981
Jenkins, Edwin G., 4432
Jenkins, Sidney, 2061
Jennings, John M., 2906
Jennings, Lawrence C., 3562
Jennings, Robert B., 4550
Jennings, Robert L., 3869
Jensen, Axel C., 3917
Jeppson, Joseph H., 2858
Jerzewiak, R.M., 1514
Jessup, Michael H., 3501
Johanningmeier, Erwin V., 4463
Johns, Lorenzo M., 2714
Johns, Robert, 3676
Johnson, Adolph, Jr., 3294
Johnson, Alandus C., 555
Johnson, Alvin D., 363
Johnson, Clarence S., 3614
Johnson, Daniel T., 591
Johnson, Edward R., 3955
Johnson, Elinor C., 613

Johnson, Ellen E., 876
Johnson, Francis M., 325
Johnson, Halvin S., 2488
Johnson, Helen R., 828
Johnson, Henry C., Jr., 690
Johnson, James G., 376
Johnson, Jesse B., 992
Johnson, John L., 232
Johnson, Lauren T., 877
Johnson, Lee A., 202
Johnson, Lillian P., 3295
Johnson, Loaz W., 163
Johnson, Max R., 841
Johnson, Ronald E., 933
Johnson, Ronald M., 691
Johnson, Roy J., 2603
Johnson, Ruth M., 1327
Johnson, Ted D., 98
Johnson, Vernon E., 4008
Johnson, William R., 3061
Johnston, Judy A., 2304
Johnston, Ruth V., 4464
Jolt, Harvey A., 1667
Jones Anglin, I. Patricia, 1078
Jones, Alan H., 1328
Jones, Albert H., 282
Jones, Bertis L., 3791
Jones, Cloyde C., 997
Jones, Daniel P., 4527
Jones, Doris E.G., 2779
Jones, Flora M., 965
Jones, Glendell A., 2701
Jones, Horace R., 4312
Jones, Ivan L., Jr., 258
Jones, James H., 807
Jones, John A., 1012
Jones, John C., 2522
Jones, Katharine G., 4313
Jones, Kenneth M., 4214
Jones, Lawrence N., 4122
Jones, Lewis L., 878
Jones, Lewis N., 2604
Jones, Marilyn, 2174
Jones, Marjorie F., 1839
Jones, Mary A., 3682
Jones, Nathen E., 846
Jones, Ralph W., 2749
Jones, Richard B., 4045
Jones, Robert A., 1242
Jones, Ruth, 1739
Jones, Thomas P., 819
Jones, Vance H., 3956
Jordahl, Donald C., 672
Jordan, Harold M., 3659
Jordan, Kathryn S.N., 3502
Jorgensen, Sharalee C., 240
Josephson, Harold, 1740
Jowers, Jonnie, 1982
Joyce, Walter E., 377

Judd, Ronnie D., 1003
Junod, Alfred E., 4009
Justis, Joel A., 667

Kahler, Arthur D., 912
Kahler, Conrad A., 944
Kahn, Albert S., 1154
Kain, Margaret N., 303
Kaiser, Gertrude E., 592
Kalapos, Stephen A., Jr., 3503
Kalb, John M., 469
Kaledin, Arthur D., 1186
Kaley, Jack, 847
Kalme, Albert P., 3027
Kaluzynski, Thomas A., 4521
Kamins, Robert W., 1302
Kane, Patricia L., 3615
Kansfield, Norman J., 3957-3958
Kanter, David R., 1354
Kao, Lin-Ying, 1741
Kaplan, Anne C., 3677
Kappel, Vernon E., 1022
Karier, Clarence J., 3870
Karlen, Janice M., 1583
Karnoutsos, Carmela A., 4057
Karr, Joan M., 1329
Kartendick, James J., 1110
Kassen, Tex, 2214
Kato, Mother Ayako, 1824
Katz, Lee P., 1262
Kaufman, Arnold, 3356
Kaufman, Martin, 4086
Kaufmann, Christopher A., 2466
Kearney, Anna R., 3381
Kearney, June F., 2007
Keating, James M., 1742
Keck, George R., 1515
Keck, Judith D., 450
Keefe, Robert J., 2100
Keels, Oliver M., 4314
Keenan, Hubert J., 1861
Keenan, James P., III, 3348
Keene, Charles J., Jr., 2564
Keeney, Elizabeth B., 4215
Kegley, Charles F., 2067
Kegley, Tracy M., 2538
Kellam, Nettie L., 2759
Keller, Dorothy J., 1901
Keller, Jean, 194
Keller, Jim L., 92
Kellog, John A., 786
Kellogg, Richard A., 2886
Kelly, Carl R., 4123
Kelly, Edward J., 3504
Kelly, Gale L., 3037
Kelly, Samuel E., 3296
Kelly, Sister Thomas A., 349

Kelsey, Harry E., Jr., 321
Kelsey, Roger R., 1398
Kelton, Allen, 2539
Kendall, Philip E., 4504
Kenneally, Finbar, 127
Kennedy, Arthur W., 3871
Kennedy, Elizabeth C., 2510
Kennedy, Gerald J., 2442
Kennedy, Harold W., 3168
Kennedy, Peter E., 378
Kennedy, Sister M. St. Mel, 3563
Kennedy, Steele M., 1187
Kennedy, Walter A., Jr., 2458
Kennel, Pauline G., 734
Kennelly, Edward F., 1624
Kennett, Sister Marguerite E., 350
Kenney, Daniel J., S.J., 1501
Kent, Lori A., 3792
Kepner, Charles W., 2279
Kernan, John N., 2828
Kerr, James W., 283
Kerr, Kenneth M., 3186
Kerr, Norwood A., 28
Kerr-Tener, Janet C., 4058
Kersey, Harry A., Jr., 692
Kershner, James W., 1887
Kersten, Evelyn S., 3743
Kett, Joseph F., 4087
Kevles, Daniel J., 4216
Keyser, Bernard D., 4124
Khan, Muhammad, 3133
Kidd, Charles V., 3587
Kiefer, Elva, 128
Kievit, KarenAnn, 470
Killion, Mead W., 1276
Kilman, Gail A., 4551
Kimball, Bruce A., 3939
Kincheloe, Joe L., 4173
King, Diane, 2321
King, James B., 3616
King, JoAnn, 442
King, John L., 1489
King, Kermit C., 164
King, Lauriston R., 4059
King, Lovern C., 3907
Kinlaw, Howard M., 2460
Kinnison, William A., 2008
Kinsey, Dan C., 2101
Kinsey, Daniel C., 2102
Kinzie, Glenn L., 4315
Kinzig, Elizabeth S., 2074
Kiracofe, Edgar S., 2887
Kirby, Jack R., 4316
Kirby, Madge B., 1084
Kirby, Maurice W., 1541
Kirby, Ronald F., 668
Kirchoff, Kim A., 934
Kirkendall, Richard S., 3169
Kirkpatrick, Wyona J., 4552

Kissiah, Herman C., 3617
Kittell, Janet R., 1330
Kittelson, David, 569
Kitzhaber, Albert R., 3660
Klags, Alfred D., 2770
Klaperman, Gilbert, 1907
Klausman, Grant J., 310
Klegon, Douglas A., 4088
Klein, Christa R., 1668
Klein, Mary E., 832
Klein, Melvyn S., 2167
Klein, Sarah J., 1108
Klepper, William M., II, 3134
Kletzly, Brother Paul F., 3531
Kline, William A., 3505
Kling, Frederick W., 2936
Klingerman, E.M., 2418
Klopf, Gordon J., 3062
Klotz, Richard R., 2326
Klotzberger, Edward L., 1827
Klotzburger, Katherine M., 1703
Knauf, Vincent H., 3063
Knight, George W., 3918
Knighten, Loma, 1049
Knights, Paul A., 3793
Kniker, Charles R., 1669
Knoer, Sister Mary M.A., 3959
Knoff, Gerald E., 379
Knowles, Robert L., 3794
Knutson, Keith A., 3085
Kobasky, Michael G., 480
Koch, Gail A., 3690
Koch, Konrad K., Jr., 2215
Koch, Ruth M., 1743
Koch, Sister Madeline M., 1454
Koelsch, William A., 1188
Kofmehl, William E., Jr., 4010
Kohlenberg, Randy B., 2216
Kohler, Francis J., 879
Kohlstedt, Sally L.G., 4217
Kohr, Russell V., 1189
Kolhoff, Kathleen E., 2198
Kolzow, Virden J., 939
Konopnicki, William S., 69
Kopecky, Paul J., Jr., 3795
Korcheck, Stephen J., 421
Korff, J. Michael, 284
Korsgaard, Ross P., 1534
Koudelka, Janet B., 1095
Kovacic, Charles R., 2136
Kraft, Sister M.I., 2305
Kralovec, Dalibor W., 2383
Kramer, Urban J., 1507
Krampitz, Sydney D., 3744
Krankling, James D., 3225
Kraske, Gary E., 3960
Krasnick, Phyllis D., 1787
Kraus, Joe W., 3961
Kraus, John D., Jr., 4011

Krick, Gerald R., 1190
Krieg, Cynthia J., 439
Kromenaker, Joseph G., 645
Krueger, Hanna E., 3044
Kruszynski, Eugene S., 233
Kruytbosch, Carlos E., 4180
Kubik, Jan B., 3174
Kujawa, Rose Marie, 1293
Kulesz, John M., Jr., 2654
Kun, Cecilia R., 1670
Kunz, Calvin S., 2829
Kupersanin, Michael, 2313
Kurland, Gerald, 1744
Kurtz, John L., 749
Kuslan, Louis, 4218
Kuykendall, Dean W., 3919
Kuznick, Peter J., 4219
Kwik, Robert J., 4220
Kyle, Judy M., 2137

La Boone, Elizabeth, 543
La Bougty, High O., 234
La Fauci, Horatio M., 3691
Labaj, Joseph J., S.J., 1502
LaBan, Frank K., 935
Labecki, Geraldine, 3745
LaBud, Verona, 1794
Lackey, Sue A., 669
Lacy, Edmund E., 4163
Lacy, George R., 2679
Ladd, Robert M., 1059
LaFollette, Marcel E.C., 4221
Lagemann, Ellen C., 4553
Lagow, Larry D., 750
Lahey, Judith, 353
Lain, Gayle R., 3472
Laine, Joseph B., 3661
Laird, David B., Jr., 1331
Laird, Ray A., 2605
LaMagdeleine, Donald R., 3382
Lamb, Jane A., 4365
Lamb, Wallace E., 1871
Lancaster, James D., 42
Land, Carroll B., 3226
Landrus, Wilfred M., 2989
Lane, Genevieve, 4465
Lane, John J., 664
Lane, Marilyn A., 2231
Lane, Robert W., 1472
Lane, Ulysses S., 1046
Lang, Charles L., 3170
Lang, Daniel W., 1841
Lang, Elizabeth H., 3408
Lang, Martin A., 3401
Lang, William C., 880
Lang, William L., 3297
Lanier, Raphael O., 451, 2606

Lanphier, David N., 3872
Lansman, Quentin C., 4125
Lantz, Charles P., 593
Lapradd, Charles W., 3683
Large, Larry D., 2232
Large, Margaret S., 1263
Larkin, Charles W., Jr., 1080
Larsen, Dale R., 1568
Larsen, Lawrence H., 3064
Larson, Arlin, 2103
Larson, Gary O., 3588
Larson, Magali S., 4089
Larson, Robert L, 1745
Larson, Sexton, 1376
Lash, Frederick M., 2973
Laska, Lewis L., 2511
Laska, Vera, 646
Lasko, Richard, 3873
Lassiter, Wright L., Jr., 57
Lathrop, Ruth H., 1028
Lau, Estelle P.O., 3047
Laudine, Sister Mary, 215
Lauffer, Carolyn, 3618
Laughlin, Lynn A., 936
Laurent, David, 2433
Lavery, Thomas F., 2439
Lawn, Evan, 3402
Lawrence, Cora J., 2998
Lawrence, Evan J., 1590
Lawrence, Irene J., 4317
Lawrence, Marie K., 3962
Lawrence, Paul R., 3227
Lawrence, Robert R., 3874
Lawson, Allen L, 228
Lawson, Hal A., 3746
Lawton, Edward M., Jr., 1746
Lawton, Willie O., 422
Layton, Donald B., 3187
Layton, Edwin T., 4090
Lazar, Stephen H., 4409
Lazzell, Carleen C., 1643
Le Duc, Thomas H.A., 1143
Leach, Eugene E., 4318
Leach, Georgia B., 4466
Leaf, Carol A., 3747
Leahy, John F., Jr., 2009
LeBlanc, M. Elizabeth, 3692
Lebowitz, Carl F., 1835
Lee, Arthur O., Jr., 1369
Lee, Charles M., 2168
Lee, Dorothy E., 3357
Lee, James L., 853
Lee, Joe B., 2760
Lee, Julius W., Jr., 3684
Lee, Kathryn H., 2414
Lee, Lurline M., 90
Lee, Michael M.S., 3963
Lee, Robert C., 3619
Lee, Robert E., 1551

Lee, William R., 1747
Leeds, Sylvia K., 401
Leedy, Paul D., 3506
Leef, Audrey J.V., 1598
Lees, Sondra, 2859
Lefcourt, Robert, 4319
Lefebvre, Jeanne M., 3135
Lehmann, Joyce W., 1693
Leighninger, Leslie H., 4320
Leister, Terry G., 2974
Leland, Richard W., 285
Lelon, Thomas C., 740
Lendrim, Frank T., 2104
Lenn, Marjorie P., 4410
Lenoue, Bernard J., 820
Leonard, A. Leslie, 1715
Leonard, Janet G., 1595
Lesesne, Joab M., Jr., 2459
Leslie, Mary E., 3228
Leslie, William B., 2280
Lester, Jeanette A., 4514
Lester, Paul F., 693
Lester, Robin D., 647
Levine, David O., 3796
Levitt, Leon, 270
Levy, David C., 1840
Levy, John W., 506
Levy, Richard M., 4091
Levy, Roland G., 8
Lewis, Alvin F., 957
Lewis, Elmer C., 3298
Lewis, Guy M., 3229
Lewis, John S., Jr., 3875
Lewis, John, Jr., 2048
Lewis, Lenore L., 342
Lewis, Linda A., 2075
Lewis, Stanley J., 2512
Lewis, William J., 4467
Lewitter, Sidney R., 1591
Lezotte, Ruth A., 1303
Li, Shu-Tang, 4411
Lide, Anne, 507
Liebenau, Jonathan M., 2281
Lieuallen, Roy E., 4060
Light, John J., 2010
Lightfoot, Frank K., 9
Likins, Jeanne M., 1072
Lincoln, Winfred J., 1644
Lindberg, Paul M., 1363
Linderman, Winifred B., 1748
Lindgren, Frank E., 271
Lindsay, Allan G., 1281
Lindsey, William H., 2453
Linehan, Joseph A., 3383
Lipping, Alar, 1191
Lisherness, Nancy L., 3620
List, Barbara T., 1966
Little, Faye M., 2688
Little, Monroe H., Jr., 3299

Littlefied, Henry W., 3442
Liu, Yung-Szi, 1332
Lively, Roger M., 491
Livingston, Inez B., 4412
Lizardi, Marie M., 2422
Loberger, Gordon J., 3621
Lobuts, John F., Jr., 423
Lochra, Albert P., 1917
Lofthus, Richard R., 1992
Logsdon, Guy W., 2227
Lokensgard, Erik, 854
Long, Curtiss M., 471
Long, Douglas E., 1712
Long, Emmett T., Jr., 129
Long, Howard O., 2472
Long, Watt A., 2257
Longenecker, Justin G., 4413
Loomis, Burt W., 678
Lopiccolo, John, 1029
Lorance, Robert T., 22
Lord, Jerome E., 343
Lord-Wood, June, 1749
Loren, Morris J., 3911
Lorensen, Frederick H., 3473
Loso, Idelia, 1364
Lottick, Kenneth V., 3797
Louden, Lois M.R., 3649
Loughlin, William A., Jr., 354
Lourie, Stephen J., 3685
Loveless, William A., 3403
Lovett, Warren P., 556
Low, Mortimer E., 311
Lowell, Maurice W., 3065
Lowell, Mildred H., 808, 3964
Lowenstein, Arlene J., 2391
Lowery, Paul J., 842
Lowman, Harmon L., 4468
Lozo, John P., 2282
Lubeck, Dennis R., 1455
Lucas, Aubrey K., 1406
Lucas, Christopher J., 3098
Luckett, George R., 1114
Luebke, William R., Jr., 241
Luetmer, Nora, 1365
Luker, Richard M., 2105
Lunbeck, Elizabeth, 1131
Lunceford, Charles R., 483
Lundean, Joel W., 620
Lunger, H.J., 1004
Lunsford, Andrea A., 3507
Lunsford, Walter C., 3230
Lunt, Sally H., 1231
Lurie, Edward, 1192
Lykes, Richard W., 3136
Lynn, Harlan C., 1490
Lynn, Louis A.A., 1013
Lyon, Bruce W., 3589
Lyon, Mona L., 1566
Lyons, John O., 3622

Lyons, Mack D., 3940

Mabry, Mary V., 2789
MacDougall, James A., 1193
MacEachen, John, 1750
Machesney, John D., 3015
Mack, Henry W., 1155
MacKay, Vera A., 809
Mackaye, Ruth C., 3590
MacKenzie, Blair L., 1804
Mackey, James A., 1030
Maclaren, Sharon A., 3443
MacLeish, Marlene Y., 3300
MacMillan, Genevieve, 4554
MacMitchell, T. Leslie, 3532
Macy, William K., 3066
Maddalena, Lucille A., 2298
Madden, Richard H., 2138
Madsen, David L, 4022
Magnuson, Roger P., 1264
Magruder, Edith M.C., 4126
Mahan, L.D.J., 1505
Maiden, Arthur L., 3188
Maiden, Marvin, 2888
Mailer, Julia H., 3067
Maitland, Christine C., 130
Malek-Madani, Firouz, 4379
Malick, Herbert, 3154
Mallon, Arthur, 1671
Mallonee, Richard C., II, 4222
Malloy, Thomas A., Jr., 1132
Malnekoff, Jon L., 235
Malone, Dumas, 2473
Malone, Mark H., 58
Malone, Thomas L, 3701
Maloney, Edward F., 1672
Maloney, Sara E., 4321
Mangun, Vernon L., 1133
Manilla, Sunday J., 1353
Mann, Aubrey E., 1636
Mann, George L, 1456
Mann, Gordon C., 938
Mann, Harold W., 529
Mann, Lawrence R., 3189
Manning, Randolph, 424
Manning, Robert N., 3662
Mansfield, Henry, 131
Mansfield, Stephen S., 2907
Manzer, Edna L, 1134
Manzo, Elizabeth, 1584
Marble, Robert F., 486
Marciano, John D., 1795
Marcom, Robert, 2607
Marden, David L, 4061
Marderosian, Haig D., 1159
Mariner, P.M., 2091
Markle, David H., 364

Marley, Owen G., 1751
Marlin, Bernard, 1243
Marlow, T. Stuart, 2354
Maroscher, Albert C., 2684
Marotta, Gary M., 4062
Marsh, Allan T., 416
Marsh, Joseph T., 724
Marsh, Josephine P., 4555
Marshall, David C., 1014
Marshall, Max L., 4322
Marshall, Philip C., 4323
Martens, Alice, 4127
Martin, Curtis A., 4469
Martin, David W., 1681
Martin, Doris M., 2715
Martin, James L., 2695
Martin, John C., 3231
Martin, John P., 2338
Martin, Margaret I., 3748
Martin, Robert E., 816
Martin, Robert G., 3444
Martin, Rochelle, 4092
Martin, Theodora P., 4556
Martin, Thomas S., 3232
Martinelli, Fred M., 2139
Martus, Charles T., 1967
Marvelli, Alan L., 1135
Marwah, Surinder K., 4470
Maskin, Melvin R., 3301
Mason, Frank M., 2768
Mason, Peter W., 4324
Mason, Robert L., 3233
Massengale, Robert G., 4128
Masson, Margaret W., 3409
Masteller, Larry T., 1277
Maszkiewicz, Ruth A., 2392
Matassarin-Jacobs, Esther R., 3749
Matejski, Myrtle P., 1101
Matheny, Dave, 919
Matheson, Robert G., 3508
Mathews, Alice E., 3410
Mathews, Ben A., 2804
Mathews, Brother S.G., 2060
Mathews, Forrest D., 4063
Mathis, Emily D., 1407
Mathis, Gerald R., 544
Mathis, Robert R., 2748
Matthews, Alfred T., 810
Matthews, Alfred W., 2981
Matthews, Emily P., 1683
Matthews, Herbert C., 2063
Matthews, Lamoyne M., 433
Mattice, Howard L., 1673
Mattingly, Paul H., 4093
Mattox, Fount W., 101
Maul, Ray C., 905
Maust, Earl M., 3876
Mavrogenes, Nancy A., 648
Maxwell, Bernice J., 545

Maxwell, Grace R., 3798
Maxwell, Howard B., 3175
Maxwell, Margaret N.F., 1333
May, John B., 94
May, Russell A., 3509
Maybee, Harper C., 1265
Mayer, Gary H., 2790
Mayer, Gerard E., 322
Mayo, Helen N., 1053
McAlduff, William H., 1522
McAllister, Ethel M., 1848
McAlmon, Victoria M., 225
McBride, Don W., 4129
McBride, Esther B., 4325
McBride, Jack E., 2217
McBride, James C., 2691
McBride, Sara A., 481
McBride, Ullysses, 3302
McCadden, Joseph J., 2283
McCaffrey, Donna T., 2437
McCaffrey, Katherine R., 1628
McCain, Clara E., 2655
McCain, John W., Jr., 2449
McCamey, Marion B., 4515
McCann, Maurice J., 3591
McCarrell, Lamar K., 3877
McCarren, Edgar P., 3384
McCarthy, Harry B., 1066
McCarthy, John R., 3303
McCarthy, Joseph J., 3304
McCarthy, Robert E., 694
McCaughey, Robert A.P., 1194
McCaughey-Oreszak, Leona D., 1230
McCaul, Robert L., Jr., 508
McClarty, Edward L., 242
McCleary, Iva D., 4471
McClintock, David H., 3641
McCloy, Frank D., 4130
McColl, M.C., 2372
McCollom, Marvin G., 23
McCollom, Stewart F., 3088
McConnell, John J., 3234
McConnell, Leona B., 2197
McCoy, Connie M., 2205
McCoy, Walter J., 3305
McCracken, Charles W., 2092
McCrary, Delwin W., 2849
McCulley, Kathleen M., 1388
McCune, Robert P., 4223
McDannel, James H., 3799
McDermott, Genevieve A., 132
McDermott, Louis M., 181
McDermott, Maria C., 4472
McDonald, Cleveland, 2046
McDougall, Daniel J., 3099
McDowell, Henderson, 2673
McFadden, Daniel H., 2393
McFall, Kenneth, 2037
McFarland, M.M., 2299

McFarland, William E., 2210
McGee, Leo, 3306
McGehee, Larry T., 4070
McGinnis, Frederick A., 2172
McGinnis, Howard J., 3016, 4071
McGinnis, Robert S., Jr., 1752
McGivern, James G., 4224
McGlon, Charles A., 4326
McGovern, James H., 2434
McGovern, Sister Mary V., 2355
McGowan, Frank, 3965
McGowan, James E., 1694
McGrath, Earl J., 3137
McGrath, Gary L., 1389
McGrath, Gerard M., 1753
McGrath, Robert M., 1151
McGurk, Josephine H., 1704
McHargue, Robert M., 226
McHugh, Thomas F., 2373
McIlwain, James L., 261
McIntire, George R., 2241
McIntyre, Calvin M., 3038
McIntyre, Dorothy P., 1918
McIvers, William D., 3941
McKay, Robert B., 344
McKean, John R.O., 1905
McKee, Earl S., 962
McKenna, Jon F., 594
McKenzie, Pearle, 2477
McKevitt, Gerald, 263
McKinney, Robert Q., 3445
McKinney, Robert, 3800
McKirdy, Charles R., 1136
McKnight, Arnold W., 434
McKnight, Richard P., 1575
McKown, Harry C., 3155
McLaughlin, Marvin L., 2697
McLeroy, Nellie M., 2608
McMahon, Aileen, 2681
McMahon, Ernest E., 3510
McMaster, Robert K., 881
McMasters, Richard K., 1888
McMenemy, Agnes C., 1266
McMillan, Joseph T., 3307
McMillan, William A., 3308
McMullen, Charles H., 649
McMullen, Harvey M., 1991
McMurdock, Bertha J., 1457
McMurray, Howard J., 3068
McMurtry, George W., 1458
McNeely, Richard I., 3404
McNeer, James B., 2908
McNeil, James H., 546
McNeil, William K., 4327
McNeill, Clayton, 1067
McNulty, Helen P., 2173
McPeake, Thomas E., 3702
McPheeters, Alphonso A., 526
McPherson, Linda M.G., 4557

McReynolds, Billy, 3344
McSweeney, John P., 1552
McTaggart, John B., 2314
McVey, William E., 3511
Mead, George W., 1377
Meador, William R., 1633
Meagher, Walter J., 1158
Mealy, Franklin R., 3446
Means, Richard L., 4328
Measells, Dewitt T., Jr., 1429
Meckler, Alan M., 3564
Medeiros, Frank A., 286
Medlin, Stuart B., 2889
Mees, Carl F., 595
Mehl, Warren R., 3966
Meighan, Cecilia, 3385
Meinert, Charles W., 2076
Meinert, James D., 2233
Meinhard, Robert W., 882
Meisterheim, Matthew J., 596
Melchor, Beulah H., 435
Melebeck, Claude B., Jr., 1031
Melendy, Earle R., 3878
Melosh, Barbara, 3750
Meltzer, Gilbert W., 1803
Melville, Keith E., 4329
Mendenhall, William R., 4433
Mendola, James J., Jr., 1267
Meredith, Cameron W., 1334
Meredith, Thomas C., 4414
Meriwether, Colyer, 2450
Merlino, Maxine O., 133
Merrill, George D., 3920
Merritt, Judy M., 10
Merritt, Raymond H., 4225
Merryman, John E., Sr., 2328
Merwin, Bruce W., 906
Meservy, Royal R., 4131
Messersmith, Lloyd E., 3447
Messina, Salvatore M., 2330
Messinger, Milton A., 3703
Metzger, Jerome C., 3474
Metzger, John, 751
Metzger, Loya F., 3100
Metzger, Walter P., 3349
Meyer, Donald H., 3879
Meyer, Edward L., 2486
Meyer, Roy F., 1366
Meyerend, Maude H., 2374
Meyers, Judith K., 2025
Mezoff, Earl R., 2284
Michael, Robert L., 2011
Michalik, Craig A., 4370
Michelson, Donald D., 380
Michener, A.O., 2356
Michener, Roger E., 1056
Middlebrooks, Deloris J., 1570
Midgette, Nancy S., 4226
Milacek, Barbara R., 4227

Mileham, Hazel B., 1459, 4132
Miles, Dorothy W., 2656
Millamed, Israel S., 1705
Millbrooke, Anne M., 4228
Miller, Blanche, 883
Miller, Donald G., 673
Miller, Edward A., Jr., 332
Miller, Enid, 597
Miller, Francis J., 2031
Miller, Frederick R., 2609
Miller, Gary E., 3693
Miller, George M., 40
Miller, Guy H., 4133
Miller, Howard S., 4181
Miller, Lawrence A., 3967
Miller, Lloyd D., 1112
Miller, Lucy H., 3751
Miller, Margaret, 563
Miller, Michael H., 4380
Miller, Richard E., Jr., 3968
Miller, Richard V., 1674
Miller, Richard, 2967
Miller, Robert W., 2716
Miller, Sandra K., 2140
Miller, Stephen S., 417
Miller, Virginia P., 1371
Miller, William C., 1495
Millican, Alta, 45
Milligram, Emerson N., 3358
Millman, Howard L., 3116
Mills, George H., 2982
Mills, Thomas J., 2252
Milner, Orlin, 940
Minnick, Walter C., 3011
Miranti, Paul J., Jr., 3359
Mirwis, Allan N., 3969
Mitchell, Joseph T., 1968
Mitchell, Merle, 4229
Mitchell, Reavis L., Jr., 3309
Mitchell, Theodore R., 3171
Mitchell, Yetta G., 2809
Mitchem, Arnold L., 3049
Mix, Mary D., 489
Mize, Richard L., 1947
Moak, Franklin E., 1754
Mock-Morgan, Mavera E., 1755
Moeder, Monica (Sister), 913
Moffatt, Georgabell H., 811
Mohler, Samuel R., 2909
Mohr, Eleanor S., 2692
Mohr, Joland E., 4072
Moldow, Gloria M., 406
Molen, Clarence T., Jr., 897
Molitor, Clarence W., 2114
Moll, Clarence R., 2416
Molloy, Peter M., 1889
Moloney, Louis C., 2791
Molster, Jean L., 3880
Molyneux, Robert E., 3970

Monahan, Danno R., 1483
Mondale, Clarence C., 3686
Mondschein, Eric S., 3801
Money, Mary G., 985
Moniba, Harry F., 59
Montalto, Nicholas V., 3908
Montgomery, Douglas B., 134
Montgomery, James R., 2574-2575
Moomaw, Leon A., 1540
Moon, Clyde L., 452
Mooney, Donald J., 1852
Moore, Albert A., 2077
Moore, David W., 1756
Moore, Elif A., 2771
Moore, Ernest W., 4134
Moore, Gail E., 188
Moore, Gay G., 1969
Moore, George H., 900
Moore, Hastings, 650
Moore, Irene, 3623
Moore, Kathryn S.M., 1195
Moore, LeRoy, Jr., 1849
Moore, Ralph R., 4505
Moorhead, Patrick H., 742
Moran, Kaye D., 4415
Morgan, Alda C.M., 3101
Morgan, Charles C., 549
Morgan, Clarence M., 765
Morgan, Kenimer H., 2540
Morgan, Ruth H., 794
Morgan, William H., 4164
Morgenroth, George W., 1585
Morris, Barbara L., 1856
Morris, Harold W., 4026
Morris, Marilyn L., 213
Morris, Rita M., 1196
Morris, Stephen A., 3642
Morris, William M., 189
Morris, William S., 4506
Morrison, Betty L., 1043
Morrison, James L., Jr., 1890
Morrissey, Robert S., 2218
Morrow, Anne H., 29
Morton, Albert R., 1061
Mosch, Theodore R., 3592
Moseley, Carolyn, 2610
Mosher, Bryan J., 1675
Mosher, E.R., 4473
Mosley, Calvin N., 1197
Moten, Sarah E.P., 3310
Motley, Daniel E., 2910
Mould, Michael W., 3235
Mountney, Virginia R., 3881
Mouritsen, Russell H., 2860
Movrich, Ronald F., 3997
Mowder, Barbara J., 679
Muck, Steven J., 218
Mulder, John M., 1611
Mulka, John S., 2285

Mullen, Kathryn R., 2792
Mullins, James L., 3971
Mullins, Lula L., 2611
Munford, James K., 3138
Munn, Robert F., 3031
Munson, Corliss D., 1394
Murdoch, M.C., 165
Murdock, Mary E., 1198
Murdock, Patrick M., 2990
Murphee, Herbert C., 35
Murphy, Donald J., 4064
Murphy, Ella L., 1939
Murphy, Jean M., 999
Murphy, John P., 3921
Murphy, Kathleen M., 3386
Murphy, Mary E., 1199
Murray, Catherine A., 1757
Murray, Floyd B., 1553
Murray, Neil D., 2234
Muscatell, Toni G.P., 453
Musser, Adah, 2093
Muto, Albert H., 166
Mwonyonyi, Isaya, 4073
Myers, Clara A., 2331
Myres, William V., 381
Myricks, Noel, 3475

Nabors, D.J., Jr., 3663
Nader, Samuel J., 3236
Nakireru, Alexander O., 3345
Nalley, Charles G., Jr., 4012
Napoli, Donald S., 4330
Narel, Ronald A., 3624
Nash, Evelyn M., 1420
Nass, Deanna R., 3102
Navarre, Jane P., 2012
Nawaz, Muhammad, 4474
Nayebkhail, Mohammad Y., 3802
Naylor, Natalie A., 3190
Neel, George W., 2315
Neeley, William G., III, 3512
Neff, William B., 2394
Neiger, Helen M., 2261
Neil, Robert G., 2525
Neill, Henry R., 2302
Nelsen, Randle W., 3803
Nelson, Allen E., 3752
Nelson, Amy G., 988
Nelson, Clinton E., 1200
Nelson, Clyde K., 2404
Nelson, Darryl P., 203
Nelson, David P., 304
Nelson, Dorwin R., 812
Nelson, Fred A., 135
Nelson, Karen C., 3103
Nelson, Torlef, 2975
Nelson-Jones, Richard C., 3694

Nenninger, Timothy K., 907
Nester, William R., Jr., 2051
Nethers, John L., 2026
Neumann, Florence M., 1676
Neve, Paul E., 3882
Neville, John P., 3346
Newcomb, Joan I., 2141
Newcomer, Joe C., 1118
Newman, Christy M., 4516
Newman, George C., 2027
Newman, V., 2705
Newsome, George L., Jr., 3804
Newton, James H., 2723
Nicholas, Freddie W., 3311
Nicholas, William E., III, 4528
Nichols, Edward L., 3625
Nichols, Mary E., 1081, 1430
Nichols, Scott G., 2300
Nicholson, James M., Jr., 1987
Nickerson, Francis B., 2235
Niehaus, Earl F., 1021
Nielson, Dean C., 579
Noall, Sandra H., 2824
Noble, David F., 4094
Noe, Minnie A., 2693
Noffsinger, Mark G., 1335
Nolan, John P., 382
Nolen, Claude B., 2954
Nonacs, Merija, 986
Noone, Bernard J., 3387
Norbrey, Grace V.H., 2945
Noroian, Elizabeth L., 2395
Norris, Clarence W., Jr., 2751
Norris, Larry B., 3448
Norris, Timmerman H., 11
North, Richard B., 2260
Norton, John O., 2417
Norwood, William F., 3998
Nostrand, Geraldine S., 4046
Notestein, Robert B., 383
Novak, Steven J., 4381
Novolony, George, 3237
Novotny, Marianne K.H., 1554
Nozicka, George J., 4182
Numark, Eleanor J., 4331
Nunley, Joe E., 2524
Nunn, E.S., 2188
Nunn, Norman L., 4434
Nuss, Elizabeth F., 884
Nutter, Larry W., 2189
Nye, Roger H., 1891
Nyikos, Michael S., 1336
Nystrom, Richard K., 236

O'Brien, Dorothy A., 3883
O'Brien, James P., 2830
O'Brien, John J., 3388

O'Brien, Kenneth B., Jr., 3476
O'Connor, John A., 1201
O'Connor, Thomas F., 384
O'Connor, Thomas J., 36
O'Dell, DeForest, 4332
O'Donnell, John M., 4333
O'Hara, Leo J., 2286
O'Leary, Dennis J., 80
O'Mara, Francis L., Jr., 1160
O'Neill, Norman W., 2793
O'Neill, Sister Margaret A., 830
O'Reilly, Edmund P., 262
O'Shea, Joseph A., 651
Oakley, Jesse R., 3449
Ofiesh, Gabriel D., 4334
Ogilvie, Charles F., 3104
Ogle, Merle F., 326
Oh, Song J., 1903
Ohles, John F., 1808
Okin, Susan M., 4558
Olauson, Clarence R., 2831
Olcott, Ruth H., 3805
Oliphant, James O., 2978
Oliver, Henry L., 573
Oliver, Mary C., 2519
Olmstead, Madeline, 4559
Olsen, Obed M., 2501
Olsen, Richard A., 1202
Olsen, Richard N., 1758
Olson, Donald O., 1555
Olson, Gordon B., 1990
Olson, Ralph D., 567
Onorato, Ronald J., 2345
Orbach, Noreen R.F., 4095
Orlando, Vincent A., 2057
Orr, Billy M., 2565
Orr, Helen A., 2915
Orr, John C., 598
Orr, Kenneth B., 3565
Orr, Robert S., 3972
Orsini, Joseph E., 4135
Ortega-Wheless, Ludivina G., 2612
Ortenzio, Paul J., 3806
Orth, Andrew P., 3695
Ortiz, Hewtan S., 2142
Osborne, John T., 2410
Osborne, Ruby O., 2911
Osysko, Edmund, 1759
Ottinger, Richard E., 30
Otto, Leroy W., 221
Ottoson, Ronald, 725
Oullette, Vernon A., 167
Overby, George R., 3117
Overstreet, Earle L., 2865
Overton, Edward F., 2918
Overturf, Donald S., 1647
Overy, David H., 2938
Owen, Helen R., 1500
Owen, Stephen P., 3139

Owens, Hugh M., S.J., 1499
Owens, Robert L., II, 3312
Owings, Vivian B., 1105
Oziri, Ihemadubuinroya, 4335

Paciorek, Loretta A., 1892
Page, Barbara A.S., 3140
Page, John C., 1503
Page, Patricia A., 1629
Palais, Elliott S., 1815
Palcic, James L., 472
Palinchak, Robert S., 3450
Palmer, Barbara H., 3566
Palmer, James F., 2657
Palmieri, Patricia A., 1238
Palmquist, Eben O., 4336
Paltridge, James G., 136
Panchaud, Frances L., 1203
Pangburn, Jessie M., 4475
Pannell, William P., 12
Panzer, Vern A., 3884
Pappas, Richard J., 1290
Parham, Paul M., 3973
Parietti, Elizabeth S., 3753
Parish, William A., 4047
Park, Hun, 137
Parker, Clara M., 4476
Parker, Craig B., 237
Parker, Edith H., 2613
Parker, Franklin, 2541
Parker, Giles E., 3238
Parker, Harris H., 1877
Parker, Lockie, 4560
Parker, Paul C., 3650
Parker, Paul E., 766
Parkman, Aubrey L., 1850
Parks, Deborah Z., 2762
Parks, Walter W., 1556
Parle, Grace, 1516
Parr, James H., 782
Parrish, William S., 2456
Parry, Alicia H., 1872
Parsons, Jerry L., 1690
Parsons, Nellie F., 1493
Partridge, Arthur R., 3704
Partridge, Ronald R., 3191
Pate, James A., 24, 43
Patience, Alice, 60
Patrick, Harold L., 695
Patterson, Charles E., 967
Patterson, Joseph N., 3313
Patterson, Richard H., 1479
Patterson, Robert M., 652
Patton, B., 2614
Patton, June O., 558
Paul, Gary N., 287
Paul, Norma A., 599

Paul, Roschelle Z., 168
Pauli, Kenneth W., 3922
Paxman, Marlys E., 272
Paylor, Mary M., 454
Payne, John W., 2794
Payne, Joseph A., 3314
Payne, Mary E., 977
Payton, Philip W., 3513
Peach, Larry D., 3567
Pearce, Donald C., 2890
Pearsall, Thelma F., 1948
Pearson, Robert W., 3754
Pease, Harold W., 2832
Pease, Norval F., 4507
Peavy, Robert D., 3755
Peck, Richard C., 4477
Pedtke, Dorothy A.H., 712
Pefley, Wallace B., 2722
Peirce, Henry B., Jr., 1226
Pelton, Carol N., 3045
Pence, James W., Jr., 2955
Penn, John S., 3069
Penney, Grace J., 2219
Penrod, Michael R., 4382
Peo, John R., 3626
Perea, Jacob E., 209
Perkins, Iris J., 1047
Perkins, Richard W., 767
Perkins, Theodore E., 1937
Perlman, Daniel H., 741
Pernal, Michael E., 345
Pernick, Martin S., 4096
Perrin, Porter G., 3664
Perrins, Barbara C., 3974
Perry, Charles M., 1337
Perry, Eugene H., 1144
Perry, Raymond J., 362
Persico, Connell F., 210
Person, Peter P., 3807
Pesci, Frank B., 1068
Peters, David E., 1809
Peters, William R., 2375
Petersen, Vesta, 3975
Peterson, Charles E., Jr., 717
Peterson, Daniel E., 2999
Peterson, Elof R., 885
Peterson, Hazel C., 1233
Peterson, Howard W., 1032
Peterson, Karl G., 1796
Peterson, Kenneth G., 169
Peterson, Lawrence L., 4048
Peterson, Mildred J., 4097
Peterson, Orville C., 4136
Petit, Judith L., 2739
Petree, Colbert G., 2576
Petrovich, Janice R., 2423
Pettiss, John O., 1041
Pevey, Wayne, 2795
Pfanner, Daniel J., 3315

Pfeiffer, Clyde E., 248
Phelan, Arthur E., 238
Phelph, Margaret S., 2513
Phelps, Marianne R., 4383
Phelps, Ralph A., Jr., 2615
Phillips, Claude A., 1460
Phillips, Richard C., 3514
Phillips, Robert L., 3347
Philo, L.C., 4137
Picklesimer, Dorman, Jr., 2038
Piemonte, Robert V., 3756
Pierro, Armstead A., 3316
Pierson, Charles L., 752
Pihl, Cedric H., 190
Pilver, Erika E., 346
Pinckney, George H., Jr., 2833
Pinkard, Elfred A., 2058
Pinkston, Dorothy, 3757
Pinkston, Esther K., 2287
Piper, Emilie S., 1797
Pittard, Homer, 2560
Pittet, Marcel, 3070
Pittman, Jacquelyn, 3758
Pitts, James H., 4435
Plath, Paul J., 713
Plough, James H., 3389
Plugge, Domis E., 3885
Pollak, Peter G., 3039
Pollard, Lucille A., 4561
Pollingue, Alice B., 25
Pollitt, Frank C., 2754
Pollock, Edward W., 1338
Poole, Charles P., 62
Pope, Christie F., 1919
Pope, Emma, 2616
Pope, Linda T., 327
Pope, Louis B., 1920
Pope, Richard M., 1477
Pope, Wilbur A., 2732
Poret, George C., 2542
Porter, Charlotte M., 2380
Porter, Earl W., 1934
Porter, George H., 3451
Porter, James L., 2253
Porter, Louise M., 403
Portman, David N., 3162
Potter, Jessica C., 3000
Potts, David B., 4138
Powell, Arthur G., 1204
Powell, Benjamin E., 3976
Powell, John B., III, 1033
Powell, John T., 3239
Powell, Mae M., 2769
Powell, Ruth A., 3020
Prahl, Marie R., 1284
Pratte, Richard N., 347
Preer, Jean L., 3317
Prendergast, Michael L., 385
Prescott, Thomas B., 2685-2686

Preville, Joseph R., 360
Price, Hugh, 1637
Price, Paula, 473
Price, Rebecca R., 3568
Price, Robert M., 4436
Price, Robert P., 1205
Priest, Jimmie R., 2816
Priestley, Alice E.A., 1902
Prince, John F., 70
Pritchard, Pamela, 2143
Prochnow, Larry A., 1367
Proctor, Mamie M., 2773
Proctor, Samuel, 482
Pruitt, Franklin B., 4337
Pruitt, Harvie M., 2617
Pruitt, Nero, 138
Pugh, Darrell L., 3192
Pugh, David W., 1645
Pugsley, Sharon G., 2861
Pullen, Carol F., 696
Pullum, Fred D., 509
Purchard, Dora, 4437
Puthoff, Martilu, 3705
Pyeatt, Margaret F., 1527
Pyles, Henry M., 978

Qualls, J. Winfield, 2554
Quatroche, John R., 2288
Quenzel, Carrol, 3105
Quick, Donald M., 1268
Quillen, Herbert N., 2728

Rabe, William F., 3141
Rachut, Marie P., 886
Racz, Ernest B., 1145
Rader, Benjamin G., 3071
Radford, Neil A., 3977
Radner, Sanford, 3886
Ragsdale, Annie L., 547
Rahe, Herbert E., 768
Rainsburger, Richard A., 2013
Rainsford, George N., 3593
Ralson, Hugh E., 2733
Ramsay, John T., Jr., 3240
Ramsey, Berkley C., 517
Ramsey, Harold E., 2144
Rand, Albert N., 4230
Randall, Joyce L., 1292
Randolph, Scott K., 1760
Randolph, Stephen P., 1069
Randolph, Victor R., 600
Randolph, William L., 2618
Ranker, Irene K., 139
Ranson, Leonard B., 1206
Rappaport, Margaret M., 4384

Rashid-Farokhi, Helen E., 510
Rasmussen, E. Keith, 914
Ratcliffe, Thomas E., Jr., 697
Rauch, Julia B., 2289
Ravitch, Harold, 653
Rawlings, Wyatt, 715
Rawls, Ruth E., 2643
Ray, Harold L., 386
Ray, Mauldin A., 2552
Read, James C., 1431
Reagan, Gaylord B.L., 3706
Rediger, Joseph L., 4338
Reed, Charles R., 4174
Reed, Deward H., 1634
Reed, Donald E., 490
Reed, George R., 1278
Reed, Germaine M., 1034
Reed, Glenn A., 3707
Reed, John D., 4416
Reed, Larry W., 1761
Reed, Lawrence L., 3040
Reed, Lloyd D., 2869
Reed, Marian E., 4478
Reed, Myer S., Jr., 4165
Reed, Neville F., 2357
Rees, Arland B., 4417
Rees, Frances, 564
Reeve, Frank D., 1646
Reeves, Dorothy E., 3540
Regier, Bernard W., 3887
Reichert, Stephen B., Jr., 140
Reichmuth, Roger E., 991
Reid, Alban E., 141
Reid, Hubert D., 3452
Reid, John Y., 1762
Reid, Robert H., 3515
Reilly, Patricia M., 2891
Reilly, William J., 1862
Reinert, Paul C., 3569
Reinke, Earl F., 4156
Reitzer, Paul G., 3808
Renberg, James B., 2658
Renfer, Rudolf A., 2668
Renner, William F., 698
Rennie, Thomas P., 1107
Rentschler, David M., 2415
Reveley, David R., 2956
Reverby, Susan M., 3759
Revkin, Amelia S., 2426
Reynolds, Helen M., 3978
Reynolds, Margaret M., 958
Reynolds, Thomas U., 1416
Rhoads, Lester, 3241
Rhoda, Leonard G., 2834
Rhoda, Richard G., 2514
Rhodes, Dent M., 4479
Rhodes, Francis A., 455
Rhodes, James L., 2796
Rhodes, Jess D., 576

Rhodes, Mary, 1476
Riccio, Gregory J., 714
Riccitelli, Santo J., 2427
Riccomini, Donald R., 387
Rice, Abbott E., 1572
Rice, Jessie P., 4480
Rice, Kathleen G., 1442
Rice, P. Jeannine, 2078
Rich, George E., 1612
Rich, Thomas R., 2170
Richards, Alden LeG., 3809
Richards, John D., 1893
Richards, Robert O., Jr., 3142
Richards, Timothy J., 615
Richardson, Charles R., 2687
Richardson, Cora E., 2043
Richardson, Ellen R., 2332
Richardson, Frederick, 2454
Richardson, Janice K., 3760
Richardson, John A., 2259
Richardson, John V., Jr., 654
Richardson, Orvin T., 3942
Richter, Suzanne L., 3931
Rickenbach, Robert L., 3242
Ricker, Paul A., 1494
Rickman, Claude R., 3516
Riddell, Steven G., 182
Riddle, Billy R., 2674
Riddles, Willard P., 312
Rideout, Roger R., 1156
Rider, Manning C., 488
Ried, Paul E., 1207
Riekse, Robert J., 1285
Riffe, Terri D., 75
Riley, Mary A., 621
Riley, Mary L., 3999
Rilling, Alexander W., 4013
Rimington, David B., 2835
Rincon, Frank L., 3810
Ringenberg, William C., 1269
Ritchie, Gladys W., 4385
Ritchie, Linda C.S., 1557
Ritzenhein, Donald, 1361
Rives, Ralph H., 2892
Roach, Helen P., 1763
Roach, John K., 4481
Roane, Florence L., 460
Roark, Daniel B., 2619
Robarts, James R., 4339
Robb, Dale W., 2079
Robb, Mary M., 4497
Robert, Edward B., 2543
Roberts, Charlie W., Jr., 1035
Roberts, Francis X., 1691
Roberts, Norene A.D., 1390
Robertson, David F., 3243
Robertson, Henry M., 4438
Robertson, Mary P.P., 3118
Robertson, Neville L., 3811

Robey, Margaret D., 4508
Robinson, Blackwell P., 1970
Robinson, Chester H., 4482
Robinson, Giles, 273
Robinson, Ivor J., 824
Robinson, Joseph, 3453
Robinson, Omelia T., 3318
Robinson, Ray E., 1106
Robinson, Walter G., Jr., 3319
Robinson, William H., 2922
Robison, Richard W., 2836
Roblee, Dana B., 4483
Robson, David W., 3411
Roby, Lorene M., 2763
Rocker, Jack L., 3761
Rockwell, Jean A., 1586
Rockwell, Leroy, 1558
Roda, Alfonso P., 4139
Rodabaugh, James H., 2080-2081
Rodehorst, Wayne L., 1270
Rodes, Harold P., 388
Rodgers, Elise A., 2957
Rodgers, Rosemary T., 413
Rodnitzky, Jerome L., 699
Rodrigo, Arambawattage D., 3244
Roeske, Clarence E., 3923
Rogers, Clara L., 1208
Rogers, James F., 3812
Rogers, James T., 2115
Rogers, Nancy L.D., 4562
Rogers, Walter P., 1798, 2106
Rogers, William F., 2014
Rohfeld, Rae W., 1764
Rohrer, Daniel, 2107
Rolnick, Stanley R., 3106
Roloff, Ronald W., 1397
Romer, Robert D., 3517
Romney, Leonard S., 4340
Roop, Jeane, 3024
Root-Bernstein, Robert S., 4231
Roper, Dwight D., 211
Rose, Doreen D., 170
Rose, Harry E., 989
Rose, Richard M., 511
Rosell, Garth M., 2108
Rosenbaum, Judy J., 3320
Rosenberg, Helen, 1680
Rosenbrier, Gilbert M., 4386
Rosene, James, 31
Rosenstock, Sheldon A., 2145
Rosenthal, Irving, 1706
Rosenthal, Michael L., 1620
Rosentreter, Frederick M., 3072
Rosinski, Bernard J., 3390
Ross, Andrea L., 1935
Ross, Donald K., 3073
Ross, Dorothy, 1157
Ross, James A., 2068
Ross, Margery R., 1271

Ross, Naomi V., 3594
Ross, Norma, 1816
Ross, Raymond S., 3050
Ross, William R., 330
Rosskopf, Lea A., 1480
Rota, Tiziana, 1227
Rothberg, Morey D., 4341
Rothenberg, Marc, 4232
Rothenberger, Katharine, 813
Rothman, Norman C., 553
Rothstein, William G., 4098
Rothwell, William J., 3245
Rouleau, Christine R., 1036
Roundy, Jerry C., 580
Rountree, George W., 557
Rouse, Roscoe, Jr., 2659
Rowan, Jonnie, 2817
Rowan, Milton, 4233
Rowe, Elizabeth, 1060
Rowe, Roy H., Jr., 1921
Rowen, William A., 1904
Rowland, David A., 13
Rowland, Eugenia, 195
Rowland, James, 171
Roy, Victor L., 1015
Royster Horn, Juana R., 3001
Ruane, Joseph W., 1111
Ruderman, Laurie P., 2044
Rudolph, Charles F., Jr., 1244
Rudy, S. Willis, 1707
Ruffin, Mary B., 3979
Ruger, Marcus C., Jr., 3543
Rulifson, John R., 3002
Rulon, Philip R., 2211
Rumbolz, Harry H., 2958
Rumjahn, Miriam C., 655
Runda, Robert L., 829
Runge, Janis M., 3813
Runkel, H. John, 3932
Runkle, Raymond J., 3246
Runquist, Kenneth, 1235
Rush, N. Orwin, 1054
Russ, Anne J., 1906
Russell, John C., 2146
Russell, Miriam L., 1945
Russell, Tom S., 1571
Rutherford, Joann K., 3247
Rutkowski, Edward, 4342
Rutledge, Lawrence A., 3454
Ryan, Edmund G., 1121-1122
Ryan, James E., 142
Ryan, John E., 2147
Ryan, Michael G., 577
Ryder, William H., 2946

Sabock, Ralph J., 2148
Sack, Allen L., 3248

Sack, Saul, 2290
Sackmary, Benjamin D., 4234
Sadler, Esther A., 887
Sadnytzky, Nicholas O.O., 3814
Sage, George H., 250
Sahm, Jay H., 1587
Sahraie, Hashem; Sahraie, Janet, 1765
Salie, Robert D., 1209
Salinas, Anna, 3980
Salisbury, Harland R., 3455
Salley, Charles L., 1023
Salls, Donald J., 14
Salwak, Stanley F., 1137
Salyard, Ann B., 3163
Samec, Charles E., 1146
Sammis, George F., Jr., 1055
Sampson, Bill A., 2236
Sampson, Harold P., 2490
Sandborn, William C., 2339
Sandel, Mildred J., 2717
Sanders, Gabe, 3107
Sanders, James W., 601
Sanders, Jane A., 3003
Sanders, Marlin C., 456
Sandle, Floyd L., 3321
Sands, Gene C., 333
Sanford, Paul L., 2451
Santee, J.F., 2254
Santee, Joseph F., 2237
Saslaw, Rita S., 4418
Satneck, Walter J., 399
Satterfield, Virginia, 512
Saunders, Bruce D., 1096
Saunders, Harold H., 4343
Saunders, Pearl I., 3888
Saunders, Robert C., 1339
Savage, Nancy, 2238
Savage, Willinda H., 1340
Saviers, Samuel H., 2064
Sawers, William K., 3391
Sawyer, Robert M., 1461
Sawyer, William E., 3924
Sayre, Mildred B., 3533
Scarborough, David K., 2412
Scarborough, John A.L., 2797
Schaap, Eleanor H., 288
Schachner, Marcia K., 2396
Schaefer, Donald G., 2844
Schaehrer, Peter C., 3108
Schaffer, Edward W., 1843
Schanke, Robert A., 2707
Schaper, Florence W., 4344
Schatte, Curtis E., 2764
Scheetz, Mary J., 831
Scheibner, Helen L., 769
Scheinman, Muriel, 700
Schieb, Gwendolyn P., 3412
Schiller, Preston L., 4099
Schindbeck, David J., 760

Schink, Ronald J., 2175
Schisler, Charles H., 1630
Schlafmann, Norman J., 1272
Schlauch, Gustav H., 2976
Schlaver, David E., 821
Schleich, Miriam, 3518
Schlesinger, Sue H., 4419
Schley, Ruth, 3981
Schlichting, Harry F., 656
Schlifke, William H., 1820
Schmidt, George P., 4074
Schmidt, Inge, 289
Schmidt, William, 947
Schmiel, Eugene D., 2052
Schmitthenner, John W., 1814
Schmitz, Mary P., 4175
Schmotter, James W., 4166
Schmunk, Paul L., 1766
Schnapp, Mary M., Sr., 2032
Schneider, Donald O., 3413
Schneider, Lydia E., 197
Schnell, Rudolph L., 4387
Schnur, Sidney, 4000
Schock, Eldon D., 4176
Schoen, Walter T.J., 1817
Schoenberger, Karen C., 2912
Schoenhals, Lawrence R., 4140
Scholz, Carol K., 3627
Schott, Charles J., 3595
Schrader, Alvin M., 4345
Schrader, Shirley L., 1341
Schreiber, Lee L., 2346
Schreiber, Stephen T., 4388
Schubert, Florence M., 3762
Schudson, Michael S., 4100
Schufletowski, Frank W., 3570
Schulken, Emma W., 4420
Schultz, Susan F., 4235
Schulz, John A., 2239
Schumacher, Billy G., 2664
Schutter, Howard N., 3628
Schwager, Sally, 1210
Schwalm, Vernon F., 4177
Schwaneger, Henry., 397
Schwarberg, W.D., 2053
Schwartfeger, Sylvia, 3087
Schwartz, Rachel C., 1847
Schwartz, Rudolph, 4014
Schwartzwalder, Wayne W., 3032
Schwegler, John S., 3109
Schweikert, Roman J., 2171
Schwerner, Stephen A., 4421
Scott, Ellen, 1005
Scott, Frank L., 204
Scott, Gregory M., 3322
Scott, Richard P., 3982
Scott, Tom, 1971
Scott, William J., 1138
Scovel, Raleigh D., 1604

Scudiere, Paul J., 1677
Scully, James A., 2015
Seamster, Frederick C., 4484
Searcy, Sylvia C.L., 2555
Sears, Jesse B., 3678
Seaton, Chadwick L., 3629
Seaton, Leslie T., 1289
Seavey, Marceta J., 3983
Sebaly, Avis L., 1273
Sedlak, Michael W., 735
Seetharaman, Arumbavur N., 1236
Segner, Kenyon B., II, 1922
Seidel, Robert W., 143
Seller, M. Charles, 4157
Semmes, David H., 3074
Semple, Anne R., 2206
Senkier, Robert J., 1767
Serinko, Regis J., 2303
Servos, John W., 4236
Sesney, John W., 3544
Sevick, Charles V., 487
Sevy, Barbara, 2405
Seward, Doris M., 1873
Sewell, Tom S., 2620
Sexton, John E., 1211
Shackelford, Walter M., 1432
Shackson, Marian, 1287
Shafer, Henry B., 3984, 4101
Shaffer, Lowell D., 2291
Shank, Russell, 4237
Shankland, Wilbur M., 1462
Shannon, Edith R., 1588
Shannon, Samuel H., 2567
Shapiro, Harvey S., 4065
Shapiro, Ira G., 3143
Shapiro, Max A., 3912
Shaughnessy, Thomas E., 4015
Shaw, Otto E., 2190
Shaw, Ralph R., 4238
Shawen, Neil M., 2959
Shay, John E., Jr., 4422
Shea, Charlotte K., 1228
Shea, Whitney J., 1818
Sheahan, Dorothy A., 3763
Shealy, Cyrus S., 2476
Sheehan, Michael T., 2376
Sheehan, Patrick M., 1212
Sheehan, Roberta A., 1152
Sheets, Norman L., 3017
Shehee, Blanche A., 513
Shelburne, James C., 334
Shelton, William E., 2621
Shennon, Ella W., 1342
Shepherd, Robert E., 3323
Sheppard, Charles P., 1115
Sheppard, Lydia D., 559
Sherard, Catherine, 514
Sherer, Robert G., Jr., 15
Shereshewsky, Murray S., 1613

Sheridan, Phyllis B., 1768
Sherman, John, 1594
Sherockman, Andrew A., 837
Sherratt, Gerald R., 2847
Sherwood, Philip K., 770
Sherwood, Sidney, 1863
Shields, Elizabeth A., 3764
Shields, JoAnn B., 4346
Shiflett, Orvin L., 3985
Shilling, Katheryn T., 2489
Shinn, Marion L., 570
Shipp, Frederic T., 144
Shirley, Betty L., 825
Shockley, Ethel V., 2622
Shoemaker, Alice, 3164
Shoen, Harriet H., 3545
Shores, Louis S., 4522
Shores, Louis, 3986
Shoub, Ralph D., 3815
Shuchman, Hedvah L., 355
Shults, Fredrick D., 2109
Shultz, Alva T., 4347
Sidar, Jean W., 1621
Sidnell, Robert G., Jr., 2811
Sievers, Camille G., 3249
Sikes, William M., 46
Sillars, Malcolm S., 252
Sills, James H., Jr., 402
Silva, Sister Frances C., 2169
Silver, George, 1589
Silverman, Peter H., 548
Simeone, Angela M., 4563
Simmons, Joseph D., 2568
Simmons, S.A., 4564
Simon, Henry W., 3889
Simon, Martin P., 1539
Simpson, Lowell, 3193
Sims, Edward R., 2329
Sims, Frank K., 2464
Simson, Sharon J.P., 2377
Sinclair, Joseph B., 2318
Sinclair, Oran L., 2660
Singer, Claude C., 4239
Singleton, Edward M., 2474
Sisco, Sue L.P., 2718
Siske, James H., 3687
Sitter, Clara L., 2798
Sizemore, Virginia L., 3019
Skelton, Phillip D., 107
Skelton, Robert H., 4027
Skinner, Albert T., 1682
Skipper, James E., 2149
Skirvin, Emmett E., Jr., 205
Sklar, Bernard, 3075
Skoog, Rodney A., 1372
Skyrm, Richard D., 2110
Sladek, Lyle V., 2492
Slavens, Thomas P., 848, 1878
Sliney, Bruce M., 2095

Sloan, James C., 908
Sloan, Patricia E., 3765
Slonaker, Arthur G., 3026
Small, Herbert G., 191
Smallwood, Frances, 93
Smallwood, Mary L., 4498
Smart, Ronald E., 274
Smawley, Robert B., 3519
Smeby, Myrtle V., 3456
Smedley, Margaret A., 3909
Smit, Pamela R., 1829
Smith, Aine P., 2893
Smith, Alan M., 2894
Smith, Allan B., 356
Smith, Andrew W., 3890
Smith, Anthony R., 1343
Smith, Boyce O., 519
Smith, Charles L., 1923
Smith, Charles R., Jr., 3630
Smith, Clustor Q., 2623
Smith, Dale C., 4001
Smith, Dolores F., 959
Smith, Dora, 172
Smith, Dorothy J., 2295
Smith, Earle R., 32
Smith, Faye E., 1304
Smith, Francis W., 4066
Smith, Gilbert E., III, 3596
Smith, Glenn R., 313
Smith, Gregory L., 3051
Smith, Henry J., 297
Smith, Herbert E., 4240
Smith, J.W., 2719
Smith, James S., 1070
Smith, Janet F., 2515
Smith, Jay T., Sr., 1412
Smith, Jesse G., 2663
Smith, Jessie C., 3987
Smith, Jessie M., 3360
Smith, Keith L., 2837-2838
Smith, Lamar, 3324
Smith, Lewis I., 2675
Smith, Marjory A.I., 3891
Smith, Mark C., 4348
Smith, Mazine H., 2991
Smith, Melvin, 602
Smith, Michael D., 3076
Smith, Mildred P., 4565
Smith, Morris E., 183
Smith, Nila B., 3520
Smith, Nina B., 3766
Smith, Paul R.G., 771
Smith, Peggy C., 3816
Smith, Peter P., 2872
Smith, Raymond E., 1769
Smith, Robert M., 1213
Smith, Ronald A., 3041
Smith, Russell T., 2913
Smith, Terry W., 2378

Smith, Thaddeus T., 948
Smith, Travis E., 960
Smith, Walter L., 457
Smith, Willard G., 4141
Smith, Willard W., 3414
Smith, William S., 290
Smith, Willis L., 2731
Smola, Bonnie K., 843
Smolich, Robert S., 3457
Snarr, Otto W., 4485
Snowden, Gary L., 2624
Snyder, Sam R., 1344
Soare, Warren G., 3250
Sobolik, Gayle A., 3361
Sokal, Michael M., 1770
Sollinger, Charles E., 3892
Solomon, Alan L., 3194
Sonnedecker, Glenn A., 3767
Sonner, Ray V., 2928
Sorensen, Willis C., 4241
Souder, Marian J., 2054
Soulier, Sister Catherine F., 1716
South, Oron P., 4349
Spainhower, James I., 1463
Spalding, Sharon B., 2740
Sparhawk, Ruth M., 3251
Sparks, Claud G., 1345
Sparks, Robbie S., 33
Spector, Ronald H., 2443
Speidel, Charles M., 2358
Spence, Judson C., Sr., 3817
Spencer, Louise W., 3534
Spencer, Thomas M., Jr., 2735
Sperduto, Frank V., 1622
Spiegle, Edward F., 1528
Spindle, Oran R., 4142
Spindt, Herman A., 173
Spiro, Bernard, 335
Spofford, Timothy J., 1421
Sponberg, Adryn L., 3252
Sprague, Harry A., 4486
Sprankle, Dale R., 1279
Spratt, Bessie W., 855
Springer, Clair G., 2258
Sproul, Christine, 3651
Stachiw, Jaroslaw D., 4242
Stack, Elizabeth C., 3521
Stafford, Frances J., 4350
Stagg, Paul, 3253
Stahl, Wayne K., 603
Staib, Mary P., 3631
Stallings, Charles W., 3325
Stallman, Abraham M., 1708
Stambaugh, Ben F., Jr., 1799
Stameshkin, David M., 2870
Stankiewicz, Mary Ann, 1874
Stanley, Ellen L., 787
Stanley, Larry D., 961
Stanton, Charles M., 145

Star, Bonnie S., 3893
Stark, Cruce, 1408
Stark, Grace W., 1409
Stark, Lois, 2359
Startz, Milton, 1709
Stathis, John C., 2558
Stathis-Ochoa, Roberta A., 4439
Staton, Mary L., 4487
Staud, Margaret C., 4243
Stavely, Martha R., 291
Stavish, Emanuel, 1614
Steckman, Mildred C., 314
Steelman, Bobby J., 95
Stefanov, Jan J., 1491
Stegath, William B., 1346
Stegenga, Preston J., 1288
Stein, Charles W., 3522
Stein, David T., 1464
Stein, John H., 2065
Stein, Lloyd E., 657
Steiner, Bernard C., 1071
Steinger, Charles S., 492
Steinhauser, Richard G., 963
Stentz, Oren W., 2156
Steph, Harlan J., 3535
Stephens, Cline B., Jr., 4366
Stephens, Harold H., 920
Stephens, Raphael W., III, 2553
Sterling, Jo Ann J., 665
Stetar, Joseph M., 3818
Stevens, Eugene H., Jr., 247
Stevens, Glenn R., 1305
Stevens, William H., III, 2979
Stevenson, Louise L., 389
Stevenson, Perry L., 3571
Stevenson, William I., 2625
Stevenson, William J., 4389
Stewart, Charles J., 2487
Stewart, Gloria P., 348
Stewart, Nathaniel J., 1710
Stewart, Ralph E., 1492
Stewart, Richard A., 1436
Stillman, Rachel B., 4529
Stillwell, Hamilton, 3362
Stine, George F., 2360
Stinehart, James S., 888
Stites, Francis N., 1576
Stiver, Harry E., Jr., 1559
Stoeckel, Althea L., 3415
Stomfay-Stitz, Aline M., 726
Stompler, Russell, 4016
Stone, Bruce W., 1139
Stone, Charles A., 4488
Stone, Helen W., 909
Stone, Marie K., 658
Stooke, David E., 4102
Storey, Bertha M., 3458
Storie, Catharine, 3988
Storm, Harrie P., 1119

Storr, Richard J., 3708
Story, Donna K., 844
Stout, Billy H., 2561
Stout, Loreen W., 2292
Stoutenburg, Herbert N., Jr., 1355
Stracka, Daniel, 753
Strain, Sibyl M., 4566
Stranges, John B., 1771
Strauss, Lovell H., 3989
Strimer, Robert M., 2016
Stritter, Frank T., 1897
Strobel, Eugene C., Jr., 1357
Strobel, Marian E., 4567
Strong, Evelyn R., 2191
Strother, Martha D., 2702
Struthers, Frederick R., 3459
Struthers, Robert E., 2839
Stryker, Mabel K., 941
Stuart, Mary C., 174
Stubblefield, Harold W., 3165
Stumpf, Wippert A., 659
Sturchio, Jeffrey L., 4244
Sturgeon, Angie H., 3460
Sturtevant, Charles C., 419
Styons, Robert B., 515
Suelflow, Roy A., 1475
Suen, Ming T., 701
Suhrie, Eleanor B., 2397
Sullivan, John E., 3326
Sullivan, Patricia A., 351
Sullivan, R. Mark, 358
Summer, Pepi, 1692
Summers, Kurt, 2069
Summers, Victoria F., 1239
Summerscales, William, 1772
Summersette, John F., 522
Sundstrand, Lyndon D., 3632
Super, Sister Dolores, 3894
Super, Stacia I., 4351
Sussman, Diane, 1685
Sutton, Robert B., 3110
Sutton, William S., 2157
Svob, Roberts S., 76
Swadener, Marc, 814
Swann, John P., 4183
Swanson, Jon W., 3679
Swanson, Phyllis R., 622
Swanson, Richardson A., 702
Swartz, Jack H., 192
Swarz, Ilona P., 1214
Swets, Marinus M., 1286
Swingle, Marilyn R., 474
Swisher, Randall S., 4390
Swiss, Deborah J., 1057
Sylvester, Blaine E., 2862
Syme, Eric D., 3461
Synan, Harold V., 527
Synnott, Marcia G., 3156
Szymczak, Donald R., 743

Tachikawa, Akira, 1224
Tade, Wilma J.D., 674
Tadie, Nancy B., 420
Talbot, Gordon G., 3119
Talbott, Laurence F., 4245
Taliaferro, Cecil R., 2965
Taliaferro, William, 2626
Talley, Kate, 2665
Tanner, Carol M., 2960
Tanner, Louis E., 2223
Tarlton, Shirley M., 1975
Tata, Samba S., 3327
Tatum, Beulah B., 4489
Taub, Andrew, 3895
Taylor, Bernard A., 921
Taylor, Charles W., 2316, 4143
Taylor, Cyrus B., 3328
Taylor, Ethelyn P., 2840
Taylor, George D., 4440
Taylor, Luciann W., 2720
Taylor, Prince A., Jr., 531
Taylor, Walter C., 2463
Taylor, William W., 1347
Teele, Arthur E., 1924
Temin, Charlotte B., 3523
Temple, Ronald J., 3462
Tergerson, Charles J., 4352
Terrell, Darrell, 1215
Terry, William E., 2774
Tewell, Fred, 1037
Tewksbury, Donald G., 3819
Texter, Merry E., 3896
Thackery, John, 4423
Thames, Anna-Marie, 146
Thelin, John R., 3820
Thomas, Arnold R., 3897
Thomas, Dale O., 3254
Thomas, George W., 1039
Thomas, Gregory, 3329
Thomas, Katherine E., 3898
Thomas, Mary M., 2741
Thomas, Milton H., 1773
Thomas, Ota, 3665
Thomas, Richard K., 475
Thomasson, Arnold L., 4490
Thomison, Dennis V., 3990
Thompkins, Robert E., 3330
Thompson, Bertha B., 2082
Thompson, Jay C., Jr., 772
Thompson, Jo Ann G., 3821
Thompson, John F., 3463
Thompson, Kenneth D., 3255
Thompson, Lloyd K., 2627
Thompson, Mary M., 3524
Thompson, Sister Mary M., 1097
Thompson, Wade H., Jr., 778

Thompson, Willard C., 3925
Thomson, Mary, 3768
Thornburgh, Daniel E., 736
Thornton, David H., 3331
Thornton, Thurle C., Jr., 3004
Thorpe, Judith L., 1972
Throne, Mildred, 889
Thurber, Evangeline, 3926
Thurber, John H., 1543
Thurman, Francis A., 2935
Thurmond, Raymond C., 3256
Tidwell, Frank R., 2850
Tiffin, Gerald C., 4144
Tift, Thomas N., 604
Tiger, Dennis D., 2293
Tilley, Winthrop, 4246
Timmons, David R., 2192
Tingey, Joseph W., 2923
Tinsley, Sammy J., 1434
Tipps, Garland E., 1635
Tipton, Elizabeth H., 1079
Tisdale, Thomas T., 1423
Titowsky, Bernard, 3077
Tobacco, Charles T., 3005
Tobey, Ronald C., 4247
Tobias, Marilyn I., 1577
Toepfer, Kenneth H., 1774
Toles, Caesar F., 4367
Tolles, Bryant F., Jr., 3177
Tolley, Jerry R., 1938
Tolman, William H., 2428
Tolson, Billy J., 17
Tomikel, John, 4248
Tomlan, Michael A., 4103
Tomlinson, Marie G., 2765
Tompson, Horace R., 2628
Tong, Curtis W., 2111
Toole, Robert C., 2556
Tootle, Randolph F., 1348
Topping, Leonard W., 2919
Torney, John A., 3257
Torres, Maximino D., 722
Torsey, Kathleen E., 4353
Tostberg, Robert E., 605
Totaro, Joseph V., 390
Toto, Charles, 147
Towler, Daniel L., 4167
Townsend, Lucy F., 739
Towry, Inez C., 1042
Trapp, Leonard Y., 4145
Trares, Thomas F., 756
Travers, Harold E., 328
Travers, Paul D., 3822
Travis, William G., 4354
Traxler, Joseph M., 754
Traylor, Judy A.G., 4441
Treacy, Robert E., 239
Tremonti, Joseph B., 3392
Trice, Ethel P., 2544

Triebwasser, Marc A., 4355
Triggs, Frances O., 4442
Trimpe, Dale W., 606
Trindale, Armando D., 292
Trout, Douglas G., 4146
Troutman, R. Dwight, 2399
Truby, Roy E., 571
Trueheart, William E., 3332
Truman, Margot, 2500
Truscott, Natalie A., 1805
Trusz, Andrew R., 1678
Tucker, Jennie S., 2112
Tucker, John M., 2113
Tucker, Kenneth W., 3258
Tucker, Louis L., 391-392
Tufano, Alfred G., 3078
Turk-Roge, Janet L.C., 937
Turlington, Terry T., 1504
Turnbach, Catherine R., 2340
Turner, Edna M., 4249
Turner, Eula D., 275
Turner, Theodore B., III, 3633
Turner, William L., 2379
Turrentine, Mrs. Richard J., 3709
Tutt, Celestine C., 1775
Tuttle, John G., 4250
Tuttle, William M., Jr., 1216
Twohy, David W., 2083
Tyler, Frances L., 1414
Tyler, Kenneth D., 727
Tyran, Cynthia J., 1979
Tyree, Lawrence W., 458

Ulbrickson, Alvin E., 3006
Ulrich, Robert J., 3042
Umberson, George E., 3899
Underwood, Harold L, 34
Unruh, Alice E., 783
Urata, James H., 184
Usher, Mildred M., 476

Valade, William J.A., 1274
Valenti, Paul B., 2245
Valentine, Sister M., 2327
Valenzuela, Harvey, 1638
Valla, Joseph P., 2361
Vallance, Harvard F., 2028
Van Arsdall, James E., 1560
Van Bibber, Edward C., 3259
Van Camp, Leonard W., 3900
Van de Water, Peter E., 1349
Van de Wetering, Maxine S., 4251
Van Horn, Harold E., 2435
Van Horn, James E., 16
Van Houten, Peter S., 175

Van Loan, Lillian S., 2246
Vance, Maurice M., 3079
VanderGriend, Ward M., 2841
Vanderhoof, Wesley E., 393
VanderMeer, Barbara G., 3634
Vandever, William T., Jr., 4147
VanEyck, Daniel K., 1350
Vanlandingham, Karen E., 560
Vanvalkenburgh, Lloyd L., 1275
Varnado, Otto S., 1016
Vaughan, George B., 2895
Vaughan, John E., 4148
Vaughn, William H., 968
Vaughn, William P., 4067
Veasey, Columbus, Jr., 4252
Veith, Donald P., 3666
Venuto, Louis J., 2362
Vermilya, Nancy C., 2163
Verner, William S., 206
Veron, Gale, 3260
Veysey, Laurence R., 3823
Vick, Mildred W., 2721
Vincent, Audrey W., 1237
Vittum, Henry E., 1623
Vlahos, Michael E., 2444
Vogt, Peter J., 2084
Voigt, Harry R., 1930
Vokes, Lee S., 148
Volberg, Rachel A., 4253
Vollmar, Edward R., 3393
Vollmar, William J., 2150
Voltmer, Carl D., 3261
Von Conrad, Georgia B., 1482
Vosper, James M., 1542
Vujnovich, Miles M., 1410

Waage, James, 896
Waas, Lulu M., 4568
Wack, John T., 822
Wacker, Hazel M., 3769
Waddell, Frederick J., 2629
Waddell, John N., 1776
Wade, Louise H., 1020
Wadell, Keith A., 755
Wadsworth, Emily C., 723
Wadsworth, L.E., 1465
Waffle, Eugene M., 2545
Wagner, Hilda S., 1229
Wagner, Lloyd F., 2333
Wagner, Marta, 3824
Wagoner, Jennings L., Jr., 4424
Wainwright, Frank N., 227
Wake, Orville W., 2927
Waldo, Michael J., 3991
Waldorf, James A., 728
Waldrip, William L., 100
Waldron, Calvin H., 1777

Walker, Franklin T., 1778
Walker, Mary M.J., 729
Walker, Phillip N., 3007
Walker, Thomas T., 2703
Wall, Charles C., 2961
Wall, William L., 2017
Wallace, Jeffry J., 1864
Wallace, Percival E., 2644
Wallace, Sylvia F., 3080
Wallenfeldt, Evert C., 3081
Waller, Charlie F., 2753
Waller, Fred, 2502
Wallis, Judith M., 942
Wallisch, William J., Jr., 336
Walsh, James P., 176
Walsh, Mary R., 1140
Walsh, Thomas R., 1561
Walsh, Walter, 2931
Walter, Edwin C., 4149
Walter, Judith M., 1779
Walter, Maila L. K., 1217
Wanamaker, John F., 4254
Wang, Peter Y.K., 3262
Wang, Shu-ching Y., 1218
Wangberg, Martha I., 890
Wangensteen, Margaret R., 1391
Warch, Richard, 394
Ward, Arthur, 2382
Ward, Earl R., 910
Ward, Natalie J.S., 251
Ward, Richard H., 2516
Warden, James E., 2899
Wardrip, Mark A., 177
Ware, Bettie A., 1240
Ware, Lowry P., 660
Warford, Malcolm L., 4150
Warlick, Kenneth R., 1925
Warner, Frank L., 1051
Warner, Gordon, 149
Warren, Constancia, 1711
Warren, E.N., 2255
Warren, J.I., 2630
Warren, Nagueyalti, 523
Warren, Shirley C., 3008
Warriner, David R., 815
Washington, Walter, 1441
Washke, Paul R., 3770
Waters, Rudolph E., 3333
Watkins, Bari J., 4517
Watkins, Mary B.S., 2569
Watson, James E., 178
Watson, Jan C., 1977
Watson, Robert J., 2401
Watson, Rollin J., 3572
Wayland, John T., 395
Weakley, Margaret E., 2962
Weatherford, Terry L., 703
Weatherhead, Arthur C., 4104
Weaver, Mary L., 3652

Weaver, R.G., 398
Weaver, Samuel H., 3597
Webb, David L., 3643
Webb, Lester A., 1894, 4017
Webb, Russell F., 2631
Webber, Robert S., 3635
Weber, Ralph E., 823
Webster, David S., 3825
Webster, Randolph W., 1306
Wechsler, Harold S., 3157
Wedertz, Gilbert C., 179
Weeks, Sandra R., 2807
Wegener, Frank C., 4049
Weidenbach, Amelia R., 891
Weidman, John M., 2220
Weil, Oscar A., Jr., 716
Weinberg, Julius, 3082
Weiner, Charles I., 443
Weintraub, Arnold, 1563
Weintraub, Stanley A., 3901
Weiss, Janice H., 3363
Weitekamp, Raymond, 414
Welch, Eloise T., 3334
Welch, Frank G., 150
Welch, Joe B., 2698
Welch, Joseph E., 1147
Welch, Myron D., 1307
Welch, Robert W., 3927
Welch, Tony J., 2842
Weller, L. David, Jr., 856
Wells, Donald A., 719
Wells, Margaret C., 1875
Wemple, Quincy A., 607
Wentz, Richard E., 2363
Wenzke, Annabelle S., 396
Werdinger, Jeffrey, 1245
Wert, Robert J., 1219
West, Earle H., 2436
West, Francis M., 2520
Westbay, William W., 307
Westerberg, Virginia M., 892
Westhaver, Steven J., 2676
Westin, Richard B., 1926
Westlake, Richard K., 3263
Westphaf, Leonard W., 1506
Wetzel, Charles J., 3653
Weyer, Frank E., 1535
Whalen, Mary G., 817
Wheadon, Rosetta F.D., 1466
Wheadon, William C., 4184
Wheatley, Steven C., 4002
Whistler, Harvey S., 1780
White, Annie Mae V., 2725
White, Clarence, Jr., 3335
White, Estelle E., 3166
White, Irle E., 2256
White, Jacqueline A., 2158
White, Katherine E., 1308
White, Katherine H., 3336

White, Maxwell O., 4356
White, Michael A., 2632, 2661
White, Woodie T., 661
Whitehead, John S., 3405
Whitehead, Marie H., 2729
Whitmer, Edith F., 3826
Whitney, Herbert C., 1075
Whitson, William W., 2409
Whittemore, Richard F., 1781
Whittington, Russell, Jr., 4255
Wiberg, Charles E., 1392
Wicker, William W., 3992
Wickiser, Ralph L., 608
Wiebe, David U., 911
Wiebe, Jeffrey J., 757
Wiegandt, Don B., 1309
Wierwillie, Donald E., 916
Wilbanks, Floy F., 2780
Wilbee, Victor R., 1351
Wilbur, Barbara, 2914
Wilcox, Lucile E., 704
Wilcox, Reba W., 2863
Wilder, Joan K., 1220
Wildman, Edward L., 2666
Wiley, Wayne H., 2963
Wilgus, Billy E., 2030
Wilkins, Orin L., 2193
Wilkinson, Carl W., III, 2461
Wilkinson, Jean L., 3012
Willbern, Glen D., 2750
Willers, Jack C., 2799
Willey, Darrell S., 2864
Williams, Ann L., 2941
Williams, Barbara J., 3993
Williams, Brenda G., 1038
Williams, C.W., 2337
Williams, Cartus R., 1517
Williams, David A., 2633
Williams, David, 3195
Williams, Earl F., 2662
Williams, Earl R., 104
Williams, Glenn D., 2018
Williams, Hobie L., 524
Williams, Howard D., 1714
Williams, Howard R., 2045
Williams, John A., 196
Williams, John R., 1536
Williams, Lea E., 3337
Williams, Marjorie G., 922
Williams, Mary M., 2980
Williams, Mima A., 2669
Williams, Omer S., 3144
Williams, Robert L., 305
Williams, Sallye L., 4569
Williams, Samuel A., 1679
Williams, Sidney A., 2742
Williamson, Graydon G., 3033
Williamson, Phyllis M.D., 1058
Willis, H. Warren, 415

Willmon, Jesse C., 26
Willoughby, Avalee, 44
Willoughby, Glenn E., 2977
Wills, Elbert V., 4357
Wills, Lynette A.H., 2546
Willson, John P., 1782
Willson, Michael W., 71
Wilmarth, David L., 4256
Wilson, Ann E.J., 4491
Wilson, Ben Jr., 2745
Wilson, Douglas, 2085
Wilson, Ella M., 3028
Wilson, Ellen G., 3827
Wilson, George D., 3338
Wilson, George P., Jr., 2964
Wilson, Henrietta, 3009
Wilson, Herman K., III, 2475
Wilson, Jettie L., 38
Wilson, Karl K., 4358
Wilson, Lois M., 1352
Wilson, M. Debora, 3394
Wilson, Marlene, 2019
Wilson, Maureen P., 3902
Wilson, Robert A., 705
Wilson, Robert, Jr., 1017
Wilson, S.K., 3416
Wilson, Wilbert R., 1102
Wims, Lu D., 2020
Winckler, Paul A., 1783
Windrow, John E., 2547
Wine, Margaret A.M., 893
Winegarden, Neil A., 4509
Wing, Lucy F., 3828
Wing, Mary J., 1973
Wing, Roger L., 706
Wingard, Kathleen M., 2480
Winkleman, Gerald G., 4151
Winn, Evelyn B., 2457
Winn, Janet B., 4359
Winship, Frank L., 1565, 2634
Winston, Chauncey G., 773
Winston, Eric V.A., 1310
Winters, Elmer A., 1784
Winters, Marilyn B., 3525
Winton, George P., Jr., 1895
Wisneski, Carl A., 3526
Wisor, Harold C., 2336
Witherington, Henry C., 2517
Witt, Michael J., 2523
Wkovich, Steven R., 1221
Woelfel, Norman, 3829
Woerlin, George W., 3264
Woerman, Melodie B., 3395
Wofford, Kate V., 4492
Wolf, Donald L., 707
Wolf, Harold H., 3265
Wolf, Hugh A., 3464
Wolf, Ruth B., 4443
Wolfe, Thomas H., 2800

Woo, Kun K., 4360
Wood, Chester W., 1368
Wood, Edwin K., 2221
Wood, Joyce L., 2086
Wood, Thomas C., 3120
Woodburn, Ethelbert C., 2484
Woodburn, James A., 774
Woodburn, Robert O., 2896
Woodbury, Darwin S., 2846
Woodnick, Michael L., 1161
Woodruff, Joe H., 2225
Woodward, George R., 3091
Woodward, Mary T., 2772
Woodyard, William T., 337
Woofter, James A., 2055
Woolums, Edward C., 4023
Woomer, Dale W., 2294
Wooten, Rebecca G., 2559
Wooten, Samuel R., 1980
Wootton, Ralph T., 2635
Workman, George L., 1498
Worner, Lloyd E., 1518
Worthington, Leland G., 1103
Wortman, Leonore, 1828
Woytanowitz, George M., 3527
Wray, Mary E., 2364
Wrenn, Jack, 1936
Wright, Chester W., 3339
Wright, Clare B., 2194
Wright, Irvin L., 3417
Wright, Jerry J., 2039
Wright, R.D., 2088
Wright, Richard G., 3465
Wurseter, Stephen H., 662
Wyer, Jean C., 3830
Wygant, Foster L., 1785
Wyllie, Robert H., 357
Wyneland, John L., 609

Xenakis, William A., 293

Yakely, Leon, 3831
Yanagihara, Hikaru, 4152
Yarborough, Legrand I., 2452
Yarcho, Yvonne V., 294
Yarish, La Vera M., 459
Yazawa, Melvin M., 3418
Yeaney, Darrell W., 4178
Yearnd, Moretta A., 894
Yenawine, Wayne S., 708
Yerby, Frank G., 3340
Yevish, Irving A., 3636
Yin, Tsi-chieh L., 3943
Young, Alfred C., 295
Young, Alfred, 4050

Young, Burns B., 4493
Young, James M., 3903
Young, James N., 3598
Young, Jerry G., 1467
Young, Matt N., 4153
Young, Virgil M., 572
Young, Wade P., 1927
Young, William L., 2021
Youngberg, Elizabeth M., 264
Youngquist, Bernard E., 1393
Younker, Donna L., 2636
Yulish, Stephen M., 4051

Zaheer, Mohammad, 3364
Zahorsky, Arthur, 2493
Zaidenberg, Arthur, 1222
Zam, Gerard A., 2022

Zeigler, Earle F., 3771
Ziegenfuss, George, 1786
Zielonka, Alfred W., 3904
Ziemba, Walter J., 3121
Zimbalist, Sidney E., 4361
Zimmer, Agatho P., 3832
Zimmerman, Joan G., 4425
Zimmerman, Norman A., 3083
Zimmerman, William D., 1800
Zimring, Fred R., 2406
Zingale, Donald P., 3772
Ziporyn, Terra D., 4105
Zschoche, Sue, 4570
Zubatsky, David E., 3994
Zuckerman, Harriet A., 4257
Zuersher, Dorothy J.S., 1896
Zunzer, Robert F., 663
Zusman, Ami, 151
Zwerman, Gilda N., 3145

SUBJECT INDEX

[Numbers refer to entry numbers]

Abilene Christian University, 2637-2641
Academic freedom, 120, 150, 161, 171, 231, 293,
    1344, 1997, 2322, 2406, 2413, 2447, 2786,
    2963, 3003, 3092-3110, 3471, 3628
Academies, 3493
Accounting, 1010, 3356, 3359, 3638
Accreditation, 117, 2940, 3111-3121, 3285, 3365,
    3447, 3857
Accrediting Association of Bible Colleges, 3119
Adams State College, 305
Adams, Herbert B., 1091-1093, 1096
Adelphi University, 1680
Administration, 63, 121, 210, 247, 257, 260, 295,
    332, 333, 346, 515, 576, 598, 624, 649, 705,
    711, 741-742, 747, 766, 778, 791, 810, 818,
    870, 872, 969, 1008, 1104, 1184, 1205, 1219,
    1330, 1336, 1352-1353, 1355, 1387, 1390,
    1464, 1495, 1575, 1582, 1589, 1592, 1653-
    1654, 1712, 1857, 1875, 1893, 1955, 2020,
    2055, 2069, 2086, 2156, 2215, 2388, 2419,
    2426, 2514, 2529, 2548, 2553, 2578, 2626,
    2853, 2861, 2893, 2925, 3038, 3055-3056,
    3068, 3122-3145, 3173, 3191, 3223, 3282,
    3293, 3322, 3415, 3465, 3484, 3510, 3668,
    3698, 3742, 3931, 4052, 4073, 4440, 4480,
    4531
Admissions, 10, 156, 336, 388, 767, 1059, 1073,
    1197, 1644, 1711, 2254, 2470, 2912, 3146-
    3157, 3545, 3935
Adrian College, 1267
Adult education, 50, 535, 542, 615, 626, 795, 1511,
    1587, 1950, 1951, 2386, 2837, 3158-3166,
    3306, 4519
Affirmative action, 1399
Afghanistan, 1765
AFL-CIO, 4511
Africa, 2335
African Methodist Episcopal Church, 3307
African Methodist Episcopal higher education, 553,
    1944, 2172, 3289
Agassiz, Louis, 1192
Age of Fable, 3843
Agricultural education, 28, 96, 165, 505, 595, 852,
    1027, 1048, 1103, 1126, 1296, 1298, 1393,
    1417, 1425, 1621, 1792, 1794, 1927, 1948-
    1949, 2211, 2355, 2356, 2452, 2567, 2755,
    2762, 2765, 2802, 2848, 2942, 2969, 2990,
    3053, 3167-3171, 3643, 4194
Agriculture, 3643

Ainsworth, Dorothy S., 1233
Air University, 17
Akron, University of, 2023, 4522
Alabama, 1-60, 4063
Alabama Collegiate Conference, 9
Alabama State University, 18
Alabama, University of, 19-26
Alaska, 61-64
Alaska Methodist University, 63
Albany State College, 516-517
Albany (University), State University of New York,
    1681
Albertus Magnus College, 349
Alberty, Harold B., 2121
Albion College, 1267, 1276-1279
Albuquerque, NM, 1641
Alcorn State University, 1411-1412
Alderman, Edwin A., 2963
Alexander City State Junior College, 27
Allegheny College, 2295
Allport, Gordon, 4273
Alma College, 1267
Alma White College, 1590
Almira College, 672
Alumni, 331, 424, 987, 1011, 1048, 1212, 1426,
    1571, 1692, 1722, 1741, 1899, 2085, 2300,
    2761, 2764, 2832, 3172-3175, 3413, 3651,
    4374, 4532, 4536-4537
Amarillo College, 2642
Amateur Athletic Union of the United States, 3209
American Academy of Physical Education, 3747,
    3755
American Association for Health, Physical Education,
    and Recreation, 3770
American Association of Junior Colleges, 3424, 3454
American Association of Scientific Workers, 4212
American Association of Theological Schools, 3111
American Association of University Professors, 1392,
    2406, 3095, 3101, 3186, 3441
American Association of University Women, 1404,
    2614
American Baptist Association, 4108
American College for Girls, 3651
American College in Rome, 411
American College of Sports Medicine, 3197
American College Personnel Association, 4433,
    4436
American College Public Relations Association, 4157
American College Society, 3988

American College Testing Program, 3543
American College Theatre Festival, 3872
American Education Society, 3190
American Educational Theatre Association, 3854
American Federation of Teachers, 4514
American Federation of Teachers (Los Angeles), 115
American Football Coaches Association, 3213
American Historical Association, 4268, 4315, 4336
American Historical Review, 4356
American Indians, 62, 2195, 2198, 2923, 3417,
    4024-4027
American Institute of Certified Public Accountants,
    3359
American Institute of Sacred Literature, 626
American Journal of Nursing, 3720
American Library Association, 3990, 3994
American Literature, 1935
American Missionary Association, 3313, 3334
American Philosophical Society, 4208
American Public Health Association, 3726
American Social Science Association, 4301
American Society for Public Administration, 3192
American Theological Library Association, 3966
Amherst College, 1141-1147, 1735, 3173, 3250
Amherst Project, 3505
Anderson College (IN), 761, 775
Anderson College (SC), 2453
Anderson, Carl L., 3713
Anderson, Rasmus B., 3060
Anderson, William G., 386
Anderson-Broaddus College, 3014
Andover Newton Theological Seminary, 1148
Andreen, Gustav, 610
Andrew College, 518
Andrew Female College, 519
Andrews University, 1267, 1280-1281, 4507
Andrews, Elisha B., 2432
Angell, James B., 1351, 4424
Angelo State University, 2643
Ann Arbor Human Rights Party, 1343
Anna T. Jeans Foundation, 3672
Anne Arundel Community College, 1072
Annhurst College, 350
Anthropology, 405, 2781
Antioch College, 2024-2028
Archaeology, 2781
Architecture, 236, 438, 463, 737, 1643, 3176-3177,
    3944, 3949, 3953, 3978, 4091-4092, 4103-4104
Archives, 436, 4264
Arden Club, 2736
Arizona, 65-82
Arizona Music Educators Assocation, 71
Arizona State University, 72-74
Arizona, University of, 75-76
Arkansas, 83-107, 3433
Arkansas City Junior College, 912
Arkansas College, 91
Arkansas State University, 92-93
Arkansas, University of, 94-95

Arkansas, University of (Pine Bluff), 96-98
Armstrong, Samuel C., 2920
Art education, 98, 416, 524, 700, 746, 937, 1112,
    1152, 1172, 1326, 1693, 1702, 1729, 1755,
    1839, 1867, 1874, 2345-2346, 2374, 2811,
    2844, 3588, 3858, 3860, 3867, 3883, 4450,
    4466
Arthur D. Little Management Education Institute,
    3696
Articulation, 10, 131, 2235, 2607, 3502, 3884, 4283
Asbury College, 962-963
Ashland College, 2029-2030
Aslin, Neil C., 1489
Assembly of God higher education, 2746, 2980
Associated Colleges of Central Kansas, 903
Associated Colleges of Indiana, 770-771
Association for Higher Education, 3798
Association for the Advancement of Science, 4217
Association of American Universities, 3188
Association of College and Secondary Schools for
    Negroes, 3314
Association of College and Research Libraries, 3952
Association of Research Libraries, 3965
Association of Texas Colleges, 2600
Association of University Summer Sessions, 3509
Associations and societies, 3115, 3178-3195, 3264,
    3799, 4185, 4482
Astronomy, 1901-1902, 4204, 4232, 4545
Athenaeum of Ohio, 2031-2032
Athens, GA, 504
Athletics, 9, 44, 75-76, 92, 148, 186, 189, 192, 198-
    199, 202-203, 206, 220, 232, 255, 260-261,
    279, 305, 326, 378, 434, 461, 467, 471, 476,
    539, 575, 579, 593, 628, 647, 666-668, 676,
    680-681, 683, 687, 689, 694-696, 703, 705-707,
    710, 725, 776, 792, 847, 882, 912, 914-915,
    917, 921, 926, 928-929, 940, 944, 976, 1036,
    1191, 1249, 1277, 1279, 1291, 1309, 1312,
    1330, 1336, 1339, 1342, 1372-1373, 1377,
    1411, 1437-1438, 1467, 1492, 1498, 1504,
    1524, 1616, 1641, 1694, 1786, 1802, 1914,
    1936, 1938, 1967, 1971, 1982, 1985-1986,
    1996, 2007, 2011, 2016-2017, 2020, 2030,
    2035-2036, 2039, 2061, 2066, 2074, 2077,
    2109, 2111, 2118, 2122-2123, 2127, 2129,
    2132-2133, 2136, 2139, 2142, 2144, 2147,
    2152, 2174, 2203, 2207, 2217, 2240, 2245,
    2251, 2253, 2255, 2274, 2313, 2316, 2319,
    2347-2349, 2351-2354, 2358-2359, 2361, 2390,
    2412, 2481, 2493, 2499, 2522, 2561, 2569-
    2570, 2572, 2596, 2704, 2708-2709, 2720,
    2776-2777, 2825, 2828, 2830, 2833, 2842,
    2846, 2849, 2856, 2862, 2865, 2887, 2967,
    2997, 3004-3006, 3030, 3032, 3076, 3090,
    3196-3265, 3735, 3772
Atlanta University, 520-524, 558
Atlanta University Center, 560
Atlantic Coast Conference, 3205
Auburn Community College, State University of New

York, 1682
Auburn University, 28-34, 2780
Audiology, 4084
Audiovisual, 311, 799, 1384, 2972, 3052, 3500, 3969
Augustana College (IL), 610-613
Augustana College (SD), 2485-2486
Austin College, 2644
Austin Peay State University, 2518
Austin, Gilbert, 4353
Averett College, 2893, 2897-2898
Axtell, George E., 3783
Ayres, Brown, 2574
Azusa Pacific College, 152

Babbitt, Irving, 1166, 3870
Bache, Alexander, A., 2318
Bacone College, 2195
Bagley, William C., 4463
Bailey, Liberty H., 1794
Bakersfield College, 153
Baldwin, Alice M., 1931
Baldwin, Theron, 717
Baldwin-Wallace College, 2004, 2033-2034
Ball State University, 776-778
Baltimore City College, 1073
Baltimore Junior College, 1074-1075
Baltimore, MD, 1062
Bands, 308
Bank Street College of Education, 1683
Baptist higher education, 7, 39, 41-44, 106, 552,
    559, 788, 825, 970-972, 993-995, 1023, 1291,
    1414, 1424, 1505, 1633, 1946, 1982, 1986-
    1987, 2046, 2204, 2314, 2454, 2460-2461,
    2464, 2490, 2516, 2521-2522, 2554-2555,
    2601, 2608, 2624, 2645-2662, 2670, 2680,
    2682-2686, 2703, 2728, 2748, 2897-2898,
    2965, 3104, 3267, 4108, 4113, 4116, 4124,
    4126, 4138, 4147, 4326, 4505
Barnard College, 351, 1778-1779, 3710
Barnard, Frederick A.P., 1725, 4070
Barth, John, 3633
Barzun, Jacques, 1733, 1756
Bascom, John, 1242
Baseball, 189, 198, 668, 707, 2039, 2122, 2319,
    2354, 2499, 2830, 2862, 3265
Basketball, 192, 579, 666, 687, 710, 912, 929, 940,
    1504, 2035, 2142, 2245, 2319, 2352, 2499,
    2570, 2776, 3030, 3090, 3225, 3234
Baton Rouge, LA, 1026
Baylor University, 21, 2635, 2645-2662, 2796, 4346
Baylor, R.E.B., 2624, 2649
Beard, Charles A., 1766
Beecher, Edward, 4070
Behaviorism, 1086
Belhaven College, 1413
Belknap College, 1572
Bell County, TX, 2585

Bell, Daniel, 1756
Bell, Goodloe H., 1281
Belleville Junior College, 614-615
Bellow, Saul, 3633
Beloit College, 251, 4425
Bemidji State University, 1369
Bemis, Edward W., 2042
Benedict College, 2454
Benedictine College, 913
Benedictine higher education, 2986, 3394
Bennett Law, 3042
Bennett, Charles A., 618
Bennington College, 2867-2868
Benton, Guy P., 2084
Berea College, 964-965, 4150
Berkeley, CA, 154
Berkeley, University of California, 154-179, 1683
Bessey, Charles E., 1561
Beth Medrash Govoho, 1591
Bethany Biblical Seminary, 616
Bethany College (KS), 610, 914
Bethany College (WV), 3014
Bethany Nazarene College (OK), 2196-2197
Bethany, OK, 2197
Bethel College (IN), 779
Bethel College (KS), 911, 915
Bethel College (KY), 966
Bethel College (TN), 2519
Bethune-Cookman College, 460
Bibliographies, 1887, 2044, 3794
Big Eight Conference, 3200
Big Ten, 3252, 3261
Bilbo, Theodore G., 1427
Bilingualism, 3902
Biology, 1085, 1245, 2380, 4192, 4194, 4205, 4210,
    4213, 4230
Birmingham-Southern College, 21
Bisection, 3502
Bishop College, 2602
Bishop, Curtis V., 2897
Bishop, William W., 1345
Black higher education, 15, 48-60, 90, 209, 313, 399,
    404, 428-429, 431-435, 440, 451-452, 457, 462,
    472, 484, 495, 509, 514, 517, 520, 523-524,
    529, 548, 552-555, 558, 763, 901, 951, 974,
    979, 984, 1014, 1017, 1019-1020, 1047, 1076-
    1078, 1310, 1420, 1431, 1441, 1455-1457,
    1481, 1886, 1911-1912, 1915, 1924-1926,
    1939, 1944, 1968, 1981, 2058, 2098, 2119,
    2143, 2157, 2172, 2179, 2191, 2199, 2287,
    2306, 2335, 2451, 2503, 2506, 2510, 2550,
    2562, 2588, 2602, 2606, 2615, 2627, 2633,
    2751, 2876, 2879, 2920-2921, 2923, 3001,
    3019, 3028, 3207, 3232, 3266-3340, 3672,
    3765, 3815, 4050, 4441
Black Mountain College, 1928
Black studies, 2157
Blackwell, Elizabeth, 4545
Blair, James, 2904, 2909-2910

Blaisdell, James A., 251
Blake, Anna S.C., 259
Bleyer, W.G., 3073
Bloomsburg University of Pennsylvania, 2296
Blount College, 35
Blue Mountain College, 1414
Bluefield State College, 3018
Boaz, Hiram A., 2598
Bode, Boyd H., 2121
Bogue, Jesse P., 2869
Boise State University, 573
Bolton, Frances P., 2041
Bolton, Frederick E., 3002
Books, 613, 1333, 2798, 3816, 3961, 3979, 4238
Bookstores, 4413
Boston College, 1149-1150
Boston Conservatory of Music, 1151
Boston Museum School, 1152
Boston University, 1153-1155
Boston, MA, 1134, 1139-1140, 4001
Botany, 1561, 1794, 4202, 4215, 4253
Bowditch, Henry P., 1180
Bowdoin College, 1056-1058, 1148
Bowdon College, 525
Bowerman, William J., 2251
Bowers, Ethel, 4331
Bowie State College, 1076-1079
Bowling Green Business University, 967
Bowling Green State University, 1995, 2035-2039
Bowman, John B., 978
Bowne, Borden P., 1155
Boxing, 2361, 3255
Boyd, David, 1034
Boyd, David R., 2218
Boylston Chair of Rhetoric and Oratory, 1207
Bradley University, 617-618
Bray, Reverend Thomas, 4159
Breckinridge, Robert J., 968
Bresee, Phineas F., 249
Brethren of the Common Life, 4119
Bridgeport, University of, 386
Bridgewater College (VA), 2899
Briggs, Thomas H., 1751
Brigham Young University, 2825-2841
Brigham, Albert P., 1713
Broadcasting, 31, 134, 216, 242, 453, 478, 491, 749,
    794, 886, 1283, 1297, 1302, 1304, 1309, 1338,
    1346, 1485, 1490, 1551, 1558, 1805, 1859,
    2003, 2068, 2070, 2072, 2075, 2138, 2494,
    2497-2498, 2654, 3069, 3341-3347, 3864, 4347
Broadus, John A., 993
Brockport (College), State University of New York,
    1684
Brooklyn College, City University of New York, 1685
Brooks, Cleanth, 1026
Brooks, Eugene C., 1962
Brooks, Samuel P., 2645, 2658, 2660
Brooks, William K., 1085
Brookwood Labor College, 4510

Brown University, 381, 1142, 1144-1145, 2429-2436,
    3851, 4256, 4296, 4341
Brown v. Board of Education, 3336
Brown, John, 104
Brumbaugh, Martin G., 2330
Bryan, William L., 802
Bryn Mawr College, 1776, 1783, 1931, 2297-2298,
    3710
Buchanan, John L., 94
Buchtel, Henry, 318
Bucknell University, 2280, 2299-2300
Buffalo (College), State University of New York, 1686
Buffalo (University), State University of New York,
    1687-1692, 1762
Buffalo Fine Arts Academy, 1693
Bulfinch, Thomas, 3843
Burgess, John W., 1735
Burleson College, 2663
Burleson, Rufus C., 2652
Burnham, William, 1343
Burns, James A., 3381
Burritt College (TN), 2520
Burroughs, William, 3633
Burrowes, Thomas H., 2356
Business and education, 1264, 3122, 3145, 3348-
    3349, 3974, 3977, 4244, 4263, 4379, 4548
Business education, 80, 225, 671, 735, 867, 967,
    1042, 1050, 1164, 1213, 1586, 1715, 1767,
    1835, 1838, 2049, 2212, 2244, 2293-2294,
    2674, 3350-3364, 3696, 4481
Butler University, 278, 281, 288, 290, 780, 805, 1153
Butler, Nicholas M., 1781

Cabell, Joseph C., 2960
Calculus, 4229
Calendar, academic, 3484
California, 108-300
California Association of Student Councils, 132
California Institute of Technology, 180, 286
California Maritime Academy, 181
California Polytechnic State University, 182-183
California State College (San Bernardino), 125, 184
California State University, 130
California State University (Chico), 185-192
California State University (Fresno), 193-195
California State University (Hayward), 196
California State University (Long Beach), 146
California State University (Northridge), 197
California State University (San Diego), 198-206
California State University (San Francisco), 170,
    207-211
California University of Pennsylvania, 2301-2303
California, University of, 125, 145-146, 154-179, 229-
    239, 259-262, 351, 737, 1683, 2530, 3432,
    3438, 3980, 4044, 4369
Callahan County, TX, 2631
Calvin College, 1267

Cambridge University, 3416
Campus closure, 358
Canada, 1678, 3711, 3813, 4500
Canfield, James H., 1548
Canisius College, 1694
Canterbury College, 781
Capen, Samuel P., 1689
Cardinal Stritch College, 3043
Carl Sandburg College, 619
Carleton College, 4425
Carlyle, Thomas, 3562
Carnegie Corporation, 3977
Carnegie Foundation for the Advancement of
    Teaching, 3667
Carnegie Institution, 407, 4235, 4296, 4341
Carnegie Mellon University, 2304
Carr-Burdette College, 2664
Carroll College (WI), 3044-3045
Carson-Newman College, 2521-2522
Carter, Thomas M., 1278
Case Western Reserve University, 2040-2045, 2799,
    4351
Casper College, 3088
Catawba College, 4168
Catholic Educational Association, 3389
Catholic higher education, 117, 122, 127, 256-257,
    263, 292, 349-350, 360-361, 408-415, 425-427,
    444-445, 582, 599, 601, 664-665, 714, 720,
    817-823, 830-832, 913, 958, 996, 998-999,
    1043, 1081, 1097, 1108-1111, 1120-1122,
    1149, 1158, 1162, 1259, 1271, 1283, 1293,
    1365, 1370, 1395, 1397, 1405, 1454, 1473,
    1483, 1499, 1501-1502, 1507, 1521, 1541-
    1542, 1579, 1582, 1624, 1668, 1672-1673,
    1694, 1716, 1806, 1823-1825, 1852, 1854-
    1856, 2031-2032, 2062, 2169, 2173, 2242,
    2305, 2309-2313, 2327, 2332, 2340, 2399,
    2437, 2523, 2931, 2984-2986, 3043, 3048-
    3050, 3304, 3365-3395, 3531, 3959, 4472
Catholic University of America, 408-415
Cattell, James M., 1770, 3101
Cedar Crest College, 4168
Cedarville College, 2046
Centenary College of Louisiana, 1018
Center for Research and Education in American
    Liberties, 1769
Central Intercollegiate Athletic Association, 3207,
    3231
Central Methodist College, 1468-1469
Central Michigan University, 1263, 1268, 1282
Central Missouri State University, 1470-1472
Central Normal College, 782-783
Central Plains Academy, 2604
Central Plains College and Conservatory of Music,
    2604
Central State University, 432, 2047
Central University of Iowa, 845
Certification, 117, 600
Certification, teacher, 66, 111, 114, 456, 905, 1011,

1053, 1649, 2448, 4487
Chadron State College, 1537
Chamberlin, Thomas C., 4235
Chambers, Will G., 2267
Chandler, Charles F., 1745
Chapelle, Howard I., 442
Chapin, F. Stuart, 1378
Chapman College, 212-213, 264
Character education, 4051
Charles County Community College, 1080
Charters, Werrett W., 2145-2146
Chattanooga, TN, 2512
Chattanooga, University of, 2564
Chautauqua, 1669
Chemistry, 382, 1040, 1621, 1745, 1773, 2045,
    2117, 4191, 4195, 4206, 4231, 4236, 4244,
    4527
Cherry, H.H., 952
Chestnut Hill College, 2305
Cheyney University of Pennsylvania, 2287, 2306-
    2308
Chicago Lutheran Theological Seminary, 620
Chicago State University, 621-622
Chicago, IL, 582, 601, 605, 633
Chicago, University of, 597, 623-663, 804, 1069,
    1086-1087, 1784, 2044, 3080, 3203, 3251,
    3432, 3438, 3946, 4033, 4044-4045, 4235
China, 373, 1332, 1741, 4411
Christ College Irvine, 214
Christian Brothers College (MO), 1473
Christian Brothers College (TN), 2523, 4459
Christian Scientist higher education, 737
Chronicle of Higher Education, 3781
Church and state, 124, 713, 806, 2447, 3396-3405,
    3473, 4160-4161, 4170, 4173
Church College of Hawaii, 567
Church of Christ higher education, 101, 670, 1439-
    1440, 1477, 1937-1938, 2257, 2316, 2410,
    2525, 2554-2555, 2625, 2637-2641, 4153
Church of God higher education, 297, 775, 2453,
    2551-2553
Church of the Brethren higher education, 939, 2029-
    2030, 2330, 2899
Cincinnati Conservatory of Music, 2048
Cincinnati, OH, 2001
Cincinnati, University of, 2015, 2049-2055, 4522
Citadel, the, 2449
Citizenship education, 4265
City University of New York, 1695-1711
Civil Liberties Educational Foundation, 1769
Civil rights movement, 560
Civil War, 42, 529, 763, 1009, 1425, 1450, 1664,
    1882, 1884, 1895, 1924, 2052, 2098-2099,
    2429, 2621, 3306, 3766, 4067, 4524, 4529
Clap, Thomas, 391-392
Clare McPhee Laboratory School, 1554
Claremont College (NC), 1929
Claremont University Center and Claremont
    Graduate School, 125, 215, 251

Clarendon College, 2665
Clark College (GA), 526
Clark County, GA, 504
Clark University, 1156-1157, 1689
Clark, Felton G., 1047
Clarke Memorial College, 1415-1416
Clarke School for the Deaf, 1135
Classics, 837, 1750, 1860, 2949, 2953, 3835, 3843, 3880, 3885
Clements, William L., 1333
Clemson University, 2449
Cleveland College, 2056
Cliburn, Van, 2695
Clifford Seminary, 2455
Clinton County, NY, 1844
Co-education, 336, 547, 887, 1150, 1237, 2863, 2951, 3530, 4398, 4406, 4411-4412, 4536, 4562
Cobleskill (College), State University of New York, 1712
Coffman, Lotus D., 1380
Coker College, 2456
Colby College, 623
Cold War, 171, 2406, 3003, 3099, 3102, 3108, 4056, 4061
Colgate University, 1713-1714, 2436
College Band Directors National Association, 3873
College Entrance Examination Board, 3150, 3532, 3545
College for the Children of the Infidels, 4025
College Misericordia, 2309
College of Charleston, 4522
College of Eastern Utah, 2842
College of Emporia, 916
College of Great Falls, 1521
College of Insurance, 1715
College of Music of Cincinnati, 2057
College of Notre Dame of Maryland, 1081
College of San Mateo, 216
College of Santa Fe, 4459
College of St. Francis (IL), 664-665
College of St. Francis Xavier (NY), 1668
College of St. Rose, 1716
College of St. Thomas (MN), 1370
College of the Desert, 217
College of the Holy Cross (MA), 1158
College of the Ozarks, 99
College of William & Mary, 2900-2914, 2949, 2953, 2968, 4256, 4395, 4402, 4498
College of Wooster, 2058
College Physical Education Association, 3728
Colonial higher education, 347, 369, 372, 381, 391-392, 394, 435, 498, 508, 591, 1127-1128, 1136, 1173, 1179, 1183-1184, 1186, 1195-1196, 1205, 1212, 1443, 1575, 1584, 1606, 1612-1613, 1648, 1663, 1728, 1730, 1737, 1752, 1757, 1763, 1811, 1896, 2264-2265, 2365, 2369, 2374, 2375, 2378-2379, 2434, 2445, 2511, 2884, 2894, 2902, 2904-2906, 2909-

2910, 2958, 3159, 3177, 3193, 3284, 3371, 3386, 3388, 3406-3418, 3490, 3664-3665, 3786, 3814, 3819, 3832, 3851, 3865, 3901, 3961, 3975, 3979, 3986, 4015, 4025, 4030-4031, 4116, 4133, 4147, 4166, 4202, 4240, 4246, 4300, 4303, 4319, 4379, 4407, 4420, 4496, 4498, 4539
Colorado, 301-337, 3393
Colorado College, 306-307, 3245
Colorado Seminary, 319
Colorado Women's College, 315
Colorado, University of, 308-314, 1518, 1747
Colorado, University of (Denver), 313
Columbia College (MO), 1474
Columbia College (SC), 2457
Columbia Theological Seminary, 2468
Columbia Union College, 1082
Columbia University, 351, 618, 644, 1654, 1717-1786, 3101, 3175, 3193, 3405, 3408, 3710, 3946, 3963, 3981, 4033, 4070, 4256, 4316, 4421, 4463
Columbia, MO, 4564
Columbiad, 1721
Colvin, George, 981
Colvin, Valerie, 2209
Comer, Braxton B., 4
Commencements, 2378
Commonwealth College, 100, 4510
Communications, 534, 1734, 3358, 3361
Communism, 2406, 3101
Community College of the Air Force, 36
Community colleges, 2, 5, 12, 13, 16, 27, 34, 36, 64, 67, 69-70, 78, 81, 85, 88, 112, 116, 118-119, 125, 137-138, 140-141, 144, 148, 224-225, 227, 229, 241-242, 248, 258, 301-302, 317, 329-330, 339, 344, 348, 448, 457-459, 483-484, 491, 497, 499-500, 503, 515, 530, 561, 584-585, 588, 596, 602, 604, 609, 614, 617, 757, 840-841, 842, 909, 912, 961, 1068, 1070, 1072, 1074-1075, 1080, 1107, 1123, 1137, 1138, 1163, 1247, 1254, 1270, 1274, 1276, 1285, 1290, 1292, 1353, 1357, 1364, 1366, 1403, 1407-1408, 1417, 1423, 1441, 1444, 1459, 1465-1466, 1494, 1509, 1529, 1532, 1569, 1655, 1658, 1682, 1809, 1820, 1851, 1858, 1862, 1917, 1922, 1950, 1951, 2002, 2009, 2018, 2021, 2059, 2189-2190, 2192-2193, 2325-2326, 2338, 2427, 2476, 2515, 2551, 2562, 2582, 2586, 2589, 2592-2593, 2595, 2597, 2601, 2605, 2607, 2609, 2611, 2618-2620, 2622, 2625-2626, 2630, 2677, 2688, 2692, 2696, 2723, 2726, 2733-2734, 2743, 2751, 2757-2758, 2810-2811, 2818, 2821, 2867, 2869, 2880-2881, 2885, 2890, 2893, 2895, 2897-2898, 2970, 2974, 2976-2977, 3088, 3235, 3364, 3377, 3392, 3419-3465, 3483, 3649, 4025, 4508
Community service, 2, 402, 1262, 1348, 1364, 1789, 2002, 2113, 2390, 2690, 2928, 3791, 4066,

4154, 4299
Comparative education, 125, 3813
Computers, 4250
Conant, James B., 1216
Concentration, undergraduate, 3480, 3513
Concord College, 3019
Concordia College (NC), 1930
Concordia Seminary, 1475
Concordia Teachers College, 1538-1539
Concrete College, 2666
Confederate University, 4524
Conference of Faculty Representatives, 3239
Congregational Christian higher education, 556-557
Connecticut, 338-396, 3364
Connecticut College, 351
Connecticut, University of, 343, 352-357
Connecticut, University of (Torrington), 358
Conservation, 307, 1869
Continuing education, 81, 149, 615, 1033, 1099,
     1586, 2386, 2513, 2932, 3491, 3510, 3718,
     4519
Conwell, Russell H., 2404
Cook County, IL, 595
Cook, George H., 1621
Coolidge, Archibald C., 1202
Cooper Union, 1787
Cooper, Oscar H., 2635
Cooper, Peter, 1787
Cooper, Thomas, 2473
Cooperative education, 119, 1791, 2049, 3481
Cooperative extension service, 3170, 3916
Copiah-Lincoln Agricultural High School and Junior
     College, 1417
Corcoran School of Art, 416
Cornell University, 1652, 1788-1800, 3127, 3805,
     3853, 4220, 4424
Correspondence study, 3495
Cortland (College), State University of New York,
     1801-1802
Cotner University, 1540
Cottey College, 1476
Council for Administrative Leadership, 3133
Council for the Advancement of Small Colleges,
     3799
Counseling, 538, 1253, 2840, 4430, 4474, 4531,
     4533, 4543
Counts, George S., 644
Courts, 455, 548, 1027, 1258, 1260, 1573, 1656,
     1690, 3096-3097, 3277, 3292, 3317, 3336,
     3397, 3464, 3466-3476, 3547, 3550, 3554-
     3555, 3567, 4415-4416, 4516, 4562
Cowley, W.H., 1812
Cox, Jacob D., 2052
Crane Junior College, 3457
Creighton University, 1541-1542
Cremin, Lawrence, 1760
Crew, 3006, 3257
Criticism, 290, 629, 801, 1819, 3114, 3147, 3552,
     3707, 3997, 4002, 4047

Cross country, 2828
Cuba, 487
Cubberley, Ellwood P., 280, 282
Culture, 241, 811, 1157, 1171, 1234, 1337, 1387,
     1842, 2811, 3177, 3540, 3820, 3905, 3960,
     4225, 4397, 4425
Cumberland Female College, 2524
Cumberland University School of Law, 41
Curriculum, 51, 73, 84, 123, 153, 155, 181, 225, 283,
     291, 320, 327, 335, 337, 367, 390, 479, 486,
     488, 497, 506, 553, 565, 648, 658, 673, 709,
     715, 723, 739, 788, 820, 838, 850, 855-856,
     894, 900, 906, 999, 1015, 1023, 1112, 1115,
     1132, 1147, 1170, 1225, 1235, 1265, 1319,
     1352, 1403, 1407, 1415, 1480-1481, 1508,
     1595, 1610, 1623, 1666, 1681, 1696-1697,
     1705, 1708, 1727, 1729, 1750, 1767, 1819,
     1876, 1897, 1915, 1928, 2041, 2049, 2121,
     2124, 2150, 2213, 2261, 2275, 2284, 2345,
     2350, 2439, 2466, 2568, 2591, 2689, 2718,
     2725, 2787, 2848, 2914, 2956, 3012, 3057,
     3129, 3160, 3179, 3283, 3287, 3293, 3296,
     3302, 3308, 3324, 3328, 3342, 3344, 3401,
     3444, 3451, 3477-3527, 3557, 3667, 3673,
     3738, 3757, 3837, 3847, 3849, 3861, 3867,
     3890, 3893, 3898, 3906, 3913, 3935, 3937,
     3942, 3943, 4038, 4041, 4155, 4172, 4202,
     4283, 4314, 4334, 4403, 4453, 4455, 4457,
     4464, 4486, 4504
Curry, Jabez L.M., 4467, 4477, 4480
Curry, Samuel S., 4353
Cuyahoga Community College, 2059
Cytology, 4210

Dabney, Robert L., 2938
Daggett, Naphtali, 369
Dakota State College, 2487
Dakota Wesleyan University, 2488-2489
Dallas College, 2667
Dallas County, TX, 2597, 2618
Dallas Theological Seminary, 2668
Dana, James D., 385
Dance, 1240, 2805, 2807, 2841, 3839, 3860, 3883
Daniel Baker College, 2669
Danville Theological Seminary, 968
Dargan, Edwin J., 995
Dartmouth College, 1573-1577, 3193, 3405, 3665
Darwin, Charles, 2468, 4198
David Lipscomb College, 2525
Davie, William R., 1970
Davis and Elkins College, 3014
Davis, Angela, 231
Davis, Jerome, 3101
Dawson, William L., 58
Day, James R., 1872
Dayton, University of, 2060
Deaf education, 1135

Dean of men, 2252, 3528-3529, 3531, 3535
Dean of students, 1306, 3532
Dean of women, 813, 1931, 3386, 3530, 3533-3534
Deans, 813, 878, 1306, 1620, 1931, 2252, 3386,
    3528-3535, 4431, 4531, 4533
Debate, 19, 252, 473, 590, 597, 730, 863, 932, 1037,
    1159, 1301, 1361, 1506, 1555, 2038, 2158,
    2753, 2892, 3050, 3654-3656, 3658-3666
Degrees, 108, 709, 728, 843, 1292, 1570, 2716,
    2891, 2954, 2956, 3118, 3146, 3478, 3490,
    3515, 3648, 3700-3703, 3709, 3768, 3849,
    3855, 3871, 3881, 3942, 4222
Delaware, 397-403
Delaware State College, 399
Delaware, University of, 400-402
Della Plain Male and Female Institute, 2604
Delta Pi Epsilon, 3680
Delta Psi Kappa, 3681
Demiashkevich, Michael J., 2534
Denison University, 2000, 2061
Denmark, 414
Denmark, Annie D., 2453
Dental education, 789, 891, 1066, 1447, 1516, 1692,
    2372, 2446, 3730, 3736, 4095
Denver, University of, 316-322, 3973
DePauw University, 784-786
Desegregation, 484, 548, 554, 984, 1077, 1455,
    1955, 2058, 2143, 2503, 2923, 3013, 3028,
    3266, 3272, 3277, 3281, 3317, 3336, 4052
Detroit, MI, 1320, 1357-1358
Detroit, University of, 1271, 1283
Developmental education, 25, 244, 418-420, 459,
    1135, 2019, 4465
Dew, Thomas R., 2907
Dewey, John, 239, 1340, 1683, 4033, 4200
Dewey, Melvil, 3963
Dickinson College, 2473
Dickinson, Emily, 3841
Diemer, George W., 1470
Disciples of Christ higher education, 212-213, 264,
    780, 1000-1005, 1439-1440, 1474, 1477, 2063-
    2065, 2243, 2693, 2766-2767, 2768-2769,
    2927, 3298, 4144
Distributive education, 3494
District of Columbia, 404-445
District of Columbia, University of the, 417
Dixie College, 2843
Dixie Conference, 3217
Dixon v. Alabama, 3466, 3471
Dodd, William E., 660
Dormitories, 2134, 2156, 2792, 4409-4410, 4412,
    4422
Douglass, Harl R., 314
Dow Company, 3075
Dow, Arthur W., 1755
Downs, Robert B., 701
Doyle, Price, 991
Drake University, 846-848, 1153
Drama, 29, 201, 273, 277, 289, 294, 401, 409, 420,

466, 545, 574, 604, 625, 675, 688, 731, 785,
    793, 800, 829, 935, 942-943, 1017, 1020, 1051,
    1226, 1229, 1256, 1282, 1295, 1311, 1316,
    1321, 1347, 1354, 1379, 1382, 1472, 1559,
    1680, 1870, 2151, 2153, 2162, 2225, 2238,
    2256, 2429, 2489, 2496, 2609, 2634, 2676,
    2695, 2699-2700, 2707, 2717, 2740, 2795,
    2827, 2831, 2854, 2859, 2992, 3007, 3067,
    3321, 3340, 3557, 3833, 3842, 3844, 3847,
    3854, 3857, 3861, 3872, 3885, 3889, 3891
Draper, Andrew S., 691
Dresslar, Fletcher B., 2530
Drury College, 1477
DuBois, W.E.B., 523, 3294
Dufau, Louis, 1022
Duggan, Anne S., 2807
Duke University, 1931-1935, 1962, 3818
Dumbarton Oaks, 1215
Dunham, Barrows, 2406
Duquesne University, 2310-2313
Dwight, Timothy, 396

Earlham College, 787, 4378
East St. Louis, MO, 1466
East Texas Baptist College, 2670
East Texas State University, 2671-2676
Eastern Baptist Theological Seminary, 2314
Eastern Collegiate Athletic Conference, 3210
Eastern Connecticut State College, 359
Eastern Illinois University, 666-669, 1751
Eastern Kentucky University, 969
Eastern Michigan University, 1263, 1268
Eastern New Mexico University, 1636
Eastern Washington University, 2978
Easton, David, 2974
Eaton, Amos, 1848
Eby, Frederick, 2796
Ecology, 307, 1869, 4210
Economics, 1709, 2042, 2742, 2949, 2953, 3015,
    3071, 3453, 3811, 4303, 4305, 4357, 4379,
    4548
Eden Theological Seminary, 1083
Edgecliff College, 2062
Edinboro University of Pennsylvania, 2315
Education as discipline, 23, 26, 129, 139, 230, 232-
    233, 245, 270, 274, 276, 280, 282, 285, 291,
    312, 314, 328, 424, 468, 479, 534, 536, 582,
    630, 648, 655-656, 658, 661, 727, 803, 827,
    1092, 1191, 1204, 1273, 1282, 1334, 1348,
    1353, 1380, 1395, 1486, 1489, 1502, 1508,
    1523, 1528, 1592, 1619, 1687, 1704, 1727,
    1751, 1760, 1777, 1784, 1860, 1928, 2143,
    2154, 2168, 2248, 2260, 2267, 2389, 2394,
    2469, 2475, 2488, 2513, 2763, 2799, 2829,
    2853, 2954, 3002, 3087, 3091, 3521, 3702,
    3704, 3783, 3809, 3983, 4259, 4271, 4277,

4285, 4287, 4295, 4307, 4329, 4339, 4342, 4344, 4352, 4360, 4456
Education Commission of the States, 3187
Educational Policies Commission, 3806
Edwards, Richard, 678
Edwards, William J., 3280
Egan, Maurice F., 414
Eggleston, Joseph D., Jr., 2918
Egypt, 3651
Eisenhower College, 1762
Eisenhower, Dwight D., 3780, 4058
El Camino College, 218
El Paso Junior College, 2677
Elective system, 1352, 3482, 3746
Eliot, Charles W., 1176-1178, 1191, 1198, 1201, 1208, 1211, 1220, 3127, 3853, 4424
Elliott, Edward C., 827
Ellis, Alexander C., 2799
Elmhurst College, 670, 4168
Elmira College, 1803, 3566, 3710
Elon College, 1937-1938
Ely, Richard T., 3071
Emerson College, 1159-1161
Emerson, Charles W., 1161
Emerson, Ralph W., 1187, 3853
Emmanuel College (GA), 527
Emmanuel College (MA), 1162
Emory and Henry College, 94, 2915
Emory University, 528-529
Empire State College, State University of New York, 1804
Empire State Federation of Teachers, 1674
Empire State FM School of the Air, 1805
Emporia State University, 917-922
Enderis, Dorothy, 4331
Endowments, 179, 1189, 3011
Engineering, 4094, 4098
Engineering education, 131, 854, 857, 2125, 2317, 2871, 2948, 4090-4091, 4189-4190, 4193, 4199-4220, 4222, 4224-4225, 4237-4238, 4242, 4249, 4305
England, 2914, 3537, 3649, 3821, 4147
English, 380, 414, 1169, 1171, 1178, 1610, 1699, 1720, 1726, 1778, 2004, 2304, 2429, 2433, 2587, 2711, 2787, 2994, 3153, 3507, 3599-3602, 3604-3636, 3666, 3838, 3841, 3843, 3848-3849, 3856, 3874-3875, 3884, 3886, 3888-3889, 3901, 4082, 4497
Enrollment, 486, 1073, 2691, 3640
Entomology, 4241
Entrance requirements, 10, 156, 336, 388, 767, 1059, 1073, 1644, 1711, 2254, 2261, 2470, 3146-3147, 3545, 3935
Episcopal higher education, 1985, 2478, 2563-2564, 2933, 2935, 4152
Erskine College, 2458-2459
Essentialist Committee for the Advancement of American Education, 4038
Essex County College, 1592

European influence, 1069, 1318, 1352, 1612, 1730, 2910, 2914, 3110, 3536-3540, 3645, 3821, 3822, 4284
Evangelical higher education, 718-719, 761, 2363, 4125, 4150, 4168, 4173
Evans, John, 321
Evelyn College for Women, 1593
Evergreen State College, 2979
Evolution theory, 2468, 4198
Ewell, Benjamin S., 2900
Examinations, 163, 356, 1303, 2261, 2711, 3150, 3541-3545, 4491, 4498
Exchange programs, 3905
Expenses, 1300, 2691, 3573, 4400
Experimental colleges, 1142, 1145, 1683, 1817, 1837, 1841, 2198
Exploration, 1315
Extension education, 23, 164, 480, 592, 595, 637, 798, 858, 1294, 1358, 1560, 1617, 1642, 2219, 2441, 2969, 3072, 3085, 3170, 3501, 3511, 3527, 3916

Faculty, 120, 130, 150, 161, 171, 231, 293, 320, 633, 741, 872, 1077, 1088, 1260, 1317, 1336, 1344, 1368, 1392, 1659, 1701, 1717, 1735, 1753, 1756, 1997, 2086, 2191, 2217, 2322, 2406, 2413, 2443, 2483, 2786, 2788, 2963, 2995, 3003, 3075-3076, 3092-3093, 3095-3110, 3123, 3138, 3161, 3169, 3186, 3239, 3268, 3293, 3322, 3349, 3366, 3441, 3471, 3475, 3510, 3536, 3546-3572, 3600-3601, 3604, 3608-3609, 3611, 3616, 3621, 3625, 3628, 3631, 3789, 3800, 3824, 3826, 3940, 4031, 4062, 4064, 4066, 4154, 4259, 4299, 4303, 4470, 4483, 4512-4514, 4517, 4525, 4528, 4534-4535, 4541, 4561, 4563
Fairfield University, 360
Fairmont State College, 3020
Falcone, Leonard, 1307
Farnsworth, Charles H., 1747
Fayetteville State University, 1939
Federal aid, 5, 417, 419-420, 584, 598, 1252, 1534, 2013, 2022, 2355, 2613, 3167, 3189, 3332, 3396-3397, 3403, 3473, 3505, 3573-3598, 3643, 3737, 3802, 3929, 4053, 4055, 4058-4059, 4145, 4182, 4184, 4207, 4252, 4288, 4401, 4409
Federal control, 577, 2322, 3097, 3426
Federal institutions, 3490
Federation of American Scientists, 4212
Fee, John G., 965
Feinberg Law, 1690
Fencing, 694
Ferguson, James, 2793
Ferrum College, 2916
Fess, Simeon D., 2026
Fiction, higher education in, 3599-3636, 4102

Finances, 86, 565, 606, 771, 885, 1179, 1252, 1257, 1356, 1387, 1589, 2013, 2139, 2194, 2270, 2421, 2449, 2592, 2594, 2673, 2691, 2734, 2886, 3011, 3378, 3428, 3594, 3637-3643, 3729, 3949, 3972, 3982, 3989, 4139, 4179, 4363, 4365, 4366, 4400, 4520

Financial aid, 510, 748, 1197, 1675, 2210, 2877, 3252, 3312, 3584, 3586, 3589, 3637, 3642, 4391, 4401

Findlay College, 1995

Fine arts, 524, 700, 937, 1240, 1319, 1326, 1693, 1729, 1785, 1867, 1874, 2345-2346, 2374, 2805, 2807, 2811, 3325, 3588, 3839, 3860, 3867, 3883, 3934, 4450

Finley, John H., 1861

Finney, Charles G., 2105, 2108

First Amendment, 3467, 4416

Fish, Carl R., 3070

Fisher Junior College, 1163

Fisk University, 2526-2527, 3307

Fisk, Wilbur, 364

Fiske, Daniel W., 1790

Fiske, John, 1200

Flaming Rainbow University, 2198

Flexner Report, 2001

Flexner, Abraham, 2001, 3997, 4002, 4036, 4045

Flint Junior College, 1254, 1284

Flipper, Henry O., 1886

Flora MacDonald College, 1983

Florida, 446-492

Florida Agricultural & Mechanical University, 461-462

Florida Southern College, 463

Florida State University, 464-476

Florida, University of, 477-482

Floyd Junior College, 530

Floydada Presbyterian Academy, 2604

Flynt, Henry, 1173

Folwell, William W., 3432

Football, 203, 232, 255, 579, 647, 681, 696, 847, 912, 926, 976, 1277, 1312, 1616, 1936, 2011, 2132, 2152, 2174, 2251, 2255, 2319, 2348, 2351, 2499, 2596, 2833, 2997, 3032, 3203-3204, 3213-3214, 3220, 3229, 3231, 3237, 3248, 3251, 3258, 3260

Fordham University, 1806

Foreign higher education, 59, 411, 1659, 1678, 1765, 1857, 2127, 2914, 3110, 3538-3539, 3644-3653, 3675, 3778, 3813, 3822, 4147, 4411, 4474, 4500

Foreign language and literature, 390, 837, 865, 1166, 1670, 1696, 1790, 1959, 2528, 3060, 3834, 3865, 3893, 4460

Foreign policy, 4064

Foreign students, 487, 646, 1288, 1332, 1722, 1741, 2335, 3807, 4420

Forensics, 252, 409, 473, 481, 590, 679, 730, 863, 932, 943, 1037, 1301, 1361, 1391, 1506, 1537, 1564, 1865, 2038, 2073, 2158, 2753, 2766, 2775, 2892, 3050, 3654-3666, 4260, 4279,

4292, 4293, 4304, 4312, 4326

Forestry, 307, 1869

Fort Hays State University, 923-924

Foundations, 179, 771, 822, 1328, 1769, 2005, 2013, 2210, 2436, 2541, 2543, 3276, 3337, 3371, 3429, 3639, 3667-3679, 4179, 4223, 4233, 4449, 4452, 4467, 4477, 4480

Fourteenth Amendment, 3469-3470

Fox, Albert C., 3048

Framingham, MA, 1199

Franck, James, 1069

Frank, Glenn, 3064-3065

Franklin and Marshall College, 2280, 2316, 4168

Franklin College (TX), 2678

Franklin College of Indiana, 788

Franklin County, TN, 2509, 2563

Franklin Institute, 2317-2318

Franklin Pierce College, 1578

Franklin, Benjamin, 1896

Franklin, Bruce, 293, 3101

Fraternities, 1187, 1963, 2855, 3680-3687, 3956, 4418

Fredonia (College), State University of New York, 1807-1808

French language, 1166

Freud, Sigmund, 3996

Frissell, Hollis B., 2921

Fromm, Erich, 4273

Fuller, O. Anderson, 1481

Fuller, Thomas O., 3280

Fund raising, 2005, 2013, 2139, 4139

Furman University, 2460-2461, 4346

Furman, Richard, 2460

Gale, George W., 1871

Gallager, E.C., 2207

Gallaudet College, 418-420

Gammon Theological Seminary, 526, 531, 550

Gannon, Robert I., 1806

Gannon, Sister Ann I., 720

Garrison, S. Olin, 1628

Geertz, Clifford, 4273

Gehrkens, Karl W., 2104

Gem City Business College, 671

General education, 423, 475, 1174, 1241, 1833, 2742, 2944, 3009, 3262, 3673, 3688-3695, 4350

Genesee Community College, 1809

Geneseo (College), State University of New York, 1810

Genetics, 4210

Geneva College, 2319-2320

Geography, 1188, 1196, 1713, 4302, 4358, 4445

Geology, 1621, 1708, 1713, 2362, 3080, 3603, 4186-4187, 4228, 4235, 4248

George Peabody College for Teachers, 727, 2472, 2528-2547, 4070

George Peabody Fund, 2436, 2541, 4467, 4477, 4480
George Washington University, 421-424, 2460
Georgetown College (KY), 970-972
Georgetown University, 425-427
Georgia, 493-566, 4063, 4505, 4565
Georgia College, 532
Georgia Southern College, 533
Georgia, University of, 534-548
German language, 1696, 3865
Germany, 1069, 1318, 1352, 1659, 3536, 3538, 3645, 3653, 4116, 4284
Ghost colleges, 948
G.I. Bill, 3592
Gibbs, Wolcott, 1773
Gifted programs, 3516
Gildersleeve, Basil L., 1088
Gilman, Daniel C., 167, 1089-1090, 1094, 3127, 4424
Glee clubs, 3897
Glenville State College, 3021
Goals, 320, 1259, 1433, 1953, 2103, 2690, 2950, 3134, 3149, 3168, 3357, 3373, 3406, 3407, 3409, 3422, 3519, 3739, 3793, 3796, 3806, 3820, 3823, 3941, 4093, 4350, 4449-4450, 4481, 4555
Golf, 199, 683, 1986
Gonzales College, 2679
Goodnight College, 2680
Goodwin, John E., 3980
Goose-Step, 4028
Gordon Military College, 549
Goshen College, 761, 3457
Göttingen University, 3645
Goucher College, 1084, 3710
Governance, 63, 121, 210, 247, 257, 295, 332-333, 346, 515, 576, 649, 711, 741, 747, 766, 778, 791, 810, 818, 870, 872, 969, 1008, 1104, 1184, 1205, 1219, 1336, 1352-1353, 1355, 1387, 1464, 1495, 1575, 1582, 1592, 1653-1654, 1712, 1857, 1893, 1955, 2055, 2069, 2156, 2215, 2419, 2426, 2514, 2529, 2548, 2553, 2578, 2626, 2861, 2893, 2925, 3016, 3038, 3055-3056, 3068, 3122-3145, 3173, 3191, 3223, 3282, 3293, 3322, 3415, 3465, 3510, 3698, 3742, 3931, 4052, 4073, 4440
Governors, 1067
Graceland College, 849
Grading policies, 2261, 3541-3542, 4498
Graduate education, 25, 108, 125, 155, 312, 541, 552, 644, 654, 728, 759, 797, 874, 878, 891, 907, 1050, 1089, 1091, 1119, 1135, 1214, 1225, 1329, 1332, 1401, 1426, 1486, 1501, 1516, 1635, 1722, 1767, 1799, 1875, 2168, 2350, 2377, 2385, 2513, 2536, 2546, 2571, 2682, 2764, 2779, 2800, 2829, 2853, 2877, 2954, 2957, 3033, 3059, 3127, 3300, 3356, 3526, 3583, 3696-3709, 3717, 3753, 3758, 3855, 3871, 4013, 4121, 4285

Grambling State University, 1019-1020
Grand Canyon College, 77
Grand Rapids Junior College, 1254, 1285
Grand Valley State College, 1286
Gratz College, 2321
Graves, Frank P., 1860
Gray, William S., 648
Grayson College, 2681
Great Awakening, 372, 1185, 1613, 4174
Great Books, 4041
Great Britain, 2910, 3540, 3648, 3652, 3675
Great Depression, 1294, 1996, 3565, 3595, 3643, 4154, 4348, 4380, 4428, 4429, 4520
Greek language, 837
Green Mountain Junior College, 2869
Green, Ashbel, 1607
Green, Edith, 3594
Greene, Evarts B., 4316
Greenland, 1315
Greenville College, 672-674
Greenwood Female College, 2462
Gregory, John M., 692
Grinnell College, 850-851, 4425
Grove City College, 2322-2324
Guerry, Alexander, 2564
Guidance, 1920, 2006, 3687, 4426, 4437, 4443
Guild, Rueben A., 2431
Guilford College, 1940
Gulf Park College for Women, 1418
Gullickson, Otta A.S., 3024
Gustavson, Reuben G., 1552
Gustavus Adolphus College, 1371-1372
Gymnastics, 467, 689, 3206, 3246, 3250

Hadley, Herbert S., 1518
Hagerstown Junior College, 2325
Hall, G. Stanley, 1156-1157
Hamilton College (NY), 1811-1812, 3173
Hampden-Sydney College, 2900, 2917-2919
Hampton Institute, 2920-2923, 3307
Handicapped students, 4399
Hardin-Simmons University, 2635, 2682-2687
Harding University, 101
Harper, William R., 635, 639, 642, 3432, 3438
Harris, James W., 245
Harris-Stowe State College, 1478-1480
Hartvigsen, Milton F., 2834
Hartwick College, 1813-1814
Harvard University, 1164-1222, 1350, 1773, 3127, 3156, 3174, 3248, 3250, 3405, 3665, 3805, 3853, 3870, 3946, 3979, 4256, 4422, 4424, 4498
Hasselquist, T.N., 611
Hastings College, 1543
Haven, Erastus O., 1351
Hawaii, 567-569
Hawaii, University of, 568-569

Hayakawa, Samuel, 170
Hayes, Carlton J.H., 1736, 1782
Hayes, Rutherford B., 2130
Haygood, Atticus G., 529
Heacock, Joe D., 2748
Health sciences, 14, 30, 44, 185, 194, 221-223, 235,
    250, 275, 355, 368, 421, 430, 454, 464, 509,
    539, 575, 589, 622, 628, 680, 769, 777, 789,
    828, 843-844, 882-883, 891, 977, 1065-1066,
    1098, 1147, 1233, 1235-1236, 1239, 1263,
    1266, 1292, 1327, 1342, 1385, 1402, 1419,
    1447, 1482, 1503, 1516, 1522, 1570, 1627,
    1679, 1718, 1724, 1788, 1826, 1956, 1977,
    2041, 2053-2054, 2063, 2074, 2088, 2090-
    2091, 2100-2102, 2111, 2114, 2118, 2120,
    2133, 2135, 2146, 2148, 2155, 2159, 2201,
    2209, 2214, 2229, 2247, 2281, 2302, 2311,
    2359, 2364, 2371-2372, 2381, 2385, 2395,
    2397, 2446, 2479, 2527, 2544, 2568, 2572,
    2591, 2616, 2671, 2714, 2718, 2721, 2784,
    2824, 2834, 2850, 2857, 2887, 2943, 2991,
    2993, 2998, 3008, 3018, 3029, 3197, 3256,
    3262, 3316, 3696, 3705, 3710-3772, 4078,
    4095, 4544
Heart Greek Theatre, 177
Heaton, Alma, 2841
Hehir, Martin A., 2312
Heidelberg College, 2004, 4168
Henderson State University, 102-103
Henry, Joseph, 443
Hershey Junior College, 2326
Hesston College, 904, 911
Heyliger, Victor, 3245
Hickey, Mary A., 3722
Higher Education Act of 1965, 84, 1262, 2308, 3580,
    3577, 3598
Higher education, general, 2106, 2373, 2796, 3634,
    3773-3832, 4392, 4493
Highland Park Junior College, 1254
Hill, David J., 1850
Hill, Leslie P., 2306
Hill, Walter B., 544
Hillquit, Morris, 1847
Hillsboro College (KS), 904
Hillsboro Junior College (TX), 2688
Hillsdale College, 1267
Hindsley, Mark H., 684
Hiram College, 2063-2065
Hispanic American Historical Review, 1935
Hispanic higher education, 722
History as discipline, 233, 282, 286, 371, 432, 441,
    660, 851, 873, 925, 1091, 1093, 1096, 1146,
    1168, 1202, 1243, 1698, 1719, 1732-1733,
    1736, 1740, 1756, 1764, 1766, 1771, 1782,
    1829, 1866, 1879, 1915, 1931, 1952, 2131,
    2213, 2432, 2783, 2801, 3040, 3070, 3077,
    3309, 3505, 3513, 3545, 4239, 4264, 4266,
    4268-4269, 4277-4278, 4281, 4283, 4287-4288,
    4290, 4296, 4313-4316, 4323, 4327, 4336-

    4337, 4341, 4349-4350, 4356
History of higher education, 4287
Hitchcock, Edward, 1147
Hiwassee College, 2548
Hockey, 3245
Hofstadter, Richard, 1719, 1756
Hofstra University, 1815-1817
Holism, 4429
Holley, Horace, 1003, 4070
Hollis professorship of divinity, 1189
Hollis, Florence, 4351
Holmes, George F., 2949, 2953
Holocaust, 3653
Holy Cross College (DC), 3381
Holy Family College (PA), 2327
Home economics, 51, 592, 855, 1686, 4309, 4311,
    4545
Homeopathy, 4086
Honors programs, 2387, 3150, 3516, 3522
Hood College, 4168
Hoole, William S., 21
Hoover Institution, 287
Hope College, 1267, 1287-1289
Hopkins, Mark, 1244
Hospitals, 3759
Hottzclaw, William H., 3280
Houghton College, 1818
Housing, 2134, 2156, 2792, 4409-4410, 4412, 4422
Houston, David F., 2794
Houston, University of, 2689-2692
Howard Payne College, 1468-1469
Howard University, 428-435, 2047, 3283
Howe Institute, 3280
Hudson, Winthrop, 1206
Huff, George A., 680
Hughes, Glenn, 2992
Humanities, 73, 836, 1750, 3588, 3677, 3823, 3833-
    3904, 3933, 4189, 4324
Humboldt State University, 219-220
Hunt, Harriot, 4545
Hunter College, City University of New York, 1819,
    4522
Huntingdon College, 37
Huston-Tillotson College, 2602
Hutchins, Robert M., 629, 632, 636, 645, 653, 657,
    663, 4044-4045

Idaho, 570-580
Idaho Education Association, 571
Idaho State University, 574
Idaho, University of, 575-577
Illinois, 581-760, 3303, 3733, 4364
Illinois Association for Professional Preparation in
    Health, Physical Education & Recreation, 589
Illinois Board of Higher Education, 603
Illinois College, 583, 587, 4070
Illinois Intercollegiate Athletic Conference, 593

Illinois State University, 583, 587, 675-679
Illinois Wesleyan University, 709-710
Illinois, University of, 467, 583, 587, 680-708, 804,
    1759, 2121, 3245, 3674, 3914, 4316, 4463
Immigrants, 1288, 1659, 3653, 3807, 3815
In Loco Parentis, 4396, 4404-4405, 4415, 4417,
    4424
Independent study, 3522, 3524
Indian River Junior Community College, 483
Indiana, 761-837, 3303, 4364
Indiana Dental College, 789
Indiana State University, 790-794, 3880
Indiana University, 278, 281, 288, 290, 795-815
Indiana University of Pennsylvania, 2272, 2296,
    2328-2329
Indiana Vocational Technical College, 816
Indiana, PA, 2272
Industrial arts, 191, 205, 325, 1496, 1785, 1910,
    2301, 2343, 2710, 2806, 3353
Industrial technology, 2125
Industry, 1221, 2281, 3145, 3743, 4252, 4263
Insurance, 1715
Integration, 484, 548, 554, 984, 1077, 1455, 1955,
    2058, 2503, 2923, 3013, 3028, 3266, 3272,
    3277, 3281, 3317, 3336, 4052
Inter-Varsity Christian Fellowship, 4122
Intercollegiate Socialist Society, 3039, 4057, 4377
Intercultural education, 722, 745, 750, 809, 1695,
    1832, 3822, 3905-3909
Interdenominational Theological Center, 550
International education, 26, 753, 2208, 2373
International relations, 3778, 4064, 4526
International Teaching Service Bureau, 1754
Iowa, 838-900, 3733
Iowa State University, 852-856, 1561
Iowa Wesleyan College, 839
Iowa, University of, 857-894, 3002, 3973, 4322

Jackson Community College, 1290
Jackson State University, 1419-1421
Jackson, Andrew, 3831, 4060
Jacksonville State University, 38
James Madison University, 2924
Jameson, J. Franklin, 4296, 4341
Jamestown Community College, 1820
Japan, 2127
Jarvis Christian College, 2602, 2693
Jeans, Anna T., 3672
Jefferson College (LA), 1021
Jefferson College (MS), 1422
Jefferson, Thomas, 2896, 2950, 2952, 2958-2959,
    2963, 4030, 4034, 4060
Jersey City State College, 1594
Jesuit higher education, 122, 263, 426-427, 1120-
    1122, 1668, 1806, 3366, 3373, 3378, 3391,
    3393
Jewish higher education, 1062, 1591, 1657, 1907,

    2321, 3910-3912
John A. Logan College, 711
John Brown University, 104
John F. Slater Fund, 3672
John Fletcher College, 895
Johns Hopkins University, 371, 623, 1085-1096,
    1156-1157, 3071, 3127, 4296, 4341, 4424
Johnson C. Smith University, 1941-1942
Johnson, Alexander, 1628
Johnson, Lyndon B., 3579, 4058
Johnson, Samuel, 1728, 1752
Johnstone, Edward R., 1628
Joliet Junior College, 3457
Jones County Junior College, 1423
Jones, Laurence C., 3280
Jordan, David S., 278, 281, 288, 290, 805, 3432
Journal of Higher Education, 1812
Journalism, 611, 922, 1861, 3064, 4082, 4100
Journalism about higher education, 586, 933, 1721,
    1812, 1954, 3126, 3158, 3295, 3387, 3421,
    3548, 3553, 3558, 3568, 3683, 3779, 3781,
    3794, 3817, 4105, 4221, 4230, 4378, 4421
Journalism education, 736, 1484, 1706, 2789, 2790,
    3065, 3073, 4322, 4332, 4347, 4421
Judson College, 39
Juilliard School, 1758, 1821
Julius Rosenwald Fund, 3669
Jung, Carl, 4273
Juniata College, 2330
Junior College Journal, 3421
Justin Morrill College, 1305

Kalamazoo College, 692, 1267, 1271, 1291
Kansas, 901-948, 3840
Kansas City, KS, 901
Kansas City, MO, 1447
Kansas Community Junior College, 909
Kansas Wesleyan, 938
Kansas, University of, 925-937
Karpovich, Peter V., 1236
Kaskaskia College, 712
Kean College of New Jersey, 1595
Keane, John J., 408
Kearney State College, 1544
Kefauver, Grayson N., 276, 285
Keller, Charles, 1243
Kennedy, John F., 4058
Kent State University, 2066-2069
Kentucky, 949-1007, 2170-2171, 3303
Kentucky Southern College, 973
Kentucky State University, 974-975
Kentucky, University of, 976-978
Kenyon College, 2000
Kerr, Clark, 157, 170-171, 174, 4044
Kerr, Harrison, 2216
Kesey, Ken, 3633
Kidd, Robert F., 3022

Kidd-Key College, 2694
Kilgore College, 2695
King, Martin L., Jr., 3335
Kinley, David, 685
Kiphuth, Robert J.H., 378
Kirk, John R., 1497
Kleinsmid, Rufus B., 269
Knapp, Bradford, 2780
Knox College, 581, 713, 1735, 1861, 4425
Kondratieff Theory, 4379, 4548
Koos, Leonard V., 630
Korean War, 2076
Krohn, Ernst C., 1515
Kuehn, Ruth P., 2397
Kutztown University, 2331

La Grange College, 551
La Salle College (PA), 2332, 4459
Labor market, 3830
Labor movement, 4511, 4517
Labor studies, 1618
Laboratory schools, 187, 238-239, 640-641, 656,
    698, 786, 875, 884, 893-894, 1030, 1268, 1554,
    1560, 2185
Lacrosse, 3201, 3224
Lafayette College (PA), 2296, 2333
Laidler, Harry W., 4057
Lake Erie College, 2004, 2012
Lake Forest College, 4378
Lakeland College, 4168
Lamar University, 2696-2698
Lambuth College, 2549
Land, Adelle, 1687
Land-grant institutions, 65, 116, 343, 577, 583, 587,
    827, 1387, 1531, 1561, 1781, 1798, 1949,
    2008, 2022, 2357, 2440, 2613, 2945, 2988,
    3189, 3278, 3282, 3287-3288, 3293, 3311,
    3326, 3328, 3331-3332, 3339, 3582, 3823,
    3913-3927, 3987, 3993, 4006, 4040, 4053,
    4072, 4532
Landes, James H., 2687
Lane College, 2550, 3286, 4150
Lane Theological Seminary (OH), 1148
Lane, Isaac, 2550, 3286
Lange, Alexis F., 3432, 3438
Langston University, 2199
Langston, John M., 429
Languages, ancient, 94, 1088, 1750
Languages, modern, 390, 865, 890, 1697, 1879,
    3902, 3904, 4460
Languages, romance, 1166, 1697
Lansing Community College, 1292
Latin, 1545
Latin America, 745, 1959, 4064
Latter-Day Saints higher education, 849, 2820, 2822,
    2825-2841, 3844, 4024, 4107, 4129, 4131,
    4148, 4451

Law, 1127, 1128, 1573, 1648, 2445, 3615, 3895,
    4077, 4079-4080, 4085, 4088, 4100
Lawrence University, 2435, 3046-3047
Lawther, Ethel L.M., 1977
Lea, Henry, 2366
Learned societies, 1139, 1829, 3190, 3988, 4501
Lebanon Valley College, 2334
Lectures, 290, 374, 443, 636, 1200, 2637, 2641,
    4273
Lee College (TN), 2551-2553
Lee, Edwin A., 234
Lee, Stephen D., 1425
Legal decisions, 1, 455, 548, 602, 1027, 1258, 1260,
    1690, 2182, 3096, 3097, 3277, 3292, 3317,
    3336, 3397, 3464, 3466-3547, 3550, 3554-
    3555, 3567, 4054, 4415, 4516
Legal education, 41, 109, 158, 256, 353, 366, 429,
    634, 983, 1127-1128, 1136, 1517, 1581, 1648,
    1692, 1980, 2052, 2445, 2511, 2773, 2894,
    2905, 2939, 3061, 3962, 3971, 4077, 4080,
    4085, 4088, 4319
Legislation, 1, 5, 11, 84, 151, 154, 175, 301, 332,
    345, 446, 455, 515, 584, 598, 600, 602-603,
    772, 949, 1008, 1027, 1257, 1258, 1262, 1272,
    1331, 1387, 1406, 1446, 1451, 1656, 1674,
    1690, 1701, 1746, 1769, 1921, 2059, 2182,
    2213, 2263, 2292, 2308, 2357, 2440, 2449,
    3042, 3055, 3081, 3109, 3189, 3199, 3278,
    3431, 3445, 3459, 3475, 3576-3577, 3590-
    3592, 3639, 3758, 3905, 3917, 3920-3921,
    3924, 3926-3932, 4053, 4056, 4288, 4401
Leith, Charles K., 3080
Lemieux, Albert A., 2984
LeMoyne-Owen College, 2554-2555
Lenox College, 862
Leverett, John, 1186
Lew Wentz Foundation, 2210
Lewis and Clark College, 2238
Lewis University, 664, 4459
Liberal arts, 113, 156, 367, 490, 581, 714, 788, 868-
    869, 1256, 1305, 1354, 1681, 1811, 1876,
    2000, 2284, 2893, 2987, 3019, 3057, 3240,
    3355, 3366, 3477, 3641, 3823, 3840, 3869,
    3876, 3906, 3933-3943, 3968, 3989, 4039-
    4040, 4203, 4259, 4378
Liberalism, 320, 1756, 1849, 3939, 4039-4040
Liberia, 59
Librarians, 21, 365, 437, 439, 686, 701, 1089, 1168,
    1345, 1388, 1776, 1783, 1790, 2043-2044,
    2113, 3945, 3963, 3973, 3980, 4078, 4180
Libraries, 8, 82, 112, 169, 172, 215, 287, 342, 349-
    350, 353, 361, 365-366, 384, 400, 425, 431,
    436-438, 444, 477, 485, 512, 543, 613, 616,
    620, 624, 649, 697, 704, 708, 787, 808, 848,
    889, 920, 922, 980, 983, 986, 1005, 1049,
    1054, 1056, 1081-1082, 1084, 1095, 1105,
    1108, 1114, 1117, 1120, 1141, 1168, 1181,
    1202, 1215, 1218, 1313, 1333, 1370-1371,
    1383, 1388, 1397, 1430, 1488, 1515, 1606,

1640, 1651, 1665, 1685, 1691, 1710, 1739,
1748-1749, 1775-1776, 1790, 1811, 1816,
1824, 1828-1829, 1831, 1872, 1878, 1892,
1900, 1903, 1937, 1940-1941, 1948, 1956-
1957, 1959-1960, 1964-1966, 1969, 1975,
1987, 2023, 2025, 2033, 2040, 2060, 2064-
2065, 2087, 2093, 2112, 2126, 2149, 2160,
2163, 2169, 2175, 2295, 2299, 2305, 2314,
2327, 2332-2333, 2337, 2366, 2368, 2372,
2374, 2405, 2407, 2410, 2418, 2429, 2431,
2433, 2526, 2533, 2594, 2646, 2659, 2760,
2773, 2785, 2791, 2798, 2906, 2915, 2933,
2962, 2988, 3000, 3014, 3021-3022, 3031,
3040, 3044, 3086, 3182, 3184-3185, 3193,
3274, 3288, 3926, 3944-3994, 4127, 4180,
4264
Library education, 654, 686, 1388, 1783, 1973, 2043-
2044, 3058, 3947, 3963, 3985, 4345
Library of Congress, 436-439, 1345, 4296, 4341
Limestone College, 2463
Lincoln University, 462, 1461, 1481, 2287, 2335,
3283
Lindsay, Inabel B., 433
Lindsley, John B., 2547
Lindsley, Philip, 4070
Linfield College, 2240
Linguistics, 4461
Linwood College, 1943
Literary societies, 19, 481, 590, 812, 1669, 2064-
2065, 2073, 2107, 2646, 2955, 3063, 3182,
3184-3185, 3193, 3991
Literature, 387, 626, 890, 1026, 1169, 1171, 1182,
1319, 1610, 1645, 1699, 1720, 1726, 1750,
1778, 1903, 2004, 2433, 3599, 3600-3602,
3604-3636, 3821, 3841, 3843, 3849, 3856,
3874-3875, 3884, 3888-3889, 3895, 3898,
3901, 3903, 4082, 4102, 4497
Little, Charles E., 2528
Little, Clarence C., 1350
Littlefield College, 2604
Livingston University, 40
Livingstone College, 1944, 3286
Lobbyists, 4059
Lock Haven University of Pennsylvania, 2336
Lockney Christian College, 2604
Loma Linda University, 221, 1280
Loma Linda University (Lasierra), 222-223
Lon Morris College, 2699-2702
Long Island University, 1822
Longwood College, 2925-2926
Los Angeles City College, 224
Los Angeles Community College District, 146
Los Angeles Junior College, 225
Los Angeles Pierce College, 226
Los Angeles Southwest College, 227
Los Angeles Trade Technical College, 228
Los Angeles, CA, 109, 128
Los Angeles, University of California, 146, 229-239,
351, 3980

Louisburg College, 1945
Louisiana, 1008-1051, 3433, 3954
Louisiana College, 1022-1023
Louisiana State University, 1024-1038
Louisiana Tech University, 1039
Louisville Municipal College, 979, 984
Louisville, University of, 979-986, 4522
Low, Seth, 1742, 1744
Lowell, Abbott L., 1193
Lowell, James R., 1181
Lowrey, Lawrence T., 1414
Lowrey, Sara, 4346
Loyalty oath, 120, 161
Loyola College (MD), 1097
Loyola University of Chicago, 714
Lutheran higher education, 610-613, 620, 835, 1363,
1371-1372, 1398, 1464, 1482, 1538-1539,
1903-1904, 1992, 1998, 2337, 2465-2466,
2485-2486, 2601, 2770-2771, 3869, 3882, 4106
Lutheran Medical Center School of Nursing, 1482
Lutheran Theological Seminary, 2337
Lutkin, Peter C., 734
Luzerne County Community College, 2338
Lynchburg College, 2927

MacBride, Thomas H., 862
MacDougall, Curtis D., 736
Mackey, A.B., 2578
MacLean, George E., 876
Macy, Jesse, 851
Madison College (PA), 2339
Madison College (VA), 2928
Madison, James, 2924
Madonna College, 1293
Mahan, Dennis H., 1885
Mailer, Norman, 3633
Main Currents in American Thought, 2994
Maine, 1052-1061
Maine, University of, 1060
Maine, University of (Augusta), 1059
Maine, University of (Portland-Gorham), 1061
Malin, James C., 925
Manhattan College, 1823, 4459
Manhattan School of Music, 1758
Manhattanville College, 1824
Mankato State University, 1373-1377
Manly, Basil, 24
Manly, Basil, II, 971
Mann, Horace, 2024
Mann, Matthew, II, 1339
Mare, Paul, 3870
Marian College, 817
Marietta College, 2000
Marillac College, 1483
Marion College (IN), 761
Marion College (VA), 2929
Maritime preservation, 442

Marketing, 3351
Markham, Edwin, 1903
Marquette University, 3048-3050
Mars Hill College, 1946
Marshall College (TN), 2556
Marshall University (WV), 3022-3024
Martin, Herbert, 881
Marx, Karl, 3443
Mary Hardin-Baylor College, 2703
Mary Sharp College, 2509
Mary Washington College, 2930
Marygrove College, 1271
Maryland, 1062-1122
Maryland, University of, 1098-1103
Marymount College of Virginia, 2931
Marymount Manhattan College, 1825
Marywood College, 2340
Massachusetts, 1123-1245, 3364
Massachusetts General Hospital Institute of Health
    Professions, 3696
Massachusetts Institute of Technology, 1223-1224
Massachusetts, University of, 1225-1226
Mathematics, 631, 814, 1598, 2900, 4203, 4229,
    4255
Mathews, Shailer, 662
Mattern, David E., 1325
Maybeck, Bernard R., 737
Mayo, Elton, 1221
Mayville State College, 1991
McCarthy, Joseph, 171, 2406, 3099, 3102, 3108
McCord, Mary L., 2740
McCorkle, Samuel E., 1961
McCune School of Music and Art, 2844
McDiarmed, Errett W., 1388
McDonald, Howard S., 2835
McGlothlin, William J., 2461
McGrath, Earl J., 1762
McGuffey, William H., 2015
McKendree College, 715-716
McKenzie, Robert T., 2371
McLemore, Richard A., 1424
McMurry College, 2704-2705
McMurry, Charles A., 727
McPherson College, 939
Media, 84, 311, 354, 799, 1384, 3052, 3500, 3526,
    3969
Medical College of Louisiana, 1040
Medical College of Pennsylvania, 2341
Medical education, 155, 272, 365, 406, 762, 959,
    986, 1040, 1095, 1101, 1134, 1140, 1180,
    1214, 1329, 1400, 1426, 1462, 1692, 1780,
    1828, 1897, 1933, 2001, 2120, 2265, 2286,
    2341, 2368, 2377, 2392, 2405, 2407, 2565,
    2939-2940, 2957, 2962, 3197, 3300, 3696,
    3995-4002, 4036, 4045, 4081, 4083, 4097,
    4099, 4101, 4545
Medicine, 386, 501, 1131, 1147, 1236, 1448, 1663,
    1667, 1788, 2111, 2281, 3602, 3714, 3737,
    3754, 3999, 4081, 4086-4087, 4096, 4102,
    4105, 4194, 4262, 4538
Meiklejohn, Alexander, 1142, 1144-1145
Melby, Ernest O., 1830
Memphis State University, 2513, 2557-2559
Mennonite higher education, 904, 911, 915, 946-947,
    3748, 3876
Mental retardation, 4444
Meredith, James, 1431
Mergers, 257, 490, 664, 1654, 1840, 2555, 3055-
    3056, 3132
Metheny, Eleanor, 275
Methodist higher education, 37, 63, 83, 103, 105,
    243-245, 316, 319-320, 322, 364, 460, 463,
    526, 528, 551, 554-555, 562-564, 672-674,
    709-710, 715-716, 784-786, 839, 896, 938,
    943-944, 1006, 1018, 1117-1119, 1276-1279,
    1468-1469, 1565, 1931-1935, 2033-2034,
    2087-2088, 2115, 2159-2163, 2241, 2261,
    2268, 2295, 2334, 2457, 2549-2550, 2590,
    2598, 2601, 2611, 2704-2705, 2737-2741,
    2749-2750, 2803-2804, 2915-2916, 2934,
    2968, 2981-2983, 3104, 3286, 3308, 3512,
    4110-4111, 4115, 4120, 4128, 4132, 4136,
    4140-4141, 4143, 4145
Methodist University of Portland, 2241
Metropolitan Museum of Art, 1729
Miami Alumni Association, 2085
Miami University (OH), 2015, 2070-2086
Miami, University of, 485-487
Miami-Dade Junior College, 484
Michigan, 1246-1361
Michigan Intercollegiate Athletic Association, 1249
Michigan State University, 1271, 1294-1310, 1830
Michigan, University of, 1311-1352, 1789, 1796,
    1798, 2542, 3175, 3245, 3432, 3674, 3805,
    4369, 4422, 4424, 4498
Michigan, University of (Dearborn), 1314
Michigan, University of (Flint), 1314
Micropublishing, 3564
Microscope, 4227
Middle States Association of College and Secondary
    Schools, 3951
Middle Tennessee State University, 2560
Middlebury College, 2870, 4378
Midland College, 2706-2707
Midwest Association of Student Financial Aid
    Administrators, 3642
Military education, 17, 36, 331-337, 362, 549, 853,
    907, 1024, 1032, 1034, 1113-1116, 1547, 1571,
    1639, 1855, 1880-1896, 2150, 2249, 2408-
    2409, 2416-2417, 2442-2444, 2573, 2684,
    2871, 3279, 3281, 3846, 4003-4017, 4042
Miller, Albert, 2836
Miller, George T., 2928
Millersville University of Pennsylvania, 2342-2343
Milligan College (TN), 2561
Mills College, 3710
Mills, C. Wright, 1756
Mills, Caleb, 837

Millsaps College, 1410
Milton College, 3051
Milwaukee-Downer College, 3047
Miner Teachers' College, 440
Minnesota, 1362-1398
Minnesota, University of, 314, 630, 1378-1393, 3914, 4369
Minnesota, University of (Morris), 1394
Minnich, Harvey C., 2083
Minorities, 209, 3208
Miracosta College, 240
Missionary higher education, 779, 2526-2527
Mississippi, 1399-1442
Mississippi College, 1424
Mississippi State University, 1425
Mississippi Valley State University, 1433-1434
Mississippi, University of, 1426-1432, 1725, 2949, 2953, 3818
Missouri, 1443-1519, 3840
Missouri Dental College, 1516
Missouri Inter-Collegiate Athletic Association, 1467
Missouri Valley College, 1493
Missouri, University of, 1461, 1484-1492, 1860, 2145-2146, 4322
Mitchell College, 1947
Mitchell, Elmer D., 1342
Mitchell, Lucy S., 1683
Mitchell, Maria, 1901-1902, 4545
Moberly Area Junior College, 1494
Modern Language Association of America, 3904
Modesto Junior College, 241-242
Montana, 1520-1528
Montana State University, 1522, 1830
Montana, University of, 827, 1523-1525, 1830
Montclair State College, 1596-1598
Montgomery, AL, 2503
Montgomery, E.W., 70
Monticello Seminary, 717
Moody Bible Institute, 718-719
Moody, D.L., 719
Moore, Ernest C., 233
Moore, James, 1002
Moravian higher education, 1909
Morehead State University, 987-989
Morehouse College, 552, 3275
Morehouse School of Religion, 550
Morgan State University, 1104-1105, 3283
Morgan, Arthur E., 2027
Morison, Samuel, 1206
Morley, Edward W., 2045
Morningside College, 896
Morphology, 1085
Morrill Act, 577, 583, 587, 1387, 1949, 2008, 2022, 2357, 2440, 3278, 3582, 3913-3914, 3917-3918, 3920-3924, 3926-3927, 4053
Morrill, Justin S., 3917, 3927
Morris Brown College, 553
Morris College, 2464
Morris Harvey College, 3025

Morris, Delyte W., 754
Morris, Don H., 2639
Morristown College, 2562
Mott, Frank L., 4322
Mount Angel Seminary, 2242
Mount Holyoke College, 1227-1229, 3710, 4498
Mount Union College, 2087-2088
Mountain State Athletic Conference, 3233
Mudge, Isadore G., 1776
Mundelein College for Women, 720
Murphy, Howard A., 1758
Murray State University, 990-991
Museums, 441, 879, 1152, 1172, 1224, 1729, 2781
Musgrave, Ray S., 1410
Music, 2429, 2819
Music education, 71, 97, 168, 200, 237, 265, 271, 274, 308, 310, 370, 428, 436, 474, 578, 669, 674, 684, 693, 734, 752, 845-846, 849, 866, 877-888, 901, 909, 927, 930, 934, 936, 985, 991, 1035, 1038, 1106, 1151, 1156, 1265, 1307, 1325, 1341, 1481, 1515, 1525, 1629-1630, 1666, 1747, 1749, 1758, 1761, 1807, 1821, 1836, 1845, 1968, 1995, 2034, 2048, 2054, 2057, 2104, 2110, 2199, 2216, 2329, 2334, 2415, 2433, 2505, 2576, 2603, 2656, 2695, 2716, 2722, 2816, 2836, 2844, 2891, 2903, 2946, 3023, 3046, 3066, 3194, 3324, 3837, 3840, 3845-3846, 3852, 3855, 3859, 3862-3864, 3866, 3868-3869, 3871, 3873, 3876-3878, 3881-3882, 3887, 3890, 3892, 3894, 3896-3897, 3899-3900, 3945
Muskingum College, 2089-2093

Nabakov, Vladimir, 3633
Nacubo College, 57
Nader, Ralph, 4390
Naismith, James, 929
Nashville, TN, 2503, 2505
National Association for Women Deans, Administrators, and Counselors, 3533, 4531, 4533
National Academy of Design, 1729
National Assembly for Teaching the Principles of the Bill of Rights, 1769
National Association for Music Therapy, 3194
National Association of Intercollegiate Athletics, 3222, 3226
National Association of Personnel Workers, 4441
National Association of State Universities and Land-Grant Colleges, 3189
National Business Education Association, 3350
National Catholic Educational Association, 3384
National Collegiate Athletic Association, 3209, 3211-3212, 3219, 3227, 3230, 3253, 3260
National Council for Accreditation of Teacher Education, 3117
National Council of Teachers of English, 3886
National Defense Education Act, 598, 3109, 4056

National Defense Student Loan, 3584
National Education Association, 1781
National Endowment for the Humanities, 3677
National Institute of Education, 4329
National Junior College Athletic Association, 3235
National Lawyers Guild, 4077
National League of Nursing Education, 3756
National Normal University, 2094
National Organization for Public Health Nursing,
    3732
National Science Foundation, 814, 4223, 4233, 4449
National Teacher Examination Program, 4491
National University, 4018-4023
National War College, 4008
National Youth Administration, 1913
Native Americans, 61, 62, 2195, 2198, 2923, 3417,
    4024-4027
Nativism, 3385
Navajo Community College, 78, 4025
Nazarene higher education, 249, 1495, 2196-2197,
    2578-2579, 4134, 4137, 4142
Nazarene Theological Seminary, 1495
Nazareth College, 1271
Nazism, 1659
Nearing, Scott, 3101
Nebraska, 1529-1568
Nebraska Wesleyan University, 1564-1565
Nebraska, University of, 1545-1561, 3082, 3973
Nebraska, University of (Omaha), 1562-1563
Neff, Pat M., 2645, 2647, 2653, 2657
Netherlands, 1288
Nevada, 1569-1571
Nevada, University of, 1571
New Brunswick Theological Seminary, 1599
New College, 490
New Deal, 3169, 3301, 3595, 4154
New England, 1224, 2440, 3177, 3364, 3463, 3922,
    3944, 4093, 4166, 4251
New Hampshire, 1572-1579
New Jersey, 1580-1630
New Mexico, 1631-1647, 3393
New Mexico Highlands University, 1637-1638
New Mexico Military Institute, 1639
New Mexico Quarterly, 1645
New Mexico State University, 1640
New Mexico, University of, 1641-1646
New Paltz (College), State University of New York,
    1826-1827
New School for Social Research, 1732, 1764, 1840
New York, 1648-1907
New York Academy of Medicine, 1828
New York State Teachers Association, 1650, 1674
New York Times, 1861, 3779
New York University, 1352, 1654, 1830-1835, 3783
New York, City University of, 1662, 1685, 1695-1711,
    1773, 1819, 1861, 4421, 4522
New York, NY, 1662, 1665, 1673, 1676, 4001
New York, State University of, 1681-1682, 1684,
    1686-1692, 1712, 1762, 1801-1802, 1807-1808,

1810, 1826-1827, 1837, 1843-1845, 1851,
    1857-1864, 1897, 4463
New York-Historical Society, 1829
Newark, University of, 1600
Newberry College, 2465-2466
Newman Movement, 3376
Newton Theological Institution, 2436
Nichols, Frederick G., 1164
Nichols, John H., 2111
Niles' Weekly Register, 3817
Nixon, Richard M., 4055
Nobel laureates, 1069, 4257
Normal schools, 3, 74, 133, 142, 324, 359, 621, 675-
    679, 724, 764, 782-783, 897, 910, 923, 988,
    1041, 1055, 1063-1064, 1076, 1078, 1112,
    1132-1133, 1273, 1374, 1376, 1527, 1637,
    1660, 1801, 1844, 1961, 1991, 2037, 2094,
    2228, 2273, 2275-2276, 2303, 2328, 2342,
    2400-2401, 2438, 2487, 2558, 2567, 2724-
    2725, 2730, 2882, 2930, 2978, 3010, 3036,
    3041, 3948, 4218, 4447, 4453, 4473, 4490
North Carolina, 1908-1987, 4192, 4565
North Carolina Agricultural & Technical State
    University, 1948
North Carolina State Intercollegiate Athletic
    Conference, 1914
North Carolina State University, 1949-1951
North Carolina, University of, 1952-1973, 3818
North Carolina, University of (Boone), 1974
North Carolina, University of (Charlotte), 1975
North Carolina, University of (Greensboro), 1976-
    1977
North Central Association of College and Secondary
    Schools, 773, 3112-3113, 3121, 3181, 3183,
    3195, 3489
North Central Intercollegiate Athletic Conference,
    3263
North Central Technical College, 2095
North Dakota, 1988-1994
North Dakota, University of, 1992
North Newton College, 904
North Texas State University, 21, 2708-2721
Northeast Missouri State University, 1496
Northeastern Illinois University, 721-723
Northeastern Oklahoma University, 2200
Northern Arizona University, 79-80
Northern Colorado, University of, 323-328
Northern Illinois University, 724-729
Northern Iowa, University of, 897
Northern Michigan University, 1268, 1271
Northern Montana College, 1526
Northwest Christian College, 2243
Northwest College of the Assemblies of God, 2980
Northwest Missouri State University, 1497-1498
Northwest Territory, 717, 3797, 3918, 4171, 4176-
    4177
Northwestern College (IA), 898
Northwestern Oklahoma State University, 2201-2203
Northwestern State University of Louisiana, 1041-

1042
Northwestern University, 321, 597, 702, 730-736,
    1830, 3071, 3783
Norwich University, 2871-2872
Notre Dame, University of, 414, 818-823, 3381
Nott, Eliphalet, 4070
Nursing, 2229, 3732, 3766
Nursing education, 221, 368, 430, 454, 777, 828,
    843-844, 1065, 1266, 1292, 1482, 1570, 1724,
    1788, 2041, 2229, 2311, 2395, 2397, 2591,
    2616, 2784, 2824, 2998, 3711-3712, 3714,
    3717, 3719-3720, 3722, 3724, 3727, 3738,
    3740, 3742-3745, 3749-3751, 3753, 3756,
    3758-3759, 3762-3765, 3768

O'Connell, Dennis J., 411
O'Shea, Michael V., 3078
Oakland City College (IN), 824-825
Oakland College (MS), 1435
Oakland Community College (MI), 1353
Oakland University (MI), 1354-1355
Oberlin College, 2000, 2004, 2096-2113, 4150
Objectives, 320, 1259, 1433, 1953, 2103, 2690,
    2950, 3134, 3149, 3168, 3357, 3373, 3406-
    3407, 3409, 3422, 3517, 3739, 3793, 3796,
    3806, 3820, 3823, 3941, 4093, 4350, 4449-
    4450, 4481, 4555
Oceanography, 1245
Octavo School of Musical Art, 1836
Ogden College, 992
Oglethorpe University, 2468
Ohio, 1995-2175, 3303
Ohio Athletic Conference, 2020
Ohio Council for Education, 2014
Ohio Foundation of Independent Colleges, 2005
Ohio Northern University, 2114-2115
Ohio State University, 655, 658, 1860,111, 2116-
    2150
Ohio University, 2015, 2151-2158, 3880
Ohio Wesleyan University, 2004, 2159-2160, 4378
Oklahoma, 2176-2227, 3433
Oklahoma Association of Negro Teachers, 2191
Oklahoma Baptist University, 2204
Oklahoma City University, 2205
Oklahoma Presbyterian College, 2206
Oklahoma State University, 2207-2211, 2780
Oklahoma, University of, 1339, 2212-2221, 2994
Okolona College, 1436
Old Dominion University, 2932
Old Jefferson College, 2344
Old Westbury (College), State University of New
    York, 1837
Old Willie Halsell College, 2222
Olympics, 2569
Ombudsman, 801, 4408
Optometry, 1667
Oregon, 2228-2261

Oregon State Scholarship Commission, 2233
Oregon State University, 2234, 2244-2246, 3713
Oregon, University of, 314, 2234, 2247-2256
Osburn, Burl N., 2343
Osteopathy, 3995, 4081
Oswego (College), State University of New York,
    4463
Otterbein College, 2161-2163
Our Lady of Holy Cross College (LA), 1043
Owen College, 2555

Pacific Coast Conference, 232
Pacific Union College, 246, 4507
Pacific University, 2257
Pacific, University of the, 243-245, 3203, 3251
Packard Junior College, 1838
Packard, Silas S., 1838
Paine College, 554-555
Pakistan, 4474
Palmer, George H., 1203
Palomar College, 247
Panola College, 2722
Paris Junior College, 2723
Park College, 1445
Park, Rosemary, 351
Parrington, Vernon L., 2994
Parsons College, 899
Parsons School of Design, 1839-1840
Partridge, Alden, 1894, 2871
Pasadena Junior College, 248
Paterno, Joseph V., 2348
Pathology, 4099
Paul Quinn College, 2602
Payne, Daniel A., 3286
Payne, William H., 2542
Peabody Conservatory of Music, 1106
Peabody, George, 2538, 2541
Penn School, 2467
Penniman, Josiah H., 2370
Pennsylvania, 2262-2418
Pennsylvania Academy of the Fine Arts, 2345-2346
Pennsylvania State Athletic Conference, 2274
Pennsylvania State University, 2267, 2347-2364
Pennsylvania State University (Altoona), 2291
Pennsylvania, University of, 702, 1221, 1732, 1764,
    1770, 1860, 2265, 2330, 2365-2379, 2473,
    3101, 3408, 3981, 4256
Pensacola Junior College, 458
Pentecostal higher education, 4109, 4135
People's College, 1841
People's Institute, 1842
Peppe, Michael, 2133
Peru State College, 1566
Pharmaceutical education, 1402, 2146, 2381, 3718,
    3767
Pharmacy, 2281, 4183
Phelps, William F., 380

Phi Beta Kappa, 1187, 3686
Phi Delta Kappa, 2855, 3684
Philadelphia Academy of Natural Sciences, 2380
Philadelphia College of Pharmacy, 2381
Philadelphia College of Textiles and Science, 2382
Philadelphia School of Pedagogy, 2383
Philadelphia, PA, 2264, 2286, 2289, 2346, 4001
Philander Smith College, 105
Philanthropy, 179, 771, 822, 1328, 2005, 2013,
    2210, 2289, 2541, 2543, 3276, 3371, 3423,
    3429, 3639, 3667-3679, 3972, 3977, 4002,
    4054, 4179, 4181, 4223, 4449, 4452
Phillips School of Theology, 550
Philomath College, 2258
Philosophy, 375, 657, 802, 836, 881, 1142, 1145,
    1155, 1185, 1200, 1203, 1207, 1211, 1242,
    1337, 1340, 1380, 1751, 1871, 2121, 2796,
    3836, 3850-3851, 3879, 4066, 4558
Philosophy of education, 412, 577, 583, 587, 629,
    645, 653, 663, 1074, 1130, 1166, 1177, 1223,
    1243, 1280, 1486, 1508, 1605, 1611, 1614,
    1784, 1796, 1819, 2024, 2103, 2109, 2205,
    2306, 2583, 2645, 2718, 2799, 2876, 2896,
    2950, 2952, 2958, 2979, 2986, 3035, 3144,
    3149, 3312, 3315, 3373, 3521, 3539, 3695,
    3773, 3780, 3803, 3840, 3913, 3915, 4028-
    4051, 4065, 4200, 4259, 4304, 4348, 4424,
    4435, 4446
Phoenix College, 81-82
Phoenix College District, 70
Physical education, 14, 30, 44, 93, 185, 194, 222,
    235, 250, 275, 386, 421, 464, 467, 509, 539,
    575, 589, 622, 628, 680, 882-883, 929, 977,
    1098, 1147, 1191, 1233, 1235-1236, 1239,
    1312, 1327, 1342, 1385, 1411, 1419, 1503,
    1522, 1627, 1679, 1718, 1826, 1977, 1996,
    2053, 2061, 2063, 2074, 2088, 2090-2091,
    2100, 2102, 2111, 2114, 2118, 2133, 2135,
    2148, 2155, 2159, 2201, 2203, 2209, 2214,
    2247, 2302, 2359, 2364, 2371, 2479, 2481,
    2527, 2544, 2568, 2572, 2671, 2714, 2718,
    2834, 2850, 2857, 2887, 2991, 2993, 3008,
    3018, 3029, 3250, 3256, 3262, 3316, 3705,
    3710, 3715-3716, 3721, 3725, 3728, 3731,
    3733-3735, 3739, 3741, 3746-3748, 3752,
    3754-3755, 3761, 3769-3772, 4544
Physical plant, 463, 859, 3953
Physical therapy, 3757, 3760
Physics, 143, 407, 443, 1069, 1175, 1217, 4196,
    4216
Physiology, 1180, 3713
Piedmont College, 556-557
Pinesville (College), State University of New York,
    1843
Piney Woods School, 3280
Pittsburg State University (KS), 940-942
Pittsburgh, PA, 2268
Pittsburgh, University of, 2145-2146, 2267, 2384-
    2397

Pittsburgh, University of (Johnstown), 2291
Planning and evaluation, 26, 57, 651, 658, 816,
    1549, 2009, 2055, 2124, 2719, 3018, 3118,
    3427
Plattsburgh (College), State University of New York,
    1844
Poetry, 1026, 1169, 1720, 1903, 2429, 2433, 3603,
    3635, 3841, 3889
Point Loma Nazarene College, 249
Point Park College, 2398
Political science, 178, 383, 851, 1705, 1735, 4284,
    4300, 4343, 4355, 4558
Politics and social policy, 11, 120, 151, 154, 161,
    346, 355, 446, 492, 494, 496, 501, 594, 608,
    949, 952, 955, 1008, 1067, 1124, 1129, 1212,
    1216, 1257, 1272, 1331, 1343, 1387, 1399,
    1406, 1427, 1463, 1536, 1659, 1662, 1746,
    1769, 1795, 1847, 1880, 1921, 2042, 2130,
    2234, 2269, 2425, 2618, 2875, 2943, 2979,
    2996, 3003, 3015, 3037, 3042, 3054, 3059,
    3075, 3081, 3092, 3108, 3169, 3189, 3278,
    3317, 3349, 3408, 3415, 3418, 3443, 3453,
    3551, 3574, 3579, 3580-3581, 3586, 3590-
    3592, 3595-3598, 3653, 3772, 3778, 3802,
    3826, 3917, 3927-3930, 3960, 4002, 4028,
    4052-4067, 4079-4080, 4089, 4219, 4233,
    4247, 4266, 4297, 4319, 4373-4374, 4377,
    4389, 4390, 4419, 4421, 4517, 4526, 4528,
    4562, 4567
Polytechnic institutes, 180-183, 617, 1039, 1223,
    1234, 1514, 1848, 1889, 2010, 2779, 2804,
    2935, 2942, 4240
Pomona College, 250-251
Pope Pius XII, 361
Port Huron Junior College, 1254
Porter, James D., 2529
Porter, Noah, 375, 377
Portland State University, 2259
Portland, University of, 2238
Potsdam (College), State University of New York,
    1845
Prairie View Agricultural & Mechanical University,
    2724-2725
Pratt Institute, 1755
Presbyterian higher education, 46, 91, 99, 945, 968,
    1413, 1493, 1535, 1543, 1613, 1941, 1942,
    1978, 1979, 1983-1984, 2058, 2089-2093,
    2206, 2279, 2319-2320, 2322-2324, 2418,
    2458-2459, 2519, 2580, 2644, 2772, 2866,
    2917-2919, 3044-3045, 3104, 3330, 3508,
    4112, 4114, 4123, 4133, 4146, 4354, 4503
Presidency (U.S.), 1880
Presidents, 3123, 3139, 4068-4074, 4167
Press, 4416
Preston, Ann, 2341
Price, Hartley D., 467
Price, Joseph C., 3286
Prince George's Community College, 1107
Princeton Theological Seminary, 1601-1604

Princeton University, 443, 1605-1614, 1861, 2280, 3156, 3174-3175, 3193, 3250, 3851, 3981, 4256, 4421
Principia College, 737
Prisoner education, 744
Private institutions, 13, 135, 510, 766, 1163, 1463, 1677, 1918, 2005, 2263, 2421, 2512, 3131, 3431, 3433, 3469, 3477, 3769, 3801, 3810, 3906, 4184, 4362-4363, 4417, 4516
Procter, William, Jr., 2381
Professionalization, 907, 1087, 1128-1129, 1180, 1222, 1231, 1317, 1650, 1885, 3078, 3133, 3143, 3158, 3166, 3359, 3425, 3448, 3465, 3526, 3689, 3712, 3838, 3947, 4080, 4088, 4091, 4180, 4190, 4294, 4298-4299, 4301, 4308, 4330-4331, 4433, 4530
Professions, 355, 405-406, 501, 1010, 1127-1128, 1134, 1136, 1140, 1266, 1402, 1448, 1648, 1663, 2012, 2170-2171, 2229, 2286, 2341, 2445-2446, 2894, 3359, 3627, 3719, 3727, 3732, 3736, 3749-3750, 3766, 3789, 3815, 3996, 4075-4105, 4215, 4220, 4225-4226, 4242, 4251, 4320, 4330, 4523, 4538, 4543, 4545, 4549
Progressive Education Association, 3179
Progressivism, 239, 633, 1744, 1842, 2278, 4200, 4370, 4542
Project Upward Bound, 3577
Propaganda, 4266
Protestant Episcopal Theological Seminary, 2933
Protestant higher education, 591, 1250, 1269, 1367, 1669, 2889, 3957, 3958, 4106-4153, 4176-4178, 4325, 4328
Providence College, 2437
Psychiatry, 321, 1131, 2396, 3627, 3724, 3758, 3762, 3996, 4075, 4083, 4465
Psychology, 546, 1086, 1087, 1157, 1221, 1378, 1410, 1770, 2763, 3081, 3521, 4258, 4272, 4275, 4280, 4291, 4295, 4330, 4333-4334, 4338, 4351, 4430, 4478, 4523
Public administration, 1299, 3192
Public health, 1667, 3713, 3719, 3723, 3726, 3732, 3737, 4078
Public Interest Research Group, 4390
Public Law 874, 3932
Public relations, 699, 3287, 4154-4157
Publishing, 166, 4237
Puerto Rico, 2419-2425, 1695, 1832
Puerto Rico, University of, 2424-2425, 3650
Puget Sound, University of, 2981-2982
Purdue University, 826-829
Putnam, Herbert, 439

Quachita Baptist College, 106
Quaker higher education, 152, 300, 787, 900, 1940, 2402-2403, 4118
Queens College (NC), 1978-1979

Quincy, Josiah, 1194

Radcliffe College, 1197, 1210, 3710
Radio, 31, 242, 478, 749, 794, 886, 1297, 1302, 1309, 1346, 1490, 1551, 1805, 1859, 2075, 2138, 2494, 2497, 2654, 3069, 3341, 3343-3344, 3346-3347
Raley, John W., 2204
Rand School of Social Science, 1846-1847
Randolph-Macon College, 660, 2934
Randolph-Macon Woman's College, 4551
Ranger Junior College, 2726
Ratchford, Fannie, 2798
Read, Daniel, 3880
Reading, 648, 729, 1403, 3497, 3499, 3504, 3506, 3517-3518, 3520, 4461
Rebellions, student, 145, 154, 162, 210, 560, 682, 933, 1183, 1308, 1310, 1343, 1421, 1638, 1717, 1795, 1868, 1972, 2066-2067, 2234, 2425, 3054, 3059, 4371-4390
Recreation education, 44, 204, 539, 589, 1419, 1522, 1802, 2390, 2568, 2709, 2841, 3120, 3143, 3705, 3716, 3735, 3752, 3770, 4331
Redlands, University of, 125, 252
Reference service, 3968
Reformed Church in America, 1289
Reformed Church in America higher education, 845, 898, 1287-1288
Regis College, 1230
Religion, 7, 363, 372, 626, 650, 662, 713, 806, 1143, 1211-1212, 1224, 1320, 1351, 1611, 1898, 2079, 2096, 2624, 2826, 2858, 2909-2910, 2982, 3101, 3397, 3399, 3401, 3404, 3417, 3551, 3782, 3809, 3819, 4035, 4037, 4158-4167, 4251, 4273, 4358
Religious colleges, 113, 297, 719, 761, 834, 1248, 1256, 1269, 1367, 2193, 2551, 2627, 2889, 3014, 3104, 3113, 3119, 3313, 3366, 3369, 3389, 3403, 3473, 4141, 4144, 4168-4169, 4171, 4173, 4175-4177, 4500, 4502
Religious education, 599, 895, 1148, 1877, 2177-2178, 2747, 3330, 3400, 3402, 4113, 4170, 4172, 4174, 4178
Remedial education, 1550, 3496-3497, 3499, 3506-3507, 3523
Rensselaer Polytechnic Institute, 1621, 1848
Research, 143, 165, 265, 271, 443, 656, 708, 1215, 1508, 1768-1769, 1831, 2145-2146, 2781, 3574, 3579, 3587, 3701, 3737, 3952, 3965, 3994, 4179-4184, 4199, 4204, 4207, 4233, 4252, 4260, 4285, 4329, 4361, 4390, 4527
Reynolds, Bertha C., 1232
Rhetoric, 290, 590, 632, 636, 863, 932, 1207, 1275, 1301, 1322, 1361, 1506, 1564, 2038, 2158, 2587, 2637, 2766, 2892, 2955, 3654-3666, 3833, 3901
Rhode Island, 2426-2444, 3364

Rhode Island Board of Regents, 2426
Rhode Island College, 2438-2439
Rhode Island, University of, 2440-2441
Rice University, 2727
Rice, John H., 2917
Richards, Ellen S., 4545
Richardson, Loche, 1865
Richmond College (VA), 2949, 2953
Richmond Female Institute (VA), 971
Richmond Hill Law School (NC), 1980
Richmond, University of, 4467, 4477, 4480
Rickover, Hyman G., 4042
Ricks College, 578-580
Riddell, John L., 1040
Rider College, 1615
Rio Grande College, 2164
Rio Hondo College, 253
Riverside, University of California, 125
Rivier College, 1579
Robert College, 3646-3647
Robinson, James H., 1732, 1764
Rochester Theological Seminary, 1849
Rochester, University of, 1850
Rockford College, 738-739, 3710
Rockhurst College, 1499
Rocky Mountain Athletic Conference, 3238
Rollins College, 488
Roosevelt University, 740-741
Roosevelt, Franklin D., 3595
Root, Azariah S., 2113
Rosenwald, Julius, 3669
Ross, Edward A., 3082
ROTC, 1032, 1547, 1571, 1855, 2249, 2573, 2684,
    4004, 4007, 4009, 4016
Rowing, 3006, 3257
Ruffner, Henry, 2966
Ruffner, William H., 2926
Rufi, John, 1486
Rugg, Harold, 1784
Rush Medical College, 321
Rush, Benjamin, 2265
Rush, James, 4353
Rush, Ralph E., 274
Rusk Baptist College (TX), 2728-2729
Ruskin College, 1500
Russell, Harry L., 3053
Russell, James E., 1774
Russian language, 1670
Rutgers Preparatory School, 1622
Rutgers University, 1616-1623, 3108, 4256
Ruthven, Alexander G., 1349
Ryan, James H., 415

Sabin, Ellen C., 3047
Sacramento Junior College, 254
Sacramento State College, 255, 3090
Sailing, 3241

Saint Andrew's Society of New York, 1730
Saint Louis University, 1501-1502
Saint Mary's College (MN), 1395
Saint Mary-of-the-Woods College (IN), 830
Saint Paul's College (VA), 2935
Salaries, 2626, 4303
Salem College, 3014
Sam Houston State University, 2730-2731
Samford University, 41-44, 4467, 4477, 4480
San Antonio College, 2732
San Antonio Junior College, 2733
San Bernardino Valley Community College, 125
San Diego College for Women, 257
San Diego, University of, 256-257
San Jacinto College, 2734-2735
San Jose State University, 145
San Luis Obispo Junior College, 258
Sandburg, Carl, 619
Sanders, Henry R., 232
Santa Barbara, University of California, 259-262
Santa Clara, University of, 263
Savannah State College, 558
Scandinavia, 3060
Schenectady (College), State University of New
    York, 1851
Scholarly publications, 387, 1187, 1935, 2994, 3102,
    3542, 3564, 3941, 4356
Scholarships and fellowships, 642, 1090, 2233,
    2538, 3323, 3586, 3706
Scholastic performance, 3208, 3262, 3541, 3825
School for Social Workers, 1231
School of Social Studies (CA), 1142, 1144-1145
Schumpeter, Joseph, 4303
Schurman, Jacob G., 1793
Sciences, 180, 182, 617, 627, 879, 1011, 1139,
    1222, 1224, 1234, 1315, 1319, 1367, 1514,
    1663, 1669, 1869, 2050, 2264, 2289, 2318,
    2380, 2382, 2727, 2779, 2804, 3578, 3697,
    3823, 3856, 4162, 4181, 4185-4257, 4293,
    4449
Scientists, 278, 281, 290, 385, 805, 1040, 1069,
    1167, 1175, 1180, 1192, 1217, 1561, 1621,
    1745, 1773, 1848, 1901-1902, 2045, 2468,
    3053, 3080, 3653, 4201, 4204, 4211-4212,
    4214-4215, 4219, 4221, 4527, 4545
Scotland, 1612, 1730, 2914
Sears, Barnas, 2436
Seashore, Carl E., 878
Seattle Pacific College, 2983
Seattle Seminary, 2983
Seattle University, 2984-2985
Seattle, WA, 2973
Seeds, Corinne, 239
Segregation, 3, 548, 1012, 1034, 1063-1064, 1076,
    1916, 1926, 3019, 3292, 4489
Selecman, Charles C., 2738
Selvidge, Robert W., 1487
Seminaries, 127, 319, 376, 526, 531, 550, 613, 616,
    620, 718, 775, 968, 993-995, 1083, 1121-1122,

1148, 1276, 1475, 1495, 1599, 1601-1604, 1814, 1849, 1878, 1919, 2242, 2263, 2314, 2337, 2455, 2668, 2748, 2933, 2936, 2938, 2983, 3104, 3111-3113, 3365, 3390, 3910, 3957-3958, 3966, 4120, 4127, 4130, 4151, 4326, 4451, 4499, 4503-4504, 4506, 4508
Seminars, 1738
Seminole Junior College, 2223
Servicemen's Readjustment Act, 772, 3576, 4401
Seth Low Junior College, 1723
Seth War College, 2604
Seton Hall University, 1624
Seton Hill College, 2399
Seven Seas, University of the, 264
Seventh-Day Adventist higher education, 126, 221-223, 246, 1082, 1280-1281, 3866, 4117, 4139, 4149
Sexology, 807, 4308
Shahan, Thomas J., 410
Shakespeare, William, 3889
Shaler, Nathaniel S., 1167
Sharp, Katharine, 686
Shaw College at Detroit, 1356
Shaw University, 1981-1982
Shawnee College, 2165
Sheldon Jackson Junior College, 64
Shelton, Everett F., 3090
Shepherd College, 3026
Shera, Jesse, 2044
Sheridan College, 3089
Shimer College, 742
Shippensburg University of Pennsylvania, 2400
Shorter College, 559
Shotwell, James T., 1740, 1771
Shurter, Edwin D., 2788
Siena College, 1852
Sill, Anna P., 739
Silliman College, 1044
Silliman, Benjamin, 382
Sinclair, Upton, 4028
Sioux Falls College, 2490
Sisters of Bethany, 3395
Skidmore College, 1853
Skyline Athletic Conference, 3238
Slater, John F., 3672
Slaught, Ellsworth, 631
Slavery, 42, 429, 462, 763, 965, 2096-2099, 2907, 3284, 3297, 3303, 3306, 3319, 3334
Slippery Rock University, 2401
Small, Albion W., 623
Smith College, 1135, 1232-1233, 3566, 3710, 4351
Smith, David S., 370
Smith, Henry L, 803
Smith, Samuel S., 1607
Smith, William, 2365, 2375
Smithsonian Institution, 441-443
Snead Junior College, 45
Snedden, David, 1727
Snow College, 2845-2846

Snow Hill Institute, 3280
Snow, C.P., 3562
Snyder, Jonathan L., 1296
Soccer, 2017, 2036, 2349, 3196, 3202
Social Gospel, 2096-2097
Social sciences, 348, 860, 873, 1170, 1213, 1386, 1396, 1846-1847, 1915, 2853, 3039, 3292, 3538, 3704, 3934-4035, 4189, 4223, 4258-4361, 4541
Social work, 433, 493, 521, 1131, 1190, 1231-1232, 1271, 1448, 1775, 2422, 3380, 4078, 4261, 4267, 4276, 4286, 4298, 4310, 4320-4321, 4325, 4340, 4351, 4361
Socialism, 1847, 2996, 3039, 3443, 4057, 4377
Society for Public Health Education Inc., 3723
Society for the Promotion of College and Theological Education at the West, 4501
Sociology, 623, 638, 652, 804, 1221, 1242, 1759, 2949, 2953, 3082, 3644, 4065, 4098, 4165, 4234, 4257, 4270, 4274, 4297, 4306, 4317, 4328, 4335, 4338, 4343-4354, 4359
Soule, Martha E.L., 539
South Atlantic Quarterly, 1935
South Carolina, 2445-2480, 3954, 4192, 4505, 4565
South Carolina College, 2468, 2470
South Carolina, University of, 2449, 2469-2475, 3818
South Dakota, 2481-2502
South Dakota Intercollegiate Athletic Conference, 2481
South Dakota School of Mines and Technology, 2491
South Dakota State University, 2492-2493
South Dakota, University of, 2494-2500
South Dakota, University of (Springfield), 2501
South Florida, University of, 489-490
South, University of the, 1778, 2563-2564
Southeast Missouri State University, 1503-1504
Southeastern Conference, 3215, 3236, 3249
Southeastern Illinois College, 743
Southeastern Louisiana College, 1045
Southeastern Massachusetts University, 1234
Southern Arkansas University, 107
Southern Association of Colleges and Secondary Schools, 8, 3178, 3285, 3858
Southern Baptist Convention, 2682-2685, 2703, 4126
Southern Baptist Theological Seminary, 971, 993-995, 2461
Southern California, University of, 265-275
Southern College Personnal Association, 4432
Southern Farmers' Alliance, 3171
Southern Illinois University, 644, 744-754, 3783
Southern Illinois University, Edwardsville, 755
Southern Intercollegiate Gymnastic League, 3206
Southern Methodist University, 2736-2742
Southern Mississippi, University of, 1410, 1437-1438
Southern Seminary, 2936
Southern Seminary Junior College, 2893
Southern University and Agricultural & Mechanical

College, 1046-1047
Southern Utah State College, 2847
Southwest Baptist College, 1505
Southwest Missouri State University, 1506
Southwest Texas Junior College, 2743
Southwest Texas State University, 2744-2745
Southwestern Assemblies of God College, 2746
Southwestern Baptist Theological Seminary, 2747-2748
Southwestern College, 943-944
Southwestern Louisiana, University of, 1048-1049
Southwestern Oklahoma State University, 2224-2225
Southwestern University, 2749-2750
Soviet Union, 4290
Spain, 1782
Spalding, John L., 412
Spanish-American War, 4062
Spartanburg Junior College, 2476
Special education, 25
Specialization, 3787
Speech education, 22, 91, 244, 294, 374, 409, 426,
    465, 498, 568, 590, 731, 768, 784, 896, 919,
    943, 1020, 1028-1029, 1031, 1039, 1058, 1060,
    1311, 1322, 1391, 1445, 1471, 1537, 1543-
    1544, 1550, 1563, 1680, 1747, 1763, 1865,
    2029, 2078, 2137, 2162, 2202, 2238, 2486,
    2490-2492, 2500-2501, 2587, 2617, 2638,
    2707, 2717, 2740, 2767, 2775, 2788, 2839,
    2964, 3025, 3062, 4260, 4262, 4279, 4289,
    4292-4293, 4304, 4312, 4326, 4346, 4353
Speech pathology, 4084
Spelman College, 560
Spofford, Ainsworth R., 437
Springfield College (IL), 756
Springfield College (MA), 1235-1236
St. Andrews Presbyterian College, 1983-1984
St. Augustine's College, 1985
St. Bonaventure University, 1854-1855
St. Cloud State University, 1396
St. Cloud, MN, 1365
St. Francis College (IN), 831
St. Francis Xavier College (MO), 1507
St. John's College (MD), 1108
St. John's University (MN), 1397
St. John's University (NY), 1668, 1856
St. John, Lynn W., 2118
St. Joseph College (CT), 361
St. Joseph's College (KY), 996
St. Joseph's College (MD), 1109
St. Lawrence University, 4378
St. Louis, MO, 1444, 1448-1449, 1456, 1462
St. Martin's College, 2986
St. Mary's College (CA), 4459
St. Mary's College (IN), 832
St. Mary's College (MD), 1110-1111
St. Mary's College (MN), 4459
St. Olaf College, 1398
St. Petersburg Junior College, 491
St. Petersburg, University of, 492

St. Philip's College, 2751
Stagg, Amos A., 3203, 3251
Stanford University, 145, 276-295, 805, 1812, 3082,
    3101, 3432
Stanton, Madeline E., 365
State aid and coordination, 4, 11, 69, 87, 114, 120-
    123, 131, 135-136, 148, 161, 303-304, 338,
    340, 449, 455, 492, 510, 513, 548, 571, 585,
    593-594, 603, 606, 771, 950, 953-955, 1067,
    1124, 1252, 1257-1258, 1272, 1331, 1362,
    1427, 1446, 1452, 1463, 1520, 1536, 1653,
    1664, 1675, 1677-1678, 1791, 1911, 1918,
    1921, 1989, 2009, 2013-2014, 2182, 2190,
    2194, 2232-2233, 2235, 2239, 2263, 2269-
    2271, 2274, 2287-2288, 2393, 2426, 2483,
    2508, 2584, 2612, 2629, 2823, 2861, 2875,
    2877, 2882, 2886, 2975, 3016, 3037, 3068,
    3332, 3396, 3398, 3414, 3930, 4145, 4362-
    4367, 4485
State Historical Society of Wisconsin, 3040
State system, 134, 175, 446, 469, 548, 1653, 1926,
    1990, 2181, 2277, 2292, 2426, 2474, 2514,
    2517, 3055-3056, 4173, 4364
State university, 2037, 2507, 3068, 3124, 3976,
    4073, 4170, 4368-4370
State University of New York, 1857-1864
Statistics about higher education, 3202, 3249, 3270,
    3390, 3814, 3989, 4197, 4282
Stearns, Eben S., 2545
Steidle, Edward, 2362
Stephen F. Austin State University, 2752-2753
Stephens College, 1508, 2145-2146
Sterling College, 945
Sterling, J.E. Wallace, 286
Stiles, Ezra, 381
Stillman College, 23, 46
Stone, Jared, 881
Stone, Mode L., 468
Stonewall Jackson College, 2937
Stout, Florence O., 977
Stowe, Calvin E., 1148
Straight, Willard, 1797
Student activism, 145, 154, 162, 210, 560, 682, 933,
    1183, 1308, 1310, 1343, 1421, 1638, 1717,
    1795, 1868, 1972, 2066-2067, 2234, 2425,
    2996, 3054, 3059, 4371-4390
Student discipline, 1195, 3466, 4407, 4417
Student life, 132, 153, 204, 223, 284, 362, 481, 511,
    520, 748, 810, 812-813, 821, 871, 888, 1195,
    1197, 1306, 1335, 1476, 1555, 1620, 1757,
    1797, 1800, 1868, 1873, 1893, 1898, 1905,
    1931, 2064-2065, 2071, 2073, 2076, 2107,
    2119, 2134, 2140-2141, 2143, 2156, 2252,
    2285, 2297, 2360, 2388, 2782, 2792, 2955,
    2961, 3001, 3063, 3074, 3182, 3184-3185,
    3193, 3269, 3299, 3324, 3386, 3468-3469,
    3528-3535, 3573, 3575, 3583, 3589, 3610,
    3617, 3624, 3629, 3637, 3642, 3874, 3877,
    3897, 4158, 4164, 4387, 4391-4425, 4438,

4441, 4443, 4542
Student Nonviolent Coordinating Committee, 4373
Student organizations and government, 132, 284,
    308, 472, 511, 684, 732, 888, 930, 1307, 1335,
    1731, 1797, 1815, 3038, 3074, 3084, 3324,
    3859, 3863, 3869, 3877-3878, 3897, 4373,
    4377, 4387, 4390, 4403, 4418-4419, 4440-4441
Student personnel services, 52, 113, 538, 778, 1253,
    1597, 1743, 1862, 1875, 1893, 1920, 2006,
    2051, 2092, 2141, 2360, 2840, 2989, 3687,
    4376, 4426-4443, 4474, 4543
Students for a Democratic Society, 1795, 4389
Sue Bennett College, 997
Sul Ross State University, 2754
Summer sessions, 814, 1029, 1323, 1553, 1557,
    2298, 3066, 3488, 3509, 3899
Summerland College, 2477
Sumner, William G., 383
Supreme Court, 3467-3470, 3473, 3476
Sutherland, Edwin, 804
Swain, David L., 1958
Swarthmore College, 2280, 2402-2403
Swedish higher education, 3807
Swimming, 378, 695, 1339, 2133, 2147, 3004, 3243
Syracuse University, 1865-1875

Tabor College, 911, 946-947
Talladega College, 3275
Talmadge, Herman, 496
Tannenbaum, Frank, 1738
Tappan, Henry P., 1318, 1337, 1351-1352, 3432
Tarleton State University, 2755-2756
Tate, William K., 2472
Taxonomy, 4210
Taylor Law, 1656
Taylor University, 761
Taylor, Thomas H., 1468
Teacher education, 3, 14, 20, 25, 38, 47, 68, 72, 74,
    95-96, 111, 117, 133, 142, 187, 193, 207, 219-
    220, 259, 262, 324, 326, 338, 340, 347, 359,
    398, 440, 447, 450, 460, 487, 489, 533, 536,
    599, 618, 621, 640, 648, 675, 677-679, 690,
    724, 764-765, 782-783, 786, 790, 792-794, 833,
    856, 884, 897, 909, 918-924, 941-942, 960,
    963, 988, 990, 1007, 1011-1013, 1015, 1030,
    1041, 1053, 1055, 1061, 1063-1064, 1076,
    1078, 1112, 1129, 1132-1133, 1135, 1154,
    1225, 1235, 1241, 1246, 1268, 1273, 1278,
    1374, 1376, 1409, 1432, 1453, 1458, 1460,
    1478-1480, 1491, 1496-1498, 1527, 1530,
    1538-1539, 1544, 1554, 1556, 1566-1567,
    1584, 1588, 1596-1597, 1625-1627, 1634,
    1637, 1660-1661, 1671, 1679, 1681, 1686,
    1688, 1718, 1733-1734, 1739, 1741, 1743,
    1754-1755, 1761, 1765, 1774, 1785, 1801,
    1808, 1826-1827, 1834, 1844, 1874, 1908,
    1939, 1961, 1991, 1993, 1999, 2012, 2032,

2037, 2083, 2094, 2170-2171, 2185, 2202,
    2228, 2236-2237, 2262, 2266-2267, 2273,
    2275-2276, 2302-2304, 2306-2307, 2315, 2328,
    2331, 2336, 2342, 2383, 2387, 2400-2401,
    2438-2439, 2482, 2484, 2487, 2501, 2504-
    2505, 2513, 2528-2547, 2557-2558, 2560,
    2567, 2571, 2628, 2636, 2672-2673, 2675,
    2708-2709, 2713-2715, 2718-2721, 2724-2725,
    2730-2731, 2744-2745, 2752, 2754, 2815,
    2817, 2864, 2879, 2882, 2888, 2925, 2928,
    2930, 2971-2972, 2978, 2986, 3008, 3010,
    3017, 3019, 3034, 3036, 3041, 3078, 3116-
    3117, 3354, 3360, 3534, 3544, 3563, 3571,
    3733, 3858, 3862, 3890, 3948, 4071, 4150,
    4205, 4218, 4288, 4307, 4342, 4444-4493,
    4544
Teachers College of Indianapolis, 833
Teachers College of Kansas City, 1470
Teaching, general, 900, 1650, 2004, 2131, 3520,
    3618, 3892, 4340, 4494-4498, 4557
Technical and Vocational Training Assistance Act,
    3578
Technical education, 96, 116, 138, 180, 182-183,
    191, 205, 225, 228, 325, 335, 441, 505, 514,
    570, 617-618, 816, 1027, 1034, 1138, 1206,
    1223-1224, 1234, 1247, 1270, 1412, 1496,
    1514, 1585, 1785, 1848, 1889, 1910, 1948-
    1949, 2010, 2050, 2095, 2211, 2301, 2343,
    2382, 2491, 2567, 2697, 2710, 2725, 2727,
    2762, 2765, 2779, 2804, 2806, 2935, 2942,
    3167, 3328, 3353, 3462, 3578, 3696, 3909,
    4222, 4240, 4242, 4245
Teilhard de Chardin, Pierre, 3391
Television, 134, 453, 491, 749, 1283, 1304, 1338,
    1485, 1558, 2072, 2494, 2498, 3345, 4347
Temple Junior College, 2757-2758
Temple University, 1762, 2404-2406
Tennessee, 2503-2581
Tennessee Medical College, 2565
Tennessee State University, 2566-2569
Tennessee, University of, 2513, 2570-2576
Tennessee, University of (Martin), 2577
Tennis, 206, 683
Tenure, 293, 1260, 1583, 2626, 3100, 3103, 3475,
    3547, 3555, 3567, 3569
Terrill College, 2509
Terry, Dwight H., 4273
Texas, 2582-2817, 3433
Texas Agricultural & Industrial University, 2759-2760
Texas Agricultural & Industrial University (Corpus
    Christi), 2607
Texas Agricultural & Mechanical University, 2761-
    2765, 2794
Texas Christian University, 2766-2769
Texas College, 2602
Texas Eastern University, 2607
Texas Lutheran College, 2770-2771
Texas Presbyterian College, 2772
Texas Southern University, 2606, 2773-2774

Texas Technological University, 2775-2780
Texas Wesleyan College, 2598, 2803-2804
Texas Woman's University, 2598, 2805-2807
Texas, University of, 2781-2800, 3980
Texas, University of (Arlington), 2801-2802
Texas, University of (Permian Basin), 2607
Text books, 3309, 3358, 3361-3662, 3833, 3841,
    3862, 3901, 3912, 4195, 4243, 4269, 4290,
    4353, 4355, 4358
Thayer, Sylvanus, 1887
Theater, 29, 177, 249, 273, 277, 289, 294, 401, 409,
    420, 466, 545, 574, 604, 625, 675, 688, 731,
    785, 793, 800, 829, 935, 942-943, 1017, 1020,
    1051, 1226, 1229, 1256, 1282, 1295, 1311,
    1316, 1321, 1347, 1354, 1379, 1382, 1472,
    1559, 1680, 1870, 2151, 2153, 2162, 2225,
    2238, 2256, 2429, 2489, 2496, 2609, 2634,
    2676, 2695, 2699-2700, 2707, 2717, 2740,
    2795, 2819, 2827, 2831, 2854, 2859, 2992,
    3007, 3067, 3321, 3340, 3557, 3833, 3842,
    3844, 3847, 3854, 3857, 3861, 3872, 3885,
    3889, 3891
Theological education, 127, 319, 374, 376, 379, 389,
    393, 395, 413, 526, 531, 550, 610, 613, 616,
    620, 635, 717-719, 775, 968, 993-995, 1083,
    1121-1122, 1148, 1189, 1276, 1475, 1495,
    1599, 1601-1604, 1612, 1752, 1814, 1849,
    1871, 1878, 1919, 2032, 2108, 2242, 2263,
    2314, 2337, 2455, 2461, 2468, 2641, 2668,
    2748, 2917, 2933, 2936, 2938, 2983, 3111-
    3113, 3119, 3190, 3365, 3370, 3390, 3910,
    3957-3958, 3966, 4120, 4125, 4127, 4130,
    4151, 4166, 4326, 4451, 4499-4509
Third World, 208
Thomas Jefferson University, 2407
Thomas More College, 998-999
Thomas, Theodore, 1780
Thoreau, Henry D., 1182
Three Rivers Community College, 1509
Thurston, Robert H., 4220
Tidwell, Robert E., 23
Tilton v. Richardson, 3473
Time, 3126
Toledo, University of, 1995, 2166-2168, 4522
Tougaloo College, 1439-1440
Towson State University, 1112
Track and field, 186, 250, 261, 471, 667, 706, 928,
    1967, 2144, 2251, 2253, 2353, 2499, 2777,
    2825, 2828, 3005, 3230
Transylvania University, 1000-1005, 4070
Trent, William P., 1778
Trenton State College, 1625-1627
Trevecca Nazarene College, 2578-2579
Trilling, Lionel, 1756
Trinidad State Junior College, 329-330
Trinity College (DC), 444-445
Trinity College (NC), 1932, 1934
Trinity Junior College (IL), 757
Trinity University (TX), 2808-2809

Troy State University, 47
Truett McConnell Junior College, 561
Truman, Harry S., 3591, 3597, 4058
Trustees, 741, 747, 978, 1575, 1582, 1871, 2069,
    3123, 3131-3132
Tufts University, 1237, 1689, 1860
Tuition, 1300, 3573, 3640, 4400
Tulane University, 1050-1051
Tulsa, University of, 2226-2227
Turkey, 3646-3647
Turner Theological Seminary, 550
Turner, Jonathan B., 583, 587
Tusculum College, 2580
Tuskegee Institute, 48-60, 462, 3275, 3280, 4050
Tutoring, 2141, 3496, 3507, 3523
Tuve, Merle A., 407
Tyler Junior College, 2810-2811
Tyler, Alice S., 2043
Tyler, Ralph W., 655, 658

Union Christian College, 834
Union College (KY), 1006
Union College (NE), 1533
Union College (NY), 1745, 1876, 3173, 4070
Union for Experimenting Colleges and Universities,
    2198
Union School of Religion, 1877
Union Seminary, 2938
Union Theological Seminary, 1878
Unions, 115, 130, 208, 1266, 1359, 1392, 1583,
    1618, 1656, 1674, 2483, 2599, 3322, 3362,
    3441, 3546, 4510-4517, 4550
Unitarian higher education, 1185, 1211
United Negro College Fund, 3337
United States Air Force, 331-337, 1032, 2573, 3245,
    3846, 4005, 4009, 4012, 4014
United States Air Force Academy, 331-337, 3245-
    3846
United States Army, 907, 1880-1896, 2052, 2408-
    2409, 2871, 3764, 4003-4004, 4010, 4012,
    4014
United States Army War College, 2408-2409
United States Coast Guard Academy, 362
United States Constitution, 1769, 3467-3470, 3473,
    3475-3476, 3801
United States International University, 3783
United States Merchant Marine Academy, 1879
United States Military Academy, 1880-1896, 2871,
    4003
United States Naval Academy, 1113-1115, 4042
United States Naval Institute, 1116
United States Naval War College, 2442-2444
United States Navy, 1113-1116, 2442-2444, 4012-
    4013, 4042
United States Office of Education, 3136, 3426
University City, MO, 1455
University Council for Educational Administration,

3191
University presses, 166, 1935
Upper Iowa College, 839
Upstate Medical Center, State University of New
    York, 1897
Urban university, 224, 227, 1262, 1654, 1671, 1831,
    2055, 3301, 3462, 4518-4522
Ursinus College, 2410, 4168
Ursuline College, 2169
Utah, 2818-2866
Utah State University, 2848-2850, 3713
Utah, University of, 2851-2864
Utica Institute, 3280
Utica Junior College, 1441
Utopianism, 1648, 3856, 3903

Valley City State College, 1993-1994
Valparaiso University, 835
Van Hise, Charles R., 3035, 3079, 3081, 4032
Van Vleck, J.H., 1175
Vanderbilt University, 232, 2528-2547, 3818
Vassar College, 1652, 1898-1902, 3566, 3710, 4421
Vaux, Roberts, 2283
Veblen, Thorstein, 4047
Ventura College, 296
Vermont, 2867-2872, 3917, 3927
Vermont, University of, 2084
Veterans, 486, 772, 815, 1125, 3576, 3592, 3722,
    4262, 4401
Veterinary education, 2943
Vietnam, 750
Vietnam War, 1972
Vincennes University, 280, 282, 836
Vincent, John, 237
Vineland Training School (NJ), 1628
Virginia, 2873-2968, 4565
Virginia Commonwealth University, 2939-2941
Virginia Intermont College, 2893
Virginia Polytechnic Institute and State University,
    2918, 2926, 2942-2943
Virginia State University, 2944-2946
Virginia Union University, 2965
Virginia, University of, 2947-2964, 3805, 4030, 4402
Volleyball, 3244
Volunteers, 3523
Voorhees College, 2478

Wabash College, 837
Wabash Valley College, 758
Waco University, 2812
Wadsworth family (NY), 1810
Wagner College, 1903-1904
Wake Forest University, 1986-1987
Walker, Francis A., 1223
Waller, David J., Jr., 2296

Wang Institute of Graduate Studies, 3696
War and higher education, 42, 287, 486, 726, 815,
    1125, 1214, 1216, 1659, 1772, 2071, 2076,
    2221, 2797, 3083, 3279, 3653, 4061-4062,
    4266, 4375, 4401, 4523-4529
Ward, Winifred, 731
Warren, Earl, 3468
Warren, Robert P., 1026
Waseda University, 2127
Washington, 2969-3012
Washington and Jefferson College, 2411-2412, 4402
Washington and Lee University, 2926, 2966-2967
Washington College (MD), 2375
Washington College (TN), 2581
Washington State University, 2987-2991
Washington University, 1455, 1510-1518, 2794
Washington, Booker T., 53, 59-60, 3280, 3294, 4050
Washington, University of, 630, 1860, 2992-3009,
    3108
Watson, John B., 1086-1087
Wayland, Francis, 2430-2431
Wayne County Community College, 1357
Wayne State University, 1358-1361, 4522
Webb, Walter P., 2801
Weber State College, 2865
Wellesley College, 1238-1240, 3566, 3710
Wells College, 1905-1906, 3710
Wendell, Barrett, 1171
Weniger, Charles E., 4507
Wentz, Lew, 2210
Wesley College, 2813
Wesley, Charles H., 432, 2047
Wesley, Edgar B., 1386
Wesleyan Church of America higher education, 1818
Wesleyan College (GA), 562-564, 4551
Wesleyan Female College (DE), 403
Wesleyan Female Institute (VA), 2968
Wesleyan University (CT), 363-364, 2435
Wessington Springs College, 2502
West Chester University, 2413-2415
West Coast Christian College, 297
West Florida, University of, 458
West Indies, University of, 3650
West Los Angeles College, 298
West Texas State University, 2814-2817
West Virginia, 3013-3033
West Virginia State College, 3013, 3027-3028
West Virginia University, 3029-3033
West Virginia Wesleyan College, 3014
Western Athletic Conference, 3238
Western College (MO), 1519
Western College (OH), 2012
Western Kentucky University, 1007
Western Literary Institute, 2170-2171
Western Maryland College, 1117-1119
Western Michigan University, 1263, 1268, 1271,
    1273
Western Montana College, 1527-1528
Western New Mexico University, 1647

Western Oregon State College, 2260
Western Personnel Organization, 4439
Western University (KS), 948
Western Washington University, 3010
Westfield State College, 1241
Westminster Choir College (NJ), 1629-1630
Westminster College (UT), 2866
Westminster Foundation, 3671
Westmont College, 299
Wham, John P., 751
Wheaton College (IL), 581, 759
White, Andrew D., 1789, 1796, 1798, 1800, 3127, 3853, 4424
White, Ellen G., 1280
White, Emerson, 826
White, Eva W., 4331
White, William A., 922
White, William R., 2645
Whitman College, 3011-3012
Whittier College, 300
Whitworth College for Women, 1442
Wichita State University, 4522
Wickersham, James P., 2342
Widener College, 2416-2417
Wilberforce University, 432, 2172, 3286, 3307
Wiles, Kimball, 479
Wiley College, 2602
Willamette University, 2261
William Jewell College, 804, 1445
William Penn College, 900
Williams College, 1242-1244, 3173
Williams, John D., 1431
Williams, Jonathan, 1896
Williams, Walter, 1484
Williamson, Charles C., 1783
Wilson College, 2418
Wilson, Louis R., 1960, 1969
Wilson, Woodrow, 1605, 1609, 1611, 1614
Winchester Normal School, 2509
Winsor, Justin, 1168
Winston Churchill College, 760
Winthrop College (SC), 2449, 2472, 2479
Wisconsin, 3034-3087, 3733
Wisconsin Idea, 3035, 4032
Wisconsin State University Conference, 3041
Wisconsin Student Association, 3038
Wisconsin, University of, 827, 1142, 1144-1145, 1175, 2121, 3035, 3041, 3052-3083, 3674, 3805, 3880, 4235
Wisconsin, University of (La Crosse), 3084-3085
Wisconsin, University of (Oshkosh), 3086-3087
Witherspoon, John, 1607, 1612
Wofford College, 3818
Wolfe, Sister M. Madelena, 832
Woman's College of Due West, 2480
Women, 37, 74-75, 146, 185, 194, 220, 279, 291, 315, 336, 341, 351, 403, 406, 444-445, 476, 502, 513, 519, 532, 547, 551, 560, 562-564, 717, 720, 732, 739, 883, 887, 1084, 1134,

1140, 1150, 1209-1210, 1227-1229, 1232-1233, 1237-1240, 1327, 1381, 1385, 1404, 1418, 1442, 1476, 1483, 1508, 1524, 1593, 1683, 1692, 1703, 1779, 1873, 1875, 1898-1902, 1905-1906, 1909, 1916, 1919, 1931, 1965, 1979, 2007, 2012, 2043, 2086, 2090, 2107, 2116, 2123, 2135, 2148, 2155, 2297-2298, 2341, 2364, 2397, 2399, 2453, 2462, 2480, 2524, 2546, 2569, 2572, 2583, 2614, 2703, 2708, 2803, 2805-2806, 2851-2852, 2860, 2863, 2878, 2883, 2893, 2897-2898, 2930, 2951, 2968, 2991, 2995, 3008, 3029, 3047, 3199, 3221, 3223, 3228, 3247, 3249, 3318, 3368-3369, 3372, 3491, 3549, 3566, 3601, 3620, 3631, 3651, 3682, 3710, 3725, 3727, 3733-3734, 3764, 3766, 3815, 4092, 4095, 4249, 4331, 4398, 4406, 4411-4412, 4472, 4530-4570
Women's Athletic Association, 279
Women's Educational and Industrial Union, 4550
Women's studies, 146
Women's study clubs, 4556
Woodberry, George E., 1726
Woodrow, James, 2468
Woods Hole Marine Biological Laboratory, 1245
Woodson, Carter G., 4050
Woodstock College, 1120-1122
Woodward, C. Vann, 371
Woody, Thomas, 2373
Wooster College, 2118
Work People's College, 4510
Work-study, 3583
Worker education, 1847
World War I, 1772, 2221, 2797, 3083, 4266, 4523, 4525, 4527-4528
World War II, 486, 815, 1125, 1214, 1216, 1659, 2071, 3279, 3574, 3653, 4083, 4401, 4526
Wrestling, 579, 1373, 2207, 2347, 2358, 2849, 2856, 2967, 3198, 3216, 3233, 3242, 3254
Wright, Richard R., Sr., 558
Wriston, Henry M., 2435
Writing, 1178, 3361, 3838, 3888
Wyer, Malcolm G., 3973
Wyoming, 3088-3091
Wyoming, University of, 1860, 3090-3091
Wythe, George, 2905

Xavier University, 2173

Yale University, 343, 365-396, 610, 635, 644, 3101, 3156, 3174-3175, 3193, 3248, 3250, 3405, 3408, 3665, 3851, 3946, 3979, 4256, 4498
Yearbooks, 4423
Yeshiva University, 1907
York College (NE), 1567-1568

Yorke, Peter C., 176
Yost, Fielding H., 1312
Young Harris College, 565-566
Young Men's Christian Association, 2947, 3180,
    4164
Young, Brigham, 2822
Young, Nathan B., 462

Youngstown State University, 2174-2175

Zahm, John A, 823
Znaniecki, Florian, 1759
Zoology, 1167, 1224, 4243

About the Compiler

Arthur P. Young is Dean of University Libraries and professor, The University of Rhode Island. He has published *Books for Sammies: The American Library Association and World War I* (1981) and *American Library History: A Bibliography of Dissertations and Theses* (1988). More than two dozen articles have appeared in such journals as *College & Research Libraries, Journal of Library History, Library Quarterly,* and *RQ.*